100 Great War Movies

The Real History behind the Films

ROBERT NIEMI

ABC-CLIO™

An Imprint of ABC-CLIO, LLC
Santa Barbara, California • Denver, Colorado

Library of Congress Cataloging-in-Publication Data
Names: Niemi, Robert, author.
Title: 100 great war movies : the real history behind the films / Robert Niemi.
Other titles: Hundred great war movies | One hundred great war movies
Description: Santa Barbara, California : ABC-CLIO, [2018] | Includes bibliographical
     references and index.
Identifiers: LCCN 2017053745 (print) | LCCN 2018005576 (ebook) |
     ISBN 9781440833861 (ebook) | ISBN 9781440833854 (hardcopy : alk. paper)
Subjects: LCSH: War films—History and criticism.
Classification: LCC PN1995.9.W3 (ebook) | LCC PN1995.9.W3 N54 2018 (print) |
     DDC 791.43/658—dc23
LC record available at https://lccn.loc.gov/2017053745

ISBN: 978-1-4408-3385-4 (print)
          978-1-4408-3386-1 (ebook)

22 21 20 19 18   1 2 3 4 5

This book is also available as an eBook.

ABC-CLIO
An Imprint of ABC-CLIO, LLC

ABC-CLIO, LLC
130 Cremona Drive, P.O. Box 1911
Santa Barbara, California 93116-1911
www.abc-clio.com

This book is printed on acid-free paper ∞

Manufactured in the United States of America

This one is for Connie, who put up with an MIA husband,
With far too many hours logged at his computer . . .

Also dedicated to the memory of

Alfred A. Niemi, Sr. (1915–2005), 20th Air Force, Guam, Mariana Islands,
World War II

Kenneth A. Niemi (1929–2014), 3rd Ranger Infantry Company (Airborne),
Korean War

They Served Their Country with Honor

Contents

Introduction

The War Film

Even if this were not an American-made book by an American writer for a mostly American readership, the lion's share of films covered herein would still emanate from the United States of America. That's because the United States has been an extraordinarily bellicose nation since its inception, at war 222 of its 241 years to date (92 percent of the time). This being the case, American society has always had an outsized reverence for the force of arms and all things military—regarded in the popular imagination as the only true and sacrosanct test of authentic masculinity, courage, and patriotism. Accordingly, Americans have an abiding passion for war films. That's why we make so many of them and why American war films consistently rank among the world's most accomplished and popular films, ethical and political considerations notwithstanding.

Though always a crowd-pleaser, the war film genre is an inherently schizoid one. In an earlier era, war films often functioned as jingoistic propaganda or de facto recruitment vehicles (there is a long history of the Department of Defense providing material support for war films for which it approves). In more recent decades increasingly jaded tastes and political complications have spawned war films that mostly traffic in the high-octane machismo of martial glory—putatively apolitical but ideologically suspect upon closer examination. On the other side of the schism are anti-war films, which attempt to characterize war more realistically—as, at best, an unavoidable tragedy in service to a good cause (e.g., to end slavery or defeat fascism) or, at worst, a senseless orgy of death and destruction that only benefits corrupt ruling elites, war profiteers, and undertakers. And it gets more complicated still, because the divide between the tendency to romanticize or condemn war is often blurred *within* each war film, insofar as the cinematic depiction of combat typically comes off as thrilling entertainment that often amounts to a pornography of violence, a tendency famously identified by Francois Truffaut, who wrote: "It seems to me that war films, even pacifist, even the best, willingly or not, glorify war. A film that truly shows war, battles, almost necessarily exalts war—unless it is a matter of parody . . . The effective war film is often the one where the action begins after the war, when there is nothing but ruins and desolation everywhere . . . War should not be shown as an accepted fact, inevitable, imponderable, but rather as a human decision, made by a small group of men . . . After having shown those who give the orders, one should show those who receive them, and their reactions (the simple soldiers)" (quoted in French, 2006).

All too often, war films implicitly serve an oppressive social order by making the worst of human evils palatable to impressionable young men "ardent for some desperate glory," as Wilfred Owen put it. They do so by making mortal combat a sanitized and fascinating aural-visual spectacle, viewed in the comfort and safety of the Cineplex auditorium or the family living room or on one's iPhone, far removed from the squalor, stench, terrifying dangers, and agonies of the real thing. At the same time, conventional war films often afford short shrift to the wider context in which combat occurs. Refusing to address why a war is being fought (and for whose benefit), many war films are really narrowly focused survivalist pictures that show soldiers fighting for one reason and one reason only: to stay alive and to ensure that their brothers-in-arms survive—a morally unassailable rationale to be sure, but one that also involves a pernicious kind of political myopia that needs to be interrogated and called out. (Though well-made and often gripping, films like *Black Hawk Down*, *We Were Soldiers*, *American Sniper*, and *Lone Survivor* are guilty of ideological evasions and historical misrepresentations that subliminally glorify the business of war by glorifying the warrior, an equation that is by no means inevitable, or even logical.)

On the other side of the divide, the greatest war films are always *anti*-war films, especially the ones that emanate from actual combat veterans who have known the true face of war and wish to educate the uninitiated to its horrors, for example, Erich Maria Remarque (*All Quiet on the Western Front*), Humphrey Cobb (*Paths of Glory*), Pierre Schoendoerffer (*The 317th Platoon*), Kurt Vonnegut (*Slaughterhouse-Five*), Lothar-Günther Buchheim (*Das Boot*), James Carabatsos (*Hamburger Hill*), and Oliver Stone (*Platoon*), among many others. Films based in the real experience of combat veterans are obviously better able to represent war's deadly mayhem without making it an exhilarating advertisement for more of the same in real life—though no film is immune to grossly distorted viewer reception.

In sum, the war film genre is extremely variegated, rife with contradictions, and layered with ideological complexities that have been treated in depth in dozens of academic studies. The aim of this book is more modest: to present a wide sampling of the best of the genre and to provide sufficient background information about how the film came into existence and how it relates to the real history it purports to represent in either broad or very specific terms—the two things that most often stimulate viewer curiosity.

Selection Criteria

Though many selections for the greatest war films are obvious (e.g., *Lawrence of Arabia*, *The Bridge on the River Kwai*), no two people could ever agree as to the top 100 entries in the war film genre. Tastes vary, as do underlying ideological biases and agendas. At any rate, the film list I compiled for this book derives from a lifetime as a film buff, 30 years teaching film at the college level, writing several film books, taking suggestions from friends and colleagues, and doing extensive research, including a thorough review of the "best of" lists compiled by other film critics and historians. Readers might find a few of the selections herein quirky and may strenuously object to certain omissions (e.g., *Casablanca* or *Gone with the Wind*, which are essentially wartime romances). All I can say is that I have tried my best to produce a book that is broadly representative of the genre in all its variety and complexity.

As for selection criteria, the two main guiding principles established from the outset is that (1) all the selections be full-length, sound-era fiction films made between 1930 and the present and (2) that each film be widely recognized as a superior example of the genre, not necessarily in terms of technical quality (though that's an important criteria), but in terms of a meaningful and emotionally compelling narrative. I've excluded war-related television docudrama mini-series (e.g., Steven Spielberg's *Band of Brothers*) and/or documentaries and documentary miniseries (e.g., PBS's *Vietnam: A Television History*; Ken Burns' *The Civil War* and his WWII series, *The War*, etc.). Documentaries and miniseries are vital parts of the cinema on war but they would require their own full-length studies. On the other hand, I have defined the war film genre quite broadly. Contained herein are not just ground combat films but selections from other war movie subgenres (e.g., POW movies, submarine movies, aviation movies, guerilla war movies, homefront movies, Holocaust movies, etc.) that treat war from a variety of perspectives and include an array of national cinemas—mostly United States, but also films from the United Kingdom, France, Germany, Russia, Japan, Australia, the Netherlands, Poland, and Finland. More than half of these war films deal with the Second World War—a skewed list to be sure—but justifiable because WWII was the largest and bloodiest armed conflict in human history. As such, it has spawned the lion's share of notable war films.

Format

Each film entry is divided into six parts. The first part, "Synopsis," provides a capsule description of the film. The second part, "Background," focuses on the creative genesis and development of the film. If based in history, a brief outline of the historical event is also included. Script writing, funding, casting, and other aspects of the pre-production process are also often considered. The third part of the entry, "Production," deals with the circumstances surrounding principal photography (i.e., where, when, and how the film was shot). The "Plot Summary" provides a detailed plot summary and identifies the main actors and their characters in the film. The fifth part, "Reception," provides release dates, box office information, awards, and an overview of the critical response. The sixth part, "Reel History Versus Real History," discusses the film's degree of historical accuracy in treating the specific military event it was based upon, or more generally, the war in which the film is set.

Does Historical Accuracy Matter in War Movies?

Regarding war films that purport to convey real history, the answer is yes, it does matter. Historical literacy is abysmal in the United States and almost equally poor the world over. Most people do not read history books; they get what little historical awareness they have through movies and, to a lesser extent, through television and the Internet. That being the case, war movies referencing real wars (or firmly rooted in the history of real battles and campaigns) will be the only means through which the majority of the populace have any acquaintance with or understanding of a particular war or battle. Playing the devil's advocate, one might well argue that historically inaccurate war movies are of no great consequence; lots of people harbor misinformed or just plain wrong historical impressions they got from movies—so what?

Actually, movies can have considerable sociopolitical impact in the real world. Historian Andrew E. Larsen cites the case of Mel Gibson's *Braveheart*: a grossly inaccurate war movie that "has been credited with having a very substantial impact on Scottish politics in the mid-1990s. It was released in 1995, and two years later Scotland overwhelmingly voted in favor of a proposal to establish a Scottish Parliament. It has been credited with significantly encouraging Scottish nationalism and has been accused to encouraging Anglophobia in Scotland. The film's relentlessly negative depiction of the English as vicious rapists is wildly wrong, but very effective." Larsen also cites *The Battle of Kosovo* (1989), a Yugoslav historical drama/war film filmed in Serbia that depicts the historical Battle of Kosovo between medieval Serbia and the Ottoman Empire, which took place on 15 June 1389. Larsen notes that Serbian President Slobodan Milosevic used showings of the film "as way to whip up Serbian support for his brutal treatment of the Kosovar Albanians in the 1990s" (Larsen, 2014). Another example of war movies shaping a nation's cultural climate is the raft of Vietnam War films released in the 1970s and 1980s. These movies presented a series of competing narratives about the meaning of the war and the character of the U.S. Vietnam veteran as America struggled mightily to reconcile itself to the war's bitter legacy. Nagging popular stereotypes about post-traumatic stress disorder (PTSD)–deranged Vietnam veterans largely derive from exaggerated cinematic representations, for example, *The Deer Hunter* (1978) or *Apocalypse Now* (1979).

The historical integrity of war movies *does* matter but begs another question: Is a high level of historical accuracy really possible? The answer, most often, is no. Past events are not only unrepeatable but also, in many ways, unknowable—or at least subject to lots of subjective interpretation. Any cinematic re-creation of an historical event—whether it be a fictional narrative imposed on a real setting or an attempt to accurately retell a slice of military history—is inevitably going to be the product of selective analysis, guesswork, speculation, and fantasy based on a complex welter of disparate and often contradictory sources and influenced by the filmmaker's biases and political agenda. The other problem facing historical reenactment in war movies (or any kind of movie based in history) is that cinematic narrative requisites are frequently incompatible with historical accuracy. Like all Hollywood genre movies, war movies generally require a hero or two, a villain or villains, a few supporting characters, a carefully plotted three-act narrative arc, a Manichean moral schema that clearly identifies the good guys (our side) from the bad guys (usually a faceless and ruthless enemy), and a definitive resolution (victory, defeat, or mere survival). Real battles in real wars involve hundreds or even thousands of combatants and do not readily lend themselves to tidy narrative plotting, easily identified heroes and villains, black and white moral oppositions, or pat endings that tie up loose ends. War movies based in actual history can offer compelling storylines or they can stay close to the known historical facts; they can seldom do both—although there are a select few war films that achieve dramatic impact and an unusually high level of historical accuracy, for example, James Carabatsos' *Hamburger Hill* (1987), Pekka Parikka's *The Winter War* (1989), Roman Polanski's *The Pianist* (2002), and Bernd Eichinger's *Downfall* (2004).

ALL QUIET ON THE WESTERN FRONT (1930)

Synopsis
All Quiet on the Western Front is an American Pre-Code anti-war epic based on the famous World War I novel by Erich Maria Remarque. Adapted by Maxwell Anderson, George Abbott, and Del Andrews and directed by Lewis Milestone, the film stars Lew Ayres, Louis Wolheim, John Wray, Arnold Lucy, and Ben Alexander. It recounts the harrowing experiences of a German Army frontline infantry company during the First World War.

Background
A decade after the end of World War I former German soldier Erich Maria Remarque (1898–1970) turned his grueling frontline experiences with the 2nd Guards Reserve Division at Hem-Lenglet, France, into *Im Westen nichts Neues* [*Nothing New in the West*]: a searing anti-war novel first serialized in 1928 in the Berlin-based liberal daily newspaper, *Vossische Zeitung*. Published in book form on 29 January 1929, Remarque's novel took the world by storm, selling 2.5 million copies in 22 languages in its first 18 months in print. Little, Brown & Sons published the first U.S. edition on 1 June 1929 under the title, *All Quiet on the Western Front*. Soon after its U.S. publication, Universal Pictures producer Carl Laemmle purchased the film rights for $20,000 ($286,000 in 2017 dollars) and put his 21-year-old son, Carl Laemmle, Jr., in charge of production—a move met with amused skepticism throughout the film industry, but Carl Jr. proved equal to the task. He wisely hired eminent playwrights Maxwell Anderson and George Abbott to adapt the novel to the screen, former Signal Corps filmmaker Lewis Milestone to direct, and the distinguished German cinematographer, Arthur Edeson, to shoot the picture.

Production
Filming began on Armistice Day 1929—exactly 11 years after the end of the war and less than two weeks after the stock market crash that precipitated the Great Depression. As the first major epic of the talkie period, *All Quiet on the Western Front* proved to be a costly and difficult undertaking involving lots of logistical hurdles. Shooting occurred at various locations in southern California. Village scenes were shot at a set built on Universal's backlot, but most of the filming took place at the Irvine Ranch, 50 miles southeast of Los Angeles, where trenches and a shell-pocked battlefield were constructed. To ensure verisimilitude, hundreds of real French and German uniforms were imported from Europe at great expense. Because American

soldiers were prohibited from wearing the uniforms of a foreign power, Laemmle couldn't rely on the U.S. Army as a source of extras; he had to scour greater Los Angeles to recruit some 2,000 of them. All were WWI veterans, many of them German, but also of various other nationalities. The shoot was supposed to run for 48 days but ended up taking 99 days, resulting in numerous cost overruns, mostly for salaries, wardrobe, set construction, and lighting. Originally slated to cost $891,000, the film came in at $1.4 million, or 39 percent, over budget; however, this money was later recouped by brisk box office business.

Plot Summary

The film opens at a gymnasium (boys' secondary school) in Germany at the outbreak of the First World War in 1914. Professor Kantorek (Arnold Lucy) gives a bombastic speech about the glory of military service and "saving the Fatherland," prompting his entire class to enlist. After basic training, the new recruits arrive at the front, but one of them is killed before they can reach their post. On night patrol, veteran soldier Stanislaus "Kat" Katczinsky (Louis Wolheim) instructs the "schoolboys" to hit the ground to better survive incoming artillery shells. The unit strings barbed wire and tries to avoid shells. Flares light up the night sky as the enemy tries to spot them, machine guns rattle, and shelling begins. Behn (Walter Browne Rogers) is killed by machine-gun fire. Franz Kemmerich (Ben Alexander) runs out to retrieve Behn but later realizes that he's been carrying a corpse. Back in the bunker, the soldiers play cards and fend off rats. Others scream and shake uncontrollably, unnerved by the constant shelling. Kemmerich panics, runs out of the trench, and is badly wounded. Suddenly the shelling ends and the men are ordered out to man the trenches and repel an enemy attack. Hundreds of French soldiers run toward the trenches. Despite heavy losses, the enemy reaches the German trenches, where hand-to-hand combat ensues. Overwhelmed, the Germans retreat to a second line of defense and then launch a counterattack that proves unsuccessful. The men of 2nd Company return from the battle and line up for a meal. Ginger, the cook (William Irving), refuses to feed them until the entire company arrives. The men explain that they are all that is left of the company—only 80 of the original 150—but Ginger remains adamant. Lt. Bertinck (G. Pat Collins) arrives and orders the cook to feed his men. After eating, they hear that they have been ordered to return to the front the next day. The men speculate about who needs the war more: the Kaiser or the arms manufacturers. Katczinsky suggests roping off a field and stripping the kings and their ministers down to their underwear and letting them fight it out with clubs. Five of the men visit their wounded friend Kemmerich and find him in poor shape, and Müller (Russell Gleason) informs Kemmerich that his right leg has been amputated. Kemmerich rues the fact that he will never become a forester, and Paul Bäumer (Lew Ayres) tries to comfort him. Kemmerich asks Paul to give his boots to Müller, who has asked for them, and then dies. Paul leaves the dressing station and brings Müller Kemmerich's boots. Müller is pleased to return to the front in such fine boots. During a scene in a cemetery, Paul stabs a French soldier (Raymond Griffith) and is then trapped in a shell crater for the night as the soldier slowly dies. As the night wears on, Paul attempts in vain to save the soldier's life. After the man dies, Paul weeps and begs forgiveness from the dead body.

A German soldier, Paul Bäumer (Lew Ayers), subdues a French soldier (Raymond Griffith) in a still from Lewis Milestone's anti-war classic, *All Quiet on the Western Front* (1930). (Universal Pictures/Photofest)

Later, Paul manages to return to the German lines. After a day off, the soldiers return to the frontline. Paul sustains serious injuries and is brought to a Catholic hospital along with his friend Albert Kropp (William Bakewell). Kropp's leg is subsequently amputated. Paul's wounds result in a furlough, and Paul returns home. Oblivious as to the real goings-on at the front, the townspeople are stupidly patriotic. Paul visits Kantorek's classroom and finds the teacher extolling the "glory of war." Disgusted, Paul returns to the frontline and learns that only a few members of the 2nd Company have survived, including Tjaden (Slim Summerville), who informs Paul that Katczinsky is still alive. Paul searches for Katczinsky and finds him wounded in the ankle by an aerial bomb. As Paul carries Katczinsky to a field hospital, a plane drops another bomb, killing Katczinsky. Paul is unaware that his friend is dead until he reaches the field hospital—a revelation that fills him with grief. In the final scene, Paul watches a butterfly from his trench on the frontlines. Paul stretches his arm out towards the butterfly and is hit with a bullet from an enemy sniper. The final shot shows the 2nd Company arriving at the front, fading out to the image of a cemetery.

Reception
Lavishly praised by critics, a major hit at the box office, and the winner of the third Best Picture and Best Director Oscars, the film fared less well in Europe and

elsewhere due to its anti-war message. When it premiered at the Mozart Cinema in Berlin on 5 December 1930 Adolf Hitler's future propaganda minister, Joseph Goebbels, bought up a block of 300 tickets for Nazi Stormtroopers who proceeded to ruin the screening by releasing white mice, throwing smoke bombs and sneezing powder, and shouting "Jewish film!" Six days later, the Weimar chief film censor caved in to the Nazis and banned the film. After Hitler came to power in 1933 the Nazis banned and burned Remarque's novel and its sequel, *Der Weg zurück* [*The Road Back*] (1931), along with scores of other books deemed subversive and "un-German." Needless to say, *All Quiet* was banned in Nazi Germany throughout the 12-year lifespan of the Third Reich. It was finally re-released in West Germany in April 1952. The film was also banned in Italy, Austria, and France in 1931, sanctions that would remain in place for many decades.

Reel History Versus Real History

Shot in black and white with the primitive sound equipment available in 1929–1930, *All Quiet on the Western Front* lacks the sophisticated sound, special effects, and simulated Technicolor gore that characterizes more recent war films. Nonetheless, *All Quiet* achieves a high degree of accuracy in its depiction of life and death in the trenches during the First World War. Uniforms, weapons, the look of the trenches and battlefield, military deportment, combat tactics, and the soldiers' psychology all ring true, despite a few minor continuity lapses and acting that sometimes tends toward exaggeration in facial gestures and body language (a holdover from silent film stylistics). Milestone's masterpiece remains one of greatest anti-war films ever made. Delbert Mann's 1979 made-for-TV version starring Richard Thomas was also well received.

AMERICAN SNIPER (2014)

Synopsis

American Sniper is an American biopic/war drama directed by Clint Eastwood and loosely adapted by Jason Hall from *American Sniper: The Autobiography of the Most Lethal Sniper in U.S. Military History* (2012) by Chris Kyle, co-written with Scott McEwen and Jim DeFelice. The film recounts the life of Kyle, a sniper credited with 255 kills from four tours of duty in the Iraq War, 160 of which were officially confirmed. Although Kyle was celebrated for his successes as a combat marksman, his military service took a heavy toll on his personal and family life.

Background

Christopher Scott "Chris" Kyle (1974–2013) was a rancher, professional bronco rodeo rider, and U.S. Navy SEAL from Odessa, Texas. During four tours of duty in Iraq (2003–2009) Kyle (aka "Legend" and "The Devil of Ramadi") became the deadliest combat sniper in U.S. military history with 160 confirmed kills. After 10 years in the U.S. Navy, Kyle took his discharge in 2009; moved to Midlothian, Texas, with his wife, Taya, and two children; and co-founded Craft International, a tactical training company for U.S. military and law enforcement personnel. On 2 January 2012 William Morrow published Kyle's memoir (co-written with Scott McEwen and Jim DeFelice): *American Sniper: The Autobiography of the Most Lethal Sniper in U.S. Military History,* a book that stayed on *The New York Times* bestseller list for over nine months. Screenwriter Jason Hall—who had been working with Chris Kyle on a Kyle biopic script since March 2010—successfully pitched the project to actor Bradley Cooper. On the strength of Cooper's involvement, Warner Bros. teamed with Cooper's production company to purchase the rights from Chris Kyle on 24 May 2012. On 2 February 2013, the day after Hall finished a first draft of the screenplay, Chris Kyle and a friend named Chad Littlefield set out to take ex-Marine Eddie Ray Routh to a shooting range in Glen Rose, Texas, as post-traumatic stress disorder (PTSD) therapy. Before they reached the range Routh, 25, shot both men dead in order to steal Kyle's customized pickup truck. (Routh was subsequently convicted of the double homicide and sentenced to life without parole.) Shortly after Kyle's murder Steven Spielberg signed on as director but quit the project three months later after he and the studio couldn't come to a budget agreement. In September 2013 Clint Eastwood took over as director, and Cooper began a rigorous, six-month diet and exercise regimen to transform himself into a credible likeness of the heavier and more muscled Chris Kyle. He also watched dozens of hours of home movies that Kyle's widow lent him to master Kyle's demeanor and body language.

Production

On 14 March 2014, Sienna Miller was cast as Kyle's wife, Taya. By the end of March most of the rest of the principal cast had been hired. Principal photography began on 31 March 2014 in Los Angeles and then relocated to Rabat, northern Morocco, for 12 days of location shooting. From 23 April to 6 May shooting took place at a simulated Iraqi village at the Blue Cloud Movie Ranch in Santa Clarita, California. In the latter half of May domestic scenes were shot in Culver City and Los Angeles. The 44-day shoot wrapped on schedule in early June in order to meet the film's limited-release Christmas 2014 deadline. Notorious for being a very fast-working—some would say slapdash—director, Clint Eastwood kept to his customary six or fewer takes per shot (usually two or three). Also typical for Eastwood was the minimal amount of time he spent on rehearsal—a good thing in some instances, because it can enhance spontaneity in actors, but it can just as easily result in some shoddy performances.

Plot Summary

Chris Kyle's father, Wayne (Ben Reed), teaches the youngster how to shoot a rifle and also teaches him that the world is composed of wolves (predators), sheep (prey), and sheepdogs (protectors of the weak) and that the strong and righteous assign themselves to the third category. Years later, Kyle is a rodeo cowboy when he watches a news story about the U.S. embassy bombings (7 August 1998) and immediately decides to join the U.S. Navy. After rigorous training, he becomes a U.S. Navy SEAL sniper. Kyle meets Taya Renae (Sienna Miller) in a San Diego bar, they marry, and he is sent to Iraq after the 9/11 attacks. Kyle is a talented sniper, earning the nickname "Legend" for his numerous kills. As he hunts for al-Qaeda leader Abu Musab al-Zarqawi, Kyle pays a family $100,000 to lead the SEALs to "The Butcher" (Mido Hamada), al-Zarqawi's right-hand man. Despite careful planning, The Butcher's sniper captures and restrains Kyle while The Butcher kills the father and son who helped the SEALs. Kyle returns home for the birth of his son, but is preoccupied with the haunting memories of combat. Taya begs Kyle to put his energy into his family, but he soon leaves for a second tour. After the second tour, Kyle returns home again, this time to a newborn daughter. He is even more alienated from his loved ones. On his third tour, despite injuries inflicted by a Dragunov sniper rifle, Kyle and his unit choose to continue their mission. On his fourth tour of duty, Kyle is assigned to take out "Mustafa" (Sammy Sheik), a skilled enemy sniper killing U.S. Army combat engineers. Perched on a rooftop, Kyle spots Mustafa and kills him with a shot from his Lapua .388 rifle at a distance of 2,100 yards (1.2 miles), but the shot reveals his team's position to the enemy, and swarms of armed insurgents attack. Luckily, the team escapes under the cover of a sandstorm, but Kyle sustains an injury and is almost left for dead. Kyle goes home, but is on edge and incapable of adjusting to civilian life. He copes by coaching wounded or PTSD-afflicted veterans at a shooting range. Eventually, he settles in to life at home. On 2 February 2013, Kyle brings a veteran to a shooting range. On-screen subtitles reveal: "Kyle was killed that day by a veteran he was trying to help," followed by archival news footage of thousands of people lining his funeral procession while thousands more are shown attending his memorial service on 11 February 2013 at Cowboys [now known as AT&T] Stadium in Arlington, Texas.

Reception

American Sniper proved to be a huge hit at the box office. On its opening weekend (16–18 January 2015) in wide release (3,555 theaters) the film posted more than $89 million in ticket sales. By the end of its 27-week run in June it had earned $547.4 million in worldwide grosses—almost 11 times its $59 million production budget. As for official accolades, *American Sniper* garnered six Oscar nominations and won an Oscar for Best Sound. But *American Sniper* also ignited fierce debate among film critics, pundits, bloggers, and the general public as to its merits and putative meaning. Conservatives heaped praise on the film as a fitting tribute to Chris Kyle's combat exploits and as a stirring paean to U.S. military service. More centrist voices judged the film a balanced and poignant rendering of the devastating effects of war on soldiers and their families. Some critics on the Left denounced *American Sniper* as a simple-minded infomercial for American xenophobia and colonialist militarism and machismo. Perhaps the most astute appraisal, though, was rendered by journalist Matt Taibbi in a review for *Rolling Stone* (2015): "The really dangerous part of this film is that it turns into a referendum on the character of a single soldier. It's an unwinnable argument in either direction. We end up talking about Chris Kyle and his dilemmas, and not about the [Donald] Rumsfelds and [Dick] Cheneys and other officials up the chain [of command] who put Kyle and his high-powered rifle on rooftops in Iraq and asked him to shoot women and children. They're the real villains in this movie, but the controversy has mostly been over just how much of a 'hero' Chris Kyle really was."

Reel History Versus Real History

American Sniper depicts Chris Kyle joining the SEALs after watching TV news coverage of the U.S. embassy bombings in Dar es Salaam, Tanzania, and Nairobi, Kenya, on 7 August 1998. In point of fact, these events had nothing to do with Kyle's enlistment in 1999. The film also shows the United States invading Iraq right after the 9/11 attacks in 2001, implying causality between the two events; in reality Iraq had nothing to do with 9/11 (most of the hijackers were Saudis). There was a sniper known as Mustafa but Kyle never encountered him. The dueling snipers motif was a script element added by Steven Spielberg that was probably copied from or inspired by Jean-Jacques Annaud's *Enemy at the Gates* (2001). The terrorist depicted as The Butcher might be loosely based on Ismail Hafidh al-Lami, known as Abu Deraa ("Father of the Shield"), blamed for thousands of Iraqi deaths. Although the film alters Kyle's book in significant ways, Chris Kyle's own veracity has proven to be highly suspect. In 2014 Jesse Ventura sued Kyle's estate for defamation and was paid $1.84 million in damages. In TV interviews in 2012 Kyle stated that he assaulted Ventura in a bar in 2006 after Ventura made negative comments about the Navy SEALs and their role in Iraq. Ventura has vehemently denied ever meeting Kyle. Kyle also told a writer that he had gunned down two carjackers in Dallas in January 2010 but there is no police record of this crime. Kyle also stated that he and a fellow sniper went to the top of the Superdome in New Orleans after Hurricane Katrina in 2005 and shot some 30 civilians he thought were looting or otherwise making trouble—another story that proved to be entirely apocryphal.

APOCALYPSE NOW (1979)

Synopsis

Apocalypse Now is an American Vietnam War epic directed and produced by Francis Ford Coppola and co-written by Coppola and John Milius, with voice-over narration written by Vietnam veteran, Michael Herr. Starring Marlon Brando, Martin Sheen, Robert Duvall, Frederic Forrest, Albert Hall, Sam Bottoms, Larry Fishburne, and Dennis Hopper, the film transposes Joseph Conrad's novella, *Heart of Darkness* (1899) to the Vietnam War as it follows Capt. Benjamin L. Willard (Sheen) on a secret mission to assassinate Col. Kurtz (Brando), a renegade American officer who has presumably gone insane and formed his own guerilla army.

Background

Filmmaker John Milius tried to volunteer for military service during the Vietnam War but was rejected because of an asthmatic condition. While he was working as an assistant for Francis Ford Coppola on *The Rain People* (1969), Milius began to write a script that transposed Joseph Conrad's *Heart of Darkness* to the Vietnam

Martin Sheen as Capt. Benjamin L. Willard (left) and Frederic Forrest as Engineman 3rd Class Jay "Chef" Hicks as they venture into the stronghold of renegade Col. Walter E. Kurtz (played by Marlon Brando, not pictured) in a scene from Francis Ford Coppola's *Apocalypse Now* (1979). (United Artists/Photofest)

War and used Conrad's story of a white trader's mad exploits in Africa as the template for an allegory about America in Vietnam. Milius finished a first draft on 5 December 1969, but the controversial nature of the Vietnam War delayed production for several years, during which Milius wrote nine more drafts and changed the title from "The Psychedelic Soldier" to "Apocalypse Now" (a mocking reference to the hippie slogan, "Nirvana Now"). In the spring of 1974, Coppola undertook pre-production in earnest. By the latter months of 1975 he had finished a revised version of Milius's script. He would continue to revise throughout the shoot, ultimately using Werner Herzog's conquistador epic *Aguirre, the Wrath of God* (1972) and Michael Herr's bestselling Vietnam War memoir, *Dispatches* (1977), as additional sources of inspiration. After the resounding success of *The Godfather,* Parts I (1972) and II (1974), Coppola managed to secure financing from United Artists and distributors in the amount of $15.5 million—a modest budget for a complex, large-scale project. He scouted locations in New Zealand but finally opted to shoot the film in the Philippines, where labor was cheap and President Ferdinand Marcos could be counted on to supply military equipment, especially helicopters.

Production
Apocalypse Now is legendary for having a protracted and chaotic production history. At the outset, Francis Ford Coppola struggled to cast the role of Capt.

Willard. Robert Redford, Jack Nicholson, Steve McQueen, James Caan, and Al Pacino all refused the part, probably because it involved 14 weeks of location shooting in fetid Philippine jungles. Harvey Keitel (*Mean Streets*) accepted the role of Willard, and production began in March 1976, but just a week into the shoot Coppola fired Keitel and replaced him with Martin Sheen. Marlon Brando ultimately took on the role of Kurtz—for the exorbitant fee of $3.5 million for 20 days work (i.e., $175,000 a day). In late May, about seven weeks into the shoot, Typhoon Olga destroyed sets and halted production for six weeks while they were rebuilt, putting the movie $2 million over budget. When production resumed that summer, Marlon Brando presented more problems for Coppola when he arrived on set weighing some 300 pounds and clueless about the role he was supposed to play. Valuable time was wasted as Brando and Coppola improvised Kurtz's lines and Brando's corpulence forced Coppola to dress him in black and shoot him mostly in close-up and deep shadow to obscure his bulk. By the end of the year Coppola had a rough cut of his movie assembled but still needed to improvise an ending. Filming in the Philippines resumed in February 1977 and continued until 5 March 1977 when Martin Sheen, then in the throes of severe alcoholism, had a near-fatal heart attack, which delayed production for another six weeks while he recuperated. The shoot finally wrapped on 21 May 1977. Coppola's cinematographer, Vittorio Storaro, shot an unprecedented 1.5 million feet of film: 550 hours of raw footage that was eventually edited down to a film running 153 minutes (making for an unheard of 216:1 shooting ratio). What was supposed to be accomplished in 14 weeks took 14 *months* and ran $16 million over budget—more than double the original projection—forcing an often-frantic Coppola to subsidize the project with millions of dollars of his own money. Post-production complications with editing, sound mixing, and voice-over narration delayed the movie's release until the Cannes Film Festival on 10 May 1979, more than three years after the start of principal photography and a full decade after Coppola commissioned Milius to write the script. During a press conference at Cannes Coppola waxed grandiloquently: "My film is not about Vietnam. It *is* Vietnam. The way we made it is the way Americans were in Vietnam. We had too much money, too much equipment and little by little we went insane."

Plot Summary

The setting is the Vietnam War, c.1969. An opening montage establishes Army Capt. Benjamin Willard (Martin Sheen) as deeply troubled, likely suffering from post-traumatic stress disorder (PTSD). On leave in Saigon, Willard is summoned to a communications security (COMSEC) intelligence briefing in Nha Trang, where Gen. Corman (G. D. Spradlin), Col. Lucas (Harrison Ford), and CIA agent R. E. Moore (Jerry Zeismer) order Willard to terminate Special Forces ("Green Beret") Col. Walter E. Kurtz (Marlon Brando) "with extreme prejudice" (Kurtz has become a dangerous renegade and formed his own Montagnard army inside Cambodia). After reluctantly accepting the mission Willard joins a Navy PBR [river patrol boat] heading upriver, commanded by Chief Petty Officer George Phillips "Chief" (Albert Hall) and manned by Gunner's Mates Lance (Sam Bottoms), "Chef" (Frederic Forrest), and "Mr. Clean" (Laurence Fishburne). They soon rendezvous with Lt. Col.

Bill Kilgore (Robert Duvall), a macho 1st Cavalry commander and surfing enthu-siast, who gets them past the Nùng River's Viet Cong–held coastal entrance at "Charlie's Point" by conducting a helicopter raid on the enemy village there to the accompaniment of Wagner's "Ride of the Valkyries" on loudspeakers. Further up the Nùng the PBR stops at a supply depot for diesel fuel and the men watch a night-time United Service Organizations (USO) show featuring Playboy bunnies that quickly dissolves into chaos as lustful soldiers try to get to the showgirls. The PBR eventually reaches the American-held Do Lung Bridge at night, which is under enemy attack. Failing to find the U.S. commander of the bridge outpost in all the confusion, Willard orders Chief to continue upriver. The next day, Willard learns from a radio dispatch that Capt. Richard M. Colby (Scott Glenn) was sent on an earlier mission identical to Willard's but joined Kurtz rather than kill him. Mean-while, Lance sets off a smoke grenade that inadvertently alerts enemy soldiers on shore, and Mr. Clean is killed in the ensuing firefight. Chief is hit by a spear released by native tribesmen and tries to kill Willard. Willard finishes him off, and Lance disposes of Chief's body in the river. Willard shares his plan with Chef and the two continue on together. When the PBR arrives at Kurtz's compound Willard encounters a manic freelance photojournalist (Dennis Hopper) who praises Kurtz extravagantly. Returning to the PBR, Willard and Lance soon depart, telling Chef to initiate an airstrike on Kurtz if the pair fails to return—a futile safeguard because Chef is soon decapitated by Kurtz's men. Willard is captured, caged, and then brought before Kurtz in a darkened temple where he is lectured by Kurtz on war, life, and the fanaticism of the Viet Cong who cut off the arms of children newly inoculated by the Americans. That night, Willard enters Kurtz's chamber and attacks him with a machete. Quoting directly from *Heart of Darkness*, Kurtz whis-pers "The horror, the horror" and dies. When Willard leaves the compound, Kurtz's minions bow down to him but Willard refuses to supplant Kurtz as their new demi-god; he leads Lance to the boat and they depart downriver as the screen fades to black.

Reception
Apocalypse Now shared the Palme d'Or for Best Film with Volker Schlöndorff's *The Tin Drum* at the 1979 Cannes Film Festival and earned eight Oscar nominations, winning two (for Best Sound and Best Cinematography). It also did well at the box office, earning $81.2 million, and received almost universal accolades from film critics. The American Film Institute (AFI) ranks *Apocalypse Now* as 30th among the best 100 films ever made. On the other hand, critics remain divided as to whether the movie is pro-war or anti-war. For example, Col. Kilgore's Wagnerian helicopter attack on the enemy village comes off as exhilarating, and if Kurtz is supposed to represent war's perversion of the human spirit, his rendition by Brando achieves a certain tragic grandeur that seems to undermine the film's putative anti-war message.

Reel History Versus Real History
Apocalypse Now is entirely fictional; none of the events depicted—including the mass dismemberment incident recounted by Kurtz—actually happened.

Capt. Willard and Col. Kurtz are based on the central characters in Conrad's *Heart of Darkness* but Coppola has admitted that Kurtz was also loosely based on Col. Robert B. Rheault (1925–2013), 5th Special Forces Group, whose 1969 arrest over the murder of suspected double agent Thai Khac Chuyen in Nha Trang generated a scandal known as the "Green Beret Affair." The Nùng [Vietnamese for "Hot"] River is fictional but seems to correspond to either the Tonle-Sap River or the Mekong River (or its tributary, the Bassac River). These are the only rivers that run though Cambodia into Vietnam before they empty into the South China Sea in South Vietnam's Mekong Delta. The Viet Cong–held village at "Charlie's Point" would therefore have to be located in the Delta, an area controlled by Army of the Republic of Vietnam (ARVN) and U.S. forces, which would preclude its existence by definition. The U.S. base supply depot at Hau Phat is also fictional, as is the Lo Dung Bridge. As for the film's depiction of U.S. military operations in Vietnam, combat veteran Reginald "Malik" Edwards (Pfc., U.S. Marines) delivered a scathing judgment on the film's gross historical inaccuracies in Wallace Terry's *Bloods: An Oral History of the Vietnam War* (1984): "*Apocalypse Now* didn't tell the truth. It wasn't real. I guess it was a great thing for the country to get off on, but it didn't remind me of anything I saw. I can't understand how you would have a bridge lit up like a Christmas tree. A USO show at night? Guys attacking the women on stage. That made no sense. I never saw us reach a point where no one was in charge of a unit . . . If you don't know anything you know the chain of command. And the helicopter attack on the village? F—in' ridiculous. You couldn't hear music coming out of a helicopter. And attacking a beach in helicopters was just out of the question. The planes and napalm would go in first. Then, the helicopters would be eased in after the fact . . . By making us look insane the people who made that movie [were] somehow relieving themselves of what they asked us to do over there. But we were not insane . . . We were not ignorant. We knew what we were doing. I mean, we were crazy but it's built into the culture." Coppola and Milius were well intentioned in trying to characterize the Vietnam War as insanity, but as Edwards rightly notes, the filmmakers erroneously characterize the combatants themselves—not their overlords—as epitomizing the geopolitical psychosis that was Vietnam: simple-minded hyperbole that makes for gripping allegorical cinema but obscures deeper truths regarding American imperialism and cultural hubris.

ARMY OF SHADOWS [FRENCH: *L'ARMÉE DES OMBRES*] (1969)

Synopsis

Army of Shadows is a French film directed by Jean-Pierre Melville that is a cinematic adaptation of Joseph Kessel's 1943 book of the same title, which blends Kessel's own experiences as a member of the French Resistance (called the Maquis in rural areas) with fictionalized material. The film follows a small group of heroic Resistance fighters on and between covert hit-and-run missions as they attempt to evade the capture and likely execution by the Germans.

Background

Former Resistance fighter turned filmmaker Jean-Pierre Melville (real name: Jean-Pierre Grumbach, 1917–1973) read Joseph Kessel's seminal novel about the French Resistance, *L'armée des ombres* (Charlot, Algiers, 1943), at the time of its publication and was haunted by its authenticity and evocative power. Twenty-five years later, when Melville finally managed to adapt Kessel's book to the screen, he created a tense, somber noir masterpiece of epic length that is vividly naturalistic, yet rife with ambiguity and infused with a tragic sense of futility.

Production

Generously budgeted at 8,175,000 francs, *Army of Shadows* was filmed at Boulogne Studios in the Boulogne-Billancourt district, a Paris suburb, and on location in Nice and various other sites in Paris. Shot in color by world-class cinematographer Pierre Lhomme, *Army of Shadows* was brilliantly edited by Françoise Bonnot, who won an Oscar for her work on Costa-Gavras' *Z* (1969).

Plot Summary

In October 1942 Vichy police arrest Philippe Gerbier (Lino Ventura), a civil engineer and the head of a Resistance cell. He is imprisoned in a concentration camp and then moved to Gestapo headquarters at the Hôtel Majestic in Paris for interrogation, where he makes a daring escape by killing a guard. Gerbier travels to Marseilles where he and three of his men—Félix Lepercq (Paul Crauchet), Guillaume Vermersch, aka "Le Bison" (Christian Barbier), and Claude Ullmann, aka "Le Masque" (Claude Mann)—are forced to kill one of their own members, Paul Dounat (Alain Libolt), for having betrayed Gerbier. The men brutally strangle the young agent. Thereafter Lepercq recruits an old friend in a bar, a former pilot named Jean-François Jardie (Jean-Pierre Cassel). On his initial mission to Paris, Jardie meets Mathilde (Simone Signoret), a bourgeois housewife who is actually one of Gerbier's key operatives. Gerbier then travels to the Free French headquarters in London in a British submarine. En route, Gerbier meets Luc Jardie, a leader in the Resistance—a fact unknown to his brother, Jean-François. Once in London, Gerbier sets up a network of support for the resistance, but after discovering that the Gestapo has taken Lepercq to a Gestapo prison in Leon, he ends his trip and returns to France. Mathilde forms a plan to save Lepercq and shares it with Jean-François Jardie. As a result, Jean-Francois sends an anonymous letter to the Gestapo turning himself in to get close to Lepercq. The two become cellmates and sustain unbearable wounds from torture. Disguised as a German nurse and two Wehrmacht soldiers, Mathilde, Le Masque, and Le Bison use forged papers to get Lepercq transferred, but their scheme fails when Lepercq is deemed unfit to be moved. Jean-François takes pity on Lepercq and supplies him with his single cyanide pill. Despite Mathilde begging him to flee to London, Gerbier is captured in a raid and handed over to the Germans. Mathilde's team rescues Gerbier at the last moment, before execution. He then isolates himself in a farmhouse in the countryside. Luc Jardie asks his advice following the arrest of Mathilde, but goes into hiding when Le Masque and Le Bison arrive. Gerbier orders Mathilde's execution but Le Bison refuses. Jardie emerges and convinces Le Bison that Mathilde is incapable of suicide; they must kill her. Jardie and his team find Mathilde in Paris and Le Bison kills her. The film ends with intertitles that confirm the fate of the four main characters. All are either dead via suicide or eliminated by the Nazis.

Reception

At the time of its initial release in France (12 September 1969), *Army of Shadows* did fairly well at the box office, but France's leading (neo-Marxist) film journals, *Positif* and *Cahiers du cinéma*, denounced the film as a reactionary Gaullist nostalgia piece, an inaccurate characterization and somewhat beside the point, insofar as de Gaulle had resigned the presidency of France six months earlier, after a decade in office. *Army of Shadows* did not see theatrical release in the United States until 37 years later. In 1996 *Cahiers du cinéma* published *Le Cinéma selon Melville*, a reappraisal of Melville's work by Rui Nogueira that led to a painstaking digital restoration at the Eclair Laboratories in Paris in 2004 by StudioCanal's Béatrice Valbin-Constant under the supervision of the film's original cinematographer, Pierre Lhomme. Released by Rialto Pictures in 2006, the film won almost universal critical acclaim in the United States and appeared in many critics' annual top 10 lists.

Reel History Versus Real History

In Kessel's novel, much of the action is based on real events, but almost all the characters in *Army of Shadows* are composites of real people, which was necessary camouflage, as the war was still raging when the book was published and identities had to be protected. A faithful adaptation of the novel, Melville's film also disguises the real persons involved. For example, Luc Jardie is based on Jean Moulin (1899–1943), a nationally recognized hero of the Resistance who died at the hands of the Gestapo. Mathilde, Simone Signoret's character, is a composite of three real-life Resistance members: Lucie Bernard Aubrac (1912–2007), Dominique Persky Desanti (1920–2011), and Signoret's makeup artist, Maud Begon. Apart from these devices, Melville's film captures the aura of isolation, paranoia, and secrecy that is pervasive in any clandestine war.

ATTACK! (1956)

Synopsis

Attack! is an American war drama set in Europe during the final months of World War II. Adapted by James Poe from Norman Brooks's 1954 play, *Fragile Fox*, directed by Robert Aldrich and starring Jack Palance, Eddie Albert, Lee Marvin, William Smithers, Robert Strauss, Richard Jaeckel, Buddy Ebsen, and Peter van Eyck, the film recounts the story of a frontline combat unit led by a cowardly captain (Albert) who clashes with a tougher subordinate (Palance) over the fate of their rifle company in a combat situation.

Background

Keen to make a WWII movie, independent director-producer Robert Aldrich (*Kiss Me, Deadly*) tried but failed to secure the rights for Irwin Shaw's *The Young Lions* (directed by Edward Dmytryk for 20th Century Fox in 1958) and Norman Mailer's *The Naked and the Dead* (directed by Raoul Walsh for Warner Bros., also in 1958). Aldrich did obtain the rights to Norman Brooks's controversial Broadway play, *Fragile Fox* (1954), a work he pronounced "ahead of its time, in terms of being anti-war, anti-military" (Arnold and Miller, 2004). What Aldrich saw as strengths, the U.S. Department of Defense (DOD) found unacceptable after vetting James Poe's script, which revolves around a combat unit jeopardized by a cowardly officer during the Battle of the Bulge. Anxious to uphold American military prestige in the depths of the Cold War, the DOD refused to loan Aldrich U.S. Army equipment and soldiers as extras—and even refused to let him use stock U.S. Signal Corps combat footage. Frustrated but undaunted, Aldrich bought a tank for $1,000, rented another one from 20th Century Fox, and worked with a small cast of 19 actors (all of them WWII veterans) to represent a 100-man company of infantry.

Production

An independent production that ultimately cost $810,000 (mostly funded by bank loans but $35,000 in budget overruns were covered by United Artists), *Attack!* was shot in 25 working days (16 January–15 February 1956) at RKO-Pathé and Universal Studios, Universal's "Little Europe" backlot, and at Albertson (aka Russell) Ranch in Triunfo, northwest of Los Angeles. The film's modest budget and outlier status is evident in its shaky production values. The two tanks used in *Attack!* are conspicuously poor imitations of German panzers, the combat action is less than convincing, and aside from some fake snow, the mise-en-scène looks suspiciously warm and dry—nothing like the Ardennes in the bitter cold, fog, and heavy snow that prevailed in the winter of 1944–1945. Fortunately, a taut script and fine, though sometimes strident acting more than compensate for shaky production values. Ironically, Eddie Albert, who plays the cowardly Erskine Cooney, was considered a true war hero and was awarded the Bronze Star with Combat "V." During his tenure as pilot of a Coast Guard landing craft, Albert saved 47 stranded Marines and oversaw the rescue of 30 other Marines who were enduring enemy fire.

Plot Summary

Fragile Fox is a U.S. Army rifle company occupying a town in Belgium near the frontline in 1944. They are "led" by Capt. Erskine Cooney (Eddie Albert), a conniving coward who freezes under fire. Cooney's position is the result of a kindness paid by battalion commander Lt. Col. Clyde Bartlett (Lee Marvin), a longtime friend of the Cooney family. Cooney's ineptitude is causing morale problems and aggravating Platoon Leader Lt. Joe Costa (Jack Palance), a brave and resourceful combat soldier respected by his men. Cooney's capable executive officer, Lt. Harold Woodruff (William Smithers), struggles to keep the peace between Cooney and Costa while he tries to get Cooney reassigned to a rear echelon desk job. When the Germans initiate the Battle of the Bulge, Cooney is ordered to take the town of

La Nelle. Without knowing the whereabouts of the German soldiers, Cooney refuses to commit the whole company to a coordinated attack and orders Costa to lead a reconnaissance probe over open ground. Costa agrees as long as he is promised reinforcements if his men are fired upon. As they approach La Nelle, a dug-in SS unit opens fire on Costa's platoon. With most of his men killed or wounded, Costa and his fellow survivors seek shelter in a farmhouse. Costa calls for reinforcements but Cooney panics, ignores Woodruff's pleas, and turns to drink. When panzers appear, Costa and his men are forced to retreat. Costa tells Woodruff over the radio to warn Cooney that he's "coming back!" Costa goes missing, but almost all other soldiers make it back to base. The men are not afraid to show their displeasure: Bernstein (Robert Strauss) spits at Cooney's feet and Sgt. Tolliver (Buddy Ebsen) refuses to drink with him, telling him that where he comes from "We don't drink with another man unless we respect him." Woodruff and Cooney are told to hold their position, but Woodruff threatens to make a formal complaint to Gen. Parsons, the colonel's superior, over Cooney's poor decisions. A drunken, distraught Cooney tells Woodruff that his father beat him to "make a man" out of him and that Bartlett gave him his command as a favor to Cooney's father. At this point Costa suddenly reappears, determined to exact vengeance on Cooney, but a renewed German attack sends him back into combat. Costa grabs a bazooka and knocks out a German tank, only to have his arm flattened by its treads. A handful of men, including Woodruff, Sgt. Tolliver, and a wounded Pvt. Bernstein, take refuge in a basement. Costa suddenly appears, and bleeding profusely from his crushed arm, falls over and dies before he can kill Cooney. Cooney then suggests that the rest of the men surrender. When Cooney goes to leave the cellar, Woodruff shoots him and then insists that Tolliver place him under arrest. Instead, they take turns shooting Cooney to share responsibility. Bartlett arrives with reinforcements and the Germans retreat; then Woodruff is promoted to captain and given charge of Fox Company after the company claims that Cooney was killed by the enemy. Bartlett voices his plan to nominate Cooney for the Distinguished Service Cross, enraging Woodruff and causing him to accuse Bartlett of corruption. Unfazed, Bartlett reminds Woodruff that he (Woodruff) has too much to lose if he goes public. Calling his bluff, Woodruff gets on the radio to call General Parsons.

Reception

Scandalized by its subject matter, the Department of Defense banned *Attack!* from U.S. military bases, prompting Rep. Charles Melvin Price (D-Illinois), a member of the House Armed Services Committee, to charge the DOD with censorship. The American Veterans Committee, a liberal veterans organization, also denounced the military's "Pollyanna policy." A month before the film's national release Clare Booth Luce, ambassador to Italy (and a staunchly conservative Republican), caused further controversy when she boycotted that year's Venice Film Festival because *Attack!* was one of the films being featured. Her snub was repudiated by the festival jury, which bestowed the Pasinetti Award on Aldrich's film for best foreign entry. Critics and the film-going public likewise sided with Robert Aldrich. *Attack!* opened in major American cities in October 1956 to excellent reviews and solid box office returns and recouped its production costs more than twice over.

Reel History Versus Real History

The movie is fictional but its culminating incident—the deliberate killing of an army officer by fellow soldiers—has lots of historical precedent. Mutinous behavior is often associated with the Vietnam War (in the course of the war an estimated 1,000 officers and noncommissioned officers (NCOs) were "fragged," resulting in about 100 deaths and 700 injuries) but such things have, of course, occurred in all American wars. Before the United States desegregated its military in 1948, mutinies were most often racially motivated. Anti-segregation protests by African American servicemen deemed "mutinies" mostly occurred stateside during World War II at Dale Mabry Field (Florida), Fort Bragg (North Carolina), Camp Robinson (Arkansas), Camp Davis (North Carolina), Camp Lee (Virginia), Fort Dix (New Jersey), Freeman Army Field (Indiana), and other bases. Black soldiers fired on white soldiers in mutinies at Camp Claiborne (Louisiana) and Brookley Air Force Base (Alabama), and at least one mutiny occurred in a combat theater. Though it does not address the most common cause of mutiny during World War II *Attack!* does constitute a salutary move away from the knee-jerk triumphalism of wartime war films and a healthy break with Cold War ideology by daring to suggest that "The Good War" wasn't all good and that the military establishment mirrors the injustices of society as a whole—a theme explored with great efficacy by Stanley Kubrick's WWI-era *Paths of Glory* (1957).

BALLAD OF A SOLDIER [RUSSIAN: *BALLADA O SOLDATE*] (1959)

Synopsis

Ballad of a Soldier is a Soviet war film directed by Grigori Chukhray and starring Vladimir Ivashov and Zhanna Prokhorenko. Set during World War II, the film is about the adventures of Alexei Skvortsov (Ivashov), a 19-year-old Red Army soldier who travels home from the front on a six-day leave to reunite with his mother and repair the roof of their homestead—his reward for knocking out two Nazi panzers.

Background

Drafted into the Soviet Army in 1939, Grigor Chukhray (1921–2001) initially served as a signalman with the 134th Rifle Division. Soon after Nazi Germany invaded the USSR in the summer of 1941, Chukhray volunteered to join an airborne unit. Thereafter he participated in numerous battles, including the defense of Stalingrad. He was wounded four times, much decorated, and eventually promoted to lieutenant. After the war, Chukhray studied filmmaking at the All-Union State Institute of Cinematography (now known as the Gerasimov Institute) in Moscow; joined the state studio, Mosfilm, in 1955; and made *The Forty-First* (1956), a well-received film adaptation of Boris Lavrenyov's 1926 anti-Stalinist novel. Chukhray then drew on his own war experiences to co-write (with Valentin Yezhov) and direct *Ballad of a Soldier*, his moving tribute to the estimated 8.7 million Soviet soldiers killed in World War II.

Production

Chukhray originally wanted to make a film about the Battle of Stalingrad but he was unable to secure funding and the army's help, so he sought to make *Ballad of a Soldier* instead. When he presented his script to Alexander S. Federov, head of production at the Cinematography Council, for state approval in 1957, Chukhray met with a cool reception. The screenplay centered on the six-day leave of a young soldier who goes home to repair the roof on the family homestead before returning to the front. Federov found the story "trifling" and advised Chukhray not to produce the film. Soon thereafter, Soviet premier Nikita Khrushchev delivered a series of nationalistic speeches (collected and published on 28 August 1957 as *For Close Ties between Literature and Art and the Life of the People*). In the words of Chukhray himself, Khrushchev urged Soviet artists to make accessible patriotic art reflecting "the contemporary relevance and beauty of Russia." Though the Arts Council found *Ballad of a Soldier* insufficiently patriotic, it allowed Chukhray to proceed with the film's production, "but without much enthusiasm" and on a slim budget. Following the lead of the cultural commissars, camerawoman Era Saveleyev organized members of the crew in refusing to work on the film because it contradicted Khrushchev's vaunted "socialist realism." Unfazed, Chukhray replaced Saveleyev with Vladimir Nikolayev, hired a new crew, and proceeded to make the film, which starred two young, unknown actors in the lead roles.

Plot Summary

A peasant woman wanders through her village and glances down a dirt road while a voice-over informs viewers that the woman's son was killed during the war and buried far from his home. Cut to the battlefront as a scared 19-year-old private named Alexei Nikolayevich Skvortsov (Vladimir Ivashov) singlehandedly knocks out two German panzers with a PTRS-41 anti-tank rifle. His commanding general (Nikolay Kryuchkov) tries to award him a medal, but Alyosha requests a visit to his mother and their homestead, which is in need of repairs. Alyosha is allowed a six-day reprieve and journeys home: a trip that reveals to him the utter devastation caused by the war. When Alyosha tries to gain passage on an army supply train, he is stopped by Gavrilkin (Alexandr Kuznetsov), a sentry. Alyosha bribes Gavrilkin with a can of beef and is allowed to board the freight car. A young woman named Shura (Zhanna Prokhorenko) sneaks on to the train as well, but the sight of Alyosha terrifies her and Alyosha has to stop her from trying to jump off the speeding train. She eventually reveals that she is heading to visit her fiancé, a pilot who has been hospitalized. Soon Shura loses her fear and warms up to Alyosha, but Gavrilkin discovers her, initiating another bribe from Alyosha. Surprisingly, when the lieutenant (Yevgeny Teterin) becomes aware of the stowaways, he allows them to remain on the train and even goes so far as to force Gavrilkin to return his bribe. At one stop, when Alyosha disembarks for water, the train moves on without him on board. A female trucker (Valentina Telegrina) gives him a ride to the next station, but he arrives to find that he has already missed the train. However, Shura is at the station, waiting for him. After completing an errand for a friend, Shura and Alyosha part ways. During their goodbyes, Shura reveals that she has been lying—she has no other man to visit. As his train pulls away, Alyosha realized that Shura's confession was one of love. His train is then halted by a bombed bridge and subsequently attacked by German Stuka dive-bombers. In desperation, Alyosha takes a raft across the river and hitches a ride home to his village of Sosnovka. Alyosha is only able to visit with his dear mother for a few moments before he has to return to the frontlines. His mother is determined to wait for him to return once again. A voice-over confirms that although he had potential, Alyosha will always be remembered, simply, as a Russian soldier and nothing more.

Reception

Vladimir Surin, director-general of Mosfilm, didn't like *Ballad of a Soldier* because it depicted the Soviet Army without the usual heroic solemnity, showed a woman being unfaithful to her husband, and most egregiously, killed off its hero: narrative sins that would have been met with opprobrium by Hollywood as well. Influential film director Sergei Gerasimov also panned the film in *Pravda*, though he hadn't seen it. Written off as a failed effort, *Ballad of a Soldier* was released, but not in large cities; exhibition was confined to farmers' collectives and workers' clubs in the countryside. Then something unexpected happened. Alexei Adzhubei, *Pravda*'s editor-in-chief (and Khrushchev's son-in-law), administered a nationwide questionnaire asking "Which recent film have you liked best?" From all over the hinterlands the surprising answer was *Ballad of a Soldier*. The film's popularity with ordinary folk prompted an official reassessment. Gerasimov finally saw the film and praised it extravagantly. Khrushchev was also shown the film, liked it, and ordered that it be entered into competition at the 1960 Cannes Film Festival, where it won a special prize for its "high humanism and outstanding quality." Released in the West, *Ballad of a Soldier* went on to receive Oscar and BAFTA nominations and the praise of New York film critics for its evocation of genuine emotion and its gentle lyricism.

Reel History Versus Real History

Grigory Chukhray drew on his own extensive experiences in the war to make *Ballad of a Soldier* an inarguably authentic rendition of life at and behind the frontlines. The film's aura of authenticity is only marred by the obviously phony-looking air attack on the train near the movie's end that was the best Chukhray could do on the paltry production budget he was allotted. He requested supplementary funds to reshoot the scene but was turned down on the grounds that the film would probably not be successful anyway.

BATTLE OF ALGIERS, THE [ITALIAN: *LA BATTAGLIA DI ALGERI*] (1966)

Synopsis

The Battle of Algiers is an Italian-Algerian war film co-written and directed by Gillo Pontecorvo and starring Jean Martin and Saadi Yacef. Shot in mock cinema vérité style on location in Algiers and scored by Ennio Morricone, the film recounts the so-called Battle of Algiers during the Algerian War (1954–1962) of independence against the French colonialist government in North Africa.

Background

Though it ended in military stalemate, the Algerian War of Independence (1954–1962) resulted in political victory for Algeria's nationalist movement, Front de Libération Nationale (FLN); after 132 years of French colonial rule, Algeria became a sovereign nation on 2 July 1962. Earlier that year Italian film director Gillo Pontecorvo and screenwriter Franco Solinas, equipped with fake journalists' credentials, traveled to Algiers to meet with FLN leaders and do research for a film on the war. Solinas subsequently wrote "Parà": a script developed with Paul Newman in mind about a former French paratrooper covering the conflict as a journalist who grows disillusioned with his country's brutal counterinsurgency tactics. Two years later Salah Baazi, an FLN official, met with Pontecorvo and Solinas in Italy to further pursue their Algerian War film project. Baazi subsequently rejected "Parà" as not sufficiently centered on the Algerian people and countered with a script by Saadi Yacef, a former FLN military commander, based on Yacef's own book (*Souvenirs de la Bataille d'Alger* [*Memories of the Battle of Algiers*] 1962) that details a year-long episode in the war known as the "Battle of Algiers" (1957–1958). Pontecorvo found Yacef's script "sickeningly propagandistic" so he and Solinas set out to write an entirely new screenplay, closely based on true events but striving for a more even-handed treatment that avoided partisan extremes in either the French or Algerian direction. The Algerians subsidized six months of research and location scouting in Algiers, during which Pontecorvo and Solinas interviewed hundreds of eyewitnesses. They also visited Paris, studied documents and newsreels, and interviewed French army veterans who had served in Algiers. Five major revisions of the script were produced before both sides were satisfied. By 1965 Pontecorvo had forged a co-production deal between Casbah Films, an Algerian company co-owned by Yacef and the state, and Igor Film, an Italian firm owned by Antonio Musu, Pontecorvo's production manager on his previous film, *Kapò* (1960).

Production

Influenced by Italian neorealism, Pontecorvo and his cinematographer, Marcello Gatti, took pains to mimic the raw immediacy of newsreel and Direct Cinema documentaries. Using techniques already perfected during the shooting of his previous film, *Kapò* (1960), they shot in black and white, with 16-mm handheld cameras, in natural light. To simulate the look of newsreel footage shot hastily in uncontrolled conditions—a high level of graininess and image contrast—Gatti and Pontecorvo made new negatives from the positive images. They then made new, rougher positive prints from those that were then blown up to 35 mm. As for actors, Pontecorvo mostly cast Algerian Arabs or Kabyles (a Berber ethnic group native to Kabylia in northern Algeria) who had no professional acting experience. The only professional actor in the film was Jean Martin, who played Col. Mathieu. A French actor who had worked mostly in theater, Martin had fought with the Maquis in World War II and had been a paratrooper during the Indochina War, military credentials that lent his performance a high degree of authenticity.

Plot Summary

The film opens in Algiers in 1957. A group of French troops have completed a round of torture during their interrogation of an Algerian prisoner. The interrogation has proved successful, and the troops travel to an address given up by the tortured Algerian. One of the four key leaders of the FLN and his fellow crew members are masked by a fake wall. Col. Mathieu (Jean Martin) demands that the leader, Ali la Pointe, emerge from his hiding place, as he is the only one of the leaders still alive. Next we see a flashback to Algiers in 1954; the National Liberation Front (FLN) calls its members to take arms and fight for independence. Ali la Pointe, aka Ali

Omar (Brahim Haggiag), a petty criminal with a lengthy record, is arrested. Five months later, la Pointe leaves prison and joins the battle for independence. The FLN tasks him with an assassination assignment: to kill a French cop obtaining information about the FLN from an Algerian informant. La Pointe is armed with a gun at the last moment, but attempting to fire the weapon he finds that nothing happens. In a panic, la Pointe takes down the police officer and flees the scene. Returning to the FLN, la Pointe angrily asks why he was set up to fail. Djafar (Yacef Saadi) reveals that this is a hazing ritual for new recruits to confirm that they will actually fire a weapon when ordered to and remain loyal to the FLN. The FLN, led in part by la Pointe, spends the next several months exercising its power; banning alcohol, drugs, and prostitution, attacking police stations; bombing French civilians; and inciting an organized retaliation effort by French officials. By 10 January 1957, French troops enter Algiers with the aim of wiping out the FLN. Jean Charrot serves as inspector general and organizes the battle against FLN operatives while General Carelle maintains order in Algiers. Lt. Col. Philippe Matthieu is ordered to lead the daily offensives against the FLN. Matthieu's plan is straightforward: ebb the flow of FLN attacks by apprehending FLN members, torturing them for names, and then using each bit of information gathered to create a full organizational chart. Once they determine the hierarchy, then their troops can move to kill the FLN leaders. A few weeks later, a general strike occurs in Algiers. La Point is informed that those striking would incur the wrath of the French, who were looking to round up agitators. Four days into the strike, French soldiers begin capturing, torturing, and interrogating Algerians suspected of involvement with the FLN. As a result, the organizational chart begins to take shape. By February, Matthieu has zeroed in on the four main leaders of the movement: Si Murad, Ramel, Jaffar, and Ali La Pointe. He commands that the four men be apprehended and jailed. Jaffar, hearing of the French plans to round up FNL leadership, suggests that he and his fellow leaders split up. Several factions of their movement are dead or out of contact, so they are forced to build up the fourth section and make plans to reorganize. The FLN continue to wreak havoc, detonating a bomb at a race track and leaving numerous French civilians dead or wounded. By March, French reporters demand answers from a now-captive Mr. Ben M'Hidi. The reporters also question Col. Matthieu regarding his torture techniques employed in Algiers. The colonel, trying to save face, lies and says that they are not torturing the Algerians, despite the fact that French soldiers are using water torture, electric shocks, and blow torch burns to the skin and are hanging hog-tied people upside-down. The Algerians respond with drive-by shootings of French civilians on the street. In late summer, Ramel and Si Murad are apprehended, and by early fall, French forces corner Jaffar and blow up a building in order to finalize his death. La Pointe, now the final FNL leader still alive, joins with a few other FNL supporters to organize the bombing of several French locations. The flashback ends and brings viewers back to the present. Colonel Matthieu and his squadron order la Pointe and his supporters to abandon their hiding place. The group refuses to yield their position, and the French forces begin to set up explosive devices. La Pointe is given a final chance to surrender, but he will not turn himself in. As a result, the French bombs are set off and the building housing la Pointe is brought to the ground. La Pointe and his followers are all killed. This violence is followed by two years of peace in Algiers, until more fighting breaks out in the mountains in winter of 1960. 21 December 1960 marks the final day of demonstrations, and by July 1962, after two more years of struggle, the Algerian nation is born.

Reception

The Battle of Algiers had its premiere at the Venice Film Festival on 31 August 1966 (where it won the Golden Lion) and its premiere in Algiers on 27 October 1966. It was first screened in the Unites States on 20 September 1967. The film was initially banned in France as "incendiary"; it wasn't shown until October 1970 and wasn't screened in Spain until 1978, three years after Francisco Franco's death. A restored version was released in Italy in April 1999, and then extended versions were released in Hong Kong (May 2000) and in the UK (December 2003). The *Battle of Algiers* was re-released in the United States on 9 January 2004 and screened at the Cannes Film Festival, 15 May 2004. For its 50th anniversary, a digitally restored version was screened at the Venice Film Festival, then at the Toronto and New York film festivals. There are no accurate records of lifetime box office proceeds, but they have been modest.

Reel History Versus Real History

Historians are in general agreement that *The Battle of Algiers* is true to history in the chronology and most of its particulars of the events it depicts. One commentator, British historian-screenwriter Alex von Tunzelmann, calls the film "a masterpiece of historical accuracy" and notes that the principal characters are all based on real people (though some are composites). Tunzelmann also observes that the "film's inclusion of female and underage militants, while apparently shocking to many viewers, is accurate. If anything, women like Zohra Drif, Samia Lakhdari, Djamila Bouhired and Hassiba Ben Bouali played a more significant role than the film allows them" (von Tunzelmann, 2009). British journalist Martin Evans offers a dissenting opinion. He begins by pointing out that calling the conflict in Algiers a "battle" is a misnomer: "This was not urban warfare on a grand scale like Stalingrad in 1942 or even the Irish Easter uprising of 1916. There was no sustained street-to-street combat. Rather the confrontation took the form of short bursts of fighting at close quarters, interspersed with the bombing of civilians on the FLN side and mass round-ups and torture on the French side." Although Evans concedes that "much of the film's narrative follows the facts in a brutally honest manner," he charges that it "also diverges from the facts" and elides "the role of the Algerian Communists, who supplied the bomb making expertise to the FLN, or the rival MNA [Mouvement National Algérien/Algerian People's Party], still an important political force in early 1957. Equally, the bitter divisions within the FLN are ignored, as in the case of Abbane Ramdane who is absent as an historical figure. Instead Pontecorvo presents the war uniquely in terms of the FLN against the French paratroopers" (Evans, 2012).

BATTLEGROUND (1949)

Synopsis

Scripted by WWII combat veteran Robert Pirosh; directed by William Wellman; and starring Van Johnson, John Hodiak, James Whitmore, Ricardo Montalbán, and George Murphy, *Battleground* is an American war film about a company of the 327th Glider Infantry Regiment, 101st Airborne Division, surrounded by German forces and holding out at Bastogne during the Battle of the Bulge in World War II.

Background

Robert Pirosh (1910–1989), Hollywood writer and producer and, later, creator of the popular 1960s *Combat!* TV series, was uniquely qualified to make *Battleground*, a film about the Siege of Bastogne (20–27 December 1944) during the Battle of the Bulge. Pirosh served in World War II as a master sergeant with the 35th Infantry Division, saw action in the Ardennes and Rhineland campaigns, and was awarded a Bronze Star. During the Battle of the Bulge Pirosh led a patrol into Bastogne to help relieve surrounded American forces there. After the war he used material from his wartime journal to develop a screenplay that presented Bastogne from the infantryman's point of view, but he had to wait a few years before the war (film)-weary public was ready for a postwar combat film. *Battleground* became an RKO property in 1947 but was shelved by studio owner Howard Hughes, a decision that caused production head Dore Schary to resign. When Schary went to MGM, he purchased the rights to the script from RKO, over the objections of Louis B. Mayer, who believed that the public was tired of war films. MGM signed Robert Taylor, Keenan Wynn, and John Hodiak, and the project was budgeted at $2 million. Twenty veterans of the 101st were hired to train the actors and to appear in the film as extras. Lt. Col. Harry Kinnard, deputy divisional commander of the 101st at Bastogne, was hired on as the film's technical advisor. Director William Wellman put the cast through two weeks of military training, but Robert Taylor, a former navy officer, dropped out, and Van Johnson replaced him.

Production

Battleground was shot in 44 days between 5 April and 3 June 1949 at several sets: a replica of Bastogne, refashioned from an Italian village set built on a United Artists (UA) studio backlot for *The Story of G.I. Joe* (1944); a faux pine forest in the Ardennes, built on a UA sound stage using 528 real trees; and on location in northern California, Oregon, and at Fort Lewis, near Tacoma, Washington, which was used for the tank sequence showing the relief of the 101st Airborne by Patton's Third Army. Shooting went faster than anticipated, taking 20 fewer days than planned. This time savings was in part due to Schary's creative filming methods—he often processed film right after it was shot, then had scenes cut together so that they were available for preview two days after being shot. The film came in almost $100,000 under budget.

Plot Summary

In December 1944, new replacements Jim Layton (Marshall Thompson) and William J. Hooper (Scotty Beckett) are dispensed to different companies in the 327th Glider Infantry Regiment, 101st Airborne Division. Holley (Van Johnson) returns to his unit after recovering from an injury. The squadron is set to go on leave, but is instead sent to the frontlines to fight off German forces in the Ardennes Forest. After stopping for a night in Bastogne, Belgium, Sgt. Kinnie (James Whitmore) orders his men to settle in at multiple locations at the town borders. While guarding a roadblock during the night, Holley, Layton, and "Kipp" Kippton (Douglas Fowley) are surprised by German soldiers who are dressed as American G.I.s. The German soldiers blow up a bridge. A snowstorm greets the squad the next morning. Roderigues (Ricardo Montalbán) delights in the snow, though a fellow soldier, "Pop" Stazak (George Murphy), remains unfazed. Layton discovers that his friend Hooper has been killed by German mortar rounds, and Kinnie sounds the alarm about the German infiltration. A patrol heads out—Holley, Roderigues, and Jarvess (John Hodiak)—to comb through the woods, but before they get far, the Germans attack and the platoon panics. Bettis (Richard Jaeckel) runs for cover, Holley's patrol battles against the infiltrators, and Roderigues is injured in the firefight, left unable to walk. Holley tries to hide Roderigues beneath a jeep while the men continue to ward off the German fire, but Roderigues freezes to death before his platoon can retrieve him. Two soldiers are sent off to a field hospital, and Holley is named the new squadron leader along with Layton. Pop Stazak is grouped with Hansan (Herbert Anderson). The squadron discovers, by reading *Stars and Stripes*, that theirs is a "heroic stand," and Kippton confirms that the 101st is fully surrounded. The 3rd Platoon falls victim to an attack at first light, and as they are overwhelmed, Hansan sustains an injury and Holley flees the scene in panic. After facing his embarrassment at being cowardly in front of his inferiors, Holley counterattacks. Later, while on guard duty, the squad meets a group of German soldiers who have arrived beneath a "flag of truce" to present terms of surrender to Brigadier General Anthony McAuliffe. McAuliffe shocks and confuses the Germans with his famous reply, "Nuts!" Foggy weather grounds Allied transport aircraft, and the squad is short of supplies. That night, Luftwaffe planes bomb Bastogne and Denise is killed. The "walking wounded," Hansan included, are summoned to the frontlines in a last-ditch effort to defend the town. Bettis lets fear get the better of him and delays his return, dooming himself to the cruel fate of a bomb destroying the house he is staying in. The fog finally lifts, and Allied fighters attack the Germans, enabling the 101st to hold. When the siege lifts, Kinnie leads the successful survivors toward a well-deserved respite from the lines. The film ends with a group of fresh troops marching in to replace those going on leave, with the war veterans chanting the refrain from "Jody" as they leave the battleground.

Reception

Battleground went into general domestic release on 20 January 1950—just five years after the events it depicted. Contrary to Louis B. Mayer's dour predictions, the movie made a healthy profit and won an Oscar nomination for Best Picture. Critical notices were mixed but mostly positive. Bosley Crowther praised *Battleground* as "a smashing pictorial re-creation of the way that this last [war was] for the dirty and frightened foot-soldier who got caught in a filthy deal. Here is the unadorned image of the misery, the agony, the grief and the still irrepressible humor and dauntless mockery of the American GI" (Crowther, 1949). On the other hand, John McCarten found the movie "constantly reiterating the idiosyncrasies of its characters," a tendency that rendered the film "pretty monotonous" in McCarten's view, but he also noted that "there are plenty of rousing battle scenes" (McCarten, 1949).

Reel History Versus Real History

Although the film is a fictionalized and very narrowly focused version of the siege of Bastogne, it is highly accurate with one major exception. There were no Germans disguised as American soldiers around Bastogne. *Unternehmen Greif* (Operation Griffin), as it was designated, only operated in front of the 6th SS Panzer Army at the start of the German offensive, many miles to the north. Another minor but deliberate inaccuracy: the 327th Glider Infantry Regiment did not have an Item Company (glider regiments consisted of two battalions, with each battalion having four companies, A-D and E-H). The film's producers created a fictitious unit to allow for artistic license and not have veterans object to inaccuracies.

BEASTS OF NO NATION (2015)

Synopsis

Beasts of No Nation is an American war drama written, co-produced, and directed by Cary Joji Fukunaga (who also acted as the film's cinematographer). Based on the 2005 novel of the same title by Uzodinma Iweala, the film—shot in Ghana and starring Idris Elba, Abraham Attah, Ama K. Abebrese, Grace Nortey, David Dontoh, and Opeyemi Fagbohungbe—is about a young boy who becomes a child soldier in a genocidal war wracking his unnamed country in West Africa.

Background

While he was an undergraduate at UCal Santa Cruz in the late 1990s filmmaker Cary Joji Fukunaga (*True Detective*) began studying the plight of child soldiers involved in civil wars in Africa in an effort to develop a film script on the subject. After six years of research, including a solo trip to Sierra Leone in 2003, Fukunaga discovered Uzodinma Iweala's novel, *Beasts of No Nation* (2005) and realized he had found the story vehicle for which he had been searching. Focus Features optioned the rights to Iweala's book for Fukunaga in early 2006, and he wrote the first draft of a screen adaptation toward the end of that year, using Joseph Campbell's 12 Stages of The Hero's Journey as his narrative template (an approach advocated in a widely circulated development memo by Christopher Vogler, subsequently turned into a book entitled *The Writer's Journey: Mythic Structure For Writers*, 2007). Eight years would pass before Fukunaga had the time and money to turn his script into a film. Funding was put together from various sources: Red Crown Productions,

Primary Productions, Parliament of Owls, Participant Media, and Mammoth Entertainment. Originally budgeted at $4.3 million, *Beasts of No Nation* ultimately came in at $6 million.

Production

Encouraged by producers to shoot his film in South Africa, which has tax incentives and a well-established filmmaking infrastructure, Cary Fukunaga insisted on shooting in Ghana to achieve greater verisimilitude. Securing permissions from the Ghanaian military, transporting three dozen crew members to remote locations (Koforidua and Ezile Bay) in Eastern Ghana and keeping them fed and housed, finding child actors to play his boy soldiers all proved to be enormous logistical challenges that Fukunaga was able to meet, despite battling monsoon rains, contracting malaria, having equipment stolen and extras imprisoned—and even having one of his co-stars, Idris Elba, narrowly escape death after accidently falling off a cliff.

Plot Summary

A young boy named Agu (Abraham Attah) lives in a small village in West Africa with his parents, older brother, and two younger siblings in an unnamed country overtaken by civil war. When rebels associated with the military approach Agu's village, terrified villagers flee to the country's capital. Agu's father (Kobina Amissa-Sam) is able to arrange safe transport for his wife (Ama K. Abebrese) and their youngest child (Vera Nyarkoah Antwi), but he has to stay behind himself with Agu and his eldest son (Francis Weddey). Government forces rout the rebels in fighting at Agu's village. They then round up the remaining villagers as suspected rebels. Just before being shot, Agu's father tells his sons to run. The two boys try to escape into the jungle, but Agu's brother is killed. Agu is eventually dragooned into a rebel faction known as the NDF. The Commandant (Idris Elba), Agu's battalion commander, takes Agu under his wing, and Agu befriends another NDF child soldier, a mute boy named Strika (Emmanuel Nii Adom Quaye). After being raped by the Commandant, Agu is comforted by Strika, also a rape victim. An older soldier named Preacher (Teibu Owusu Achcampong) gives Agu a hallucinogen called "brown-brown." Agu and Strika participate in a series of bloody battles as the battalion captures several villages and kills scores of innocent men, women, and children—"success" that earns them a summons to NDF headquarters to meet the Supreme Commander, Dada Goodblood (Jude Akuwudike). The soldiers (except for Agu and Strika) spend the night at a brothel, and one of the prostitutes shoots the lieutenant, badly wounding him. In retaliation, the Commandant and his followers kill the women and abandon the city to the battalion. Now on the run from their own faction, as well as the United Nations (UN) and government forces, the battalion is decimated by airstrikes and Strika is killed in an ambush. The remnants of the battalion shelter at a gold mine. After the ammunition runs out, Preacher, now the Commandant's lieutenant, calls for the soldiers to surrender to the UN. The Commandant initially refuses, but Agu persuades him to relent.

The soldiers surrender and are taken into custody by UN troops, leaving the Commandant alone and raving. Afterwards, the battalion's boy soldiers are sent to a missionary school in a safe area. Haunted by what he has done and experienced, Agu shies away from the other children, who are carefree and innocent. Eventually Agu confesses to Amy, the school's counselor (Gifty Mawena Sossavi), that he has seen and done "terrible things" and is afraid she will think he is "some sort of beast or a devil," but also says that he once had a family and that he was loved. In the final scene Agu decides to join the other boys as they swim and play in the ocean.

Reception

After paying $12 million for the movie's distribution rights, Netflix simultaneously released *Beasts of No Nation* on its streaming platform and in selected theaters the weekend of 17–18 October 2015. The theatrical release was to allow the film to qualify for Oscar nominations, but it received none (though it did earn many other awards, including an Independent Spirit Award). The movie also bombed at the box office, earning only $90,777 for a two-week run in 31 theaters, a not-unexpected result insofar as Netflix subscribers could more conveniently watch it at home—and many did; Netflix subsequently reported 3 million views among its 50 million members. For the most part, *Beasts* met with critical acclaim, with reviewers describing the film as "chilling," "ultra-violent," and "hard to watch" but also "honest," "eye-opening," and "powerful." Some critics, however, found the movie too relentlessly graphic while lacking in real depth: "Cary Joji Fukunaga's artistry registers less as psychological imprint than as a measure of his professional bona fides" (Gonzalez, 2015). Others noted that the film's power tends to dissipate by its third act: "We march through pillage and rape, and the Commandant tightens his power through abuse of his youthful charges; meanwhile, the film itself, supped full of horrors, begins to sicken and dwindle" (Lane, 2005).

Reel History Versus Real History

Canadian Lt. Gen. Romeo Dellaire, former commander of the UN Assistance Mission for Rwanda (UNAMIR) during its genocidal civil war in 1994, judged *Beasts of No Nation* too simplistic: "It's the classic *Blood Diamond* story of disaster in Africa but it doesn't give an analysis of the situation. There was a lot missing. I'm not against the film. Cinema is an extraordinary tool [but] I think the film could have done more to show the indoctrination of the children, and the psychological battles. It needs to be more nuanced than just African kids with AK47s" (Alexander, 2015). Helen Morton, director of advocacy for War Child, an international children's war relief agency, further notes that the movie's exclusive depiction of boy soldiers obscures another reality: "Forty per cent of child soldiers are girls, and few films ever portray that. Girls are combatants—and in growing numbers. They are forced to do things that are beyond even a child's imagination, and often recruited as sex slaves" (Alexander, 2015). A related criticism, voiced by Zeba Blay, is that the movie reinforces popular stereotypes of Africa as a monolithic "site of misery and pain" (Blay, 2015).

BENEATH HILL 60 (2010)

Synopsis

Adapted from war diaries by David Roach and directed by Jeremy Sims, *Beneath Hill 60* is an Australian war drama set during World War I. The film tells the story of the 1st Australian Tunneling Company's efforts to dig a series of tunnels underneath Hill 60 in the Ypres Salient on the Western Front in order to plant high-explosive mines meant to disrupt German defenses and aid a British offensive in 1917.

Background

Beneath Hill 60 owes its genesis to Ross J. Thomas, a mining engineer and World War I history buff from Townsville, Queensland, Australia. In 1992 Thomas chanced to discover the war diary of Capt. Oliver Holmes Woodward (1885–1966) of the 1st Australian Tunneling Company, a WWI unit that helped to plant and detonate 19 mines (totaling 447 tons of explosives) beneath German lines that opened the Battle of Messines (7–14 June 1917) in Flanders, Belgium. The resulting explosion was immense—it blew the top off Wytschaete Ridge and killed an estimated 10,000 German defenders—but did not result in a war-winning strategic advantage as was hoped; the Allies took what was left of Hill 60, but the Germans retook it a few months later. Though the Hill 60 operation was not militarily decisive, the hitherto unknown story of the tunnelers was the stuff of high drama. Thomas eventually met with documentary director-producer Bill Leimbach (*Gallipoli: The Untold Stories*) and quickly convinced him that Woodward's story was worthy of filmic treatment. Leimbach made Thomas executive producer, hired Jeremy Hartley Sims (*Last Train to Freo*) to direct a documentary, and hired David Roach (*Young Einstein*) to write a screenplay based on Woodward's diary, with additional research culled from Canberra's Australian War Memorial Archives. During the pre-production stage, the filmmakers deemed the material suitable for a feature-length docudrama. By the end of 2008 they had cast the film and raised most of what eventually became an 8.1 million AUD ($7.8 million USD) budget. Screen Australia, the government's film funding agency, furnished 81 percent of the budget, and various Townsville businesses pledged the other 19 percent and also provided key filming locations and earth-moving equipment, gratis, and the army supplied period artillery.

Production

Under the working titles *The Silence* and *The Silence Beneath*, filming in and around Townsville took place over a 40-day period (20 July–28 August 2009). A crew led by production designer Clayton Jauncey and art director Sam Hobbs transformed a sloping Townsville paddock into a section of the Western Front, complete with more than 500 meters of trenches. For logistical and safety reasons, the tunnel scenes were shot in above-ground simulated tunnels constructed in a large shed.

Plot Summary

Oliver Woodward (Brendan Cowell), a 30-year-old Australian copper miner and metallurgist, falls in love with Marjorie Moffat Waddell (Bella Heathcote), a woman 10 years his junior, but romance must wait. Under pressure to enlist, especially from Waddell's father, William (Gerald Lepkowski), Woodward takes a commission to lead the newly formed 1st Australian Tunneling Company, an auxiliary unit supporting Britain's Royal Engineers. On the Western Front, Woodward meets Frank Tiffin (Harrison Gilbertson), a young, shell-shocked Australian soldier (the underaged Tiffin initially served as a stretcher bearer, where he was given a front-row seat to the devastation of trench warfare). Woodward reassigns Tom Dwyer (Duncan Young) and Norman Morris (Gyton Grantley) to relieve Tiffin. When two German tunnelers break through into the tunnel the Allies are digging beneath the German lines, Morris and Dwyer kill the Germans but a German mine explodes, collapsing the tunnel on top of them. Morris is rescued by the other sappers but Dwyer is killed. Thereafter, Woodward is assigned the task of destroying the Red House, a German fort raining enfilade fire on the British trenches, by planting explosives beneath it. His commanding officer, Col. Wilson Rutledge (Chris Haywood), asks the work to be completed immediately. Sgt. Bill Fraser (Steve Le Marquand), Morris, and Woodward cross No Man's Land, reach the Red House, and bury the explosives beneath the building. On their way back to British lines, the soldiers realize that their wire reel isn't long enough, so Morris is forced to go ahead to grab the detonator. As they await Morris's return, the men find a fatally injured Lt. Robert Clayton (Leon Ford). Morris successfully returns with the detonator, and the Red House is blown up. The troops are called to the Belgian frontlines, and when they arrive, Tiffin, Walter, and Bacon are sprayed with German gunfire. Bacon sacrifices himself for his comrades, running ahead to distract the Germans so that Tiffin and Walter make it to the British lines. The unit continues on to Hill 60. For months, Canadian engineers have dug tunnels underneath the Messines Ridge, embedding nearly a million pounds of high explosives in the form of 21 massive mines within the soil. Woodward and his platoon are told to maintain and protect the tunnels, and Woodward engineers a drainage shaft to keep the explosives dry while also constructing diversion tunnels. Sneddon meets his fate in one of those tunnels after Rutledge orders him to enter it despite the report that Germans would soon be setting off their own explosives. The Germans discover their scheme and begin to dig toward the primary tunnel. The Australians counter with an attack tunnel and blow up the exploratory shaft minutes before they are discovered. Unfortunately, a portion of their tunnel collapses, trapping Tiffin. His comrade, Sgt. Fraser, races through the trenches to halt the explosions in the mines, but Woodward refuses his impassioned pleas; the operation is more important than a single man. Knowing full well he is killing Tiffin, Woodward sets off the mines in a massive explosion that begins the Battle of Messines. The scene shifts to Australia, where Woodward marries Marjorie in 1920 and the surviving members of the unit are there to celebrate his wedding.

Reception

After a red carpet premiere in Townsville on 15 April 2010, *Beneath Hill 60* opened nationally the next day and ultimately brought in a total of 9.6 million (AUD) ($6.8 million USD) in foreign and domestic box offices—solid returns perhaps representing a modest profit after advertising and promotion costs were deducted. The film garnered 16 AACTA Award nominations among other nominations and awards. The film did not attract much attention outside of Australia, but most of the reviews by Australian film critics were positive—although Margaret Pomerantz damned the film with faint praise: "Perhaps the tension of the situation is not exploited quite as much as one would hope but this is an ambitious project that will resonate" (Pomerantz, 2010).

Reel History Versus Real History

Closely based on Woodward's unpublished war diary and other war archive documents, *Beneath Hill 60* achieves a high degree of historical accuracy in its depiction of equipment, weapons, and uniforms; the look and feel of the trenches and tunnels; and the events depicted. It also manages to adopt a tone of quiet realism that avoids nationalistic self-congratulation (though flashbacks detailing Woodward's courtship of Marjorie Waddell slow the pace of the narrative). The film does, however, engage in considerable poetic license in its depiction of Frank Tiffin. There was a sapper named Frederick "Frank" Matterson Tiffin in the 1st Tunneling Company, but he survived the war and died an old man in 1962. Little else is known about him. In the film Tiffin evolves from frightened boy, to intrepid soldier, to martyr-hero—pure fiction designed to elicit the maximum emotional audience reaction when Woodward is forced to sacrifice him to complete the mission. Viewers watching Bill Fraser's frantic run through the trenches to try and stop the detonation will be reminded of a similar scene in Peter Weir's *Gallipoli* (1981), when Frank Dunne (Mel Gibson) runs through the trenches in a desperate, futile effort to stop a suicidal assault that will kill his best friend, Archy Hamilton (Mark Lee).

BIG RED ONE, THE (1980; RESTORED VERSION, 2004)

Synopsis

The Big Red One is an American war epic starring Lee Marvin and Mark Hamill and written and directed by Samuel Fuller, based on his own combat experiences as a soldier with the 1st Infantry Division (aka "The Big Red One"), from fighting in North Africa, through the D-Day invasion of Normandy, until Germany's surrender in May 1945.

Background

During World War II, Samuel Fuller (1912–1997) enlisted in the U.S. Army in 1942 and was assigned to the 16th Infantry Regiment, 1st Infantry Division (aka "the Big Red One"). Fuller saw combat in every major European campaign and was awarded the Bronze Star, the Silver Star, and the Purple Heart. After the war Sam Fuller became a pulp fiction writer and then a filmmaker specializing in B-movies, but making a film based on his own war experiences was never far from his mind. By 1958 he had a "Big Red One" script completed. John Wayne got wind of the project and asked Fuller if he could star in the movie, but Oscar Dystel, head of Bantam Books, encouraged Fuller to write a book instead of doing a movie. In the end Fuller did neither because he could not formulate a coherent narrative (Peary, 2012, p. 79). In 1974 director-producer Peter Bogdanovich, a close friend of Fuller's who had been hearing his war stories for years, offered to produce Fuller's "Big Red One" film and persuaded Paramount studio head Frank Yablans to option the property. Yablans paid Fuller $5,000 to write a new script. By the time Fuller had it completed, Yablans had left Paramount and been replaced by Robert Evans, who let the option lapse. Ultimately Lorimar, a new mini-studio specializing in TV production, took over the project but repeatedly scaled down its projected budget, from $12 million to just $4 million, precluding some planned location shooting in Tunisia and Yugoslavia (now Slovenia). Gene Corman, Roger Corman's brother, replaced Bogdanovich as producer. As was always Fuller's intention, U.S. Marine Corps WWII veteran Lee Marvin was hired to play the iconic lead role of the sergeant. The only other big name was Mark Hamill (*Star Wars*), who played Pvt. Griff. Robert Carradine (who also appeared in *Star Wars*) played Zab, a cigar-chomping private representing a WWII-era Fuller.

Production

Principal photography took place in the spring and summer months of 1978. Directing battle scenes with a loaded .45 pistol in his hand, Fuller would fire into the air after a take to remind his actors of the mortal gravity of combat. Castle scenes were filmed in Ireland and winter forest scenes were shot in California's Sierra Madre Mountains, but most of the film was shot at various locations in Israel, with Nazi soldiers played by Jewish extras (paid $11 per day), wearing yarmulkes under their helmets. A quarry at Rosh Ha'ayin near Tel Aviv doubled for the Kasserine Pass in Tunisia; a Roman amphitheater at Beit She'an near the Israel-Jordan border stood in for the El Djem Coliseum in Tunisia; North African and European beach invasion scenes were shot on beaches at Caesarea and Netanya, midway between Haifa and Tel Aviv; Sicilian village scenes were shot in Haifa; and an abandoned armory at Schneller Army Base in Jerusalem stood in for Falkenau concentration camp, its swastikas hidden from the religious school opposite. The shoot went well, but postproduction proved exceedingly rocky. Fuller eventually assembled a four-and-a-half-hour rough cut, but Lorimar executives rejected it as not "epic" enough in content to warrant its lengthy running time. They took the editing away from Fuller and hired journeyman editor Morton Tubor to cut the film down to 113 minutes, leaving 60 percent of Fuller's rough cut on the cutting room floor. They also hired composer Bodie Chandler (*Futureworld*) to write a score without consulting Fuller: another indignity that Fuller had to accept because his contract did not grant him final cut.

Plot Summary

A boldface title added to the 2004 version reads: "This is a fictional life based on factual death." The film then begins in black and white on 11 November 1918 (Armistice Day, World War I). A private (Lee Marvin) kills a German soldier who walked toward him in a pose of surrender. Back at his headquarters, the private, a member of the 1st Division, is informed that the "war's been over for four hours." The film then shifts ahead to November 1942, when the same man, now a sergeant in the "Big Red One," leads his five-man rifle squad (1st Platoon, I Company of the 3rd Battalion, 16th Infantry Regiment) through Northern Africa. Over the next two years the squad fights in Sicily, storms Omaha Beach at D-Day, and helps to liberate France (even battling Germans garrisoned inside a mental asylum with the unsolicited help of a mental patient who commandeers a machine gun and ironically declares himself "sane" and therefore qualified to fight). The squad also takes part in the invasion of Germany and the liberation of one of the Nazi death camps at war's end. Simultaneously, the sergeant's German counterpart, a noncommissioned officer (NCO) named Schroeder (Siegfried Rauch), fights in the same skirmishes from the other side, showing unending loyalty to his country and to Hitler. As the American forces continue across France, the unit passes the spot where the sergeant killed the conceding German soldier 26 years earlier. A First World War monument now stands at the site, and Pvt. Johnson (Kelly Ward) naively mistakes it for a newly minted *WWII* memorial—a bitter irony not lost on the sergeant. The unit concludes its tour with the liberation of the Falkenau concentration camp. Afterwards, Schroeder surprises the sergeant in the woods at night in an attempt to surrender. The sergeant, having just buried a small child released from the concentration camp, stabs Schroeder. The sergeant's unit arrives, informing him that the war was over "about four hours ago." As the squad leaves the area, Pvt. Griff (Mark Hamill) sees that Schroeder is alive. The sergeant and his unit then scramble to save the German soldier's life on their way back to camp.

Reception

The Big Red One premiered at the 33rd Cannes Film Festival in May 1980 and was released in the United States on 18 July. For a film that had been drastically abridged in the editing process and consigned to limited distribution, it did quite well at the box office ($7.2 million gross) and elicited glowing critical notices. For example, the anonymous reviewer for *Variety* called it "a terrific war yarn, a picture of palpable raw power which manages both intense intimacy and great scope at the same time" (31 December 1979). Vincent Canby also offered praise: "The movie's battle footage is mostly small-scale but terrifically effective, especially in a sequence devoted to the 1944 landings at Omaha Beach in Normandy, which is as good as anything in *The Longest Day*. Mr. Fuller's characters aren't very interesting but, in this case, banality has a point. These really are ordinary guys and not the wildly representative ones seen in most Hollywood war movies. More important, one is always aware of the soldiers' sense of isolation even in the midst of battle and of the endlessness of their task. If they survive one battle, their only reward is to be able to fight another" (Canby, 1980). In his posthumously published memoirs,

Fuller confessed to being "thrilled by the almost universal esteem. Yet I can't stop thinking about my four-and-a-half-hour version of the movie, which is somewhere in the vaults at Warner Brothers, who bought the rights several years ago" (Fuller, 2002, p. 482). In 2004, eight years after Fuller's death, film critic/historian Richard Schickel brought Fuller's unrealized dream of a director's cut to fruition. Using 70,000 feet of vault footage and Fuller's original shooting script as a guide, Schickel produced *The Big Red One: The Reconstruction*: a 158-minute version that removes a gratuitous voice-over device and restores 45 minutes of missing content, allowing for more depth and scope, more detailed characterizations, and a more meaningful narrative shape than was evident in the original theatrical release in 1980. Reviews this time were even more enthusiastic. Roger Ebert awarded the film four out of four stars and wrote, "The restored [The] Big Red One is able to suggest the scope and duration of the war, the way it's one damned thing after another, the distances traveled, the pile-up of experiences that are numbing most of the time but occasionally produce an episode as perfect as a short story" (Ebert, 2004).

Reel History Versus Real History

In the words of military historian Clayton Odie Sheffield, "*The Big Red One* is historically accurate in the macro sense, but incorporates a good deal of dramatic license" (Sheffield, 2001, p. 117). Sheffield then goes on to enumerate some of the film's embellishments or omissions. For example, in depicting the 1st Infantry Division's landings near Oran, Algeria (8 November 1942), the movie shows French troops reading American leaflets that urge nonresistance, which is actually not possible because the landings took place at 0100 hours—too dark for any defender to read a leaflet. It also shows the Vichy commander initiating a brief exchange of gunfire, resulting in a few casualties on both sides, after which the French and American soldiers join each other and celebrate their union on the beach. Sheffield says: "In all accounts from the 16th Regiment sector, resistance was either non-existent or light and unorganized, and there were no beach reunions commemorating a cease-fire with the joining of two armies in a truce" (Sheffield, 2001, p. 118). Sheffield also notes that the 16th Regiment "was hit with winter rains and snow while deployed in the Kasserine Pass area," but the movie depicts almost no inclement weather (Sheffield, 2001, pp. 118–119). Sheffield finds the movie's depiction of action in Sicily credible but notes a number of chronological and tactical inaccuracies in the film's rendition of the landings at Normandy on D-Day. He further notes that insofar as *The Big Red One* "provides very little replication of large combat formations of soldiers," it does not need to feature much heavy equipment (Sheffield, 2001, p. 121). As was true of other cash-strapped WWII productions (e.g., *The Battle of the Bulge*), Fuller deploys M4 Sherman tanks with German decals to stand in for German panzers, but Sheffield finds the discrepancy "irrelevant." Finally, some critics thought Lee Marvin, 54 at the time of the film shoot in 1978, was too old to play a WWII U.S. Army sergeant. Yet he was just a few years older than his own father, Lamont Walter Marvin (1896–1971), who was a sergeant in World War II in his late forties. Indeed, after the film came out, Marvin told an interviewer, "I really played my father" (Johnson, p. 39).

BLACK HAWK DOWN (2001)

Synopsis
Black Hawk Down is an American combat film co-produced and directed by Ridley Scott, from a screenplay by Ken Nolan, based on the eponymous 1999 nonfiction book by Mark Bowden. Book and film recount a 1993 raid in Mogadishu, Somalia, by the U.S. military that devolved into a desperate fight for survival known as the Battle of Mogadishu. The film features a large ensemble cast that includes Josh Hartnett, Ewan McGregor, Eric Bana, Tom Sizemore, William Fichtner, Jason Isaacs, Tom Hardy, and Sam Shepard.

Background
On 3 October 1993, "Task Force Ranger," a 160-man, U.N.-affiliated U.S. military detachment, conducted a raid in the center of war-torn Mogadishu, Somalia. Its mission—to capture two lieutenants of Habr Gidr clan leader Mohamed Farrah Aidid—went disastrously awry when the task force encountered fierce resistance from hundreds of armed civilian Somali National Alliance (SNA) fighters. Surrounded and pinned down for almost 14 hours, the Americans took heavy casualties (18 dead, 73 wounded) before being evacuated by an armored relief convoy early Monday morning on 4 October In the aftermath of what became known as the Battle of Mogadishu, news reports showed jubilant Somalis dragging the body of a dead and nearly naked U.S. soldier through the streets of Mogadishu—an image that horrified the American public and rocked the Clinton administration (though American media outlets did not bother to report that over 1,000 Somalis also died in the same battle). To mollify critics Clinton fired Les Aspin, his secretary of defense, and demoted Gen. William F. Garrison, the officer in charge of the disastrous operation. Anxious to discover what went wrong, journalist Mark Bowden traveled to Mogadishu, interviewed participants on both sides, and reviewed voluminous Army records. His painstaking account of the incident was first published as a series of 29 articles in *The Philadelphia Enquirer* in 1997 and later turned into a critically acclaimed bestseller, *Black Hawk Down: A Story of Modern War* (1999). Director Simon West (*Con Air*) suggested to Hollywood mega-producer Jerry Bruckheimer (*Top Gun, Pearl Harbor*) that he secure the film rights and let West direct. Bruckheimer did buy the film rights but hired Ridley Scott (*Alien, Blade Runner*) to direct after West took on another film project. Though Ken Nolan received sole credit for the screenplay, Mark Bowden wrote the initial adaptation, Nolan rewrote Bowden's version, Steven Gaghan did another rewrite, Steven Zaillian and Ezna Sands rewrote most of Gaghan and Nolan's work, and then Nolan did a final rewrite. For purposes of dramatic streamlining but also for ideological reasons, what had been a fuller characterization of the combatants and the political context was pared back and soldiers' expressions of ambivalence regarding the mission were excised altogether.

Production
Crucial to the project was the full cooperation of the American military establishment, which Ridley Scott sought and won quid pro quo. For a $3 million fee and

script approval rights, the Department of Defense (DOD) supplied numerous consultants and the requisite war matériel, including Black Hawk helicopters and the pilots to fly them. The DOD also arranged for military training of the actors. The 40 actors playing Army Rangers took a one-week crash course at Fort Benning, Georgia, while the 15 Delta Force actors took a two-week course from the 1st Special Warfare Training Group at Fort Bragg, North Carolina. Mogadishu survivor Michael Durant and other Little Bird and Black Hawk pilots briefed Ron Eldard and the actors playing 160th SOAR helicopter pilots at Fort Campbell, Kentucky. "They [the DOD] saw this as a recruitment film," Scott later avowed. Scott and his team initially scouted Amman, Jordan, as their principal location, but the city was too built up and not on the coast, as is Mogadishu. They ended up shooting the film in Morocco, where Scott had shot parts of *Gladiator* in 1999. Filming took place in the cities of Rabat, Salé, and Kénitra, Morocco, between March and June 2001.

Plot Summary

In 1993, following the start of a civil war in Somalia, the United Nations conducted military peacekeeping operations there. When it withdrew most of its forces, Mogadishu-based militia loyal to Mohamed Farrah Aidid declared war on the remaining UN personnel. In response, U.S. Army Rangers, Delta Force counterterrorist specialists, and 160th SOAR airmen are deployed to capture Omar Salad Elmi and Abdi Hassan Awale Qeybdiid, two of Aidid's top advisors. Delta Force troops take Aidid's lieutenants prisoner within the building, but the Rangers and helicopters chaperoning the convoy are hit by intense fire, while SSG Matt Eversmann's (Josh Hartnett) Chalk Four is mistakenly let off a block away. Pfc. Todd Blackburn (Orlando Bloom) fractures his spine after a fall out of a Black Hawk helicopter, so SSG Jeff Struecker (Brian Van Holt) takes a few Humvees and moves to rescue Blackburn. As Struecker breaks away from the convoy, Sgt. Dominick Pilla (Danny Hoch) is shot and killed. Black Hawk Super Six-One piloted by CWO Clifton "Elvis" Wolcott (Jeremy Piven) is shot from the air by a rocket-propelled grenade (RPG). The pilots perish in the aftermath, and the crew chiefs sustain injuries. Ordered to reach the crash site and evacuate survivors and fatalities, LTC Danny McKnight's (Tom Sizemore) Humvee column sustains heavy casualties in a failed attempt to reach it. In the meantime, a set of Ranger Chalks, including Eversmann's unit, arrive at the Super Six-One crash site and form a barrier around the wounded men and deceased pilots and wait for extraction. As they wait, Super Six-Four, piloted by CWO Michael Durant (Ron Eldard), is gunned down and sent crashing to the road, blocks away from Super Six-One. Heavy gunfire keeps ground troops from accessing the crash sites and leaves all Rangers without backup. A pair of Delta Force snipers are dropped into the Super Six-One site and find Durant alive. Unfortunately, the crash site is infiltrated by enemy combatants: Shughart and Gordon are killed, and Durant is captured. McKnight's column decides against proceeding to the Six-One crash site and instead returns to the base. The men regroup and devise a plan to rescue the Rangers and pilots, led by Major General William F. Garrison (Sam Shepard), commander of Task Force Ranger, who sends an LTC (Steven Ford) to request back-up reinforcements from the 10th Mountain Division. Following sunset, Aidid's militia forces attack the Americans cornered at Super Six-One's crash site. AH-6J Little Bird light helicopter gunships manage to hold off the swarming Somali militants throughout the night with strafing runs and rocket attacks. Shortly after sunrise the 10th Mountain Division's relief column reaches the crash site and rescues the American soldiers.

Reception
Rushed into wide release (3,100 theaters) four months after 9/11 to capitalize on American patriotic fervor, *Black Hawk Down* ran from mid-January to mid-April 2002. The movie grossed $108.6 million domestically and another $64.3 million overseas for a worldwide total of $172.9 million—at least $35 million in profits over and above production, advertising, and promotion costs. Nominated for four Oscars, *Black Hawk Down* won two (for Best Editing and Best Sound) and also fared well with most film critics, who praised the film's frenetic, nonstop action—impeccably edited, tightly framed, and uncannily realistic. There were, however, dissenting voices. Film critic Elvis Mitchell described *Black Hawk Down* as "accomplished but meaningless" and took the movie to task for a "lack of characterization [that] converts the Somalis into a pack of snarling dark-skinned beasts, gleefully pulling the Americans from their downed aircraft and stripping them. Intended or not, it reeks of glumly staged racism" (Mitchell, 2001).

Reel History Versus Real History
Though it accurately depicts the course of the Battle of Mogadishu, *Black Hawk Down* skimps on the broader context. In so doing it largely reduces a complex geopolitical reckoning to a 144-minute firefight. At the insistence of the Pentagon, the movie also elides a U.S. soldier involved in the battle named John "Stebby" Stebbins (renamed in the movie as "John Grimes"). In 1999 SPC Stebbins was convicted by court-martial for repeatedly raping his own six-year-old daughter, a domestic atrocity that was also a PR nightmare the DOD was anxious to suppress. Other elisions can be chalked up to the usual narrative and cultural imperatives that define Hollywood cinema. Ergo, the movie condenses 100 key figures in Bowden's book down to 39 and includes only one African American actor and no Somali actors. Conversely, the film features soldiers wearing helmets with their last names on them, a fictional device deployed by Ridley Scott to help the viewing audience distinguish among the many characters.

BORN ON THE FOURTH OF JULY (1989)

Synopsis
Born on the Fourth of July is an American biopic/war drama based on the best-selling autobiography of the same title by Vietnam War veteran Ron Kovic (played by Tom Cruise in the film) that traces Kovic's evolution from soldier to anti-war activist. Vietnam veteran Oliver Stone co-wrote the screenplay with Kovic and also co-produced and directed the film, which is the second installment in Stone's trilogy

of films about the Vietnam War, following *Platoon* (1986) and preceding *Heaven & Earth* (1993).

Background

Vietnam combat veteran turned filmmaker Oliver Stone (*Platoon*) read Ron Kovic's best-selling autobiography *Born on the Fourth of July* (McGraw-Hill, 1976) and decided he had to make it into a movie. Stone and Kovic had similar stories: both men had once been gung-ho American patriots who became bitterly disillusioned with nationalism and war by their military service in Vietnam. After Stone bought the rights to Kovic's book in 1977, the two men became close friends and collaborated on a screen adaptation. A movie version to be produced by Martin Bregman, directed by William Friedkin (later replaced by Daniel Petrie), and starring Al Pacino was supposed to begin production in the summer of 1978, but despite a budget of only $6 million, funding fell through. Stone promised a crestfallen Kovic that he would someday make the picture when he was in a position to do so. Ten years later, after the huge success of his first Vietnam movie, *Platoon* (1986), Stone was able to keep his promise. Now considered bankable, Stone secured a production deal with Universal Pictures as director and co-producer with his frequent collaborator, A. Kitman Ho. Having achieved superstar status with *Top Gun* (1986), Tom Cruise, 27 at the time, was cast as Ron Kovic.

Production

Given the movie's anti-war and anti-establishment slant in the jingoistic Reagan era, Universal executives were dubious about its box office potential. Accordingly, they set the budget at a modest $14 million. To economize, most of the cast contracted to receive a percentage of the profits in lieu of a salary up front (a highly lucrative deal, as it turned out). Thirteen years after the fall of Saigon, U.S.-Vietnam relations were still strained, so Stone could not shoot the film in Vietnam. As he had done with *Platoon*, Stone opted to shoot his Vietnam scenes in the Philippines. Most of the scenes set in Massapequa, Long Island (Ron Kovic's hometown), and at the 1972 Republican National Convention in Miami were actually shot in Dallas, Texas. Wanting to understand Kovic's life as a paraplegic, Cruise obtained a wheelchair and stayed in it for many weeks. Stone, following suit, accompanied Kovic on public outings to see how paraplegics in wheelchairs were treated by the general public. After viewing a rough cut of the movie, Universal execs, heretofore parsimonious, ordered the final scene—of Kovic delivering a speech at the 1976 Democratic National Convention—to be reshot with a much larger crowd (6,000 extras instead of the 600 Stone had on hand). The $500,000 reshoot was done in a single day at the L.A. Forum.

Plot Summary

In Massapequa, Long Island, in the summer of 1956, 10-year-old Ron Kovic (Bryan Larkin) plays war games in the woods and attends a Fourth of July parade. An idealistic patriot, Kovic (Tom Cruise) enlists in the Marines in 1964 at the age of 18. He almost skips his high school prom after failing to secure a date with his love interest, Donna (Kyra Sedgwick), but decides to go at the last minute and ends up dancing with her on his last night before boot camp. Three years later, in October 1967, Kovic is a Marine sergeant on his second tour of duty in Vietnam. His unit kills several Vietnamese civilians, mistakenly believing them to be Viet Cong. Then Kovic accidentally kills a member of his own platoon, a new arrival named Wilson (Michael Compotaro). Four months later, during the Tet Offensive, Kovic is critically wounded in a firefight. Rendered a paraplegic, he spends several months recovering at a decrepit, rat-infested Veterans Administration (VA) hospital in the Bronx. Returning home disabled in 1969, Kovic succumbs to despair and alcoholism. During a Fourth of July parade, Kovic shows signs of post-traumatic stress disorder (PTSD) when he is deeply unnerved by the sound of firecrackers exploding. Asked to give a speech, he gets overcome by emotion and is forced to leave the stage. Kovic meets up with a high school friend, Timmy Burns (Frank Whaley), who is also an injured serviceman, and swaps stories about wartime experiences. Later, Kovic visits Donna at her college in Syracuse, New York, but the two are separated as she and other student demonstrators are arrested for standing against the Vietnam War. Back home, Kovic finds himself in a bar, close to blows with a WWII veteran. Afterwards, Kovic argues passionately with his mother, and his father sends him to Mexico. He arrives in "The Village of the Sun" (i.e., the town of Ajijic in the state of Jalisco, Mexico), a safe space for injured Vietnam veterans. There Kovic has his initial sexual encounter with a prostitute and befriends another dissolute wheelchair-bound veteran named Charlie (Willem Dafoe). Going back to Long Island, Kovic visits Wilson's family and confesses his responsibility for Wilson's death. Kovic then joins Vietnam Veterans against the War (VVAW) and attends the 1972 Republican National Convention in Miami. He shares his Vietnam experience with a reporter and speaks out against the Vietnam War, enraging the Nixon supporters at the convention. Security guards remove him from the hall. Four years later Kovic's struggles are finally vindicated when he is invited to speak at the 1976 Democratic National Convention and publishes his autobiography, *Born on the Fourth of July*.

Reception

Released just before Christmas 1989, *Born on the Fourth of July* grossed $5.3 million by the third week of its run, ranking #1 at the box office. The film went on to earn $70 million domestically and $91 million overseas for a total of $161 million in worldwide ticket sales—a smash hit, considering that the film's production budget was less than 10 percent of that sum. Among many other accolades *Born* nearly swept the Golden Globe Awards and received eight Oscar nominations, with Oliver Stone winning for Best Director and David Brenner and Joe Hutshing winning for Best Editing. Likewise, the critical response was overwhelmingly favorable, though not unanimous. For example, Jonathan Rosenbaum felt that the film's ending cheapened its otherwise somber message: "The movie's conventional showbiz finale, brimming with false uplift, implies that the traumas of other mutilated and disillusioned Vietnam veterans can easily be overcome if they write books and turn themselves into celebrities" (Rosenbaum, J., n.d.).

Reel History Versus Real History

The movie follows Kovic's autobiography faithfully, but, to heighten melodrama, it does resort to falsification in at least two major ways. In reality Kyra Sedgwick's character, Donna, never existed. The prom scene, Ron's visit to Syracuse, his personal involvement in the protest, and police crack-down—none of these events actually happened, though Kovic did watch the demonstration on television. In his memoir he recalls being outraged by the treatment of the protestors; their victimization reminded him of the way he and his fellow veterans had been treated after they returned home. In the movie Ron Kovic is shown visiting Wilson's parents and widow and confessing to them that he accidentally killed Wilson in combat. In reality, the meeting never took place. Kovic did admit to the shooting in his book—a far cry from an in-person apology and obviously not cinematic.

BRAVEHEART (1995)

Synopsis

Braveheart is an American war epic directed by and starring Mel Gibson, who portrays William Wallace, a late 13th-century Scottish warrior who led the Scots in the First War of Scottish Independence against King Edward I of England. Adapted for the screen by Randall Wallace, the film derives from Scottish poet Blind Harry's epic poem *The Actes and Deidis of the Illustre and Vallyeant Campioun Schir William Wallace*.

William Wallace (Mel Gibson, right) leads the Scots in a 13th-century war for independence from England in Gibson's *Braveheart* (1995). (20th Century Fox/Photofest)

Background

On vacation in Scotland in 1983, screenwriter Randall Wallace got the idea for *Braveheart* when he encountered a statue of Sir William Wallace (1270–1305) at Edinburgh Castle and learned from a Black Watch guard that Wallace was Scotland's greatest hero: a medieval warrior-leader who gloriously defied British rule, at least for a time. In 1988 Wallace wrote the first draft of a script for an epic biopic of his namesake (no relation), based on *The Actes and Deidis of the Illustre and Vallyeant Campioun Schir William Wallace* (more commonly known as *The Wallace*), an epic poem by Scottish poet Blind Harry (c.1440–1492). Written some 170 years after Wallace's death, *The Wallace* mostly traffics in patriotic myth. Randall Wallace used Blind Harry's poem indiscriminately and salted it with a good deal more romanticized balderdash. Wallace sold the script to MGM/UA in 1992. When studio chief Alan Ladd Jr. was ousted from MGM in July 1993, he was allowed to take *Braveheart* with him when he re-established his independent firm, The Ladd Company. The project lay fallow for a year, during which time Mel Gibson, who had initially passed on the project, changed his mind and offered to direct the picture if he could radically revise the script. Though he would have preferred young Jason Patric as Wallace, Gibson eventually agreed to star in the movie as well. During pre-production negotiations with Paramount, Gibson waived his salary—usually $10 to $12 million a movie—in lieu of a share of the gross profits and had his own production company, Icon Entertainment, put in $15 million toward a projected budget of $60 million. Hedging its bets, Paramount Pictures opted to acquire only U.S. and Canada distribution rights on the condition that 20th Century Fox acquire the foreign rights. Paramount ultimately put in $17 million and 20th Century Fox contributed $43 million, after overruns pushed the final production cost up to $75 million.

Production

The grueling 105-day shoot began on 6 June 1994 (the 50th anniversary of D-Day) and ended on 22 September 1994. During the first six weeks the scenes covering William Wallace's early years were shot on location in Glen Nevis in the Scottish highlands, where it rained almost every day. From mid-July to late August the major battle scenes were shot on the Curragh Plains, about 30 miles southwest of Dublin, Ireland. The opposing armies were played by 1,500 reserve members of the Irish Defence Forces (IDF). With 1,400 extras for some scenes, it took hours to get everyone through costume, makeup, and armoring. The Battle of Stirling Bridge took six weeks to film (though the actual battle in 1297 took only an hour or two). Gibson used hundreds of extras, many real horses, and a couple of mechanical horses for shots showing horses being felled in battle (the animatronic beasts weighed 200 pounds and were fueled by nitrogen cylinders that propelled them at 30 mph on 20-foot tracks). Using nine cameras, cinematographer John Toll shot roughly half a million feet of film for the Stirling battle sequence that was later edited down to only seven minutes of screen time. During editing, a few frames were removed at various points in the combat sequences to produce a jarring effect and accentuate the frenzied violence. After test screenings elicited audience revulsion at scenes like Wallace's graphically depicted disembowelment, Gibson and his editor, Steven Rosenblum, cut out the most brutal parts to avoid the expensive stigma of NC-17 from the Motion Picture Association of America (MPAA); the final version was rated R for "brutal medieval warfare."

Plot Summary

After the death of King Alexander III of Scotland in 1280, King Edward "Longshanks" (Patrick McGoohan) invades and conquers Scotland. Surviving the deaths of his father and brother, Young William Wallace (James Robinson) is ferried out of his home country and taught by his Uncle Argyle (Brian Cox). Years later, Longshanks grants his noblemen land and privileges in Scotland. An older Wallace (Mel Gibson) comes back to Scotland and secretly marries his childhood sweetheart Murron MacClannough (Catherine McCormack). After Murron is murdered by the British, Wallace seeks vengeance and leads his clan against the local English garrison. Word of Wallace's actions against the British reaches his fellow Scots, and clans near and far pledge allegiance to his rebellion. Longshanks then commands his son, Prince Edward (Peter Hanly), to neutralize Wallace. Wallace proves a victorious leader, winning the Battle of Stirling Bridge and obliterating the city of York, killing Longshanks's nephew in the process. Wallace turns to Robert the Bruce (Angus Macfadyen), the son of nobleman Robert the Elder and in the running for the crown, for assistance. However, Robert proves to be under his father's control, acquiescing to the Elder's wishes by submitting to the English in a play for the throne. Meanwhile, concerned by the possibility of Wallace's outright rebellion, Longshanks enlists the help of his son's wife, Isabelle of France (Sophie Marceau), to open negotiations with Wallace. Isabelle sets a meeting with Wallace and becomes quickly infatuated with him. Unmoved, Wallace begs the Scottish royals to strike against Isabelle's forces. Longshanks takes to the battlefield and confronts the Scots at Falkirk where noblemen Lochlan (John Murtagh) and Mornay (Alun Armstrong), betray Wallace and lose the fight for the Scots. Not one to allow betrayal, Wallace kills Lochlan and Mornay and finds his vengeance in a seven-year war against English forces. Isabelle proves a comrade in arms and a lover with whom Wallace has an affair. Robert the Younger attempts to open the lines of communication by setting a meeting with Wallace in Scotland, but he is thwarted by his father, who has colluded with other royals to apprehend Wallace and deliver him to English forces. Robert is disgusted by his father's deceit and disowns Robert the Elder. Once in London, Wallace is accused of high treason and subsequently sentenced to public torture and death by beheading. Throughout his torture, Wallace does not acknowledge the English king. As the crowds beg for mercy, the magistrate offers Wallace a deal: if Wallace himself asks for mercy, then he will be gifted with a swift death. However, not to be manipulated, Wallace shouts "Freedom!" seconds before his decapitation. Wallace embraces a final comfort of seeing a vision of Murron's face within the crowd before he perishes. In 1314, Robert the Bruce has been named king of Scotland. However, rather than bow to English rule, Bruce shocks the English by battling against them and eventually securing freedom for Scotland.

Reception

Though no run-away blockbuster, *Braveheart* proved to be a solid hit at the box office. During its initial domestic run (19 May–24 August. 1995; widest release: 2,037 theaters), the movie earned a respectable $60 million. Paramount re-released *Braveheart* twice: on 15 September 1995 and again on 16 February 1996, after it was nominated for 10 Oscars. By 9 June 1996, the final day of its year-long run in North America, *Braveheart* had earned $75.6 million—just past the break-even mark—but an additional $134.8 million in foreign box office receipts pushed the total gross to $210.4 million. Released on VHS in March 1996, *Braveheart* topped all video rentals that year. In addition to strong box office showings, *Braveheart* was showered with awards: 7 BAFTA nominations (and 3 wins); 4 Golden Globe nominations (Mel Gibson won for Best Director); and 10 Academy Award nominations (and 5 wins, for Best Picture, Best Director, Best Cinematography, Best Sound Editing, and Best Makeup). President Bill Clinton enjoyed *Braveheart* so much he watched it twice in three days in May 1995. Reviews were, likewise, mostly approving. Film critics praised the movie for its epic scale, rousing battle sequences, and emotional earnestness, but more than a few found *Braveheart* overwrought and excessively violent (i.e., a trite Mel Gibson vanity project).

Reel History Versus Real History

Of all the films ever made that purport to be based in actual history, *Braveheart* ranks as the most egregiously inaccurate. In the opening scene a caption indicates that the year is 1280 while a voice-over claims that Scottish King Alexander III has died without leaving a male heir, thus creating a power vacuum filled by English King Edward I ("Longshanks"), whose troops are occupying Scotland. King Alexander III actually died in 1286, and the English did not invade Scotland until 1296, during the reign of John Balliol (appointed over Robert the Bruce by Edward I, who acted as arbitrator of the succession). The Scottish rebellion broke out in 1297, when William Wallace was 27 years old; Scotland had been free and at peace when he was a child. The movie also mangles chronology in its depiction of Princess Isabella. She could not have warned Wallace about the upcoming Battle of Falkirk (22 July 1298) because she was only three years old at the time and still living in France. Indeed, Isabella never knew Wallace or King Edward I. She first arrived in England and married Edward II in January 1308—three years after Wallace's execution and six months after the death of King Edward I. Likewise, the film's characterizations of King Edward I as a ruthless psychopath and his son, Prince Edward, as a homosexual are historically dubious at best. Longshanks was a hardened warrior-king but not demonical. Rumors of Edward II's alleged homosexuality stem from his close friendship with a courtier named Piers Gaveston, 1st Earl of Cornwall (c.1284–1312), but an intimate relationship has never been proven. In the movie King Edward I murders Phillip, his son's gay lover (based on Gaveston), by nonchalantly throwing him out a high castle window—a scene that amused audiences but angered gay activists, who found it homophobic. William Wallace is portrayed in the film as hailing from a family of peasant farmers. In actuality Wallace's father was a minor nobleman. The movie depicts the English as executing Wallace's wife, thus providing Wallace with a deeply personal motive for rebelling against them. This is pure fiction; there is no record of Wallace having been married. Even Mel Gibson's physiognomy and age are wrong. Wallace was reputed to have been tall (perhaps 6'5") and heavily muscled. He would have been in his late twenties to mid-thirties during the uprising against England. Standing a trim 5'11" and 38 years of age at the time of filming, Mel Gibson was a half-foot shorter than Wallace, much slighter of build, and somewhat older. The movie's depiction of the Battle of Stirling Bridge is also wildly inaccurate, mainly because it features no bridge—the crucial tactical fulcrum that enabled the Scots to cut off half the English Army and slaughter those enemy troops that made it across the bridge. Woad, the blue war paint prominently displayed in the film's battle scenes, had not been used by Scottish warriors since the end of the Roman era, that is, some 800 years before the events depicted in the film. The movie depicts several clans that comprise Wallace's army as dressed alike in their representative clan tartans, but the use of distinctive kilts and tartan patterns did not emerge until the Victorian era, 600 years later. Furthermore, many Scots were offended by the film's portrayal of Robert the Bruce, who is also considered a national hero.

BREAKER MORANT (1980)

Synopsis

Breaker Morant is an Australian war film directed by Bruce Beresford, who also co-wrote the screenplay. Based on Kenneth G. Ross's eponymous play (1978), the film dramatizes the 1902 court martial of Lts. Harry Morant, Peter Handcock, and George Witton, Australians serving in the British Army during the Second Anglo-Boer War accused of murdering captured enemy combatants and an unarmed civilian in the Northern Transvaal.

Background

Since his court-martial and execution by the British for alleged war crimes committed during the Boer War, Harry "Breaker" Harbord Morant (1864–1902) has been an Australian folk hero rivaling the legendary bushranger, Ned Kelly. Morant's legend was firmly established in 1907 by *Scapegoats of the Empire*, an exculpatory tome written by his surviving co-defendant, George Witton (1874–1942). In the 1970s the legend was revived in a small way by writer Kit Denton with a novel based on Morant's life entitled *The Breaker* (1973) and by neophyte filmmaker Frank Shields' low-budget documentary, also entitled *The Breaker* (1974). Of greater cultural impact in Australia was *Breaker Morant*, a two-act play by Kenneth G. Ross that ran at the Athenaeum Theatre in Melbourne in 1978 and was a critical and commercial success, so much so that Ross turned his play script into a screenplay. As film historian Graham Daseler notes, filmmaker Bruce Beresford (*The Getting of Wisdom*) "had two scripts to work from. One was Ross's play, the other a screenplay by David Stevens and Jonathan Hardy. Beresford scrapped both, considering them each too generous to the defendants, and traveled to the Imperial War Museum in London to conduct fresh research. After he returned, he began his own script, building his dramatic structure around the trial (as the play had also done) but widening his field of vision to reveal what Ross, in his stage production, never could: the interior world of the characters" (Daseler, 2013).

Production

American actor Rod Steiger was Bruce Beresford's first choice to play Harry "Breaker" Morant. Later, Australian actor Terence Donovan (who played Morant in the original stage production) was considered, but Beresford decided he needed a more famous actor in the role (Donovan was cast as Capt. Simon Hunt). The part ultimately went to English actor Edward Woodward—a casting choice resented by some Australian Actors Equity members, even though Woodward bore an uncanny resemblance to Morant. The Major Thomas role was originally offered to Bryan Brown before it went to Jack Thompson (Brown ended up playing Lt. Handcock). Though set in the high veldt of South Africa, *Breaker Morant* was filmed in and around Burra, South Australia, on the edge of the Great Desert, 100 miles north of Adelaide. *Breaker Morant* was made on a shoestring budget of 800,000 AUD. The Australian Film Commission contributed 400,000 AUD, and the South Australia Film Corporation (SAFC) put up another 250,000 AUD. The remaining funds were provided by Seven Network and PACT Productions and raised privately.

Plot Summary

In 1902, during the Second Boer War, three officers of the Bushveldt Carbineers (aka BVC, a 320-man Australian irregular mounted infantry regiment)—Lieutenants Harry Morant (Edward Woodward), Peter Handcock (Bryan Brown), and George Witton (Lewis Fitz-Gerald)—are arrested by the British and charged with murdering Boer prisoners-of-war and Reverend C.A.D. Heese, a German missionary. Major Charles Bolton (Rod Mullinar) prosecutes the court-martial while Major J. F. Thomas (Jack Thompson), a solicitor from New South Wales in civilian life, acts as defense counsel. After a number of damning character witnesses testify, Bolton focuses on the shooting of Floris Visser (Michael Procanin), a wounded Boer prisoner, in order to avenge the torture, death, and mutilation of BVC Capt. Simon Hunt (Terence Donovan), a close friend of Morant. Major Thomas argues that standing orders existed to shoot "all Boers captured wearing khaki," but Morant damages his own defense by defiant testimony on the witness stand. The next day, Bolton turns to the shooting of the six Boers. BVC Capt. Alfred Taylor (John Waters) testifies that Lord Kitchener issued orders that no more Boer prisoners were to be taken alive. On cross-examination, Bolton nullifies Taylor's testimony by forcing him to admit that he is also awaiting court-martial for shooting prisoners. Other witnesses testify that Morant had six Boer guerrillas lined up and shot after they had surrendered. Major Thomas demands that Kitchener be summoned. Lt.-Col. Denny (Charles "Bud" Tingwell) and Major Bolton try to dissuade Major Thomas from pressing the matter, but he persists. At any rate, Kitchener has since reversed himself. Rather than "total war," he now advocates peace with the Afrikaners—a stance necessitating that a few soldiers will need to be sacrificed for all the war crimes committed by the British Army. Kitchener's surrogate Col. Hamilton (Vincent Ball) takes the stand and denies ever having relayed a take-no-prisoners order from Kitchener to the BVC. The trial then examines the murder of Rev. Heese. After leaving Fort Edward in a horse-drawn buggy, Heese was later found shot to death along the road. Bolton accuses Morant of ordering Handcock to kill Heese to prevent him from informing the BVC's commander of Morant's plans to kill his Boer prisoners. On the stand, Morant denies the allegation, as does Handcock, who claims that he was visiting the homes of two married Afrikaner women that day for sex. Major Thomas produces signed depositions from the women to corroborate Handcock's alibi. During a lull in the trial, Handcock admits to Witton that he did indeed shoot Heese before visiting his two lady friends. When Witton asks if Major Thomas knows, Morant tells him that there is no reason for Thomas to know. Despite an impassioned closing argument by Major Thomas, the defendants are found guilty of shooting the prisoners but acquitted of murdering Rev. Heese. The next morning the defendants are sentenced to death, but Witton's sentence is commuted to "life in penal servitude." Major Thomas hurries to Kitchener's headquarters to plead for commutations for Morant and Handcock, only to learn that Kitchener has already left and that both the British and Australian governments have publicly affirmed the verdict and sentences. He also learns that a peace conference is in the offing and that the troops will soon be going home. At dawn the next morning Morant and Handcock are put before a firing squad. Morant, defiant to the end, refuses the comfort of clergy and a blindfold (as does Handcock). The firing squad musters as Morant's poem, "Butchered to Make a Dutchmen's Holiday," is recited in voice-over. Just before they fire their fatal volley Morant shouts, "Shoot straight, you bastards! Don't make a mess of it!"

Reception

Breaker Morant proved to be the most popular indigenous movie released in Australia up to that time, grossing 4.7 million AUD at the box office (the equivalent of almost $50 million in 2017 U.S. dollars). After screenings at Cannes, the New York Film Festival, and other venues, the movie received international acclaim, rave reviews from critics, and 18 AACTA Award nominations, winning 15 of them, plus an Oscar nomination for Best Adapted Screenplay, a Palme d'Or nomination at Cannes, and a win at Cannes for Best Supporting Actor (Jack Thompson). *Breaker Morant* also inaugurated Bruce Beresford's career as a film director of international stature and is now recognized as one of the key works of the Australian Film Renaissance of the 1970s and 1980s.

Reel History Versus Real History

In order to enlist optimal viewer empathy for Morant, Handcock, and Witton, *Breaker Morant* alters history in large and small ways. For example, it depicts Lord Kitchener as demanding convictions for the killing of Rev. Heese so as to appease Germany and keep it from entering the Boer War on the side of the Afrikaners. In actuality, Germany did not officially protest the murder of Heese. Though ethnically German, Heese was born in Cape Colony (present-day South Africa), so he was technically a British subject. Besides misrepresenting the geopolitical context, the movie omits the three other defendants who were also on trial with Morant, Handcock, and Witton: Lt. Henry Picton, a British-born BVC officer, charged with participating in the shooting of Floris Visser (found guilty of manslaughter and cashiered from the British Army); Capt. Alfred Taylor, the Irish-born commander of military intelligence at Fort Edward, accused of ordering Lt. Handcock to murder B. J. van Buuren, an Afrikaner BVC trooper who had objected to the shooting of prisoners, also accused of the murder of six unarmed Afrikaners and the theft of their money and livestock (acquitted on a technicality); and Major Robert W. Lenehan, the Australian Field Commander of BVC, accused of covering up the murder of Trooper van Buuren (found guilty and reprimanded). *Breaker Morant* also mischaracterizes the enlisted men at Fort Edward who testify against Morant, Handcock, and Witton as British-born malcontents motivated by personal grudges against their Australian officers. In reality, the 15 enlisted men at Fort Edward who signed an accusatory letter were Australians stirred by genuine disgust for the war crimes they had personally witnessed. Furthermore, the movie portrays the prosecution as single-mindedly bloodthirsty while neglecting to note that Morant and Handcock actually rejected offers of immunity from prosecution if they would agree to testify against Capt. Taylor and Major Lenehan for issuing take-no-prisoners orders. The effect of all these changes is to encourage viewers (especially Australian viewers) to see the defendants as martyrs to British political intrigue and injustice rather than guilty of war crimes, which they most assuredly were. Somewhat disingenuously, Bruce Beresford has since deplored the fact that *Breaker Morant* has been widely misconstrued "as a film about poor Australians who were framed by the Brits." In a 1999 interview with Australian film critic Peter Malone, Beresford said, "The film never pretended for a moment that they weren't guilty. It said they are guilty. But what was interesting about it was that it analyzed why men in this situation would behave as they had never behaved before in their lives. It's the pressures that are put to bear on people in war time . . . That was what I was interested in examining" (Malone, 1980).

BRIDGE, THE [GERMAN: *DIE BRÜCKE*] (1959)

Synopsis
Die Brücke (*The Bridge*) is a West German war film directed by Austrian filmmaker Bernhard Wicki. Based on an actual event fictionalized by Gregor Dorfmeister in a 1958 novel of the same title, the film tells the story of a small squad of German teenagers who assume the futile task of defending a bridge against the Allies in the closing days of World War II in Europe.

Background
Toward the end of World War II Manfred Gregor Dorfmeister turned 16, so he was inducted into the Volkssturm (People's Army) in his hometown of Bad Tölz, Bavaria, a resort hamlet about 30 miles south of Munich. On 1 May 1945—the day after

Hitler's suicide and a week before Germany's surrender—Dorfmeister and four other 16-year-old draftees were ordered to defend a bridge in the forest 12 miles south of town. The next day American tanks spearheading an advance by the U.S. 141st Infantry Regiment (36th Infantry Division) approached the bridge. The Americans were fired upon by the Volkssturm boys. The lead tank was knocked out and a crewman badly, perhaps fatally, wounded. In the ensuing firefight, two of the five German boys were killed while Dorfmeister and the other two survivors of the skirmish fled back to Bad Tölz through the woods. When they arrived in town a few hours later, they were ordered by two Feldjägers (military policemen) to man a machine-gun nest and defend Tölzer Isar Bridge. After the Feldjägers left, Dorfmeister opted to go home, but his two comrades stayed to fight; they were killed before the town fell to the Americans. Thirteen years later, Dorfmeister, writing under the pseudonym of Manfred Gregor, expressed lingering feelings of guilt and grief by writing *Die Brücke* [*The Bridge*] (1958), a fictionalized account of the incident that became a bestseller in West Germany and was translated into 15 languages. Producers Hermann Schwerin and Jochen Schwerin secured the film rights and hired Austrian filmmaker Bernhard Wicki to direct a movie version. Wicki and cowriters Michael Mansfeld and Karl-Wilhelm Vivier wrote the adaptation.

Production

Die Brücke was shot in black and white in the fall of 1958 at Florian-Geyer-Brücke [Florian Geyer Bridge] (demolished in 1991 and replaced in 1995) and at other locations in Cham, Bavaria, a town 150 miles northeast of Bad Tölz. None of the three M24 Chaffee light tanks shown in the movie are real. Because the newly formed Bundeswehr (postwar German Army) still did not have any tanks in 1959, Bernhard Wicki had to have wooden models constructed and then placed on top of truck chassis (the truck wheels can clearly been seen under the body of each "tank").

Plot Summary

In the final days of World War II, U.S. forces close in on a small Bavarian town. In the town's school, seven boisterous 16-year-old boys are teasing girls, following the receding battle front on a wall map, and reading love passages from *Romeo and Juliet* in their English class. Walter Forst (Michael Hinz) is deeply resentful of his arrogant father (Hans Elwenspoek), the local Nazi Party Ortsgruppenleiter (local group leader), who has chosen to send his wife away to a safe location and save himself using the excuse of a Volkssturm meeting. Sigi Bernhard (Günther Hoffmann) refuses to let his mother send him out of town to avoid danger. Karl Horber (Karl Michael Balzer) is infatuated with Barbara (Edeltraut Elsner), his father's young assistant at the hair salon, and is bewildered once he sees the two meeting romantically. Klaus Hager (Volker Lechtenbrink) does not notice that his classmate, Franziska (Cordula Trantow), has feelings for him. Jürgen Borchert (Frank Glaubrecht), whose father was a German soldier who died in battle, struggles to do justice to his father's legacy. To their surprise, the young men are assigned to a local army platoon, and they are forced to deploy after only a single day in the barracks. As they prepare to depart, the boys' teacher asks Fröhlich

(Heinz Spitzner), the Kompaniechef (company commander)—a former teacher who has just lost his son in action—to keep them out of the war so they won't be sacrificed pointlessly. The commander assigns the boys to the defense of a local bridge (slated for demolition anyway), under the command of Cpl. Heilmann (Günter Pfitzmann), a veteran Unteroffizier. The young men hunker down as Heilmann leaves to alert the demolition squad, but on his way, Heilmann is confused for a deserter by a German patrol and goes into a panic. Instead of communicating his purpose, he attempts to flee and is shot by the Feldegendarmerie patrolmen. The boys are thus left on their own, on the bridge, without a way to contact their unit. The boys decide to remain in position until receiving official orders to pull back. At dawn an American fighter plane drops a bomb near the bridge, killing Sigi, who had stubbornly refused to take cover as he had endured endless mockery for what his friends contended was cowardice. The death of their friend stuns the boys as they scramble to set up positions against three American tanks and accompanying troops. Walter uses Panzerfausts to obliterate two of the tanks, but soon overwhelmed, he is killed in action. Karl kills a G.I., but is immediately the victim of intense machine-gun fire. Klaus is unable to cope with Karl's death and sprints forward into American gunfire. Finally, the last American tank and remaining soldiers do retreat, and Hans and Albert, the only boys still alive, realize that they have temporarily stalled the American advance. A German demolition squadron arrives on the scene, and one of the leading officers chastises the two remaining boys, sarcastically referring to them as "fools" and "fine heroes." Hans goes mad once he sees that his friends have perished for nothing, and he threatens the German officer. Before the officer can shoot him, Albert fires at Hans instead. Hans dies in a last round of machine-gun fire, and Albert goes home, alone. A single sentence appears before the end credits: "This event occurred on April 27, 1945. It was so unimportant that it was never mentioned in any war communique."

Reception

Released in West Germany on 22 October 1959, *Die Brücke* won five awards at the 1960 German Film Awards, including Outstanding Feature Film. At the Mar del Plata Film Festival in Argentina in March 1960, *Die Brücke* beat out 25 other films to win Best Film in International Competition and also won the FIPRESCI Prize (tied with Alfonso Corona Blake's *Verano violento*). At the 5th Valladolid International Film Festival in Seminci, Spain (April 1960), the film won the Silver Spike (i.e., second place behind François Truffaut's *The 400 Blows*). It also received the Golden Globe Award for Best Foreign Language Film, the National Board of Review Award for Best Foreign Language Film, and a nomination for the Academy Award for Best Foreign Language Film (but lost to Marcel Camus' *Black Orpheus*). Not surprisingly, reviews, both contemporary and more recent, continue to heap praise on *Die Brücke* as an exemplary anti-war film. In the words of Bosley Crowther, "Withal, Herr Wicki has constructed an intense and compelling film, notable for its cinematic sharpness and its concentrated emotional drive" (Crowther, 1961).

Reel History Versus Real History

Though based on a real incident as noted earlier, *Die Brücke,* both the film and the novel it closely follows, concentrates the action to one bridge, adds two more Volkssturm boys, makes them all classmates and friends, provides backstories to particularize them, and greatly embellishes and complicates the action. All of these fictional elements were added on to the original and rather banal incident in order to attain maximum irony and pathos and to underscore the senseless futility of the boys' deaths in a war that was long lost and almost over. Decades since its original release, the ersatz tanks and ramping up of melodrama may strike more sophisticated audiences as somewhat jejune, but *Die Brücke* still works because its anti-war message remains imminently valid. A made-for-German-TV remake of *Die Brücke,* directed by Wolfgang Panzer, appeared in 2008 but is widely regarded as inferior to the original version.

BRIDGE ON THE RIVER KWAI, THE (1957)

Synopsis

The Bridge on the River Kwai is a British-American war epic directed by David Lean and starring William Holden, Jack Hawkins, and Alec Guinness and featuring Sessue Hayakawa. Based on the novel *Le pont de la Rivière Kwaï* (1952) by Pierre Boulle (also the author of *Planet of the Apes*), the film is fictional but uses the construction of the Burma Railway in 1942–1943 for its historical setting.

Background

A Frenchman working on British rubber plantations in Malaya, Pierre Boulle (1912–1994) enlisted in the French army when World War II broke out in 1939. In 1941, a year after the fall of France, Boulle served as a secret agent with the resistance movement in China, Burma, and French Indochina (Vietnam). In 1943, he was captured by Vichy loyalists on the Mekong River and spent the rest of the war in forced labor as a prisoner of war (POW) in Hanoi. In 1949 Boulle returned to France and wrote *Le pont de la Rivière Kwaï* (1952; English-language edition: *The Bridge over the River Kwai*, 1954). A fictional story placed in a historical setting, *Kwai* was inspired by the building of a bridge, but actually there were two parallel bridges: a bypass bridge made of wood (designated Q-654) and another bridge made of steel and concrete (designated 277)—and they were situated on the less poetically named Mae Klong River, near the city of Katchanburi, Thailand, in the province of the same name. These bridges were erected during the construction of the Burma-Siam Railway (aka "Death Railway"), a 415-km (258-mile) rail link between Bangkok, Thailand, and Rangoon, Burma, used by the Empire of Japan to move troops and supplies. More than 180,000 Southeast Asian civilians ("romusha") and 60,000 Allied POWs were conscripted by the Japanese to work on the railway and its bridges. Of that number over 100,000 Asian workers and 12,621 Allied POWs died during its construction (15 September 1942—17 October 1943). After Boulle's novel became an international bestseller, Carl Foreman (*High Noon*), a blacklisted

Co-stars (from left) Alec Guinness, William Holden, and Jack Hawkins pose in front of the fabled bridge during the filming of David Lean's *The Bridge on the River Kwai* (1957). (Columbia Pictures/Photofest)

American screenwriter self-exiled in London, optioned the film rights. American producer Sam Spiegel (*On the Waterfront*) was also captivated by Boulle's book. He met with Foreman, bought the screen rights for $7,000, and hired him to write an adaptation for $10,000. Columbia Pictures agreed to finance a film version, and Spiegel insisted that an American character be added to the script to enhance the film's domestic appeal. Spiegel then considered various directors: Fred Zinnemann, Howard Hawks, William Wyler, John Ford, Carol Reed, and Orson Welles. All either turned down the assignment or were rejected by Spiegel. Katherine Hepburn recommended David Lean (*In Which We Serve*), a British "art house" director who had yet to make a Hollywood wide-screen epic. Spiegel hired him in February 1956. Lean read Foreman's script and disliked it intensely, feeling it strayed too far from the spirit of Boulle's novel. Inevitably, friction developed between Foreman and Lean as they tried to work out a new version of the script in the ensuing months. In the meantime Spiegel, Lean, and Jack Hildyard, Lean's cinematographer, scouted the actual bridge location in Siam (as Thailand was then called) but rejected it as too remote for a large-scale movie production. The bridge site they eventually chose was located on the Masleliya Oya, a tributary of the Kelani Ganga River near Kitulga, Ceylon (present-day Sri Lanka). An abandoned stone quarry near Mahara, eight miles northeast of Colombo, the capital city, was chosen for the site of the POW camp (in the film, it is adjacent to the bridge). In 1956 hundreds of Sinhalese workers, assisted by 48 elephants, built the camp's numerous bamboo huts and then undertook the construction of the wooden trestle bridge itself. An enormous structure 425 feet long and 90 feet high, built from locally harvested timber, the bridge was completed in January 1957 at a cost of $52,085. In the end, after five months of troubled collaboration on the script, Lean fired Foreman in late June 1956. Sam Spiegel then brought in screenwriter Calder Willingham (*Paths of Glory*), but after just two weeks of trying to work with Lean, Willingham quit. In early September Spiegel sent a third screenwriter to Ceylon: Michael Wilson (*Friendly Persuasion*). The third time was the charm; Wilson and Lean began to produce a workable script but then another problem emerged. Lean initially wanted Charles Laughton for the key role of British Lt. Col. Nicholson but Laughton was in poor shape—simply too fat to play a half-starved POW. After much cajoling by Lean, Alec Guinness took the part. Spiegel wanted Cary Grant to play Shears but Lean, who preferred William Holden, prevailed. A big star after his Oscar win for *Stalag 17* (1953), Holden commanded top dollar; he signed a $300,000 contract that also guaranteed 10 percent of the box office receipts, a payout that ultimately amounted to $3.9 million ($34 million in 2017 dollars). For the role of Col. Saito, the Japanese camp commandant, Lean coaxed 68-year-old Sessue Hayakawa out of retirement. Both British and Japanese military advisors were also hired to ensure a reasonable degree of authenticity.

Production

After a 10-month pre-production phase, principal photography took more than 8 months (November 1956–May 1957) in the jungle in high heat and humidity—a grueling shoot made even more unpleasant by Lean's imperious directorial methods that alienated most of the cast and crew, especially Alec Guinness. The crucial moment of the production—the filming of the bridge being blown up—was supposed to take place on Sunday, 10 March 1957. Unfortunately, cameraman Freddy Ford forgot to signal that he had made it to safety after setting his camera, forcing Lean to abort the take. With the explosion called off, the train (a steam locomotive and six cars) proceeded across the bridge unimpeded. It ended up bursting through a sand barrier and then crashing into a generator on the far side of the bridge. The train was not damaged but it was derailed. Put back on the tracks with the assistance of elephants, the train was soon returned to its starting point. The next morning the bridge was successfully blown sky high, pitching the train into the river, as planned—a spectacular scene witnessed by S.W.R.D. Bandaranaike, Prime Minister of Ceylon, and other government dignitaries. Afterward, a second near-catastrophe occurred when all the film footage of the bridge explosion disappeared in transit from Ceylon to London. Ordinarily, the film would have been sent to London by sea, but the Suez Crisis necessitated air freight shipment instead. When the film canisters failed to arrive in London, a frantic worldwide search was undertaken. A week later the film was discovered, sitting in the sun on an airport tarmac in Cairo. Almost miraculously, none of the footage had been damaged by the intense heat.

Plot Summary

In early 1943, World War II British captives are brought to a Japanese POW camp in Burma. The man in charge, Col. Saito (Sessue Hayakawa), tells the captives that they will be constructing a rail bridge over the River Kwai in order to link Bangkok with Rangoon. The head British official, Lt. Col. Nicholson (Alec Guinness), tries to avoid the manual labor by citing examples from the Geneva Conventions, but the next morning, all enlisted soldiers are forced to report to work. Nicholson tells his own officers to stay behind in protest, and Saito warns that he will have the men executed should they refuse their work orders. Nicholson does not budge. Major Clipton (James Donald), a British medical officer, steps in, threatening Saito by saying that he can't kill an entire group of officers with so many witnesses. Furious, Saito punishes the men by leaving them to stand outside for the day, amidst the unbearable heat. When night falls, the disobedient officers are confined to a punishment hut and Nicholson is confined to a locked iron box. In the meantime, U.S. Navy Commander Shears (William Holden) breaks free from the camp. Despite his injuries, he finds a nearby village whose residents help him to escape via boat. Back at the camp, the POWs work as slowly and ineffectively as possible in order to undermine the Japanese captors, knowing that if Saito is unable to build the bridge by his assigned deadline, he will be forced to commit ritual suicide. In a play to save his own life, Saito creates an excuse for the delay by proclaiming a general amnesty to celebrate the Japanese victories in the Russo-Japanese War, which releases the British soldiers from their work. Nicholson uses the reprieve to look over his men's work and is appalled to find that they have been doing such a poor job. While some of his fellow squad members rail against him, Nicholson works with Capt. Reeves (Peter Williams) and Major Hughes (John Boxer) to plan and execute the creation of a sturdy, working bridge in order to bolster his unit's confidence and morale. The men choose a better site for the bridge downstream. Meanwhile, the escaped Shears recuperates in a hospital bed, cared for by a steadfast nurse (Ann Sears), when British Major Warden (Jack Hawkins) arrives and tells him that the United States Navy has commissioned him to join three other British soldiers to obliterate the bridge being built by his comrades before they can complete construction. Shears is hesitant at first, but upon hearing that he can retain an officer's title, eventually agrees to "volunteer" for the mission. Back at the river, Nicholson encourages his unit to complete the construction of the bridge by their intended deadline to prove the dedication and hard work of the British Army. Three paratroopers survive the jump and arrive at the drop point, and Warden, Shears, and Canadian Lt. Joyce (Geoffrey Horne) get to the river before the bridge is put into active use. In the dark, Shears and Joyce rig the bridge towers with explosives beneath the water line. The men then wait to blow up the bridge until the next day, when a train full of enemy soldiers and dignitaries are scheduled to cross it by train. The next morning, the three soldiers panic when they notice that the water level has gone down, leaving the wires from their explosives in plain sight. Nicholson sees the exposed wire and tells Saito, and the two run down to the bridge to examine it. Joyce, who stands by the detonator, runs out and brutally kills Saito with a knife. In shock, Nicholson calls for backup and wrestles Joyce to the ground to stop him from detonating the bomb. Joyce informs Nicholson that he is also a British officer and was sent to eliminate the bridge. Joyce is killed by the Japanese, and Shears is fatally shot while swimming across the river. Nicholson recognizes his friend and exclaims, "What have I done?" Warden fires his mortar at Nicholson, who then throws himself on the detonator just in time to blow up the bridge that he has just completed and watch the train careen into the river.

Reception

The Bridge on the River Kwai had its world premiere in London on 2 October 1957 and opened in the United States on 14 December 1957. With its catchy theme song ("Colonel Bogey March"), exotic setting, engrossing story, and stunning wide-screen cinematography, the movie was a huge commercial success, posting $33.3 million ($290 million in 2017 dollars) in worldwide box office receipts against a $3 million production budget. Nominated for eight Oscars, it won seven: Best Picture (Sam Spiegel); Best Director (David Lean); Best Actor (Alec Guinness); Best Adapted Screenplay (Michael Wilson, Carl Foreman, and Pierre Boulle); Best Music, Scoring (Malcolm Arnold); Best Film Editing (Peter Taylor); and Best Cinematography (Jack Hildyard). The movie also won three BAFTAs, three Golden Globes, three New York Film Critics Circle Awards, and a Grammy. With few exceptions, contemporary American reviews tended to be extravagant, for example, Bosley Crowther's: "Brilliant is the word, and no other, to describe the quality of skills that have gone into the making of this picture, from the writing of the script out of a novel by the Frenchman Pierre Boulle, to direction, performance, photographing, editing and application of a musical score" (Crowther, 1957). British critics were typically more circumspect in their appraisal. For example, the anonymous reviewer for *The Times* wrote, "When one remembers *A Walk in the Sun*, or even *The Red Badge of Courage* [*Bridge on the River Kwai*] is no masterpiece . . . There is too much suspicion of appeal to a world market for distribution, too great a readiness to be deflected by the sirens of Cinemascope and Technicolor, although these are splendidly exploited at times" (2 October 1957).

Real History Versus Reel History

Actual conditions under which Allied POWs toiled were infinitely worse than what is depicted in the film, and the real bridges took far longer to build. The film's more egregious inaccuracy, though, is its depiction of the British POW commander. Julie Summers, the granddaughter of Nicholson's real-life counterpart, Lt. Col. (later Brigadier) Sir Philip John Denton Toosey (1904–1975), reports that when her grandfather "first saw the film and he saw the ridiculous stormy row between Saito and Nicholson, he turned round to his daughter and he said, 'That was never like that. You could never have confronted the Japanese and caused them to lose face. That would have been fatal, I would not have survived'" (quoted by Summers, 2012). Once Lt. Col. Nicholson bends Saito to his will, Nicholson's nationalistic hubris drives him to unwittingly collaborate with the Japanese by building them an excellent railway bridge in record time. This, also, is far from the historical truth. Lt. Col. Toosey was not confrontational, but he was no collaborationist either (a characterization fabricated by Pierre Boulle to cast aspersions on traitors with France's Vichy government). In fact, Toosey was much the opposite, doing everything in his power to protect his men while surreptitiously delaying and sabotaging construction. For example, he had his men collect and deploy large numbers of termites to eat away at wooden bridge structures and saw to it that the concrete was mixed poorly. Likewise, the movie's depiction of Saito also slanders his real-life counterpart—a Japanese officer at the camp named Risaburo Saito, who was actually a sergeant-major, second in command, and not at all like Sessue Hayakawa's Col. Saito. Indeed, the real Saito had great respect for Lt. Col. Toosey and was, by all accounts, an unusually humane guard. The movie also erroneously portrays the Japanese as incapable of proper bridge design and in need of British expertise. In reality, the Japanese army had excellent engineers. At the end of the movie the wooden bridge is destroyed by commandos almost immediately after its completion. In actuality, the wooden bridge was bombed and rebuilt seven times between 1943 and 1945. Completed on 1 May 1943, the concrete and steel bridge (Bridge 277) remained intact more than for two years, until it was destroyed in June 1945 by B-24 liberators from the U.S. 458th Heavy Bombardment Group. As reparations after the war, the Japanese rebuilt the bridge, which still stands today.

BRIDGE TOO FAR, A (1977)

Synopsis
A Bridge Too Far is a World War II epic based on the 1974 book of the same title by Cornelius Ryan. Produced by Joseph E. and Richard P. Levine, adapted by William Goldman, and directed by Richard Attenborough, the film tells the story of the failure of Operation Market Garden, an ambitious Allied attempt to seize several bridges in the occupied Netherlands in order to outflank German defenses and end the war in Europe by Christmas of 1944.

Background
On 17 September 1974 Simon & Schuster published *A Bridge Too Far*, a 672-page epic by WWII historian Cornelius Ryan (*The Longest Day*) that recounted the story of Operation Market Garden (17–25 September 1944), Field Marshall Montgomery's failed attempt to hasten the end of the war by landing paratroopers behind German lines in the Nazi-occupied Netherlands in a bid to outflank the Siegfried Line and reach the Rhine. Published on the 30th anniversary of Market Garden, Ryan's magisterial tome garnered glowing reviews and earned over a million dollars in sales. Sadly, its author did not survive long after his final success; he died from prostate cancer five weeks after publication—but not before expressing the wish to movie mogul Joseph E. Levine that it be made into a film. Not affiliated with a studio, Levine raised money by selling advance distribution rights, but eventually put in $10 million of his own money. Riskier still, pre-production planning was done without a script; William Goldman's adaptation would not be completed until November 1975.

Production

During the film's 16-month pre-production phase, Levine hired Geoffrey Unsworth as his cinematographer and Richard Attenborough to direct (though Attenborough had directed only two films, both flops: a WWI-era musical and a biopic on Winston Churchill). Levine's production team put together a formidable air fleet: 11 WWII-era C-47 Dakota transport planes (from Portugal, Djibouti, Denmark, and Finland); 4 T-6 Texan/SNJ/Harvard fighter planes, an Auster III, and a Spitfire Mk IX. Levine also secured an international all-star cast that would rival the all-star cast of *The Longest Day* (1963)—Dirk Bogarde, James Caan, Michael Caine, Sean Connery, Edward Fox, Elliott Gould, Anthony Hopkins, Gene Hackman, Hardy Krüger, Ryan O'Neal, Laurence Olivier, Robert Redford, Maximilian Schell, and Liv Ullmann—for the film's 14 featured roles. Levine's first choice to play Kate Ter Horst (Ullmann's role) was Audrey Hepburn, who was a 15-year-old girl living in the Netherlands during Market Garden, but Hepburn's agent asked for $750,000 for six days work—too much even for Levine. Steve McQueen also wanted too much money: $3 million for three days work. Location shooting in Holland lasted the six months that weather conditions were favorable, starting in April 1976 and wrapping in October. In Attenborough's capable hands, the movie came in on schedule and under budget. It premiered on 15 June 1977, which was Levine's target date from the outset—a remarkable feat for a large-scale project employing 130 actors and hundreds of extras, 100 technicians, airplanes, tanks, and numerous other vehicles used in lengthy, large-scale, pre-CGI combat sequences.

Plot Summary

Concocted by British Field Marshall Bernard Montgomery, Operation Market Garden prescribed a combined airborne ("Market") and ground ("Garden") assault, a plan calling for 35,000 paratroopers to be flown from bases in England and dropped behind enemy lines in the Netherlands. Their mission is to secure bridges along a north-south road and hold them for 48 hours so that an armored column advancing north from the Allied frontline in Belgium will be able to reach Arnhem, 100 kilometers (60 miles) deep into German-held territory. The British 1st Airborne Division, commanded by Maj.-Gen. Roy Urquhart (Sean Connery), supported by a Polish airborne brigade under Gen. Stanisław Sosabowski (Gene Hackman), is to land in drop zones east and west of Arnhem and to secure both sides of the bridge there. Farther south, the U.S. 82nd Airborne Division under Brig. Gen. James Gavin (Ryan O'Neill) is to land near Nijmegen and secure its bridge and approaches. The U.S. 101st Airborne Division under Maj. Gen. Maxwell Taylor (Paul Maxwell) is tasked with securing the road and bridges around Eindhoven. The XXX Armoured Corps under Lt. Gen. Brian Horrocks (Edward Fox) is to advance north, cross the bridges captured by the American paratroopers, and reach Arnhem two days after the drop. When Gen. Urquhart briefs his officers, some of them balk at landing so far from their objective (up to 13 kilometers, to avoid German anti-aircraft fire), but Urquhart assures them that German resistance in the area will be negligible—despite the fact that recon photos and reports from the Dutch resistance indicate panzers near Arnhem. Lt. Gen. Frederick Browning (Dirk Bogarde) ignores these reports because he is not willing to contravene Montgomery. In a similar fashion,

British officers quash reports that the portable radios used by the paratroopers will probably not work across the long distances from the drop zones to the Arnhem Bridge. The airborne drops on 17 September 1944 go well, but the Son Bridge near Eindhoven is blown up by the Germans just before the 101st Airborne can get to it. Stiff German resistance, the narrowness of the sometimes raised road (dubbed "Hell's Highway"), and the need to construct a Bailey bridge all combine to stymie the advance of the XXX Corps. At Nijmegen, units of the 82nd Airborne cross the Waal River in canvas-and-wood assault boats under withering fire. Eventually the bridge is captured. At Arnhem the situation begins to deteriorate. As predicted, the radios are useless, and many of the jeeps needed to quickly reach the Arnhem Bridge never arrive by glider or are destroyed in action. The Germans overrun the British supply drop zones and launch an armored attack over the bridge being held at one end by British units under the command of Lt. Col. John Frost (Anthony Hopkins). The British manage to hold their positions but incur mounting casualties. Delayed by ground fog in England, Sosabowski's men join the battle too late to reinforce the British. After days of fierce house-to-house fighting, Urquhart's lightly armed troops are forced to surrender or retreat with staggering losses. When Urquhart returns to British HQ, he confronts Browning about the fiasco that was Market Garden and Browning sheepishly replies, "Well, as you know, I always felt we tried to go a bridge too far." In the final scene, a Dutch woman (Liv Ullmann) abandons her badly damaged home, which was used as a hospital by the British. Passing through the front yard, which has been converted into a makeshift graveyard, she and her children walk along the high riverbank with her father, an elderly doctor (Laurence Olivier), pushing some salvaged household items in a wheelbarrow.

Reception

Posting $50.7 million in ticket sales against a $27 million production budget, *A Bridge Too Far* did well at the box office—but for a three-hour WWII epic with an outsized cast of A-list movie stars, not as well as was hoped. Ignored at Oscar time, the movie drew mixed reviews from critics. Typical is the judgment of Vincent Canby, who found *A Bridge* "massive, shapeless, often unexpectedly moving, confusing, sad, vivid and very, very long" (Canby, 16 June 1977). As Canby notes, the sheer length and complexity of the film—lots of cross-cutting between disparate locales and too many players to allow for much character development (or viewer identification)—doubtless left audiences shell-shocked. Furthermore, the movie did something that few war films dare: it recounted an Allied military disaster of epic proportions, which was depressing fare for a film genre that usually serves up triumphalist scenarios.

Reel History Versus Real History

Allowing for the usual streamlining to achieve narrative coherence, William Goldman's script closely follows Cornelius Ryan's painstaking account of Market Garden. Accordingly, *A Bridge Too Far* achieves a high degree of historical accuracy. Inaccuracies tend to be minor. Some paratroopers are shown jumping "clean fatigue," that is, without weapons or equipment; the parachutes used are of a type not available in 1944; the 2nd SS Panzer Corps is referred to as the 2nd SS Panzer Division, etc. (Murray, 2013, pp. 14–18). Curiously, Market Garden's architect, Field Marshall Montgomery, is not depicted in the film, though he is quoted by Lt. Gen. Browning as judging Market Garden "90 percent successful"—a patently ridiculous claim. Browning's statement about "a bridge too far" was actually made during the planning stages, not after the battle, as depicted in the film.

CASUALTIES OF WAR (1989)

Synopsis

Casualties of War is an American war crime drama directed by Brian De Palma and starring Michael J. Fox and Sean Penn. The screenplay by David Rabe is based on the Incident on Hill 192 during the Vietnam War: the 1966 kidnapping, gang rape, and murder of a Vietnamese woman by four American soldiers, who were subsequently court-martialed and convicted, based on the damning testimony of the fifth member of the squad who refused to participate.

Background

On 18–19 November 1966, during the Vietnam War, four members of Charlie Company, 2nd Battalion (Airborne), 8th Cavalry Regiment, 1st Cavalry Division, kidnapped a 21-year-old Vietnamese woman named Phan Thi Mao, gang-raped her, and then murdered her. Pfc. Robert M. Storeby, the fifth member of the squad, refused to participate. Despite threats to his own life, Storeby reported the atrocity to superiors and ultimately testified against his brothers-in-arms, which resulted in their being court-martialed, dishonorably discharged, and receiving prison terms from eight years to life in prison. What became known as the "Incident on Hill 192" gained notoriety after journalist Daniel Lang published an exhaustive 29,000-word account entitled "Casualties of War" in *The New Yorker* (18 October 1969), subsequently published as a slim paperback with the same title. West German filmmaker Michael Verhoeven's 79-minute Brechtian docudrama based on the incident (and rather cryptically entitled *O.K.*) appeared the following year. (When it was listed for competition at the 1970 Berlin Film Festival, the jury president, American director George Stevens, resigned after failing to have the film excluded as anti-American. In the ensuing row, the entire jury resigned without bestowing any prizes.) Also in 1970, producer David Susskind bought the film rights for Warner Bros. The studio hired Jack Clayton to direct and journalist Pete Hamill to write a script but Hamill's script was rejected, and the film did not materialize. In 1979, when Susskind tried to revive the project for ABC-TV—again without success—playwright David Rabe mentioned it to Brian De Palma, who had read Lang's *New Yorker* article a decade earlier and had been haunted by it. De Palma wanted to make the picture but could not secure studio backing. By 1985 Rabe had written a new script, and Michael J. Fox and Sean Penn had signed on as actors—almost enough impetus to attract financing from Paramount but not quite. After the resounding box office success of Vietnam War films—*Coming Home*

(1978), *The Deer Hunter* (1978), *Apocalypse Now* (1979), *Platoon* (1986), and *Full Metal Jacket* (1987)—and with De Palma a hot director after scoring a major hit with *The Untouchables* (1987), Dawn Steel (Columbia's new studio head) green-lit the project, confident that it, too, would be a moneymaker.

Production

Except for bookend scenes shot in San Francisco, *Casualties of War* was filmed on location in Thailand from late March to early July 1988. To achieve verisimilitude De Palma's technical advisor (also Oliver Stone's advisor on *Platoon*), Vietnam Marine veteran Dale Dye (who also has a small part in the film) had the actors eat C-rations, sent them on forced marches carrying M-60 machine guns or an M-79 grenade launcher, and had them learn to fieldstrip their M-16 rifles for the first two weeks on location. Ubiquitous snakes, insects, and the intense tropical heat and humidity made the four-month shoot a grueling experience.

Plot Summary

Most of the film unfolds as the flashback-nightmare of Max Eriksson (Michael J. Fox), a Vietnam veteran who falls asleep on a Muni Metro train in San Francisco. On nighttime patrol, Lt. Reilly's (Ving Rhames) platoon is attacked by the Viet Cong after a soldier panics and exposes their position. Soon thereafter Eriksson walks over an abandoned Viet Cong tunnel. It collapses, trapping him. He is rescued by his squad leader, Sgt. Tony Meserve (Sean Penn). While on break near a river village in the Central Highlands, the unit comes under fire, and one of Meserve's friends, the squad's radio operator Spec 4 "Brownie" Brown (Erik King), is fatally wounded, a death that deeply affects Meserve. Back at their barracks at Wolfe Base, Pfc. Antonio Dìaz (John Leguizamo) arrives as Brownie's replacement. Sent back out on a long-range recon patrol, an embittered Meserve orders the squad to kidnap a Vietnamese girl for sex. Eriksson tries to dissuade his comrades, but Meserve, Cpl. Thomas E. Clark (Don Patrick Harvey), and Pfc. Herbert Hatcher (John C. Reilly) ignore him. After sunset, the troops kidnap a young Vietnamese villager named Than Thi Oahn (Thuy Thu Le) and take her with them on patrol. The squad later shelters in an abandoned hooch where Meserve, Clark, and Hatcher confront Erikkson and Dìaz, pressuring them to join in the victimization of Than. To placate the others Dìaz decides to go along with the rape. Erikkson, now outnumbered four to one, is asked to stand guard while the other squad members rape Than. At dawn, Erikkson is left to watch over Than while the other troops position themselves by a railroad bridge near a Viet Cong river supply depot. Erikkson decides to go against his orders and bring Than back to her family, but Meserve sends Clark to get Erikkson and Than, thus thwarting Erikkson's plan. Meserve commands Dìaz to radio for air support so that the squad can attack the depot and then goes a step further by ordering Dìaz to stab Than to death. To rescue Than, Eriksson fires his weapon and gives away their position to enemy combatants. During the battle that follows, Than and Eriksson attempt to flee, but Meserve takes down Eriksson with his gun. Eriksson is left to watch, helpless, as his squad members exterminate Than and leave her to fall off of the bridge. Following the firefight, Eriksson awakens in a field hospital and relays his story to a friend, Rowan (Jack Gwaltney). Rowan encourages Erikkson to relay his story to their superiors, Lt. Reilly and the company commander, Capt. Hill (Dale Dye). However, rather than take corrective action, both Reilly and Hill choose to sweep the situation under the carpet and reassign Erikkson to a position digging tunnels. The other four squad members are split up and reassigned to other units as well. Later that evening after Clark tries to "frag" (assassinate) him, Eriksson, armed with a shovel, confronts Meserve and his men, who back off. After Eriksson meets with Capt. Kirk (Sam Robards), a chaplain, and tells him the story of Than's grim fate, an investigation is launched and the four men involved in Than's rape and murder are court-martialed. Clark is sentenced to life in prison, Hatcher receives 15 years hard labor, Meserve receives 10 years hard labor, and Dìaz receives 8 years. At the end of the film, Eriksson awakens from his Vietnam flashback still on the train he was riding at the outset of the film. Seated nearby is a Vietnamese American student who resembles Than. She leaves behind a scarf as she disembarks at Dolores Park, and Eriksson runs after her to return it. She thanks him politely and turns away and adds that he's had a bad dream as he gazes thoughtfully over a peaceful scene.

Reception

In 1,487 theaters by mid-August 1989, *Casualties of War* grossed $5.2 million at the box office the first week of its release but quickly faded. If audiences were expecting a rousing war picture, they got anti-war gothic horror instead. Ultimately the movie was not profitable; it earned only $18.7 million but cost $22.5 million to make and probably another $5 to $10 million to market: a net loss of at least $9 million, perhaps more. Reviews were largely positive but *Casualties* ignited protests by some Vietnam veterans' groups, who judged it an exploitative work that perpetuated popular stereotypes of Vietnam soldiers as rapists and murderers (Kastor, 1989, C1). Adding some credibility to their claims, screenwriter David Rabe disassociated himself from the movie, citing "creative differences" with De Palma, probably having to do with fabricated action scenes not in the original source material and a concocted "happy ending."

Reel History Versus Real History

Except for the victim's name, which is correctly reported, Daniel Lang used fictional names throughout his account of the Incident on Hill 192. The movie version uses Lang's pseudonyms with a few slight variations (e.g., Sven Eriksson, the Robert Storeby character, becomes Max Eriksson). It also gets the kernel of the story right: the five-day recon patrol, the abandoned hooch, the rape and murder of a Vietnamese peasant girl, the one righteous dissenter and witness, the initial reluctance to prosecute, the subsequent court-martial (actually there were four), and the sentencing. But *Casualties of War* also resorts to considerable embellishment and omission in its rendition of the events. In reality Storeby was not rescued from a hole by his squad leader (whose real name was Sgt. David E. Gervase). The squad's radioman was not killed. In actuality Gervase and his men did not make a spur-of-the-moment decision in the midst of a firefight to kill their victim; they planned to kill her from the outset. Other circumstances surrounding the rape and murder of Phan Thi Mao are also fictionalized. The assault on the riverside supply depot is entirely fictional and quite absurd; an attack on a key enemy position by a four-man squad, ushered in by helicopter airstrikes, is tactically preposterous. As the movie depicts, Mao was stabbed and then shot, but in the bushes off a hillside trail as she tried to crawl away, not from a cinematically spectacular bridge. Storeby's squad mates did not try to kill him afterwards, nor did he assert his manliness by fending them off; they were not allowed access to him after allegations were filed. Finally the film omits the fact that Storeby faced intense harassment by defense attorneys during the courts-martial, and all the sentences handed down were drastically reduced on appeal.

COME AND SEE [RUSSIAN: *IDI I SMOTRI*] (1985)

Synopsis
Come and See is a Soviet war drama directed by Elem Klimov, with a screenplay by Klimov and Ales Adamovich, starring Aleksei Kravchenko and Olga Mironova. Set during the German occupation of Byelorussia during the Second World War, the film follows a traumatized young boy as he witnesses a series of Nazi atrocities.

Background
As a teenager Ales Adamovich (1927–1994) fought with Belarusian partisans against the Nazis in World War II. Some 25 years after the war ended, Adamovich and fellow writers Yanka Bryl and Vladimir Kolesnik visited the sites of many of the 628 Belarusian villages that had been razed by the Nazis after the German defeat at Stalingrad in 1943. Gathering firsthand accounts by survivors, the trio published a compilation of those stories entitled *Ya iz Pylayushchey Derevni* [*I Am from the Burning Village*] (1972). Adamovich also published *Khatyn* (1971), a novel based on the same topic. Commissioned by Goskino USSR, the Soviet state cinema agency, to make a film that would commemorate the "Great Victory" of 1945, Russian filmmaker Elem Klimov (1933–2003) collaborated with Ales Adamovich to write a screenplay about the Nazi genocide in Belorussia (present-day Belarus), based primarily on Adamovich's novel. Pyotr Masherov, First Secretary of the Communist Party of Belarus, himself a partisan veteran, was highly supportive of Klimov's film. However, just before filming was slated to begin in Minsk in 1977, state censors led by Goskino Vice President Boris Pavlenok and film critic Dal Orlov demanded drastic screenplay revisions that Klimov refused to make. In the face of official intransigence Klimov suffered a nervous breakdown but persisted. After seven years of intensive lobbying, Soviet cinema bureaucrats finally capitulated and authorized production in 1984. The only change that Klimov had to make was to alter the title, from "Kill Hitler" to *Come and See*, a phrase derived from the New Testament Revelation of St. John the Divine 6:1: "And I saw when the Lamb opened one of the seals, and I heard, as it were the noise of thunder, one of the four beasts [of the Apocalypse] saying, Come and see."

Production

Come and See was shot in sequence over a period of nine months in 1984. To achieve maximum realism Klimov employed lots of Steadicam shots and often loaded the guns used in the film with live ammunition, as opposed to blanks. Aleksey Kravchenko, the 13-year-old nonactor who played Flyora, mentions in interviews that bullets sometimes passed just millimeters above his head in certain scenes. Worried that the extreme rigors of the shoot might drive Kravchenko mad, Klimov tried unsuccessfully to have the boy hypnotized to inoculate him emotionally. As it was, Kravchenko stayed sane but returned to school thin and prematurely grey.

Plot Summary

In 1943 two Belorussian boys, hoping to join the Soviet partisan forces, dig up a battlefield for abandoned weapons. One of the boys, Flyora (Aleksey Kravchenko), finds a rifle. The next day he is conscripted but when the partisans move on, their commander, Kosach (Liubomiras Laucevičius), orders Flyora to stay behind. Upset and angry, Flyora enters the refugee camp and encounters Glasha (Olga Mironova), an attractive but demented woman in love with Kosach who thinks that Flyora is Kosach. Suddenly the camp is shelled (shattering Flyora's eardrums) and then attacked by German paratroopers. Flyora and Glasha hide themselves in the woods, then flee to Flyora's house only to find it empty. Flyora refuses to think his family killed, so he instead convinces himself that they have sought refuge in an island across from the bog. Fleeing the village, Glasha spies a pile of half-naked corpses in a pile behind the house, but chooses not to inform Flyora. At first Flyora is incapable of accepting the truth, but an encounter with other villagers who have run from the Nazis leaves him convinced that his family is actually dead. Flyora blames himself, but a partisan named Roubej (Vladas Bagdonas) helps him to move forward and search for food. At sunset, Roubej and Flyora steal a cow from a Nazi-occupied village, but Roubej and the stolen cow are shot by Germans as they run across a field. Flyora attempts to steal a horse and cart, but the owner of the cart stops him but then decides to assist the thief by helping him to obtain false identification. Their plans are interrupted when a German einsatzkommando [mobile killing squad] arrives and surrounds the village. Flyora tries to alert the townsfolk of the impending attack, but he is rounded up by the German soldiers. Flyora exits the church by jumping out a high window, but is caught and forced to watch as Wehrmacht soldiers light the church building on fire with the villagers locked inside. A German soldier then puts a gun to Flyora's head for a photograph. Flyora leaves the village and discovers that partisan soldiers have surprised the Germans in a counterattack. After retrieving his coat and weapon, Flyora encounters a bloodied woman who is dazed after being raped and sees that his comrades have successfully imprisoned 11 Germans and their associates. The associates cover the German soldiers with gasoline, but the partisan soldiers shoot the Germans before the fire is lit. As the partisan forces depart, Flyora finds a portrait of Adolf Hitler in a puddle. In a surreal sequence, Flyora shoots at the picture, causing time to unwind in reverse and all the horrors of the war to be undone. The film ends with Flyora joining the other partisan soldiers in their march through the forest in the snow.

Reception

Come and See was a box office smash in the Soviet Union, racking up a phenomenal 28.9 million admissions. The film won the Golden Prize at the 14th Moscow Film International Festival and the FIPRESCI [International Federation of Film Critics] Award. It also garnered high praise from film critics throughout the world, many of whom rank *Come and See* as one of the greatest films ever made. According to Klimov, the movie's strange blend of nightmarish surrealism and ferociously graphic depictions of unspeakable atrocities proved overwhelming for some audience members who had lived through the events dramatized; they had to be carted away in ambulances.

Reel History Versus Real History

The film's anchoring narrative—Flyora's hellish, mind-bending coming of age—is fictional, but most of the events depicted in *Come and See* are based on eyewitness accounts, though they are sometimes embellished. For example, to achieve maximal demonization of the enemy, Klimov engages in hyperbole regarding the look and behavior of the German soldiers, especially during the bizarrely carnivalesque Perekhody massacre scene. The Germans are dressed in weird motley à la *Mad Max* and depicted as a mob of ravening, rampaging monsters. Yet, in a way, the historical reality is even more chilling; the Nazis were disciplined killers who carried out acts of genocide in a matter-of-fact manner. Nonetheless, *Come and See* gets its basic scenario right. During an after-screening discussion in Germany, an elderly man stood up and said: "I was a soldier of the Wehrmacht; moreover, an officer . . . I traveled through all of Poland and Belarus, finally reaching [the] Ukraine. I will testify: everything that is told in this film is the truth. And the most frightening and shameful thing for me is that this film will be seen by my children and grandchildren" (http://www.classicartfilms.com/come-and-see-1985).

COURAGE UNDER FIRE (1996)

Synopsis

Courage Under Fire is an American war film written by Vietnam veteran Patrick Sheane Duncan, directed by Edward Zwick, and starring Denzel Washington and Meg Ryan. The second collaboration between Washington and Zwick after *Glory* (1989), *Courage Under Fire* is a *Rashomon*-like investigation into the Gulf War combat death of a female Medevac helicopter pilot being considered for the Medal of Honor.

Background

A few years after the First Persian Gulf War (1990–1991) Patrick Sheane Duncan (*84 Charlie MoPic*) wrote novel and screenplay versions of *Courage Under Fire*, a *Rashomon*-like narrative inspired by the downing of a Black Hawk helicopter in Mogadishu, Somalia, on 3 October 1993 that resulted in two U.S. Army Rangers being awarded the Medal of Honor posthumously (an incident later dramatized in

Ridley Scott's *Black Hawk Down*, 2001). Duncan's script recounts an investigation into the Gulf War combat death of a female Medevac helicopter pilot being considered for the Medal of Honor. On 27 January 1995 Patrick Duncan's agent, Mary Kimmel, sold his spec script to 20th Century Fox for $1 million—$2 million if it got produced, which it immediately was. Budgeting for a $50 million production, the studio considered Tom Hanks and Harrison Ford before hiring Denzel Washington to play the lead male role. Meg Ryan was hired to play the female lead, and the two actors were paid $10 and $6 million, respectively. Washington persuaded the studio to hire Edward Zwick (with whom he worked on *Glory*) to direct, and frequent Coen brothers' director of photography Roger Deakins was hired to shoot the picture.

Production

In the nine-month pre-production lead-up to the start of the shoot on 16 October 1995, the studio sought script approval from the Department of Defense (DOD) so as to be allowed to rent Abrams tanks, Bradley Fighting Vehicles (BFVs), and a fleet of Apache and Blackhawk helicopters—and thereby save $1 million in production costs. Five successive revisions of the script were submitted to the Army's Public Affairs Office in L.A. between March and September 1995, but all were rejected for putting the military in an unfavorable light (e.g., depictions of a small unit mutiny, the de facto murder of an officer, cover-ups, etc.). Denied U.S. military support, Zwick had to import 11 surplus British Centurion tanks (shipped to Vancouver from Australia and then trucked to Texas), where sheet metal was added to make them resemble M1A1 Abrams tanks. To prepare for his role, Denzel Washington visited with members of the 1st Battalion, 12th Cavalry Regiment, an armored unit stationed at Fort Hood in Killeen, Texas. Matt Damon, then 25 and still a relative unknown, went to far greater Method Acting lengths to nail his on-screen transformation from a healthy combat medic to an anguished vet suffering from post-traumatic stress disorder (PTSD) and heroin addiction (depicted in just one scene, albeit a crucial one, late in the film). In order to look sufficiently gaunt and wasted, Damon put himself on a near-starvation diet and ran 13 miles a day. He lost 50 pounds and suffered adrenal gland damage and other health problems that took months of medication to repair.

Plot Summary

During the First Gulf War (1991), Lt. Col. Nat Serling (Denzel Washington) accidentally takes out one of his own tanks in the midst of a chaotic nighttime battle, killing his friend Capt. Boylar (Tim Ransom). The U.S. Army covers up the incident and transfers a remorseful and alcoholic Serling to a desk job. Later, Serling has to relive his own "friendly fire" event when he is tasked with deciding whether or not Capt. Karen Emma Walden (Meg Ryan) deserved to be the first woman to receive a (posthumous) Medal of Honor for valor in combat (the Medal of Honor had been awarded to a woman, Dr. Mary Edwards Walker, 1832–1919, an American Civil War doctor—but not for combat heroics). Walden commanded a crew on a Medevac Huey called in to save the injured soldiers from a shot-down Black

Hawk helicopter. En route to the crash, Walden came face to face with an enemy T-54 tank. She and her fellow soldiers destroyed the enemy tank, but Walder's helicopter was gunned down. The next day, when the two downed crews are finally rescued, Walden is reported dead. Reviewing the testimonies of Walden's crew, Serling notices inconsistencies between them. Specialist Andrew Ilario (Matt Damon) expresses high praise for Walden, but Staff Sgt. John Monfriez (Lou Diamond Phillips) pronounces Walden to be a coward and states that he, Monfriez, eliminated the enemy tank. Other members of the crew prove incapable of testifying due to their injuries. The crew of the Black Hawk mentions hearing M16 gunshots, but Ilario and Monfriez deny that shots were ever fired. Feeling pressure from his superiors to wrap things up, Serling instead leaks the story to a reporter, Tony Gartner (Scott Glenn), hoping to prevent another cover-up. Serling presses Monfriez during a car ride, and the shaken officer forces Serling out of the car at gunpoint before killing himself by colliding with an oncoming train. Serling is able to track down Ilario, however, who finally tells the true story. Wanting to flee and leave Rady (Tim Guinee) behind, Monfriez shot Walden in the stomach during a firefight with the enemy, either accidentally or deliberately. Though wounded, Walden covered her crew's retreat with an M16 the next morning, expecting to be rescued later, but Monfriez told his rescuers that Walden was already dead. As a result A-10 Warthogs dropped napalm on the entire area, finishing off Walden. Ilario was too frightened to tell the truth, and Altameyer was too injured to speak. Serling presents his final report to Hershberg, and Walden's young daughter, Anne Marie (Christina Stojanovich), receives the Medal of Honor in her mother's behalf at a White House ceremony. Later, Serling meets with Capt. Boylar's parents (Richard Venture and Diane Baker) and confesses about the true manner of their son's death. The Boylars tell Serling he must forgive himself. The final scene reveals that Capt. Walden was the pilot who evacuated Boylar's body after Serling's friendly fire incident.

Reception

Running for seven weeks in the summer of 1996 (12 July–22 August; widest release: 2,000 theaters), *Courage Under Fire* was a solid box office hit, grossing over $59 million domestically and $41.8 million in foreign markets for a worldwide gross of $100.9 million, representing a $40 million profit. Reviews were mostly positive, though not effusive. For example, Richard von Busack characterized Edward Zwick as a liberal making a war movie who, perforce, "alternates between deploring violence and succumbing to the excitement of battle." In von Busack's view, *Courage Under Fire* "acknowledges the hellishness of war while admiring the erectness of the officer's spine. The film is stalemated. It's politically neutral, not questioning the various diplomatic missteps on the part of the United States that encouraged Sadaam Hussein to think he could get away with annexing Kuwait" (von Busack, 1996).

Reel History Versus Real History

Denied DOD cooperation, Edward Zwick had to use Bell AH-1 Cobra helicopters instead of Black Hawks, though Cobras were sometimes used in the Gulf War. Capt.

Walden's UH-1H Medevac helicopter goes into action without a gunship escort—something that would never occur in a real combat zone. Nor would Sgt. Monfriez have been allowed to carry an automatic weapon on a Red Cross–marked Medevac helicopter; U.S. military law prohibits such weapons on ambulance vehicles of any kind (though sidearms for personal protection are allowed). Similarly, Walden's attack on the Iraqi tank with a Huey fuel bladder is logistically absurd and a blatant violation of the Law of Armed Conflict (LOAC) and the Geneva Conventions, which define medical personnel as noncombatants forbidden from engaging in hostilities. Rather than being awarded a Medal of Honor, Meg Ryan's Capt. Karen Walden would likely have been court-martialed, had she lived.

CROSS OF IRON (1977)

Synopsis
Cross of Iron is a British-German war film directed by Sam Peckinpah that stars James Coburn and features Maximilian Schell, James Mason, and David Warner. The film follows a Wehrmacht platoon fighting on the Eastern Front in World War II as the Germans try to stem Soviet advances on the Taman Peninsula in late 1943. The film focuses on the class conflict between an aristocratic Prussian officer without battle experience who covets the Iron Cross and a cynical, battle-hardened infantry NCO. The screenplay was based on *The Willing Flesh* by Willi Heinrich, a novel published in 1956 that is loosely based on the true story of Werhmacht soldier Johann Schwerdfeger.

Background
German WWII Eastern Front veteran Willi Heinrich (1920–2005) began writing novels after the war. His first and most famous book, *Das Geduldige Fleisch* [*The Willing Flesh*], about retreating Wehrmacht soldiers embroiled in the Battle of Krymskaya in the Crimea (April 1943), was published in 1955. In 1975 Wolf C. Hartwig, a West German producer of low-budget soft porn exploitation movies eager to break into mainstream filmmaking, decided to try and film Heinrich's novel. He sent director Sam Peckinpah a copy of the book, retitled *The Cross of Iron* in the 1956 English-language edition. Intrigued by the subject matter, Peckinpah agreed to make a movie version for a $300,000 director's fee, plus another $100,000 and 5 percent on the back end, if the film proved to be profitable. Hartwig hired Julius Epstein (*Casablanca*) to write a screenplay, but Peckinpah rejected it as too convoluted and cliché-ridden and hired James Hamilton, a Korean War veteran, to write a new script and Walter Kelley (*Pat Garrett & Billy the Kid*) to collaborate on rewrites after viewing numerous Nazi and Allied newsreels at film archives in Koblenz and London, respectively (Weddle, 2000, pp. 504–506).

Production
A joint Anglo-German production (EMI Films/ITC Entertainment, London and Rapid Films GmbH, Munich), *Cross of Iron* was plagued from the outset by financial

and logistical problems. Wolf Hartwig had budgeted $4 million to make the movie but had managed to secure only a fraction of that sum when pre-production commenced. The Yugoslav government promised to supply WWII-era war matériel—including airplanes, 15 Soviet T-34 tanks, and German MG42 machine guns and MP40 submachine guns—but much of this equipment was not yet available by the start of the shoot, causing considerable delays. Once under way, the production was hobbled by Hartwig's penny-pinching ineptitude as a producer and by Sam Peckinpah's alcoholism. According to biographer David Weddle, Peckinpah steadily drank 180-proof slivovitz throughout the shoot. For two or three weeks at a time he could control his intake enough to function but would then go on benders and have blackouts that would render him dysfunctional for several days: a pattern that resulted in highly uneven filmmaking. To save money, the film was mostly shot in northern Yugoslavia (present-day Slovenia) around Obrov and Zagreb, and in Trieste, Italy, and Savudrija, Croatia. Interior shots were completed at Pinewood Studios in London. Nonetheless, various delays and interruptions resulted in $2 million in cost overruns. Out of money, Hartwig and co-producer Alex Winitsky tried to shut down production before the final scene could be filmed on 6 July 1976 (the 89th day of a shoot that began on 29 March). An irate James Coburn ejected the pair from the set, and he and Peckinpah improvised a closing scene to complete the picture.

Plot Summary

The opening credit sequence features black-and-white prewar and war scenes, accompanied by Franz Wiedemann's popular children's song "Hänschen klein" ("Little Hans"). The film proper (in color) begins with a Wehrmacht platoon led by Sergeant Rolf Steiner (James Coburn) raiding a Russian outpost. Steiner and his men wipe out the enemy position and capture a Russian boy-soldier (Slavko Štimac). Captain Stransky (Maximilian Schell), an effete, aristocratic Prussian officer, is assigned as the battalion leader at the Kuban bridgehead on the Taman Peninsula, Eastern Front, in 1943. Stransky boasts to both Col. Brandt (James Mason) and his adjutant, Captain Kiesel (David Warner), that he went out for the posting in Russia with the specific aim of earning the Iron Cross. Upon their initial meeting, Stransky commands Sgt. Steiner to kill a young Russian prisoner in accordance with a standing order. Steiner fails to shoot the prisoner, and as Stransky sets out to follow the order himself, Corporal Schnurrbart (Fred Stillkrauth) steps in and saves the boy's life. Later, Stransky promotes Steiner to Senior Sergeant. Steiner then releases the young Russian prisoner, only to see the child disposed of by his own side. During the attack, Stransky takes shelter in a bunker, revealing his cowardice. Meanwhile, Lt. Meyer (Igor Galo), who commanded Steiner's company, is eliminated during the counterattack. Steiner sustains injuries during the attack while attempting to save a German soldier and is released to a hospital to convalesce. While at the hospital, Steiner sees visions of the dead, including the face of the Russian youth who he released. Upon recovering, he is given the option to go on leave, but chooses to rejoin his squadron. Meeting up with his men, Steiner hears that Stransky has been taking credit for leading the counterattack, refusing to credit Meyer, and has consequently been nominated for the Iron Cross. Stransky named as witnesses Lt. Triebig (Roger Fritz), who he blackmailed with his knowledge of Triebig's homosexuality, and Steiner. Stransky implores Steiner to back up his story, but Steiner makes no promises. When questioned by Brandt, Steiner bitterly claims that he abhors military officers on principle and asks for some time to fully consider his reply. In the interim, Stansky is told that his patrol must pull back, but he fails to let Steiner know, thus forsaking Steiner's entire platoon. As Steiner's men come to the German frontlines, they send word ahead in the hopes of avoiding friendly fire. Stransky deviously mentions to Triebig that Steiner and his men could be "mistaken" for Russian soldiers, if they should choose to kill them. As a result, Triebig commands his troops to fire upon the Germans; only Steiner and two of his men survive. Steiner kills Triebig and then searches for Stransky. The Soviet forces unleash a forceful assault, and Brandt both emboldens the troops into a counterattack and calls for the immediate evacuation of Kiesel. In the midst of the battle, a song plays until the ending credits. Steiner locates Stransky, but decides to leave him alive, giving him a weapon for battle to see "where the crosses of iron grow." Stransky takes on Steiner's "challenge," and the pair go into battle. The movie ends with Stransky failing to properly reload his weapon and being wounded by a Soviet soldier (Sweeney MacArthur), who looks similar to the young Russian released by Steiner in the beginning of the film. Stransky audaciously begs Steiner for assistance, and Steiner's laughter carries viewers to the end credits.

Reception

Initially released in Europe and Japan in the early months of 1977, *Cross of Iron* did well at the box office, particularly in Germany. Released in the United States mid-May of that year, the movie tanked commercially and reviews were mixed. Some American critics praised the film as an effective anti-war movie that signaled Peckinpah's comeback, whereas others were dismissive. For example, David Rosenbaum pronounced it "worse than your typical blow-'em-up war movie because it is pretentious" (Rosenbaum, 1977) and the anonymous reviewer for *Variety* termed it "well but conventionally cast, technically impressive, but ultimately violence-fixated" (1 January 1977). After seeing the film, Orson Welles cabled Peckinpah, praising *Cross of Iron* as "the best war film he had seen about the ordinary enlisted man since *All Quiet on the Western Front*" (Seydor, 1995, p. 20). Director Quentin Tarantino, a Peckinpah fan, cites the film as one of his favorite WWII movies and acknowledges it as a key influence on his decision to make *Inglorious Basterds* (2009).

Reel History Versus Real History

The battle action in *Cross of Iron* is fictional and generic and is not meant to represent any specific engagements on the Eastern Front in 1943. However, author Willi Heinrich did base Sgt. Rolf Steiner, the lead character of his novel, *Das Geduldige Fleisch*, on Johann Schwerdfeger (1914–2015). A stalwart German noncommissioned officer, Schwerdfeger enlisted in the Wehrmacht in 1935, joined Jäger Regiment 228 of the 101st Jäger Division in June 1942, fought in the Don Bend at Rostov and Maykop in the Caucasus, and took part in the German retreat through the Kuban bridgehead and the Taman Peninsula—the setting of Heinrich's novel and Peckinpah's film. On 17 May 1943, Feldwebel (deputy platoon leader) Schwerdfeger was awarded the *Ritterkreuz* (Knight's Cross of the Iron Cross). In April 1944, in the breakout from Hube's Pocket, he was severely wounded—as is Steiner in the movie—and had Oak Leaves added to his Knight's Cross on 14 May 1944. At 6'2" and 48 years old in 1976, James Coburn was both much taller and much older than his real-life counterpart; Johann Schwerdfeger was of average height and only 28 in the summer of 1943.

CRUEL SEA, THE (1953)

Synopsis

The Cruel Sea is a British war film based on the bestselling novel of the same title by former naval officer Nicholas Monsarrat. Produced by Leslie Norman; directed by Charles Frend; and starring Jack Hawkins, Donald Sinden, Denholm Elliott, and Stanley Baker, the film tells the story of the Battle of the Atlantic by focusing on life aboard two Royal Navy corvettes.

Background

A classic account of WWII's Battle of the Atlantic from the British perspective, Nicholas Monsarrat's novel, *The Cruel Sea* (Cassell, 1951), sold over 2 million copies in two years. Monsarrat knew his subject well. An officer in the Royal Navy throughout the war, he served on three different corvettes and two frigates protecting Allied shipping from German U-boats in the North Atlantic, kept meticulous notes on his experiences, and wrote three books on convoy escort duty before penning *The Cruel Sea*. Michael Balcon's Ealing Studios purchased the screen rights shortly after the book's publication and hired Eric Ambler, famed espionage novelist and screenwriter, to adapt *The Cruel Sea* to the screen. Ambler took Monsarrat's 416-page book and by the usual compression and distillation techniques, turned it into a taut script that avoided jingoism and the "war is hell" clichés that mar lesser war films. Indeed, the film's central dramatic premise is the somber notion that everyone who fought became more dehumanized and morally coarsened as the war dragged on. Also fortuitous was the hiring of Charles Frend to direct; having made wartime propaganda films and docudramas, Frend was particularly well suited to the material.

Production

Ealing Studios had the full cooperation of the Admiralty but faced major logistical problems at the outset: how to obtain a Flower-class Royal Navy corvette that would serve as the story's fictional HMS *Compass Rose* (K49). Almost all 231 of these small (950-ton) anti-submarine escort ships that survived the war (36 were lost in action) had either been scrapped already or sold off to other navies after the war ended. Fortunately, one of the film's technical advisors, Capt. Jack Broome, DSC RN, located one such ship, *The Coreopsis* (K32)—a badly disheveled wartime loaner to the Royal Hellenic Navy—in Malta, where it was awaiting breaking. After undergoing repairs, K32 steamed back to England under its own power in June 1952, where it was refurbished and transformed into the *Compass Rose*, with the majority of filming taking place on board (the ship was scrapped a year later). HMS *Saltash Castle*, the other ship featured in Monsarrat's novel, was portrayed in the film by Castle-class corvette HMS *Portchester Castle* (F362, scrapped in 1958). Both ships used for filming were based at Devonport, near Plymouth (southeast of London), with the River Tamar and Plymouth Sound standing in for the River Mersey in Liverpool. The scenes of the ships at sea were filmed in the English Channel just out of sight of land in summer waters generally too calm to effectively portray conditions on the Atlantic Ocean in winter, so, for those scenes, the ships were taken to a tidal race off the tip of the Island of Portland. Though close to shore, a sand bar and a number of converging tidal streams provided the roiling seas needed for proper verisimilitude. Englishman Donald Sinden was initially cast as the cowardly James Bennett (an Australian in the book), and Welshman Stanley Baker was cast as Keith Lockhart (based on Monsarrat) but the actors eventually swapped roles. The dramatic handling of the film's key sequence was also a source of some consternation. When the *Compass Rose*'s ASDIC (sonar) detects what is suspected to be a U-boat lurking directly beneath a group of British sailors treading water after their ship has been sunk, Ericson must decide instantly whether to sacrifice those sailors by dropping depth charges. He does so, but in a night scene that immediately follows, a drunken and inconsolable Ericson shares his emotional trauma with Lockhart. After viewing the rushes of the scene, Michael Balcon asked Charles Frend to reshoot it with Jack Hawkins directed to play his part with the usual British stoicism and emotional reserve. Balcon liked the results but two days later, after another viewing, the scene was reshot again, with a bit more feeling. Ironically, and to Hawkins' amusement, the original take was the one that ended up in the film's final version.

Plot Summary

Set in the fall of 1939, as the Battle of the Atlantic begins, Lt.-Commander George Ericson (Jack Hawkins), a British Merchant Navy and Royal Naval Reserve officer, is called to active duty and given command of HMS *Compass Rose*, a newly built Flower-class corvette intended for convoy escort duties. His newly commissioned sublieutenants, Lockhart (Donald Sinden) and Ferraby (John Stratton), are inexperienced. Ericson's first lieutenant ("No. 1") is James Bennett (Stanley Baker), a cowardly, hectoring martinet. Drawbacks notwithstanding, the *Compass Rose* makes numerous escort runs in the North Atlantic, often in terrible weather, and its men soon coalesce into a tough and competent fighting force. With the fall of France in May 1940, French ports become available to the U-boats, enabling them to attack convoys anywhere in the Atlantic Ocean. Now the bad weather works to Allied advantage; the U-boats cannot attack convoys in rough seas. After Bennett is put ashore with a duodenal ulcer, Lockhart is promoted to No. 1, and the *Compass Rose* continues to cross the Atlantic escorting convoys, but despite the best efforts of the escorts, many merchant vessels are sunk and scores of sailors lost. After nearly three years on the water, the *Compass Rose* falls victim to a torpedo attack and sinks. Forced to abandon ship, most of the crew drown or die from hypothermia. Taking to a couple of rubber life rafts, Ericson survives along with Lockhart and a few sailors. Ericson is promoted to commander, and with Lockhart as his first officer, takes command of the HMS *Saltash Castle*. With Ericson leading an anti-submarine escort group they continue their escort duties. Late in the war, while serving with the Arctic convoys, they track and ultimately destroy *U-53* [a U-boat actually sunk by Tribal-class destroyer HMS *Gurkha* on 23 February 1940 with the loss of all 42 hands]. As the war ends in May 1945 *Saltash Castle* returns to port, sailing past the surrendered but still formidable U-boat fleet, prompting Ericson to reflect on the fact that his commands were only able to sink two enemy subs over a more than five-year period.

Reception

Released in the UK on 26 March 1953, *The Cruel Sea* was the most successful movie at the British box office that year and made Jack Hawkins a genuine movie star with British audiences. It also earned £215,000 in the United States, a high figure for British movies at the time. The film garnered three BAFTA nominations and one Oscar nomination, and reviews were positive. For example, the anonymous reviewer for *The Times* wrote, "Ealing Studios have translated Nicholas Monsarrat's *The Cruel Sea* into a fine film—[as] thrilling and authentic as the book which has excited nearly 4,000,000 readers in 18 months . . . tells a moving story without embellishment or blarney" (25 March 1953). Alexander Walker acknowledged the film's authenticity but felt it lacked dramatic impact. In his view it was "professionally executed but short on intensity, emotion and the cruelty of the sea, which is termed the villain of this piece" (Walker, 11 August 1953).

Reel History Versus Real History

The general consensus by Royal Navy WWII veterans and historians is that *The Cruel Sea*, though fictional in terms of the specific events it portrays, is a very credible depiction of life on British convoy-escorts during the Second World War. The film captures, with understated realism, the harsh living conditions on board these cramped vessels, the often horrendous weather, the endless tedium of war patrols, and the stark terror of battle.

DAM BUSTERS, THE (1955)

Synopsis
The Dam Busters is a British war film based on *The Dam Busters* (1951) by Paul Brickhill and *Enemy Coast Ahead* (1946) by Guy Gibson. Directed by Michael Anderson and starring Michael Redgrave and Richard Todd, the film tells the true story of Operation Chastise: a mission carried out by the Royal Air Force's (RAF's) 617 Squadron of bombers that attacked the Möhne, Eder, and Sorpe dams in Germany's Ruhr region with a bouncing bomb specially designed by Barnes Wallis.

Background
On a daring secret mission dubbed "Operation Chastise" (16–17 May 1943) 19 Lancaster bombers of the RAF's 617 Squadron attacked three huge dams—the Sorpe, Möhne, and Edersee—in Germany's industrial Ruhr valley in order to disrupt the German war effort. The bombs used were a unique spherical "bouncing bomb" developed by Barnes Wallis (1887–1979), a Vickers engineer. Though the Sorpe Dam sustained only minor damage, the Möhne and Edersee dams were breached, causing catastrophic flooding that destroyed two hydroelectric power stations and damaged or destroyed other power stations, factories, and mines and drowned an estimated 1,600 civilians. The Germans managed to minimize the damage by rapid repairs, but full industrial production in the Ruhr did not return to normal until September. The leader of the raid, Wing Commander Guy Gibson, died in a plane crash in September 1944 but not before writing *Enemy Coast Ahead*. Posthumously published by Michael Joseph Ltd. in 1946, Gibson's memoir included a RAF-censored account of the so-called "Dam Busters raid." Four years later Paul Brickhill, a former Royal Australian Air Force (RAAF) pilot and author of *The Great Escape* (1950), published *The Dam Busters* (1951), a bestselling account of the raid. In October 1951 Robert Clark of the Associated British Picture Corporation (ABPC) purchased the film rights as a star vehicle for actor Richard Todd and hired R. C. Sheriff to write a script based on a treatment by ABPC production supervisor Bill Whittaker and script editor Walter Mycroft. Sheriff had the script completed by October 1952.

Production
The Dam Busters was filmed from mid-April to mid-July 1954 at various locations in England. The flight sequences were shot using four real Avro Lancaster B.VII bombers that had to be taken out of storage and modified (i.e., their mid-upper

gun turrets were removed to mimic 617 Squadron's special-purpose aircraft). The planes, supplied by the RAF, cost £130 per hour to run—a tenth of the film's production costs. The long, narrow reservoirs in the Upper Derwent Valley, Derbyshire, a few miles west of Sheffield—the test area for the real raids—stood in for the Ruhr valley for the film. Coastal scenes were shot between Skegness and King's Lynn, Norfolk, on the English Channel, and additional aerial footage was shot north of Windermere, in the Lake District. The film set some scenes at RAF Scampton, where the real raid was launched, but most ground location shooting took place at still-operational RAF Hemswell, just north of Scampton and 55 flight miles due east of the Upper Derwent Valley. Several obsolete Avro Lincolns mothballed at Hemswell prior to being broken up were used to double for additional 617 Squadron Lancasters on the ground. Active-duty RAF pilots based at Hemswell flew the Lancasters during filming.

Plot Summary

At the start of World War II, Barnes Wallis (Michael Redgrave), a British aeronautical engineer, works to come up with a way to destabilize German dams in order to disrupt the flow of their industry. In addition to his work for the Ministry of Aircraft Production and his position at Vickers, Wallis toils away to invent a buoyant bomb capable of dodging torpedo nets by skimming over the water's surface. In theory, when the bomb would reach the dam, it would have to sink before detonation in order to pack the most punch and cause the most destruction. Wallis deduces that the bomb's delivery plane would have to fly very close to the water in order to allow the bomb to skim across effectively. Wallis brings his ideas to the ministry and is turned down due to an inability to produce newly proposed weapons. Not to be thwarted easily, Wallis meets with Sir Arthur "Bomber" Harris (Basil Sydney), the head of RAF Bomber Command, in order to procure the resources necessary to create his bombs. Hesitant at first, Harris eventually approves Wallis's plans, and Prime Minister Winston Churchill (not depicted on screen) authorizes the project. A special unit of bombers is assembled, to be led by Wing Commander Guy Gibson (Richard Todd). Gibson puts together a tried-and-true team with experience flying at lower altitudes. As the pilots train, Wallis perfects his bomb, pushing through setbacks and recalculating drop altitudes. Weeks away from the mission date, Wallis works out the kinks and provides the bombers with a working explosive. The bombers fly low and attack the dams as planned. Although eight Lancasters and on-board crew members perish, two dams are successfully breached.

Reception

The Dam Busters premiered at the Empire Theatre, Leicester Square, London on 16 May 1955 (the 12th anniversary of the raid), with Princess Margaret and 617 Squadron veterans and family members in attendance. UK box office numbers are unknown, but the *London Times* reported that *The Dam Busters* was the "most profitable film" in Great Britain in 1955 (*The Times*, 29 December 1955). Contemporary notices on both sides of the Atlantic were uniformly adulatory. The anonymous reviewer for the *London Times* (17 May 1955) termed *The Dam Busters* "a film of unusual merit." Brigid Murnaghan called it "a motion picture that must be seen" (Murnaghan, 9 November 1955).

Reel History Versus Real History

For the most part, *The Dam Busters* achieves a high degree of historical accuracy but does tweak the facts for dramatic purposes. Barnes Wallis's achievements as an aviation engineer are slightly exaggerated (e.g., he wasn't the chief designer of the Vickers Wellington bomber). The movie also exaggerates the bureaucratic opposition that Wallis faced. He was not directly opposed, merely ignored, until a chance encounter with a key Air Ministry official won him permission to build and test prototypes of his experimental bomb. Nor did the idea of bombing the dams originate with Wallis; they were already identified as important targets by the Air Ministry before the war. The film also romanticizes Guy Gibson by showing that all of Gibson's crew from 106 Squadron volunteered to follow him to his new command. Actually, only his wireless operator, Robert Hutchinson, went with him to 617 Squadron. The real Guy Gibson was unpopular with his men. In a 2013 interview, George "Johnny" Johnson, the last surviving Dam Busters aviator, said that "one of [Gibson's] major failings was he couldn't bring himself down to the lower crews. He mixed very well with senior officers, particularly those above him and with the senior officers immediately below him but even with the junior officers he had difficulty. With the NCO's he just didn't want to know. He was bombastic, he was arrogant . . . He was a strict disciplinarian" (Jepps, 2013). The film shows Gibson devising a spotlights altimeter after visiting a theater. Actually Benjamin Lockspeiser of the Ministry of Aircraft Production suggested the method— already in use by RAF Coastal Command aircraft for some time—after Gibson requested they solve the problem.

DAS BOOT [THE BOAT] (1981)

Synopsis

Das Boot is a German submarine film produced by Günter Rohrbach, written and directed by Wolfgang Petersen, and starring Jürgen Prochnow, Herbert Grönemeyer, and Klaus Wennemann. Adapted from Lothar-Günther Buchheim's 1973 novel of the same title, the film is set during World War II and follows U-96, a Type VIIC–class U-boat, and its crew on a war patrol.

Background

Lothar-Günther Buchheim (1918–2007) was a German painter, photographer, and writer who served as a war correspondent in Hitler's Kriegsmarine during World War II. Twenty-eight years after the end of the war Buchheim published *Das Boot* (1973), a novel based on his experiences aboard a Type VIIC–class U-boat. Bavaria Filmstadt bought the screen rights to *Das Boot* in 1976. Envisioning a large-scale production with an international profile, Bavaria initially sought Hollywood prestige and expertise. In the early stages of development John Sturges (*The Great Escape*) was hired to direct and Robert Redford was signed on to play the U-Boat captain. By 1978 Don Siegel had replaced Sturges as director and Paul Newman had replaced Redford in the lead role, but Buchheim and the producers at Bavaria rejected the American script and the project ground to a halt. In 1979 Bavaria's new studio head, Günter Rohrbach, decided to entrust *Das Boot* to a fellow German: director Wolfgang Petersen. Heinrich Lehmann-Willenbrock (1911–1986), the captain of U-96 (the boat on which Buchheim served), and Hans-Joachim Krug, former first officer on U-219, were hired as consultants. Planning twin projects—a feature film and a TV mini-series cut from the same material—Bavaria shared production with two German public television stations, the BBC, and public broadcasting outlets in Austria and Italy. The budget was set at 25 million Deutschmarks (about $12 million USD), making *Das Boot* the most expensive German film up to that time (Haase, 2007, pp. 74–75).

Production

Wolfgang Petersen's guiding principle in making *Das Boot* was to achieve the highest possible degree of authenticity and realism. He would have preferred to film inside a real U-boat, but the only surviving VIIC–class U-boat is U-995, a museum ship since 1972 that is located near Kiel, on the Baltic Sea, that could not be used for filming. Instead, Petersen and his crew constructed a number of U-boat models at Bavaria Filmstadt, two of which were full-size mock-ups of a Type VIIC boat: one for interior scenes and another for exterior scenes. The interior mock-up was mounted on a huge, hydraulically powered scaffold dubbed "Die Wippe" ("The Seesaw") that was suspended 5 meters (16.4 feet) off the floor and could be shaken, rocked, or tilted 45 degrees to simulate dives, surfacing, or depth-charge attacks. The mock-up for full shots of the U-boat's exterior was the requisite 225 feet long and propelled by a small engine. Additionally, a mock-up of the U-boat's conning tower was set up in a water tank in the studio for more tightly framed shots. To heighten realism and a claustrophobic atmosphere, Petersen opted not to remove a side wall of the mock-up that would have opened up the field of view; interior shots were filmed by cinematographer Jost Vacano using a handheld 35-mm Arriflex with gyroscopic stabilizers—a smaller-scale Steadicam Vacano invented so that he could navigate the cramped interior spaces of the mock-up (Vacano wore a bicycle helmet and padding to minimize injury). Location shooting included segments shot in the still-extant bombproof U-boat bunkers at La Pallice, France. During the shoot in 1980 the full-size U-boat mock-up for exterior shots broke apart and sank. It was later raised, patched together, and sunk again on purpose in *Das Boot*'s final scene (and was also used in Steven Spielberg's *Raiders of the Lost Ark*, 1981). The night approach to Vigo, Spain, was filmed using miniatures of merchant ships. The climactic air raid scene required 200 French extras and a million deutschmarks' worth of explosives. A French aeronautical club supplied vintage U.S. planes to masquerade as British warplanes.

Plot Summary

Lt. Werner (Herbert Grönemeyer) is assigned as a war correspondent to U-96 in October 1941. The night before they depart on a war patrol he meets its captain (Jürgen Prochnow), chief engineer (Klaus Wennemann), and the crew in a French bordello. The next morning, U-96 sails out of La Rochelle. After many uneventful days, the crew is excited when another U-boat locates an enemy convoy. U-96 targets a British destroyer, but the destroyer spots its periscope and attacks with depth charges. The boat makes a narrow escape. A storm rages for nearly a month, during which time U-96 comes across another U-boat in raging seas. Following the storm, U-96 attacks a British convoy, sinking two ships with torpedoes, but it is spotted by a destroyer and has to dive below its rated limit to evade depth charges. During the depth-charge attack, Obermaschinist (chief mechanic) Johann (Erwin Leder) panics and has to be restrained on threat of being shot. Despite damages, the boat surfaces under the night sky. A torpedoed enemy tanker is still afloat and burning, so they shoot again, realizing afterwards that there are sailors still on board. Helplessly, they watch as the burning, terrified sailors throw themselves overboard and attempt to swim toward their boat. However, the captain, in line with his orders to avoid taking prisoners, commands his men to back the boat away from the desperate sailors. The U-boat is ordered to sail on to La Spezia, Italy, through the Strait of Gibraltar, a narrow sea passage heavily guarded by the Royal Navy. The U-boat docks in Vigo, Spain, and meets up with the SS *Weser* for a resupply, and then embarks for Italy. As the crew approaches Gibraltar, they are strafed

Obermaschinist (Chief Mechanic) Johann (Erwin Leder) tends the engines of U-96 in Wolfgang Petersen's *Das Boot* (1981). (Triumph Releasing Corporation/Photofest)

by a British fighter plane, and the boat's navigator, Kriechbaum (Bernd Tauber), is badly wounded. U-96 crash dives but when it attempts to level off, the controls do not respond and the boat continues to descend into the depths. Just before being crushed by the tremendous atmospheric pressure, the boat lands on an undersea shelf at the depth of 280 meters (918.6 feet). Over the next 16 hours Johann works feverishly to make repairs to the electric batteries to restore propulsion before the oxygen runs out. He is ultimately successful. The boat is able to surface and returns to La Rochelle. At dawn, shortly after Kriechbaum is brought to land and placed on an ambulance, Allied planes bomb and strafe the base, decimating most of the crew. After the raid, Werner finds the captain mortally wounded and clinging to an iron mooring bollard on the dock as he watches his battered U-boat sink at its berth. Just after the boat disappears under the water, the captain collapses and dies. Werner rushes to his body and surveys the grim scene with tears in his eyes.

Reception

Das Boot was released in West Germany on 17 September 1981. By the end of its run, the movie had posted almost $85 million in ticket sales, making it the highest-grossing German film up to that time. At the 55th Academy Awards (1983), *Das Boot* was nominated for six Oscars: Best Director, Best Adapted Screenplay, Best Cinematography, Best Film Editing, Best Sound, and Best Sound Editing—the most Academy Award nominations for a German film to date. Almost all reviews were highly favorable. Critics typically characterized the movie as "brilliant," "authentic," "gripping," "tense," and "claustrophobic." One critic (Cole Smithey) went so far as to call the viewing of *Das Boot* "a religious experience."

Reel History Versus Real History

Das Boot is a fictionalized account of U-96's seventh war patrol under the command of Kptlt. Heinrich Lehmann-Willenbrock (who, at 29 in the fall of 1941, was a decade younger than Jürgen Prochnow in 1980 and a stockier man lacking Prochnow's craggy intensity). All the other wardroom officers are also based on real people. The real sub was at sea for 41 days, departing St. Nazaire, France, on 27 October 1941 and returning to St. Nazaire on 6 December 1941. The first depth-charge attack on U-96 depicted in the movie corresponds to an actual incident. About 500 miles off the Irish coast on 31 October 1941, U-96 attacked Convoy OS.10 during a full moon and sank the Dutch freighter SS *Bennekom* at 22.47 hours (there were 8 dead and 46 survivors). Giving chase, the British escort sloop HMS *Lulworth* drove U-96 under water with gunfire and then dropped 27 depth charges, but the U-boat escaped undamaged. As depicted in *Das Boot*, U-96 rendezvoused with the interned German cargo ship *Bessel* (called *Wesser* in the film) at 22:03 hours in the neutral port of Vigo, Spain, on 27 November 1941 and sailed again at 04:00 hours. In the movie U-96 is attacked and nearly sunk while attempting to pass through the Straits of Gibraltar. Its crew subsequently endures 16 hours at near-crush depth while repairs are made. In real life U-96 was indeed attacked and heavily damaged by two bombs dropped from a British Swordfish biplane as it approached the Straits of Gibraltar (at 22:35 hours on 30 November 1941). U-96 dove and remained submerged for only 6 hours, not 16, before returning to its base at St. Nazaire for repairs (in early December, not at Christmastime, as in the movie). The Allied air raid on the U-boat base and the sinking of U-96 as it returns home is a complete fabrication, obviously concocted to convey the utter futility of war (U-96 actually survived most of the war; it was decommissioned when it was sunk by the U.S. Eighth Air Force in the port of Wilhelmshaven on 30 March 1945). Allied air attacks on the U-boat facilities in France did not commence until October 1942, a full year after the film's time frame.

DAWN PATROL, THE [AKA FLIGHT COMMANDER] (1930; REMADE 1938)

Synopsis

The Dawn Patrol is an American Pre-Code World War I film directed by Howard Hawks (a former World War I flight instructor). Starring Richard Barthelmess and Douglas Fairbanks Jr., the film follows the fighter pilots of the 59th British Squadron of the Royal Flying Corps as they cope with the stresses of combat on an almost daily basis. When it was remade in 1938 under the same title, the original was renamed *Flight Commander*.

Background

The Dawn Patrol originates with John Monk Saunders (1897–1940), an Oxford-educated Rhodes Scholar and U.S. Army Air Service flight instructor in Florida during the First World War whose great regret in life was not being able to secure an air combat posting to France during the war. A screenwriter specializing in aviation pictures, Saunders wrote the treatment for William Wellman's *Wings* (1927), the film that won the first Academy Award for Best Picture in 1929. That same year director Howard Hawks—himself a WWI Army Air Corps veteran who served in France—asked Saunders to write a story for an aviation movie that would serve as a starring vehicle for Ronald Colman, with Samuel Goldwyn as producer. Drawing on the recollections of humorist Irvin S. Cobb, who had known WWI Royal Flying Corps (RFC) pilots, and from his own conversations with British and Canadian ex-fighter pilots during his time at Oxford (1919–1920), Saunders wrote an 18-page treatment entitled "The Flight Commander" that dramatized the stoical fatalism and comradery exhibited by fliers facing death daily. Hawks purchased Saunders' story for $10,000, then sold it for the same amount to First National-Vitaphone, a newly acquired Warner Bros. subsidiary, after Goldwyn passed on it. First National provided a $600,000 production budget. With the change in studios Ronald Colman was eliminated as the possible star of the movie; Hawks cast *Wings* star Richard Barthelmess in his stead and Douglas Fairbanks Jr. in the supporting role of what would be Hawks's first "talkie." Hawks then hired Seton I. Miller to turn Saunders' story into a screenplay and later hired Dan Totheroh—a WWI combat veteran—to polish dialogue. Hawks also hired many of the pilots and cameramen who had just worked on Howard Hughes' WWI aviation epic, *Hell's Angels* (1930).

Production

The shoot for *The Dawn Patrol* started on 28 February 1930. The English airdrome scenes were shot during the first three weeks of March at Van Nuys Airport, 15 miles northwest of Hollywood. The German airdrome sequence was then shot over a four-day period at Newhall, Santa Clarita, and Sherwood Forest, California. Aerial dogfight sequences were shot by Elmer Dyer (the first aerial cinematographer) with a high-speed Akeley "Pancake" camera from the observer's rear cockpit of a biplane. These scenes were shot in April and May in the skies above the San Fernando Valley with some two dozen stunt aviators, carefully drilled to choreograph complicated maneuvers safely. It did not escape the notice of Howard Hughes that the climactic raid on a German ammo dump in *The Dawn Patrol* was patently similar to a scene in *Hell's Angels* (Hughes had a spy employed on Hawks's set). Hughes officially objected, but the scene was shot as written after producer Hal Wallis refused to make any changes. The 13-week shoot was concluded in early June. Postproduction was rushed through and finished in just two months so that *The Dawn Patrol* could preempt the general release date of its direct competitor, *Hell's Angels*—which it did by 11 weeks.

Plot Summary

A foreword in captions sets the scene: "The late fall of 1915 in France, when a great country was forced to entrust its salvation to youth—pitifully young, inexperienced, bewildered—but gloriously reckless with patriotism—proud and eager to rush hopelessly into combat against the veteran warriors of the enemy." A brief aerial combat sequence follows, in which an RFC pilot is shot down and killed. The pilots of the 59th British Squadron of the Royal Flying Corps deal with the psychological stress of combat in a variety of ways, but mostly they resort to gallows humor and nightly rounds of boisterous singing and drinking. The two top pilots in "A Flight," Capt. Dick Courtney (Richard Barthelmess) and Lt. Douglas Scott (Douglas Fairbanks, Jr.), loathe their superior officer, Brand (Neil Hamilton). They blame their commander for ordering ill-trained new flyers into the air in less-than-ideal planes. Unbeknownst to the bitter pilots, Brand has gone back and forth with their high command in order to secure extra practice time in the air for the newer flight recruits. Unfortunately, not wanting to lose their reputation as superior air fighters, Brand's superiors order the new recruits into combat as soon as they report to their frontline base. Back at the base, Brand is forced to drink alone due to his being ostracized by his men and begins to suffer a mental break as a result. The situation intensifies as an incredibly capable German flight team led by von Richter (Howard Hawks) positions itself directly opposite from the British base. The British flight crew suffers the loss of numerous veterans, meaning that the ranks are composed of newer and newer pilots who don't stand a chance against the more experienced Germans. Von Richter taunts the inexperienced pilots, and Courtney and Scott retaliate by going against Brand's orders and launching an attack on the German airdrome. Afterwards, Brand is forced to return to headquarters while Courtney assumes command of the squadron. Newly in charge, Courtney discovers that Brand was fighting to give inexperienced pilots more time to train, but was being rebuffed. Courtney feels the full responsibility of sending newer pilots into active duty after being forced to send Donny (William Janney), Scott's brother, on a mission before he is ready—an act that results in Donny's death. Brand arrives back on base with a veritable suicide mission for his pilots that will send them behind enemy lines. As the new squadron commander, Courtney is not allowed to participate in the mission. Enraged over the death of his brother, Scott volunteers for the mission, but Courtney plies him with drink and takes his spot in order to make amends. Courtney shoots down von Richter but is then shot down and killed by another German pilot. The film ends with Scott assuming command of the unit and reading orders to even newer recruits.

Reception

Premiering on 10 July 1930, when sound films were still an exciting novelty, *The Dawn Patrol* did well at the box office and garnered glowing reviews but further aggravated Howard Hughes, who sued the filmmakers for plagiarizing *Hell's Angels*. Hughes soon changed his mind, however, and dropped his lawsuit. He even invited Hawks to play golf with him and ended securing an agreement from Hawks to co-produce and direct *Scarface* (1932), his pre-Code gangster classic with Paul Muni. The success of *The Dawn Patrol* in 1930 spawned a remake eight years later, with Errol Flynn as Capt. Courtney, David Niven as Lt. Scott, and Basil Rathbone as Major Brand. The 1938 version recycles the script and the aerial combat footage of the earlier film but supplements both with some new material. In keeping with the better sound equipment available in 1938, dialogue was slightly expanded—mainly with anti-war sentiments appropriate to the temper of the times—and improved by a more naturalistic acting style that lent the remake a smoother feel. Like its predecessor, the second *Dawn Patrol* was a box office and critical success. Critics and film historians are divided as to which version is superior, though IMDb ratings rank the 1930 version slightly higher than the 1938 version.

Reel History Versus Real History

Though inspired by aviators' stories, *The Dawn Patrol* is not specifically based on any true events. In keeping with its purely fictional character, the film makes no references to any battles, units, or famous names connected with the war. There was a 59th Squadron in the RFC but it was not formed until 1 August 1916 and did not enter frontline service in France until February 1917–more than a year after the temporal setting of the film. The movie does, however, depict the chaotic maelstrom of WWI air combat in a realistic manner. It also accurately represents the reality of combat for RFC pilots in the first two years of the war, when inexperienced recruits flying inferior airplanes took exceedingly high casualty rates. For example, during the Somme campaign (July–November 1916), the RFC lost 800 aircraft and 252 aviators. RFC ineffectiveness and lopsided losses against German Fokkers continued until the summer of 1917, when the introduction of new and better planes (e.g., the Sopwith Camel and the Bristol F.2B fighter) allowed the RFC to begin to achieve fighting parity with the enemy and drastically reduce losses. Scott and Courtney's attack on the German aerodrome was perhaps inspired by a similar attack mounted by WWI Canada's top flying ace, William Avery "Billy" Bishop (1894–1956). On 2 June 1917 Bishop flew a solo mission behind enemy lines to attack a German aerodrome. Though there were no corroborating witnesses, Bishop claimed that he shot down three enemy aircraft that were taking off to attack him and destroyed several more on the ground. For this feat, he was awarded the Victoria Cross (VC), only one of two without witnesses to the alleged action. Author Brereton Greenhous contends that Bishop was "a brave flier—and a consummate, bold liar" who regularly embellished his exploits. He further argues that Bishop's attack on the German aerodrome likely never happened (Greenhous, 2002, p. 13).

DEER HUNTER, THE (1978)

Synopsis

The Deer Hunter is an American Vietnam War epic co-written and directed by Michael Cimino about a trio of Russian-American steelworkers (played by Robert De Niro, Christopher Walken, and John Savage) who are wounded physically, psychologically, and emotionally by their horrific experiences in Vietnam.

Five blue-collar buddies played by (left to right) Christopher Walken, Robert DeNiro, Chuck Aspegren, John Savage, and John Cazale emerge from their shift at the steel mill in Clairton, Pennsylvania, in an early scene from Michael Cimino's Vietnam War epic, *The Deer Hunter* (1978). (Universal Pictures/Photofest)

Background

The Deer Hunter began as a story idea by actor/screenwriter Quinn K. Redeker, circa 1971. After reading an article about a man who was filmed playing Russian roulette, Redeker filed the incident away as an idea for a film script. In 1974 he called fellow screenwriter Louis A. Garfinkle and proposed that they collaborate on a screenplay, mentioning the Russian roulette motif among other story ideas. Garfinkle found it compelling and, in February 1975, the two writers completed "The Man Who Came to Play," a spec script about a gambler who comes to Las Vegas to play Russian roulette. They soon sold the property to producers Barry Spikings and Michael Deeley of British Lion (later absorbed by EMI) for $19,000. In November 1976, writer/director Michael Cimino (*Thunderbolt and Lightfoot*) was hired to rewrite the script and insert the Russian roulette element into a Vietnam War scenario. Cimino then subcontracted with screenwriter Deric Washburn to produce a revised draft. Without doing any research or interviewing any Vietnam vets, Washburn wrote a new screenplay in one month and was duly dismissed from any further participation in the development process. Soon thereafter, Cimino put only his own name on Washburn's script, failing to credit its real author (Washburn took the matter to the Writers Guild for arbitration and was eventually accorded sole credit for the screenplay and a co-credit for the film's story). After hiring Vilmos Zsigmond as his cinematographer, Cimino signed Robert De Niro for the lead role of Michael, and through De Niro's influence, the rest of the main cast: Christopher Walken, John Savage, Meryl Streep, and Streep's boyfriend, John Cazale (diagnosed with lung cancer in March 1977, Cazale was dying during production and would pass away at age 42 on 13 March 1978, almost nine months before the film's premiere). Shortly before the start of the shoot, Cimino took his principal players to Weirton, West Virginia, a location that would partly substitute for Clairton, Pennsylvania, the film's stateside setting. The cast stayed in Weirton a week, soaking up atmosphere. As Walken recalls, "We went to a real Russian wedding, huge, with food and dancing. We traveled in the same car together, so by the time we did start shooting we had some real camaraderie going, which I hadn't done in a movie before" (quoted in Biskind, 2008).

Production

The Deer Hunter shoot lasted more than six months (June 1977–January 1978). Most of the Clairton scenes were actually shot in Ohio: the opening steel mill scenes were filmed at US Steel's Central Furnaces on the Monongahela River in Cleveland; the wedding scene, which took five days to film, was shot at St. Theodosius Russian Orthodox Cathedral, in Cleveland (with Fr. Stephen Kopestonsky, the cathedral's actual pastor, presiding); the raucous wedding banquet scene was filmed at nearby Lemko Hall (originally slated for 21 minutes of screen time, it ended up running 51 minutes); the bar scene was filmed at a set constructed inside an empty storefront in Mingo Junction, Ohio; Veterans Administration (VA) hospital scenes were filmed at a real VA hospital in Cleveland; other street, mill, road, and cemetery scenes were shot in Steubenville, Struthers, and McKeesport, Ohio (over the Monongahela from Clairton), in Clairton and Pittsburgh, Pennsylvania; and in

Follansbee and Weirton, West Virginia. The deer hunting scenes were shot in the Heather Meadows area of Mount Baker-Snoqualmie National Forest and at Nooksack Falls in the North Cascades range of Washington State—2,700 miles from Clairton but visually spectacular (the deer was actually an elk, which is not indigenous in the Eastern states). The Vietnam scenes were filmed on location in Thailand during the second half of the six-month shoot. The production's liaison in Thailand was General Kriangsak Chomanan, head of the Thai military, who provided the film with army vehicles, weapons, and aircraft—but had to take it all back, at least temporarily, because he needed the war matériel to stage a coup on 20 October 1977. Bangkok substituted for Saigon. The harrowing prisoner of war (POW) camp scenes were shot on the famous River Kwai, in the Katchanburi district of northern Thailand, near the Burmese border, and took an entire month to shoot. A perfectionist notorious for shooting large numbers of takes, Cimino was already well over budget when he started the Thailand portion of the production. Bad weather and logistical difficulties doubled the duration of the shoot there, from two to four months. Originally allotted $8 million for production, *The Deer Hunter* ended up costing $13 million ($52.5 million in 2017 dollars).

Plot Summary

[Act I] The setting is Clairton, Pennsylvania, at the end of 1967. A group of Russian American steel workers—Michael "Mike" Vronsky (Robert De Niro), Steven Pushkov (John Savage), and Nikanor "Nick" Chevotarevich (Christopher Walken), along with friends and co-workers Stan (John Cazale) and Peter "Axel" Axelrod (Chuck Aspegren) and local bar owner and friend John Welsh (George Dzundza)—ready themselves for marriage and military assignments. Before Mike, Steven, and Nick leave for basic training, Steven and a pregnant Angela (Rutanya Alda) have a Russian Orthodox wedding. All the while, Mike tries to cover up the fact that he is in love with Nick's girlfriend, Linda (Meryl Streep). While enjoying the wedding reception, the men notice a lone Green Beret (U.S. Army Special Forces) sitting at the bar. Mike tells the soldier that he and his friends are headed to Vietnam, and the Green Beret toasts them saying, unnervingly, "F— it." Linda and Nick get engaged after she catches the bride's bouquet. Nick later makes Mike promise not to leave him in the combat zone if anything should happen. The friends go hunting the next day, and Mike gets frustrated with Stan, who is unprepared and shows no respect for what Mike considers a sacred ritual. Mike kills a deer with a single, well-aimed rifle shot. [Act II] In Vietnam, U.S. soldiers attack an enemy village with napalm. Mike, a staff sergeant, watches a North Vietnamese Army (NVA) operative kill a woman with a baby and then kills the operative. Simultaneously, a group of "Huey" helicopters delivers a number of American infantry troops to the combat zone, including Nick and Steven. Mike, Steven, and Nick reunite, but are soon taken prisoner by enemy combatants and sent to a POW camp. The sadistic guards have the POWs play Russian roulette, gambling on the outcome. Mike, Steven, and Nick all play, but Steven is unable to play against Mike and shoots at the air instead. As a result, the guards cage Steven underwater with rats. Mike and Nick plot an escape, convincing the guards to let them play with extra bullets and then turning on their enemies. Nick and Mike kill the guards and rescue Steven; then the trio floats down the river in search of rescue. Although an American helicopter unit spots them, Nick is the only one who can make it aboard. Steven, weak from his torture, slides back into the water, and Mike goes in after him. Mike manages to get Steven to the riverbank and then carries him through the jungle to the American lines. Meanwhile, Nick convalesces in a field hospital in Saigon, battling against post-traumatic stress disorder (PTSD) and worrying about the fate of his friends. After his wounds heal, Nick leaves the hospital and goes absent without leave (AWOL). He walks through Saigon's red-light district and into a gambling den. Mike is also in the den, watching a game of Russian roulette but not participating. Nick enters the game, and Mike notices his friend and senses that he is not acting like himself. Nick takes the gun and fires it at another player before turning the gun on himself. Nick survives, but is driven away by Julien Grinda (Pierre Segui) before Mike can catch him. [Act III] Stateside, Mike arrives home, but he is unable to embrace the friends who wait for him with a "welcome home" banner outside the house. He and Linda spend time together the next day, thinking that they've lost Nick forever. Mike also visits Angela, but she is cold and clearly depressed. She tells Mike that Steven is at a VA hospital. Upon reaching the VA hospital, Mike realizes that Steven has had both legs amputated and is paralyzed. Steven tells Mike that an anonymous source in Saigon has been mailing him money and that he suspects the source to be Nick. Mike delivers Steven to Angela, then goes back to Saigon in search of Nick just before it falls to the communists [late April 1975]. Mike discovers Nick gambling, but Nick appears to be ignorant of who Mike is and where he comes from. Nick tries to jog his friend's memory using a game of Russian roulette, but Nick is too far gone. To keep him away from the gun, Mike grabs Nick's arms, revealing scars that are obviously heroin tracks. Nick finally recognizes Mike, smiles, and tells him he wants to take "one [more] shot." Nick then raises the gun to his head and pulls the trigger. This time a live round is in the gun's top chamber and, to Mike's horror, Nick kills himself. [Epilogue] Mike has brought his body home, making good his promise. After gathering for Nick's funeral and burial, they all repair to John's bar and sing "God Bless America," as Mike lifts a toast in Nick's honor.

Reception

To qualify for Oscar nominations, *The Deer Hunter* was released for a week in New York and Los Angeles (8–15 December 1978). The film then went into wide release on 23 February 1979, just after nominations were announced. A resounding commercial and critical success, *The Deer Hunter* grossed nearly $50 million at the box office and earned nine Academy Award nominations, nine BAFTA nominations, and six Golden Globe nominations. It went on to win five Oscars—for Best Picture, Best Director, Best Supporting Actor (Christopher Walken), Best Film Editing, and Best Sound. But the movie also generated a firestorm of controversy for its depiction of the Viet Cong as bloodthirsty sadists who used Russian roulette as an instrument of torture on American POWs. At Oscar night (9 April 1979) 13 members of Vietnam Veterans against the War (VVAW) staged a leafleting protest against the film outside the Dorothy Chandler Pavilion in Los Angeles. In a press interview, VVAW member Randy Rowland said, "Having John Wayne give the Best Picture Award to *The Deer Hunter* was just too much. I'm convinced that John Wayne knew the film would win, because it carries on the John Wayne tradition. It's *The Green Berets* of the 1970s. It puts the shoe on the wrong foot, turning the Vietnamese into the aggressors and war criminals. It's a racist view and lays the basis for future wars. At the end of the film, when the survivors sing 'God Bless America,' I was shaking with rage" (Hartl, p. 69). Further aggravating matters, Cimino lied about his military service while promoting the film, falsely claiming he had been a Green Beret medic in Vietnam at the time of the Tet Offensive in 1968: a claim debunked in the April 1979 issue of *Harper's* magazine by Tom Buckley, a former Vietnam correspondent for *The New York Times*. Lost in all the outrage over the film's reckless deployment of the Russian roulette metaphor, however, was the recognition that *The Deer Hunter* does make a valid point; that the war wreaked havoc on the white working class that supplied the bulk of American troops in Vietnam, an insight proffered some years later by USC English professor Rick Berg: "What we see [in the film's culminating "God Bless America" scene] is a community shattered by Vietnam, trying to express a deeply rooted nationalism, with all its ironies and contradictions. These people, then, are not merely the inheritors of simple freedoms, but the constructors of a history that has both made and unmade them. Like the Vietnamese, they are the ignorant and innocent victims of a war being waged against exploited peoples by exploited people" (Berg, 1986, p. 120).

Reel History Versus Real History

As a cinematic representation of ethnic working-class life in America, c.1967–1975, *The Deer Hunter* has considerable merit. As a Vietnam War movie, it is a pure fiction that perpetrates gross historical inaccuracies. Though the North Vietnamese treated American POWs brutally, there is not a single documented instance of either the Viet Cong or NVA forcing American POWs to play Russian roulette for their captors' amusement. Likewise, there is no evidence that Russian roulette gambling dens existed in Saigon during the Vietnam War—or have ever existed anywhere, for that matter. The film's timeline is also deeply suspect. Nick starts playing Russian roulette on a regular basis no later than 1968, yet he is still alive when Michael tries to rescue him in April 1975: a miraculous feat of survival on Nick's part that beggars logic. Finally, the movie's exclusive focus on white working-class soldiers, although perfectly valid, presents a skewed ethnographic depiction of the American experience in Vietnam. Despite being barely visible in the film, 12.6 percent of the soldiers in Vietnam were African American. Overrepresented in combat situations, African Americans accounted for 15.1 percent of the war's American casualties while comprising only 11 percent of the population: a historical reality that cannot be extrapolated from *The Deer Hunter*.

DEFIANCE (2008)

Synopsis
Defiance is an American war film directed by Edward Zwick. With a screenplay by Zwick and Clayton Frohman based on Nechama Tec's book, *Defiance: The Bielski Partisans* (1993), *Defiance* tells the story of the Bielski partisans: a group led by Belarusian Jewish brothers who saved hundreds of Jews in Nazi-occupied Belarus during the Second World War. The film stars Daniel Craig as Tuvia Bielski, Liev Schreiber as Zus Bielski, Jamie Bell as Asael Bielski, and George MacKay as Aron Bielski.

Background
Alexander Zeisal "Zus" Bielski (1912–1995) was one of the four legendary Bielski brothers: Jewish partisans who rescued some 1,200 Jews from Nazi extermination in Belarus during World War II. When Zus Bielski died in New York City 50 years after the war ended, screenwriter Clayton Frohman read his obituary in the *New York Times* and brought Bielski's story to the attention of his boyhood friend, film director Edward Zwick (*Glory*). Convinced that the story of the Bielski brothers would provide a powerful counternarrative to the widespread belief that Jews passively succumbed to Nazi genocide, Frohman and Zwick set out to bring the Bielski saga to the screen. Serendipitously, Holocaust historian/survivor Nechama Tec (University of Connecticut) had recently published the definitive history of the Bielski brothers—*Defiance: The Bielski Partisans* (1993). Zwick acquired the film rights to Dr. Tec's book, and he and Frohman collaborated on a screen adaptation, but it would take a decade to bring the project to fruition; the Hollywood studios were not interested in financing a Holocaust-themed picture certain to be a grim, if not grueling, viewing experience. After actor Daniel Craig was cast in the lead role in May 2006, Zwick secured $32 million from Canadian film financing mogul Don Starr's Grosvenor Park Productions. With Craig signed and financing in place, Zwick's production company, Bedford Falls Productions, was able to sell U.S. and Canadian distribution rights to Paramount Vantage. The following August, Liev Schreiber, Jamie Bell, Alexa Davalos, and Tomas Arana were cast.

Production
Zwick and his co-producer, Pieter Jan Brugge, considered shooting the movie in Canada, but labor costs were prohibitive. They then pondered Poland or Romania, where labor costs are low, but could not find the requisite forest setting close to a major city needed to lodge production offices, cast, and crew (Dapkus, E.20). Ultimately they chose to shoot in eastern Lithuania, at a forest site close to Vilnius, the nation's capital city, and just 100 miles from the actual locations of the Bielski partisan camps in Belarus. As it turned out, some locals who acted as extras in the film were descended from families the Bielski partisans had rescued. According to Zwick, the shoot was an arduous one: "To work at northern latitudes is to be acutely aware of winter's approach. By September there was frost on the ground. By mid-October we were knee-deep in snow. By November dawn wasn't until 8 a.m., and

the pale sun began to fade by 3. Despite our sophisticated outerwear, we were always cold." But Zwick was always cognizant that the real people being depicted had had it far worse: "Yet for three long winters, with subzero temperatures and a mind-numbing wind off the Baltic that brought Hitler's assault on Russia to a frost-bitten halt, the Bielski partisans wrapped themselves in skins and rags, braved starvation and dug burrows into the hillsides, living like moles" (Zwick, 2008, AR7). The shoot began in late August 2007 and wrapped in early December so Daniel Craig could move on to his next job, reprising his role as James Bond in *Quantum of Solace*.

Plot Summary

The film opens with an on-screen notation: "A true story." It is August 1941, and Nazi einsatzgruppen (task forces) are systematically killing Jews throughout the Eastern European territories just conquered by the Wehrmacht. Those who are not among the dead or left to struggle in ghettos include the Polish Jewish Bielski brothers: Tuvia (Daniel Craig), Zus (Liev Schreiber), Asael (Jamie Bell), and Aron (George MacKay). Their parents have been killed off by the police, who acted under the influence of German commands. Vowing to avenge their parents, the Bielski brothers retreat to the primeval Naliboki Forest in northwestern Belarus. The brothers discover other Jews attempting to escape the Germans and take on a leadership role among them. The brothers spend the next year protecting and caring for an ever-growing population of refugees, moving their location any time that the local police discover their whereabouts. During this time, Tuvia murders the Belarussian police captain (Sigitas Rackys) who carried out his parents' deaths and also eliminates the captain's sons (Vaidas Kublinskas and Valentin Novopolskij) when they try to stop the attack. The brothers stage small-scale raids and ambushes on the German soldiers, but Tuvia is pained by the Jewish casualties and considers a different approach. Tuvia and Zus disagree about how to proceed as fighting in the forest continues. Zus sees the defeat of the German militia as a primary and all-important goal that supersedes surviving the German occupation. Zus sees Tuvia's "politics of diplomacy" as too soft and chooses to join a Soviet unit, though the transition isn't a smooth one. The Soviet unit has preconceived notions about Jewish soldiers that Zus is forced to rail against. Tuvia ("Our revenge is to live") defends his ever-growing camp and deals with such hardships as starvation, disease, and in-fighting among camp members. Zus's new Soviet unit makes a pact with Tuvia's camp, agreeing to protect the Jewish camp members in exchange for supplies. Following a difficult winter, the camp discovers that the Germans have hit upon their location and are planning a large-scale attack. When the Soviets withdraw their support, the Jews are forced to flee their camp just as German dive-bombers begin their attack. Asael and a small group of fellow camp members attempt to hold the Germans off, but they are unable to adequately defend their ground. Almost the entire small group perishes in the attack. When the situation seems hopeless, Zus and his partisan troops attack the Germans from behind, leaving the Soviets to rescue the Jewish camp. The surviving camp members flee to the forest, and on-screen text states that the group grew to 1,200 people who survived for two more years, building an entire refugee city in a push for survival. The film ends with photographs of the real Bielski brothers and details their life histories. Original photographs of the real-life persons are shown, including Tuvia in his Polish Army uniform, and their ultimate fates are shared: Asael joined the Soviet Army and was soon killed in action, never getting to see the child he fathered; and Tuvia, Zus, and Aron survived the war and emigrated to America to form a successful trucking firm in New York City.

Reception

During its 17 weeks (16 January to 30 April 2009) in wide release in the United States, *Defiance* earned $28.6 million at the box office. Foreign box office receipts came in at $22.5 million. Ultimately, *Defiance* made $51.5 million—almost $20 million more than its production budget—but with marketing costs (now usually about 50% of production costs) added in, net profits were probably a modest $5 million or less. Along with a mediocre box office showing, *Defiance* was met with mixed reviews from film critics. Typically ambivalent was Peter Rainer. On the one hand he praised the film "as a piece of historical redress" that does "a great service . . . in bringing this narrative to the screen." On the other hand, Rainer found *Defiance* excessively didactic in tone: "Too much is spelled out for us; too many speeches have a stentorian heft. Do we really need to hear Tuvia announce, Moses-like, that his communal goal is to 'live free, like human beings, for as long as we can'?" (Rainer, 17 January 2009).

Reel History Versus Real History

Belarusian critics noted a lack of Belarusian language within the film and also noted that whereas the Soviet partisans in the movie sing a "Belarusian" folk song, real partisan soldiers from that area would've been more likely to sing Russian ballads. In addition, some Soviet partisan veterans claimed that the film contained a number of historical inaccuracies. Some reviews, as in Poland, criticized the film for ignoring the Bielski partisans' crimes against the local population. In one scene it is stated that there may be an epidemic of typhus and that ampicillin was needed. The action takes place approximately 17 years before this drug was available.

DOWNFALL [GERMAN: *DER UNTERGANG*] (2004)

Synopsis

Downfall is a German-, Italian-, and Austrian-funded war drama depicting the bizarre final 10 days in the life of Adolf Hitler (played by Bruno Ganz), hunkered down in his Berlin Führerbunker in late April 1945 as the Red Army closes in to seal his doom. Based on several eyewitness histories, the film was written and produced by Bernd Eichinger and directed by Oliver Hirschbiegel.

Background

Having produced Hans-Jürgen Syberberg's seven-hour visionary epic, *Hitler-ein Film aus Deutschland* [*Hitler: A Film from Germany*] (1977), Bernd Eichinger had long wanted to make a more mainstream film about Adolf Hitler. Developments in 2002 gave him the fresh source material he needed. Traudl Junge, Hitler's personal secretary from 1942 to 1945, wrote a memoir in 1947–1948 but left it unpublished for more than half a century. Elderly and suffering from terminal cancer in 2001, Junge was finally persuaded by her friend, Anne Frank biographer Melissa Müller, to let her book, *Bis Zur Letzten Stunde* [*Until the Final Hour*], be published and to be interviewed for a documentary film by Austrian artist André Heller. Junge's book came out on 1 January 2002, and Heller's film, *Im toten Winkel—Hitlers Sekretärin* [*Blind Spot: Hitler's Secretary*], was released six weeks later. Soon thereafter historian Joachim Fest published a more objective account of the same events: *Der Untergang: Hitler und das Ende des Dritten Reiches* [*Downfall: Hitler and the End of the Third Reich*]. Sensing the time was finally right for a docudrama on Hitler—a subject heretofore taboo in Germany—Eichinger wrote a screenplay that detailed the last 10 days of Hitler's life in the bunker, based primarily on Junge and Fest, but also drawing on a number of other sources: Albert Speer's *Inside the Third Reich* (1969); Gerhard Boldt's *Hitler's Last Days: An Eye-Witness Account* (first English translation 1973); Siegfried Knappe's 1992 memoir, *Soldat: Reflections of a German Soldier, 1936–1949* (1992); and Dr. Ernst-Günther Schenck's *Das Notlazarett unter der Reichskanzlei: Ein Arzt erlebt Hitlers Ende in Berlin* [*Field Hospital Under the Reich Chancellery: A Doctor Experiences Hitler's End in Berlin*] (1995). After completing a script, Eichinger sent it to director Oliver Hirschbiegel, who agreed to take on the project. Soon thereafter, acclaimed Swiss actor Bruno Ganz (*Wings of Desire*) was cast as Hitler. To prepare for the role, Ganz researched the part by visiting a hospital to study patients with Parkinson's disease (from which Hitler suffered). He also studied an 11-minute tape recording of Hitler in private conversation with Finnish Field Marshal Carl Gustaf Mannerheim secretly made in June 1942. Hirschbiegel also made every effort to achieve authenticity, especially with regard to the look of the Führerbunker. As he told interviewer Carlo Cavagna, "The bunker was constructed at the Bavaria Studios in Munich, following precisely the floor plan. What you see is really how it looked . . . I told them I wanted it exactly the way it was, and did thorough research about even where the table stood, and the position of the chairs, and things like that. And, furthermore, it was a fixed set. You couldn't take walls out. I couldn't remove anything, really. There was no, 'Let's take out that wall and use a long lens.' So it was like we were shooting in the [actual] bunker" (Cavagna, 2005).

Production

Principal photography of *Downfall* took place over a 12-week period (12 August–15 November 2003). All the interior scenes inside Hitler's Wolf's Lair in East Prussia and in the Berlin Führerbunker were shot on sets constructed at Bavaria Studios near Munich. Ironically, Hirschbiegel chose St. Petersburg, Russia, to stand in for war-torn Berlin. On certain streets of the city the architecture was virtually indistinguishable from Hitler's capital because St. Petersburg's early 18th-century buildings had been designed by such German architects as Leo von Klenze and Georg Peter Bärenz. The filmmakers found a street with empty buildings and obtained permission to block it off for many weeks. There they built a façade of the war-torn Reich Chancellery and installed Berlin-style street lamps, signs, WWII bombing rubble, wrecked vehicles, etc. They were even permitted to dig up the pavement to create defensive trenches, foxholes, and shell craters. Russians acted as extras, portraying both German and Russian soldiers.

Plot Summary

The film begins with an interview clip from *Blind Spot: Hitler's Secretary* (2002), featuring the real Traudl Junge (1920–2002) expressing her remorse for admiring Hitler in her youth. Then the film proper begins, showing a courtly Adolf Hitler (Bruno Ganz) hiring Frl. Junge (Alexandra Maria Lara) as his secretary at the Wolf's Lair in East Prussia in November 1942. The story skips ahead almost two and half years later, to 20 April 1945 (Hitler's 56th birthday) during the Battle of Berlin. A nearby artillery blast awakens Traudl, Frau Gerda Christian (Birgit Minichmayr), and Frl. Constanze Manziarly (Bettina Redlich), Hitler's vegetarian cook. In the Führerbunker, Hitler enquires as to the source of the shelling. Gen. Wilhelm Burgdorf (Justus von Dohnányi) informs him that Berlin is under artillery attack, and Gen. Karl Koller (Hans H. Steinberg) further reports the shelling as indicating that the Red Army is just miles away from the center of the city. In the midst of Hitler's birthday celebration, two of his officers, SS chief Heinrich Himmler (Ulrich Noethen) and SS adjutant Hermann Fegelein (Thomas Kretschmann), implore their commander to flee from Berlin, but Hitler decides to stay. In a Berlin street some members of Hitler Youth are preparing an 88-mm flak gun for anti-tank defense. Peter Kranz (Donevan Gunia), a member of the Hitler Youth, ignores the pleas of his disabled father (Karl Kranzkowski) when he asks him to desert and save himself. Elsewhere in the city, a physician (Christian Berkel) decides to stay in the face of an evacuation order, persuading an SS general to allow him to continue his work. Eva Braun throws a wild party in the Reich Chancellery featuring loud music, raucous dancing, and copious amounts of alcohol: a surreal bacchanal that ends abruptly when a Russian artillery shell blows out the windows, causing the celebrants to flee back to the Führerbunker. The next day, Gen. Helmuth Weidling (Michael Mendl) is condemned to execution for commanding his troops to retreat west. However, after he explains that there has been a misunderstanding, Weidling is promoted by Field Marshal Wilhelm Keitel (Dieter Mann) to supervise the defense of Berlin. During a military conference Hitler orders a counterattack by Felix Steiner's combat group to check the Soviet advance. Generals Krebs and Jodl reluctantly inform him that Steiner's forces are too weak to mount any such attack. Dismissing everyone from the room except for Keitel, Jodl, Krebs, and Burgdorf, Hitler flies into a towering rage against his generals' alleged treacherousness and incompetence. After his anger is spent, Hitler concedes that he has lost the war, but still refuses to leave Berlin. Instead, he is intent on remaining in his city and committing suicide. After seeing hapless Volkssturm conscripts needlessly slaughtered in battle, Gen. Mohnke confronts Joseph Goebbels (Ulrich Matthes). Goebbels admits to Mohnke that he does not feel badly for the fallen civilians for they sketched out their fate when they first sided with Hitler. Minister of Armaments Albert Speer (Heino Ferch) pays a farewell visit to Hitler and admits that he has failed to follow the "scorched earth policy" commands. Displeased, Hitler does not shake Speer's hand when he leaves. At dinner, Hitler flies into a rage when he discovers that Himmler has colluded with Count Folke Bernadotte to work out the terms of Hitler's surrender. Hitler demands that von Greim and his mistress, test pilot Hanna Reitsch (Anna Thalbach), retrieve Himmler and his adjutant, Hermann Fegelein (Thomas Kretschmann). Upon finding out that Fegelein has deserted, Hitler orders his execution. Reichsphysician SS Ernst-Robert Grawitz (Christian Hoening), the head of the German Red Cross who infamously performed human medical experiments for the Nazis, begs Hitler's permission to leave Berlin. When Hitler denies his request, Grawitz kills himself along with his family by setting off a pair of hand grenades over dinner. That night, Fegelein is arrested and executed. Mohnke reports that the Red Army is only 300 to 400 meters from the Reich Chancellery. Hitler reassures his officers that he'll order Gen. Walther Wenck's 12th Army to break off from the Western Front and march east to join the fight against the Soviets—an absurd, unworkable proposition. After midnight (29 April 1945), Hitler communicates his last will and testament to Traudl and then marries Eva Braun as a show of gratitude for her loyalty. Finally accepting that the situation is hopeless, Hitler decides to commit suicide to avoid capture. Hitler consumes a last meal and says his goodbyes. He hands his Golden Party Badge Number 1 to Magda Goebbels, who pleads with Hitler to flee Berlin. Instead, Hitler remains and kills himself off-screen. Eva Braun also commits suicide. Their bodies are carried out of the bunker and cremated in a shell crater in the Chancellery garden. Magda and Joseph Goebbels follow suit, murdering their own children and killing themselves off-screen. Military staff members evacuate the bunker, but Krebs and Burgdorf also give in to suicide. Weidling broadcasts to the city that Hitler is dead and declares that he will be seeking an immediate ceasefire. Traudl, Gerda, and the remaining SS troops join Schenck, Mohnke, and Günsche as they try to flee the city. Meanwhile, the child soldiers have all been killed—except for Peter, who discovers that his parents have been executed. With Red Army soldiers approaching, Traudl decides to leave the bunker. She and Peter join up and make their way through the ruined streets, avoiding Russian soldiers. At a bridge, Peter finds a discarded bicycle. They both get on it—Peter sitting "side saddle" on the top tube while Traudl pedals—and the pair bicycle away from Berlin. An epilogue describes the fates of the other Führerbunker inhabitants, and the film ends with a final excerpt from Heller's documentary.

Reception

Downfall premiered in Munich on 8 September 2004 and went into wide release in Germany and Austria a week later. The movie was also showcased at a number of international film festivals, and an extended version was shown in two parts on German television in October 2005. Final box office numbers were impressive; *Downfall* made $93.6 million against an estimated production cost of €13.5 million ($15.9 million). The film also garnered many film awards, including a 2005 Oscar nomination for Best Foreign Language Film of the Year. Reviews were mostly positive; many were adulatory. Hitler biographer Ian Kershaw exemplified affirmative opinion when he extolled the film as a "superb reconstruction" and avowed that he "could not imagine how a film of Hitler's last days could possibly be better done." Kershaw also added his voice to a chorus of praise for Bruno Ganz's performance: "Of all the screen depictions of the Führer . . . this is the only one which to me is compelling. Part of this is the voice. Ganz has Hitler's voice to near perfection. It is chillingly authentic" (Kershaw, 2004). Still, some critics panned the film. For example, J. Hoberman found it both "grimly self-important and inescapably trivializing" (Hoberman, 2005). The most scathing critique of *Downfall* was rendered by another German filmmaker, Wim Wenders. For Wenders, the movie seems to adopt young Traudl Junge's naïve point of view: enthrallment to Hitler's charisma not sufficiently countered by the bookend clips of the real Junge repudiating her younger self. Wenders also objected to Hirschbiegel's decision to *not* show Hitler and Goebbels in the act of committing suicide: "Why can't we see Hitler and Goebbels dying? Are they not becoming mythical figures by not exhibiting them? Why do they deserve so worthy an outlet, while all the other good and bad Germans are [graphically] killed? . . . The film has no opinion on anything, especially of fascism or Hitler . . . so the seducer and the victim find themselves united once again in the arbitrary lack of attitude that makes this film so incredibly annoying. [This] lack of narrative [slant] leads the audience into a black hole, in which they are induced (almost) imperceptibly to see [history] this time somehow from the perspective of the perpetrators, at least with a benevolent understanding for them" (Wenders, 2004).

Reel History Versus Real History

In general terms *Downfall* ranks as one of the most historically accurate films ever made. It does, however, rearrange the order of some of the events and resorts to some streamlining. Furthermore, Peter Franz, the Hitler Youth boy decorated by Hitler, is a fictional character, so his joining up with Traudl Junge to flee Berlin is also a fabrication. In reality, Junge did not escape Berlin so easily. After hiding out in a cellar for a week with other Führerbunker refugees, Junge was arrested by the Soviets on 9 May 1945, imprisoned and interrogated for the next five months, and later hospitalized with diphtheria. She returned to Munich, her home town, in 1946.

DUNKIRK (2017)

Synopsis

Dunkirk is a war film written, co-produced, and directed by Christopher Nolan. A co-production between the United Kingdom, the United States, France, and the Netherlands, the film depicts the successful May 1940 evacuation of more than 300,000 Allied (mostly British) troops from the beaches of Dunkirk, thus avoiding capture or annihilation by the victorious Nazi forces that surrounded them during the fall of France in the early part of the Second World War.

Background

When Hitler's armies overran the Low Countries and outflanked France in May 1940, the British Expeditionary Force (BEF) and remnants of Belgian forces

Allied troops nervously await evacuation in Christopher Nolan's *Dunkirk* (2017). (Warner Bros./Photofest)

and three French armies were forced to retreat to France's Atlantic coast. By 20 May these troops found themselves cut off and threatened with annihilation on the beaches at Dunkirk, whereupon Winston Churchill's Cabinet hatched "Operation Dynamo": the evacuation of the BEF back to England by sea. The massive undertaking began a week later, on 27 May, and continued until 4 June. Over that nine-day period 861 Allied vessels—of which 693 were British, mostly requisitioned private boats—rescued 338,226 Allied troops (198,000 British and 140,000 French, Polish, and Belgian soldiers). Though it was a major turning point of the Second World War because it enabled Britain to fight on, the Dunkirk evacuation was hardly an unqualified success. As Churchill put it, "Wars are not won by evacuations." The British had to abandon all their vehicles and heavy guns and equipment: enough to outfit eight to ten divisions. They also lost 84 Royal Air Force (RAF) planes and 240 naval vessels (including six destroyers) during the Dunkirk evacuation. Nor did everyone make it out. A rearguard force of 5,000 British and 35,000 French troops had to be left behind, were subsequently captured, and were consigned to slave labor in Germany for the duration of the war—a grim aftermath not widely reported. A moral victory in an otherwise disastrous phase of the war for the Allies, the so-called "Miracle of Dunkirk" received its first cinematic dramatization in almost 50 years with Christopher Nolan's *Dunkirk* (2017). Nolan first conceived of such a film in 1995, when he and his then-girlfriend (now wife)

Emma Thomas, hired a small yacht to sail the 26 miles from England to Dunkirk—a Channel crossing that proved to be unexpectedly arduous. Almost 20 years and a string of highly successful films (e.g., *Memento*, the *Batman* trilogy, *Interstellar*) later, Nolan felt he was ready to take on an epic-scale war film. He started by reading firsthand accounts by Dunkirk survivors at the Imperial War Museum and also relied on *Forgotten Voices of Dunkirk* (Ebery, 2010): an oral history compiled by historian Joshua Levine, who was hired as the film's historical advisor. Nolan and Levine also interviewed a number of elderly Dunkirk veterans in person. After researching the battle, Nolan decided to make a film that would use fictive characters and concentrate, à la Hitchcock, on building suspense insofar as the evacuation was a tense race against time. He also opted to emphasize chaos and danger by creating a nonlinear narrative structure that crosscuts between three perspectives—land, sea, and air—though not in the conventional way that would indicate actions in each sphere happening simultaneously. To further concentrate mood, Nolan kept the emphasis on visual storytelling; dialogue is so sparse that the screenplay came in at only 76 pages, whereas the film's running time clocked in at a modest 106 minutes: Nolan's shortest film to date.

Production

In keeping with his preference for analog over digital formats and to achieve optimal image quality, Nolan shot 75 percent of the movie using 15/70-mm IMAX film (the other 25 percent was shot using Super Panavision 65-mm film). Nolan also refrained from using computer-generated imagery (CGI). Other than a few "name" actors (e.g., Kenneth Branagh, Mark Rylance, Tom Hardy), Nolan decided to cast young unknowns in key roles. Principal photography began at Dunkirk—with a film crew of 200, hundreds of extras, and some 50 boats—on 23 May 2016, almost 76 years to the day that the actual evacuation began. After a month of filming on Dunkirk's beaches and dunes, the shoot moved to The Ijsselmeer, a closed-off inland bay in the central Netherlands, to film scenes supposedly taking place at sea. In late July the production then moved to Dorset, England, to film the departure and arrival of Mr. Dawson's boat, *Moonstone*, at Weymouth harbor (set-dressed to look like 1940). Related scenes of evacuees being put on trains after disembarkation were filmed at nearby Swanage Railway Station. Thereafter, some interior filming took place at Warner Bros. studios in Burbank, California, while additional exterior scenes were shot at Point Vicente Interpretive Center and Lighthouse, Rancho Palos Verdes, a location remote enough to allow for loud simulated gunfire and explosions. Fifteen weeks of filming concluded on 2 September 2016.

Plot Summary

[I. The Mole] Tommy (Fionn Whitehead), a young British private, walks the streets of Dunkirk with fellow soldiers as German leaflets fall on them from the sky, informing them that they are surrounded and should surrender. Suddenly shots ring out. Though all of his comrades are killed as they try to seek cover, Tommy makes it to an Allied-held street barricade. He soon arrives at the beach and meets Gibson (Aneurin Barnard), another young soldier, who is burying a dead soldier in the sand. After the two silently bond, they pick up a wounded soldier on a stretcher and rush him to a departing hospital ship as a pretext for their own escape. Ordered off the ship after delivering the wounded soldier, the two men then hide under the pier, ready to try and stow away, but the ship is suddenly bombed and sunk by a German Stuka dive-bomber. The two men manage to save Alex (Harry Styles), a young soldier. The trio gets on another vessel that night, but it is sunk by a German U-boat. Gibson saves Alex and Tommy from drowning, and they find a way back to shore. The next day, they board a small beached trawler with a group of soldiers from the Argyll and Sutherland Highlanders and wait inside its hold for the tide to come in and refloat the boat out to sea. However, the boat is not within the British perimeter, and the Germans shoot at it for target practice. When the tide eventually rises, there are so many bullet holes in the boat's hull that it cannot stay afloat. Alex then makes allegations that Gibson—who has remained mute— is a German spy and must leave to balance the ship. Tommy comes to his aid, but Gibson admits that his true heritage is French—he has co-opted the identity of a British soldier. The ship begins to sink and the troops evacuate, but as they do, Gibson gets tangled in a chain and drowns. Alex and Tommy eventually board Mr. Dawson's (Mark Rylance) boat and return home to a hero's welcome by citizens. [II. The Sea] At a dock in England, Mr. Dawson, a middle-aged civilian sailor, decides not to turn over his boat to the Royal Navy to evacuate soldiers from Dunkirk but opts instead to sail it himself, with the assistance of his 17-year-old son, Peter (Tom Glynn-Carney), and Peter's friend (George Barry Keoghan). On their trip across the English Channel, they encounter a shivering, shell-shocked soldier (Cillian Murphy), the sole survivor of a U-boat attack, huddled on the stern of his mostly submerged vessel. The soldier climbs aboard but once he realizes they are heading to Dunkirk, he attempts to turn the boat around. A scuffle ensues; George is knocked below decks and sustains a severe head injury. When a Spitfire ditches in the water nearby, Mr. Dawson insists on helping the pilot, Collins (Jack Lowden), who is stuck in his cockpit by a damaged canopy as the plane sinks. After they free Collins and help him aboard the boat, Peter reveals that his older brother, now dead, was a Hurricane pilot. Mr. Dawson later saves the lives of several soldiers, including Alex and Tommy. George dies from his injury, but Peter decides against telling the shivering soldier about this, insisting that George will fine. They eventually reach England, and Mr. Dawson is celebrated for his heroics as George's body is removed from the boat. The local paper later labels 17-year-old George a "Dunkirk hero." [III. The Air] In the skies over the English Channel, three Spitfire pilots—Farrier (Tom Hardy), Collins, and their unnamed leader—approach Dunkirk. The leader is the first to go in a dogfight with a Luftwaffe fighter plane. Continuing east, Farrier and Collins are successful in taking down a Nazi plane, but Collins' Spitfire is fired upon and he crashes into the sea. Farrier continues alone. Though low on fuel, he guards the skies over the Dunkirk beaches, getting applause from all the soldiers—even Commander Bolton (Kenneth Branagh), the highest-ranking officer on the beach. Out of fuel, Collins cranks down his landing gear by hand and lands his plane on the beach north of Dunkirk, sets it on fire, and is taken prisoner by German soldiers.

Reception

After its London premiere on 13 July 2017, with director, actors, Prince Harry, and Dunkirk veterans in attendance, *Dunkirk* was screened at the Galway Film Fleadh [Festival] on 16 July. It was then released in most of Europe on 19 July and in the United States and many other countries worldwide on 21 July. Budgeted at $100 million, *Dunkirk* was an expensive film to make, but the filmmakers' summer blockbuster release strategy—unusual for what was considered a niche market film—paid off handsomely; *Dunkirk* (widest release: 4,014 theaters) recouped all of its production costs in its first weekend in theaters and ultimately earned $525 million by its closing date (23 Nov. 2017). Most reviews were overwhelmingly positive. As was typical of many film critics, Philip Kemp praised the film's straightforward narrative style: "With *Dunkirk*, [Christopher Nolan's] first film dealing with a real-life event, the director has shifted out of cerebral overdrive and rediscovered a welcome directness and simplicity. A lot of the time, in fact, it's what he doesn't do that makes the film so powerful. The payoff, in terms of sheer emotional and visceral impact, is immense" (Kemp, 2017). Manhola Dargis called *Dunkirk* "a movie that is insistently humanizing despite its monumentality, a balance that is as much a political choice as an aesthetic one" (Dargis, 2017).

Reel History Versus Real History

As the film correctly shows, most aerial combat occurred away from the beaches, giving stranded BEF soldiers the false impression that the RAF was sitting out the fight—though it is true that Britain conserved planes and ships to oppose an anticipated Nazi invasion. Yet insofar as Christopher Nolan concentrates on re-creating the subjective experience of the evacuation through a few fictional characters (mostly British), the movie eschews any systematic presentation of the larger military/political context. Made by an Anglo-American director and financed with American money, *Dunkirk* largely omits the French. Viewers will get the false impression that only the BEF was evacuated but 120,000 French soldiers and 20,000 Polish and Belgian soldiers were also rescued. Even more galling to the French was the movie's failure to depict France's role in making the evacuation possible by holding off the Germans. In a blistering critique of the Anglo-Saxon bias of *Dunkirk*, French film critic Jacques Mandelbaum posed a series of rhetorical questions: "Where are the other 40,000 [French troops] who sacrificed themselves to defend the city against a superior enemy in arms and in numbers? Where are the members of the First Army, who, abandoned by their allies . . . nevertheless prevent[ed] several divisions of the Wehrmacht from [marching into] Dunkirk? Where is Dunkerque, half destroyed by the bombardments, but rendered here invisible?" (Mandelbaum, 2017). Where indeed? *Dunkirk* also elides the colonial soldiers from Britain's empire in South Asia (mostly Indian and Pakistani troops) who fought at Dunkirk. As Yasmin Khan notes, "The myth of Dunkirk reinforces the idea that Britain stood alone. It is a political tool in the hands of those who would separate British history from European history and who want to reinforce the myths that underpin Brexit" (Khan, 2017). With elisions come distortions. The film's focus on the intrepid Mr. Dawson gives viewers the erroneous notion that the so-called "Little Ships of Dunkirk," the 700 private boats that helped rescue the BEF, were skippered by their civilian owners. A few were, but most were turned over to the Admiralty and manned by Royal Navy crews. Nolan's use of fictional or composite characters also met with criticism, especially in the case of Kenneth Branagh's character, Commander Bolton, who seems to have been modeled on at least two Royal Navy officers: Captain (later Admiral) William "Bill" Tennant (1890–1963) and James Campbell Clouston (1900–1940), pier-master of "the mole." Clouston organized and regulated the flow of men along the mole into the waiting ships for five days and nights. He was killed the last night of the evacuation. Clouston's son Dane, 78, got in touch with the film's producers in January 2017 to ask if his late father could be credited, but was told it was not possible to honor every hero. Dane Clouston told the *Daily Mail*: "I was quite upset he is not referred to by his proper name" (Adams, 2017).

E

84 CHARLIE MOPIC [AKA 84C MOPIC] (1989)

Synopsis
Written and directed by Vietnam veteran Patrick Sheane Duncan, *84 Charlie MoPic* is an independently produced American combat drama set during the Vietnam War about a small, stealthy long-range reconnaissance patrol (LRRP) (pronounced "lurp") that probes deep into enemy-held territory to gather intelligence. The story is told through the eyes of an army motion picture (MoPic) cameraman who has been assigned to make a documentary about the patrol.

Background
Patrick Sheane Duncan served in Vietnam with the U.S. Army's 173rd Airborne Brigade ("Sky Soldiers") in 1968–1969, was twice wounded in combat, and earned a Bronze Star for bravery. Some years after his military service, Duncan began to write spec scripts. The idea for *84C MoPic* occurred to Duncan in 1983 while he waited in traffic that had piled up due to an accident on the highway. A TV news cameraman arrived on the scene and began to shoot footage as he wandered amid the wreckage. "I watched him go up to a woman who was sitting on a hillside. He stuck the camera in her bleeding face. It was horribly intimate. I said, 'Aha, this is the way to do my film'" (Norman, p. H15). Duncan wrote the screenplay in five days, but couldn't find a director who understood his vision for the film. He decided to learn how to direct himself at Robert Redford's Sundance Institute. With Sundance cachet and the success of other Vietnam movies, Duncan and his producer, Michael Nolin, were finally able to find financing five years after the script was completed.

Production
84C MoPic was shot (in Super 16 mm) in Southern California with a crew of 30, on a budget of just over $1 million. Prior to start of the shoot (which lasted only 17 days: 9–27 May 1988), Vietnam veteran Capt. Russ "Gunny" Thurman, USMC, Retired (also the technical advisor for *Vietnam War Stories*) conducted a week-long training course for the movie's seven actors playing members of a long-range reconnaissance patrol with the 173rd Airborne Brigade. Thurman taught the men reconnaissance techniques; stealth in the field; camouflage discipline; and the use of small arms, including M-16A1 rifles, an M-60 machine gun, and the M-79 grenade launcher. Because the story involved the patrol running into an enemy ambush, Thurman drilled the actors until they were intimately familiar with their weapons and could reload them quickly and correctly in a combat situation.

Plot Summary

The setting is a remote U.S. Army base in the Central Highlands, South Vietnam, 1969. For a training film, an 84C MoPic (Motion Picture Specialist) (Byron James) is assigned to a squad of six soldiers about to embark on a three-day Long-Range Reconnaissance Patrol: Sgt. "OD" O'Donigan (Richard Brooks), Lt. "LT" Drewery (Jonathan Emerson), Pvt. "Easy" Easley (Nicholas Cascone), SPEC/4 "Pretty Boy" Baldwin (Jason Tomlins), SPEC/4 "Hammer" Thorpe (Christopher Burgard) and "Cracker" (Glenn Morshower). The men board a Huey helicopter, are flown to a drop-off site, disembark, and begin to move into the jungle. During a rest break OD discovers that Easy is packing marijuana. Noting that the acrid smell of the smoke could give away their position, OD dumps the offending substance on the ground. The next morning Pretty Boy tells MoPic that he was mistaken for dead after an enemy mortar round hit close by. He also tells MoPic he's been incredibly lucky (e.g., a bullet hit him in the helmet and merely creased his hair). In another filmed interview Cracker tells MoPic he came from a large, poor "white trash" family in South Carolina so he enlisted to have a career and take advantage of educational and retirement benefits. His working-class philosophy is "Do your job," right or wrong, to put food on the table. Asked if he resents being led by a black man, Cracker angrily asserts his admiration and brotherly love for OD and stops the interview. After encountering a booby trap, they leave the trail and duck out of sight just as an enemy patrol passes close by. Soon thereafter, the squad spots a North Vietnamese Army (NVA) unit of about 20 soldiers, and OD hatches a plan to attack them. Easy interviews LT on camera; LT says he sees the army as a big corporation where the "advancement potential is enormous." The men set up a booby trap on the trail with a grenade and tripwire to "out-Chuck Chuck." The squad discovers the NVA force they've been surveilling has grown overnight to the size of a regiment. Easy gets on the radio and transmits map coordinates for an artillery barrage and airstrike. LT declares the LRRP mission completed and radios to arrange for a rendezvous with a helicopter at a nearby village. On the way back, the squad decides to attack a small squad of enemy soldiers, killing five of the Viet Cong, but one remains alive, instigating a heated debate. Pretty Boy wants to finish him off, but LT wants to bring him back for interrogation; OD sides with LT. Just then, the squad comes under heavy small arms fire. Pretty Boy is hit, stranded in the open, and hit several more times. Hammer tries to rescue him but is also wounded. The squad is pinned down and cannot get to Pretty Boy so OD decides to put him out of his misery. After the skirmish ends, OD removes Pretty Boy's dog tags and tapes one of them into his mouth. The squad can carry back only one body; Americans never leave their dead behind, so OD demands that LT kill their wounded Viet Cong prisoner. LT stabs the man but does not kill him; OD finishes the job. The squad moves out but is soon ambushed. OD takes a bullet to the stomach but Cracker takes three rounds to the abdomen and quickly dies. OD wraps up the corpses of Pretty Boy and Cracker and tells his surviving squad mates that "We'll send a chopper back for them." On camera, Hammer speculates that luck migrates from one soldier to another and he now feels that he has Pretty Boy's luck for surviving the ambush. Overcome by dread, Easy begins to panic, but OD promises to take care of him. As OD weakens from his wound, LT tries to take over but OD insists on walking point. As they move out Hammer is killed by a booby trap. The four survivors enter the village of their rendezvous destination but find it deserted and burning, with civilians lying dead on the ground. The men hunker down and await the helicopter but come under intense fire just as it arrives. OD, LT, and Easy make it to the chopper but MoPic is shot and killed trying to reach it, making the film just seen "found footage."

Reception

84 Charlie MoPic premiered at the Sundance Film Festival in January 1989, where it received a Grand Jury Prize nomination. A shoestring independent production, the movie had a very limited theatrical release through New Century Vista in March–April 1989 (just $154,264 in ticket sales). Principal revenues came from the sale of cable TV broadcast rights to Cinemax and sales rights to Columbia Pictures Home Entertainment for the VHS tape market. Besides the Sundance nomination, *84 Charlie MoPic* was nominated for two 1990 Independent Spirit Awards. Reviews were mostly positive. For Mike Pearson (Scripps-Howard), *84 Charlie MoPic* achieved "a haunting level of realism and resonance" (Pearson, 1989, p. 66). Roger Ebert gave the film a qualified "thumbs up": "The strength here is that the movie seems to happen as we watch it. The tradeoff is that the director has less freedom to pick and choose his shots for dramatic effect; once he establishes the point of view, he's stuck with it [but] . . . It is a brave and original attempt to record nothing more or less than the actual daily experience of a unit on patrol, drawn out of the memories of men who were there" (Ebert, 1989).

Reel History Versus Real History

Long-range reconnaissance patrols (LRRPs) were common during the Vietnam War: 23,000 were conducted, and they accounted for some 10,000 enemy killed in action (KIA) through ambushes, airstrikes, and artillery. The LRRP depicted in *84 Charlie MoPic* is credible in terms of its mission, size, configuration, and the armaments carried. As is depicted in the movie, LRRPs were recon missions conducted by squads of five to eight men, led by a seasoned noncommissioned officer (NCO), and lightly armed for mobility's sake. Still, cinematic imperatives clash with historical realism in a number of ways. By their very nature, LRRPs were expected to be stealthy. This meant taping down equipment, using hand signals, and talking as little and as quietly as possible to elude detection and avoiding contact with the enemy. The soldiers on recon patrol in *84 Charlie MoPic* talk constantly and loudly, making for compelling storytelling but poor verisimilitude. The squad's fateful decision to engage an enemy unit rather than going around it enlivens the action but constitutes another violation of verisimilitude. Furthermore, as of February 1969, all U.S. Army LRRP units were folded into the newly formed 75th Infantry Regiment (Rangers), so a LRRP by a unit from the 173rd Airborne Brigade would have been unlikely. As for a lone Army cameraman accompanying a LRRP for the purposes of making a training film—this, too, is highly unlikely. The U.S. Army Signal Corps has been making training films since the 1930s but all of them have been produced under controlled conditions far away from combat zones. Despite

84 Charlie MoPic's violations of realism, Gordon L. Rottman, a widely published military author who served in the 5th Special Forces Group in Vietnam in 1969–1970, rates *84 Charlie MoPic* as one of the most historically accurate films about the Vietnam War (Rottman, p. 58).

EMPIRE OF THE SUN (1987)

Synopsis

Empire of the Sun is an American war film/coming-of-age drama based on J. G. Ballard's semi-autobiographical novel that bears the same title. Directed by Steven Spielberg and starring John Malkovich, Miranda Richardson, Nigel Havers, and Christian Bale, the film recounts the saga of Jamie "Jim" Graham, a British boy who goes from living in wealthy circumstances in Shanghai to becoming a prisoner of war in a Japanese internment camp during World War II.

Background

Born and raised in the Shanghai International Settlement in China, acclaimed British writer J. G. Ballard (1930–2009) lived through the Japanese occupation that started the day after Pearl Harbor and ended shortly before Japan's surrender on 2 September 1945. Some 40 years later Ballard wrote *Empire of the Sun* (Gollancz, 1984), a quasi-autobiographical novel derived from his boyhood years living under Japanese rule, mostly at the Lunghua Civil Assembly Center, a Japanese internment camp in Shanghai. Short-listed for the Man Booker Prize, Ballard's novel garnered rave reviews, earned Ballard an estimated £500,000 in royalties, and attracted the attention of Hollywood. Warner Bros. purchased the film rights and hired Harold Becker to direct, Robert Shapiro to produce, and playwright Tom Stoppard to write the screen adaptation in collaboration with Ballard. After Becker dropped out, David Lean was hired to direct, and Steven Spielberg took over as producer. Lean worked on pre-production for a year and a half before finally ceding the directorial reins to Spielberg, who had a closer personal affinity to the project that stemmed from his interest in coming-of-age stories and a lifelong fascination with World War II (his father had been a radio operator on B-25 Mitchell bombers in the China-Burma Theater). Spielberg then hired Menno Meyjes (*The Color Purple*) to do an uncredited rewrite before Stoppard was rehired to write a fourth and final draft, that is, the shooting script (completed on 2 February 1987).

Production

After his casting team vetted over 4,000 hopefuls, Steven Spielberg hired Christian Bale, a 13-year-old British actor from Wales, to play the lead role of Jamie Graham. The shoot for *Empire of the Sun* took place in England, Spain, and China and lasted 100 days (1 March to 24 June 1987). While some scenes were filmed at Elstree Studios in Hertfordshire, southern England, the interior shots of the Graham family home in Shanghai were filmed in a bungalow at Sunningdale, England, and exterior shots were filmed at a house in Knutsford, a town near Manchester, England. After a year of negotiations with Shanghai Film Studios and China Film Co-Production Corporation in 1985, the filmmakers were granted permission for a three-week shoot in Shanghai in March 1987. Signs were altered to traditional Chinese characters, entire city blocks near the Huangpu River waterfront were closed off for filming, and over 5,000 local extras were used for the chaotic mob scene where Jamie is separated from his mother. Members of the People's Liberation Army were enlisted to play Japanese soldiers. The Lunghua detention center set was built inside the abandoned Beckton Gas Works in East London (where Stanley Kubrick filmed the Vietnam scenes for *Full Metal Jacket* in 1986). The Suzhou Creek prison camp set was built near Jerez, 80 miles northwest of Seville, in southwest Spain. Four Harvard SNJ (aka North American T-6 Texan) trainer aircraft were modified in France to resemble Mitsubishi A6M Zeros. Three restored North American P-51D Mustang fighter planes—two from Stephen Grey's The Fighter Collection and one from Ray Hanna's Old Flying Machine Company (both based at Duxford Airfield, Cambridgeshire, England)—were flown in the film. Hanna and his son, Mark, and Michael "Hoof" Proudfoot of The Fighter Collection flew the P-51s for a complex and spectacular air-raid scene on the Japanese base adjacent to the Suzhou Creek Internment Camp that took over 10 days to film (later reshot at considerable expense in Trebujena, Spain because Spielberg felt the original lacked authenticity). Large-scale remote control flying models were also used, including an 18-foot wingspan B-29 used for the supply drop scene. Industrial Light & Magic designed the visual effects sequences with some computer-generated imagery (CGI) also used for the Nagasaki atomic bomb flash. J. G. Ballard makes a cameo appearance at the costume party scene.

Plot Summary

During Japan's invasion of China, young Jamie Graham (Christian Bale) is enjoying the privileged life of an upper-class British expatriate in the Shanghai International Settlement. After they attack Pearl Harbor, the Japanese occupy Shanghai's foreign settlements. In the chaos that ensues, Jamie is separated from his parents. He returns to their deserted home but is forced to venture into the city after the food runs out. Jamie attempts to turn himself in to a group of Japanese militiamen, but he is turned away. He is then taken in by Basie (John Malkovich)—a stranded American ship's steward and a hustler—and his partner-in-crime, Frank Demarest (Joe Pantoliano), who nicknames him "Jim." To mollify Basie and Frank, Jamie leads them back to his neighborhood where they can loot valuables. At Jamie's old house, the trio is arrested by Japanese soldiers and taken to Lunghua Civilian Assembly Center outside Shanghai for processing. Soon thereafter a truck arrives to take some internees to the Suzhou Creek Internment Camp. Basie is among those selected to go. Jamie is not, but he convinces the soldiers to take him along. When he reaches the camp, Jim walks to the airfield and watches workers fixing up a squadron of Mitsubishi A6M Zero fighters and trades salutes with fighter pilots. Later, resourceful Jim survives in the camp by running a lucrative trading network, involving even the camp's commander, Sgt. Nagata (Masatô Ibu). Dr. Rawlins (Nigel Havers), the camp's British doctor, becomes Jim's surrogate father and mentor. In the aftermath of a bombing raid, Sgt. Nagata commands that the prisoners' hospital be obliterated, but changes course when Jim asks for forgiveness. Through the barbed wire fencing, Jim befriends a teenaged Kamikaze pilot trainee (Takatarô Kataoka). He also visits Basie in the American prisoner of war (POW) barracks. Basie tasks Jim with setting up snare traps on the perimeter of the camp's wire (a way to test the area for land mines as Basie is plotting to escape). When the work is completed, Basie lets Jim join him in the American barracks. One morning Jim salutes departing Kamikaze pilots by singing "Suo Gân," a traditional Welsh lullaby. The base is suddenly attacked by a flight of USAAF P-51 Mustang fighters. Overjoyed at the sight, Jim climbs up a pagoda for a better vantage point. Dr. Rawlins follows Jim in order to rescue him, whereupon Jim becomes emotional because he is unable to remember his parents' faces. The Japanese evacuate the camp, and Basie escapes during the confusion, leaving Jim behind though he had promised to take Jim with him. During their evacuation march, many of the camp's prisoners die from exhaustion, disease, and starvation. Arriving at a football stadium near Nantao, Jim recognizes his parents' Packard among war booty looted by the Japanese. Waking up next to a young woman's corpse, Jim witnesses the bright flash from the atomic bombing of Nagasaki hundreds of miles to the East (9 August 1945). Jim slips away from the group, wanders back to Suzhou Creek, and soon learns that Japan has surrendered and the war is over. He also encounters the young kamikaze Japanese pilot trainee he befriended earlier. Basie reappears with a group of armed Americans who have arrived to loot airdropped Red Cross containers. Jim's young friend is about to cut a mango for Jim with his katana (samurai sword) when one of the Americans, mistakenly believing Jim to be in harm's way, murders the Japanese youth. Basie volunteers to help Jim locate his parents, but Jim opts to stay behind. Jim is located by American soldiers and brought to an orphanage, where he is finally reunited with his mother and father.

Reception

During its seven-week run in the United States and Canada (11 December 1987– 28 January 1988; widest release: 673 theaters), *Empire of the Sun* took in $22.2 million. It earned an additional $44.5 million in other countries, for a worldwide total of $66.7 million—almost double its $35 million production budget—but was still considered a box office flop, especially by Spielberg standards; *Empire of the Sun* ranks near the bottom of Spielberg's 30-film oeuvre for box office revenues. The movie did rack up lots of award nominations—two Golden Globes and six Oscars—and won three BAFTA Awards (for cinematography, sound design, and music score). In keeping with tepid box office and award results, reviews were mixed. Janet Maslin credited Spielberg for infusing the film with "a visual splendor, a heroic adventurousness and an immense scope that make it unforgettable" (Maslin, 1987). Conversely, Desson Howe found the movie visually "flashy" but ultimately rather puerile: "In a way, Spielberg is to film what Michael Jackson is to pop. Both grew up within their respective arts rather than in real life, their human growth on perpetual hold. Thus, we're doomed to watching (or hearing) their endless perspectives on the ways of childhood" (Howe, 1987).

Reel History Versus Real History

The film mostly follows its source material, J. G. Ballard's novel, quite faithfully, but Ballard himself had already strayed far from the actual facts of his own biography in writing *Empire of the Sun*. In book and movie the Ballard figure, Jamie Graham, is separated from his parents in the chaos that ensues after the Japanese takeover of Shanghai's International Settlement. The settlement was indeed occupied by the Japanese the day after Pearl Harbor, but the Ballard family continued to live in their home at 31A Amherst Avenue in the British Concession for another 16 months after 8 December 1941, and young James Graham ("J. G.") Ballard was never separated from his family during the war. In March 1943 Ballard, his parents, and his four-year-old sister were interned with other foreign civilians at the Lunghua Camp in the south of the city (now Shanghai Zhongxue). They lived together in a small room in G Block and remained at Lunghua with 2,000 other internees until the end of the war in late August 1945: a period of two and a half years that Ballard would later remember as "largely happy" (J.G. Ballard, 2009). The movie's depiction of Jim's scuffling time alone in Shanghai, his entanglement with Basie, his later interment at Suzhou Creek Camp, his evacuation to Nantao, the killing of the young kamikaze pilot—all these events are pure fiction that lend the narrative greater drama and provide a basis for Jim's maturation process. As depicted in the movie, however, there were American air raids on Japanese positions near the camp, and at the end of the war a B-29 dropped relief supplies by canisters attached to parachutes for the hungry internees.

ENEMY AT THE GATES (2001)

Synopsis

Enemy at the Gates is a French-American war film written and directed by Jean-Jacques Annaud and based on William Craig's *Enemy at the Gates: The Battle for Stalingrad* (1973): a history of the World War II battle in the winter of 1942–1943. The film's main character (played by Jude Law) is a fictionalized version of Soviet sniper Vassili Zaitsev, who engages in a snipers' duel with Major Erwin König, a crack Wehrmacht sniper (played by Ed Harris).

Background

Russian snipers played an important role in World War II, especially during the decisive Battle of Stalingrad (23 August 1942–2 February 1943), where they picked off over 1,200 German officers and noncommissioned officers (NCOs). The most celebrated of these snipers was Chief Master Sergeant Vassili Grigoryevich Zaitsev (1915–1991), aka "Zayats" ("The Hare"), 2nd Battalion, 1047th Rifle Regiment, 284th Tomsk Rifle Division. In a 38-day period (10 November–17 December 1942) Zaitsev, a Siberian hunter from the Urals using a standard-issue Mosin-Nagant rifle with a 4× scope, was credited with 225 verified kills (11 of them enemy snipers), many at distances over 1,000 meters. For his prowess as a marksman Zaitsev was named a Hero of the Soviet Union and awarded four Orders of Lenin. Legendary in his own country, Zaitsev's name filtered to the West thanks to two books: William Craig's nonfiction book, *Enemy at the Gates: The Battle for Stalingrad* (Reader's Digest Press, 1973) and David L. Robbins' historical novel, *War of the Rats* (Bantam Books, 1999). Russian newspaper accounts during the war and Sgt. Zaitsev's own memoir, *Zapiski Snaypera* [*A Sniper's Notes*] (1956), tell of a snipers' duel at Stalingrad between Zaitsev and a German officer named Heinz Thorvald (aka Major Erwin König) that Zaitsev won, a story that has never been either verified or disproven (*Enemy at the Gates* devotes a mere three pages to this incident, whereas Robbins' novel is entirely centered on it). Fascinated by the anecdote "of a lonely man fighting against the devil," French filmmaker Jean Jacques Annaud (*The Name of the Rose*) co-wrote a screen adaptation with frequent collaborator, Alain Godard, allegedly based on William Craig's cursory account. Budgeted at $86 million, *Enemy at the Gates* was the most expensive American production to be shot in Europe up to that time. Paramount Pictures co-financed the movie with Mandalay Pictures and CP Medien AG, a German tax shelter fund. Paramount handled domestic distribution while Mandalay pre-sold the movie to overseas distributors.

Production

Searching for locations to build Stalingrad sets Annaud, producer John D. Schofield, and production designer Wolf Kroeger conducted a search of Europe before they settled on three sites in eastern Germany: an abandoned factory in the industrial town of Rudersdorf (where scenes with König, the German sharpshooter played by Ed Harris, were filmed); a deserted military barracks in the village of Krampnitz (where Stalingrad's Red Square was re-created); and a new lake created from a former opencast lignite mine near the village of Pritzen, south of Brandenburg (where Volga River scenes were shot). The building of the Red Square set took five months (October 1999–February 2000). The massive set included exterior ruins of the Pravda printing plant, the Gorky Theatre, the Univermag department store, and Stalingrad's most iconic landmark: the Barmaley Fountain, a statue depicting a circle of six children dancing around a crocodile. Principal photography took place between mid-January 2000 and May 2000, with final interior scenes filmed at Babelsberg Studio, outside Berlin.

Plot Summary

In the fall of 1942 Vassili Zaitsev (Jude Law), a former shepherd from the Ural Mountains, is fighting on the frontlines during the Battle of Stalingrad. During a suicidal frontal assault on German positions, Zaitsev uses his superior skills as a marksman to kill five Germans, saving himself and Commissar Danilov (Joseph Fiennes). Nikita Khrushchev (Bob Hoskins), who comes to Stalingrad to bolster the city defenses, sees a need for improving the overall morale of the citizens. Danilov, a senior lieutenant, argues that Russians are in need of heroes to pin their hopes on. To this end, Danilov churns out stories lauding Zaitsev's accomplishments in the army newspaper, labeling him a national hero. To complicate matters, Zaitsev and Danilov both become infatuated with Tania Chernova (Rachel Weisz), a private in the Stalingrad militia who is moved from the frontlines to a small intelligence unit. As German forces deal with gunfire from unceasing Soviet snipers, German Major Erwin König (Ed Harris) is sent to Stalingrad to murder Zaitsev as a propaganda coup. The major, an expert sniper, entices Zaitsev into a trap and then eliminates a pair of Zaitsev's comrades. Zaitsev escapes. When the Red Army high command discovers König's mission, they send a former student, Koulikov (Ron Perlman), to assist him with the murder. However, König kills his former student instead. Sacha (Gabriel Marshall-Thomson), a young Soviet boy, passes König false information about Zaitsev's whereabouts, which allows Zaitsev a chance to ambush the major. Zaitsev aims to trick König and injures him, but a thieving German soldier steals his sniper log. After seeing the log, the German command believes Zaitsev to be dead, but König suspects that his enemy still lives. König's dog tags are stripped from him to prevent Russian propaganda from profiting if he is shot. Tania and Zaitsev fall in love and consummate their romance. When König sees Tania and Zaitsev at an ambush area, he becomes certain that Sasha is working for both sides. As a result, he kills Sasha and hangs his body in public to agitate Zaitsev. Zaitsev asks Tania and Danilov to usher Sasha's mother (Eva Mattes) away from the city, but Tania is left wounded. As Zaitsev waits to surprise König, Danilov reveals himself in order to instigate a shooting match with König. Mistaking Danilov for Zaitsev, König inspects the body and realized his error too late—he is in Zaitsev's sights. He turns to face Zaitsev and doffs his hat in tribute to his opponent's skill just before Zaitsev shoots him. Two months later, after the German forces have surrendered, Zaitsev finds Tania recovering in a field hospital.

Reception

Paramount planned to release *Enemy at the Gates* on 22 December 2000 as a possible awards contender, but the film was pushed back twice (to 23 February and then to 16 March). Against the wishes of Mandalay, German distributor Constantin arranged to have *Enemy at the Gates* premier at the Berlin Film Festival on 7 February 2001, where it was roundly booed by the audience. It subsequently had poor box office returns in Germany and was savaged by German film critics, who regarded it as a Hollywood-style glorification of war. During its 12-week North American run (16 March–21 June 2001; widest release: 1,724 theaters), the movie earned $51.4 million at the box office while receipts from foreign markets totaled $45.5 million. Worldwide, *Enemy at the Gates* earned almost $97 million, but against an $86 million production budget, it was deemed a flop. Reviews were mixed. Peter Travers observed that "Annaud's film boasts harrowing battle scenes as Russian relief troops are bombarded while crossing the River Volga and Stalingrad itself is battered by air and sea while tanks and soldiers overrun its streets. In the shell of the city, Vassili and König face off in a duel of wits that is meant to mirror the larger battle. Any flaws in execution pale against those moments when the film brings history to vital life" (Travers, 2001). Giving *Enemy at the Gates* three out of four stars, Roger Ebert decried the romance subplot as "soppy," but noted that when the movie focuses on the duel between Zaitsev and König, it "works with rare concentration" (Ebert, 2001).

Reel History Versus Real History

Enemy at the Gates is a loose blending of broad fact and pure fiction. There was most certainly a Battle of Stalingrad and a Russian sniper named Vassili Zaitsev. However, Danilov and Tania Chernova are fictional, as is, of course, the entire romance subplot. Zaitsev's duel with the German sniper, Major König, is also probably apocryphal, likely a morale-boosting propaganda concoction that became a national legend. There was never a German sniper school at Zossen, and there is no extant record of a German sniper named either Heinz Thorvald or König—but, then again, lots of Nazi military service records were destroyed during the war. Russian WWII historian Valeriy Potopov (who hated the film) also notes Danilov could not have been a commissar throughout the entire movie because the Institute of Commissars was abolished in the Red Army as early as 9 October 1942.

EUROPA EUROPA [GERMAN TITLE: *HITLERJUNGE SALOMON*] (1990)

Synopsis

A French-Polish co-production, *Europa Europa* is a war film directed by Agnieszka Holland. Starring Marco Hofschneider, the film is based on the 1989 autobiography of Solomon Perel, a German Jewish youth who pretended to be a Nazi to escape the Holocaust.

Background

After a health scare in 1983 Holocaust survivor Solomon "Solly" Perel began to write his memoirs: an incredible story of survival he had kept under wraps for almost 40 years. In the preface to the English-language edition of *Europa Europa,* Perel admits that "he could no longer suppress the trauma . . . To free myself of it I had to write it all down—to get it off my chest" (Perel, 1999, p. xii). Polish Jewish film producer Artur Brauner (*Morituri*), a native of Łódź, also a Holocaust survivor, learned of Perel's book well before its publication, secured the film rights, and asked director Agnieszka Holland, with whom he had just collaborated on another Holocaust film—*Angry Harvest* (1985)—to direct the film. Working closely with Solomon Perel, Holland wrote the screen adaptation, with help from Paul Hengge (*Angry Harvest*). Brauner's own production company, Central Cinema Compagnie-Film GmbH (CCC), joined forces with Les Films du Losange (France) and two Polish companies—Telmar Film International Ltd. and Zespol Filmowy "Perspektywa"—to finance the project. Holland wanted to cast German actor René Hofschneider in the lead role, but it took three years to put financing in place, by which time Hofschneider was 29 and a bit old for the role, so Holland cast his younger brother Marco instead. Rene ended up playing Solomon Perel's older brother Isaak.

Production

Europa Europa was filmed (in German) in Poland over a four-month period in the summer and fall of 1989. Interior scenes were shot at FilmPolski's Studio, Filmowe Perspektywain, in Warsaw while exteriors were filmed in Lódz and environs, for example, at the Jewish Cemetery; in the Plac Koscielny (Church Square); on the Przybyszewskiego, one of the main east-west streets in the city center (the trolley scene through the Lódz Ghetto); at an abandoned factory (the Hitler Youth combat scene near the end of the film), etc.

Plot Summary

Solomon Perel (Marco Hofschneider) and his family live in Nazi Germany. On the eve of Perel's bar mitzvah, Kristallnacht (Nov. 9–10, 1938) occurs. As Nazis stone the house, Solomon escapes from a bath and hides naked in a barrel in an adjacent alley. The next morning a neighbor gives him a new coat with a swastika-laden armband. Clothed, he returns home, only to find that his sister Bertha (Marta Sandrowicz) has been killed by the Nazis. Solly's father (Klaus Abramowsky), who was born in Łódź, Poland, decides to return there, taking his family with him, that is, his wife (Michèle Gleizer), Solomon, and two other sons: David (Piotr Kozlowski) and Isaak (René Hofschneider). In Łódź Perel enjoys a brief affair with Basia (Nathalie Schmidt), a cinema cashier, but his halcyon interlude ends when the Nazis invade Poland, starting World War II. Perel's family decides he and his brother should move farther east. Isaak and Solomon flee but are separated, and Solomon is placed in a Soviet orphanage with other refugees from Poland. He lives there for two years, joins the Komsomol, and undergoes Communist indoctrination. He develops a romantic interest in Inna (Delphine Forest), an attractive young teacher who stands up for him when school administrators uncover his bourgeois social class. When Germany invades the Soviet Union, all of the children are evacuated from the orphanage, but Solomon is left behind during an air attack. He discards his identity papers and tells the Germans who capture him that he is "Josef Peters," a *Volksdeutscher* (ethnic German) from a Baltic German family. When the Germans capture Yakov Dzhugashvili, Stalin's son, Solomon helps by translating Russian. They call him "Jupp" (a baby name) and adopt him as an auxiliary. Fluent in German and Russian, Solly becomes an interpreter but is still in grave danger; he must stay modestly covered, lest anyone see his circumcised penis and realize that he is Jewish. Robert (André Wilms), a homosexual soldier, catches sight of Jupp while he is bathing, however, the pair become friends when they realize that they both carry secrets that would lead to death, should the Nazis find out. Not long after, Robert is killed in battle. While attempting to reach the Soviet lines, Jupp goes across a bridge and unwittingly brings a German unit along with him. The Soviets are forced to surrender, and the Germans praise Jupp for his heroics. Jupp is then sent to the elite Hitler Youth Academy in Braunschweig to receive a full Nazi education. While at school, "Peters" is labeled a combat hero. He still struggles to hide his circumcision, and Solomon uses string and rubber bands to simulate a foreskin: efforts that result in an excruciatingly painful infection. He successfully dodges a medical exam by feigning a toothache, but then has to have a healthy tooth pulled without the aid of medication. Girls from the Bund Deutscher Mädel (BDM, League of German Girls, the female equivalent of the Hitler Youth) serve meals at the academy. BDM girl Leni (Julie Delpy) becomes infatuated with Jupp and strongly hints that she would happily bear Jupp's child, but after she makes an anti-Semitic remark he slaps her and they break up. Afterwards, while serving at a factory to support the war effort, Jupp and his fellow students discover that the Sixth Army has been destroyed at Stalingrad. Solly decides to visit Leni's mother (Halina Labonarska) and tells her he's Jewish but she does not betray him. When she tells him Leni is pregnant, Solomon concludes that the father of the child is one of his classmates, a friend named Gerd (Ashley Wanninger). Solomon's charade as an "Aryan" German begins to crumble when he is summoned to Gestapo offices and cannot produce a Certificate of Racial Purity. An ensuing investigation will expose him, but just as he leaves the building, it is destroyed by Allied bombs, killing Gerd in the bargain. As the Red Army closes in on Berlin, the Hitler Youth at the school are sent to the front. Perel surrenders and tells his captors he's a Jew but they don't believe that any Jew would have survived. They are about to have Solomon shot when his brother Isaak, who has just left a concentration camp, stops the shooting and saves his brother's life. Solly soon moves to the British Mandate of Palestine, the future state of Israel, and finally lives his Jewish heritage. The films ends with a shot of the real Solomon Perel, who is now 65 years old, performing a Jewish folk song ("Hine Ma Tov," Psalm 133:1).

Reception

Europa Europa had its European premiere in Paris on 14 November 1990 and simultaneous East and West Coast American openings in New York City and in Seattle on 28 June 1991. Well received in the United States, the movie garnered good reviews, received a Golden Globe Award for Best Foreign Language Film, and grossed $5.6 million at the box office: respectable returns for a subtitled foreign film on a downbeat topic. American Jewish associations and concentration camp survivors also praised the film. *Europa Europa's* reception in Germany was another matter entirely, however. A comic-absurd picaresque journey through the Holocaust that featured an amoral protagonist who survives through deception, collaboration, and pure luck, the movie went against postwar Germany's lofty moral protocols regarding Jewish victimhood and national guilt. In the words of film scholar Lawrence Baron, "*Europa Europa's* multicultural message, multinational origins, and discomforting synthesis of comic, sensual, and violent elements hurt its reception in the newly reunified Germany" (Baron, 2005, pp. 87–88). To add insult to critical opprobrium and dismal box office returns, the German Export Film Union decided not to submit *Europa Europa* for Oscar consideration as Best Foreign Film. The snub provoked a protest letter signed by Germany's leading filmmakers, including Volker Schlöndorff (*The Tin Drum*), Wolfgang Petersen (*Das Boot*), and Michael Verhoeven (*The Nasty Girl*). More alarmingly, Claude Lanzmann, maker of the acclaimed Holocaust documentary *Shoah* (1985), denounced Holland as an anti-Semite, even though the Nazi death camps claimed both of her Jewish father's parents (her mother was Catholic). Holland defended herself, saying, "I respect him enormously for *Shoah*, but he's an incredibly unpleasant man [and] a megalo-maniac" (Tong, 1990). As for Solomon Perel, he loved the movie and watched it at least 200 times.

Reel History Versus Real History

For the most part, Agnieszka Holland's film version of Solomon Perel's autobiography stays close to the self-reported facts of Perel's life during the war, but *Europa Europa* does indulge in cinematic embellishment. For dramatic effect, the movie depicts Solomon's sister, Bertha, as being killed by the Nazis during Kristallnacht in 1938. Actually, she was killed by the Nazis in 1945, during the death march from Stutthof concentration camp. The perfectly timed bombing of the Russian orphanage, signaling the German invasion of the Soviet Union, did not happen as such. Nor did the aerial bombing of the Gestapo offices in Braunschweig occur a second after Solomon Perel left them (though the city was bombed in 42 separate Allied air raids between 1940 and 1945). Holland also had Perel and his Hitler Youth comrades fighting the Red Army in Berlin. In actuality, he was captured by American forces on the Western Front. The film's more serious distortion, though, is its failure to represent Perel's internalized anti-Semitism—passing as a Nazi among Nazis went on for too long for him not to have fascist attitudes take hold. As a result, Perel admits that he has been plagued with a dual consciousness that is both Jewish and anti-Jewish. In a 1992 interview, Perel said, "To this day I have a tangle of two souls in one body. By this I mean to say that the road to Josef, the Hitler Youth that I was for four years, was very short and easy. But the way back to the Jew in me . . . was much harder" (Diehl, 1992). In her zeal to tell Perel's story objectively, Holland suppresses this somber truth.

F

FLAGS OF OUR FATHERS (2006)

Synopsis

An American war film adapted by William Broyles, Jr. and Paul Haggis from the book of the same title by James Bradley and Ron Powers (2000), *Flags of Our Fathers* recounts the story of the five Marines and one Navy Corpsman who raised the American flag on Mount Suribachi during the World War II Battle of Iwo Jima. Directed, co-produced, and scored by Clint Eastwood, the film examines how the event changed the lives of the surviving flag raisers.

Background

On 23 February 1945 Associated Press photographer Joe Rosenthal took a hasty snapshot of five U.S. Marines and a sailor raising the American flag on the summit of Iwo Jima's Mount Suribachi, signaling a key moment in wresting the island from the Japanese (though the flag-raising photographed by Rosenthal was actually the second one with a larger flag, not the first, and the Battle of Iwo Jima would rage on for another 31 days). Published in the *New York Times* two days later and then picked up by hundreds of U.S. newspapers, the photograph won Rosenthal a Pulitzer Prize and quickly became, for Americans, the most iconic image of World War II—reproduced on 150 million 3¢ postage stamps, 1.2 million war bond drive posters, and 5,000 billboards in 1945 and later immortalized by the Marine Corps War Memorial in Arlington Ridge Park, Virginia: a colossal sculpture by Felix de Weldon dedicated in 1954 that features bronze figures of the six flag raisers 32 feet tall. Almost 49 years after the battle, James Bradley, son of John "Doc" Bradley (1923–1994), a medic on Iwo Jima, discovered a letter postmarked 26 February 1945 that his father wrote mentioning his own involvement in the flag raising: a startling revelation that inspired Bradley to co-author, with Ron Powers, *Flags of Our Fathers* (Bantam, 2000), a compelling account of the battle and how the three surviving flag raisers fared afterwards. The book spent 46 weeks on the *New York Times* nonfiction bestseller list, 6 weeks at the number-one spot. A month after its publication, Steven Spielberg acquired the option on the film rights for DreamWorks Pictures and hired screenwriter William Broyles, Jr. (*Jarhead*) to write a screen adaptation. Actor-director Clint Eastwood read the book in 2003, liked it, and wanted to make a movie version. On 26 February 2004, at the Academy Awards Governors Ball, Eastwood and Spielberg conversed with each other about *Flags of Our Fathers* and Spielberg suggested that he produce and Eastwood direct, an arrangement formalized that July. Thereafter, Eastwood brought in Paul Haggis

(*Million Dollar Baby*) to do a rewrite that was completed in late October 2004. Reading about the Battle of Iwo Jima from the Japanese perspective—especially that of the island's garrison commander, Lt. Gen. Tadamichi Kuribayashi—Eastwood decided to film *Letters from Iwo Jima,* a companion film shot entirely in Japanese.

Production

Jared Leto was originally cast as Rene Gagnon but dropped out due to scheduling issues. With the exception of Barry Pepper, Paul Walker, and Harve Presnell, the large cast—nearly 100 speaking parts—was composed of unknowns. Filming took place over a 58-day period in far-flung locations in the winter of 2005–2006. Eastwood made a scouting trip to Iwo Jima in April 2005 but determined it was too remote for a large-scale film production. Instead, the battle scenes were shot on Reykjanes, a volcanic peninsula in Iceland that featured black sand beaches and craters almost identical in appearance to Iwo Jima. A couple of scenes were shot at Universal Studios' backlot, but most of the stateside scenes were shot at various locations in Pasadena, Los Angeles, Chicago, and at the USMC War Memorial in Arlington, Virginia. A bond drive scene supposedly taking place at Soldier Field in Chicago was actually filmed at the Rose Bowl in Pasadena, using lots of computer-generated imagery (CGI) (though exterior shots of the real stadium were also used). Shooting ended early in 2006. The shoot for the movie's companion piece, *Letters from Iwo Jima,* began in March 2006.

Plot Summary

The three surviving US servicemen who were the flag raisers at Iwo Jima—Marine Pfcs. Ira Hayes (Adam Beach) and Rene Gagnon (Jesse Bradford) and Navy Corpsman John "Doc" Bradley (Ryan Phillippe)—are celebrated as heroes in a U.S. war bond drive. They reflect on their experiences during and after the war via a series of flashbacks. After training at Camp Tarawa in Hawaii (October 1944), the 28th Marine Regiment (5th Marine Division) joins an invading armada headed for Iwo Jima, a small island off Japan's mainland. To soften Japanese resistance, the Navy shells Iwo Jima for three days. Sgt. Mike Strank (Barry Pepper) is put in charge of Second Platoon. On the fourth day of the battle—19 February 1945—the Marines land on Iwo Jima in Higgins boats. They meet no immediate resistance but then, all at once, Japanese heavy artillery and machine guns open fire on the advancing Marines. The beaches are secured, but casualties are heavy. After two days of fierce fighting, the Marines mount an assault on Mount Suribachi. Doc saves the lives of several Marines under fire, earning the Navy Cross in the process. After a dogged fight, the mountain is secured. On 23 February Sgt. Hank Hansen (Paul Walker) is ordered to scale Mount Suribachi. His squad reaches the summit and hoists the American flag atop Suribachi. Secretary of the Navy James Forrestal (Michael Cumpsty) sees the flag as he reaches the beach and asks to keep the flag himself. However, Col. Chandler Johnson (Robert Patrick) counters that his own 2nd Battalion is more deserving of the flag than Forrestal. Rene Gagnon is sent up with Second Platoon to replace the first (smaller) flag with a second one intended for Forrestal. Mike, Doc, Ira, Rene, and two other marines—Cpl. Harlon Block

(Benjamin Walker) and Pfc. Franklin Sousley (Joseph Cross) are photographed by Joe Rosenthal as they send up the second flag. On 1 March Mike is hit by "friendly fire" and dies from his wounds. Later that day Hank and Harlon are also killed in action. Two nights later (4 March), while Doc tends to an injured soldier, Ralph "Iggy" Ignatowski (Jamie Bell) is kidnapped by the Japanese and pulled through an underground tunnel. Doc finds his mutilated body a few days later. On 21 March a mortally wounded Franklin Sousley dies in Ira Hayes' arms. Three squad members remain: Doc Bradley, Ira Hayes, and Rene Gagnon. A few days after Sousley's death, Doc is injured and returns home. On 26 March the Battle of Iwo Jima ends in American victory (but at a grave price: 6,700 dead and 19,000 wounded). Joe Rosenthal's photograph appears in newspapers throughout the country. Rene Gagnon is asked to name the six men in the photo: he identifies himself, Mike Strank, Doc Bradley, and Franklin Sousley, but misidentifies Harlon Block as Hank Hansen. Gagnon identifies Ira Hayes as the final man in the photograph, but Hayes says that it isn't him, but Harlon Block in the photo. Gagnon asks Hayes to reevaluate, mentioning that, as flag raisers, this denial will send them both home, but Gagnon refuses to give in and threatens Gagnon's life if he dares to name Hayes in the photograph. Gagnon does eventually name Ira Hayes as the sixth man in the photograph. Bradley, Hayes, and Gagnon are then sent stateside to raise money for the war effort. Hayes calls the bond drive a joke, but Bud Gerber (John Slattery) of the Treasury Department disciplines them and admits that the U.S. government is nearly bankrupt; if the bond drive fails, the United States will be forced to abandon the Pacific and all their sacrifices will be in vain. The three agree not to tell anyone that Hank Hansen was not in the photograph. As the trio is sent around the country on their fundraising tour, Ira Hayes suffers from survivor's guilt and the lingering effects of battle fatigue and also faces blatant bigotry as a Pima Indian. In the throes of alcoholism, Hayes vomits one night in front of Gen. Vandegrift (Chris Bauer), commandant of the Marine Corps; Vandegrift orders him sent back to his unit. After the war, the three survivors return home. Ira Hayes hitchhikes to Texas to see Harlon Block's family and tell Harlon's father that his son was indeed in the famous photograph. At the dedication of the USMC War Memorial in 1954 the three surviving flag raisers see each other one last time. The next year Ira Hayes dies of exposure after a night of heavy drinking. That same year Doc Bradley visits Iggy Ignatowski's mother to tell her how her son died. Rene Gagnon attempts to begin a professional life in the business sector, but finds that the offers he received during the bond drive have been rescinded and spends the rest of his life as a janitor. Doc, however, finds success as the owner and director of a funeral home. In 1994, close to death, Doc relays his vivid tale to his son, James.

Reception
Released 20 October 2006, *Flags of Our Fathers* ran for eight weeks (widest release: 1,876 theaters) and earned $33.6 million in gross domestic box office receipts. Exhibition in foreign markets (November 2006–March 2007) earned another $32.3 million, for a grand total of $65.9 million: disappointing results but probably inevitable because (a) the film lacked star power and (b) it presented a dishearteningly

revisionist depiction of "The Good War," showing the U.S. government cynically exploiting military heroism for propaganda and fundraising purposes. After theaters took their percentage of the gross and P&A (promotion and advertising) expenses were deducted, both co-producing studios—Paramount and DreamWorks—ended up in the red. Originally budgeted at $80 million, *Flags* would have lost far more money had Clint Eastwood not completed the film well ahead of schedule and under budget, bringing it in for only $55 million. Though it flopped at the box office, *Flags* enjoyed strong sales on the U.S. home video market, grossing $45 million. Reviews were mostly affirmative, some adulatory. Roger Ebert gave the film four out of four stars and praised Eastwood's two-film project as "one of the most visionary of all efforts to depict the reality and meaning of battle. The battle scenes, alternating between close-up combat and awesome aerial shots of the bombardment and landing, are lean, violent, horrifying. His cinematographer, Tom Stern, wisely bleeds his palette of bright colors and creates a dry, hot, desolate feeling; there should be nothing scenic about the film's look" (Ebert, 2007). Philip French found *Flags of Our Fathers* to be "touched by greatness. It argues that soldiers may go into battle for country and glory but they always end up fighting for the survival of themselves and their comrades" (French, 2006).

Reel History Versus Real History

Historians concur that Bradley and Powers' book is a well-researched and accurate rendition of the Battle of Iwo Jima; the 7th War Loan Drive (aka "Iwo Jima Tour," May–July 1945); and the postwar lives of Ira Hayes, Rene Gagnon, and Doc Bradley. Likewise, Eastwood's film version is a faithful adaptation of its source material. Interviewed by Robert Siegel on National Public Radio on 19 October 2006 regarding the film's historical accuracy, Charles D. "Chuck" Melson, Chief Historian of the U.S. Marine Corps, found the film to be quite true to life, describing the war bond drive, the ships coming to Iwo Jima, the beachside invasion and resulting chaos, and the flag raising. Asked by Siegel if the movie was accurate or exaggerating when it dramatized Rosenthal's photograph as "the very fulcrum on which public support for the war effort in 1945 rested," Melson answered, "I think it would take a social historian to really pin that one down" (Siegel, 2006). Melson's judicious answer notwithstanding, the movie does exaggerate the importance of the Rosenthal photograph in winning the war in the Pacific. The United States would have prosecuted the war to its conclusion, whatever the success or failure of the 7th War Loan Drive. Fortunately, the Drive far exceeded expectations by raising over $26 billion ($353 billion in 2017 dollars)—an astonishing sum of money.

FROM HERE TO ETERNITY (1953)

Synopsis

From Here to Eternity is a military drama directed by Fred Zinnemann and based on the 1951 novel of the same title by James Jones. The film dramatizes the lives of three U.S. Army soldiers (played by Burt Lancaster, Montgomery Clift, and Frank Sinatra) who are stationed in Honolulu, Hawaii, in the months leading up to the Japanese attack on Pearl Harbor.

Background

Published in 1951, James Jones' 861 page debut novel, *From Here to Eternity* presented a shockingly caustic depiction of army life at Schofield Barracks in Honolulu, Hawaii, just before the Japanese attack on Pearl Harbor. A revisionist take on the U.S. military in the midst of the Korean War, Jones' book stirred controversy but it also generated sales of nearly a quarter million copies and went on to win the third annual National Book Award in 1952. A couple of weeks after the book's publication Columbia Pictures mogul Harry Cohn purchased the film rights for $85,000, but due to its sheer length, narrative complexity, and scandalous content, the majority opinion was that *From Here to Eternity* was unfilmable; the project was quickly dubbed "Cohn's folly." Indeed, Cohn and his production team had to overcome daunting challenges, not least of which was producing a viable script that would get past Production Code restrictions and also win the crucial cooperation of the Department of Defense (DOD). Cohn hired James Jones to write a screen adaptation of his own novel, but Jones could not come up with a workable script, so Cohn hired screenwriter Daniel Taradash (*Knock on Any Door*) in his stead. Initially, the Pentagon was adamant about refusing to cooperate with Columbia, given the fact that Jones' novel was bitterly anti-authoritarian and anti-military. Eventually producer E. Maurice "Buddy" Adler, a lieutenant colonel in the U.S. Army Signal Corps during World War II, was able to win grudging DOD approval by agreeing to two key script changes: (a) Fatso Judson's sadistic treatment of Angelo Maggio in the stockade could not be depicted on screen; and (b) Judson's cruelty had to be characterized as the aberrant behavior of a sick individual, not routine Army policy at that time, as depicted in Jones' novel. Director Fred Zinnemann (*High Noon*) and Taradash took the first concession in stride, coming to the conclusion that Maggio's death in Prewitt's arms would be a more effective way to convey his suffering at Fatso's hands. They were less sanguine about the second change, however. In the novel, Capt. Holmes is promoted to major, a plot point the filmmakers found to be suitably ironic, but the Pentagon also insisted that a scene be added showing Holmes confronted by his superiors and given the choice of resigning from service or facing a court-martial—an unctuous departure from the novel that Zinnemann later characterized as "the worst moment in the film" (Zinnemann, 1992). Casting also proved to be an arduous process, fraught with initial missteps. Harry Cohn wanted Humphrey Bogart to play Sgt. Warden. Bogart was still a major star in 1951 but as a craggy-faced 52-year-old, he wasn't anyone's idea of a sexy leading man. Cohn wanted to hire Joan Crawford to play Karen Holmes but rescinded the deal after Crawford carped about second billing and insisted on being filmed by her own cameraman. The Warden role soon went to Burt Lancaster and the Karen role went to Deborah Kerr, a 30-year-old Scottish actress. Cohn's first choice for Prewitt was Aldo Ray, but Zinnemann wanted Montgomery Clift as Prewitt. He threatened to resign if Ray was hired, so Clift got the role. Both Cohn and Zinnemann wanted Eli Wallach to play Angelo Maggio, but Wallach had to turn down the role due to a scheduling conflict. According to a myth popularized by Francis Ford Coppola's *The Godfather* (1972), Frank Sinatra was given the Maggio part only after his Mafia associates strong-armed the film's director. Though he certainly had lifelong Mafia connections, Frank Sinatra won the Maggio part in a more prosaic fashion: he lobbied hard for it in order to extricate himself from a career slump. After agreeing to a pay cut (to a $1,000 a week), Sinatra eventually overcame Cohn's skepticism about his acting abilities and got the coveted role.

Production

Some filming took place on sets constructed on Columbia's backlot (e.g., the New Congress Club), but most of *From Here to Eternity* was shot on location in Honolulu, Hawaii, in 41 work days between 7 March and 5 May 1953. Settings include various buildings within Schofield Barracks at Fort Shafter; the Royal Hawaiian Hotel; Kuhio Beach Park, Waikiki Beach; Waialae Golf Course; and Hālona Beach Cove on the southeastern tip of the island (where the famous scene featuring Warden and Karen kissing in the surf was filmed).

Plot Summary

In 1941, Pvt. Robert E. Lee "Prew" Prewitt (Montgomery Clift), a career soldier and bugler, transfers to Company G at Schofield Barracks on the island of Oahu, Hawaii. Having heard that Prewitt is a gifted middleweight boxer, Capt. Dana "Dynamite" Holmes (Philip Ober) tries to convince him to be a part of his team, but Prewitt won't join the regiment. Prewitt has given up boxing, in part due to his overwhelming guilt for having injured his sparring partner. In an effort to change Prewitt's mind, Holmes makes life difficult for the boxer by ordering court-martial papers. However, First Sergeant Milton Warden (Burt Lancaster) suggests using punishment to influence Prewitt. As the other noncommissioned officers (NCOs) follow Holmes' lead, Prewitt finds his only support in Private Angelo Maggio (Frank Sinatra). To make matters worse, Warden begins a sordid affair with Holmes' wife Karen (Deborah Kerr). As their relationship deepens, Warden asks Karen about her previous affairs, which have been communicated to him by another officer, to see if she will be honest with him. Karen admits to multiple infidelities and tells Warden about her miscarriage. She also reveals that Holmes has also had multiple trysts during the course of their marriage. Due to Holmes' negligence during her medical emergency, Karen is unable to bear any more children. Karen entices Warden with an offer of a future marriage: if Warden attains the title of an officer, then she can divorce Holmes. As he considers this proposal, Warden allows Prewitt the weekend off. Prewitt visits Lorene (Donna Reed), an escort attempting to move up the social ladder, whom he has come to care for. After a fight breaks out that initiates an internal investigation, Holmes' scheme against Prewitt is discovered and the base commander orders a court-martial. Holmes resigns as a result. Maggio, who has been placed in a stockade, escapes only to die moments later next to Prewitt while telling his friend of how Judson abused him. Prewitt reacts by angrily tracking down Judson and killing him with a switchblade. He is wounded during his attack and seeks shelter at Lorene's house. The Pearl Harbor attack of 7 December 1941 emboldens Prewitt to return to his company, but he is mistakenly killed by a soldier guarding the fort. Meanwhile, Karen leaves Warden after discovering that he is not applying to become an officer, boarding a boat with her husband back to the mainland. Lorene and Karen meet on the ship, where Lorene tells Karen about her fiancé. Though Karen recognizes Prewitt's name, she keeps the information to herself.

Reception

Released on 5 August 1953—just nine days after the end of the Korean War—*From Here to Eternity* proved to be a runaway box office smash. Made for only $2 million, the movie grossed $30.5 million, making it the third top-grossing film of 1953. Adjusted for inflation, its box office gross would exceed $277 million in 2017 dollars. Likewise, the movie was showered with awards. Nominated for 12 Oscars, it won 8 statuettes for Best Picture (Buddy Adler); Best Director (Fred Zinnemann); Best Writing, Screenplay (Daniel Taradash); Best Supporting Actor (Frank Sinatra); Best Supporting Actress (Donna Reed); Best Cinematography (Black-and-White) (Burnett Guffey); Best Film Editing (William A. Lyon); and Best Sound (Recording) (John P. Livadary). Reviews were mostly glowing. Film critic Abe H. Weiler expressed the majority opinion when he noted that the film version of *From Here to Eternity* "naturally lacks the depth and fullness" of the book [but] "this dramatization of phases of the military life in a peacetime army . . . captures the essential spirit of the James Jones study. And, as a job of editing, emending, re-arranging and purifying a volume bristling with brutality and obscenities, *From Here to Eternity* stands as a shining example of truly professional moviemaking" (Weiler, 1953). Conversely, Manny Farber detected a studied show business slickness that worked against real verisimilitude: "*From Here to Eternity* happens to be fourteen-carat entertainment. The main trouble is that it is too entertaining for a film in which love affairs flounder, one sweet guy is beaten to death, and a man of high principles is mistaken for a saboteur and killed . . . When the soldiers get drunk, the scene is treated in a funny, unbelievable way. When Clift blows his bugle, it is done with a hammy intensity that tries to mimic Louie Armstrong at his showiest. When Lancaster and Kerr are being passionate, on the beach, it is done in patterned action that reeks with a phony Hollywood glamour. The result is a gripping movie that often makes you wish its director, Zinnemann, knew as much about American life as he does about the art of telling a story with a camera" (*The Nation*, 29 August 1953).

Reel History Versus Real History

Author James Jones clearly based "Prew" Prewitt, the troubled nonconformist, on himself and distilled his own life in the Army from 1939 to 1944 into the months at Schofield Barracks leading up to Pearl Harbor that is the book's setting. In effect, *From Here to Eternity* was censored twice before it reached the screen—once by Jones himself and a second time by the filmmakers. The original version of the

U.S. Army Sgt. Milton Warden (Burt Lancaster) and Karen Holmes (Deborah Kerr), his commanding officer's wife, kiss in the surf near Honolulu in a famous moment from Fred Zinnemann's *From Here to Eternity* (1953). (Columbia Pictures/Photofest)

novel featured graphic depictions of homosexual activity between servicemen and civilians in Honolulu. Jones was forced to excise most of these passages to get his book published. As Jones' daughter, Kaylie, points out, in the original manuscript the number of soldiers "hanging out in the gay bars is . . . staggering; in fact, there are so many of them that the Army launches a (very quiet) investigation. One soldier, Bloom, realizes he enjoys sex with men, and is so terrified and ashamed of being gay and of being called on it, that he commits suicide. The sin and the shame, it seems, are not associated with the act itself or even in getting paid for it, but in whether or not a soldier enjoys it. My father saw the total hypocrisy and ridiculousness of this and Bloom's death is portrayed as a tragedy, absurd and unnecessary" (Jones, 2009). Already pre-censored, *From Here to Eternity* underwent another round of censorship before it reached movie screens. Its violence whitewashed for the cinema per DOD wishes, the novel's language and sexual content also underwent cleansing so the movie would not run afoul of Motion Picture Production Code restrictions. In the novel, the New Congress Hotel is clearly a brothel and Lorene is definitely a prostitute—seedy realities the film obscures by transforming the hotel into the New Congress *Club*, suggestive of a more wholesome USO-type facility, and turning Lorene into a kind of hospitality hostess. Any filmic reference to the homosexuality that was rife in Honolulu in 1941 was, of course, still out of the question in 1953, as per the Hays Code: "Sex perversion or any reference to it is forbidden."

FULL METAL JACKET (1987)

Synopsis

Full Metal Jacket is a British-American war film produced and directed by Stanley Kubrick. The film's screenplay was adapted by Kubrick, Michael Herr, and Gustav Hasford from Hasford's novel, *The Short-Timers* (1979). It follows a platoon of U.S. Marines through boot camp at Parris Island and then into combat in the Vietnam War during the Tet Offensive in 1968.

Background

Alabama native Gustav "Gus" Hasford (1947–1993) joined the U.S. Marine Corps in 1966 and served a 10-month tour of duty (November 1967 to August 1968) in Vietnam as a combat correspondent, where he covered the Battle of Huê, which took place in March 1968, during the Tet Offensive. In the decade that followed, Hasford wrote some two dozen drafts of a Vietnam War novel that was eventually published as *The Short-Timers* (Harper & Row, 1979; Bantam pbk. edition, 1980). Though critically acclaimed, the book sold modestly and was soon remaindered. Following *The Shining* (1980), director Stanley Kubrick pondered a Holocaust picture but finally decided to make another war film (his third, after *Fear and Desire*, 1953, and *Paths of Glory*, 1957) and sought out a creative collaboration with Michael Herr (Vietnam War correspondent, author of *Dispatches*, 1979, technical advisor for Coppola's *Apocalypse Now*). In 1982 Kubrick discovered Hasford's novel through a notice in *Kirkus Reviews*, read it, and decided that it presented the kind of bitterly sardonic perspective on war that he was seeking. Kubrick bought the film rights from Hasford through an intermediary and proceeded to collaborate on a screen adaptation with Michael Herr. As he had done with Herr, Kubrick carried on a series of long-distance telephone conversations with Hasford before all three men finally met at Kubrick's Hertfordshire estate on 17 January 1985. Repelled by Hasford's intimidatingly brash demeanor, Kubrick barred him from the set and never met with him again, though the trio continued to collaborate on rewrites of the script by phone and mail. Kubrick also refused to give Hasford full credit as a co-screenwriter, igniting a bitter dispute that Hasford eventually won by threatening to publicly embarrass Kubrick for cheating a Vietnam veteran.

Production

Stanley Kubrick initially hoped to cast Anthony Michael Hall (*The Breakfast Club*) as Pvt. Joker but negotiations stretching over eight months ended in failure. Matthew Modine, who had already starred in two Vietnam War–themed movies—Robert Altman's *Streamers* (1983) and Alan Parker's *Birdy* (1984)—was cast in the lead role. The drill instructor role went to the film's technical advisor, R. Lee Ermey, a Vietnam vet and Parris Island drill instructor who had acted in other Vietnam

War films (Sidney Furie's *The Boys in Company C*, 1978, and Coppola's *Apocalypse Now*, 1979). In Hasford's novel Private Pyle is described as "a skinny redneck" but Kubrick opted to portray him as obese. Accordingly, Vincent D'Onofrio gained 70 pounds to play him. Because Kubrick lived in Britain and was unwilling to travel, settings there masqueraded for locations in the United States and South Vietnam. The Parris Island training scenes and the air base at Da Nang were shot at Bassingbourn Barracks in Cambridgeshire, England, while the Parris Island barracks set was built inside an old asbestos factory in a London suburb. Kubrick re-created the war-torn city of Huế at the Beckton Gas Works, a square-mile complex on the River Thames near London, closed since 1969. Working from still photographs of Huế, Kubrick's production designer, Anton Furst, had buildings blown up and used a wrecking ball to knock simulated shell holes in other buildings. Signs and wall advertisements in Vietnamese and other embellishments (including 200 imported Spanish palm trees and 100,000 plastic tropical plants from Hong Kong) were added for effect. Matthew Modine called the Beckton Gas Works "an environmental disaster area" that sickened the cast and crew (Modine, 2005).

Plot Synopsis

During the Vietnam War a group of new recruits arrives at Marine Corps Recruit Depot, Parris Island, South Carolina, for 13 weeks of basic training. After having their heads shaved, they are assembled in barracks and harangued by Senior Drill Instructor Gunnery Sgt. Hartman (Lee Ermey), who insults and belittles them in order to break down their individuality and rebuild them as Marines. Among the men in the platoon are Pvts. "Snowball" Brown (Peter Edmund), James T. "Joker" Davis (Matthew Modine), "Cowboy" (Arliss Howard), and Leonard "Gomer Pyle" Lawrence (Vincent D'Onofrio), an obese, dimwitted recruit who is paired with Joker after proving himself hopelessly inept in every endeavor. Pvt. Lawrence makes improvements as the Joker works with him, but when Hartman finds an "illegal" doughnut in Lawrence's footlocker, things go downhill: Hartman states that the 75-man platoon will be punished for every mistake Lawrence makes while he is spared. One night the platoon exacts vengeance on Lawrence with a "blanket party"; they hold him down in his bed and beat him with towel-wrapped bars of soap. After this incident, Lawrence seems to become a model Marine (and a surprisingly good marksman). Hartman is impressed, but Joker recognizes signs of incipient psychosis when Lawrence begins to talk to his M-14 rifle. Following graduation, Joker is assigned to a Military Journalism unit while most of the remaining platoon members are assigned to Infantry. Having drawn Fire Watch (barracks sentry duty) on the final night at Parris Island, Joker discovers Lawrence in the latrine, looking deranged and loading his M-14 with live ammunition. Joker attempts to persuade Lawrence to return to his bunk but Lawrence starts to drill while loudly reciting the Rifleman's Creed, awakening Hartman and the rest of the platoon. Hartman confronts Lawrence and tells him to drop his weapon, whereupon Lawrence kills Hartman and then himself. The scene then switches to Da Nang, South Vietnam, in January 1968. Joker, now a corporal, is a journalist for *Stars and Stripes* who works alongside photographer Pfc. "Rafterman" (Kevyn Major Howard). Both men are afforded the opportunity to enter the battlefield when Viet Cong and North Vietnamese Army (NVA) forces launch the Tet Offensive with simultaneous attacks throughout South Vietnam. Accompanied by Rafterman, Joker is sent to Phú Bài where they meet the Lusthog Squad and Joker is reunited with Cowboy, who is now a sergeant. Joker joins Cowboy's squad as they enter the city of Huế, losing their platoon commander, Lt. Walter J. "Touchdown" Schinoski (Ed O'Ross), to enemy fire in the process. Once the Marines secure the area, American TV news journalists enter Huế and interview Marines on camera about their experiences in Vietnam and their attitudes toward the war. Cowboy takes command after squad leader "Crazy Earl" (Kieron Jecchinis) perishes. When the squad becomes disoriented Cowboy orders "Eightball" (Dorian Harewood) to scout the area. A well-hidden Viet Cong sniper opens fire, wounding Eightball while he is in an open area between buildings. The squad medic, "Doc Jay" (John Stafford), is also wounded while attempting to rescue Eightball. Cowboy tries to call in tank support but is informed that no tanks are available. When Cowboy orders a withdrawal, Animal Mother (Adam Baldwin), the squad's M-60 machine gunner, disobeys Cowboy and attempts to save his comrades, but Doc Jay and Eightball don't make it out alive. A sniper kills Cowboy, and Animal Mother takes over the squad and coordinates their attack. Entering a building, Joker discovers that the sniper is a teenage girl (Ngoc Le) with an AK-47. When he tries to shoot her, his rifle jams so Rafterman shoots her instead. As the squad converges on her, the mortally wounded sniper begs to be put out of her misery. The men argue the merits of killing her versus letting her suffer. Animal Mother decides to permit a mercy killing—but only if Joker does the killing. After some hesitancy, Joker shoots the stricken girl, and his fellow Marines congratulate him on his kill. In the final scene, the platoon moves through the city at night. Silhouetted against raging fires, the Marines sing the "Mickey Mouse March." In voice-over Joker states "I'm in a world of s— . . . yes. But I am alive. And I am not afraid."

Reception

In theaters from 26 June to 23 August 1987 (widest release 1,075 theaters), *Full Metal Jacket* earned $46.3 million at the box office, versus a production budget of $30 million: a moderate success at best. Though critical notices were largely positive, many reviewers noted the stark bifurcation between the film's gripping first half at Parris Island and its less focused and engaging second half in Vietnam. Roger Ebert probably came close to expressing the critical consensus when he wrote, "Stanley Kubrick's *Full Metal Jacket* is more like a book of short stories than a novel. Many of the passages seem self-contained, some of them are masterful and others look like they came out of the bottom drawer. This is a strangely shapeless film from the man whose work usually imposes a ferociously consistent vision on his material" (Ebert, 1987). Vincent Canby found more to admire: "*Full Metal Jacket*, Mr. Kubrick's harrowing, beautiful and characteristically eccentric new film about

Vietnam, is going to puzzle, anger and (I hope) fascinate audiences as much as any film he has made to date. The movie . . . will inevitably be compared with Oliver Stone's *Platoon*, but its narrative is far less neat and cohesive—and far more antagonistic—than Mr. Stone's film" (Canby, 1987).

Reel History Versus Real History

Marine Corps veterans attest that the boot camp portion of *Full Metal Jacket* is remarkably accurate—with certain qualifications. Half of Lee Ermey's hilariously caustic lines are derived, almost verbatim, from Hasford's novel. The rest he improvised himself; as a former Marine drill instructor, Ermey knew from whence he spoke. Though drill instructors are forbidden from hitting recruits, such incidents were not uncommon in the pre–all-volunteer era. Veterans have observed, however, that senior drill instructors tended to be less abusive than Ermey's Gunnery Sgt. Hartman; that role was reserved for junior drill instructors. Pvt. Pyle's stress-induced breakdown is a common boot camp occurrence, but no recruit has ever yet murdered his drill instructor. The Vietnam portion of the film recounting the Tet Offensive—including the Viet Cong night assault on Da Nang Air Base (29 January 1968) and the subsequent Battle of Huê—is quite accurate historically. As depicted in the film, *Stars and Stripes* reporters were under orders to put the best face on the war, writing "human interest" stories while studiously ignoring American military blunders, setbacks, or crimes against civilians. Likewise the Huê sequences ring true—even though they were filmed just outside London. As shown by a mass grave in the movie, the Viet Cong carried out atrocities in Huê. American troops did encounter snipers as they fought house to house to recapture the city in what was the only sustained urban combat during the Vietnam War. The pig-tailed young sniper is also historically credible; the Viet Cong numbered many teenaged girls among their ranks.

FURY (2014)

Synopsis

Fury is an American war film written and directed by David Ayer that stars Brad Pitt, Shia LaBeouf, Logan Lerman, Michael Peña, Jon Bernthal, and Jason Isaacs. The film depicts the combat experiences of the crew of a U.S. Army Sherman tank nicknamed "Fury" as it advances into the heart of Nazi Germany during the final days of World War II.

Background

Fury is the exclusive brainchild of Navy submarine veteran turned action picture writer-director-producer David Ayer, who researched, wrote, directed, and co-produced the film. The script that Ayer fashioned involves the trial by fire of a reluctant soldier and an Alamo-like last stand: plot elements obviously borrowed from Steven Spielberg's *Saving Private Ryan*.

Production

Most of the casting occurred in April 2013, starting with the signing of Brad Pitt to play the lead role of Wardaddy Collier. Prior to the actual shoot, David Ayer required his actors to undergo a four-month preparation process that included extensive reading in the period, crew training in a working Sherman tank, verbal and physical sparring for crew bonding purposes, and a week-long boot camp run by Navy SEALs. Principal photography lasted seven weeks (30 September–15 November 2013) and took place in and around the village of Shirburn, Oxfordshire (southcentral England), using five operational tanks, two of which—the Sherman tank dubbed "Fury" and a German Tiger I tank—were borrowed from the UK's Bovington Tank Museum in Dorset. The other Sherman tanks were rented from restorers. Already rattled by frequent sounds of gunfire and rumbling tanks, Shirburn residents were angered when Ayer ignored their pleas to suspend shooting on Remembrance Day (11 November). David Ayer was forced to make a public apology, as was Sony Corporation. To ease hard feelings, Brad Pitt made a parting gift of £1 million ($1.6 million) to the town when the shoot wrapped.

Plot Summary

During the Rhine campaign in the spring of 1945 Allied forces are making their final thrust into the heart of Nazi Germany. In their ranks is Don "Wardaddy" Collier (Brad Pitt), a U.S. Army staff sergeant commanding an M4 Sherman tank (dubbed "Fury") with the 66th Armored Regiment, 2nd Armored ("Hell on Wheels") Division. Collier's battle-seasoned crew consists of gunner Boyd "Bible" Swan (Shia LaBeouf), loader Grady "Coon-Ass" Travis (Jon Bernthal), and driver Trini "Gordo" Garcia (Michael Peña). The tank's assistant driver/bow gunner, "Red," has been killed in battle. His replacement is Norman Ellison (Logan Lerman), a new recruit trained as a typist, not a tank crewman, and, as such, the butt of fierce derision by Fury's veteran crew. Ordered to clean the tank, Ellison vomits after finding part of "Red's" face. Inexperienced and basically nonviolent, Ellison is reluctant to kill Germans, especially Hitlerjugend teenagers. When he hesitates, the platoon leader Lt. Parker (Xavier Samuel), is killed and Ellison's tank and fellow crew members are destroyed. To indoctrinate Ellison to the realities of war, Wardaddy Collier commands him to kill a captive German soldier. Ellison can't pull the trigger himself, so Collier holds the gun in Ellison's hand and makes the gun fire. The horrors continue as Ellison and Collier take over a German village. As they root through a house, the soldiers come upon two German women: Irma (Anamaria Marinca) and her younger cousin, Emma (Alicia von Rittberg). Noticing a mutual attraction between Ellison and Emma, Collier insists that Ellison make love to the young woman or he, Collier, will. Later, as the foursome is eating breakfast, the remaining members of Fury's crew enter the house, teasing the women and leaving Ellison and Collier enraged. Emma is then killed by German gunfire. Ellison begins to change, now enjoying hunting down and killing German soldiers. A four-tank platoon is given orders to hold a crossroads to ensure the safe passage of supply trains, but en route, the platoon is ambushed by the Germans. All but one of the

Sherman tanks are obliterated. Fury and his crew, now down to a single tank, proceed to the crossroads. Fury hits a landmine, and Ellison spies 300 Waffen-SS panzergrenadiers heading toward their crew. Both leader and crew decide to remain in their position and ambush the incoming German troops. The crewmen make it appear as though Fury has been knocked out and then take shelter in their tank. When the Germans arrive, the crew opens fire, inflicting heavy losses on the enemy. During the firefight, Grady, Bible, and Gordo are all killed and Collier is badly injured. Ellison and Collier attempt to retreat back to the tank. Collier is killed when SS soldiers detonate grenades in the tank, but Ellison escapes through a hatch in the bottom of the tank. Ellison hides from the German soldiers and then returns to the tank after they leave the area. Norman continues to hide as the surviving German soldiers advance. The next morning, Norman Ellison crawls back into the tank and respectfully covers Collier's body with his coat. Ellison is then found by American troops and named a hero as he glances back over the destruction caused by the war.

Reception

Fury had a successful commercial run, grossing $85.8 million in North America and $126 million in other countries for a worldwide total of $211.8 million, against a budget of $68 million: a substantial net profit, minus promotional expenses. The critical response was largely favorable, though seldom enthusiastic. Most critics found the film well-made but too narrowly focused on relentless depictions of extreme violence. Film critic Christopher Orr's critique is fairly representative of the critical consensus: "*Fury* offers a stark and unforgiving portrait of the closing days of the Good War in the European theater. Shot in hues of gray and brown, it presents a universe of steel and smoke and—most of all—mud: swimming with corpses, littered with dead trees, and endlessly crisscrossed by tank tracks. The performances are strong, and in technical terms the film is above reproach: This is almost certainly the most persuasive depiction of tank warfare yet committed to celluloid . . . The problem with the film is that, over its subsequent hour and a half, it does little more than repeatedly convey that same experience, albeit at escalating levels of mayhem" (Orr, 2014).

Reel History Versus Real History

Staff Sergeant Don Collier's nickname, "Wardaddy" references Staff Sergeant Lafayette G. "War Daddy" Pool (1919–1991), a real World War II Sherman tank ace with the 3rd Armored Division. In an 81-day period (27 June to 15 September 1944) Pool destroyed 12 enemy tanks and 258 armored vehicles and self-propelled guns and killed over 1,000 German soldiers, while taking another 250 as prisoners of war (POWs). Unlike his fictive counterpart, Pool survived the war (though he lost a leg from his last combat operation). In an interview with Nicholas Milton for *The Guardian* (Milton, 2014), Bill Betts, a British radio operator in Sherman tanks during WWII, gave *Fury* mixed reviews for historical accuracy: "*Fury* accurately portrays how superior the German tanks were. A Sherman provided you with protection against most enemy fire but against a Tiger it could easily become your coffin . . .

In open combat we never had a chance. So, like in *Fury*, we always had to be one step ahead. It was only because we could call up air strikes and had many more tanks than the Germans that we eventually won . . . I thought the film showed accurately how tough life could be in a tank, but the final scene where the crew holds out against a battalion of Waffen SS troops was too far-fetched. The Germans seemed to be used as cannon fodder. In reality they would have been battle-hardened and fanatical troops who would have easily taken out an immobile Sherman tank using Panzerfausts [single-shot anti-tank rocket launchers]. They [Fury's crew] also seemed to have an inexhaustible supply of ammunition and fuel. A Sherman tank only does five miles to the gallon so I think they would have run out long before the final showdown."

G

GALLIPOLI (1981)

Synopsis

Gallipoli is an Australian war film produced by Patricia Lovell and Robert Stigwood, directed by Peter Weir, and starring Mel Gibson and Mark Lee, who play two young men from Western Australia who enlist in the Army during the First World War and participate in the failed British effort to capture Gallipoli from the Ottoman Turks.

Background

On 2 October 1976, on a visit to the Dardanelles in northwest Turkey, Australian film director Peter Weir (*The Last Wave*) took a two-hour walk on the beaches of Gallipoli and decided that he had to make a film about the disastrous WWI British-ANZAC campaign against Ottoman Turkey that occurred there 61 years earlier. Weir subsequently wrote an outline and engaged playwright-screenwriter David Williamson to turn it into a screenplay. Weir and Williamson used C.E.W. Bean's 12-volume *Official History of Australia in the War of 1914–1918* (Australian War Memorial, 1921–43) as one of their primary sources. They also used diary excerpts and letters from soldiers who fought at Gallipoli, collected in Bill Gammage's book *The Broken Years: Australian Soldiers in the Great War* (Australian National UP, 1974; Gammage also served as the project's military advisor). Williamson crafted many script revisions before he narrowed the focus to two runners who become "mates" and comrades-in-arms. He also decided to focus the combat portion of the film on a single calamitous engagement during the Gallipoli campaign: the so-called Battle of the Nek (7 August 1915), when the 8th and 10th Regiments of the Australian 3rd Light Horse Brigade launched a series of failed bayonet attacks on Ottoman trenches that resulted in appalling losses: 238 dead and 134 wounded out of a force of 600 (a 62 percent casualty rate), while the Ottoman Turks suffered only 8 dead. Peter Weir initially secured an exclusive production deal with the South Australian Film Corporation (SAFC) but the deal was amended over "creative differences" and the SAFC ended up providing only partial funding. After raising 850,000 AUD between May 1979 and May 1980, Weir's producer, Patricia Lovell, approached media mogul Rupert Murdoch and producer Robert Stigwood, who had just formed a new film company (Associated R&R Films). They agreed to provide the rest of the funding on the proviso that the budget come in under 3 million AUD—the highest budget of an Australian film at that time. Rupert Murdoch's father, Keith Murdoch (1885–1952), a WWI journalist who visited Gallipoli in September 1915, was a leading critic of the way the British conducted the campaign.

Production

On the strength of his starring role in George Miller's *Mad Max* (1979), Mel Gibson was hired to play Frank Dunne, one of the co-leads. The other leading role, Archy Hamilton, went to Mark Lee, a 22-year-old unknown actor-musician from Sydney, after an impressive screen test. *Gallipoli* could not be filmed at Gallipoli; pine trees covered what had been open ground in 1915 so Weir's art director, Herbert Pinter, found topographically perfect locations for ANZAC Cove and the Nek: Farm Beach (now known as Gallipoli Beach) and Dutton Beach, respectively, both on the western side of lower Eyre Peninsula in South Australia, about 100 miles due west of Adelaide. Other locations included Beltana (Archy's home) and Lake Torrens (for the desert that Frank and Archy cross), also in South Australia. Scenes showing the 3rd Light Horse training in Egypt were shot in and around Cairo. Principal photography lasted 12 weeks, from mid-September to early December 1980, with the final battle scenes involving some 600 extras.

Plot Synopsis

The setting is Western Australia, May 1915. Trained by his Uncle Jack (Bill Kerr), 18-year-old stockman (rancher) Archy Hamilton (Mark Lee) proves his athletic prowess by winning a foot race, barefoot, against a horse, ridden bareback by a rival farmhand named Les McCann (Harold Hopkins). Frank Dunne (Mel Gibson), a destitute ex-railway worker and also a talented sprinter, sets his eyes on the prize money offered at a foot race in an athletics competition—and the side bets he placed on himself—but to his chagrin, he is defeated by Archy. Afterwards Frank approaches Archy in a café, and the pair decides to journey to Perth and enlist in the Australian Imperial Force (AIF) so that they can join the war in Europe. Once in Perth, they stay with Frank's father (John Murphy), an Irish immigrant. Archy convinces Frank to enlist in the Light Horse Brigade, despite the fact that Frank is unable to ride a horse. Frank ends up enlisting in the infantry instead, along with three co-workers: Bill (Robert Grubb), Barney (Tim McKenzie), and Snowy (David Argue). Frank and Archy part ways during their journeys to Egypt, but come back together once in Cairo. Frank transfers to Light Horse as a member of the dismounted infantry in Gallipoli. At Gallipoli, Frank's friends in the infantry fight in the Battle of Lone Pine (6 August 1915). Afterwards, Billy tells Frank that Barney was killed in action and that Snowy is in a hospital, badly wounded. The next day, Archy and Frank join a charge at the Nek in a supporting role to the British soldiers landing at Suvla Bay. The Light Horse regiments are then asked to take offensive action across open ground, despite the presence of Turkish gunners at the ground site. The first wave is scheduled to go over the top at 4:30 a.m., following an artillery bombardment; however, the Turks slaughter the first wave in a matter of seconds. The second wave attacks and is also annihilated. Major Barton (Bill Hunter) wants to halt the assault, but his commanding officer, Col. Robinson (John Morris), is resistant. When the phone line goes dead, Barton dispatches Frank to brigade headquarters to try and get the attack halted, but Col. Robinson insists that it continue. Lt. Gray (Peter Ford) admits to his commander, Barton, that he claimed to have sighted the marker flags, but can't recall where the information originally came from. Frank suggests going over the colonel's head and appealing to General Gardner (Graham Dow) about stopping the offensive. Frank sprints to Gardner's headquarters, and the general tells him to that he is indeed "reconsidering the whole situation." Frank sprints back to share the news with Barton, but in the interim, the phone lines have resumed functioning and Col. Robinson demands that the attack move forward. Barton leads his men over the top, Archy among the ranks. Arriving mere seconds too late to stop the attack, Frank screams in anguish. As Archy's comrades fall by the score, he drops his rifle and runs as fast toward the enemy positions as he can. The final shot is a freeze frame at the moment of Archy's death, as he is hit and hurled backward by a fusillade of bullets to the chest (a haunting image modeled after Robert Capa's famous photograph, "The Falling Soldier," taken in 1936 at the Battle of Cerro Muriano during the Spanish Civil War).

Reception

Gallipoli proved to be a box office hit in Australia, grossing 11,740,000 AUD—four times its 2.8 million AUD production budget. Box office receipts for international releases were more modest. For example, the movie earned only $5.7 million in the United States where exhibition was limited to art house cinemas. *Gallipoli* was nominated for the 1981 Australian Film Institute Awards in ten categories and won in eight of them: Best Film, Best Director, Best Actor, Best Supporting Actor, Best Screenplay, Best Cinematography, Best Sound, and Best Editing. Reviews were mostly positive, with many critics citing the film's deeply affecting lyricism atypical of war films. Janet Maslin's review nicely articulates the consensus opinion that "the film approaches the subject of war so obliquely that it can't properly be termed a war movie . . . Mr. Weir's work has a delicacy, gentleness, even wispiness that would seem not well suited to the subject. And yet his film has an uncommon beauty, warmth, and immediacy, and a touch of the mysterious, too." Maslin concludes by noting that there's "nothing pointed in Mr. Weir's decorous approach, even when the material would seem to call for toughness. But if the lush mood makes *Gallipoli* a less weighty war film than it might be, it also makes it a more airborne adventure" (*New York Times*, 28 August 1981).

Reel History Versus Real History

As the film's opening disclaimer declares, "Although based on events which took place on the Gallipoli Peninsula in 1915, the characters portrayed in this film are entirely fictitious." Mel Gibson's character, Frank, was invented from whole cloth, but the Archy Hamilton character was inspired by Pvt. Wilfred Lukin Harper of the 10th Light Horse, who died at the Battle of the Nek at the age of 25. He was described in Bean's *Official History of Australia in the War of 1914–1918* as "last seen running forward like a schoolboy in a foot-race, with all the speed he could compass." Col. Robinson's character equates to the actual brigade major (chief of staff) of the 3rd Brigade: Col. John Antill (1866–1937), an Australian Boer War veteran and a bit of a martinet. Because of Robinson's clipped, upper-class Australian accent, viewers tend to misidentify him as a British officer, even though he is wearing an AIF uniform. In point of fact, the Battle of the Nek was exclusively an Australian operation, though it was planned and ordered by British staff officers serving directly under ANZAC commander Gen. William Birdwood: Lt. Col. Andrew Skeen and Col. W. G. Braithwaite, chief of staff for Gen. Alexander Godley, one of ANZAC's divisional commanders. As Les Carlyon (*Gallipoli*, 2001) and other historians have noted, the blame for the senseless slaughter at The Nek rests squarely on the shoulders of Col. Antill and his immediate superior, 3rd Australian Light Horse Brigade commander Brigadier General Frederic Hughes (1858–1944). In the midst of the second wave, Hughes left his headquarters to observe the attack, cutting himself off from communication with Antill and the rest of his staff. After the third wave had been decimated, Hughes ordered the attack be discontinued, but not in time to save half of the fourth wave. In the film General Gardiner, Hughes' fictional counterpart, suspends the attack after the second wave. In reality the attack fell apart when half of the fourth wave charged the Turkish lines without orders and were duly cut down. The movie's Major Barton is modeled on Lt. Col. Noel Brazier, the surviving regimental commander in the trenches who attempted to get the attack cancelled. Carlyon and others have stated that the Australian attack at the Nek was in actuality a diversion for the New Zealanders' attack on Sari Bair, not the British landing at Suvla, as depicted in the film. The British were therefore not "drinking tea on the beach" while Australians died by the score—an anti-British slur popular with Australian filmgoers.

GETTYSBURG (1993)

Synopsis

Gettysburg is an American war epic written and directed by Ronald F. Maxwell, which he adapted from Michael Shaara's historical novel, *The Killer Angels* (1974). The film is about the Battle of Gettysburg (July 1863) during the American Civil War. The film stars Tom Berenger, Jeff Daniels, and Martin Sheen.

Background

In 1966 Michael Shaara (1928–1988), a former paratrooper with the 82nd Airborne Division turned Florida-based English professor and writer, visited the Gettysburg battlefield in 1966 and was inspired to write *The Killer Angels*, a novel about the famous battle (1–3 July 1863) that turned the tide of the Civil War. Completed in 1973, Shaara's book was rejected by 15 publishers before being placed with David McKay, a firm soon acquired by Random House. Published in September 1974 to good reviews, *The Killer Angels* won the 1975 Pulitzer Prize for fiction. Filmmaker Ronald F. Maxwell secured the film rights to Shaara's novel with a $10,000 down payment on a $40,000 option in 1978. Maxwell wrote a screen adaptation, but no one in Hollywood wanted to risk money on a sprawling, all-male Civil War epic. Eventually Maxwell's luck turned. Documentary filmmaker Ken Burns also read

The Killer Angels and was inspired to make *The Civil War*, his mini-series for PBS that aired in the fall of 1990 and proved to be a huge hit. Suddenly, for the first time since *Gone with the Wind* in 1939, the Civil War was back in vogue. Burns arranged for Maxwell to meet Ted Turner at a Producers Guild Awards dinner (5 March 1991). A Civil War buff, Turner greenlit Maxwell's Gettysburg movie as a TV mini-series, budgeted at $13 million. Casting began in early 1992 and was completed before the shoot began in July of that year. Robert Duvall was originally cast as Robert E. Lee but had to drop out due to scheduling conflicts. He was replaced at the last minute by Martin Sheen.

Production

Gettysburg was shot over a 10-week period (20 July–30 September 1992), mostly on set locations at Yingling Farm, three miles west of Gettysburg. Shooting on the actual battlefield was limited to just eight days, due to National Park Service restrictions and numerous large granite war monuments that interfered with sightlines. The shoot involved 100 actors and as many technicians, supplemented by some 5,000 Civil War re-enactors who came from all over the country at their own expense, equipped with their own replica firearms, uniforms, gear, and a sophisticated knowledge of the battle—an indispensable element that increased authenticity and saved the production millions of dollars. As the film took shape Ted Turner liked what he saw, so much so that he decided to release *Gettysburg* as a feature film instead of a television mini-series, one factor among several others—the cost of 70-mm prints, sound remixing, several premieres, even a block party for the townspeople of Gettysburg—causing cost overruns in post-production that increased expenses by another $7 million, bringing the total price tag to a hefty $20 million (Galbraith, p.1).

Plot Summary

The film begins in June 1863 with a voice-over, map, and images describing the progress of the (Confederate) Army of Northern Virginia, commanded by Robert E. Lee (Martin Sheen), crossing the Potomac River and marching across Maryland and into southern Pennsylvania as it invades the North. On 30 June, Confederate spy Henry Thomas Harrison (Cooper Huckabee) reports to Lt. Gen. James Longstreet (Tom Berenger), First Corps commander, that the (Union) Army of the Potomac is moving in their direction, led by Gen. George G. Meade (Richard Anderson). Lee commands his troops to stop near Gettysburg. Meanwhile, at the Union encampments near Union Mills, Maryland, Col. Joshua Lawrence Chamberlain (Jeff Daniels) of the 20th Maine is taking over the command of over 120 men from the previously disbanded 2nd Maine. In Gettysburg, Brig. Gen. John Buford (Sam Elliott) and his cavalry division spot elements of Major Gen. Henry Heth's (Warren Burton) division of Third Corps commanded by Lt. Gen. A. P. Hill (Patrick Falci) approaching the town. Buford asks I Corps (First Corps) commander Maj. Gen. John F. Reynolds (John Rothman) for reinforcements. Heth's unit meets Buford's men the next day (1 July 1863), and Second Corps, commanded by

Lt. Gen. Richard S. Ewell (Tim Scott), moves in to flank them. As the unit advances to battle, Reynolds is shot and killed by a Confederate soldier. The Union army is forced to retreat to Cemetery Ridge. Longstreet suggests that Lee and his army go on the defensive, but instead, Lee asks Ewell to secure the Union position "if practicable." Ewell expresses some uncertainty, and the armies consolidate their formations. At Confederate headquarters at Seminary Ridge, Maj. Gen. Isaac R. Trimble (William Morgan Sheppard) criticizes Ewell's hesitation to Lee's direct order and asks to be reassigned. On the second day (2 July), a brigade from the Union V Corps led by Col. Strong Vincent (Maxwell Caulfield) is sent to Little Round Top, and the 20th Maine and Chamberlain position themselves in wait for the Confederate forces. Lee meanwhile commands Longstreet to send men to capture Little Round Top and Big Round Top as well. Maj. Gen. John Bell Hood (Patrick Gorman), commanding one of the divisions, balks, telling Longstreet he will lose half his men if ordered to attack the well-defended high ground. Longstreet ignores Hood's suggestion and moves forward with the attack, and Hood sustains injuries while fighting at Devil's Den. Meanwhile, at Little Round Top, Chamberlain and the 20th Maine repel repeated attacks but begin to run out of ammunition. Improvising, Chamberlain surprises the Confederates and forces them to retreat down the hill. That evening, Lee's cavalry commander, Maj. Gen. J.E.B. "Jeb" Stuart (Joseph Fuqua), arrives on the battlefield. At the same time, Longstreet's remaining division, under Maj. Gen. George Pickett (Stephen Lang) reaches the field. On the third day (3 July) of the battle, Lee decides to order three divisions—led by Pickett, Trimble, and Brig. Gen. J. Johnston Pettigrew (George Lazenby)—to conduct a frontal assault on the center of the Union line at Cemetery Ridge. Longstreet tells Lee he thinks that the attack will fail; there is a mile of open ground to cross under massed artillery fire and the Union's II Corps' 10,500 riflemen under Maj. Gen. Winfield Scott Hancock (Brian Mallon) are deployed behind a stone wall. Nonetheless Lee orders the attack to go forward, preceded by a protracted artillery barrage intended to silence the Union guns on the ridge. Though the Confederate batteries commanded by Col. E. Porter Alexander (James Patrick Stuart) fail to make any appreciable impact on the Union guns, the attack proceeds as planned. The Confederates who survive the withering artillery fire and reach the Union lines are mowed down by point-blank volleys of cannon grapeshot and musket fire. Pickett's decimated division is forced to retreat. Meeting with Longstreet that evening, Gen. Lee decides to withdraw the remnants of his shattered army. The film ends by recounting the fates of the major figures of the battle.

Reception

Released on 8 October 1993 in 124 theaters (widest release: 240 theaters), *Gettysburg* grossed $10.7 million—very respectable box office returns for a small-scale release that featured a limited number of daily screenings (a film lasting four hours and eight minutes plus an intermission could only be screened once or twice a day). Despite strong sales in the video market after its theatrical run, *Gettysburg* still failed to earn back anywhere its $20 million production cost. Reviews were mixed. Even sympathetic notices expressed serious reservations regarding the film's sheer length, shapelessness, portentous musical score, excessive speechifying, and uneven acting. Film critic Ken Ringle voiced the majority viewpoint when he termed *Gettysburg* "the most ambitious and magnificently flawed cinematic undertaking since *Apocalypse Now*." Ringle praised the film's seriousness for attempting to explore "such weighty abstractions as duty, brotherhood, justice and liberty. And it does so at times to great effect." But Ringle also deplored "Martin Sheen's woolly-headed performance as Robert E. Lee . . . as a kind of crazed religious mystic: a Confederate Jim Jones invoking his legions to bullets instead of poisoned Kool Aid for no more clearly discernible reason" (Ringle, 1993). More than a few critics also noted that the false beards and mustaches worn by most of the principal characters were suspiciously well combed, outsized, and immobile. Indeed, the movie's unintentionally comical tonsorial excesses garnered *Gettysburg* a 1993 Stinkers Bad Movie Award for Worst Fake Beards. Conversely, most critics singled out Jeff Daniels for his brilliant and moving performance as the gallant and resourceful Col. Chamberlain at Little Round Top and rued the fact that Daniels disappeared from the picture's second half.

Reel History Versus Real History

As regarding the actual conduct of the battle, historians credit *Gettysburg* with achieving a high degree of historical accuracy, though some commentators have criticized the movie for a rather skewed emphasis as to what it chooses to dramatize. For example, the middle third of the movie focuses almost exclusively on Col. Joshua Chamberlain and the 20th Maine's successful defense of Little Round Top, while mostly ignoring heavy fighting at Cemetery and Culps hills on the Union line's northern flank that were of equal, if not greater, moment. Though it aspires to be even-handed, *Gettysburg* has also been criticized for its pro-Confederacy slant—though that perspective originates from Shaara's *Killer Angels*, which it closely follows. Nonetheless, the film's implicit racial politics remain suspect. Incredibly, among a cast of thousands, only one African American appears in *Gettysburg* in a brief background shot. Furthermore, the movie's 21,000-word script features only five passing mentions of the words "slave" or "slavery"—an unconscionable slighting of the Civil War's political underpinnings. Finally, perhaps due to the fact that it was originally intended as television fare valorizing martial glory, *Gettysburg* is a noticeably sanitized vision of Civil War combat. Through no fault of their own, the modern actors and reenactors are generally too well dressed and corpulent for the sake of verisimilitude—Lee's ragged army was starving—and on-screen bloodshed and environmental destruction are kept at palatable levels. In reality, Napoleonic military tactics (e.g., frontal attacks in close-order formations), combined with formidable mid-19th-century weaponry—large-caliber rifled muskets with effective ranges of 200 to 300 yards and highly mobile artillery pieces (average range: 1,700 yards)—inflicted grotesque injuries on a grand scale. The film conveys the kinetics of battle without really depicting its horrific carnage in a visceral way.

GLORY (1989)

Synopsis

Glory is an American war film directed by Edward Zwick and starring Matthew Broderick, Denzel Washington, Cary Elwes, and Morgan Freeman that recounts the unsuccessful Union assault on Fort Wagner by an all-black regiment during the Civil War. The screenplay was written by Kevin Jarre, based on the letters of Union Army Col. Robert Gould Shaw, Peter Burchard's novel, *One Gallant Rush* (1965), and Lincoln Kirstein's *Lay This Laurel* (1973), a compilation of photos of the monument to the 54th Massachusetts Volunteer Infantry at Boston Common.

Background

Screenwriter Kevin Jarre (1954–2011), an equestrian and a Civil War buff, knew about Robert Gould Shaw and the 54th Massachusetts Volunteer Regiment—the first black unit to fight in the Civil War—but his interest in the topic was not fully ignited until he met ballet impresario Lincoln Kirstein in Saratoga, New York, in June 1985. Kirstein had lived in Boston in the 1920s while attending Harvard and harbored a lifelong fascination with the story of Shaw and the 54th after encountering Augustus Saint-Gaudens' 1897 bronze relief Shaw memorial on the edge of Boston Common. Inspired by Kirstein's enthusiasm for the subject, Jarre read everything he could find about Shaw and the 54th, including Shaw's letters; the journal of Charlotte Forten (a black abolitionist and close friend of Shaw's); Peter Burchard's novel based on Shaw's letters, *One Gallant Rush: Robert Gould Shaw and His Brave Black Regiment* (St. Martin's 1965); and Kirstein's own book on Shaw, *Lay This Laurel* (Eakins Press, 1973). In the fall of 1985 Jarre wrote a screen adaptation in four weeks and initially placed his script with director Bruce Beresford (*Breaker Morant*), who brought in producer Freddie Fields. Fields negotiated a production deal with Columbia Pictures—but the movie stalled after Columbia Chairman David Puttnam was fired in September 1987. Freddie Fields soon struck a deal with Tri-Star Pictures, a Columbia subsidiary, and Edward Zwick replaced Beresford as director.

Production

In order to assure historical accuracy, Zwick hired Civil War historian/novelist Shelby Foote (1916–2005). Filming of *Glory* took place between 9 February and 27 April 1989, mostly in Georgia. The brief opening Battle of Antietam scenes were staged near McDonough, Georgia, near Atlanta (and 662 miles south of the battle's actual location, near Sharpsburg, Maryland), enhanced by a mock-up of the landmark Dunker Church and footage taken of the 125th anniversary reenactment of the Battle of Gettysburg in June 1988 that involved some 11,000 participants. Scenes supposedly taking place in Boston were actually filmed in Savannah, Georgia. The simulated burning of Darien, Georgia, was shot just west of Savannah, about 62 miles north of the actual town. The skirmish at James Island, South Carolina (aka Battle of Grimball's Landing, 16 June 1863), was filmed at Rose Dhu Island

(Savannah), 120 miles to the south. The climactic Second Battle of Fort Wagner was shot 60 miles south of Savannah, on Jekyll Island, 197 miles south of its actual location on Morris Island, South Carolina.

Plot Summary

During the American Civil War, Capt. Robert Gould Shaw (Matthew Broderick) is wounded at the Battle of Antietam (17 September 1862). As a result of his injuries, he returns to Boston on leave. He spends time with his family and is introduced to Frederick Douglass (Raymond St. Jacques), a former slave turned famed abolitionist. After a respite, Shaw is commissioned to command one of the first all-black regiments in the Union Army: the 54th Regiment Massachusetts Volunteer Infantry (MVI). He agrees to the commission, asking his friend, Cabot Forbes (Cary Elwes), to serve alongside him. Their first volunteer is a freeman named Thomas Searles (Andre Braugher). Other recruits sign up, including Sgt. Maj. John Rawlins (Morgan Freeman), an escaped slave named Silas Trip (Denzel Washington), freeman Jupiter Sharts (Jihmi Kennedy), and a mute young drummer boy (RonReaco Lee). Trip clashes with Searles and Rawlins intervenes. In response to the Emancipation Proclamation (22 September 1862) the Confederacy commands that all black Union soldiers captured during the war be shot and killed along with their white superiors. Thereafter the black soldiers undergo training at a camp in Reading, Massachusetts, under the tutelage of Sergeant-Major Mulcahy (John Finn), a tough, no-nonsense Irishman. After Trip supposedly deserts and is captured, Shaw orders him flogged as an example to the troops, but Trip's exposed back reveals the scars of many previous whippings as a slave, a sight that troubles Shaw, who is, after all, an ardent abolitionist. Shaw is further chagrined to learn from Rawlins that Trip had left camp to find shoes to replace his worn-out ones. Shaw further discovers that all of his men are being deprived of needed supplies by a racist quartermaster (Richard Riehle), whom he angrily confronts. Shaw also supports his men in a dispute over pay (white soldiers are paid $13 a month but black soldiers are paid only $10). When Trip urges his comrades to go without pay in protest, Shaw follows suit and earns the respect of his men. Because black soldiers are not allowed to rank as officers, Rawlins is promoted to sergeant-major: the highest rank for an enlisted man. After the 54th is trained, the unit is put under the command of Gen. Charles Garrison Harker (Bob Gunton). En route to joining the war in South Carolina, Harker's second-in-command, Col. James Montgomery (Cliff De Young), orders the 54th to sack and burn a Georgia town (11 June 1863). Shaw does not wish to follow the command, but acquiesces when his leadership role is threatened; the town of Darien, Georgia, is destroyed. Shaw pushes for his men to be allowed to join their fellow Union soldiers in battle; since being activated, they have been relegated to manual labor. Shaw eventually succeeds, and the unit fares well in their first bout of active combat on James Island, South Carolina (16 July 1863). Thomas is injured while saving Trip's life, and consequently earns his respect. Soon thereafter Brig. Gen. George Crockett Strong (Jay O. Sanders) informs Shaw and his other staff officers of a major campaign to secure Charleston Harbor, a plan that will necessitate the capture of nearby Battery Wagner on Morris Island, a fort considered impregnable. The only landward approach between salt marsh and sea is a narrow defile provided by beach; any regiment spearheading the attack is sure to suffer extreme casualties. Shaw volunteers to the 54th for that grim role. En route to the battlefield, the 54th is encouraged and cheered on by their fellow Union soldiers. The 54th forges ahead and suffers major casualties from enemy fire. As night falls, elements of the 54th cross the fort's water-filled moat under heavy fire. Col. Shaw is then shot and killed as he leads an assault on the fort's parapets. Trip carries the flag himself and encourages his unit to press on. Despite several bullet wounds, Trip raises the flag, struggling to hold it up until his last breath. Forbes leads the unit and successfully breaches the fort's defenses, but the men are quickly outnumbered and overwhelmed. Charlie Morse is killed, and Thomas is wounded. As the battle ends Forbes, Rawlins, Thomas, Jupiter, and the two color sergeants are killed. The next morning, the beach is seen riddled with the bodies of slain Union troops. The corpses are buried in a mass grave. The closing on-screen text reads: "The 54th Massachusetts lost over half its number in the assault on Ft. Wagner. The supporting white brigades also suffered heavily before withdrawing. The fort was never taken. As word of their bravery spread, Congress at last authorized the raising of black troops throughout the union. Over 180,000 volunteered. President Lincoln credited these men with helping to turn the tide of the war."

Reception

Released on 15 December 1989, *Glory* ran until 8 April 1990 (widest release 811 theaters). During its 17-week run, *Glory* managed to earn $26.8 million against a production budget of $18 million: a healthy profit. The movie also won numerous honors, including three Academy Awards: Best Actor in a Supporting Role (Denzel Washington, who was also awarded a Golden Globe); Best Cinematography (Freddie Francis), and Best Sound. Reviews were, likewise, mostly positive—though there were exceptions. For example Desson Howe noted that the film's "flaws are many, should you look for them. Scriptwriter Jarre (whose previous credit is, uh, *Rambo: First Blood Part II*) provides only a superficial sense of his characters' dreams (his script is made better by the performers); that liberal-hearted, misty-eyed giddiness (thanks chiefly to the gushy, rhapsodizing score by James Horner) frequently gets way out of hand; and Broderick, as the Boston Brahmin who leads the 54th to timeless glory, provides a certain, gee-willikers empathy, but he should probably give Neil Simon a call and see what's shaking. In this movie, he's an amiable non-presence, creating unintentionally the notion that the 54th earned their stripes despite wimpy leadership" (Howe, 1990).

Reel History Versus Real History

While *Glory* was still in theaters, Pulitzer Prize–winning Civil War historian James M. McPherson (*Battle Cry of Freedom*) addressed questions concerning its historical veracity (McPherson, 1990, pp. 22–27). McPherson noted that the movie got "most of the details right" and when it did not, there was sometimes a valid explanation. Other inaccuracies he deems "inexplicable":

The 54th began organizing in February 1863, not three months earlier. In his brief cameo role, black leader Frederick Douglass is presented as a venerable sage whose screen appearance is modeled on a photograph taken a quarter century later, when Douglass was in his 70s instead of the vigorous 45 he was in 1863. The real Robert Gould Shaw received the offer of command of the 54th by letter from Governor Andrew, borne by his father to Shaw in winter camp with his regiment (the 2nd Massachusetts) in Virginia. Rob discussed it earnestly with his father, wrestled with his conscience overnight, declined, then changed his mind a day later and accepted. In the movie, Shaw is [shown] attending an elegant drawing-room party in Boston while on furlough when Andrews offers the command; without a pause, Shaw accepts. Literal history in this case would seem to have offered greater dramatic possibilities for getting at a deeper truth than the cinematic version. (p. 27)

McPherson goes on to observe that, except for Shaw, the principal characters in the film are all fictional. Furthermore, the movie gives the impression that most of the 54th's soldiers were former slaves. In actuality most were recruited from the North and had always been free men. For McPherson these distortions amount to a missed opportunity: "A dramatic and important story about the relationship of Northern blacks to slavery and the war, and about the wartime ideals of New England culture, could have been constructed from a cast of real, historical figures." McPherson could have cited other inaccuracies or omissions as well. Col. Shaw married Anna Kneeland Haggerty 11 weeks before his death, but the movie makes no mention of this. The 54th's refusal to accept pay because of unequal rates took place long after it had left South Carolina. The movie's depiction of Gen. Harker as a middle-aged officer who condoned plunder and corruption among his subordinates is a complete fabrication. The real Harker, who died a Civil War hero at age 26 at the Battle of Kennesaw Mountain (27 June 1864), was an exemplary officer and not in the least corrupt. Yet, in spite of all these issues, James McPherson finds the story the filmmakers chose to tell "equally true" because it served to dramatize the African American "transformation from an oppressed people to a proud people."

GRAND ILLUSION [FRENCH: *LA GRANDE ILLUSION*] (1937)

Synopsis
Grand Illusion is a French war film directed by Jean Renoir, who co-wrote the screenplay with Charles Spaak, based on the actual experiences of a number of French aviators during the First World War. The story focuses on the relationship between a German prisoner of war (POW) camp commandant and a small group of captive French officers who are plotting their escape.

Background
During the First World War, Jean Renoir (son of Auguste Renoir, the great painter) became close friends with Armand Pinsard (1887–1953), another pilot in France's

Armée de l'Air (air force). Pinsard, a much-decorated ace with 27 victories in air combat, was shot down 8 February 1915 and sent to a German POW facility. He made several failed escape attempts over a year before finally succeeding by digging a tunnel under the prison wall with another inmate. Renoir and Pinsard lost touch after the war but fortuitously reconnected in 1934 when Renoir was shooting a film near Pinsard's air base outside Marseille. Renoir asked Pinsard to recount his exploits (already widely reported in newspapers during the war), compiled notes about them, and entrusted his notes to Belgian screenwriter Charles Spaak as material for a screenplay. After Renoir wrote a treatment entitled *Les evasions de Capitaine Maréchal* in the fall of 1935, Spaak developed a screenplay that drew on Pinsard's stories, Renoir's own recollections, and other memoirs written by members of the League of Wartime Escapees. After Renoir had cast Jean Gabin—France's biggest box office draw—to play Maréchal, he was able to secure a producer/distributer: Réalisation d'art cinématographique (RAC), a new firm founded by Albert Pinkovitch and Frank Rollmer. Before filming started casting, characterizations, and the script continued to evolve. The role of de Boeldieu, an aristocratic officer, was offered to Louis Jouvet and Pierre Richard-Willm before finally going to Pierre Fresnay. A late script change involved turning Maréchal's fellow prison escapee into a foreign-born Jewish officer named Rosenthal—a daring move in an era of rampant anti-Semitism and xenophobia. Another audacious move on Renoir's part was to cast Marcel Dalio (later, the croupier in *Casablanca*) as Rosenthal, an actor usually typecast as a shady or weak minor character. Most significant, though, was the last-minute casting of Erich Von Stroheim as Von Rauffenstein, the German fighter pilot turned prison commandant—an entirely new character that necessitated a complete script overhaul by Renoir and Spaak, his assistant Jacques Becker, and German technical advisor Carl Koch just days before shooting was scheduled to start.

Production

Filming of *La grande illusion* began on 13 February 1937, with a month of exterior shooting in the Alsace region (northeastern France). The first prison camp scenes were shot in the artillery barracks at Colmar built by Wilhelm II, Haut-Rhin (Upper Rhine), and the Wintersborn prison scenes were shot at the Château du Haut Koenigsbourg, Orschwiller, Bas-Rhin (Lower Rhine). The last snowy scene of the film was shot in Chamonix Valley near Mont Blanc. Location shooting was supplemented by studio work at Studios Éclair and Studios de Boulogne-Billancourt/SFP in Paris; the 78-day shoot wrapped on 15 May 1937.

Plot Summary

During the First World War, two French aviators—Capt. de Boeldieu (Pierre Fresnay), an aristocrat, and Lt. Maréchal (Jean Gabin), a Paris auto mechanic—are shot down behind enemy lines by Rittmeister von Rauffenstein (Erich von Stroheim), a German aristocrat. They survive the crash, but are captured. Upon returning to base, Rauffenstein sends a subordinate to invite the French flyers to lunch. During the meal, Rauffenstein and Boeldieu discover they inhabit the same aristocratic social circles. Boeldieu and Maréchal are then taken to a POW camp

Erich von Stroheim (left), as German fighter ace Rittmeister von Rauffenstein, greets captured World War I French aviators Captain de Boeldieu (Pierre Fresnay, right) and Lieutenant Maréchal (Jean Gabin, middle) just after shooting them down, in an early scene from Jean Renoir's *La grande illusion* (1937). (Photofest)

at Hallbach, where they meet a raucous group of French POWs who stage an impromptu vaudeville-type performance, complete with cross-dressing, after German soldiers take over Fort Douaumont at the beginning of the Battle of Verdun. As the POWs perform, news spreads that the French have taken back the fort. Maréchal shuts down the performance, and the French prisoners sing "La Marseillaise." Boeldieu and Maréchal oversee the creation of an escape tunnel, but before they can complete their work, the prisoners are transferred to separate camps. Unable to speak English, Maréchal cannot share information about the escape route, and Boeldieu and Maréchal are consistently moved around from one camp to the next. After a series of escape attempts, they finally arrive in Wintersborn, a supposedly escape-proof mountain fortress-prison commanded by Rauffenstein, who has been hurt during battle, promoted, and given a posting away from the front—much to his chagrin. At Wintersborn, Boeldieu and Maréchal are reunited with Rosenthal (Marcel Dalio), a wealthy naturalized French Jew who offers food to his compatriots. Boeldieu comes up with an escape idea; he volunteers to create a diversion to distract the guards so that Maréchal and Rosenthal can escape. After the POWs stage a ruckus, the guards order them to move to the courtyard. The guards realize that Boeldieu is absent from the group during a roll call, but he suddenly reveals himself overhead in the fortress, which causes the German guards to pursue him in a fury. During this diversion, Maréchal and Rosenthal escape through a window. Rauffenstein begs Boeldieu to turn himself in, but Boeldieu refuses. Rauffenstein is forced to shoot his fellow aristocrat, sending him to his death. Having escaped the fortress, Maréchal and Rosenthal travel on foot across Germany towards the Swiss border. The pair rest in a nearby German farmhouse and become friendly with the owner, Elsa (Dita Parlo), who has suffered many losses as a result of the war. Elsa keeps the men safe, even when a German patrol passes through. Maréchal and Elsa fall in love, but he is forced to move on once Rosenthal recovers from his injury. Maréchal tells Elsa that he will return for her and her daughter when the war ends. A German patrol spots Maréchal and Rosenthal en route to the Swiss border, but the pair crosses the border before the Germans reach them. A final long shot shows Maréchal and Rosenthal trudging through deep snow—to freedom and an uncertain future.

Reception

Released in France on 8 June 1937, *La grande illusion* proved to be a huge box office hit. Estimates vary, but the film likely sold 10 to 12 million tickets between 1937 and 1939. France's population was 42 million during this period, so it is likely that roughly one out of every four French people saw the film. Screened at the 5th Venice Biennial [Film] Exposition in August 1937, *La grande illusion* was widely hailed as a masterpiece of progressive humanism and a superlative anti-war film at a time when the Spanish Civil War was raging and the threat of fascism was menacing Europe. Naturally, Hitler's Propaganda Minister Joseph Goebbels hated the film—despite the fact that it offers a highly sympathetic portrait of a German officer. Declaring the movie "Cinematic Public Enemy Number One," Goebbels tried to intervene with Mussolini to prevent *La grande illusion* from winning a prize at Venice, but the festival jury gave it a special award for "Best Artistic Ensemble." An English-subtitled version premiered in the United States on 12 September 1938, produced solid box office returns, and was warmly received by American film critics. A favorite of FDR, who recommended that "every democratic person in the world should see this film," *La grande illusion* won the award for Best Foreign Film at the 1938 New York Film Critics Circle Awards. But Germany and Italy banned the film in November 1938, and after World War II broke out, French authorities also banned the movie "for the duration of hostilities," fearing it would adversely affect fighting morale. In August 1999, Rialto Pictures re-released the film in the United States, based on the Cinémathèque negative. In 1998 the print was restored and released as the inaugural DVD of the Criterion Collection. A new 4K digital restoration was released in 2012 to mark the 75th anniversary of the film's release.

Reel History Versus Real History

The film's depiction of POW life is a mostly accurate representation of Offizierlagers (officers' camps), of which there were 73 in Germany by the end of WWI. Living conditions for captured Allied officers were less harsh than those endured by regular troops. Offizierlagers were usually located in requisitioned buildings (e.g., castles, barracks, or hotels), rather than in tents and huts. Officers had more space per man than other ranks, beds instead of straw-filled paillasses, and dining facilities. They were exempt from work and were allowed recreational activities like theatricals. Rauffenstein is fairly typical of camp commandants, who tended to be older, sometimes disabled officers. On the other hand, the movie's depiction of the food situation at Offizierlagers is somewhat unrealistic. Even at these elite camps the diet of the prisoners was inadequate and malnutrition was widespread. Furthermore, it is highly unlikely that Boeldieu and Maréchal would have ended up at Wintersborn. Persistent escapers were usually consigned to Ingolstadt Fortress in Bavaria (the WWI equivalent to Colditz Castle). Though the story *La grande illusion* tells is fictional, Jean Renoir and Charles Spaak always maintained that it was an embellished version of the wartime experiences of Armand Pinsard. However, after the movie came out, another former aviator and POW named Jean des Vallières sued Renoir and Spaak for plagiarizing his book, *Kavalier Scharnhorst, Tender Germany* (Albin Michel, Paris, 1931). In des Vallières' book there's also a scene with cross-dressing prisoners, the same use of the song, "It Was a Small Ship," the word "verboten" (forbidden) used as a leitmotif, and a number of other exact coincidences. The case was settled out of court for an undisclosed amount.

GREAT ESCAPE, THE (1963)

Synopsis
The Great Escape is an American World War II epic produced and directed by John Sturges. It is loosely based on Paul Brickhill's 1950 book of the same title: a first-hand account of the mass escape of British prisoners of war (POWs) from Stalag Luft III in the province of Lower Silesia, Nazi Germany, in 1944.

Background
During the night and early morning hours of 24–25 March 1944, 76 Allied POWs used a 350-foot tunnel to escape from Stalag Luft III, a German POW camp in Lower Silesia near the town of Sagan (now Żagań, Poland), 100 miles southeast of Berlin. Three made it all the way home, but the rest were soon recaptured, and 50 of the 73 escapees were subsequently executed on Hitler's orders. Paul Brickhill (1916–1991), an Australian-born Spitfire pilot shot down in Tunisia and imprisoned at Stalag Luft III, was involved in the mass escape, but the Germans discovered the tunnel before Brickhill had a chance to make his own attempt—a happenstance that probably saved his life. After the war, Brickhill wrote *The Great Escape* (1950), a well-researched account of the large and complex escape operation and its aftermath that brought the incident to wide public attention. Over the next decade, Brickhill received lots of offers to sell the film rights but resisted until American film director John Sturges (*Bad Day at Black Rock*) eventually persuaded Brickhill that he would make a film true to the history. Sturges had trouble

interesting a Hollywood studio until he made *The Magnificent Seven* (1960), a hit Western based on Akira Kurasawa's *The Seven Samurai* and produced by the Mirisch Company. On the strength of that picture, the Mirisch brothers—Walter, Marvin, and Harold—agreed to back Sturges's escape movie, and United Artists signed on to distribute the picture. Sturges hired novelist-screenwriter W. R. Burnett (*The Asphalt Jungle*) to adapt Brickhill's novel to the screen and later hired James Clavell (*King Rat*), a former POW in the Pacific, to make script revisions. The original plan was to film *The Great Escape* at a POW camp set constructed in the San Gabriel Mountains near Big Bear Lake, 100 miles east of Hollywood, but Sturges ultimately opted to film in Germany to achieve greater verisimilitude, but also because the cost of hiring lots of extras at union-mandated rates in California proved prohibitive (Rubin, 2011, pp. 132–135). Most of the principal cast was signed by the spring of 1962, with one important change. Richard Harris was supposed to play role of Roger Bartlett, aka "Big X," the chief escape organizer based on RAF Squadron Leader Roger Bushell (1910–1944), but dropped out due to scheduling conflicts and was replaced by Richard Attenborough.

Production

The four-month *Great Escape* shoot at Geiselgasteig Studios outside Munich, Bavaria, started on 4 June 1962, but rainy weather forced Sturges to alter the schedule and shoot interior scenes from the middle part of the picture first. By mid-July, after six weeks of rushes, Steve McQueen became unhappy with his part, which he deemed too small and sketchy. Headstrong and intensely ambitious, McQueen really wanted to be first among equals in what was supposed to be another Sturges ensemble production. He badgered Sturges and W. R. Burnett but did not get the script rewrites he wanted, so he went on strike for six weeks. Actually fired at the end of August, McQueen stayed in the picture after negotiations with Sturges and United Artists, mediated by his agent Stan Kamen, resolved the situation, and screenwriter Ivan Moffett was brought in to beef up McQueen's role. After challenging and dangerous stunt work with motorcycles and airplanes was completed in October, the long and arduous shoot finally wrapped.

Plot Summary

It is 1943 and the Germans have moved their most escape-prone POWs to a new high-security POW camp. The commandant, Luftwaffe Col. von Luger (Hannes Messemer), tells the senior British officer, Group Captain Ramsey (James Donald), "There will be no escapes from this camp." The POWs try and fail a number of times when they first arrive, but eventually accept their fate and fall into a routine. Meanwhile, Gestapo agents Kuhn (Hans Reiser) and Preissen (Ulrich Beiger) and SS Lieutenant Dietrich (George Mikell) deliver RAF Squadron Leader Roger Bartlett, aka "Big X" (Richard Attenborough), a master escape organizer, to the camp. Bartlett is warned that if he escapes the camp again, he will be killed. Undaunted, Bartlett immediately begins to plan the greatest escape ever attempted—250 to 300 prisoners scattered all over Germany so that massive numbers of German soldiers will be relegated to searching for escapees rather than being deployed at the front. The

POWs duly organize themselves into teams, each specializing in a different aspect of the escape attempt. Flight Lieutenant Robert Hendley (James Garner) is "the scrounger" who obtains needed materials. Australian Flying Officer Louis Sedgwick (James Coburn), "the manufacturer," makes tools for digging and bellows for pumping air into the tunnels. Flight Lieutenants Danny Valinski (Charles Bronson) and William "Willie" Dickes (John Leyton) are "the tunnel kings" in charge of the actual digging. Flight Lieutenant Andrew MacDonald (Gordon Jackson) acts as intelligence officer, and Bartlett's second-in-command. Royal Navy Lt. Commander Eric Ashley-Pitt (David McCallum) is in charge of dispersal, that is, spreading the soil from the tunnels over the camp grounds, undetected. Flight Lieutenant Griffith (Robert Desmond) acts as "the tailor," creating civilian outfits out of military uniforms. Flight Lieutenant Colin Blythe (Donald Pleasence), in charge of forging German identity documents, almost goes blind from the strain on his eyes from all of his detailed work by candlelight (Hendley becomes Blythe's guide). To ensure a reasonable chance of success, the prisoners work on a trio of tunnels all at once, naming them "Tom," "Dick," and "Harry." USAAF Captain Virgil Hilts (Steve McQueen), the "Cooler King," persists in badgering the guards by trying to escape again and again while displaying an uncooperative attitude. Hilts and RAF Flying Officer Archibald Ives (Angus Lennie) devise a plan to flee through a shorter tunnel near the edge of camp, one that Bartlett agrees to with the knowledge that he can't shoot down all individual escape attempts if he hopes for his grand scheme to succeed. Hilts and Ives are promptly caught and punished. When Hilt is released from "the cooler," Bartlett asks him to use his next escape attempt to reconnoiter the area around the camp. Hilts turns Bartlett down, but helps the collective escape effort by becoming a scrounger. Hendley becomes friendly with a German patrolman named Werner (Robert Graf) and steals his ID documents in order to blackmail the hapless guard into securing materials necessary to the prisoners' escape. As "Tom" nears completion, Bartlett shuts down "Dick" and "Harry." While the POWs celebrate the July Fourth holiday, the guards find "Tom"—a major, morale-crushing setback. Ives, driven mad by isolation in "the cooler," attempts to climb the camp's barbed wire fence in full view of the guards. He is killed as a result. Not to be deterred, the POWs set back to work on "Harry." Hilts agrees to do some reconnaissance outside of the camp grounds, be recaptured, and then report on his findings so that the group can make maps to guide escapees. The final section of the tunnel is finished on time, but it ends up being 20 feet short of the woods, which were meant to provide cover. Bartlett proceeds with the escape, and Hilt devises a system for signaling the prisoners so that they can leave the tunnel between patrol sweeps. Danny, who has spent a lengthy amount of time in the tunnels, now suffers from severe claustrophobia and almost refuses to leave. In all, 76 prisoners manage to escape before the Germans catch on, but after attempts to reach neutral countries, almost all the POWs are recaptured or killed. Hendley and Blythe steal a plane to fly over the Swiss border, but the engine fails and they crash. Hendley surrenders, but Blythe, now blind, does not put his hands up and is shot dead. Bartlett is discovered at a busy railway station, but Ashely-Pitt overpowers the Gestapo agent and shoots him, only to be killed while attempting his own escape. In the commotion, Bartlett and MacDonald manage to escape, but are captured getting on a bus, when MacDonald mistakenly replies to a Gestapo agent in English. Mac-Donald is quickly arrested but Bartlett manages to escape, though he is soon recognized and arrested by SS Lieutenant Steinach (Karl-Otto Alberty). Hilts steals a motorcycle and is subsequently chased by a large contingent of German soldiers. He passes over the German-Swiss border and gets into the Neutral Zone, but then gets tangled in barbed wire and is arrested. Three trucks containing POWs go down a road and then split in different directions. The first vehicle, carrying, MacDonald, Cavendish, Haynes, and others, stops in a field, and the drivers ask the captives to exit the truck to "stretch their legs." They are killed. In total, 50 prisoners are killed and only Hendley and 9 fellow captives are brought back to the camp. Von Luger has been discharged. Only three POWs make it out of Nazi Germany. Danny and Willie row a boat to the Baltic coast and then stow away on a Swedish vessel. Sedgwick pilfers a bicycle and hides on a freight train that takes him to France, where he is brought to Spain by the French Resistance. Hilts is brought back to the camp alone in handcuffs and ends up in the cooler. USAAF Lt. Goff (Jud Taylor) grabs Hilts' baseball and glove, tossing them his way when Hilt walks by with the German guards. The guard locks Hilts in, and we hear the prisoner throwing his ball against the cell wall.

Reception

The Great Escape had its world premiere at the Odeon in Leicester Square, London, on 20 June 1963 and went into wide release in North America on the Fourth of July weekend. The movie did respectably well at the box office, grossing $11.7 million; almost triple its $4 million production budget, making it the 17th highest-grossing American film of 1963. The movie also earned a Golden Globe nomination for Best Picture and a Writers Guild of America Award nomination for Best Written American Drama (Screenplay Adaptation). Less demanding critics, like Judith Crist, found *The Great Escape* exhilarating: "A first-rate adventure film, fascinating in its detail, suspenseful in its plot, stirring in its climax and excellent in performance . . . Steve McQueen takes the honors" (Crist, 1963). As was often the case, Bosley Crowther voiced his dissent, panning the film as puerile, unrealistic, and manipulative: "Nobody is going to con me . . . into believing that the spirit of defiance in any prisoner-of-war camp anywhere was as arrogant, romantic and Rover Boyish as it is made to appear in this film. And nobody's going to induce me with shameless Hollywood cliffhanging tricks . . . to surrender my reason and my emotions to the sort of fiction fabricated here . . . It's strictly a mechanical adventure with make-believe men" (Crowther, 1963). Four years after its theatrical release CBS aired *The Great Escape* on TV (in two parts) in September 1967, exposing the film to a much wider viewing audience and cementing its stature as a classic of the POW war film genre.

Reel History Versus Real History

The Great Escape is a reasonably accurate rendition of POW life at Stalag Luft III, though living conditions were more wretched than the film suggests. The look of the camp and its environs, the tunnels, the escape organization and all its specialized functions, the actual (interrupted) escape, and its grim aftermath—all are faithfully shown. In many other ways, however, the movie is grossly inaccurate. As detailed in Brickhill's book, the actual escape operation involved some 600 POWs in specialized tasks. For narrative clarity, the film features about a dozen composite characters representing all these men: an understandable but misleading bit of streamlining. Commercial imperatives forced the filmmakers to depart from history in even more significant ways. An American-made film for an American market, *The Great Escape* numbers four A-list American movie stars—Steve McQueen, James Garner (playing a Canadian), James Coburn (playing an Australian), and Charles Bronson (playing a Pole)—among its top-billed roles. Furthermore, all the characters portrayed by the Americans survive, whereas many of the British POWs die. Captured American aviators did work on the construction of the tunnels, but by the time of the escape, all of them had been moved to a separate compound. The film's portrayal of McQueen's Virgil Hilts escaping along with his British counterparts is therefore a Hollywood fabrication, along with Hilts' motorcycle heroics, which were inserted at McQueen's request—rousing action cinema but bad history. Hilts' unflappable insouciance defined Steve McQueen's star persona, but as Bosley Crowther suggests earlier, it owed more to Hollywood than to history, though Hilts' "Cooler King" character was based on Flight Lieutenant Jackson Barrett "Barry" Mahon (1920–1999), an American-born RAF pilot who served as a technical advisor on the film. (Mahon was shot down in August 1942 and sent to Stalag Luft III. In "the cooler" after his second escape, he could not participate in the mass escape, which likely saved his life. During the film shoot McQueen took a liking to Mahon—who also once served as Errol Flynn's pilot—and asked to have Mahon's background written into the Hilts's character.) Another example of dramatic license: the film shows the retaliatory murders of the 50 recaptured escapers—but not in the manner in which they occurred. Most of the victims were actually driven to isolated spots in small groups, told to get out and stretch their legs, and were then shot through the back of the head, not machine-gunned en masse, as depicted in the film (though the Germans did that too, at Malmedy, Belgium, on 17 December 1944, when SS troopers murdered 84 American POWs during the Battle of the Bulge).

GUADALCANAL DIARY (1943)

Synopsis
Guadalcanal Diary is a World War II war film directed by Lewis Seiler, featuring Preston Foster, Lloyd Nolan, William Bendix, Richard Conte, Anthony Quinn, and Richard Jaeckel. Based on the best-selling book of the same title by Richard Tregaskis, the film recounts the fight of the United States Marines in the Battle of Guadalcanal in 1942.

Background
Richard Tregaskis (1916–1973), a 25-year-old war correspondent for International News Service, was with U.S. Marine Corps troops when they hit the beach at

Guadalcanal Island (in the Solomon Island chain) on 7 August 1942. Tregaskis stayed on to cover the first three months of their increasingly bloody struggle to wrest control of the island from Japanese forces. On 18 November Tregaskis signed a deal with Random House to publish a book culled from his newspaper dispatches entitled *Guadalcanal Diary*. In early December, 20th Century Fox purchased the film rights, winning a bidding war with the other major studios. By March 1943 Lewis Seiler had signed on as director. By early April it was announced that William Bendix would appear in the picture and that Victor McLaglen would play "Father Donnelly" and Preston Foster would take the role of "Capt. Cross." Ultimately Foster played the Donnelly character and McLaglen was given the "Col. Grayson" role but was later replaced by Minor Watson. Anthony Quinn, of Mexican Irish extraction, was cast in the heroic role of "Soose Alvarez" in order to help improve the public image of the United States in Latin American countries. An added selling point for Quinn is that he closely resembled Sgt. Frank Few from Buckeye, Arizona, who was one of the heroes of Guadalcanal. Eddie Acuff's character, "Tex McIlvoy," was based on Gunnery Sgt. Charles E. Angus, a Marine rifleman famous for his marksmanship on Guadalcanal. The studio won the crucial cooperation of the War Department on the condition that the script, based on "Marines in the Pacific," a treatment by George Bricker and Herman Ruby, be completely revised for historical accuracy. The studio complied, assigning Lamar Trotti and Jerome Cady, with uncredited contributions by Kenneth Gamet and Waldo Salt, to rewrite the film so that it faithfully followed Tregaskis's book. The only major departure was to focus the narrative on a single unit of Marines instead of depicting the entire campaign. For its part, the U.S. military supplied 5,000 Marines, 1,000 soldiers, 300 sailors, a transport ship, landing craft, tanks, planes, guns, etc. (Stanley, 1943).

Production

The beach landing scenes in *Guadalcanal Diary* were shot at Catalina Island off the California coast, but most of the movie was filmed at Camp Pendleton, near Oceanside, California (about 90 miles south of Los Angeles), between mid-May and late July 1943—less than a year after the events it depicts. Many of the Marines stationed there were filmed while on maneuvers, and many of them appeared in the picture in small speaking parts or as extras. The shoot was overseen by two (uncredited) technical advisors: Lt. James W. Hurlbut, a Marine Corps war correspondent who was at Guadalcanal with Tregaskis, and Capt. Clarence Martin, who fought at Guadalcanal with the first detachment of Marines.

Plot Summary

Throughout the film, voice-over narration is supplied by Reed Hadley (the war correspondent based on Richard Tregaskis), who describes the action and gives important dates. On 26 July 1942, a transport ship carrying a large contingent of Marines sails through the South Pacific. Sailing under sealed orders, the men make the most of the 11 days they have left at sea by singing, writing letters, and conversing with the war correspondent traveling with them. The men include Father Donnelly (Preston Foster), Col. Wallace E. Grayson (Minor Watson), Capt. Jim Cross

(Roy Roberts), Capt. Davis (Richard Conte), Sgt. Hook Malone (Lloyd Nolan), Corp. Aloysius "Taxi" Potts (William Bendix), Pvt. Jesus "Soose" Alvarez (Anthony Quinn), and Pvt. Johnny "Chicken" Anderson (Richard Jaeckel). Grayson discovers that the men are being sent to Guadalcanal in the Solomon Islands (northwest of Australia) and that other troops are being deployed to Tulagi. Cross and Davis organize the upcoming landings, and Donnelly bolsters the troops. While Cross and Davis plan the landing of the first two companies, Donnelly goes below to encourage the men. On 7 August 1942, the Marines land on Tulagi against stiff enemy resistance but land on Guadalcanal uncontested. There they quickly secure the airfield, make camp, and post lookouts for the enemy, but Japanese snipers, lurking in the jungle, soon pick off American soldiers one by one. Davis falls ill, and Capt. Cross commands a group of soldiers to look into a native's tip that a unit of Japanese soldiers is prepared to surrender. As the troops proceed, they are assaulted in the water by a Japanese submarine and the survivors are pinned down by machine-gun fire once they land on the beach. The men dig in and form a defensive perimeter but are soon decimated. Only Soose survives, after jumping into the ocean and swimming back to the main camp. Seeking vengeance, Col. Grayson leads a successful attack on Matanikau in force. Thereafter, the soldiers are engaged in a series of skirmishes and subjected to constant aerial attacks. Henderson airfield is rebuilt over the next few weeks, allowing supplies and reinforcements in to the region. On 10 November 1942, several units of Marines under the command of Col. Grayson begin a major offensive with the aim of destabilizing Japanese soldiers. Soose dies in battle, but Johnny Anderson is able to kill the men who attack him, leaving the Marines victorious. On 10 December 1942 U.S. Army troops relieve the Marines.

Reception

Released on 17 November 1943, *Guadalcanal Diary* earned $3 million at the box office: 20th Century Fox's second highest-grossing movie (after *Sweet Rosie O'Grady*) of the 17 films the studio released in 1943. Most reviews commended the film as an honest and entertaining paean to the soldiers who fought at Guadalcanal, but film critic David Lardner castigated the movie as exhibiting "every cliché known to man" and for the Marines being depicted as having "altogether too soft a time" as compared to what the Marines really experienced (Lardner, 1943).

Reel History Versus Real History

Capt. Cross's ill-fated patrol is based on an actual 25-man recon patrol led by Lt. Col. Frank B. Goettge on 12 August 1942 that landed near the Matanikau River estuary, on the northwest part of the island, in a Higgins boat. The patrol was subsequently ambushed and virtually wiped out by a larger Japanese force. In the movie only "Soose" Alvarez survives, but actually three men (Sgt. Frank L. Few, Sgt. Charles C. Arndt, and Cpl. Joseph Spaulding) survived by swimming down the coast to their base at Kukum. The film inaccurately depicts the Japanese as having lured the Americans into a trap by trickery; the massacre was more the result of Goettge's poor planning. The movie also sanitizes the engagement by omitting the aftermath in which the Japanese hacked the dead and dying Marines to pieces with swords. In his review of the film published in the *New York Times* the day after it was released, film critic Bosley Crowther pointed up other aspects of the movie's shortcomings with regard to historical accuracy: "The clear weakness of this picture is that Lamar Trotti and Jerry Cady, who prepared the script, have all too freely rigged up a patent fiction to fit the pattern of a film. Baldly, they have made the implication that air support did not reach Henderson Field until Oct. 14 [1942] although the fact is that we had fighters there by mid-August. Also, they have skipped completely the battles of the Tenaru River [21 August 1942] and "The [Edson] Ridge" [12–14 September 1942] and have saved their heavy fire and fury for the big advance against the enemy on Nov. 10. And the historic episode of Captain Torge[r]son tossing dynamite into caves on Tulagi has been here attributed to a heroic sergeant and geographically transplanted to Guadalcanal" (Crowther, 18 Nov. 1943).

GUNS OF NAVARONE, THE (1961)

Synopsis
The Guns of Navarone is a British-American war film/adventure epic directed by J. Lee Thompson; produced and written by Carl Foreman; and starring Gregory Peck, David Niven, Stanley Baker, and Anthony Quinn. Based on Alistair MacLean's 1957 novel, *The Guns of Navarone*, the film is about an Allied commando unit on a perilous mission to destroy two outsized German cannons that threaten Allied naval ships in the Aegean Sea.

Background
After the spectacular sales success of *HMS Ulysses* (Collins, 1955), a novel based on his war experiences, Scotsman Alistair MacLean (1922–1987), a WWII British Royal Navy veteran, went on to publish another 27 adventure-thrillers over the next 31 years. His second novel was *The Guns of Navarone* (Collins, 1957), another bestseller, inspired by the Battle of Leros (26 September–16 November 1943) during the Dodecanese Campaign in the Aegean Sea that resulted in a German victory over Allied forces. Blacklisted screenwriter-producer Carl Foreman acquired the film rights for his own production company (Open Road Films), wrote the first draft of a screen adaptation in 1958, and secured a production deal with Columbia Pictures. Foreman hoped to sign William Holden (*The Bridge on the River Kwai*) in the lead role of Capt. Mallory but Holden wanted $750,000 and 10 percent of the gross, and so he was not hired. After a raft of "A-list" actors passed on the part, it finally went to Gregory Peck. Ironically, Peck secured the exact same deal that the studio refused Holden. By March 1960 the rest of the principal roles went to a distinguished cast: Anthony Quinn, David Niven, Anthony Quail, and Stanley Baker. Teen idol James Darren (*Gidget*) was cast for youth audience appeal. Likewise, two Greek resistance fighters who were male in the novel became women in the movie version in order to lend the picture more sex appeal. Foreman initially

signed Greek opera star Maria Callas and Roger Vadim's then-wife, Danish actress Annette Stroyberg, to these roles but both soon dropped out and were replaced by Gia Scala and Irene Papas. At 24, 26, and 34, respectively, Darren, Scala, and Papas were the only major cast members plausibly young enough to have been low-ranking combatants in WWII. Most of the other principal characters were in their mid-to-late 40s (Niven was 50)—really too old to be members of a crack commando unit. Indeed, the British press cheekily dubbed *The Guns of Navarone* "Elderly Gang Goes Off to War." Foreman signed Alexander Mackendrick (*The Ladykillers*) to direct but fired him after a quarrel "over creative differences" and replaced him with J. Lee Thompson in June 1960.

Production

Carl Foreman wanted to shoot the picture's outdoor scenes on location in Cyprus, but rumors of an impending civil war prompted him to opt for the Greek Isle of Rhodes. Initially budgeted at $2 million, the production ended up costing triple that amount due to logistical challenges: remote locations, simulated battles on land and sea, elaborate studio sets (including a mock German fortress that covered an acre and a half and stood 140 feet high), a faux shipwreck during a violent storm, complicated combat pyrotechnics with real explosives, and the need to hire a dozen U.S.-built destroyers from the Greek navy and 1,000 Greek soldiers to impersonate a German Wehrmacht regiment. The production lasted seven and a half months (March–October 1960), during which cinematographer Oswald Morris shot 67 hours of raw color footage for a film with a final cut of 2.6 hours duration—a 38-to-1 shooting ratio that was about four times the industry average in that era. The shoot on Rhodes lasted three months and was a rugged experience for all involved, but the remainder of the shoot at Shepperton Studios outside London proved to be unexpectedly grueling as well. To stage the storm-induced wreck of the commando's fishing boat under properly controlled conditions required the use of an enormous water tank (120 ft. × 100 ft. that held 250,000 gallons) inside Europe's largest sound stage at Shepperton. An adjacent supply tank held another 75,000 gallons. Over 4,200 gallons (16 tons) of water hurtled down four giant chutes onto the actors and the set while giant fans blew spray around every time Foreman yelled "Action!" (Meade, 1961, pp. E1, E5). On 26 June Peck and Quinn were injured when they were swept across the set too forcefully by one of Foreman's artificial waves. On 8 September the German fortress set that took five months to build at a cost of $280,000 partially collapsed and had to be rebuilt, causing further delays. While shooting a climactic scene in the German fortress, David Niven contracted a near-fatal case of septicemia through a cut lip while standing for hours in a flooded elevator shaft. He spent weeks in the hospital but recovered enough to shoot his remaining scenes.

Plot Summary

In 1943, the Axis powers coordinate an attack on Leros, an island where 2,000 British soldiers are stranded, to convince Turkey to join the fight. The Royal Navy is unable to retrieve the soldiers due to the radar-directed cannons situated in bomb-proof caves on Navarone. The Allied forces then bring together a group of six operatives to land on Navarone and neutralize the weapons. Major Roy Franklin (Anthony Quayle) leads the team, made up of Franklin's best friend, Corporal Miller (David Niven), a bomb expert; Captain Keith Mallory (Gregory Peck), a spy and mountaineer; Greek Col. Andrea Stavrou (Anthony Quinn); Greco-American Spyros Pappadimos (James Darren), a native of Navarone; and "Butcher" Brown (Stanley Baker), an engineer and knife expert. Posing as fishermen from Greece aboard the *Maria*, a small fishing boat, they make their way across the Aegean Sea to Navarone, killing the sailors on a German patrol vessel when it attempts to board their vessel. During the sea voyage, Mallory tells Franklin that Stavrou plans to murder him after the war is over as retribution for mistakenly killing Stavrou's spouse and children. The soldiers shipwreck on the island of Navarone during a tempest, and Mallory brings the crew up a steep cliff to safety. Franklin falls during the climb and injures his leg, which eventually becomes gangrenous. Once in the mountains, Franklin resolves to commit suicide so as not to be a burden on his comrades but Mallory saves Franklin by telling him a lie, claiming that their orders have changed and the Navy will attack the Navarone coastline, far from the gun emplacements. The unit meets up with some local resistance combatants: Spyros's sister Maria (Irene Papas) and her friend Anna (Gia Scala), who became mute after being tortured by the Germans. The troops are then taken prisoner while looking for a doctor to assist Franklin. Stavrou makes a scene during their interrogation, giving his comrades time to overtake their enemies. They get away using German uniforms, moving on without Franklin in the hopes that he will be treated for his injuries. The Germans soon inject Franklin with scopolamine (aka "Devil's Breath," a mind control drug) and he tells them the incorrect information supplied by Mallory, as anticipated; the main fort is emptied to prepare for the assault. After invading Navarone, Miller finds that the majority of his bombs have been compromised, possibly by Anna. The unit questions Anna, and she admits that she is not mute, but is actually a German informant working towards her own release. Mallory goes to kill her, but Maria beats him to it. The team splits up. Mallory and Miller make a move towards the weapons while Stavrou and Spyros come up with diversions throughout the town and Marian and Brown procure a boat to aid their escape. As the mission proceeds, Spyros and Brown are killed. Mallory and Miller are able to break into the gun emplacement, but mistakenly trip an alarm as they close the doors to the cave area. Miller rigs the guns with explosive devices and places even more explosives below the weapons on an ammunition hoist, with a trigger device set into the hoist's wheels. German soldiers force their way into the gun emplacement, but Miller and Mallory are able to escape by swimming to the boat stolen by Marian and Brown. Stavrou, badly injured, is lifted onto the boat by Mallory, which erases all ill will between them. The Germans notice the explosives on their weapons and choose to send their shells towards the Allied forces, but as the guns fire, the ammunition hoist falls low enough to trip the hidden explosives. The fortress blows up, along with all of the weapons housed within it. Mallory's unit meets up with the other British forces, but Stavrou opts to go back to Navarone with Maria. Miller and Mallory go back home, glad of their successful mission.

Reception

The Guns of Navarone had its world premiere as a Royal Command Performance on 27 April 1961 at the Odeon, Leicester Square, in London's West End, with Queen Elizabeth II and the Duke of Edinburgh in attendance. Opening in the United States in June, the film went on to gross $28.9 million in international ticket sales. After *West Side Story*, it was the second top-grossing film of 1961, earning a net profit of $18.5 million. *Guns* won two Golden Globe awards (for Best Picture and for Best Original Score) and garnered six Oscar nominations, winning for Best Special Effects. Notices were mostly favorable, but the anonymous reviewer who was at the movie's London premiere astutely noted that the film was short on meaningful characterization: "The lesson to be learned from *The Guns of Navarone* is that a well-told and exciting story does not require too many characters; nor does it need psychological undertones. It can even dispense with women. All it needs is pace and credibility" (1961, p. 18). Bosley Crowther voiced a similar judgment: "One simply wonders why Mr. Foreman, who contributed to the screen play of *The Bridge on the River Kwai*, didn't aim for more complex human drama, while setting his sights on those guns" (Crowther, 1961).

Reel History Versus Real History

There is no island called Navarone. Though perhaps inspired by the Battle of Leros, the story told by *The Guns of Navarone* is entirely fictional and more than a little far-fetched. Nonetheless, another source of inspiration for novel and film might have been Operation Brassard, the Allied invasion and capture of the island of Elba, off the west coast of Italy (17–19 June 1944). Part of that operation involved 87 men from the Free French Bataillion de Choc Commando landing at Cape Enfola in rubber dinghies, scaling the crest of the 1,300-foot Monte Tambone Ridge, and successfully taking out four gun batteries. The superguns depicted in the movie are fictional, but the Germans did possess two superguns that were used to destroy Russian fortifications during Operation Barbarossa: "Schwerer Gustav" ("Heavy Gustav") and "Dora." These were massive Krupp-made railway guns—almost twice the size of the biggest guns on WWII battleships—weighed nearly 1,350 tons, and could fire projectiles 800 mm (31.5 inches) in diameter, each weighing 7 tons, to a range of 47 kilometers (29 miles). In the movie the fictional superguns have been installed in a capacious mountain cave on a small Greek island. Their size is hard to gauge, but if they were anywhere near as huge as "Schwerer Gustav" and "Dora," such an installation would have been a logistical nightmare, if not altogether impossible.

HACKSAW RIDGE (2016)

Synopsis
Hacksaw Ridge is a biopic/war film written by Andrew Knight and Robert Schenk-kan and directed by Mel Gibson. Based on the 2004 documentary *The Conscientious Objector* and other sources, the film focuses on Desmond Doss (played by Andrew Garfield), a Seventh Day Adventist conscientious objector turned combat medic who was awarded the Medal of Honor for his heroic actions during the World War II Battle of Okinawa.

Background
During the Battle of Okinawa (1 April–22 June 1945), Pfc. Desmond T. Doss (1919–2006), a combat medic assigned with the 77th Infantry Division, risked his life to save dozens of wounded comrades, carrying them from the battlefield under heavy fire and lowering them by a rope sling down the 400-foot-high cliff face of the Maeda Escarpment (aka "Hacksaw Ridge"). During this engagement Doss was himself badly wounded. Doss's incredibly heroic actions earned him the Medal of Honor, making him the first conscientious objector to be so honored. In the 1950s Hollywood producers Darryl Zanuck and Hal B. Wallis tried to get Doss to sell them his story, but to no avail. Years later a non-Adventist named Booton Herndon wrote *The Unlikeliest Hero* (1967), a Doss biography read in 1974 by Stan Jensen, communications director for the Seventh Day Adventist Church in Canada. Convinced that Doss's saga would make a great movie, Jensen moved to Los Angeles in 1996 to be closer to the Hollywood film industry in hopes of persuading a producer to make a film about Doss. In 2001 Jensen met screenwriter-producer Gregory Crosby (grandson of Bing Crosby) during a special event at Jensen's bookstore. After reading the book Crosby agreed that it should be made into a movie. Next, Jensen and Crosby traveled to rural Georgia to convince Doss, then 82, to let them make the film. Desmond Doss had not altered his views on Hollywood; he feared that a movie would sensationalize his life and disparage his religious beliefs, but Jensen and Crosby were ultimately able to convince Doss to give his assent. Crosby wrote a treatment and he and a close friend, stunt coordinator Joel Kramer, pitched Doss's story to film producer David Permut of Permut Presentations. Permut committed to the project but it then entered a 14-year period of "development hell." The film rights changed hands several times, moving from director Terry Benedict to producer Bill Mechanic to Walden Media and then back to Bill Mechanic. Mechanic was determined to get Mel Gibson to direct the film version of Doss's

story, and although he turned it down twice (as he had when approached about directing *Braveheart* in 1995), he eventually agreed in November 2014. Simultaneously, Andrew Garfield agreed to play the main role of Desmond Doss.

Production

The filming of *Hacksaw Ridge* took place in and around Sydney, New South Wales, Australia, over 59 shooting days (29 September–17 December 2015). Properly set-dressed with period signs and cars, a street in the town of Richmond, northwest of Sydney, stood in for a street in Doss's hometown of Lynchburg, Virginia, in the 1940s. A cemetery scene was filmed at Sydney's Centennial Park. Doss's basic training scenes at Fort Jackson in 1942 were shot at Newington Armory in Sydney's Olympic Park. Some of the battlefield scenes were shot at Fox Studios' backlot in Sydney, but most were shot at a dairy farm in Bringelly, about 20 miles west of Sydney, a set that included a partial mock-up of Hacksaw Ridge. Transforming a cow pasture in Bringelly into a facsimile of the Okinawa battlefield required clear-cutting and bulldozing a 1,200-acre parcel of land, but the producers won government approval on the proviso that part of the land be rehabilitated after the shoot ended, a deal that mollified local environmentalists. For wide-angle shots of Hacksaw Ridge the filmmakers filmed cliffs near Goulburn, 120 miles southwest of Sydney. Gibson was against using computer-generated imagery (CGI) during the battle scenes, so special effects were kept at a minimum.

Plot Summary

The film opens with a young Desmond Doss (Darcy Bryce) nearly killing his brother Hal (Roman Guerriero). This experience, along with an upbringing in the church, sets Desmond on a course of nonviolence. As he becomes a young man, Doss (Andrew Garfield) charitably brings a wounded man to a nearby hospital and encounters Nurse Dorothy Schutte (Teresa Palmer). As the pair start dating, Doss voices an interest in the medical profession. After Pearl Harbor, Doss enlists in the Army. His father Tom (Hugo Weaving), an embittered alcoholic who is also a World War I veteran, is repulsed by his son's decision. Before leaving for Fort Jackson (South Carolina), Doss becomes engaged to Dorothy. Under the command of Sgt. Howell (Vince Vaughn), Doss excels in his training but becomes a pariah among the troops for steering clear of weapons and refusing to complete training on Saturdays (the Seventh-day Adventist Sabbath). Howell and Capt. Glover (Sam Worthington) try to have Doss discharged on psychiatric grounds but fail so they proceed to make Doss's life miserable so he'll quit. After finishing basic training, Doss goes on leave. While he aims to return home and marry Dorothy, he is instead arrested for refusing to carry a rifle. Dorothy pleads with Doss during her visits to prison, asking him to admit guilt so that he can be released to her without penalty. However, Doss stays true to his religious beliefs and pleads not guilty at his trial. Before Doss can be sentenced, his father, wearing his soldier's uniform, interrupts the tribunal with a letter confirming that his son's decision not to carry a gun is protected by the law. The charges are dropped, and Doss and Dorothy proceed with their marriage. Soon thereafter Doss's unit is assigned to the

77th Infantry Division and deployed to the Pacific theater. During the Battle of Okinawa, the 77th is ordered to relieve the 96th Infantry Division, whose mission is to scale and secure the Maeda Escarpment ("Hacksaw Ridge"). Although many soldiers are killed during the battle, Doss is able to save some members of his unit. After a night spent in a foxhole with a fellow soldier, Smitty (Luke Bracey), Doss and his unit face a Japanese counterattack. Smitty dies in the attack, and a number of Doss's fellow soldiers are left injured on the field. Doss comes up with a creative solution for rescuing his injured squad mates: he carries them to the edge of a cliff and lowers them to safety using a rope sling. Doss successfully saves dozens of wounded soldiers. At dawn, Doss saves Howell, and the two somehow escape from Hacksaw Ridge despite enemy fire. Capt. Glover lauds Doss for his brave efforts and confirms that the men will not move forward to their next mission without him. Doss sustains injuries from a grenade, but his unit wins their battle, and Doss makes it down the cliff with his Bible in hand. Archival footage confirms that Doss saved 75 soldiers at Hacksaw Ridge and was subsequently awarded the Medal of Honor by Pres. Harry S. Truman (12 October 1945).

Reception

Hacksaw Ridge opened on 4 November 2016 and ran until 9 March 2017 (widest release: 2,971 theaters). In those 18 weeks the movie grossed $67.2 million in North America and another $108.2 million in foreign markets, for a worldwide total of $175.3 million against a production budget of $40 million. Reviews of *Hacksaw Ridge* were overwhelmingly positive, though not without misgivings. Film critic Richard Brody found its moral sobriety superior to the patriotic naiveté of *Saving Private Ryan* but also detected troubling contradictions at its core: "When Steven Spielberg depicted the gory horrors of war in *Saving Private Ryan*, its effect was to assert that, in effect, we—their descendants—were the children of demigods, of virtual superheroes who had been through Hell on Earth to keep us safe; the idea meshes with his career-long cinematic theme and tone of filial piety. Gibson shows the same horrors with an irrepressible sense of excitement; with the best of intentions, an overt revulsion at war, and the honoring of Doss's actions, Gibson has made a movie that's nearly pathological in its love of violence—but he nonetheless counterbalances its amoral pleasures with an understanding of the psychological devastation that war wreaks" (Brody, 2016).

Reel History Versus Real History

Though Doss was nine years dead when *Hacksaw Ridge* was made, the filmmakers respected his wishes regarding authenticity and made a movie that is mostly accurate historically. With regard to Doss's motivation to eschew violence, screenwriters Robert Schenkkan, Randall Wallace (uncredited), and Andrew Knight made it more personal than religious for wider audience appeal. Schenkkan and Knight also took some liberties with the story of Doss's courtship of Dorothy Schutte and, for streamlining purposes, they omitted Doss's prior combat service in the Battle of Guam (21 July–10 August 1944) and the Battle of Leyte Gulf (17 October–26 December 1944). The movie also gives the impression that Doss's actions on

Okinawa took place during one engagement, whereas Doss's Medal of Honor citation describes his actions as taking place over three separate engagements over a 23-day period (29 April, 2 May, and 21 May 1945).

HAMBURGER HILL (1987)

Synopsis
Written and co-produced by James Carabatsos and directed by John Irvin, *Hamburger Hill* is an American war film about the siege of Ap Bia Mountain (aka "Hill 937" or "Hamburger Hill") near the Laotian border in May 1969 by U.S. forces. Though ultimately successful, the assault came at a high cost in American casualties, and the conquered position was soon abandoned because it had no strategic value.

Background
At the height of the Vietnam War, 1,800 soldiers from the U.S. Army's 3rd Battalion, 187th Infantry Regiment (part of the 3rd Brigade, 101st Airborne Division) conducted an assault on Dong Ap Bia: a 3,074-foot-high mountain situated a mile east of the Laotian border in northwestern South Vietnam. Designated Hill 937, Ap Bia was a heavily fortified enemy stronghold on steep, rugged, densely wooded terrain, defended by two North Vietnamese Army (NVA) battalions numbering at least 1,000 men. What ensued was a grueling 11-day siege (10–20 May 1969), punctuated by torrential rains, that came to be known as the Battle of Hamburger Hill. The Americans took Hill 937 but not before expending 1,000 tons of bombs, 42 tons of napalm, and 19,000 artillery rounds—and sustaining heavy casualties (70 killed; 372 wounded). Confirmed enemy dead numbered 633. Just 16 days later (5 June 1969) the U.S. Army abandoned Hill 937 because it held no strategic value: a move that generated public outrage. Screenwriter James Carabatsos served in Vietnam in 1968–1969 but was not at Hamburger Hill (he was in a military police platoon with the 1st Air Calvary Division at Quan Loi near the Cambodian border). Offended by films like *Apocalypse Now* that depicted U.S. soldiers in Vietnam as deranged war criminals or renegades, Carabatsos set out to write a film script that would highlight the extreme tenacity and valor exhibited by troops at Hamburger Hill as the best way to counter demeaning stereotypes and recuperate the Vietnam-era soldier's reputation with the American public. To ensure authenticity, Carabatsos spent years interviewing dozens of veterans who fought at Hill 937 as he developed his screenplay, which was completed in 1981. It would take Carabatsos and his co-producer, Marcia Nasatir (*The Big Chill*), another five years to find the financing that would bring his script to the screen. In the meantime British director John Irvin agreed to direct the film; Irvin had been in Vietnam in 1969, making a BBC documentary, so Carabatsos's script resonated with him.

Production
Before securing a production deal with RKO Pictures in 1986, the filmmakers hired Col. Joseph B. Covey, Jr. (U.S. Army, Retired), the actual commander of the

3rd Brigade, 101st Airborne at Hamburger Hill, as the film's technical advisor and also submitted the script to the Pentagon for vetting. Army officials suggested a series of changes for the sake of historical accuracy—and to put the U.S. military in a better light (e.g., less emphasis on soldiers patronizing prostitutes and a more upbeat ending). The filmmakers agreed and won the Department of Defense's (DOD) full support: a three-week training camp at Subic Bay Naval Base for the actors (11 then-unknowns), the use of Chinook C-47 helicopters for six days, simulated airstrikes by F-4 Phantom jets, and 30 days' availability of a UH-1 Huey helicopter (Suid, 2001, pp. 530–531). The 11-week shoot took place on the island of Luzon in the Philippines (October–December 1986)—but not before extensive site preparation. A 1,800-foot hill had to be dressed with 1,000 planted trees, five off-camera stairways were installed for access, and a large pool holding sanitized mud was constructed to ensure the actors' health (Devine, 1999, p. 267).

Plot Summary

Footage of the Vietnam Veterans Memorial in Washington, D.C., plays during the opening credit sequence. An opening prologue states: "On 10 May 1969 Troops of the 101st Airborne Division engaged the enemy at the base of Hill 937 in the A Shau Valley. Ten days and eleven bloody assaults later, the troops who fought there called it . . . HAMBURGER HILL." The film proper begins with a platoon of soldiers in combat in Vietnam in 1969, and the sequence ends with a badly wounded soldier dying on a helicopter. A platoon from B Company, 3rd Battalion, 187th Infantry receives five FNGs ("F—ing New Guys") as replacements: Joseph Beletsky (Tim Quill), who worries that he won't remember everything he has been taught; Vincent "Alphabet" Languilli (Anthony Barrile), a sex-obsessed recruit annoyed when people mispronounce his last name; David Washburn (Don Cheadle), an unassuming African American soldier; Martin Bienstock (Tommy Swerdlow), an outgoing volunteer; and Paul Galvan (Michael A. Nickles), the quietest but most capable of the new soldiers. The recruits spend their first days "in country" filling sand bags and receiving hygiene lessons before being placed in a squad commanded by Sgt. Adam Frantz (Dylan McDermott), a seasoned combat veteran who provides a crash course in combat skills. The platoon also has a new commander, Lt. Terry Eden (Tegan West), sarcastically described by Platoon Sergeant Dennis Worcester (Steven Weber) as "Palmolive f—ing soap." The platoon's machine-gun team consists of the brawny Pvt. Michael Duffy (Harry O'Reilly) and his small, bespectacled companion, Pvt. Frank "Gaigs" Gaigin (Daniel O'Shea). There are also three African American veterans in the unit: Ray Motown (Michael Boatman), Abraham "Doc" Johnson (Courtney B. Vance), and Sgt. Elliott McDaniel (Don James), a "short-timer" with less than a month left on his tour of duty. The FNGs first experience combat during an enemy mortar barrage. Frantz orders return fire that ends the attack, but several civilians are killed and one of the FNG's, Paul Galvan, is decapitated by shrapnel. Soon thereafter the troops are flown to A Shau Valley. After their arrival, the men are almost immediately fired upon and McDaniel is killed, a casualty that "Doc" Johnson bitterly blames on Frantz. The battalion is ordered to lead an assault on Hill 937 (aka "Hamburger Hill"), a position defended by a well-entrenched enemy. Between infantry assaults American warplanes drop bombs, napalm, and white phosphorus, cratering the mountain and denuding it of all its foliage. In one assault, Duffy leading the charge, comes close to breaking the enemy lines but he is killed by misdirected "friendly fire" from Huey gunships. During lulls in the fighting, members of the platoon discuss opposition to the war back home. Day after day, the shrinking platoon continues its assault on Hill 937 but cannot take the hill. The 10th assault happens during heavy rains, turning the hillside into a slippery sea of mud. Gaigin and "Doc" are shot dead, and Beletsky is injured but returns to his unit anyway. An 11th and final assault is mounted, and the remaining enemy positions near the summit are overrun but casualties soar. Murphy, Worcester, Motown, Bienstock, and Languilli are all killed and Lt. Eden is seriously wounded. Stunned by the deaths of most of his friends and comrades, a dazed Frantz is wounded during the battle. Beletsky pushes through his injuries towards the summit. Frantz also makes it to the summit and rests alongside Beletsky and Washburn as battle draws to a close. The final image is of Beletsky's haunted face as he gazes at the utter devastation below. There is constant radio chatter, but no one replies.

Reception

Released on 28 August 1987—10 months after Oliver Stone's *Platoon* and just a day after Stanley Kubrick's *Full Metal Jacket* ended its nine-week U.S. theatrical run—*Hamburger Hill* ran for a month (widest release: 814 theaters), earning $13.8 million at the box office, a fraction of what other those other two Vietnam War films earned. The movie's modest commercial performance was likely due to a number of factors: its being overshadowed by its powerful predecessors; its lacking a famous director or big-name stars; its unfashionable center-right political orientation; its restrained quasi-documentary style (devoid of allegorical flourishes or surrealism); and its bleak, brutally realistic depiction of unremitting combat ending in a Pyrrhic victory after most of the film's protagonists die. In his review for the *New York Times*, Vincent Canby focused on the movie's resolute refusal to put the battle for Hill 937 in any larger context: "It could have been made a week after the conclusion of the operation it recalls, which is both its strength and weakness, depending on how you look at it . . . The film leaves it up to the audience to decide if the war was, from the start, disastrous and futile, or if it was sabotaged by those same bleeding-heart liberals who figure so prominently in the oeuvre of Sylvester Stallone" (Canby, 28 August 1987). In his review Hal Hinson credited *Hamburger Hill* for offering "a powerful representation of the fighting" from the infantryman's point of view, but Hinson also detected "hawkish, macho posturing" in the scene where the soldiers discuss hostile attitudes toward them stateside and in another scene where Frantz castigates a film crew ('You haven't earned the right to be on this hill')." In the end, Hinson expressed grudging respect for *Hamburger Hill*: "It's a violent movie, but it doesn't have the self-satisfied, aestheticized brutality of *Full Metal Jacket*. There's a purpose to it—a sense of values. The problem is that it's tough but not tough-minded. If it had been it might have been great. Still, there's a kind of greatness in it. It takes a piece out of you" (Hinson, 1987).

Reel History Versus Real History

Because it recounts an actual battle and was painstakingly researched and written by a Vietnam veteran, *Hamburger Hill* achieves a high degree of historical accuracy. Indeed, *Hamburger Hill* has been lauded by historians and other Vietnam veterans as one of the most accurate movies ever made about the Vietnam War.

HEAVEN KNOWS, MR. ALLISON (1957)

Synopsis

Heaven Knows, Mr. Allison is a war film that tells the story of two people—a tough U.S. Marine played by Robert Mitchum and a nun played by Deborah Kerr—stuck on a Japanese-occupied island in the Pacific Ocean in the midst of World War II. The movie was adapted by John Huston and John Lee Mahin from the novel by Charles Shaw and directed by Huston.

Background

In 1952 an Australian writer named Charles Herbert Shaw (1890–1955) brought out *Heaven Knows, Mister Allison*, a novel about a tough U.S. Marine and a gentle Catholic nun stranded together on a remote island in the South Pacific during World War II who form an improbable bond and ally themselves against Japanese occupying forces. Producer Eugene Frenke optioned the film rights but let his option lapse in 1953, whereupon John Wayne and Robert Fellows tried to buy the rights, but failed. In 1954, 20th Century Fox acquired the property and initially hired William Wyler to direct and Kirk Douglas to star. A few months later, Wyler and Douglas were replaced by Anthony Mann and Clark Gable. Ultimately John Huston was hired to direct. Though the book became an international bestseller, director John Huston thought it "a very bad novel which exploited all the obvious sexual implications," but screenwriter John Lee Mahin persuaded Huston to change his mind and make a film version (Huston, 1980, p. 260). Huston and Mahin repaired to Ensenada, Mexico, in the spring of 1956 and, trading off scenes, wrote a taut screen adaptation in five or six weeks that avoided prurience and sentimentality. John Huston tried to interest Marlon Brando in the role of Cpl. Allison but Brando vacillated, so it ultimately went to Robert Mitchum, with Deborah Kerr signing on to play Sister Angela.

Production

On 1 August 1956 80 20th Century Fox crew members arrived on the island of Tobago, a southern Caribbean locale off the coast of Venezuela chosen for two reasons: it was, according to Huston, a "dead ringer for a South Seas island" and was also a location where the company could use blocked UK funds, receive British film financing, and qualify for the Eady Levy (a British tax on box office receipts used to support the film industry) (Robertson, p. 139). Native workers were hired to build a thatched-roofed village, a small church, and an elevated filming platform. The script called for a company of Japanese troops occupying the island, but then film was shot in Trinidad and Tobago, and there were no Japanese inhabitants. The filmmakers located six people who spoke Japanese in an emigrant neighborhood in Brazil and hired them to play the Japanese officers in the film. Fifty or so Chinese blue-collar workers living on the island were hired to play the remaining Japanese troops, which angered the locals because their service industry was disrupted as a result. Actual filming occurred between September and November.

Plot Summary

In the South Pacific in 1944, U.S. Marine Corporal Allison (Robert Mitchum) and his recon party are disembarking from a U.S. Navy submarine when they are spotted and fired upon by the Japanese. The submarine goes into a dive, abandoning the scouts. Allison drifts across the ocean in a raft for days on end and finally comes ashore upon an island. He comes across a desolate chapel, empty save for a single occupant: Sister Angela (Deborah Kerr), a new nun who has not taken her vows. Sister Angela arrived with a priest four days prior to Allison, with the aim of rescuing a fellow clergyman. However, they found the Japanese inhabiting the island, and the natives abandoned Sister Angela and her priest companion, who soon died. Marine and nun spend time alone in their spot on the island, but Japanese troops arrive to set up a camp, and the two newer inhabitants flee to a nearby cave. As night falls, Sister Angela and Allison witness the flashes of naval gunfire at sea. A smitten Mr. Allison declares his love for Sister Angela. Overcome, she goes out into a heavy rainstorm and becomes sick. Allison carries her back to the cave to recover, just as the Japanese soldiers return to the island. As he is retrieving blankets from the Japanese camp to warm Sister Angela, Allison is discovered and pursued by a Japanese soldier. The soldier finds the cave that Allison and Sister Angela have been hiding in and forces the pair to decide between surrender or death by grenade. Just as they are trying to find a way out of their predicament, Americans begin to bomb the island in preparation to land. Allison decides to do what he can to assist the American troops by disabling the Japanese artillery while the soldiers lie in wait in their bunkers. He successfully sabotages the Japanese weaponry and saves a number of American soldiers as a result. As the pair are rescued, Allison and Sister Angela bid each other farewell. Allison lets his love go, recognizing Sister Angela's dedication to her faith.

Reception

Released on 13 March 1957, *Heaven Knows, Mr. Allison* made $4.2 million at the box office; budgeted at $2.9 million, it was a modest financial success. Deborah Kerr's performance as Sister Angela drew Oscar and Golden Globe nominations and won her the New York Film Critics Circle Award for Best Actress. Robert Mitchum received a BAFTA nomination for Best Foreign Actor. The screenplay by John Lee Mahin and John Huston garnered Oscar and WGA Award nominations, and Huston also earned a Directors Guild Award. Reviews were good. Bosley Crowther pronounced *Heaven Knows, Mr. Allison* "a film that is stirring and entertaining," called the Tobago location "exciting" and "drenched with atmosphere," and noted that the cast "while small, [is] excellent" (Crowther, 1957).

Reel History Versus Real History

In the novel Cpl. Allison comes to the island after escaping from the Battle of Corregidor (May 1942). The film is set two years later, in 1944, when the United States was clearly winning the Pacific war—a time frame adjustment necessary to make the Marine capture of the island a more credible event. The likelihood that a U.S. Marine and a Catholic nun would end up sharing a remote island cave in the Pacific is slim to none but makes for a compelling story. Almost as unlikely is Robert Mitchum's age. He was 39 when he made the film. The average age of a U.S. Marine in WWII was about 20, and many enlisted men were in their teens.

HELL IN THE PACIFIC (1968)

Synopsis

Hell in the Pacific is a World War II film directed by John Boorman about an American soldier (Lee Marvin) stranded on a remote island in the Pacific Ocean with a Japanese soldier (Toshirō Mifune)—two sworn enemies who battle each other but must reach an accord in order to survive.

Background

After collaborating on *Point Blank* (1967) a now-esteemed neo-noir, director John Boorman and actor Lee Marvin teamed up for another film immediately thereafter: *Hell in the Pacific*, an offbeat tour de force about two soldiers—one American, the other Japanese—who fight out World War II in miniature on a deserted island. *Hell in the Pacific* (successive working titles: "The Enemy Is War," "Two Soldiers—East and West," and "The Enemy") derives from an original story by producer Reuben Bercovitch, turned into a screenplay by Alexander Jacobs and Eric Bercovici. Japanese dialogue was polished by Shinobu Hashimoto, who turned the script into a scene-chewing farce, a gambit that initially caused some major headaches for John Boorman, who couldn't get his Japanese co-star Toshirō Mifune to play his role "straight" and not for broad comic effect.

Production

Logistical problems loomed large. The movie was shot on location on Koror and other Palau islands in the isolated Caroline Islands of Micronesia, 950 miles due east of the Philippines, in spring of 1968. Cast and film crew lived aboard a ship and went to work on a Palau beach every day in a tank landing craft. Palau is near the equator, and the four-month-long shoot in 90-degree heat and high humidity was a trying experience for all involved.

Plot Summary

In 1944, after his plane is shot down at sea, an unnamed U.S. Marine pilot (Lee Marvin) lands his rubber dinghy on a remote Pacific atoll, only to discover that it is already occupied by a lone Japanese naval officer (Toshirō Mifune). After becoming aware of each other's presence on the island, the men engage in a fierce cat-and-mouse game. Eventually, the Japanese officer overpowers the American, brings him back to his camp, and ties his arms in a yoke-like harness. The American soon escapes, however, captures his lone enemy in turn, and holds him captive. Unhappy with the idea of taking a prisoner, he lets his enemy go, signaling a truce. When the Japanese officer begins building a small raft, his American counterpart gets past his skepticism and offers to help. After the raft is finished, the two set off for a collection of islands, eventually reaching land. They find the island empty, but discover a bombed Japanese camp with supplies. The two soldiers get along amiably until the Japanese soldier sees images in an old *Life* magazine that depict his people wounded, suffering, and dead. The two men then part on unhappy terms. The original version of the film's ending had Mifune's character kill two Japanese soldiers who stumble upon Marvin's character and decapitate him. The idea was eventually scrapped, and Boorman shot an ending in which Marvin and Mifune drop their truce and return to fighting each other. Executive producer Henry "Hank" G. Saperstein found Boorman's ending anti-climactic, so devised a more decisive finale that practically ruined the picture: an explosion (borrowed from another film) destroys the building and both soldiers are apparently killed. Both versions survive.

Reception

Although it features only two characters, *Hell in the Pacific* ran up $7.35 million in production costs due to its highly remote Pacific island shooting location and many work interruptions due to bad weather and the obstreperous behavior of Toshirô Mifune. Poor timing—released at the height of the Vietnam War—coupled with the film's unusual premise, lack of subtitles translating the Japanese, and equally unsatisfying alternate endings severely limited its appeal; it earned only $1.33 million in North America and $1.9 million abroad for a total of $3.23 million in worldwide box office receipts: a net loss of $4.1 million, making it one of the biggest bombs in the short history of ABC films, which soon went bankrupt.

Reel History Versus Real History

Though the one-on-one war scenario *Hell in the Pacific* depicts is highly improbable, if not altogether preposterous, the men who enacted it brought authenticity to their roles. Both co-stars, Toshirô Mifune and Lee Marvin, served in the armed forces of their respective countries during World War II. Mifune saw no action—he was a quartermaster in charge of issuing saké to kamikaze pilots—but Marvin was a much-decorated Marine combat veteran ("I" Company, 3rd Battalion, 24th Marines, 4th Marine Division). He had not been back to the Pacific since his war days 23 years earlier and was forced to face some horrific memories; Marvin's platoon was ambushed on Saipan on 18 June 1944 and nearly wiped out, and Marvin was badly wounded.

HOPE AND GLORY (1987)

Synopsis

Hope and Glory is a British comedy/drama/war film written, produced, and directed by John Boorman and based on his own boyhood experiences during World War II's London Blitz (the film's title is derived from the traditional British patriotic song "Land of Hope and Glory").

Background

Forty years after World War II British director John Boorman (*Deliverance*) wrote *Hope and Glory*, a coming-of-age script based on his own memories of family life in Surrey and later in Shepperton (both London suburbs), from the ages of six to nine (1939 to 1942), a period punctuated by The Blitz (7 September 1940–10 May 1941). Proposing an unconventional WWII film, Boorman had trouble attracting Hollywood financing. He raised part of the budget by pre-selling European rights to some 20 distributors before securing principal backing from Embassy Home Entertainment and Columbia Pictures, companies owned by Coca-Cola but sold to De Laurentiis Entertainment Group and Nelson Entertainment during pre-production—a bumpy transition that nearly derailed the project. Initially visualized as a $10 million movie, *Hope and Glory* had its studio budget trimmed to $7.5 million. Consequently Boorman was forced to defer his own fees as writer, producer, and director; cut salaries; and scale back the scope of the film, for example, eliminating black and white sequences depicting Billy Rohan's fantasies about the war (Hoyle, 2012, pp. 151–161).

Production

Hope and Glory was filmed at various locations in the Greater London area over 55 shooting days (4 August–21 October 1986). For the film's main set, crews under the direction of Boorman's production designer Tony Pratt built a 200-yard-long replica of Rosehill Avenue, Carshalton (Surrey), on the disused runway at the former Wisley Airfield, also in Surrey (10 miles southwest of the center of London). The faux street—constructed at a cost of £750,000—featured the facades of six pairs of facing semi-detached houses built on scaffolding, supplemented by cut-outs of more houses and of the London skyline in the distance. The house where the Rohans lived was fully built of brick and wood because it had to be burned down. The small backyard gardens typical of semi-detached row houses were also constructed, as were ruins of bombed buildings. The entire set covered 50 acres, making it the largest movie set built in the UK since the early 1960s. Queen's Manor Primary School, Lysia Street, Fulham (London), served as Billy's school, and The Vine Inn, Hillingdon Hill, in Uxbridge was used as the setting for Billy's father's enlistment site. Other scenes by the river were shot near Shepperton Lock.

Plot Summary

A black and white newsreel announces the start of the war, but six-year-old Billy Rohan (Sebastian Rice Edwards) prefers Hopalong Cassidy Westerns. In a voice-over (by Boorman himself) the adult Bill Rowan remembers playing in the family garden when war was declared (3 September 1939). Billy's father, Clive (David Hayman), immediately enlists, but is assigned a desk job due to his age. Left at home is Billy's mother, Grace (Sarah Miles); Billy; and his two sisters: Dawn (Sammi Davis) and Sue (Geraldine Muir). For their safety, Billy's mother decides to send Billy and Sue (ten and six years old, respectively) to live with an aunt in Australia, but at the last minute she cannot bring herself to put them on the boat train. Mac (Derrick O'Connor), Billy's father's best friend (and a former beau of Billy's mother), spends a lot of time at the Rohans' house after his own wife, Molly (Susan Wooldridge), runs off with a Polish aviator. With their own spouses out of the picture, Grace and Mac begin to fall in love again but do not act on their feelings. Meanwhile, Dawn (a teenager) sneaks out of the house at night for trysts with Cpl. Bruce Carrey (Jean-Marc Barr), a Canadian soldier, and soon finds herself pregnant. For his part, Billy joins other boys his age happily playing in and around bombed-out buildings. One day, though, while Mac and the Rohans are at the seaside, their house burns down (from an ordinary fire, not the result of a bomb blast), forcing them to go live with Grace's curmudgeonly father, George (Ian Bannen), in his bungalow on the River Thames. Billy enjoys a halcyon summer there. Madly in love with Dawn, Bruce goes absent without leave (AWOL) to marry her, but is arrested by the military police right after the wedding. Soon thereafter, Dawn gives birth to their child. At the end of the summer Billy has to return to his old school in suburban London but joyfully discovers that it has been destroyed by a stray Nazi bomb. Billy shouts, "Thank you, Adolf!" In voice-over the adult Bill recalls, "In all my life, nothing ever quite matched the perfect joy of that moment. My school lay in ruins and the river beckoned with the promise of stolen days."

Reception

Hope and Glory had its premiere on 21 August 1987 at the Montreal Film Festival. In the weeks following the film's UK premiere (3 September 1987: the 48th anniversary of the United Kingdom's entry into World War II), it was screened at film festivals in Spain, Japan, and Italy. On 17 September 1987, three weeks before *Hope and Glory* was scheduled to premiere in the United States at the New York Film Festival, Columbia CEO David Puttnam was forced to resign. Puttnam had been a strong supporter of the movie so his departure adversely affected the U.S. rollout, which was anemic at best. Columbia opened *Hope and Glory* at two theaters in New York City on 16 October 1987 and gradually expanded into a modest 100 theaters by December, but stinted on promotion and advertising (e.g., it ran no TV ads). To make matters worse, Columbia then had a dispute with one of its major distributors and the film was pulled from circulation before Christmas—except for a single theater in Greenwich Village. Luckily Columbia's new CEO, Dawn Steel, liked *Hope and Glory* and soon revived its fortunes. Just before the 1988 Oscar nominations were announced, the movie was re-released in the United States. During its second run (5 February–14 April 1988; widest release: 328 theaters), it grossed a respectable $9.7 million at the box office for a total of $10 million (international box office totals are unknown, but reports indicate that the film had brisk box office returns in the UK). Commercially successful after a slow start, *Hope and Glory* was honored with numerous film awards. These included 13 BAFTA nominations and 7 wins (for Best Actress in a Supporting Role: Susan Wooldridge; Best Actor in a Supporting Role: Ian Bannen; Best Actress: Sarah Miles; Best Cinematography: Philippe Rousselot; Best Costume Design: Shirley Russell; Best Direction: John Boorman; Best Editing: Ian Crafford); 5 Oscar nominations; and 3 Golden Globe nominations and 1 win (Best Motion Picture—Comedy or Musical). Reviews were uniformly strong.

Reel History Versus Real History

Like his fictional counterpart, Billy Rohan, John Boorman lived through The Blitz as a small boy (the Rohans are a thinly disguised version of his own family). Intimately familiar with life in suburban London during the war—his own experience, the look of the streets, the fashions, the mores, the routine war measures (e.g., food rationing, barrage balloons, air raid shelters, the effects of the bombings, etc.)— Boorman created a historically authentic movie that resonated deeply with Britons who had lived through that era. He also created a refreshingly revisionist narrative that ran counter to Britain's monolithic official history of World War II as a righteous struggle against fascism, marked by resolute national fortitude and sacrifice. As historian Geoff Eley astutely notes, "While deromanticizing the grand story of 'the people's war' ('according to folk memory . . . our last great collective achievement as a nation'), [*Hope and Glory*] also deploys a different kind of romance, namely, the private story of a young boy's entry into experience, the opening of his expanded horizons, via the interruption of ordinary life's rhythms and repetitions. The film tells this story by deliberately distancing the public script of the just and anti-fascist war, because for most ordinary experience (it implies), this was beside the point" (Eley, 2001, p. 827).

HURT LOCKER, THE (2008)

Synopsis

The Hurt Locker is an American war film written by Mark Boal; directed by Kathryn Bigelow; and starring Jeremy Renner, Anthony Mackie, Brian Geraghty, Christian Camargo, Ralph Fiennes, David Morse, and Guy Pearce. The film follows the exploits of an EOD (Explosive Ordnance Disposal) team charged with finding and neutralizing IEDs (improvised explosive devices), that is, bombs, during the Iraq War.

Background

In December 2004, after navigating a sea of Department of Defense (DOD) red tape, freelance journalist Mark Boal spent two weeks embedded with the 788th Ordnance Company, a U.S. Army EOD disposal unit based at Camp Victory in Baghdad, Iraq. During that brief period Boal accompanied Staff Sergeant Jeffrey S. Sarver and his two-man team to watch them do the incredibly dangerous job of finding and disarming IEDs planted by Iraqi insurgents. Boal subsequently published an article on the experience—"The Man in the Bomb Suit" (*Playboy*, September 2005)—and then worked with film director Kathryn Bigelow to make a fiction film based on the events he had witnessed. Boal and Bigelow collaborated on a script, originally titled "The Something Jacket," and sought $20 million in financing, but none of the major Hollywood studios were interested in a movie about an unpopular war. Instead, in the summer of 2006, they signed a $13 million deal with Nicholas Chartier's Voltage Pictures, an independent production company. Bigelow then went about assembling a cast, hiring a few "name" actors (Ralph Fiennes, David Morse, Evangeline Lilly, and Guy Pearce) but mostly casting unknowns so as not to distract viewers with famous faces and dilute verisimilitude. Jeremy Renner, cast in the film's lead role as Sgt. Will James, researched his part by spending time with an EOD team at Fort Irwin National Training Center in California. As for location, filming in Baghdad was simply too dangerous, so Amman, Jordan, was selected as its substitute. Production ran into a major snag when the Jordanians would not clear the detonation equipment and supplies needed by special effects supervisor Richard Stutsman. Just before the shoot was scheduled to begin, Bigelow was able to get a customs official to authorize release of most of the materials.

Production

Principal photography on *The Hurt Locker* took place in Amman, Jordan, over 44 days between late July and early September 2007. For cast and crew, discomfort reigned; there were no air-conditioned trailers or private bathrooms during a midsummer shoot that saw temperatures often reach 120° F. Anxious to put viewers into the thick of the action Bigelow and her British director of photography, Barry Ackroyd (*United 93*), employed an intensified sort of cinema vérité style that featured lots of subjective camera, reaction shots, tight framing, slow motion, and rapid switching between points of view. These effects were made possible by using a high-speed Phantom HD camera and up to four handheld Super 16-mm Aaton XTR-Prods to shoot the action from multiple angles simultaneously: a technique that produced over 200 hours of raw footage, edited by Chris Innis and Bob Murawski over an eight-month period down to 131 minutes (a 92:1 shooting ratio). The film's final firefight was filmed in a Palestinian refugee camp that the filmmakers were told was off limits as too dangerous, but Bigelow persisted and was given permission to shoot there.

Plot Summary

The film opens with an on-screen quotation from *War Is a Force That Gives Us Meaning*, a best-selling 2002 book by Chris Hedges, a *New York Times* war correspondent and journalist: "The rush of battle is a potent and often lethal addiction, for war is a drug." In the opening scene, in Baghdad during the Iraq War, a bomb-handling Talon robot breaks down, forcing Staff Sergeant Matthew Thompson (Guy Pearce) to get close to an IED when it is remotely detonated by cell phone, killing him. Sergeant First Class William "Will" James (Jeremy Renner), a former U.S.

Anthony Mackie (left) and Jeremy Renner play U.S. Army bomb disposal specialists during the Iraq War in Kathryn Bigelow's *The Hurt Locker* (2008). (Summit Entertainment/Photofest)

Army Ranger, arrives to replace Sgt. Thompson as the team leader of a U.S. Army EOD unit. James' team includes Sergeant J. T. Sanborn (Anthony Mackie) and Specialist Owen Eldridge (Brian Geraghty). James' unorthodox bomb disposal methods are judged reckless by Sanborn and Eldridge, and tensions mount. Meanwhile, James takes a liking to an Iraqi youth nicknamed "Beckham" (Christopher Sayegh), who tries to sell him DVDs. When they are assigned a detonation job, Sanborn thinks about murdering James by "accidentally" causing an explosion before the team is ready, and upon hearing this thought process, Eldridge is put on edge. En route to their camp, the soldiers come face to face with five gun-toting men wearing traditional Arab clothing who have gotten a flat tire. James' squad has an anxiety-ridden conversation with their leader (Ralph Fiennes), who then admits that he and his men are private contractors and British mercenaries. They also boast about having captured men pictured on the most sought-after Iraqi baseball cards. All involved in the encounter are suddenly fired upon, and while the prisoners try to escape, the mercenary leader recalls that the bounty on their heads reads "dead or alive," leading him to shoot the captives. Sanborn and James procure a borrowed Barrett M82 .50-caliber rifle and shoot down three attackers, leaving Eldridge to shoot a fourth. Later that week, during a routine warehouse sweep, James discovers the body of a young boy—whom James identifies as Beckham—in which a live bomb has been surgically implanted. During evacuation, Lt. Col. John Cambridge (Christian Camargo), the camp's kindly psychiatrist and a friend of Eldridge's, dies when an IED explodes. Eldridge takes on the blame for this loss. James is then ordered to take care of a gas tanker denotation and decides to look for the responsible party, assuming that they are still close at hand. Sanborn objects, but when James leaves, he and Eldridge reluctantly follow. Iraqi insurgents end up catching Eldridge and taking him prisoner, but James and Sanborn save his life. The next day, Beckham walks up to James, seemingly alive, and passes by silently. Eldridge blames James for his wounds. Sanborn and James' team is commanded forth on another mission, right at the final two days of their rotation. They arrive as instructed to find a peaceful, Iraqi civilian with a suicide bomb taped to his chest. James attempts to remove the bomb, but the man's vest has too many locks and, with time running out, James is forced to abandon the man to certain death. The bomb detonates. Distraught by the man's death, Sanborn tells James that he wants to go home. After Bravo Company's rotation ends, James returns home to his ex-wife Connie (Evangeline Lilly) and their infant son (they still live with him) but James quickly tires of suburban life. One night, James tells his small child that there is only a single thing that he can be sure that he loves. Soon after, James begins a new tour with a 365-day rotation.

Reception

The Hurt Locker was first screened at the Venice Film Festival on 4 September 2008. The movie was then shown at 10 other American and international film festivals over the next 10 months before its domestic wide release on 26 June 2009. *The Hurt Locker* proved to be a solid box office hit, earning $17 million in North America and another $32.2 million in foreign markets, for a total gross of $49.2 million—more than four times its production budget. The movie also won a slew of awards, including nine Academy Award nominations and six Oscars: for Best Picture (Kathryn Bigelow, Mark Boal, Nicolas Chartier, and Greg Shapiro); Best Director (Kathryn Bigelow, the first woman to win an Oscar in this category); Best Writing, Original Screenplay (Mark Boal); Best Editing (Bob Murawski and Chris Innis); Best Sound Mixing (Paul N. J. Ottosson and Ray Beckett); and Best Sound Editing (Paul N. J. Ottosson). Not surprisingly, reviews were almost universally adulatory. Roger Ebert gave it four out of four stars and wrote, "*The Hurt Locker* is a great film, an intelligent film, a film shot clearly so that we know exactly who everybody is and where they are and what they're doing and why. The camera work is at the service of the story. Bigelow knows that you can't build suspense with shots lasting one or two seconds. And you can't tell a story that way, either—not one that deals with the mystery of why a man like James seems to depend on risking his life" (Ebert, 8 July 2009). Mick LaSalle wrote, "*The Hurt Locker* has a fullness of understanding that sets it apart. On the day of its release, this one enters the pantheon of great American war films—and puts Kathryn Bigelow into the top tier of American directors" (LaSalle, 2009). Whereas the vast majority of film critics hailed the movie's technical virtuosity and lauded its apolitical emphasis on the soldier's-eye view of the Iraq War, a few critics on the Left found these tendencies ideologically suspect. In her review, Tara McElvey noted that "*The Hurt Locker* sets itself up as an anti-war film" but really functions as pro-war propaganda because it makes war an unbearably exciting and meaningful existentialist enterprise compared to "the tedium of American life, with its grocery-shopping, home repairs, and vapid consumerism . . . For all the graphic violence, bloody explosions and, literally, human butchery that is shown in the film, *The Hurt Locker* is one of the most effective recruiting vehicles for the U.S. Army that I have seen" (McElvey, 2009).

Reel History Versus Real History

Though it *seems* a convincing depiction of an EOD squad's activities during the Second Iraq War, veterans found the film rife with exaggerations and inaccuracies. In an interview with James Clark for *Task & Purpose*, a news website for veterans, Kollin Knight, an Afghanistan War veteran and former EOD technician, detailed a list of the film's misrepresentations, starting with a key scene where Sgt. Will James uncovers six 155-mm artillery shells wired together into a massive IED. Knight: "And he just lifts up six of them, all daisy-chained together for no good purpose . . . You'd never do that by hand, it's amazing that he did . . . How the f— is one arm that strong to just pick up all of these 155s?" Knight went on to note that each shell can weigh between 70 and 100 pounds. Though it makes for gripping cinema, Knight avers that a real EOD tech would never do what James did: "You don't know what you're doing, what's in there, which is why you don't just pick s— up by hand and toss it around. Which is why we stress using robots and doing things remotely and slowly and cautiously, instead of just 'Oh s—, I just found a bunch of them, I'm gonna pick them all up.'" By the same token, Knight finds the film's daredevil cowboy characterization of Will James patently absurd: "For the s— that he does he could easily lose his certification, end up in prison, or get completely removed from EOD. Realistically it wouldn't happen. He would not exist." Knight also found fault with James' nocturnal pursuit of the Iraqi professor: "Nobody does this. It simply doesn't happen. It makes no sense, and anyone who's ever served in a post-9/11 warzone probably reacted to that scene the same way: What the f—?" (Clark, 2016).

ICE COLD IN ALEX (1958)

Synopsis
Ice Cold in Alex is a British war film directed by J. Lee Thompson and starring John Mills and Anthony Quayle. Based on a 1957 novel of the same title by British Desert War veteran Christopher Landon, the film follows the perilous journey of a British military ambulance from eastern Libya to Alexandria, Egypt, after the fall of Tobruk to Rommel's Afrika Korps in May 1942.

Background
Englishman Christopher Guy Landon (1911–1961) served with the 51st Field Ambulance and the 1st South African Division in North Africa during the Second World War. After the war Landon became a novelist specializing in noir thrillers. "Escape in the Desert," a fictional story grounded in his war experiences, was serialized in six consecutive issues of *The Saturday Evening Post* (21 July–5 August 1956) and then expanded into his fourth novel, entitled *Ice Cold in Alex* (Heinemann, 1957). Associated British Picture Corporation (ABPC) secured the film rights, then hired Landon to work with staff screenwriter T. J. Morrison and script supervisor Walter Mycroft to adapt the novel to the screen, a process that coincided with Landon's turning his scenario into a full-length novel—though novel and script differ markedly. W. A. Whitaker was brought in to produce and J. Lee Thompson (*The Dam Busters*; *Guns of Navarone*) to direct. Initially the project had the support of the British military, but once it became apparent that the film would have little recruiting value, support evaporated.

Production
Ice Cold in Alex was shot mostly in Libya over a two-month period in the fall of 1957; Egypt was ruled out because of the recent Suez Crisis. The shoot in Libya was a difficult one, with cast and crew being plagued by weeks of temperatures exceeding 100°, windblown sand, and swarms of flies that were fought off with DDT, a pesticide now banned as toxic to humans. The quicksand scene was actually filmed in an ice-cold artificial bog at Elstree Studios in London—a grueling experience for Quayle and Mills. The brief love scene between Diana Murdoch and Anson toward the end of the film was originally eight minutes longer and far steamier but was largely excised, per order of the British Board of Film Censors. The famous bar scene in Alexandria at the end of the film, shot at Elstree just before Christmas 1957, required John Mills to drink real beer because ginger ale and other

substitutes didn't look authentic on film. By the 14th and final take, Mills was actually quite inebriated and had to go to his trailer and sleep it off. The film's last scene, outside the bar, was shot in the "Maidan Djzair" (Algeria Square) in Tripoli, Libya.

Plot Summary

Capt. Anson (John Mills) is an officer commanding a British Royal Army Service Corps (RASC) motor ambulance company in the Western Desert Campaign during World War II. When it becomes obvious that Tobruk is about to fall to Rommel's Afrika Korps, Anson and most of his unit are ordered to evacuate to Alexandria, hundreds of miles to the east. Joining Anson, who is suffering from exhaustion, battle fatigue, and alcoholism, are Sgt. Major Tom Pugh (Harry Andrews) and two young nurses: Diana Murdoch (Sylvia Syms) and a very panicky Denise Norton (Diane Clare), who initially has to be restrained and sedated. The vehicle they drive across the desert back to British lines is a worn-out Austin K2/Y ambulance, nicknamed "Katy." Anson loses his liquor supply at the outset; it is in the DDMS Brigadier's (Liam Redmond) command vehicle, which takes a direct hit from a German artillery shell, killing the brigadier and his staff officer (Allan Cuthbertson). When the group stops at a refueling station they come across Capt. van der Poel (Anthony Quayle), a tall and muscular Afrikaner South African Army officer carrying a large backpack. After van der Poel shows Anson three bottles of high-quality gin, Anson lets him join them. The journey proves to be extremely challenging. They have to leave the main road after a bridge is blown and are forced to traverse a minefield, with Anson and van der Poel tensely walking ahead of Katy to ferret out mines. As soon as they cross safely, they encounter an Afrika Korps detachment. Anson, who is now driving and slightly drunk, decides to try to outrun the Germans. The Germans open fire—mortally wounding nurse Norton—and soon catch up to Katy. Van der Poel, who claims to have learned German while working in Southwest Africa, is able to parlay with the enemy, who inspect their vehicle and let them go. Later, when Anson is informed that Norton has died, he is filled with remorse and admits that he's a drunk; still, he motivates himself by telling Diana Murdoch that he will buy them all ice cold lagers when they finally reach the safety of Alexandria (the "Alex" of the title). After a night's stopover, they fashion a makeshift grave marker and bury Denise Norton in the desert. Just then a German light tank loaded with infantry approaches. The Germans disarm them, inform them that Tobruk has fallen, and let them go after their officer converses with van der Poel and inspects his knapsack. Low on water, they confer. Anson suggests they travel southeast, cutting straight through the Qattara Depression in northwestern Egypt—a giant sinkhole 190 miles long that lies below sea level and is covered with salt pans, sand dunes, and salt marshes. Fearing Katy will sink in the mire, Pugh and van der Poel overrule Anson so they start out on a more circuitous route. Soon one of Katy's rear springs breaks. During its replacement, van der Poel's great strength saves the group when he briefly supports Katy (which weighs two tons) on his back when the jack collapses, averting damage that would have rendered the ambulance useless. Just then an Allied plane passes over and drops a message, informing them that the Germans have advanced east along the coast road, all the way to El Daba, 100 miles west of Alexandria. They will be intercepted and captured if they continue on their present course, so they decide to go through the Qattara Depression after all. Pugh, already troubled by van der Poel's lack of knowledge of South African Army customs, covertly follows him when he leaves the group and heads off into the desert with his pack and a spade (supposedly to dig a latrine). Pugh reports that he thinks he saw a radio antenna, but Anson cautions them against confronting van der Poel just yet. They drive on and soon arrive at Siwa Oasis, where they meet a British Long Range Desert Group (LRDG) officer (Peter Arne) disguised as an Egyptian tribesman, who arranges to supply them with water and petrol. They start driving through the Qattara Depression the next morning but have to pause when Katy begins to overheat and Anson faints from thirst and exhaustion. Later, at night, they decide to use the ambulance headlights to see what Van de Poel is really up to when he goes off with his spade and knapsack. Trying to evade the light, van der Poel steps into quicksand and starts to go under but he has the presence of mind to push his pack into the ooze—though not before the others see that it contains a radio set. They manage to save van der Poel by dragging him out with a cable attached to Katy. Afterwards, Anson deliberately throws van der Poel's South African Army uniform shirt into the quicksand—a move that puzzles Diana. The others now realize that van der Poel is a Nazi spy but they decide not to confront him. The next night, Diana seduces Anson. During the final leg of the journey Katy and her crew face a steep, sandy escarpment as they try to exit the Qattara Depression. The men take turns laboriously rotating Katy's starter hand crank in reverse in order to inch her up the slippery gradient. Almost near the top, Katy slips out of gear and descends the slope again, and the grueling, Sisyphean process must be repeated. This time, Van der Poel's superior strength is again crucial to achieving success. When they finally reach Alexandria they repair to Anson's favorite bar, where he orders his coveted cold beer. Before they have all finished their first round, a Corps of Military Police (CMP) lieutenant (Basil Hoskins) arrives to arrest Van der Poel. Anson, who had prearranged the arrest with a CMP checkpoint officer (Michael Nightingale) as they entered the city, orders him to wait until the appointed time. Anson shows his gratitude to Van der Poel by offering him a deal: if he tells Anson his name, then Anson will ensure that he is labeled as a prisoner of war (POW) rather than a spy, thus escaping execution. Van der Poel admits that his name is Hauptmann Otto Lutz and that he is an engineering officer with the 21st Panzer Division. Pugh removes Lutz's fake dog tags to keep him safe from the military police. Lutz finishes his beer, shakes hands all around, and declares that they were "all against the desert, the greater enemy. I've learned a lot about the English, so different than what I've been taught." He bids his erstwhile comrades "Auf Wiedersehen" before being driven away into captivity.

Reception

Ice Cold in Alex premiered in London on 24 June 1958 to decent box office and good reviews (e.g., the reviewer for *The London Times* called it "a realistic study of human resolution in the face of mounting adversities"). Entered into competition at the 8th Annual Berlin Film Festival shortly thereafter, the movie won the FIPRESCI Award, sharing it with Ingmar Bergman's *Smultronstället* (*Wild Strawberries*). It also received a Golden Bear nomination at the 1958 Berlin Film Festival and three BAFTA nominations in 1959. *Ice Cold in Alex* was not released in the United States until 22 March 1961—unfortunately, under the misleading title, *Desert Attack*, and in a radically truncated version (54 minutes shorter) that made it an unwatchable travesty of the original movie.

Reel History Versus Real History

Like his fictional counterparts, Anson and Pugh, author Christopher Landon was a British ambulance officer in North Africa, well familiar with Austin K2/Ys and the rigors of life in the North African desert, fighting Rommel's Afrika Korps: intimate knowledge that lent the novel and film authenticity. Nolan's original story and novel are pure fiction, but, according to Sue Harper and Vincent Porter, Nolan based Sgt. Major Pugh on a longtime friend and made him the novel's central protagonist father figure to Anson and the love interest of Sister Murdoch (Harper and Porter, 2007, p. 88). The movie makes Anson its protagonist and Diana Murdoch his love interest. The film also elides most of the backstories of the four principal characters that are provided in the novel, and both book and film contain some far-fetched thriller elements. One feature hard to credit is the notion that a German spy would attach himself to a solitary ambulance in retreat and radio back constant reports to headquarters. Highly implausible from a physics standpoint is the scene showing Katy being inched up a steep sand hill by hand cranking its starter gear in reverse after disconnecting the spark plugs. The technique could actually work on hard, level ground but the steep gradient (perhaps 20 to 25 degrees), deep sand, and the sheer weight of the ambulance (actually three tons, not two, as mentioned in the film) would abet gravity in rendering the task physically impossible.

IN WHICH WE SERVE (1942)

Synopsis

In Which We Serve is a British war film written by Noël Coward and directed by Coward and David Lean. A patriotic propaganda film made during the Second World War with the full backing of the Ministry of Information, *In Which We Serve* is a fictionalized recounting of the exploits of Lord Louis Mountbatten, commander of the destroyer HMS *Kelly*, which was sunk during the Battle of Crete (May 1941). Coward composed the film's musical score and also starred as the ship's captain.

Background

During World War II Lord Louis "Dickie" Mountbatten (1900–1979), the second cousin, once removed, of Queen Elizabeth II, commanded the British Royal Navy's 5th Destroyer Flotilla aboard his flagship, HMS *Kelly*. A K-class destroyer (1,695 tons) commissioned on 23 August 1939, *Kelly*'s ill-fated time in service lasted only one year and nine months. On 23 May 1941, during the Battle of Crete, the ship was bombed and sunk by German Stuka dive-bombers. Out of a crew of 240 men, 81 lost their lives. Capt. Mountbatten and 158 other crew members survived. Back in London six weeks later (3 July 1941) Mountbatten regaled his friend, the famed playwright Noël Coward, with the tragic story of *Kelly*'s sinking. Coward was deeply moved by Mountbatten's account, which he found "absolutely heart-breaking and so magnificent" (Coward, 2000, pp. 7–9). Days later Coward was approached by film producer Anthony Havelock-Allan of Two Cities Films. The company's founder, Filippo Del Giudice, a fervent anti-Fascist, wanted to make a propaganda film to support the British war effort and needed a well-known writer to pen the screenplay. Coward took on the assignment with the proviso that it be "a naval propaganda film" based on the *Kelly* saga, that he star in the film, and that he be given complete creative control. Coward, being a man of the theater, knew nothing about filmmaking so, at the suggestion of Carol Reed, he took on young David Lean as his co-director and hired Ronald Neame as his cinematographer. In the latter months of 1941 Coward wrote an overlong, rambling screenplay (working title: "White Ensign") that was deemed unfilmable. Lean, Neame, and Havelock-Allan worked with Coward to revise the script (uncredited), with Lean suggesting they use a flashback structure for purposes of narrative economy. Mountbatten, who remained involved with the production throughout, also advised Coward to tone down his depiction of Kinross as a wealthy landed aristocrat—a figure too obviously suggestive of Mountbatten himself.

Production

Shooting of *In Which We Serve* began on 5 February 1942 at Denham Film Studios, 10 miles northwest of London. Other locations included the naval dockyard at Plymouth (opening scene), Dunstable Downs in Bedfordshire (for a picnic scene), and Smeaton's Tower on the Plymouth Hoe seafront (for the shore leave scenes between Shorty Blake and his wife Freda). HMAS *Nepal*, an N-class Royal Australian destroyer based at Scapa Flow, "played" HMS *Torrin*. Though they were officially "co-directors," Noël Coward let David Lean take charge of the production while he focused on his own role as Capt. Kinross. After six weeks on the set, Noël Coward became bored with the mechanics of filmmaking and let Lean fully assume the directorial duties. Thereafter Coward came to the studio only when scenes in which he appeared were being filmed. At one point Mountbatten and Coward invited the royal family to the set. Their visit, reported in newsreels, lent the film valuable advance publicity. After five months of filming, principal photography ended on 27 June 1942.

Plot Summary

The film opens with a line of narration by Leslie Howard (uncredited), "This is the story of a ship," followed by footage of shipbuilding in a British dockyard. A title card reads "CRETE May 23rd 1941." HMS *Torrin* and other British destroyers fire on and sink German transports in a nighttime engagement during the Battle of Crete. The next morning *Torrin* comes under heavy attack by a flight of German Junkers 88 twin-engine bombers. After the ship takes two direct hits, it begins to sink rapidly, and Capt. Edward Kinross (Noël Coward) orders his crew to abandon ship. A group of sailors and their commanding officers find a life raft just as survivors are fired upon by German planes. The narrative moves to a series of flashbacks of the men who have made it to the raft. It begins with Capt. Kinross, who remembers a time in the summer of 1939 when a naval ship, the HMS *Torrin*, is sent into battle off the coast of Norway. During the battle, a rattled stoker (Richard Attenborough) flees from his station while Ordinary Seaman Shorty Blake (John Mills) commits to his post even after his other crew members are torpedoed. Once the ship safely harbors, Capt. Kinross lauds his crew's bravery while cautioning the sailor who abandoned his post. Back in the present, the men on the raft watch the *Torrin* begin to sink. Blake is wounded by German fire. Blake then remembers first meeting his soon-to-be wife, Freda (Kay Walsh) during his leave. It turns out that the *Torrin*'s Chief Petty Officer Walter Hardy (Bernard Miles) is her relative. When Hardy and Blake return to their posts on the water, Freda goes to live with Hardy's wife and mother-in-law. The *Torrin* assists during the Dunkirk evacuation of 1940. Meanwhile, the Luftwaffe's nightly Blitz is decimating British towns and cities. During his time at sea, Blake receives a letter with the news that Freda has given birth to the couple's son in the midst of an air raid. However, the letter also reveals that Hardy's wife and mother-in-law were killed during the very same raid. Blake breaks the awful news to Harvey, and the flashback ends. The scene recommences in the present just as the life raft survivors watch the sinking Torrin get swallowed by the sea. The men give a last "three cheers" for the *Torrin*, but German planes swoop overhead and shoot at the raft, resulting in more deaths and injuries, when suddenly another German plane rakes the raft with machine-gun fire, killing and wounding more men. On board, Capt. Kinross collects addresses from the dying sailors, and sends telegrams to relatives, letting them know the sad news about their loved ones. Kinross and his fellow survivors are ferried to a military post in Alexandria, Egypt. Kinross gives an inspiring speech to his fellow survivors, stating that the deaths of their comrades and their ship should only spur them on to fight all the harder in the next battles that they will face. Capt. Kinross shakes the hand of each man as they collect their new assignments. An epilogue in voice-over praises Britain's seamen and Capt. Kinross is shown in command of a battleship, ordering its massive main guns to open fire on the enemy.

Reception

In Which We Serve premiered on 27 September 1942 in London as a benefit for several naval charities. The movie then went into wide release throughout Great Britain to critical accolades and strong box office results. It ultimately took in 2 million pounds—more than double its production cost. Released in the United States just before Christmas 1942, *In Which We Serve* was also popular with American audiences and critics. Manny Farber pronounced it the movie of the year, and Bosley Crowther was almost grandiloquent in his praise, calling it "one of the most eloquent motion pictures of these or any other times . . . truly a picture in which the British may take a wholesome pride and we may regard as an excellent expression of British strength" (Crowther, 1942).

Reel History Versus Real History

Loosely based on Lord Mountbatten's command of the HMS *Kelly*, *In Which We Serve* is an impressively accurate representation of life (and death) aboard a Royal Navy destroyer during the Second World War. The movie also offers a realistic depiction of life on the home front, with wives missing their husbands away at war—some never to return—and with the civilian populace coping daily with the terrors of the Nazi Blitz. For added verisimilitude Lord Louis Mountbatten insisted that the film's extras be replaced with real sailors. Similarly, the troops used in the movie's Dunkirk evacuation scene were acted by real soldiers from the 5th Battalion Coldstream Guards, some who had actually taken part in the Dunkirk evacuation. The scene that depicts the cowardly young stoker deserting his post was based on a real incident that occurred on 14 December 1939 on HMS *Kelly*. A sailor panicked and left his post after the *Kelly* struck a mine, sustaining damage to her hull. After the ship was towed in, Mountbatten rounded up his crew and delivered a speech that Coward enacts almost verbatim in the film. In the scenes depicting the sinking of the *Torrin*, the Royal Air Force (RAF) contributed captured German planes flown by British pilots, normally used for battle training.

IVAN'S CHILDHOOD [RUSSIAN: IVANOVO DETSTVO] (1962)

Synopsis

Ivan's Childhood is a Soviet war film directed by Andrei Tarkovsky. Based on Vladimir Bogomolov's 1957 short story, "Ivan," the film features child actor Nikolai Burlyayev in the title role as an orphan boy turned Red Army soldier who is motivated by a desire for vengeance after the German invaders slaughter his family.

Background

When Hitler's Wehrmacht invaded the Soviet Union in June 1941 a 15-year-old schoolboy named Vladimir Bogomolov (1926–2003) joined millions of his countrymen in the desperate fight to defend his homeland. Bogomolov won medals for bravery, somehow survived the war, and went on to become a writer who specialized in "Great Patriotic War" fiction. One of his earliest stories was *Иван* [*Ivan*] (1957), a first-person Socialist Realist novella about a doomed 12-year-old orphan who becomes a Soviet army scout to avenge the death of his family at the hands of the Nazis. Commissioned by Mosfilm to write a film adaptation, screenwriter Mikhail Papava made Ivan more heroic and even gave the story a happy ending. In Papava's screenplay, entitled *Vtoraya Zhisn* [*A Second Life*], Ivan is not executed by the Germans—as he is in Bogomolov's novel—but sent to Majdanek extermination camp. Freed by the advancing Soviet army, Ivan later marries and raises a family. When film director Eduard Abalov began shooting Papava's screenplay in 1960, Bogomolov objected to Papava's bastardization of his story and insisted that the script by revised to more accurately reflect the source material. The Soviet Arts Council agreed and terminated the project in October 1960. In June 1961

Mosfilm revived the project and assigned it to Andrei Tarkovsky, a recent VGIK (Gerasimov All-Russian State Institute of Cinematography) film school graduate, who had applied to direct the film, after being told about *Ivan* by his friend, cinematographer Vadim Yusov, who would go on to shoot the picture.

Production

Shooting on location near the Dnieper River city of Kaniv, in central Ukraine, Tarkovsky had to work fast because much of the film's budget had already been used up by Eduard Abalov. From the start of the shoot to the assembly of a rough cut (16 June 1960–30 January 1961), the film took less than eight months to make. It also came in 24,000 rubles under budget, partly because Tarkovsky edited as he went along, not in post-production (Johnson and Petrie, 1994, p. 67). Though they stayed much closer to Bogomolov's narrative than Papava and Abalov, Tarkovsky and his uncredited co-screenwriter, Andre Konchalovsky, added four dream sequences and slightly surreal visual elements to limn Ivan's psychological trauma. They also added a romance subplot. Such poetic license did not sit well with Bogomolov or with the Mosfilm bureaucrats supervising the project. Over the course of the production they subjected Tarkovsky to 13 "editorial" sessions, presided over by eminent Russian literary artists and filmmakers. All sorts of changes, major and minor, were suggested, but Tarkovsky's mentor, director Mikhail Romm, was able to argue against the cutting of any footage.

Plot Summary

The setting is Soviet Russia during World War II. After a brief, idyllic dream sequence, Ivan Bondarev (Nikolai Burlyaev), a young Russian, startles awake inside a windmill and runs across a decimated landscape. He continues on through a swamp and across a sizable river. When he reaches the far bank, Russian soldiers capture him and hand him over to Lt. Galtsev (Evgeny Zharikov), who interrogates him. The boy adamantly demands that the lieutenant call "Number 51 at Headquarters" to report him. Galtsev calls the headquarters and is informed by Lt.-Col. Grayaznov (Nikolai Grinko) that the boy is to be given writing materials and left to compose a high-priority report. Grayaznov also asks that the boy be treated kindly while in Galtsev's care. Cut-together dream sequences reveal that Ivan's family has been exterminated by the Germans. Ivan managed to run away and linked up with a group of partisans, later joining Grayaznov's troops. Ivan's anger over the deaths of his family members has led him to fight on the frontline, performing recon missions for his army unit. Grayaznov and the soldiers under his command take a liking to Ivan and try to convince him to enter a military academy. However, Ivan is dead set on avenging his family and the other poor souls who died at extermination camps. With interspersed dream sequences, the film spends the majority of its time in a cellar room where the soldiers wait for new orders and Ivan anticipates his next mission. The walls of the cellar are covered with desperate messages from German prisoners. At long last, Galtsev and another soldier bring Ivan back across the river under the cover of darkness. The remaining soldiers return to the other shore. The scene shifts to Berlin after the fall of the

Third Reich. A brief montage derived from newsreel footage includes shots of the ruined Reich Chancellery, the bodies of Joseph Goebbels and his children, and German General Alfred Jodl signing the surrender documents (8 May 1945). We learn from Galtsev's voice-over narration that Capt. Kholin has been killed in action. Galtsev also finds a dossier in the rubble of a Nazi government building in Berlin showing that Ivan was captured and hanged by the Germans. In a final flashback of Ivan's childhood, he is shown playfully running a foot race against a young girl on a sunny day at the beach. When he rushes up to a dead tree, the film ends.

Reception
Released on 6 April 1962, *Ivan's Childhood* sold 16.7 million tickets in the Soviet Union, making it one of Andrei Tarkovsky's most commercially successful films. Highly praised by critics, the film shared the Golden Lion with Valerio Zurlini's *Cronaca familiar* [*Family Portrait*] at the 23rd Venice Film Festival (May 1962) and also won top director's honors at the 6th San Francisco Film Festival (November 1962). After it won the Golden Lion, Mario Alicata, the editor of *L'Unità* (the official newspaper of the Italian Communist Party), denounced the film as displaying "petit-bourgeois tendencies" whereupon Jean-Paul Sartre wrote an open letter to Alicata, defending *Ivan's Childhood* as "one of the most beautiful films I have had the privilege of seeing in the last few years" and noted that "Ivan is mad . . . is a monster; that is a little hero; in reality, he is the most innocent and touching victim of the war: this boy, whom one cannot stop loving, has been forged by the violence he has internalized" (Sartre, 1965). Ingmar Bergman, who had already made many of his greatest films, would later describe his discovery of *Ivan's Childhood* as "like a miracle." Filmmakers Krzysztof Kieślowski and Sergei Parajanov have also praised the film and cited it as a major influence on their work.

Reel History Versus Real History
Though the story that *Ivan's Childhood* tells is fictional, Vladimir Bogomolov based it on his real-life experiences as an underage combatant (he reached official recruitment age in July 1944, after having already been in combat for three full years). Bogomolov's story was not unusual. After the terrible defeats in the summer and fall of 1941, the Red Army was desperate for manpower; many underage boys—known as "sons of the regiment"—were allowed to join the army. Russian war orphans like the fictional Ivan Bondarev were supposed to be sent to orphanages but sometimes unofficially joined the Red Army or partisan units. Like Ivan, they were usually used in reconnaissance roles.

J

JARHEAD (2005)

Synopsis

Jarhead is an American war film based on former U.S. Marine Anthony Swofford's 2003 memoir of the same title. Directed by Sam Mendes and starring Jake Gyllenhaal as Swofford, with Jamie Foxx, Peter Sarsgaard, and Chris Cooper, the film recounts Swofford's five-month stint in the Persian Gulf before and during the First Gulf War in 1990–1991.

Background

Anthony Swofford, the son of a Vietnam-era Marine Corps veteran from Fairfield, California, joined the Marines in 1989 at the age of 18. On 14 August 1990, just after the start of the First Persian Gulf War (2 August 1990–28 February 1991), Swofford was deployed to Riyadh, Saudi Arabia, as part of Operation Desert Shield. He served as a scout sniper with the Surveillance and Target Acquisition (STA) Platoon of 2nd Battalion, 7th Marine Division, but was not in combat during his deployment in the Persian Gulf. On 4 March 2003—16 days before the start of "Operation Iraqi Freedom"—Scribner's published Swofford's memoir: *Jarhead: A Marine Chronicle of the Gulf War and Other Battles* (the WWII-era slang word "jarhead" derives from the "high and tight" Marine haircut that gives the head a jar-like appearance). Praised by critics for its vivid evocation of a modern soldier's life, *Jarhead* became a national bestseller. While the book was still in galley form, Swofford sold the film rights for $2 million to producers Douglas Wick and his wife, Lucy Fisher, and Universal budgeted $70 million for production. William Broyles Jr. (*Apollo 13*) was hired to write a script based on the book and had a draft finished by early 2004. In May 2004 Sam Mendes (*American Beauty*) was hired to direct. Christian Bale, Emile Hirsch, Leonardo DiCaprio, Tobey Maguire, Shane West, Josh Hartnett, and Joshua Jackson were all considered for the role of Swofford, but in late October 2004, Jake Gyllenhaal won the part. The filmmakers sought the assistance of the Department of Defense (DOD), but Pentagon officials decided the script was not a "feasible interpretation of military life."

Production

Jarhead was shot in sequence between January and May 2005. Filming began on the sound stages of Universal Studios. The first location work—the Camp Pendleton scenes—took place on George Air Force Base in Victorville, California, a decommissioned but still partially active facility about 75 miles northeast of Los Angeles. The Marine barracks scenes in Saudi Arabia were filmed in and around the Grand Salon at California State University, Channel Islands in Camarillo, California. Principal photography ended almost exactly five months after it began with filming at the 200,000-acre North Algodones Dunes Wilderness Area (aka Imperial Sand Dunes or Glamis Dunes) in southeast California, 20 miles north of the U.S.-Mexico border. Ironically, at five months, the shoot took the same amount of time that Swofford spent on the Arabian Peninsula.

Plot Summary

In 1989, Anthony "Swoff" Swofford (Jake Gyllenhaal) undergoes U.S. Marine Corps training before being stationed at Camp Pendleton (Oceanside, California). Swofford pretends to be sick to get shirk his duties, but Staff Sergeant Sykes (Jamie Foxx) sees some potential in the recruit and enrolls Swofford in his Scout Sniper course. After a grueling training regimen, the number of soldiers in the course is winnowed down to eight candidates. Swofford makes the cut and becomes a sniper. His roommate, Cpl. Alan Troy (Peter Sarsgaard), serves as spotter. During the Iraqi invasion of Kuwait, Swofford and his fellow troop members are sent to the Arabian Peninsula for Operation Desert Shield. The Marines are keyed up for battle, but are forced to wait five long months before coalition forces are fully deployed in the area and ready to attack Saddam's Iraqi Army. In the meantime, life for Swofford and his fellow Marines is monotonous. To relieve the tedium, Swofford throws a Christmas party, complete with illegal alcohol, and has Pfc. Fergus O'Donnell (Brian Geraghty) cover his watch. O'Donnell mistakenly sets off a crate of flares and wakes up the entire crew. Sykes pieces together what has happened and demotes Swofford from lance corporal to private. Demotion, humiliating duty, the intense desert sun, the tedium of daily life at the camp, and Swofford's suspicion that his girlfriend is being unfaithful drive him toward a mental collapse. Swofford pulls a rifle on O'Donnell and then makes a complete 180 and demands that O'Donnell shoot him instead. Operation Desert Storm, the U.S. led-coalition offensive to drive Iraqi forces out of Kuwait, finally begins (on 17 January 1991), and the Marines head to the Saudi Arabia–Kuwait border. Swofford discovers that Troy has a hidden criminal record, one that will get him discharged from the crew once they get home. The Marines advance through the desert, encountering no enemy resistance, but are mistakenly attacked by U.S. warplanes and sustain "friendly fire" casualties. Later, the Marines encounter the infamous "Highway of Death," a road between Kuwait and Iraq that is littered with dead, mutilated Iraqi soldiers and burned vehicles—a grotesque sight that causes Wofford to vomit. The retreating Iraqis set fire to oil wells, causing a rain of crude black oil droplets to fall from the sky. At long last, Swofford and Troy are sent on a sniper mission. Lt. Col. Kazinski (Chris Cooper), the leader of their unit, orders them to eliminate one of two Iraqi Republican Guard officers in a nearby Iraqi airfield. As Swofford goes to shoot, Major Lincoln (Dennis Haysbert) interrupts the mission and phones in an airstrike. Not wanting to see their first real mission quashed, Swofford and Troy beg to proceed, but the two are overruled and forced to watch bitterly as American warplanes bomb the Iraqi airfield. Iraqi resistance never materializes, and the First Gulf War ends after just four days. Swofford goes home on leave and finds that his girlfriend, Kristina (Brianne Davis), has moved on to a new boyfriend. We see snippets of other soldiers trying to reintegrate into civilian life, and also see Sykes serving as a first sergeant in the Iraq War. Later, O'Donnell visits Swofford and informs him of Troy's death in a car accident. Swofford attends Troy's funeral and sees some of the other men from their unit. The film ends with the group reminiscing about the war.

Reception

Jarhead opened on the weekend of 4–6 November 2005 and closed on 19 January 2006 (widest release: 2,448 theaters)—four years post-9/11, seven months after the U.S. invasion of Iraq that toppled Saddam Hussein's regime, and in the midst of deadly and relentless al Qaeda insurgency, that is, the evolving military-political catastrophe known as the Second Gulf War, against which *Jarhead* was still topical in a general sense but, at the same time, yesterday's news. During its 14-week run, the movie grossed $62.6 million in domestic box office receipts. Foreign box office receipts came in at $34.2 million, for a worldwide total of $96.8 million. After theaters took their percentage of the gross, Universal made about $53.2 million, a sum that left the studio at a considerable loss (overhead, i.e., production and worldwide P&A budgets combined, probably exceeded $100 million). Though it tanked at the box office, *Jarhead* did well on the home video market, posting over $52 million in retail sales, considerably mitigating Universal's losses. Reviews were mixed. For film critic Mick LaSalle, the movie's ambivalent perspective "feels right. The ambivalence runs deep. *Jarhead*, at least to a degree, blows the myth of the noble warrior. Yet it also suggests that a nation depends on that myth and its appeal to certain kinds of impressionable people. So that at the end of his experience, Swofford doesn't know if he's been enhanced or played for a sucker. Neither do we" (LaSalle, 2005). Writing from a radical Left perspective, Joanne Laurier criticized both book and film for lacking any meaningful perspective beyond the nihilistic machismo of young Marines: "Swofford's work, however, remains extremely limited, and open to truly deplorable interpretation, because he has failed to make any serious assessment, after more than a decade, of the Gulf War, its objective origins and consequences . . . Both film and book fail to perceive that the deep demoralization of the U.S. forces flows ultimately from their soul-destroying assignment to conquer the world on behalf of a bankrupt imperialism" (Laurier, 2005).

Reel History Versus Real History

When *Jarhead* was released, the U.S. Marine Corps Public Affairs office released a memo warning that "the movie's script is an inaccurate portrayal of Marines in general and does not provide a reasonable interpretation of military life" (quoted in Fick, 2005). Though he thought the Marines' official condemnation "a bit much," ex-Marine Fick took issue with some of the incidents depicted in *Jarhead*: "Could a Marine really be shot and killed in training without any fallout whatsoever? Would dozens of Marines celebrate the end of the war by dancing around a bonfire, gleefully firing their rifles into the night sky? Could Swofford's sniper team actually get abandoned on the battlefield, alone and forgotten? Not in my Marine Corps." Interviewed by an *L.A. Times* staff writer after seeing the film at a theater near Swofford's home base, Camp Pendleton, active-duty and retired Marines gave *Jarhead* mixed reviews. A retired Marine thought that "too often, *Jarhead* shows Swofford and his buddies acting "more like a college fraternity house than a disciplined Marine unit." However, Marines who saw the film praised it for its accurate portrayal of "Semper Fi" comradery: kinship-like bonds formed in a combat zone that last a lifetime (Perry, 2005).

JOHNNY GOT HIS GUN (1971)

Synopsis

Johnny Got His Gun is an American anti-war film written and directed by Dalton Trumbo and starring Timothy Bottoms, Kathy Fields, Marsha Hunt, Jason Robards, Donald Sutherland, and Diane Varsi. Based on Trumbo's eponymous 1939 novel, the film concerns an American World War I soldier who survives the loss of all four limbs and most of his face in a shell blast and is subsequently consigned to a living death in a military hospital.

Background

According to Dalton Trumbo, his searing anti-war novel, *Johnny Got His Gun* was inspired by newspaper accounts regarding two grievously wounded WWI soldiers, one Canadian, the other British. On a trip to Canada in August 1927 the Prince of Wales visited a military facility for soldiers and encountered a limbless and mostly faceless soldier, with whom he could only communicate by kissing the man on the forehead. The other case involved a British major who was "so torn up that he was deliberately reported missing in action. It was not until years later [1933]— after the victim had finally died alone in a military hospital, that his family learned the truth" (Flatley, p. 79). Haunted by images of intact minds trapped inside shattered bodies, Trumbo wrote *Johnny Got His Gun* in 1938, a novel about an American soldier with his face and limbs blown off but still possessed of his full mental faculties (the book's title ironically references the popular WWI recruitment song, "Over There," by George M. Cohan, which contains the opt-repeated phrase, "Johnnie get your gun"). Ironically published on 3 September 1939—just two days after the start of World War II—*Johnny Got His Gun* sold over 18,000 copies and won the National Book Award (then called the American Book Sellers Award). In 1964 Trumbo and Spanish filmmaker Luis Buñuel collaborated on a screen adaptation of *Johnny* in Mexico but by the time Trumbo had the script finished in September 1965, Buñuel's producer, Gustavo Alatriste, had run out of money so the project was scrapped. The escalating war in Vietnam once again made *Johnny Got His Gun* topical and reignited Trumbo's pacifist zeal; he pitched his script all over Hollywood but it was rejected 17 times before a production deal was signed with producer Bruce Campbell in April 1968. Though he was 63 and had never directed a film, Trumbo decided to direct. Though offered $800,000 in financing from Allied

Artists, Trumbo opted to accept a $750,000 financing package put together by a group of 25 investors led by Simon Lazarus (producer of Herbert J. Biberman's 1954 strike movie, *Salt of the Earth*) and Ben Margolis, trusted friends and associates.

Production

The shoot lasted 42 days (2 July 1970–26 August 1970), was filmed at 23 locations, and went over budget. According to an August 1971 article in *American Cinematographer*, the hospital scenes were filmed at Producers Studio on Melrose Avenue in Hollywood. A small, private lake near Lake Tahoe, California, was used for some flashback sequences. Battlefield sequences were shot in Chatsworth, California. The carnival barker scenes were filmed at El Mirage Dry Lake in the Southern Mojave Desert. The bakery was located in an abandoned factory in Culver City, California. "Christ's" carpentry shop was a shed in Highland Park, and the house in which Joe's father died, located at 55th St. in Los Angeles, was the actual house where Trumbo's father died in 1926. In post-production the film was edited down from a rough cut of over three hours to its original running time of 112 minutes, and then to 111 minutes, to qualify for a "GP" rating.

Plot Synopsis

During World War I, a badly wounded soldier is saved by a trio of surgeons (Eduard Franz, Ben Hammer, and Robert Easton), although the chief surgeon, Col. M. F. Tillery (Franz), declares that the young soldier has no higher brain functions. Tillery is determined to study the soldier as a living specimen and insists that if he had more than mere basal metabolic functions, he would not allow him to live. Unknown to Tillery or the other medical personnel, the soldier, a 20-year-old American named Joe Bonham (Timothy Bottoms), has his full mental faculties. While he lies in the hospital, drugged and swathed in bandages, Joe wonders where he is and drifts into a reverie of the night before he left for the war, when he was with his sweetheart, Kareen (Kathy Fields). Despite her pleading with him not to enlist, Joe insists that he must, and the couple makes love for the first time. Back at the hospital, Joe realizes that although he can feel his blood pumping, he cannot hear his pulse, which means that he is deaf. In great pain and sensing that he is covered with bandages, Joe surmises that he been critically wounded. Believing that he can hear a telephone ringing, Joe then remembers the night that his father (Jason Robards) died. When his mind returns to the present, Joe realizes that the stinging sensation he feels is Tillery removing the stitches from his shoulder where his right arm has been amputated. Tillery then orders the staff to keep Joe in a locked room, with the windows covered so that no one will be able to see him. Still completely covered, except for his forehead, Joe floats in a drugged state and imagines himself at the train station before he and his new buddies shipped out. They play cards with Christ (Donald Sutherland), who instructs the others, who are describing how they are going to die, to leave Joe alone when they protest that he will not actually be killed. In the hospital, Joe's sutures are removed from his hips, as both of his legs have also been amputated, and he shrieks in horror to himself. As he is overwhelmed by his inability to communicate, Joe's tenuous grasp on reality slips even more. Recalling his bucolic boyhood in Colorado, before his family moved to Los Angeles, Joe remembers his mother's religious faith and his father's love for his fishing pole. Awake again, Joe forces himself to explore his face from the inside and realizes he no longer has a tongue or teeth or even a jaw. To his horror, Joe senses he has also lost his nose, eyes, and ears; that his face is cratered from his forehead to his throat. Joe's thrashing prompts the nurse to sedate him, and as he drifts off, he has a nightmare about a rat chewing on his forehead. Unable to distinguish between dreams and reality, Joe imagines himself in Christ's carpentry shop, where he asks Christ for help. Each of Christ's suggestions fail, as Joe cannot brush the rat from his face if it is real, nor yell to awaken himself if he is having a nightmare. Joe is awakened in the hospital by the footsteps of two nurses, and the head nurse, angered that Joe is so isolated, insists that the shutters be opened so that he can have sunshine and that his bed be properly made up with sheets. Joe is thrilled by the sensory changes and constructs a scheme to track the passage of time. A year later, Joe laments that he does not know exactly how old he is, nor when the year he has counted began. Recalling the war, Joe relives the night he was wounded. In a trench with some British soldiers, Joe is writing a letter to Kareen when an officious British colonel (Maurice Dallimore) orders Cpl. Timlon (Eric Christmas) to remove the stinking corpse of an enemy soldier entangled in barbed wire nearby and give him a decent burial. Timlon and several men, Joe included, go out that night to bury the German soldier but they come under heavy artillery fire and Joe is hit by a shell. Pondering his fate, Joe then recalls his family's visit to a carnival freak show and imagines his father as a barker, advertising Joe as "The Self-Supporting Basket Case." Joe's reverie ends when a new young nurse (Diane Varsi) enters the room. Exposing Joe's chest, the sympathetic woman begins to cry, and Joe is moved to feel her tears upon his skin. The nurse prompts Joe to think of Kareen, who chastises him for leaving her pregnant and alone, although Joe assures her that in his mind, she will stay young and beautiful forever. Later, on a wintry night, the nurse begins to trace letters with her finger onto Joe's bare chest. He soon realizes that she is writing "Merry Christmas" and nods his head in affirmation. Joe is overjoyed; he now has an exact date from which to tell time. After hallucinating a Christmas celebration at the bakery at which he used to work, Joe finds himself in a forest setting where he encounters his father, who advises him to seek help by "sending a telegram" using the Morse code that he and his friend Bill learned as children, and Joe realizes he can tap out a message by nodding his head. Excited, Joe begins tapping an SOS by a series of nods, and the young nurse realizes that this is not merely an automatic muscular response. The doctor sedates Joe, but when Tillery visits the hospital, the nurse brings him to Joe's bedside. One of the other officers present recognizes Joe's SOS, and it dawns on the shocked men that Joe is not brain dead but has been completely conscious the whole time. The men, especially the chaplain, castigate Tillery for condemning Joe to such a hellish existence. When asked what he wants, Joe pleads to be exhibited to the public. The brigadier general refuses so Joe then responds, "Kill me." Although she has been ordered to sedate him, the nurse says a prayer and then clamps shut Joe's breathing tube to put him out of his misery.

Joe blesses her for releasing him from his agony, but before Joe dies, the brigadier general returns, opens the air clamp, and orders the nurse to leave. Feeling the nurse's footsteps fading away, Joe despairs. After the doctor injects him, Joe weakly continues tapping out his SOS, knowing that he is condemned to his private hell until death releases him in his old age.

Reception

After it was accepted for "out-of-competition screening only" at the 24th Cannes Film Festival (May 1971), the festival's panel of critics unanimously declared that *Johnny Got His Gun* deserved to be in the main festival. The film went on to win the Grand Prix Spécial du Jury and the FIPRESCI Prize. Director Claude LeLouche (*A Man and a Woman*), who was in attendance at its screening, wept and pronounced *Johnny* "the greatest film I've ever seen" (Haber, p. 63). Also entered at the Atlanta Film Festival five weeks later, the movie won the Golden Phoenix Award for "Best of Festival" and the Golden Dove Peace Prize. Subsequent commercial exhibition, however, was extremely limited and the film lost money. Reviews were likewise mixed. Roger Ebert liked it: "Trumbo has taken the most difficult sort of material— the story of a soldier who lost his arms, his legs, and most of his face in a World War I shell burst—and handled it, strange to say, in a way that's not so much anti-war as pro-life. Perhaps that's why I admire it" (Ebert, 1971). Film critic Walter Lowe was more ambivalent. Though he termed it "excellent and highly recommended," Lowe felt that Trumbo "got carried away" with "overly surrealistic camera work on the dream sequences," an approach that "that tended to separate the dream scenes from the memories, which is contrary to the intent of the novel, which ran dreams and memories and reality together so they were barely distinguishable from one other" (Lowe, 1971).

Reel History Versus Real History

For a soldier to lose all four limbs and his face in a bomb blast and still survive in hospital sequestration was an extreme rarity but evidently did happen; as noted earlier, the terrible injuries suffered by Joe Bonham were based on two or three actual cases. One might, however, take issue with Trumbo's depiction of Joe's medical treatment—or lack thereof. Missing limbs were replaced with prosthetic ones, and army doctors made heroic efforts to reconstruct war-shattered faces through plastic surgery. Failing that, prosthetic faces were devised. Still, it is plausible that a so-called "basket case" of the severity of Joe Bonham might have elicited the kind of sequestration and non-treatment shown in *Johnny Got His Gun*.

K

KAGEMUSHA [THE SHADOW WARRIOR] (1980)

Synopsis

Kagemusha is an epic war film by Akira Kurosawa set in the Sengoku period of Japanese history that tells the story of a petty criminal who is taught to impersonate a dying daimyō (warlord) to dissuade his enemies from attacking his now-vulnerable clan. The daimyō is based on Takeda Shingen, and the film ends by depicting the actual Battle of Nagashino in 1575.

Background

In the five years after the release of *Dersu Uzala* (1975), director Akira Kurosawa (*Seven Samurai*) worked on developing three film projects: a samurai version of *King Lear* entitled *Ran* (Japanese for Chaos); Edgar Allan Poe's "Masque of the Red Death" (never filmed); and *Kagemusha*, a screenwriting collaboration with Masato Ide about a petty thief who impersonates a feudal warlord. Kurosawa could not secure funding for *Kagemusha* in Japan until the summer of 1978, when he met with two of his greatest admirers: American directors George Lucas and Francis Ford Coppola. After Lucas and Coppola persuaded 20th Century Fox to pre-purchase foreign distribution rights for $1.5 million, Toho Co. Ltd. (Tokyo) put up the bulk of the funding: 100 million yen ($5 million). With a $6.5 million budget, *Kagemusha* was the most expensive film made in Japan up to that time. It was also the most meticulously planned. In the years spent finding financing Kurosawa made hundreds of storyboard drawings and paintings mapping out the look of every shot and scene. Location scouting for a movie set in 16th-century Japan proved to be challenging; pervasive industrialization after World War II rendered much of the country visually unsuitable for a period film. Kurosawa visited dozens of medieval castles before choosing Himeji Castle (40 miles west of Kobe, on Japan's main island of Honshu), Iga-Ueno Castle (40 miles southeast of Kyoto, also on Honshu), and Kumamoto Castle (on Japan's most southwesterly island of Kyushu). Battle scenes were filmed on Hokkaido, Japan's northernmost and least developed island, utilizing hundreds of hand-picked extras and 200 specially trained horses, flown in from the United States. Many of the riders were female members of various Japanese equestrian organizations whom Kurosawa preferred because he found them more daring than most men.

Production

As Kurosawa scholar Donald Richie notes, "Of all the films of Kurosawa, *Kagemusha* was the most disaster-ridden" (Richie, 1996, p. 205). Kurosawa's cinematographer,

Kazuo Miyagawa, had to drop out due to failing eyesight brought on by diabetes. He was replaced by Takao Saito and Masaharu Ueda (supervised by Asakazu Nakai). Next, Kurosawa and his composer, Masaru Sato, parted ways after intractable disagreements over the film's score. Sato was replaced by Shinichiro Ikebe. Then Shinaro Katsu, Japan's leading comic actor for whom Kurosawa wrote the starring roles of Shingen and the thief, quit or was fired (accounts vary) on the first day of shooting. Stage actor Tatsuya Nakadai was hired to replace Katsu. Though disrupted by a typhoon and by Nakadai falling off his horse and spending time in the hospital, the nine-month shoot in 1979 went only a week or so over schedule. For the climactic Battle of Nagashino, Kurosawa had to anaesthetize dozens of horses to simulate their having been slain on the battlefield; he had only a half-hour to shoot the battle's aftermath before the horses started to wake up. Assembling a rough cut from daily rushes as he went along, Kurosawa completed the film's final cut just three weeks after the shoot ended.

Plot Summary

During Japan's Sengoku, or "Warring States," period (c.1467–c.1603), Takeda Shingen (Tatsuya Nakadai), daimyō (i.e., feudal warlord) of the Takeda clan, meets with his brother Nobukado (Tsutomu Yamazaki) and an unnamed thief (also played by Tatsuya Nakadai) whom his brother has saved from certain death using the thief's remarkable resemblance to Shingen. The brothers decide that the thief could be an asset, as he could be used as a double for security purposes or could prove useful as a kagemusha (a political decoy). Later, Shingen's army lays siege to a castle of rival warlord Tokugawa Ieyasu (Masayuki Yui). One evening, on a visit to the battlefield, Shingen is shot by a sniper who has been tracking him. Before dying from his wound, he orders his army to withdraw and tells his officers that his death must remain a secret for three years. Meanwhile, unaware that he is dead, Shingen's rival warlords—Oda Nobunaga (Daisuke Ryū), Tokugawa Ieyasu (Masayuki Yui), and Uesugi Kenshin (Eiichi Kanakubo)—ponder the meaning and consequences of Shingen's withdrawing his army. Nobukado brings the thief to Shingen's officers, suggesting that the thief serve as a kagemusha and thus act as Shingen. However, Shingen's officers feel that the thief cannot be trusted, so he is released. The Takeda leaders dispose of Shingen's remains in Lake Suwa. Tokugawa sees the disposal of the remains and deduce that Shingen has perished. The thief overhears the spies and offers to work as a kagemusha for the Takeda clan. They accept. The spies follow the Takeda to their home, but are surprised to find the kagemusha acting as Shingen. Mimicking Shingen's every mannerism, the thief effectively fools the spies, Shingen's retinue, Takeda Katsuyori's son, and even Shingen's own grandson. During the clan council meeting, the kagemusha is instructed to listen to all of the generals until they reach an agreement and then simply agree with the generals' recommended course of action and move to dismiss the council. Shingen's son, Katsuyori (Kenichi Hagiwara), is bitter about his father's lengthy, posthumous deception, as it puts a hold on his own inheritance and rise in the clan leadership. In 1573, the Tokugawa and Oda clans assault the Takeda lands, and Katsuyori defies his general and initiates a counterattack. During the Battle of Takatenjin (1574), the kagemusha rallies the soldiers and leads them to success. Becoming overconfident after his successes, the kagemusha tries to ride Shingen's excitable horse, but is thrown to the ground. As soldiers rush to his aid, they notice that he is missing Shingen's unique battle scars. The thief is shown to be an imposter, and Katsuyori assumes his rightful place as leader of the clan. Meanwhile, Oda and Tokugawa press onward in an effort to overtake the Takeda territory. Commanding his army, Katsuyori strikes against Nobunaga, culminating in the disastrous Battle of Nagashino (28 June 1575). Takeda cavalry and infantry attack in waves, but are defeated by the Oda troops who have hidden behind stockades. The thief, now exiled, witnesses the slaughter and makes a brave show of commitment to his clan by running at the Oda frontlines with a spear. The kagemusha is badly injured and dies while trying to pull the fūrinkazan from the river (the fūrinkazan is Shingen's battle standard inscribed with "Wind, Forest, Fire, Mountain," the four phrases from Sun Tzu's *The Art of War*: "as swift as wind, as gentle as forest, as fierce as fire, as unshakable as mountain").

Reception

Released in Japan on 26 April 1980, *Kagemusha* went on to become the country's most popular film that year, grossing ¥2.7 billion at the box office (the equivalent of $13.6 million in 1980). Screened in competition at the Cannes Film Festival in May, *Kagemusha* won the Palme d'Or, sharing it with Bob Fosse's *All That Jazz*. The film premiered in the United States at the New York Film Festival on 1 October 1980 and then went into general release five days later but had poor box office returns; a three-hour epic about medieval Japan, *Kagemusha* had very limited appeal in foreign markets. It did, however, garner lots of accolades, including two Oscar nominations (for Best Foreign Language Film and Best Art Direction), a Golden Globe nomination (Best Foreign Language Film), and four BAFTA nominations, winning for Best Direction and Best Costume Design. *Kagemusha* also won France's César Award for Best Foreign Film. Critics often remarked upon the film's epic sweep, visual grandeur, and elaborate sense of pageantry but also noted its essential pessimism. As Roger Ebert noted, "Kurosawa seems to be saying that great human endeavors . . . depend entirely on large numbers of men sharing the same fantasies or beliefs. It is entirely unimportant, he seems to be suggesting, whether or not the beliefs are based on reality—all that matters is that men accept them. But when a belief is shattered, the result is confusion, destruction, and death" (Ebert, 1980).

Reel History Versus Real History

Kurosawa anchored *Kagemusha* in Japan's complex medieval history but also took considerable artistic license with his source material. As portrayed in the film, Takeda Shingen (1521–1573) was a powerful feudal lord who waged war against his rivals, Oda Nobunaga (1532–1584) and Tokugawa Ieyasu (1543–1616), for control of Kyoto, Japan's capital at that time. In the movie, Shingen is shot by a sniper and dies while laying siege to a Tokugawa clan stronghold (Noda Castle in Mikawa Province). Though it is kept secret, Shingen's death causes the Takeda clan to break off the siege and retreat. In reality Shingen died on 13 May 1573, almost three months after Noda Castle surrendered (16 February 1573), and accounts vary as to the cause of death: a sniper wound sustained during the siege, or an old war wound, or possibly from pneumonia. In the movie Shingen's corpse is submersed in Lake Suwa and his death is kept secret for three years. The historical reality is that Shingen was interred at Erin-ji Temple in what is now Kōshū, Yamanashi Prefecture. There was no interregnum during which a kagemusha impersonated the daimyō. Shingen's son, Takeda Katsuyori (1546–1582), took over as leader of the clan immediately after his father's death and, as depicted the film, defeated Tokugawa Ieyasu at the Battle of Takatenjin in 1574. As also depicted in the film, Katsuyori was decisively defeated at the Battle of Nagashino in 1575. Kurasawa's rendition of Nagashino is fairly accurate. When Katsuyori's cavalry force (numbering about 4,000) attacked, 3,000 Nobunaga riflemen, protected behind wooden stockades, opened rotating volley fire with their Tanegashima (matchlock muskets) and decimated the Takeda horsemen. When it was all over Katsuyori's army of 15,000 had suffered some 10,000 casualties. Katsuyori also lost a dozen of his generals. Nobunaga's skillful use of firearms to thwart Takeda's cavalry is often cited as a turning point in Japanese warfare, indeed the first "modern" battle. What is inaccurate about the movie version: it omits the fact that the battle took place in heavy rain—which Katsuyori erroneously thought would wet the Nobunagas' gunpowder and render their muskets useless. After his devastating loss at Nagashino, Katsuyori hung on for another seven years but his fortunes continued to decline. Katsuyori's forces were finally destroyed by the combined armies of Nobunaga and Tokugawa at the Battle of Temmokuzan in 1582. In the aftermath Katsuyori, his wife, Hojo Masako, and Nobukatsu, one of his two sons, committed ritual suicide (seppuku). Daimyōs did indeed use doubles for security purposes but the story of the thief is pure fiction.

KANAŁ (1957)

Synopsis

Kanał is a Polish war film directed by Andrzej Wajda. The second installment in Wajda's War Trilogy—preceded by *A Generation* (1954) and followed by *Ashes and Diamonds* (1958)—*Kanał* tells the story of a company of Home Army resistance fighters using the city's sewers to evade capture by the Nazis as their defensive position collapses during the 1944 Warsaw Uprising.

Background

In late July 1944, during World War II, the advancing Red Army had reached the eastern suburbs of Warsaw, Poland's capital city. The close proximity of the Russians prompted the Polish government in exile in London to order its Home Army (Polish: Armia Krajowa or AK) of resistance fighters to mount an uprising against the German occupation. By liberating Warsaw prior to full Russian involvement, the Poles hoped to bolster claims to national sovereignty before the Soviet-backed communist Polish Committee of National Liberation could assume political control of the country. Stalin, of course, had other ideas. Avid to annex Poland after Hitler's defeat, he betrayed the Polish resistance by ordering his armies to halt on the eastern banks of the Vistula River and not advance into the city to aid the Poles. This allowed the Germans time to regroup and destroy the Polish resistance, which fought for 63 days with light arms and little outside support (1 August–2 October 1944). It is estimated that the AK suffered some 22,000 casualties (16,000 killed and 6,000 wounded) and 150,000 to 200,000 civilians died. Arthur Koestler called the Soviet refusal to support the uprising "one of the major infamies of this war which will rank for the future historian on the same ethical level with [the Nazi extermination of] Lidice" (Koestler, p. 374). After the war Warsaw native Jerzy Stefan Stawiński (1921–2010)—who served as an AK company commander during the Uprising—published "Kanał" (Polish for channel or sewer) in the Polish literary journal *Twórczość* [*Creativity*]: a story based on his own, bitter experiences during the doomed struggle that he soon turned into a film script. After Stalin died in 1953, his successor, Nikita Khrushchev, relaxed censorship and other forms of political repression. "Khrushchev's Thaw" spilled over to Poland and the other Soviet client states, making a film on the Warsaw Uprising politically feasible. Even though "Kanał" refrained from indicting Russian complicity in the defeat of the Uprising, Poland's Soviet-dominated political leadership did not want it made. In the words of the film's eventual director, Andrzej Wajda, "The authorities must have realized that society would be against the movie, and would regard it as the communist voice on the subject of the Warsaw uprising . . . It preferred not to make any film on the subject of the Warsaw Uprising, even one with a point of view they could accept as their own" (quoted by James Steffen, n.d.). Submitted to the government for vetting, the script was also deemed insufficiently heroic. Eventually the film was made because Tadeusz Konwicki, a member of the screenplay commission and an official of Kadr, a new film studio, lobbied behind the scenes on its behalf.

Production

Kanał was made by P. P. Film Polski at Kadr Studios and on location in Warsaw in 1956. Some of the above-ground scenes were shot in the studio, but most were filmed on location at ruins that had not yet been demolished after the war. Scenes that comprise the film's first 45 minutes were shot at Cecilia Sniegocka Street and in an adjacent park in the Solec district, a mile northeast of Mokotów, and the 10-minute closing sequence was shot beneath Kamienne Schodki [Street of Stone Steps] and on Miadowa and Długa Streets in Warsaw's Old Town. For the scenes in the sewers, Wajda and his crew constructed an elaborate replica of the sewers, and Wajda's director of photography, Jerzy Lipman, provided the evocatively eerie noir-like chiaroscuro lighting for those episodes.

Plot Summary

During the final days of the Warsaw Uprising (late September 1944), Lt. Zadra (Wieńczysław Gliński) leads a beleaguered platoon of 43 AK soldiers and Warsaw civilians in retreat to south-central Warsaw. The composer Michał (Vladek

Sheybal) gets in touch with his family, who are elsewhere in the city. Panicked, she shares that the Germans are in her building and are coming to take her, and then she is cut off. The next day, Officer Cadet Jacek "Korab" (Tadeusz Janczar) happens upon the second-in-command, Lt. Mądry (Emil Karewicz), in bed with a local messenger girl. After apologizing, the officers go to battle against the Germans. While they hold them off, Korab is shot and wounded while cutting the guide wire of a Goliath tracked mine (a remote-controlled miniature tank full of explosives) with a shovel. With his platoon now down to 27 and covered on all sides by the Germans, Zadra is commanded to take to the sewers in order to retreat. Stokrotka (Polish for "Daisy") (Teresa Iżewska), their guide, asks Zadra to permit her to help Korab. Zadra gives his consent but Stokrotka and Korab soon get separated from the group. Korab's injuries have weakened him, and he is forced to rest before climbing up to the street. Stokrotka then directs them toward the river, and they see rays of sunlight ahead. Korab, extremely weak and near blind, is unable to see that the pair's exit is blocked by metal bars. Stokrotka confesses her love for Korab while they rest and regroup. Meanwhile, the rest of the group gets lost, as they haven't had Stokrotka to guide them. Zadra attempts to command Sgt. Kula (Tadeusz Gwiazdowski) to move the troops forward, but they refuse. Zadra and Kula lose all of their men except the mechanic, Smukły (Stanisław Mikulski). The men who have not followed Zadra and Kula get lost again and eventually end up dead or captured. Zadra, Kula, and Smukły encounter a sewer exit but it is booby-trapped by German grenades. Smukły is only able to disarm two of the three grenades; the third one explodes, killing him. Zadra and Kula finally come up from the sewer to an abandoned and bombed-out part of the city. When Kula admits that he left the other men behind, Zadra kills him and returns to the sewers to find them.

Reception

Released in Poland on 20 May 1957, *Kanał* was a punishing but ultimately cathartic experience for those who had lived through the terrible, tragic events it depicts. In the words of film critic and Warsaw Uprising survivor Stanislaw Grzelecki, "The tragedy of the people who believed to the very end that the fight they had undertaken [was] right has found disturbing expression in Wajda's film. The drama assumes a shape of a metaphor, all the more meaningful because its ordinary heroes have been, for many years, forced into the shadows, into silence, to endure the mud-slinging, false accusations and slander" (Grzelecki, 1957). Other Polish critics, not as understanding as Grzelecki, initially panned the film for its unheroic grimness. *Kanał* was screened in competition at the 10th Cannes Film Festival (May 1957), where it shared the Special Jury Prize with Ingmar Bergman's *The Seventh Seal* and received rave notices from French film critics, international recognition that prompted a more positive reassessment at home. Released in the United States in 1961, the film briefly ran in a few art house cinemas. Bosley Crowther found *Kanał* as "dismal, dark and depressing a drama of events in World War II as this reviewer has yet witnessed" (Crowther, 1961).

Reel History Versus Real History

The plot of *Kanał* is fictional but the general story it tells about the final days of the Uprising is historically very accurate. As depicted in the film, by the end of September 1944, German forces had retaken most of the city. AK fighters were holding out in five isolated pockets, including an area within the suburb of Mokotów that was less than a mile long and half a mile wide, defended by about 2,750 insurgents. On 24 September 1944 German forces mounted an offensive against the Mokotów pocket from the south. Over the next three days of heavy fighting, the Polish defense perimeter shrank to just a few blocks as advancing Germans executed wounded soldiers, even hospital personnel. On 26 September 9,000 civilians fled Mokotów during a two-hour early afternoon cease fire. That evening, as depicted in the film, some 800 resistance fighters and civilians, many wounded, started evacuating through the sewers and headed for the city center, about two miles due north (Mokotów fell the next day and the Germans captured some 1,500 remaining fighters and 5,000 civilians). As also represented in the film, some AK fighters (actually about 150) headed in the wrong direction and unwittingly climbed out of the sewers at Dworkowa Street, in German-held territory half a mile to the southeast of Mokotów; 120 of them were captured and summarily executed. A monument now stands there in their memory. Actual conditions in the sewers were every bit horrific as the film shows. In his review of the film (cited earlier), Stanislaw Grzelecki observed, "I followed the same underground road from Mokotów to the centre of town as Jerzy Stawiński, and I, like he, spent seventeen hours in the sewers. I saw and experienced enough to state that Wajda's film is telling the truth."

KILLING FIELDS, THE (1984)

Synopsis

The Killing Fields is a British war drama written by Bruce Robinson, directed by Roland Joffé and produced by David Puttnam. Starring Sam Waterston, Haing S. Ngor, Julian Sands, and John Malkovich, the film concerns the experiences of two journalists who are close friends—Cambodian Dith Pran and American Sydney Schanberg—after the Khmer Rouge take over Cambodia in the 1970s.

Background

In 1976 *New York Times* journalist Sydney Schanberg won a Pulitzer Prize for reporting on the fall of Cambodia to the genocidal Khmer Rouge in 1975. Four years later Schanberg published "The Death and Life of Dith Pran" (1980), a long article about the astonishing survival of Dith Pran, a Cambodian friend and colleague of Schanberg who managed to escape from the Khmer Rouge after a long captivity and find safety in Thailand in October 1979. British producer David Puttnam (*Chariots of Fire*) read the article and knew immediately he wanted to make a film version of Pran's story. Puttnam bought the film rights and eventually secured a $16 million budget: $8 million from Goldcrest Films (London); $4 million from foreign distributors, tax shelters, and a UK government fund; and $4 million from Warner Bros. Actor-screenwriter Bruce Robinson (*Withnail and I*) wrote a 300-page draft of a screen adaptation, which Puttnam showed to various directors (including Louis Malle and Constantin Costa-Gavras) but was particularly taken by the reaction of British TV director Roland Joffé, who said that it wasn't a war story but actually a love story between Dith Pran and Sydney Schanberg—a remark that won him his first assignment as a feature film director. Regarding the casting of an actor to play Sydney Schanberg, Warner Bros. wanted a big star but Puttnam settled on Sam Waterston. Equipped with the right ethnicity, looks, and Massachusetts accent, Waterston happily lacked the distracting baggage of a famous star. Though he had no formal acting training, Dr. Haing S. Ngor was cast as Dith Pran. A native Cambodian just two years older than Pran, Ngor had also endured and escaped from Khmer Rouge captivity; no ordinary actor could have brought more authenticity to the role.

Production

The Killing Fields was shot in fits and starts between March 1983 and August 1984, mostly on location in Thailand but also in Toronto, New York City, and California. Shots involving large helicopters in the scene where Pran's family and other international diplomats are evacuated from Phnom Penh in 1975 were actually filmed in San Diego in early 1984, almost seven months after principal photography in Thailand.

Plot Summary

The setting is Cambodia's capital, Phnom Penh, 6 August 1973. The Cambodian army is fighting a civil war with the Khmer Rouge (Communist Party of Kampuchea), a conflict instigated by the war in neighboring Vietnam. Dith Pran (Haing S. Ngor), a Cambodian photojournalist and newspaper interpreter, waits for reporter Sydney Schanberg to arrive at the airport, but is called away unexpectedly. Schanberg goes to his hotel and meets up with Al Rockoff (John Malkovich). Pran later connects with Schanberg and reveals that an American B-52 has bombed the town of Neak Leung, killing and wounding hundreds of civilians. Schanberg and Pran then travel to Neak Leung and confirm that the town has been completely decimated. Two years later, in April 1975, Phnom Penh empties its embassies, knowing the Khmer Rouge is nearby and ruthless. Schanberg arranges to evacuate Pran, his wife, and their four children; however, Pran demands to remain behind to assist his friend. Khmer Rouge forces enter and occupy the capital. Schanberg encounters Rockoff at a city parade. Afterwards, a party of Khmer Rouge fighters finds and arrests them, transporting them to a back alley in the city where captives are being executed. They are later met by a detachment of the Khmer Rouge, who immediately arrest them and take them through the city to a back alley where prisoners are being executed. Pran negotiates on behalf of his comrades and uses his sway as a Cambodian civilian to secure their release. The men go to the French Embassy for help, but the Khmer Rouge want all Cambodians handed over to them. Concerned that Pran will fall victim to imprisonment or death after the embassy is overtaken, Rockoff and British press photographer Jon Swain (Julian Sands) of

The Sunday Times try to forge a British passport for Pran, but their forgery proves ineffective when Pran's image on the passport photo fades away. Pran is handed to the Khmer Rouge. Schanberg returns to New York City and rallies support for a campaign to rescue Pran. Meanwhile, in Cambodia, Pran serves as a slave laborer under the Khmer Rouge's "Year Zero" policy: an attempt to return to the agrarian ways of the past. Pran also takes mandatory propaganda classes, getting by on his ability to fake being simple-minded. During an attempted escape, Pran comes across a pile of muddy wreckage that turns out to be rotting human bodies—part of the "killing fields" under Pol Pot, where nearly 2 million Cambodians were ruthlessly murdered. In 1976, Schanberg receives a Pulitzer Prize for his coverage in Cambodia. He assigns half of the award to Pran. At the acceptance dinner he tells the audience that half the recognition for the award belongs to Pran. Rockoff later incites Schanberg for not pursuing every possible lead in the search for Pran. Schanberg feels incredibly guilty about his failed search attempts and admits that Pran likely stayed in Cambodia because he "wanted him to stay." In Cambodia, Pran is assigned to Phat (Monirak Sisowath), the commander of a different prison compound, and charged with tending to Phat's young son (Lambool Dtangpaibool). Pran proceeds with acting like an uneducated peasant, refusing to show his captors the true breadth of his knowledge. Phat even asks Pran to take charge of his son in the event that he is killed in battle. By now, Khmer Rouge units are in the midst of a border war with Vietnam. The conflict reaches Pran's region, and a battle ensues between the Khmer Rouge of the compound and two jet fighters sent to destroy the camp. After the fighting ends (momentarily), Pran is told that Phat's son has both American money and a map that will lead the men to safety. Phat attempts to stop the younger Khmer Rouge officers from ending the lives of his friends, but he is killed in response. During the shooting, Pran and four fellow prisoners get away. The group then starts a long journey through the wilderness with Phat's younger son. Pran and his companion follow Phat's map, but the companion unknowingly trips a landmine while holding the younger child. Pran begs his companion to hand over the child, but the mine explodes, killing both man and child. Pran grieves as he presses onward. Eventually he reaches the top of an escarpment in the Dângrêk Mountains and spies a Red Cross camp near the border of Thailand. Informed of Pran's miraculous survival, Schanberg calls Pran's family with the news that Pran is alive and safe. Soon after, Schanberg travels to the Red Cross camp, is reunited with Pran, and asks Pran to forgive him. Pran answers, with a smile, "Nothing to forgive, Sydney. Nothing," as the two embrace.

Reception

The Killing Fields enjoyed substantial success at the box office; by the end of its 22-week domestic run (2 November 1984–7 April 1985) it had earned $34.6 million. The movie also won numerous awards. Nominated for seven Oscars, it won three—for Best Supporting Actor (Haing S. Ngor), Best Cinematography (Chris Menges), and Best Film Editing (Jim Clark). *The Killing Fields* also won a Golden Globe and eight BAFTAs. Reviews were mixed and not quite commensurate with the film's box office and awards success. For example, Vincent Canby wrote, "*The Killing Fields* is a faithful adaptation . . . Yet something vital is missing, and that's the emotional intensity of Mr. Schanberg's first-person prose. The movie is diffuse and wandering. It's someone telling a long, interesting story who can't get to the point" (Canby, 1984). The film's use of John Lennon's utopian anthem "Imagine" as its closing theme, underscoring the moment when Schanberg and Pran are reunited, also generated some controversy. Some commentators found the juxtaposition deeply affecting or cleverly ironic, whereas others denounced it as nauseatingly sentimental and pretentious.

Real History Versus Real History

In general terms, *The Killing Fields* is a faithful adaptation of Sydney Schanberg's account of the fall of Cambodia, his relationship with Dith Pran, and Pran's subsequent survival odyssey. Yet the movie's emphasis on the "love story" between Schanberg and Dith Pran is problematic in several ways. First of all, it tends to gloss over the political complexities that led to genocide in Cambodia. For example, Lon Nol (1913–1985), the Cambodian general whose pro-American military government ruled his country for five years (1970–75) until it was overwhelmed by the Khmer Rouge, is mentioned only once and in passing. Inexplicably, Pol Pot (1925–1998), diabolical leader of the Khmer Rouge from 1963 until 1997, is not mentioned at all. The film's focus on the relationship between Schanberg and Pran also has the effect of mostly casting them as passive victims of vague, sweeping historical forces rather than depicting them as the hardworking, risk-taking journalists that they were. And, as some film critics have noted, the film's central narrative dynamic, the story of an enduring friendship, is not entirely effective on its own terms. Furthermore, that story may be exaggerated or worse. American photojournalist Al Rockoff—the only surviving principal in Schanberg's Cambodia chronicles who refused to be involved with the film's production—has gone on record denouncing the late Sydney Schanberg as "a coward who put other people's lives in danger." Rockoff also alleges that Schanberg "used and abused Dith Pran and personally tried to have me thrown out of the safety of the French Embassy in April 1975." Rockoff also suspects that Schanberg destroyed his career as a photojournalist by having him blacklisted: "Schanberg left on the first convoy out of the French Embassy and asked me for the rolls of film that I'd shot. When I told him that I was on day rate for *Newsweek* and that he could only have the pictures they didn't want he said 'See if the *New York Times* ever runs any of your stuff again.'" In the end *Newsweek* only ran three of Rockoff's photos. Upon his return to the U.S. Rockoff was relegated to the journalistic margins, the vast majority of his work unseen (Kyne and Rockoff, p. 5). In the scene depicting Schanberg's Pulitzer Prize award night, the movie does acknowledge Rockoff's bitterly contrarian point of view and even gives it some credence, but the overall thrust of the movie contradicts Rockoff's moral indictment as a minority opinion.

KING RAT (1965)

Synopsis
King Rat is an American war film directed by Bryan Forbes, which he adapted from James Clavell's 1962 novel of the same title—which is, in turn, partly based on Clavell's own experiences as a prisoner of war (POW) at Changi Prison during the Second World War. Starring George Segal in the title role and featuring James Fox, John Mills, and Tom Courtenay, the film focuses on Cpl. King (aka "King Rat"), a wheeler-dealer American POW who incurs the enmity of Marlowe (Fox), a British officer.

Background
During World War II James Clavell (1921–1994), a captain with the British Royal Artillery, became a POW when Allied forces on the island of Java surrendered to the Japanese on 12 March 1942. Clavell spent the rest of the war—almost three and a half brutal years of near-starvation—at Changi, a notorious Japanese POW camp on Singapore. In 1953 Clavell immigrated to Hollywood from England and developed a successful career as a screenwriter but lingering war memories haunted him. In a 12-week period during the long Writers' Guild strike of 1960, Clavell wrote *King Rat*, a long fictional saga loosely based on his Changi POW ordeal 15 years earlier. After many rejections and judicious cutting and revising, *King Rat* was published in 1962 and became a critically acclaimed international bestseller. Sol Schwartz, a vice president at Columbia Pictures, purchased the film rights five months before *King Rat* was published, and British filmmaker Bryan Forbes was hired to write an adaptation and to direct the film. Columbia considered Vince Edwards, Steve McQueen, Frank Sinatra, Marlon Brando, Paul Newman, Tony Curtis, and many others for the lead role of Cpl. King but ultimately signed newcomer George Segal (*Ship of Fools*) in July 1964.

Production
Before shooting could commence, producer James Woolf had to build a realistic replica of the Changi POW camp and environs. Over a seven-week period in the summer of 1964 some 200 carpenters, electricians, and other workers constructed the concrete prison building (56 feet high and 60 feet wide), and 52 adjacent thatched huts on a seven-acre site near Westlake Village in the San Fernando Valley, about 37 miles west of Los Angeles. A half-million board feet of lumber was used, as well as 45,000 square feet of Gunite (pneumatically sprayed concrete for the prison's walls), 4,000 gallons of paint, and six miles of barbed wire. The elaborate set cost $375,000 ($2.9 million in 2017 dollars) to build. Attention to detail yielded superlative results; James Clavell visited the set and was impressed at how much it looked like the real camp at Changi. The filming of *King Rat* took place in the fall of 1964.

Plot Summary
Conditions at the Changi POW camp in Singapore are exceedingly harsh. Tropical heat and humidity, overcrowding, disease, starvation, and brutal guards

make survival a constant struggle for its 10,000 inmates. Yet U.S. Army Cpl. King (George Segal), one of only a handful of Americans among mostly British and Australian POWs, maintains his own health and even thrives. He does so by running lucrative black market schemes, one of which is to breed rats and sell them as food to his fellow prisoners, hence his nickname, "King Rat." King recruits Flight Lt. Peter Marlowe (James Fox), an upper-class British RAF officer, to act as his translator (Marlowe knows Malay and can barter with the corrupt camp guards). Marlowe grows fond of King, admiring his ruthless opportunism and cunning. King seems to respect Marlowe, but it is unclear how he truly feels about him. When Marlowe injures his arm, his new officer secures antibiotics in order to keep Marlowe's sickly limb from amputation. In contrast to Marlowe the British Provost Marshal, Lt. Robin Grey (Tom Courtenay) considers King a loathsome American renegade, immoral and conniving, and relentlessly tries to engineer King's downfall. But Grey has his own issues to resolve: one of his officers is stealing from the food rations. The officer attempts to bribe Grey, but he brings the issue to his superior, Col. George Smedley-Taylor (John Mills). Smedley-Taylor informs Grey that the officer in question has been discharged and tells him to drop the allegations. An angry Grey accuses Smedley-Taylor of collusion, but he can no longer find the altered scale weight that originally tipped him off to the corruption. Grey suspects a cover-up, but now has no proof. In an attempt to placate Grey, Smedley-Taylor offers him a promotion. The British officers are then informed that the Japanese have surrendered and that the war is over. The stunned prisoners are jubilant, save for Cpl. King, who has suddenly lost his celebrity in the camp and now must face a return to "normal" life as a civilian. As King is evacuated with his fellow American prisoners, Marlowe attempts to solidify his friendship with King. However, the two part on uncertain, unhopeful terms.

Reception

Premiering on 27 October 1965, *King Rat* reached #1 at the box office in the second weekend of its release, but the movie did not enjoy sustained commercial momentum. Though budget numbers for *King Rat* are unknown, the film made at least $6.7 million in domestic ticket sales: only a modest success. Weaned on more upbeat, patriotic POW movies (e.g., *Stalag 17* and *The Great Escape*), the moviegoing public wasn't ready for a film offering so much moral ambiguity. As for awards, director Bryan Forbes received a BAFTA nomination, and the movie garnered two Oscar nominations: one for Best Cinematography, Black-and-White (Burnett Guffey) and Best Art Direction-Set Decoration (Robert Emmet Smith and Frank Tuttle). Reviews were largely positive though many critics noted that the film was bleak fare, not suitable for the faint of heart. Bosley Crowther termed *King Rat* a "grim and lacerating picture" and declared that "anyone who can sit through it without wincing is a better man than I am, Gunga Din" (Crowther, 1965). Since its initial release *King Rat*'s critical reputation has risen dramatically, though it still remains an undeservedly obscure cult movie.

Reel History Versus Real History

King Rat is a more or less accurate rendition of its source material, but Clavell always claimed that his book was pure fiction. In the novel's preface he states, "There was a war. Changi and Outram [Road] jails in Singapore do—or did—exist. Obviously the rest of the story is fiction and no similarity to anyone living or dead exists or is intended." American historian/biographer Stanley Weintraub begs to differ, postulating that *King Rat*'s title character is likely an amalgam of at least three POWs that Clavell knew (or knew of) at Changi: Eddie MacArthur, a merchant seaman; Robert I. "Bob" Martin, a Navy crewman from the sunken USS *Houston*; and Albert L. "Buttercup" Carpenter of Battery F of the New Mexico National Guard. Of the three, Corporal King most closely resembles Buttercup Carpenter. Weintraub cites Sir Thomas Howell, RAF (Ret.), a former inmate with Clavell: "He was by no means so sinister or selfish [as Cpl. King] but [Carpenter] became a 'skillful operator' and as a result of using profits for the benefits of the prisoners he was an instrument for saving many lives as risk" (Rusinko, 1998, pp. 198–199).

LAND AND FREEDOM [SPANISH: *TIERRA Y LIBERTAD*] (1995)

Synopsis

Land and Freedom (*Tierra y libertad*) is a film directed by Ken Loach and written by Jim Allen. It follows the story of David Carr (played by Ian Hart), a member of the Communist Party of Great Britain who travels to Spain to fight for the Republican side in the Spanish Civil War (1936–1938). Joining a coalition of socialists, communists, and anarchists waging a losing struggle against Francisco Franco's fascist forces, Carr experiences political disillusionment as factions of the Left battle each other as well as the enemy.

Background

When the Soviet Union collapsed in 1991, conservative pundits in the Western democracies interpreted its demise as incontrovertible proof that capitalism was the only viable way to organize modern societies. As he recalled in a 1995 interview for the World Socialist Website (Allen, 1995), Jim Allen (British film director Ken Loach's longtime screenwriter) found this view highly disingenuous: "With the fall of Stalinism, the coming down of the Berlin Wall, the West said, 'That's it. Communism doesn't work. It's finished!' And the likes of Tony Blair and company jumped on the band wagon. 'The God has failed. Go back to your factories, your dole queues and forget it. It's the free market economy that works.' We wanted to show that communism and socialism never existed in the Soviet Union, that Stalin was a monster." After coming across a pamphlet by the International Brigades Committee in Manchester, Jim Allen persuaded Ken Loach that a Spanish Civil War film would be the most effective vehicle for debunking the myth of Stalinist Russia as a "communist" state. Over the next four years, while fundraising (from British, German, French, and Spanish sources) was in progress, Allen went to Spain to interview dozens of former members of the POUM (Partido Obrero de Unificación Marxista [the anti-Stalinist Workers' Party of Marxist Unification]), read everything he could find on the war, and frequently debated and developed ideas with Loach (Anonymous, Teachers Notes, Film Education, n.d.). The script that finally emerged was based on a number of books: Mary Low and Juan Brea's *Red Spanish Notebook* (1937), Felix Morrow's *Revolution and Counter-Revolution in Spain* (1938), Abel Paz's *The People Armed* (1976), Victor Alba and Stephen Schwartz's *Spanish Marxism Versus Soviet Communism: A History of the P.O.U.M.* (1988), and Burnett Bolloten's *The Spanish Civil War* (1991), but George Orwell's *Homage to Catalonia* (1938) was the most crucial and closely followed source.

Production

Utilizing British and Spanish actors, *Land and Freedom* was shot largely in sequence on location during the summer of 1994. The film's bookend scenes, which depict David Carr's death and funeral, were shot in Liverpool but most of the film was shot in the Maestrazgo region of Spain, a mountainous area that spans the border of Aragón and Castellon 200 miles southwest of Barcelona. Specific locations include the village of Mirambel in the Teruel province of Aragón, Morella in the province of Castelló, and Barcelona. Due to severe budget constraints, some scenes key to the history of the war originally earmarked for dramatization could only be alluded to in conversation. Among those who served as consultants to ensure historical veracity were Andy Durgan (University of Barcelona), a noted Marxist historian of the Spanish Civil War; Joan Rocabert, a POUM veteran; and Jesus Garcia, an Abraham Lincoln Brigade veteran.

Plot Summary

Land and Freedom centers on Liverpudlian Dave Carr (Ian Hart), a young, unemployed, and naïve member of the Communist Party of Great Britain (CPGB) who goes to Spain to fight on the Loyalist side. The film actually begins almost 60 years later, in present-day England. After the elderly Carr's death from a heart attack, his granddaughter Kim (Suzanne Maddock) discovers a cache of letters in an old suitcase that Carr wrote to his English girlfriend, Kitty (Angela Clarke) while he was fighting in Spain in 1936–1937. The film, mostly one extended flashback, brings those letters to dramatic life. Carr, like George Orwell, travels to Spain to join the POUM militia in August 1936 and gets some decidedly amateur military training in Barcelona. Also like Orwell, Carr is provided with an 1896 Mauser rifle (which later explodes in his face) and is sent to the stabilized Aragón front in eastern Spain where he fights lice and boredom and joins his comrades in exchanging taunts with the enemy nearby. The action picks up as Carr's militia unit captures an enemy village, but Lawrence Coogan (Tom Gilroy), a beloved comrade, is killed in the process, and a Catholic priest (Ricard Arilla) is executed for aiding the Falangists. After a heated argument, Carr's comrades decide to collectivize the estate land they have seized. From that point on, though, complications set in as Spain's Stalinist-controlled Loyalist government insists that the POUM militias integrate into a unified Popular Army—which really means submitting to the political discipline of Stalin's Comintern and betraying their revolutionary ideals. Carr's unit votes not to integrate, but Carr soon joins the Stalinists, much to the chagrin of Blanca (Rosanna Pastor), his Spanish quasi-love interest. After a brief stint in Barcelona fighting former comrades from the POUM and CNT (Confederación Nacional Del Trabajo, i.e., anarchists) over control of the city's telephone exchange (April–May 1937), a disillusioned Carr rips up his CPGB membership card and rejoins the POUM. The film concludes in mid-June 1937 with Carr's POUM militia unit having to retreat on the Huesca front due to lack of promised reinforcement by Popular Army regulars. To add insult to betrayal, Loyalist government troops show up after the battle to disarm Carr's militia unit, arresting its officers for political apostasy, and shooting Blanca (the very embodiment of revolutionary idealism) dead in the process. Blanca's funeral in Spain morphs into Dave Carr's funeral in England almost 60 years later. His granddaughter eulogizes him with two lines from William Morris's 1885 poem, "The Day Is Coming": "Come, join in the only battle wherein no man can fail,/Where whoso fadeth and dieth, yet his deed shall still prevail."

Reception

After premiering in Spain on 7 April 1995, *Land and Freedom* was screened at the 50th Cannes Film Festival in May, where it won the Prize of the Ecumenical Jury, shared the FIPRESCI Prize with Theodoros Angelopoulos' *Ulysses' Gaze*, and was nominated for Palme d'Or. It also won France's 1996 César Award for Best Foreign Film. With distribution limited to art house cinemas, combined box office gross receipts for Europe, North America, and other markets was predictably modest (about £7 million) but the film still made a decent profit, considering that its production budget was only £3 million ($4.47 million). Interestingly, *Land and Freedom* did its best business in France (in depoliticized America, it ran in only 10 theaters and made a paltry $228,000). Reviews were almost universally positive—some were adulatory. For example, film critic Philip French judged it "among the finest films of the decade" (French, 1995). Although she criticized the land-use debate scene mid-film as bringing the movie's narrative to a standstill, Caryn James nonetheless praised *Land and Freedom* "as admirable and intelligent as any film around" (James, 1995, C23). German filmmaker Wim Wenders (whose company, Road Movies, was one of the co-producers of a number of Loach films, including *Land and Freedom*) confessed that he cried "his heart out" by the end of the movie (Wenders, 2003).

Reel History Versus Real History

An inherently political war film, *Land and Freedom* rekindled the sorts of fierce partisan debates over the conduct and meaning of the Spanish Civil War that raged during the 1930s. Arguments flared over the movie's implicit premise (which is also George Orwell's central premise in *Homage to Catalonia*): that Soviet communist influence hamstrung the International Brigades and fractured and debilitated the Loyalist war effort overall, handing victory to Franco in the name of Stalinist party discipline. John Dunlop, a British International Brigade volunteer from May 1937 to December 1938, denounced *Land and Freedom* as historically inaccurate in small and large ways. After taking issue with costume anachronisms (e.g., blue jeans and Doc Martins) in the movie, Dunlop found fault with Dave Carr joining the POUM on arrival in Spain: "By November 1936 all volunteers crossing the frontier were [eventually] taken . . . to Albacete, where they were documented and received into the International Brigades. So the naive depiction of how the young Liverpool Communist Party member was persuaded by complete strangers to join the POUM militia was a virtual impossibility." Yet Dunlop's assertion is contradicted by George Orwell's experience as a British anti-fascist volunteer who joined POUM upon his arrival in Spain in December 1936. Modeled on Orwell's story, Dave Carr's POUM affiliation is used as a plot device meant to provide him (and viewers) with a critical perspective on Stalinist influence on the International Brigades. A departure from Orwell's book, which the film otherwise closely follows, has Carr temporarily joining the communists against POUM and the anarchists during the street fighting in Barcelona and then regretting his apostasy in order to dramatize the Stalinist betrayal of true revolutionary ideals. But what Orwell, Jim Allen, and Ken Loach see as totalitarian treachery that foiled hopes for a truly egalitarian society, Dunlop sees as a pragmatic closing of the ranks against a powerful fascist enemy. In Dunlop's view, "The Government with the support of the Communists [was] determined to create a unified command. This was opposed by the Anarchists and the POUM" (Dunlop, n.d.). The two views remain irreconcilable.

LAST OF THE MOHICANS, THE (1992)

Synopsis

The Last of the Mohicans is an American war epic mostly based on George B. Seitz's 1936 film adaptation of James Fenimore Cooper's eponymous 1826 novel. Directed, co-produced, and co-written by Michael Mann, the film stars Daniel Day-Lewis, Madeleine Stowe, Jodhi May, Russell Means, and Wes Studi and follows the fate of a group of British American colonials during the French and Indian War (1757).

Background

James Fenimore Cooper's novel, *The Last of the Mohicans* (1826), the second of his Leatherstocking Tales, was an improbable and turgidly written frontier adventure set in the Adirondacks during the second year of the French and Indian War (1757) that nonetheless proved to be Cooper's most popular and iconic work. Indeed, *The Last of the Mohicans* defined the image of the early American settler and Native American in the popular imagination and spawned no fewer than nine film adaptations, four TV versions, a radio version, an opera version, and three comics versions in the 20th and early 21st centuries. The best of these renditions is director Michael Mann's 1992 film version, a movie with an exceptionally long gestation period of 40 years. When Mann was a preschooler in Chicago c.1949, he saw the 1936 film version of *Last of the Mohicans* starring Randolph Scott as Hawkeye—an experience that sparked a lifelong interest in the saga. After making five feature films in the 1970s and 1980s, mostly neo-noir, Mann acquired the rights to Philip Dunne's 1936 *Last of the Mohicans* script in 1990, easily won funding approval from 20th Century-Fox, and then undertook a new adaptation, co-written with Cristopher Crowe, using Dunne's script as their template, not Cooper's novel. Mann cast Daniel Day-Lewis (who had just won an Oscar for *My Left Foot*) in the lead role as Hawkeye and then sent him to U.S. Army Col. David Webster, an officer at Fort Bragg who taught pilots wilderness survival skills. Webster took Day-Lewis to Many Hawks Special Operations Center in Pittsview, Alabama, and had him work with wilderness expert Mark A. Baker, who put him through a rigorous training program in marksmanship, hunting, trapping, and all the other proficiencies involved in living off the land—a skill set that Hawkeye would have had. Being the consummate

Method actor, Day-Lewis bulked up and worked hard to master it all, then stayed in character on set by avoiding modern technology, rolling his own cigarettes, traveling by canoe, and keeping his muzzle-loading .40-caliber Pennsylvania flintlock rifle close at hand at all times. Dale Dye of Warriors, Inc., the military advisor for *Platoon*, *Casualties of War*, and many other war films, provided technical assistance on set.

Production

For the shoot (which ran 15 weeks, from 17 June–10 October 1991), Michael Mann was a stickler for authenticity in the reproduction of period hairstyles, tattoos, beadwork, costumes, uniforms, flags, canoes, weapons, fortifications, etc. He also insisted on hiring hundreds of Native Americans to portray their colonial-era brethren, most notably Russell Means (1939–2012), an Oglala/Lakota Sioux Indian and first national director of the American Indian Movement (AIM), who portrays Hawkeye's close friend, Chingachgook, in the movie. Dennis Banks, a Chippewa Indian and a close associate of Russell Means in AIM, plays Hawkeye's friend, Ongewasgone. Wes Studi (*Dances with Wolves*), the actor who portrays the villainous Magua, is a member of the Cherokee tribe. Though Cooper's novel is set in the vicinity of Lake George, Michael Mann chose to film in the Blue Ridge Mountains near Ashville, North Carolina (900 miles to the southwest), in order to better replicate 18th-century New York State because the area around Asheville more closely resembles the untouched old-growth forests of 1757. Some scenes were shot at Biltmore, George Vanderbilt's North Carolina estate south of Asheville, while other scenes were shot in nearby DuPont State Recreational Forest. The real Fort William Henry was located on the southern end of Lake George in New York's Adirondack Mountains, but for the movie, a full-scale facsimile of the fort was built at the northern end of Lake James, in Lake James State Park, about 40 miles east of Asheville. Another set built for the movie was the Indian village where Magua takes his captives (Major Heyward and the Munro sisters). The location is 30 miles southwest of Lake James, in Chimney Rock Park. In the movie the cascading waters of Hickory Nut Falls can be seen overlooking the Indian village. It was at the top of these falls where the final fight scene between Chingachgook and Magua was filmed.

Plot Summary

It is 1757 and the French and Indian War is raging in the Adirondack Mountains. British Army Major Duncan Heyward (Steven Waddington) arrives in Albany to serve under Col. Edmund Munro (Maurice Roëves), the commander of Fort William Henry on Lake George, 60 miles due north. Heyward is ordered to bring the colonel's two daughters, Cora (Madeleine Stowe) and Alice (Jodhi May), to their waiting father. An old friend of the Munro's, Heyward professes his love to Cora and proposes to her. She leaves him without an answer. Major Heyward, the two women, and a small detachment of British soldiers march through the forest, guided by Magua (Wes Studi), a Huron warrior employed by the British as a scout, but the treacherous Magua soon leads the party into an ambush in the deep woods.

The soldiers are all killed or injured, and Heyward and the women in his care are saved by a Mohican chief named Chingachgook (Russell Means), his son Uncas (Eric Schweig), and his white, adopted son "Hawkeye" (Daniel Day-Lewis). All who ambushed the group are eliminated, excepting Magua, who escapes. The trio agrees to escort the women and Heyward to the fort. En route through the forest, Cora and Hawkeye form an attraction, as do Uncas and Alice. When they arrive near the fort, they find that it is under siege by the French and their Huron allies. The small party evades enemy soldiers and enters the fort where they are greeted by Col. Munro, who asks Major Heyward about the reinforcements he has requested but is disappointed to discover that his plea for help never made it to Fort Edward. Cora and Hawkeye sneak away for a private embrace, and Cora is forced to tell a jealous Heyward that she will not be able to become his wife. Munro denies his soldiers leave to defend their families during the fighting, but Hawkeye sets up their return journeys anyway. Hawkeye himself stays to be close to Cora and, though sentenced to death, is saved by a stroke of fate. During a parlay, French General Louis-Joseph de Montcalm (Patrice Chéreau) gives the British soldiers a chance to leave their fort honorably and return home without their guns. Munro assents to Montcalm's terms, but Magua rails against the decision. The following day, Col. Munro, his soldiers, and their women and children leave the fort and march away in a long column when Magua and his Huron warriors ambush them from the surrounding woods. Magua kills Munro and cuts out his heart. Hawkeye and the Mohicans battle through, leading Cora, Alice, and Heyward to temporary safety. Later, however, Magua and his braves capture the major and the women in a cave behind a waterfall (Hawkeye, Chingachgook, and Uncas escape by diving into the rushing waterfall—a feat of toughness and athleticism that is too much for their British companions—but Hawkeye vows to come back for them). Magua brings his captives to a Huron settlement and asks its sachem (Mike Phillips) to dictate their fates—and is interrupted by Hawkeye, who has come in alone to plead for their lives. The sachem rules that Heyward must be returned to the British, Alice given to Magua, and Cora burned alive. Hawkeye's bravery allows him to leave unscathed. However, Hawkeye tells translator Heyward to beg the sachem to let him (Hawkeye) take Cora's place. But instead, Heyward swaps his own life for Cora's life. After Cora and Hawkeye are at a safe distance, Hawkeye shoots Heyward to put him out of his misery as he burns at the stake. Chingachgook, Uncas, and Hawkeye then go after Magua's party to try and free Alice. Uncas fights Magua, but is killed by his enemy. Alice chooses to step off the cliff in an act of suicide. While Hawkeye holds Magua's remaining men at bay, Chingachgook slays Magua and avenges his son. With Hawkeye and Cora by his side, Chingachgook prays to the Great Spirit to receive Uncas, calling himself "the last of the Mohicans."

Reception

The world premiere of *The Last of the Mohicans* was in Paris (where James Fenimore Cooper lived from 1826–1833) on 26 August 1992. The film had its U.S. premiere in Los Angeles on 24 September 1992. After a 12-week theatrical run (widest release: 1,856 theaters), *Mohicans* grossed $70 million in domestic box office receipts; the foreign market gross totaled $5.5 million, so overall ticket receipts came in at $75.5 million. The movie cost $35 to $40 million to make and another $15 to $20 million to market (considered high by industry standards). In the end, 20th Century Fox earned about $15 million in initial profits on a film that cost $50 to $60 million: a moderate financial success but still impressive for a period piece (and brisk video rentals later added another $25 to $30 million to the studio coffers). Reviews were mostly positive but critics did express some reservations. For example, Desson Howe wrote: "This is the MTV version of gothic romance, a glam-opera of rugged, pretty people from long ago. Yet, by its own glossy, *Miami Vice* rules, the movie is stirring. Besides, novelist Cooper's vividly drawn savages and frontiersmen were hardly the stuff of hard-nosed realism. This movie is the Cooper pulp of its day" (Howe, 1992).

Reel History Versus Real History

The Last of the Mohicans is historical fiction; it superimposes a fictional plot onto an actual historical setting, intermingling fictional characters and events with real persons and real events. The main characters in the book and all other media versions (including Michael Mann's film) are Cooper's creations. The French and Indian War—including the siege and fall of Fort William Henry and the subsequent massacre of its evacuees—are, of course, historical realities. The movie's depiction of these events is, however, not entirely accurate. In 1757, with hostilities flaring up between Britain and France, Lt. Col. George Monro (sometimes spelled 'Munro,' 1700–1757) was placed in command of 1,500 troops and 850 colonial militiamen at Fort William Henry on Lake George in the British Province of New York. On 3 August 1757 Louis-Joseph de Montcalm, Marquis de Saint-Veran (1712–1759), leading an 8,000-man force of French Army regulars and Indian allies, began to lay siege to Fort William Henry by crossfire artillery bombardment. Effectively cut off from Gen. Daniel Webb's main British force after Webb refused to send reinforcements, Monro's small garrison stood little chance against a foe more than four times its size and with many more guns. As depicted in the film, after a week of steady battering and mounting casualties, Monro was forced to open negotiations with Montcalm on 9 August. Monro's stout defense won him generous surrender terms; he was able to negotiate safe passage for his troops (who were allowed to keep their weapons but no ammunition) to Fort Edward, about 16 miles to the south. However, Montcalm's Indian allies did not honor the terms of surrender. As Monro led his defeated troops away from Fort William Henry, the Indians attacked his column, leaving an estimated 185 dead. In the movie, Montcalm secretly meets with Magua and gives him tacit permission to massacre Monro's soldiers—a massacre that is on a much greater and deadlier scale than the actual one—and Magua personally murders Monro. Actually, there's no firm evidence that Montcalm colluded with his Indian allies to permit or abet the massacre of Monro's retreating troops, though the issue continues to be hotly debated by historians. Furthermore, Monro actually survived the massacre but died suddenly of apoplexy three months later, on 3 November 1757, at Albany. For dramatic purposes, Cooper gave Monro two daughters. In reality, he never married and had no children.

LAST SAMURAI, THE (2003)

Synopsis

The Last Samurai is an American period war epic directed and co-produced by Edward Zwick, who also co-wrote the screenplay with John Logan and Marshall Herskovitz. Tom Cruise portrays a U.S. 7th Cavalry Regiment officer who becomes a mercenary soldier battling samurai warriors in the wake of the Meiji Restoration in late 19th-century Japan.

Background

In 1992 screenwriter Michael Alan Eddy completed "West of the Rising Sun," a script about an American Civil War veteran who joins up with a samurai and helps him lead a cattle drive to a starving city in Japan. Eddy sold his script to producer Scott Kroopf of Radar Pictures in 1995. After several rewrites, Kroopf hired New Zealand–born screenwriter Vincent Ward to write another draft and co-produce the film. Both Kroopf and Ward bowed out in 1997 to pursue other projects, so Edward Zwick (*Glory*; *Courage Under Fire*) took over as director. Zwick had seen Akira Kurosawa's *The Seven Samurai* (1954) when he was a teenager in Illinois and had been fascinated by Japanese culture ever since; he saw Eddy's script as the vehicle for a Japan-themed movie he had long envisioned. Zwick spent the next two years developing "West of the Rising Sun," which went through further rewrites by Garner Simmons and Robert Schenkkan before Zwick dropped the "Rising Sun" project in favor of collaborating on a related story about the end of the feudal era in Japan with his longtime production partner Marshall Herskovitz and screenwriter John Logan (*Gladiator*). Zwick did, however, retain involvement with Kroopf and Ward at Radar Pictures. The new script that Zwick, Herskovitz, and Logan began developing in late 1999 was inspired by the 1877 Satsuma Rebellion, a revolt against Japan's imperial government by disaffected samurai led by Saigō Takamori (1828–1877). To a lesser extent Zwick and his co-writers were also influenced by the stories of Jules Brunet (1838–1911), a French army captain who fought alongside Enomoto Takeaki (1836–1908) in the Boshin War (aka Japanese Revolution, 1868–1869), a civil war between forces of the ruling Tokugawa shogunate and those seeking to return political power to the Imperial Court during the period of the Meiji Restoration. Another source was the story of Frederick Townsend Ward (1831–1862), an American mercenary who helped Westernize the Chinese army by forming and then leading the Ever Victorious Army during the Taiping Rebellion (1850–1864) until he was killed in battle. In 2000 Tom Cruise, who shared an interest in Japanese culture with Edward Zwick, signed on to play the lead role of Capt. Algren and spent almost two years in preparation for the film, including historical research, Japanese language lessons, and swordplay instruction.

Production

Filming of *The Last Samurai* took place over a seven-month period (10 October 2002–9 May 2003) in the United States, Japan, and New Zealand. The opening scene, set in San Francisco, when Algren walks past cable cars, was actually filmed on the "New York Street" set in the Warner Bros. Studios backlot in Burbank, with the view of the bay added digitally. Another early scene, where Nathan Algren is introduced to Omura, was filmed in the Moorish Room of the Castle Green Restaurant in Pasadena, California. Scenes at Katsumoto's temple were filmed at Sho-sha-zan Engyo-ji Temple in Himeji City, about 30 miles west of Kobe, Japan. Scenes supposedly taking place at the Imperial Palace of the Emperor Meiji in Tokyo were actually shot at the 400-year-old Chion-In Temple in Kyoto. The rest of the film was shot in the Taranaki region on New Zealand's North Island, a location chosen because Mount Taranaki resembles Mount Fuji, also because of copious forest and farmland resembling pre-industrial Japan. Much of the filming took place on the hillsides of the Uruti Valley, where Katsumoto's village was constructed. The port where Algren arrives in "Japan" was a set built at New Plymouth, New Zealand, and the parade ground where Algren trains the Imperial Army conscripts is at the Pukekura Sports Ground, also in New Plymouth. The "battle in the fog" was filmed in Mangamahoe Forest, just outside town. As is his custom, Tom Cruise did his own stunts for the film. Supporting actor Ken Watanabe also trained intensely and performed most of his stunts. Over 500 Japanese extras trained for 10 days at the Clifton Rugby Grounds in New Plymouth for the climactic battle scenes. Oscar-winning New Zealand costume designer Ngila Dickson and her 80-member team created the Meiji-era costumes, which included military uniforms and period dress for the American Indian wars, over 250 sets of samurai armor, and traditional dress for Japanese rural village life and street scenes.

Plot Summary

Former U.S. Army 7th Cavalry Captain Nathan Algren (Tom Cruise) is a morose alcoholic haunted by his participation in an Army massacre of Native American men, women, and children at Washita River in the Oklahoma territory during the American Indian Wars. After being fired from his job selling Winchester rifles, Algren is approached by his former commanding officer, Col. Bagley (Tony Goldwyn), with a job offer: to train the newly formed Imperial Japanese Army for Japanese businessman Omura (Masato Harada), who requires an army to suppress a samurai-led insurrection against Japan's new emperor. Despite loathing Bagley for his role in the Washita River massacre, Algren needs employment, so he takes the new assignment and sails to Japan, accompanied by his old friend, Sgt. Zebulon Gant (Billy Connolly). Upon arriving in Japan, Algren meets Simon Graham (Timothy Spall), a British translator and samurai expert. Algren soon discovers that the Imperial soldiers are not well trained and are instead conscripts with no knowledge of firearms. Before he can adequately train his men, Algren is told that samurai are staging an assault on one of Omura's railroads. Omura sends the army there, despite Algren's protests. The battle quickly turns into a rout when the conscripts panic and Gant is killed. Algren kills at least eight samurai warriors

before he is surrounded. Expecting to be killed, Algren is surprised when samurai leader Katsumoto (Ken Watanabe) decides to capture him instead and take
him to his village. Deprived of alcohol in captivity, Algren is forced into sobriety.
Though he is initially treated with disdain, Algren eventually gains the respect of
the samurai—and vice versa. As he integrates into samurai culture, Algren learns
Japanese and develops a strong identification with the samurai, who chafe at the
advent of modern technology, which has eroded traditional feudalism and rendered them declassed anachronisms. Back at the village, ninjas sneak in and
attempt to kill Katsumoto, but Algren intervenes and saves him. In the battle that
follows, Algren defends Katsumoto's family. Katsumoto meets with Emperor Meiji
(Shichinosuke Nakamura) in Tokyo, but is disappointed to see that the young
emperor is Omura's puppet. During the meeting, Omura has Katsumoto arrested
for carrying his sword and suggests that Katsumoto perform ritual suicide to gain
back his honor. He refuses. Algren also refuses Omura's offer to join his new army
and is set upon by Omura's assassins. Algren makes quick work of them. Algren
and Katsumoto's samurai arrive and find some success in their attempt to rescue
Katsumoto, but during the battle, Katsumoto's son, Nobutada (Shin Koyamada),
is wounded and then sacrifices his own life to save his comrades. Pursued by
the Imperial Army, a mourning Katsumoto contemplates the ritual suicide of
seppuku, but is dissuaded by Algren. The samurai use the Imperial Army's boastful
confidence to lure their soldiers into a trap that neutralizes the advantage of their
firearms. In the ensuing battle both sides suffer heavy casualties, but the Imperial soldiers are forced to retreat. Knowing that the soldiers are facing defeat,
Katsumoto orders a suicidal charge on horseback that breaks through Bagley's
line. Algren kills Bagley in battle but as they rush through the line, they are mowed
down by Gatling guns. The Imperial captain, who had been trained by Algren, is
horrified by the mechanized slaughter; he disregards Omura's orders and orders
all of the guns to cease firing. A dying Katsumoto finally commits seppuku with
assistance from Algren, and the soldiers present kneel down in respect for the
fallen samurai. Days later, Algren interrupts trade negotiations at the Imperial Palace in order to present the emperor with Katsumoto's sword, asking him to remember tradition in his dealings, as Katsumoto would have wanted. As a result, the
emperor turns down the trade offer. Omura protests, but the emperor takes all of
Omura's wealth and hands it out to the poor.

Reception

The Last Samurai had its world premiere at Roppongi Hills multiplex in Tokyo on
22 November 2003 and its U.S. premiere at Mann Village Theater in Los Angeles
on 1 December 2003. During its 18-week domestic run (widest release: 2,938 theaters), the movie grossed $111 million. Not surprisingly, given its setting and sub-
ject matter, *The Last Samurai* had higher box office receipts in Japan ($119 million)
than in the United States. Worldwide grosses totaled $345.6 million for a grand
total of $456.7 million, versus a $140 million production budget: a bona fide blockbuster. The critical response in Japan was generally positive. Tomomi Katsuta of *The
Mainichi Shimbun* found the film "a vast improvement over previous American

attempts to portray Japan," praising director Edward Zwick for having "researched Japanese history, cast well-known Japanese actors and consulted dialogue coaches to make sure he didn't confuse the casual and formal categories of Japanese speech." Still, Katsuta observed that even "the samurai had some vulgar attributes. Overall, the film [is] a story of an 'Americanized' or idealized version of the samurai, a story of a utopia to Americans" (Katsuta, 2004). In the United States, Roger Ebert gave the film three and a half stars out of four, saying it was "beautifully designed, intelligently written, acted with conviction, it's an uncommonly thoughtful epic" (Ebert, 2003). More discerning critics found the ideological implications of the movie suspect. As Motoko Rich notes, "Reservations about *The Last Samurai* started with reviews that castigated the movie for its stale portrayals of Japanese culture, as well as the patronizing narrative of a white man teaching the rapidly modernizing Japanese how to honor their past. Tom Long, of *The Detroit News*, wrote that '*The Last Samurai* pretends to honor a culture, but all it's really interested in is cheap sentiment, big fights and, above all, star worship. It is a sham, and further, a shame'" (quoted in Rich, 2004).

Reel History Versus Real History

As noted earlier, *The Last Samurai* draws on disparate events in 19th-century American and Japanese history, making it a mish-mash historically—vaguely true in a generalized way but inaccurate, false, or misleading in many particulars. It is most certainly true that the U.S. Army committed atrocities against Native Americans during the Indian Wars; the slaughter that Algren relives in flashback sequences throughout the film is based on two actual massacres. The first of these was the Sand Creek massacre (29 November 1864), in which a 675-man force of Colorado U.S. Volunteer Cavalry killed and mutilated an estimated 70 to 163 Native Americans of the Cheyenne tribe, about two-thirds of whom were women and children. The second, known as the Washita massacre (27 November 1868), involved an attack by 574 soldiers of Gen. George Armstrong Custer's 7th Cavalry on the same tribe at the Washita River, just west of present-day Cheyenne, Oklahoma (350 miles southeast of the Sand Creek massacre site). Custer's men killed an estimated 100 to 150, an estimated 40 to 75 of whom were women and children. Hereafter the history gets fuzzy because the film conflates elements from Japan's Boshin War (1868–1869) and the Satsuma Rebellion (1877). The fictional Nathan Algren is based on Jules Brunet, the French army captain who fought on the losing side during the Boshin War (which was also a proxy war between Britain, which backed the Imperial Court, and France, which backed the Shogunate, i.e., Japan's last feudal military government). The figure of Katsumoto, the samurai chieftain, is anachronistically based on Saigō Takamori, who led the Satsuma Rebellion eight years after the end of the Boshin War. Algren could have been at the Washita massacre and in the Boshin War, but the chronology is tight. The Boshin War ended 27 June 1869—seven months after the Washita massacre, but the film shows Algren involved in the early stages of the war, which started on 27 January 1868—exactly 10 months before Washita. Transforming the Brunet figure into an American was obviously a sop to American audiences but not good history. Although it is true that the United States' Perry Expedition (1853–1854) forced Japan to abandon its feudal ways and rapidly modernize—developments that led to the Boshin War—the movie strongly implies that the United States was the primary impetus behind Japan's Westernization and elides the actual European imperialist nations that were equally involved (Britain, the Netherlands, and France). As for Katsumoto's real-life inspiration, Saigō Takamori, he ended up committing suicide on 24 September 1877 after defeat in battle, much like his fictional counterpart. The film accurately portrays the emperor as having a reverential attitude toward Katsumoto, the Takamori figure—an attitude in line with popular sentiment; shortly after his death a statue of Takamori was erected in Ueno in northeast Tokyo. It still stands today. However, the movie is grossly inaccurate in depicting the samurai as eschewing firearms in favor of traditional weapons (e.g., swords, bows, and lances). As Akira Kurosawa shows in *Kagemusha* (1980) and *Ran* (1985), the samurai started using tanegashima (the matchlock arquebus) in the middle of the 16th century—300 years before the setting of *The Last Samurai*—and used firearms into the modern era.

LAWRENCE OF ARABIA (1962)

Synopsis
Lawrence of Arabia is a British-American war epic co-produced by Sam Spiegel and David Lean and directed by Lean, with the screenplay written by Robert Bolt and Michael Wilson. The film is based on the life of T. E. Lawrence, a British Army officer who helped lead the successful Arab revolt against Ottoman Turkey during World War I. Starring Peter O'Toole in the title role, *Lawrence of Arabia* is widely regarded as one of the greatest and most influential films in world cinema.

Background
A brilliant and remarkably capable British liaison officer with the rebel forces in the Arab Revolt against the Ottoman Empire in World War I, Thomas Edward Lawrence (1888–1935) became legendary as "Lawrence of Arabia" after his exploits were made famous by American journalist Lowell Thomas. The legend was further enhanced by Lawrence's epic autobiography, *Seven Pillars of Wisdom*, self-published in 1926, then published commercially in 1935. In January 1935 British movie mogul Alexander Korda, who had begun plans for a movie about Lawrence, met with him, but Lawrence dissuaded Korda from making his film while his subject was still alive. Ironically, T. E. Lawrence died five months later, but financial constraints and political turmoil in the Mideast caused Korda to abort the film anyway. Korda tried to revive the project in 1937, 1938, and 1949 but nothing materialized. Harry Cohn at Columbia tried again in 1952 but abandoned plans, unable to satisfy Professor A. W. Lawrence (T. E.'s younger brother and literary executor), who demanded script and casting approval. Around the same time playwright Terence Rattigan approached David Lean with another Lawrence movie script entitled "Ross" (a Lawrence alias) that focused on Lawrence's alleged homosexuality—an angle that did not meet with the approval of A. W. Lawrence. A few years later

British Captain T. E. Lawrence (Peter O'Toole) leads Arab forces against the Ottoman Turks in David Lean's World War I epic, *Lawrence of Arabia* (1962). (Columbia Pictures/ Photofest)

Rattigan revived his Lawrence project. This time he won backing from the Rank Organisation, hired Anthony Asquith as director, and cast Dirk Bogarde in the lead role, but the project was derailed in pre-production by the Iraqi Revolution (July 1958) that made filming in Iraq impossible. Having worked together on *The Bridge on the River Kwai* (1957), producer Sam Spiegel (Columbia Pictures) and David Lean decided to collaborate again. After 25 years of unrealized hopes, a T. E. Lawrence film project finally got underway on 11 February 1960, when A. W. Lawrence sold the rights to *Seven Pillars of Wisdom* to Sam Spiegel for £22,500 ($63,000). At a press conference at Claridge's six days later Spiegel launched the film and announced that Marlon Brando would play Lawrence. Having written *Bridge on the River Kwai* with Carl Foreman, blacklisted American screenwriter Michael Wilson was hired (for $100,000) to adapt *Seven Pillars* to the screen but, unable to satisfy Lean, he quit a year later. Playwright Beverley Cross did some uncredited revision work until Lean hired British TV writer Robert Bolt to rewrite the script as a character study of Lawrence. Many of the characters and scenes were contrived by Wilson but virtually all of the dialogue in the film's final cut was written by Bolt. Meanwhile, Marlon Brando changed his mind about playing Lawrence, opting instead to go to Tahiti and play Fletcher Christian in Lewis Milestone's *Mutiny on the Bounty* (1962). Lean considered Anthony Perkins and Montgomery Clift but hired

Albert Finney to play Lawrence after arranging a four-day screen test in October 1960 that cost £100,000. Unwilling to sign a mandatory long-term contract, Finney quit and was replaced by Peter O'Toole, a virtual unknown who strongly resembled Lawrence (Brownlow, 1996, p. 77). Spiegel's first choice to play Lawrence's closest friend, Sherif Ali, was the French actor Alain Delon, but Delon could not tolerate brown contact lenses, so the part ultimately went to Egyptian actor Omar Sharif.

Production

With the completion of most of the casting and extensive location scouting and preparation, shooting began at Jebel Tubeiq near the border of Jordan and Saudi Arabia on 25 June 1961, a desolate spot in the Jordanian desert 150 miles from the nearest oasis that required trucking in thousands of gallons of water per day at 8¢ per gallon. The shoot was scheduled to last 6 months but ended up taking 14 months. Lean's original intention was to shoot the entire film in Jordan, but remote desert locations, windblown sand, flies, and extreme heat (up to 130°) caused lots of cast and crew illnesses, and costs soared. After five months in Jordan, Columbia Pictures pressured Sam Spiegel to stem the financial hemorrhaging by moving the production to Spain. The first three months (January–March 1962) in Spain were spent shooting city scenes and interiors in the distinctly Moorish city of Seville. The Mudéjar pavilion of the Parque de María Luisa in Seville substituted for Jerusalem. The Plaza de España stood in for Britain's Egyptian Expeditionary Force Headquarters in Cairo. The Cairo officers' club scene, where Lawrence's young companion is refused a drink after crossing the Nefud Desert, was filmed at Palaçio Español, an arcaded building also in the Plaza de España. Various other shots of Seville's Casa de Pilatos and Alcázar were used to represent Cairo and Jerusalem. The climactic Arab council chamber scene in the town hall of Damascus was filmed at El Casino, Avenida de María Luisa. In April 1962, after three months shooting in Seville, the company moved 250 miles southeast to the port city of Almería, Andalusia, a region featuring desert terrain, and, on the coast at Cabo de Gata (Cape of the Cat), the highest and most extensive sand dunes in Europe that closely resemble the Arabian deserts. The entire company traveled to Seville by train, along with their lodging trailers, and a 48-truck convoy transported the other set pieces, costumes, and equipment. Lean had planned to film at the real Aqaba and the archaeological site at Petra, both in Jordan, but once the production moved to Spain he had Aqaba painstakingly re-created by hiring hundreds of locals from the resort town of Carbonaras to construct more than 300 period building fronts and a quarter-mile-long sea wall at a dried river bed on the Mediterranean Sea known as the Playa del Algarrobico. Lawrence's execution of Gasim, the attacks on Turkish trains, and Deraa exteriors were filmed at Genovese Beach, San Jose, on Cabo de Gata. In July 1962, after three months in Almería and environs, the company moved on to Ouarzazate, Morocco, to film the Tafas massacre, with Moroccan army troops substituting for the Turkish army. Location shooting wrapped on 17 August 1962, and the opening two scenes, shot on location in Dorset and at

St. Paul's Cathedral, were completed shortly thereafter. With regard to cinematography, Lean's director of photography, Freddie Young, shot *Lawrence of Arabia* in Super Panavision, a 70-mm version of the Panavision process used on only three previous films (*The Big Fisherman*, 1959; *Exodus*, 1960; *West Side Story*, 1961). The wide-screen format required Freddie Young to rely on longer and more fluid takes that fit with Lean's extensive use of extreme long shots, pans, and following/tracking shots. Once the shoot wrapped in August 1962 Lean and his editor, Anne V. Coates, managed to produce a final cut in four months.

Plot Summary

[Part I] The film opens on 19 May 1935 when T. E. Lawrence (Peter O'Toole), 46, is killed in a motorcycle accident near his home in Dorset, England. At his memorial service at St. Paul's Cathedral (London), a reporter (Jack Hedley) tries to gain insight into Lawrence by questioning those who knew him. The story then flashes back to Cairo during the First World War. Over the objections of General Murray (Donald Wolfit), Mr. Dryden (Claude Rains) of the Arab Bureau sends Lt. Lawrence to assess the prospects of Prince Faisal (Alec Guinness) in his revolt against the Ottoman Turks. On the journey, Lawrence's local guide drinks from a well when he isn't allowed and is killed by Sherif Ali (Omar Sharif). Col. Harry Brighton (Anthony Quayle) tells Faisal that he should pull back once defeated, but Lawrence suggests a different tack: an unannounced assault on Aqaba. Although the coastal town appears heavily guarded against an attack from the sea, it has a much weaker defense on its land borders. Sherif Ali, though unsure of Lawrence's plan, is ordered to lead a group of 50 of Faisal's men to attack Aqaba. Lawrence's troops cross the Nefud Desert, traveling day and night, towards much needed rest and water. One of Ali's men, Gasim (I. S. Johar), faints from exhaustion and falls to the ground, unbeknownst to his company, as they are traveling at night. Not wanting to leave a man behind, Lawrence goes back for Gasim, gaining the respect of Sherif Ali. Lawrence convinces the Howeitat tribal leader, Auda abu Tayi (Anthony Quinn), to go against the Turks, but he almost loses the alliance when a personal matter causes one of Ali's soldiers to murder one of Auda's men. Lawrence saves the alliance by offering to personally dispatch the killer, but is shocked to find that the murderer is none other than Gasim, the man whom he doubled back to save. Lawrence has no choice but to shoot him. The next morning, Lawrence and his Arab cohort capture Aqaba. Lawrence shares news of the victory with Dryden and the new commander, General Allenby (Jack Hawkins), and is promoted. After an intermission in the film, Lawrence initiates a guerrilla war against the Turks. Jackson Bentley (Arthur Kennedy), an American journalist, publicizes Lawrence's exploits, making him internationally famous. When Lawrence scouts the enemy-held city of Daraa with Ali, he is arrested. Alongside other Arab citizens, Lawrence is taken to the Turkish Bey (José Ferrer) where he is stripped, ogled, prodded, flogged for defiance, and otherwise tortured before being left in the street. Lawrence is deeply affected by the experience. Soon after, in Jerusalem, General Allenby persuades Lawrence to join the "big push" on Damascus. Lawrence recruits an army that is monetarily motivated to fight. They come upon a column of retreating Turkish soldiers who have just massacred the residents of Tafas. One of Lawrence's men from Tafas demands "No prisoners!" He charges the Turks alone and is shot dead. Lawrence takes up the dead man's battle cry. The result is a gruesome slaughter in which Lawrence himself gleefully participates. Lawrence's men take Damascus ahead of Allenby's forces. The Arabs then set up a council to administer the city but despite Lawrence's diplomatic efforts, they bicker constantly and get nothing done. As a result, the city is abandoned to the British. Lawrence attains the rank of colonel, but has outlived his usefulness to both Faisal and the British forces. He is ordered to return to England. As he leaves Damascus in a British staff car, his automobile is passed by a motorcycle, which kicks up a cloud of dust.

Reception

The world premiere of *Lawrence of Arabia* was a Royal Command Performance attended by Queen Elizabeth II at the Odeon, Leicester Square, London, on 10 December 1962. The movie went into wide release in the UK the next day and then opened in the United States five days later. Audience reaction was enthusiastic but reviews were mixed. Alexander Walker joined many other critics in offering high praise: "*Lawrence of Arabia* is an unprecedented kind of multimillion-dollar spectacle. Here is an epic with intellect behind it. An unforgettable display of action staged with artistry. A momentous story told with moral force. What on earth has wrought this miracle?" (Walker, 1960). Bosley Crowther panned the movie altogether: "Like the desert itself, in which most of the action in *Lawrence of Arabia* takes place, this much-heralded film about the famous British soldier-adventurer . . . is vast, awe-inspiring, beautiful with ever-changing hues, exhausting and barren of humanity. It is such a laboriously large conveyance of eye-filling outdoor spectacle—such a brilliant display of endless desert and camels and Arabs and sheiks and skirmishes with Turks and explosions and arguments with British military men—that the possibly human, moving T. E. Lawrence is lost in it. We know little more about this strange man when it is over than we did when it begins" (Crowther, 1962). Despite widespread confusion and dismay over the film's portrayal of T. E. Lawrence, *Lawrence of Arabia* did well at the box office, grossing $37.5 million in worldwide box office receipts versus a $15 million budget. It also did extremely well in the awards department, with 10 Oscar nominations and 7 wins for Best Picture (Sam Spiegel); Best Director (David Lean); Best Cinematography, Color (Freddie Young); Best Art Direction-Set Decoration, Color (John Box, John Stoll, and Dario Simoni); Best Sound (John Cox); Best Film Editing (Anne V. Coates); and Best Music, Score (Maurice Jarre). Nominated for Best Actor for a performance often cited as the greatest of all time, Peter O'Toole lost to Gregory Peck for his rendition of Atticus Finch in *To Kill a Mockingbird*. *Lawrence of Arabia* also won four BAFTA Awards and six Golden Globes. Since its initial run in 1962–1963, the film has since been restored and re-released numerous times all over the world; its stature as one of the greatest films is secure. It is worth noting, however, that despite its epic length (227 minutes), the film has no women in speaking roles: an odd feature that Molly Haskell aptly characterizes as "covert misogyny" (Haskell, 2016, p. 330).

Reel History Versus Real History

A boldly revisionist cinematic portrait of T. E. Lawrence, *Lawrence of Arabia* features some authentic content but is rife with glaring historical inaccuracies. The website *T. E. Lawrence Studies* provides an exhaustive catalog of the film's myriad misrepresentations—too many to list here (www.telstudies.org/discussion/film_tv _radio/lofa_or_sid_2.shtml). What follows is a discussion of some of the major points of contention. Peter O'Toole resembled Lawrence but critics point out that O'Toole was 6'2"—almost nine inches taller than the man he portrayed. More problematic is the movie's portrayal of Lawrence as a publicity seeker who had, in the words of Lowell Thomas, "a genius for backing into the limelight." This is debatable insofar as Lawrence assumed various aliases after the war to evade attention— yet he also wrote and published *Seven Pillars of Wisdom: A Triumph*, an enormously ambitious memoir of his WWI service, albeit privately circulated during Lawrence's lifetime. In the movie, O'Toole's extreme handsomeness, slightly effeminate manner, and total absence of a female love interest strongly suggest that Lawrence is homosexual—a surmise also made by some Lawrence biographers but contradicted by letters brought to light six years after the film came out, proving that Lawrence was actually a masochist addicted to flagellation (cf. Bruce, 1968). Ironically, the film portrays Lawrence as a sadist who took pleasure in shooting Gasim and slaughtering Turks at the Tafas Massacre. As depicted in the film, Lawrence did rescue the Arab boy, Gasim, but did not shoot him later (the movie conflates two unrelated incidents). Though otherwise quite accurate, the film's depiction of the Tafas Massacre misrepresents Lawrence's bloodlust as singularly personal. In *Seven Pillars of Wisdom* Lawrence describes a *collective* frenzy for vengeance: "In a madness born of the horror of Tafas we killed and killed, even blowing in the heads of the fallen and of the animals; as though their death and running blood could slake our agony." Beyond a skewed psychological portrait of Lawrence, the film heavily fictionalizes certain events, such as the attack on Aqaba. In reality, the taking of Aqaba was a well-planned joint land–sea operation, not a surprise initiative by Lawrence. In the movie Lawrence is made aware of and appalled by the Sykes-Picot Agreement in the late stages of the Arab Revolt. In reality Lawrence knew about Sykes-Picot—a secret treaty between Russia, France, and Britain that precluded Arab self-determination by proposing a carving up of the Ottoman Empire after its defeat—early on. His own hypocrisy in dealing with Faisal and the Arabs caused him endless pangs of conscience. The culminating Arab Council scenes are also wildly inaccurate. The council did not quickly dissolve into bickering and chaos; it remained in power in Syria from 1 October 1918 until 24 July 1920, when France deposed Faisal. When Michael Wilson's script was replaced by Bolt's character-driven version, much background material on the history of the region, the First World War, and the Arab Revolt was lost.

LETTERS FROM IWO JIMA [JAPANESE: IŌJIMA KARA NO TEGAMI] (2006)

Synopsis

Letters from Iwo Jima is a Japanese-American war film directed and co-produced by Clint Eastwood, starring Ken Watanabe and Kazunari Ninomiya. The companion piece to Eastwood's *Flags of Our Fathers*, this film depicts the World War II Battle of Iwo Jima from the Japanese perspective and is almost entirely in Japanese, although it was produced by American companies DreamWorks, Malpaso Productions, and Amblin Entertainment.

Background

A tiny Pacific island about 650 miles due south of Japan, Iwo Jima would have remained inconspicuous except that the World War II battle over its control (19 February–26 March 1945) turned out to be one of history's most savage battles. Before emerging victorious, the U.S. Marine Corps suffered 26,038 casualties (6,821 killed; 19,217 wounded) among some 70,000 soldiers deployed, whereas only 1,083 of the island's 22,786 Japanese defenders survived to be captured: a fatality rate of 95 percent. Honored cinematically by two Hollywood docudramas—*Sands of Iwo Jima* (1949) and *The Outsider* (1961)—the Battle of Iwo Jima received renewed attention with Clint Eastwood's *Flags of Our Fathers* (2006). Eastwood's original intention was to tell both the American and Japanese sides of the story, but as production developed, it became obvious that there was simply too much disparate material for one film so Eastwood decided to split it into two films. The screenplay for *Letters*, written by Paul Haggis and Iris Yamashita, was based on two sources: letters left behind by Iwo Jima's Japanese garrison commander, General Tadamichi Kuribayashi (1890–1945), and Kumiko Kakehashi's *So Sad to Fall in Battle: An Account of War*, also based on Gen. Kuribayashi's letters. *Letters from Iwo Jima* was shot right after *Flags*, and almost entirely in Japanese, despite the fact that it was produced by American film companies, as mentioned. Except for Ken Watanabe, the Japanese cast members were selected through auditions in Japan.

Production

Originally entitled "Red Sun, Black Sand" and budgeted at $19 million, *Letters from Iwo Jima* was shot over a 32-day period in the spring of 2006. Whereas Eastwood shot the Iwo Jima beach landing scenes for *Flags* in Iceland (which features black volcanic sand like Iwo Jima's), he shot the Iwo Jima beach scenes for *Letters* at Leo Carrillo State Beach in Malibu and had black sand trucked in from Pisgah Volcano, a volcanic cinder cone 321 feet high and 1,600 feet across in the Mojave Desert, about 30 miles from Barstow, California, a site also used for filming. The scenes featuring Japanese-dug caves and tunnels on Iwo Jima were actually shot in and around an old silver mine at Calico Ghost Town in Barstow. A flashback scene that shows Gen. Kuribayashi receiving a gift of a Colt .45 from an American friend at a farewell banquet at what is supposed to be the Fort Bliss Country Club near El Paso, Texas, was actually shot at the clubhouse at the Griffith Park Golf

Course in Los Angeles. The battleship USS *Texas* (BB-35), now a museum ship stationed in La Porte, Texas, was used for close-up shots of the fleet for both movies. Location filming wrapped on 8 April, and the cast and crew then headed back to Warner Bros.' Burbank Studios, where more interior scenes were shot on Stage 21. At the very end of the shoot, Eastwood, Watanabe, and a smaller group of crew members went to Iwo Jima for a single day to capture the on-location shots.

Plot Summary

In 2005, Japanese archaeologists exploring tunnels on Iwo Jima find something in the dirt. The scene shifts back 61 years, to Iwo Jima in 1944. Pfc. Saigo (Kazunari Ninomiya) and his crew dig trenches on the beach. Meanwhile, Lt. Gen. Tadamichi Kuribayashi (Ken Watanabe) arrives to assume leadership and surveys the defenses currently set up on the island [19 June 1944]. He saves Saigo and his friend Kashiwara (Takashi Yamaguchi) from a beating by Capt. Tanida (Takumi Bando) for "unpatriotic speeches" and orders the men to start digging underground defenses in Mount Suribachi. Kuribayashi and Lt. Col. Baron Takeichi Nishi (Tsuyoshi Ihara), a famous Olympic gold medalist show jumper, clash with some of the other officers, who do not agree with Kuribayashi's defense-in-depth strategy. Kuribayashi posits that the American troops will have an easier time breaking through the beach defenses and suggests that the mountain strongholds stand a better chance of keeping them out. Unclean water and malnutrition lead to multiple deaths by dysentery, including the loss of Kashiwara (Takashi Yamaguchi). Kashiwara's replacement, Superior Private Shimizu (Ryô Kase), comes under suspicion of being a Kempeitai (Military Police Corps) spy dispatched to identify and track disloyal troops. Not long after Shimizu's arrival, the Americans arrive, overwhelm the island, and attack Mount Suribachi. Ordered to retreat by Kuribayashi, the commander of the Suribachi garrison orders his soldiers to kill themselves rather than concede. However, Saigo flees with Shimizu, and the two decide to battle on. They come upon other soldiers and try to flee the mountain with Lt. Oiso under the cover of darkness. Marines discover them and kill all except Saigo and Shimizu. The Japanese counterattack, but suffer major casualties. The surviving soldiers go to meet up with Col. Nishi while Ito leaves for the U.S. lines with a trio of landmines and a plan to detonate them beneath an American tank. As the battle continues, Nishi is rendered blind by shrapnel and calls on his men to retreat. Nishi then goes into a cave and a gunshot is heard, signaling his suicide. Shimizu surrenders to the Americans, but is then shot by the man guarding him. Meanwhile, a starving Ito succumbs to despair; when found by U.S. Marines, he surrenders. Okubo is killed, but Saigo reunites with Kuribayashi, who plans a final attack. That night, during the attack, most of Kuribayashi's men perish, and although Kuribayashi is badly hurt, his aid, Fujita, carries him to safety. The following morning, to die with honor, Kuribayashi commands his aid to behead him, but a Marine shoots Fujita before he can proceed. Saigo, after burying some of the documents and letters that he was ordered to burn, comes upon Kuribayashi and, after Kuribayashi commits suicide, tearfully buries him. An American Marine discovers Kuribayashi's gun near Fujita's body and tucks it into his belt. Saigo, recognizing the gun, flies into a rage and attacks the Marine and his fellow troop members with a shovel. He is knocked out, and then awakens to see the sun setting. The film flashes forward to 2005, where archeologists finish their excavation and discover the bag of letters that Saigo buried.

Reception

Letters from Iwo Jima had its world premiere at the Budokan Arena in Tokyo on 15 November 2006. The movie went into wide release in Japan three weeks later (9 December 2006), ran until 15 April 2007, and grossed the equivalent of $42.9 million: a bona fide box office hit. The film's commercial (and critical) success in Japan was due to the fact that it was in Japanese, used Japanese actors, and presented a refreshingly respectful depiction of WWII Japanese soldiers—a far cry from the crude racist propaganda of American World War II–era war films or those made in the decades that followed, which were less crude but continued to traffic in stereotypes and often employed non-Japanese actors using incorrect Japanese grammar and non-native accents to portray Japanese characters. Put into limited release in the United States for the Christmas 2006 weekend, *Letters from Iwo Jima* ran for 21 weeks but, not surprisingly, earned only $13.75 million—a third of the Japanese box office gross. Total foreign sales of $54.9 million, combined with domestic returns, boosted the film's final take to $68.7 million—almost $50 million more than it cost to make. After *Flags of Our Fathers* underperformed at the box office, DreamWorks swapped the domestic distribution rights with Warner Bros., which held the international rights. The critical response in the United States matched the acclaim the film received in Japan, with many American film critics naming *Letters from Iwo Jima* the best film of 2006. The movie also earned a Golden Globe for Best Film in a Foreign Language and received four Academy Award nominations, winning an Oscar for Best Sound Editing.

Reel History Versus Real History

Noriko Manabe (a Japanese doctoral student in ethnomusicology at CUNY Graduate Center in 2007 who is now a music professor at Temple University) offered a summary of *Letters from Iwo Jima*'s inaccuracies, as catalogued by Japanese bloggers. Acknowledging that Japanese viewers "appreciated the film for its anti-war message, its sentimental story, and its surprisingly sympathetic stance for an American director," Manabe also noted that "an articulate minority" have taken issue with the film's historical inaccuracies, for example, all the scenes looked "too clean—those battles, let alone our cities, were far more wretched . . . Some reviewers commented that Kuribayashi's assertion that there was 'no support' was not accurate, as kamikazes (suicide pilots) had sunk several American warships . . . Several commented about the unnaturalness of the characters' behavior and dialogue ('would a low-ranking soldier like Saigo have used such rough language, in that era?') Another pointed out, 'All the mistakes in the customs of the period bothered us. Shoji screens were never used for the front door—how can you knock on paper? And young people had been wearing Western clothing, not kimonos, since the 1930s." For Manabe, "The greatest concern is that the film fails to explain why the Japanese felt the need to defend a seemingly insignificant island so fervently—the fear that the firebombing of Japanese cities, already devastating to civilians, would intensify were the Americans to gain Iwo Jima as a launching pad for air strikes. In not explaining this background, viewers felt that the film catered to the stereotype of the Japanese as lemming-like fanatics." Manabe also noted that "viewers raised objections that 'good' was being equated with being America-friendly. As one user stated, 'Only officers who had been to the U.S. are depicted as rational and smart, while all other Japanese officers are evil and barbaric, as per the American stereotype' (Manabe, 2007). Unaware of the film's many inaccuracies, most American viewers and film critics embraced *Letters from Iwo Jima* as a laudably liberal-minded revisionist war film finally humanizing an often-demonized people—which it is, to a significant degree. However, as Ms. Manabe points out, the subtle truth is that, despite its pretenses to the contrary, *Letters* remains stubbornly Amerocentric in its cultural orientation and ideological predilections.

LONE SURVIVOR (2013)

Synopsis

Lone Survivor is an American war film written and directed by Peter Berg. Based on the 2007 nonfiction book of the same title by former Navy SEAL Marcus Luttrell (co-authored with Patrick Robinson), the film dramatizes a failed U.S. Navy SEALs counterinsurgency mission in Afghanistan that turned into a desperate struggle for survival.

Background

On 27 June 2005, in the fourth year of the U.S. war in Afghanistan, the U.S. military launched Operation Red Wings, an attempt to capture or neutralize Ahmad Shah (1970–2008), a dangerous Taliban leader. The operation involved first inserting a four-man Navy SEAL reconnaissance and surveillance team into Shah's home territory, the Korangal Valley, to locate him. Unfortunately the mission quickly went awry when the SEALs ran into local herdsmen, who alerted the Taliban to their presence. The team was subsequently ambushed and all were killed—except for USN Petty Officer 2nd Class Marcus Luttrell, who was eventually rescued, but not before another eight SEALs and eight Army Airborne SOAR troopers died trying to reach the battle site when their helicopter was shot down by the Taliban. Avid to publish his own account of the disastrous mission, he hired a lawyer and searched for a ghost writer. Luttrell's lawyer connected him with Ed Victor, literary agent to the stars, who also represented Patrick Robinson, a 66-year-old British novelist specializing in maritime thrillers, including novels about Navy SEALs. After Luttrell hired Robinson, the two men met four times at Robinson's summer home on Cape Cod to hash out Luttrell's story. According to Motoko Rich, "Between visits Mr. Robinson, who never used a taped recorder, typed chapters on his computer, adding researched material and filling in facts that

Mr. Luttrell couldn't remember but that could be corroborated from other sources. The core of the book—the battle and the rescue—relied entirely on Mr. Luttrell's memory" (Rich, 2007). Over a four-month period Robinson produced a 135,000-word manuscript, the U.S. Navy reviewed and approved it as accurate, and then Robinson and Luttrell met with five publishers in New York to pitch the book. In an auction Little, Brown and Company won the contract for a seven-figure advance and rushed the book into production. Meanwhile Luttrell returned to active duty and shipped out to Iraq as part of Navy SEAL Team Five during Operation Iraqi Freedom—until further injuries forced his medical discharge from military service on 7 June 2007. Five days later, Little, Brown and Company published *Lone Survivor: The Eyewitness Account of Operation Redwing* [sic] *and the Lost Heroes of SEAL Team 10*. Showcased on NBC's *The Today Show* and touted by right-wing media pundits Glenn Beck and Michelle Malkin, *Lone Survivor* went on to become a national bestseller. Motoko Rich's aforementioned review was laudatory, but Rich went on to note, "Along with the tragic story about how Mr. Luttrell lost his comrades, the book is spiked with unabashed braggadocio and patriotism, as well as several polemical passages lashing out at the 'liberal media' for its role in sustaining military rules of engagement that prevent soldiers from killing unarmed civilians who may also be scouts or informers for terrorists." After it reached No. 1 on bestseller charts, *Lone Survivor* touched off a second bidding war in August 2007, this time between Universal, Warner Bros., DreamWorks, and Sony for the film rights, which Universal won, buying the property for $2 million up front, plus 5 percent against adjusted gross in a deal brokered by Ed Victor and Hollywood super-lawyer Alan U. Schwartz of Greenberg Traurig. Eager to make *Lone Survivor*, Peter Berg (*Friday Night Lights*) secured a deal with Universal by agreeing to direct *Battleship* (2012), a big budget sci-fi film that turned out to be a critically panned box office bomb. Berg also agreed to direct *Lone Survivor* for the minimum fee allowed by the Director's Guild of America (DGA) and convinced his principal actors—Mark Wahlberg, Taylor Kitsch, Emile Hirsch, Ben Foster, and Eric Bana—to work for reduced pay. Berg wrote the screen adaptation of *Lone Survivor* in close consultation with Marcus Luttrell, whom he had cultivated early on.

Production

The 42-day shoot on *Lone Survivor* took place in October and November 2012 in New Mexico to take advantage of a 25 percent state tax credit. The initial eight days of filming occurred at locations in the Sangre de Cristo Mountains of Santa Fe National Forest—mountains ranging from 11,000 to 12,000 feet that doubled for mountains in the Hindu Kush between Afghanistan and Pakistan. Production then moved to Chilili, New Mexico, for two weeks, where wooded areas were used to film several battle scenes. Berg's art department built sets to simulate an Afghan village occupied by Ahmad Shah's Taliban insurgents, as well as the Pashtun village where Luttrell is finally rescued. The shoot then moved to Kirtland AFB in Albuquerque, which doubled for scenes set at Bagram Airfield in Afghanistan. The shoot wrapped up on sound stages at I-25 Studios in Albuquerque for bluescreen work and interior scenes (e.g., Gulab's house and Bagram Airfield's patrol base

Camp Ouellette). Peter Berg's director of photography, Tobias Schliessler, shot the film using Red Epic digital cameras and Fujinon and Angénieux lenses. Marcus Luttrell and several other Navy SEAL veterans were on set throughout the production as technical advisors, while multiple branches of the U.S. military lent their support.

Plot Summary

In Afghanistan, Taliban leader Ahmad Shah (Yousuf Azami) is the man behind the destruction of over 20 American Marines, along with villagers and refugees who assisted the U.S. troops. A U.S. Navy SEAL team is tasked with capturing Shah. Four SEALs are dispatched to locate their target: team leader Michael P. "Murph" Murphy (Taylor Kitsch), snipers Marcus Luttrell (Mark Wahlberg) and Matthew "Axe" Axelson (Ben Foster), and communications specialist Danny Dietz (Emile Hirsch). The team is dropped into the Hindu Kush region of Afghanistan but soon encounters communications problems, which will plague the mission. When they arrive at their rendezvous point, the SEALs are spotted by a shepherd (Zarin Rahimi) and two young goat herders (Rohan Chand and Daniel Arroyo). After talking it over, the team decides not to kill the shepherd and herders and to abort their mission for the time being. However, as they turn back, Taliban fighters discover them and open fire. The team kills some of the attackers, but is quickly outnumbered. All four SEALs are wounded during the firefight, and they are forced to jump from a cliff into a ravine to escape the insurgents. They survive and press on through the woods in retreat. Dietz, near delirious due to his wounds, begins shouting and gives away the unit's position. The Taliban forces shoot and kill him. Murphy attempts to scale the cliff to find a phone signal to radio for support, and he successfully makes a call for backup before being killed by the Taliban fighters. After receiving Murphy's call, a rescue team is put in place and takes two CH-47 Chinook helicopters to the SEALs' location. During the attempted rescue, Taliban fighters gun down one of the helicopters, killing all on board. The second helicopter is forced to turn back without Luttrell and Axelson. Axelson dies attempting to find cover, and when the Taliban find Luttrell, a fighter fires a rocket-propelled grenade (RPG). Luttrell is blasted into a rock crevice, where he takes shelter. He submerges himself in a small pond, and when he surfaces, he is greeted by a local Pashtun villager, Mohammad Gulab (Ali Suliman), who takes Luttrell in and hides him while a fellow villager travels to an American air base for help. In the meantime, Taliban fighters come for Luttrell, but the villagers come to his aid. American troops arrive in helicopters, decimate the Taliban, and evacuate Luttrell back to base. The film ends with a four-minute montage, showing images of the real-life Marcus Luttrell, Mohammad Gulab, and the 19 U.S. soldiers who died during the mission. An epilogue states that the Pashtun locals assisted Luttrell as part of their code of honor.

Reception

Lone Survivor premiered at the AFI Film Festival in Los Angeles on 12 November 2013 and went into wide release on 10 January 2014. The movie proved to a box office hit; during its 17-week domestic run (widest release: 3,285 theaters), *Lone Survivor* grossed $125 million. Foreign ticket sales totaled $29.7 million, making for a total gross of $154.8 million. Reviews were, however, mixed, and some, like David Edelstein's, were highly critical. Edelstein especially faulted Peter Berg for not widening the geopolitical perspective: "The film doesn't link the absence of air support and the near-total failure of communication in the mountains to an administration that diverted personnel and precious resources from Afghanistan to the catastrophic occupation of Iraq, leaving men like Luttrell with a tragically impossible job. Nor does it suggest that one reason good guys like Luttrell and his team had such a difficult time winning 'hearts and minds' was that at places like Bagram . . . prisoners were being tortured to death by U.S. interrogators in the service of Dick Cheney's 'Dark Side' manifesto. Instead, Berg leads you to the conclusion that these Americans were just too good, too true, too respectful. Luttrell's operation—and his team's lives—might have been saved if they'd summarily executed three passing goat-herders rather than following the Rules of Engagement . . . *Lone Survivor* is a brutally effective movie, made by people who think that they're serving their country. But they're just making us coarser and more self-centered. They're perpetuating the kind of propaganda that sent the heroes of Seal Team 10 to their deaths" (Edelstein, 2014).

Reel History Versus Real History

According to Ed Darrack, author of *Victory Point: Operations Red Wings and Whalers— the Marine Corps' Battle for Freedom in Afghanistan* (2009), Patrick Robinson's book, *Lone Survivor*, contains some serious inaccuracies, omissions, and exaggerations. Darrack writes, "The (very gripping, yet extraordinarily unrealistic) narrative of a small special operations team inserted on a lonely mountain to not just surveil, but to take down the operations of one of Osama bin Laden's top men— who had hundreds of fighters with him—continued to propagate throughout the media" (Darrack, 2011, p. 62). In an exhaustively researched series of articles at their website OnViolence.com, Michael and Eric Cummings detail the film's numerous falsehoods. Early in the movie, Axelson (Ben Foster) claims that Ahmad Shah killed 20 Marines in the week before Operation Red Wings, but official casualty records show that the United States did not lose 20 Marines during that period. In the film, Marcus Luttrell literally dies of his wounds and is resuscitated by medics. In his book, Luttrell recalls that he was not in mortal danger when rescued but "reported stable and unlikely to die" (p. 352). The movie depicts Luttrell as having Ahmad Shah in his gunsights at one point. In the book, Luttrell and the SEALs never see Shah, much less aim at him. In the film, Shah's lieutenant, Taraq (Sammy Sheik) comes to the village, grabs Luttrell, and is about to behead him when he is driven off at the last minute by the local villagers firing their AK-47s. In reality, none of this happened; a wounded Luttrell was beaten by Taliban fighters but not threatened with beheading. In the film, Luttrell withstands excruciating pain when he extracts a bullet from his own leg with a knife. This never happened; in reality the bullet went through and through. The movie ends with the villagers of Kandish fending off a massive Taliban attack. The prosaic reality is that there was no attack and ensuing firefight; to scare the villagers, the Taliban merely fired into the air because they couldn't afford to lose their support. In the film, during the final (mythical) battle in the village, Marcus Luttrell stabs a Taliban attacker with a knife. In a radio interview with NPR host Rachel Martin, Luttrell admitted that he "didn't kill anybody with a knife. And I remember sitting back and laughing. I go why did you put that in there? What does that have to do with anything? I mean, the story itself, I think, is enough to where you wouldn't have to embellish anything" (NPR's *Weekend Edition Sunday*, 12 Jan. 2014). In the scene melding with the attack on the village, the American military arrives with gunships routing the Taliban and airborne troopers descending from helicopters. In reality, Luttrell's rescue was far less cinematic; U.S. Army Rangers found him in the forest, walking back to the village with Gulab.

LONGEST DAY, THE (1962)

Synopsis

The Longest Day is a war epic based on Cornelius Ryan's book *The Longest Day* (1959), a comprehensive account of the D-Day landings at Normandy on 6 June 1944, during World War II. Produced by Darryl F. Zanuck and adapted from his own book by Ryan, the film recounts the events of D-Day from a variety of perspectives.

Background

Cornelius Ryan (1920–1974), Irish-born correspondent for London's *Daily Telegraph*, was one of the many war reporters who covered Operation Overlord, the crucial Normandy landings on 6 June 1944. In 1949, on the fifth anniversary of D-Day, after attending a press reunion, Ryan was inspired to try and construct a comprehensive, minute-by-minute account of the invasion. Over most of the next decade Ryan read all 240 books published about D-Day, and he and his researchers conducted 700 interviews with survivors in North America and Europe, of which 383 accounts of D-Day were used in the text of the book. Ryan's book—*The Longest Day: 6 June 1944 D-Day*—first appeared in a condensed *Reader's Digest* version. Published by Simon & Schuster in November 1959, the big book drew excellent reviews, became a bestseller, and established Ryan as a popular historian of international stature. French producer Raoul Lévy purchased the film rights to Ryan's book on 23 March 1960 then signed a deal with Associated British Picture Corporation (ABPC) to make the movie. Ryan's pay: $100,000 for the film rights, plus $35,000 to write the screenplay. Lévy intended to start production in March 1961. Unfortunately, the project had to be aborted when ABPC could not come up with the $6 million needed. In December 1961 Hollywood mogul Darryl F. Zanuck stepped in and purchased Lévy's option for $175,000 as a last chance gamble for 20th Century Fox, which was hemorrhaging millions on its runaway production of *Cleopatra*. Zanuck's friend, Elmo Williams, wrote a film treatment, so Zanuck made him associate producer and coordinator of battle episodes. Ryan commenced on his screen adaptation but often clashed with Zanuck, forcing Williams to mediate between the two throughout the script development process (Zanuck also brought in other writers to help: David Pursall, Jack Seddon, James Jones, and Romain Gary). During pre-production, producer Frank McCarthy (*Patton*), who had worked for the U.S. War Department during World War II, arranged for military collaboration with the governments of France, Germany, the United Kingdom, and the United States. With eight major battle scenes planned, Zanuck decided to hire multiple directors—Germany's Gerd Oswald and Bernhard Wicki (*Die Brücke*), Britain's Ken Annakin, and the American Andrew "Bandy" Marton—to head their own film units and shoot simultaneously. Zanuck coordinated their efforts and also did some directing in his own right. The intent all along was to have a big star-studded cast. Zanuck was able to sign a wide swathe of mostly A-list talent: John Wayne, Robert Mitchum, Henry Fonda, Robert Ryan, Rod Steiger, Richard Todd, Richard Burton, Robert Wagner, Jeffrey Hunter, Paul Anka, Sal Mineo, Roddy McDowall, Stuart Whitman, Eddie Albert, Edmond O'Brien, Red Buttons, Peter Lawford, and Sean Connery. All the major stars were paid $25,000 except John Wayne, who insisted on $250,000, to punish producer Zanuck for referring to him as "poor John Wayne" in reference to Wayne's problems with his pet project, *The Alamo* (1960), which flopped. Zanuck hired more than 2,000 real soldiers for the film as extras.

Production

Filming of *The Longest Day* took place over a nine-month period (August 1961–16 June 1962). The film was shot at several French locations, including the Île de Ré, Saleccia beach in Saint-Florent, Haute-Corse, Port-en-Bessin-Huppain (filling in for Ouistreham), Les Studios de Boulogne in Boulogne-Billancourt in Paris and the actual locations of Pegasus Bridge near Bénouville, Calvados, Sainte-Mère-Église, and Pointe du Hoc. The U.S. Sixth Fleet provided extensive support to the production, making available many amphibious landing ships and craft for scenes filmed in Corsica. The USS *Springfield* and USS *Little Rock*, both World War II light cruisers (though updated as guided missile cruisers), were used in the shore bombardment scenes.

Plot Summary

Ryan's book is divided into three parts: The Wait, The Night, and The Day. The film follows the same format, devoting about an hour to each section. It also adds a prologue that features Field Marshall Erwin Rommel (Werner Hinz) briefing subordinates. Rommel expresses his intent to defeat the coming invasion on the beaches and declares, "For the Allies, as well as Germany," that day "will be the longest day!" The film proper begins with German intelligence intercepting a coded message that seems to indicate the invasion is now imminent, but the High Command refuses to put troops on alert. Rommel discusses the stormy weather with an aide and expects it to last another week. In England on 5 June, various vignettes show invasion troops moving from staging points or whiling away the time on land and at sea, gambling or complaining about the food, the bad weather, and the seemingly endless waiting for the appointed hour as the weather has forced repeated postponements of the invasion. Col. Thompson (Eddie Albert) tells Gen. Norman Cota (Robert Mitchum) that the operation is likely about to start, "providing the weather doesn't get any worse." Lt. Col. Benjamin "Vandy" Vandervoort (John Wayne) meets with Brig. Gen. James M. Gavin (Robert Ryan) and expresses his concern about the planned paratrooper drop zone his men have been assigned. He wants it changed but relents when Gavin informs him that the chances that Operation Overlord will commence shortly "are better than 50–50." On the German side, Gen. Erich Marcks (Richard Münch) predicts the Allies will do the unexpected and attack at Normandy (the longest distance across the English Channel) and in bad weather. Gen. Dwight Eisenhower (Henry Grace) and his top generals are briefed by Royal Air Force (RAF) meteorologist Group Capt. J. N. Stagg (Patrick Barr), who predicts a window of moderately decent weather. Ike asks Sir Bernard L. Montgomery (Trevor Reid) his opinion. Monty says, "Go! Go!" The moon and tides won't be favorable again until July so Ike decides to proceed with the invasion. Gen. Gavin briefs his pathfinder paratroopers. An RAF airborne officer demonstrates "Rupert," a paradummy decoy loaded with fireworks that go off when it lands. It is hoped that many Ruperts will divert German defenders away from real paratroopers. Vandervoort briefs his men about signaling each other with "crickets" (i.e., clickers) once they land in their drop zone. French resistance fighters are stunned to get the coded radio transmission that the invasion is on; they break out weapons and move out. The Germans intercept coded radio messages indicating the invasion will start in the next 24 hours; the 15th Army is put on alert. At midnight over Normandy, Major Howard's (Patrick Jordan) glider detachment releases from their towing planes to land. Their mission, to secure the strategically vital Pegasus Bridge on the Orne River before the Germans can blow it up, proves successful. Caen, 1:07 hours: German AA guns open up on Allied transports dropping airborne troops as German ground troops muster. The Ruperts do their job, fooling the Germans into mistakenly diverting troops. French resistance fighters cut German phone lines and team up with British airborne troopers to blow up a train carrying German reinforcements. Sainte-Mère-Église, 2:03 hours: U.S. paratroopers of the 82nd Airborne Division jump in force. One group overshoots its landing zone and lands in the town square, where they are slaughtered by waiting German troops. Pvt. John Steele (Red Buttons) lands on the pinnacle of a church tower and hangs suspended, watching in horror as the carnage unfolds below him. At a coastal bunker Wehrmacht Maj. Werner Pluskat (Hans Christian Blech) phones headquarters to report hundreds of Allied planes in the skies. Vandervoort breaks his ankle jumping and discovers that his paratroopers have missed their drop zones and are scattered all over. German Field Marshall Gerd Von Rundstedt (Paul Hartmann) requests that reserve panzer divisions be mobilized to counter the invasion, but Col. Gen. Alfred Jodl (Wolfgang Lukschy) refuses to release them without Hitler's permission—and the Fuhrer is asleep and not to be disturbed. French Cmdr. Philippe Kieffer (Christian Marquand) leads his commandos into battle. Pluskat looks out from his bunker with binoculars and suddenly sees hundreds of ships approaching. He exclaims, "The invasion—it's coming!" Soon the Allied warships begin shelling. Omaha Beach, 6:32 hours: the landings begin and German troops man fortifications and open fire. Gen. Roosevelt discovers that his troops have landed at the wrong beach, a mile and a half south of their intended destination but decides to proceed anyway. Two German fighter pilots—Col. Josef "Pips" Priller (Heinz Reincke) and his wingman—strafe Gold-Juno beaches, one of the only Luftwaffe sorties on D-Day. Allied fighters strafe a German column, and Pluskat is wounded. Point de Hoc, 7:11 hours: U.S. Army Rangers use ladders and ropes attached to grappling hooks to successfully scale the supposedly impregnable 100-foot cliffs of Point du Hoc and take the German bunkers, but discover that the big guns they were supposed to take out were never installed. Lord Lovat (Peter Lawford), accompanied by his personal bagpiper, leads reinforcements to isolated British paratroopers at the Orne River Bridge. Cmdr. Kieffer and his Free French commandos attack the seaside town of Ouistreham but meet heavy resistance. A group of nuns shows up in the middle of the battle to nurse the French wounded. Then a U.S. Army tank appears on the scene and blasts the German position to ruins, allowing the French to win the battle. Troops advance on the beaches—except for Omaha Beach, where the assault falters, held back by a cement wall that prevents the troops from advancing, but Brigadier General Cota rallies his men. Sgt. John H. Fuller (Jeffrey Hunter) blasts a clear path from the beach with a dynamite charge. An American paratrooper comes across a dead German officer who has been shot by Flying Officer David Campbell (Richard Burton), a downed and wounded RAF pilot. Burton concludes, "He's dead. I'm crippled. You're lost. I suppose it's always like that, war." The G.I. asks wistfully, "I wonder who won."

Reception

The Longest Day had its world premiere at the Palais de Chaillot in Paris on 25 September 1962, a six-hour gala event that was likely the most extravagant film opening ever staged. Detachments of British, French, and American troops stood ceremonial guard for the arrival of 2,700 guests, some of whom paid as much as $70 ($583 in 2017 dollars) for a ticket. After the screening, there were fireworks at the Eifel Tower, where Edith Piaf gave a free concert. There was also a champagne supper for 400 of the guests, which included lots of Hollywood celebrities and 10 French cabinet ministers. The film had its U.S. opening in New York on 4 October and its London opening a week later. Luckily for Darryl Zanuck and 20th Century Fox, *The Longest Day* proved to be a box office smash, grossing $39.1 million domestically and $11 million in foreign markets for a total of $50.1 million against a $10 million production budget. Reviews tended to be adulatory, like Bosley Crowther's: "The total effect of the picture is that of a huge documentary report, adorned and colored by personal details that are thrilling, amusing, ironic, sad . . . It is hard to think of a picture, aimed and constructed as this one was, doing any more or any better or leaving one feeling any more exposed to the horror of war than this one does" (Crowther, 5 October 1962). Later assessments have been more discerning and insightful, for example, Scott Macdonald's: "Despite its multiple threads, it is overlong, with too much fat hanging off the narrative, becoming bogged down early in tedious exposition, when it should be pushing forward relentlessly, as the tension and drama builds . . . since it has multiple directors

and styles . . . it crumbles under its own epic intentions and lack of cohesion"
(Macdonald, 2004).

Reel History Versus Real History

To his credit, Darryl F. Zanuck sought to preserve the depth and breadth of Cornelius Ryan's sprawling history of D-Day while also striving for historical accuracy. Accordingly, Zanuck hired Ryan to adapt his own book to the screen and also retained some two dozen military and technical advisors, most of them D-Day veterans, to ensure that uniforms, weapons, and events were properly represented. Nonetheless, a three-hour movie epic cannot be a cinematic history lesson; it also has to have commercial appeal to recoup its enormous production costs. A notable concession to this prerogative is evident in the film's casting of a plethora of big-name movie stars: distracting but not historically invalid, except in the case of John Wayne, who was absurdly miscast as Lt. Col. Benjamin Vandervoort (1917–1990), the commanding officer of the 2nd Battalion, 505th PIR - 82nd Airborne Division at D-Day. Vandervoort was a compact, athletic man 27 years of age in 1944, whereas Wayne was a lumbering 6'4" and 55 years old in 1961: 28 years older and much bigger than his real-life counterpart—a preposterous paratrooper. Other bits of Hollywood window dressing involved the casting of teen idols Paul Anka, Fabian Anthony Forte (aka Fabian), and Sal Mineo and the portrayal of French Resistance fighter Janine Gille-Boitard (1907–2001) by Zanuck's then-mistress, French bombshell Irina Demick: 12 years younger in 1961 than Boitard would have been in 1944 and far sexier, no doubt, in cleavage-revealing outfits and a modishly styled hairdo unknown to the 1940s. As for historical inaccuracies, one involves the so-called Ruperts. The paradummy decoys used at Normandy were not elaborate rubber figures and did not contain fireworks, as shown in the movie; they were stuffed forms, crudely made out of burlap. Though the film's rendition of "Operation Deadstick," the taking of Pegasus Bridge by British Glider forces, is quite accurate, it does embellish the American airborne drop at Sainte-Mère-Église for dramatic purposes. In reality, very few paratroopers landed in the town square, compared to the fairly large number in the movie, who are then slaughtered. There was, indeed, a Pvt. John Steele, who ended up hanging off a church roof. In the movie, Steel intently watches the battle below. The real Pvt. Steele played dead in order to survive, and he dangled for two hours, not six. The movie also shows paratroopers firing their weapons as they descended—not possible, according to actual paratroopers. Another inaccuracy involves the scene depicting the U.S. Army Ranger assault on Point de Hoc, which shows the Rangers mounting the cliff face with grappling hooks, ropes, and ladders. In reality, these methods largely failed; most of the Rangers resorted to scaling the cliff face by free climbing. The movie also depicts the big guns as never having been installed—not true. They were installed, but the Germans removed them from their emplacements to avoid Allied naval shelling and set them farther back, where they were later found and taken out by the Rangers. The scene depicting nuns at Ouistreham braving gunfire to nurse French commando casualties is another example of fictional license; there was no nunnery at Ouistreham.

M

MASTER AND COMMANDER: THE FAR SIDE OF THE WORLD (2003)

Synopsis

Master and Commander: The Far Side of the World is an American period war epic adapted from three novels in Patrick O'Brian's Aubrey-Maturin series by Peter Weir who also produced and directed. Set during the Napoleonic Wars, the film stars Russell Crowe as Jack Aubrey, captain in the Royal Navy, and Paul Bettany as Dr. Stephen Maturin. It follows the HMS *Surprise*, a British frigate, as it pursues the French privateer, *Acheron*, across the Pacific Ocean.

Background

The prolific English novelist, Patrick O'Brian (1914–2000), was best known for his hugely popular Aubrey-Maturin books: a series of 20 nautical historical novels published between 1969 and 1999, set during the Napoleonic Wars and centering on the friendship between Royal Navy Capt. Jack Aubrey and his ship's surgeon, Dr. Stephen Maturin, a physician, naturalist, and spy. Independent producer Sam Goldwyn, Jr. bought the film rights to O'Brian's novels in 1992, but according to Tom Rothman, chairman of 20th Century Fox, Goldwyn had trouble finding a top-flight director and actor: "Sam had many opportunities to make the film with more workmanlike directors, but he felt it was exceptional material that required an exceptional director" (de Vries, 2004, p. F1). In early 2000, director Peter Weir (*The Truman Show*) stopped by Rothman's Hollywood office to see what projects he might have for him. Rothman pitched him the Aubrey-Maturin series, a property that Weir had passed on in 1993, but this time he accepted the assignment. Researching tall ships, Weir found the *Rose*, an exact modern replica of the original HMS *Rose*, a 20-gun Royal Navy frigate built in 1757 and scuttled in 1779. The newer ship had been built in Nova Scotia, Canada, in 1970 as a dockside attraction. Even before he had a deal to make the film, Weir asked Fox to buy the *Rose*, which it did for $1.5 million; the studio later re-outfitted the ship as the HMS *Surprise* for the movie. Weir and screenwriter John Collee then set about writing a script, drawing on many novels from O'Brian's series but mostly basing their adaptation on *The Far Side of the World* (1984), a novel set during the War of 1812 that pits the *Surprise* against an American warship, the USS *Norfolk*. A key change from book to script involved setting the story in 1805 and having the *Surprise* fight a French vessel—a choice obviously made for political and commercial reasons; opposing Napoleon was more palatable than having Aubrey fight a fledgling democracy and more acceptable to American audiences. To play Jack Aubrey, Weir signed megastar Russell Crowe in late 2001. Weir and Crowe then worked closely for several weeks with the Oscar-winning screenwriter Akiva Goldsman (*A Beautiful Mind*) to flesh out the relationship between Aubrey and his friend, Dr. Maturin (played by Paul Bettany).

Production

Before principal photography began, the cast was put through a two-week boot camp where they literally learned the ropes and other nautical skills in handling early 19th-century sailing vessels. The actors were also taught swordplay and how to load and fire cannons. Because of the enormous technical complexities in depicting naval warfare in the age of sail, *Master and Commander* was an expensive production: the final price tag was a whopping $150 million. It was also a long production that stretched over a five-month period (17 June–11 November 2002) and involved some 30 actors; dozens of extras; 970 technicians of all kinds (including 70 stunt men); 2,000 costumes; and extensive use of miniatures, models, and computer-generated imagery (CGI). There was location shooting in the Galapagos Islands and at sea for 10 days, with the aforementioned *Rose* masquerading as the *Surprise*, but most exterior shots were filmed in the huge (17 million gallon) horizon tank that James Cameron had built to film *Titanic* (1997), located at Fox Baja Studios in Playas de Rosarito, Baja, Mexico. Here the filmmakers used another replica of the *Surprise*, mounted inside the horizon tank on a hydraulically controlled gimbal that allowed it pitch in all directions—gently—to simulate normal sailing and, more violently, to mimic the action of heavy seas, as in the Cape Horn sequence (which was supplemented by actual footage of stormy seas taken aboard a modern replica of Capt. James Cook's ship, HMS *Endeavour*, as it sailed around the Cape while circumnavigating the globe). For interior shots of the *Surprise* (and its nemesis, the *Acheron*) Weir had a set built for each deck in sound stages adjacent to the horizon tank at Baja. Captain Aubrey plays the violin so Russell Crowe had to learn the instrument: a task he said was the hardest thing he ever learned.

Plot Summary

An opening title card reads: "April—1805 Napoleon is master of Europe. Only the British fleet stands before him. Oceans are now battlefields." During the Napoleonic Wars, Capt. Jack Aubrey (Russell Crowe), commander of the HMS *Surprise*, a 28-gun frigate, is ordered to sink, burn, or take as a prize the French privateer *Acheron* but *Acheron* ambushes *Surprise* off the west coast of South America. *Surprise* is towed into the fog to shield itself from further enemy engagement. Aubrey's officers tell him that HMS *Surprise* is no match for *Acheron*, which has a thicker hull and many more guns; they advise Aubrey to abandon pursuit. Aubrey points out his orders are to prevent *Acheron* from plundering the British whaling fleet. He commands that the *Surprise* be repaired while still at sea. *Acheron* then attacks *Surprise* again, but Aubrey tricks the Acheron using a raft and ship's lamp and evades capture. Following the privateer south, *Surprise* rounds South America's Cape Horn in high seas. Sadly, a sailor falls overboard when part of a mast breaks off and has to be cut loose to save the ship. The *Surprise* then heads to the Galapagos Islands (885 nautical miles west of Ecuador), where Aubrey is sure that England's whaling fleet will be attacked by *Acheron*. When *Surprise* gets to the Galapagos, they find survivors from a whaling ship already sunk by *Acheron*. Aubrey decided to follow after the privateer. *Surprise* sits on a calm sea for days on end, and the crew gets cabin fever. Midshipman Hollom (Lee Ingleby), already unpopular with the crew, is named a Jonah figure (i.e., a hex on the ship). As the tension rises, Carpenter's Mate Joseph Nagel (Bryan Dick) bumps into Hollom on the deck and refuses to apologize or salute. Capt. Aubrey witnesses the offense and orders that Nagel be flogged with 12 lashes for insubordination. Hollom kills himself that night. The next morning, Aubrey holds a memorial for Hollom. The wind resumes, and *Surprise* continues to pursue the *Acheron*. The next day, Marine Capt. Howard (Chris Larkin) accidentally shoots Dr. Stephen Maturin (Paul Bettany), the ship's surgeon, in the abdomen. Aubrey abandons his pursuit of the *Acheron* and returns to the Galapagos so that his surgeon can be healed. Maturin uses a mirror and performs his own surgery. Maturin explores the island and collects samples for study, but the captain and crew soon head out to battle when they realize that *Acheron* is close at hand. Aubrey knows that he will need to come close to *Acheron* in order to board and dismantle her, so he disguises *Surprise* as a whaling ship spewing black smoke from a faux tryworks. The French ship takes the bait and moves in to capture what it thinks is a whaling vessel. *Surprise* captures *Acheron* after the crew engages in fierce hand-to-hand combat. Both ships have their damages repaired, and the captive *Acheron* is taken to Chile while *Surprise* stays in the Galapagos. As *Acheron* departs, Maturin reveals that the real ship's doctor had perished months prior: the man posing as the ship's doctor was actually the French captain. Aubrey gives the order to change course to intercept the *Acheron* and escort her to Valparaíso and for the crew to assume battle stations. The two play a piece by Luigi Boccherini as the *Surprise* turns in pursuit of the *Acheron* once more.

Reception

After the better part of a year in post-production, *Master and Commander* had its North American premiere on 14 November 2003. Staggered releases elsewhere in the world began days later and ran to March 2004. During its 26-week domestic run (widest release: 3,101 theaters), the film grossed $93.9 million. Foreign receipts came in at $118 million, for a grand total of $212 million. Deducting $30 million spent on marketing, *Master and Commander* cleared a healthy $32 million. The movie was nominated for 10 Academy Awards, winning 2 Oscars, for Best Cinematography (Russell Boyd) and Best Sound Editing (Richard King). Reviews were strong. Roger Ebert called the movie "an exuberant sea adventure told with uncommon intelligence . . . grand and glorious, and touching in its attention to its characters. Like the work of David Lean, it achieves the epic without losing sight of the human, and to see it is to be reminded of the way great action movies can rouse and exhilarate us, can affirm life instead of simply dramatizing its destruction" (Ebert, 14 November 2003). Other critics described it as "satisfying," "an expansive cinematic achievement," "a gentleman's action movie," "great storytelling," and "such fun to watch."

Reel History Versus Real History

William Mclaughlin calls *Master and Commander* "one of the most historically accurate movies of this century," but also observes that "the very first battle seems unrealistic, as the *Acheron* had such a decisive advantage that it is hard to imagine how the *Surprise* possibly escaped." Mclaughlin also points out a late, glaring mistake: "At the very end of the film, the captured *Acheron* is sent to the Spanish colonial port of Valparaíso in Chile. Not only was Valparaíso farther away than other acceptable ports, it was also still very underdeveloped by 1805. Its real growth into a port city didn't start until about a decade later. On top of this Valparaíso was Spanish and therefore allied with France and Napoleon, something Jack [Aubrey] would have known. Sending the captured ship there would be as good as giving it back to the French" (Mclaughlin, 2016). Jason Epstein's assessment of the movie's historical accuracy is far harsher. He finds it highly unlikely that the Admiralty would send "the *Surprise* across the Atlantic in the fateful year 1805 when Lord Nelson needs every frigate he can muster to defend the homeland." Epstein finds it equally unlikely that "the French [would] send the formidable *Acheron* to interfere with whalers when the combined French and Spanish fleets are preparing to gather at Toulon and Cadiz for the climactic battle that will end later that year." Furthermore, Epstein notes that anyone "familiar with the vagaries of ocean navigation will also wonder how, with global positioning technology two centuries in the future, the *Acheron* pinpoints the *Surprise* in the vast South Atlantic and through an eerie fog sends, without radar or laser technology, a thundering salvo right onto Aubrey's gun deck" (Epstein, 2003).

MEN IN WAR (1957)

Synopsis

Men in War is an American war film adapted from Van Van Praag's WWII novel, *Day Without End* (1949), directed by Anthony Mann and starring Robert Ryan and Aldo Ray as the leaders of a small detachment of U.S. Army soldiers cut off and desperately trying to rejoin their division during the Korean War. The events depicted in the film take place on one day: 6 September 1950.

Background

A former truck salesman from Queens, New York City, named Van Van Praag enlisted in the U.S. Army in 1939. Promoted through the ranks until he was commissioned a 2nd Lieutenant in 1944, Van Praag fought in France as a platoon leader, was severely wounded, and was then shipped home. In the summer of 1949 William Sloane published Van Praag's only novel, *Day Without End*, a brutal day-in-the-life account of a war-weary Army platoon on the frontline for 58 straight days since

D-Day, fighting both the enemy and severe combat fatigue while stuck in the deadly hedgerows near Saint-Lô, France. The novel won high praise by critics for its taut prose and gritty realism and was republished in paperback by Pocket Books under the title *Combat* in 1951. In 1956 director Anthony Mann bought the screen rights to *Day Without End* and (at least officially) hired veteran writer-producer Philip Yordan to turn Van Praag's novel into a film. To make the film more topical to a Cold War audience, the filmmakers decided to transpose the setting from World War II to the Korean War.

Production

Anthony Mann and co-producer Sidney Harmon hoped to secure Department of Defense (DOD) cooperation but that was denied when Pentagon officials vetted the script and found that it depicted shell shock, insubordination, and unit discipline in tatters. Without recourse to military hardware *Men in War* could feature nothing more than a couple of jeeps, explosives detonations, and a few soldiers with small arms and a bazooka or two—but that was the small-scale scenario already dictated by the novel and screenplay. The film was supposedly written by Philip Yordan but he was likely fronting for blacklisted screenwriter Ben Maddow. It was shot (in black and white) in Malibu Canyon, Janss Conejo Ranch (Conejo Valley, California), and Bronson Canyon in Griffith Park, Los Angeles, in July and August of 1956 on a production budget of $1 million.

Plot Summary

On 6 September 1950, a battle-fatigued platoon of the 24th Infantry Division finds itself cut off from its battalion and picked off, one by one, by stealthy North Korean soldiers. Led by Lt. Benson (Robert Ryan), the platoon is on its way to reunite with American forces on a distant hill when it encounters a jeep driven by 1st Cavalry Division Staff Sergeant Joseph R. "Montana" Willomet (Aldo Ray), accompanied by a shell-shocked colonel (Robert Keith) who is mute, catatonic, and strapped to his seat. After the First Battle of the Naktong Bulge (5–19 August 1950), Montana has decided he and his colonel are through with the war. Benson commandeers their jeep for his platoon's rations and ammo and for Cpl. James Zwickley (Vic Morrow), another shell-shocked combatant. As the platoon proceeds towards its rendezvous point, Montana goes against Benson's order and kills a North Korean sniper on the verge of surrender. It is discovered that the sniper was hiding a weapon in his hat. Bringing up the rear, Staff Sgt. Killian (James Edwards) is killed by a North Korean infiltrator after decorating his helmet net with daisies. Montana takes his place by the side of the road and feigns sleep, luring two lurking North Koreans into the open, where he kills them. Thereafter, Montana transforms the platoon into a functioning military unit that successfully negotiates a sniper attack, artillery barrage, and a field full of landmines—though Platoon Sergeant Nate Lewis (Nehemiah Persoff) panics and gets himself killed. Once at the hill, they find it occupied by the enemy. Montana shoots a group of enemy combatants posing as Americans after a North Korean prisoner (Victor Sen Yung) is used to flush them out and is killed by his own men. Benson leads his men in an attack but Montana and the colonel demure—until the colonel suddenly comes to his senses, joins the assault, and is fatally wounded by shrapnel from a nearby shell explosion, whereupon a chastened Montana finally joins the fight. They take out a pillbox and machine-gun nest but only Benson, Montana, and Sgt. Riordan (Phillip Pine) make it through the battle. As U.S. reinforcements approach, Benson asks Montana for the Silver Star medals meant for the colonel's men. As Benson calls out their names, Montana tosses the medals to their dead recipients.

Reception

Released in February 1957, *Men in War* was only modestly successful at the box office, earning $1.5 million—just a half million dollars more than it cost to make. Due to the film's subversively mordant stance on war and the military, contemporary reviews were likewise mixed. Conservative film critic Bosley Crowther called *Men in War* "one long display of horror and misery" and wondered "what audience, if any, should be recommended to this film" (Crowther, 20 March 1957). Conversely, film critic Edith Lindeman described *Men in War* as offering "a tight, realistic and well-knit story" (Lindeman, 1957). Jay Carmody observed that the movie dug for "truths which have been evaded or distorted in so many celluloid spectaculars on the same subject" (Carmody, 1957). Since its initial release *Men in War*'s reputation as a hidden gem of war films has grown steadily over the years.

Real History Versus Reel History

The precisely stated time frame of *Men in War* (6 September 1950) places it in the middle of the Second Battle of Naktong Bulge, an engagement between United Nations (UN) and North Korean (NK) forces (1 September–15 September 1950) that was a part of the larger Battle of Pusan Perimeter. The Second Battle at Naktong ended in victory for the United Nations after U.S. and Republic of Korea (ROK) troops repelled a strong North Korean attack. In the movie the men wear taro leaf shoulder patches indicating they're part of the 24th Infantry Division. Stationed in Japan when North Korea invaded South Korea on 25 June 1950, the 24th was indeed the first division sent to Korea to hold off the North Korean advance until more troops could arrive. It sustained extremely heavy casualties in the first two months of the war, but some of its battered elements were still on the frontlines of the Pusan Perimeter in early September, as depicted in the film. Narrowly focused on a depleted and isolated platoon, *Men in War* does not allude to or pretend to represent the battle at Naktong or any specific Korean War engagement.

MERRY CHRISTMAS, MR. LAWRENCE [JAPANESE: SENJŌ NO MERĪ KURISUMASU] (1983)

Synopsis

Merry Christmas, Mr. Lawrence is a British-Japanese war film directed by Nagisa Oshima and produced by Jeremy Thomas. Starring David Bowie, Tom Conti, Ryuichi Sakamoto, Takeshi Kitano, and Jack Thompson, the film centers on four men in a World War II Japanese prisoner of war (POW) camp: two Allied and two Japanese soldiers.

Background

Sir Laurens Jan van der Post (1906–1996) was a South African–born author and Jungian mystic, advisor to Prince Charles and Margaret Thatcher, and the godfather of Prince William, among other distinctions. After his death, however, an exposé by J.D.F. Jones—*Storyteller: The Lives of Laurens van der Post*—revealed that van der Post had been a lifelong opportunist and con man. During World War II Van der Post, who was fluent in Japanese, served in the British Army in the Dutch East Indies (present-day Indonesia) and was captured on 20 April 1942, when Java fell. Van der Post spent the remainder of the war as a POW in Japanese prison camps in Sukabumi and Bandung, both in West Java, Indonesia. After the war he wrote three books of fiction based on his prison camp experiences: *A Bar of Shadow* (1954), *The Seed and the Sower* (1963), and *The Night of the New Moon* (1970). In the early 1980s Japanese director Nagisa Ôshima (*In the Realm of the Senses*) collaborated with British screenwriter Paul Mayersburg (*The Man Who Fell to Earth*) on a script based on the first two stories in *The Seed and the Sower* and mounted a joint Anglo-Japanese film project produced by Jeremy Thomas and financed by New Zealand, British, and Japanese investors. Singer/actor Kenji Sawada was Ôshima's first choice for POW camp commandant Capt. Yonoi—a character conceived in the image of Yukio Mishima—but Sawada had to drop out due to scheduling issues. Ôshima briefly considered Tomokazu Miura for Yonoi but hired rock star Ryuichi Sakamoto because he had an androgynous appearance similar to Sawada (Sakamoto also composed the film's musical score). Samurai movie star Shintaro Katsu (*Kagemusha*) was first choice for Sgt. Hara, but the part eventually went to Takeshi Kitano. Robert Redford was allegedly considered for the role of Major Jack Celliers but Ôshima cast the more age-appropriate David Bowie after seeing him in a Japanese TV saké ad and then in a Broadway production of *The Elephant Man* in 1980. British stage actor Tom Conti was cast as van der Post's fictional counterpart (and Celliers' foil), Col. John Lawrence.

Production

Filming took place over a seven-week period (September–November 1982). The first five weeks of the shoot occurred on Rarotonga in the Cook Islands, northeast of New Zealand. Ôshima hired lots of island natives as extras (British POW extras were recruited from New Zealand). He also had a complete POW camp built, but only filmed small portions of it. Ôshima meticulously directed his Japanese actors but when it came to the British actors, they were told to "do whatever it is you people do." Ôshima worked fast; he shot only one or two takes and did not screen dailies or even make safety prints; prints of each day's shoot were shipped to his editor, Tomoyo Oshima, in Japan (she had a rough cut of the film completed within four days of Ôshima's returning to Japan at the end of the shoot). For the last two weeks of the shoot the company moved to New Zealand. Scenes were shot at Wanganui Collegiate School, doubling for a boarding school in South Africa; at

Auckland Railway Station, doubling for a station in Batavia (Jakarta); and at Mount Eden Prison, Auckland, representing Hara's prison in 1946.

Plot Summary

The film deals with the complex relationships among four men in a WWII Japanese POW camp, two Allied and two Japanese soldiers: Major Jack Celliers (David Bowie), a rebellious South African harboring a guilty secret; Captain Yonoi (Ryuichi Sakamoto), the young camp commandant; Lt. Col. John Lawrence (Tom Conti), a British officer who has lived in Japan and speaks fluent Japanese; and Sgt. Hara (Takeshi Kitano), a brutal but principled noncommissioned officer with whom Lawrence strikes up a friendship. Celliers suffers from guilt for having betrayed his younger brother while both were attending boarding school in South Africa. Conversely, Yonoi feels an overwhelming sense of shame. Having been posted to Manchuria, he was unable to be in Tokyo when his Army comrades, the "Shining Young Officers," staged a military coup d'état in 1936 (i.e., the "February 26 Incident"). When the coup failed, Yonoi's comrades were all executed, and Yonoi feels ill at ease with his own survival. Although Celliers confesses his guilty secret only to Lawrence, Capt. Yonoi senses that Celliers is a kindred spirit. Yonoi develops a homoerotic fixation with him and wants to replace British RAAF Group Capt. Hicksley (Jack Thompson) with Celliers as the prisoners' advocate. Celliers, nicknamed "Strafer" Jack for his grit, instigates acts of resistance. Yonoi's batman (personal servant) tries to eliminate Celliers, thinking him to be a terrible influence on Yonoi, but Celliers evades him and escapes. As Celliers attempts to rescue Lawrence, Yonoi intervenes, challenging Celliers to single combat and promising to free him if he wins, but Celliers refuses to fight. Yonoi's disgraced batman then commits seppuku (ritual suicide). Soon thereafter the Japanese uncover a radio in the possession of the POWs. Celliers and Lawrence are forced to take the blame and are marked for execution. During Christmas Eve 1942, an inebriated Sgt. Hara calls for Celliers and Lawrence and, to their surprise, releases the two men. Yonoi is shocked that Sgt. Hara has released both Celliers and Lawrence from their holding cells but only mildly reprimands him for exceeding his authority and has him redeployed. Hicksley demands an explanation. Furious that Hicksley has pressed him for an answer, Yonoi has the whole camp put on parade—all POWs, including the sick and wounded, are ordered to form lines outside their barracks. Capt. Yonoi then singles out Hicksley for execution by beheading. Breaking ranks, Celliers calmly walks up and places himself between Yonoi and Hicksley. Yonoi angrily shoves him aside, but Celliers gets up and impassively kisses Yonoi on each cheek. Mortified by an act that so deeply offends his bushido honor code, Yonoi reaches out for his katana against Celliers but collapses in an onrush of conflicted feelings: angry frustration, embarrassment, and his unacknowledged love for Celliers. Capt. Yonoi's soldiers immediately take over, beating and stomping Celliers for his insolence. Now compromised, Yonoi is slated for redeployment. His successor (Hideo Murota) punishes Celliers by having him buried in the ground up to his neck and left to die. When they are alone, Yonoi extracts a lock of Celliers' hair as a memento. Celliers dies soon after. In 1946, Lawrence visits Sgt. Hara, now a prisoner of the Allies. In English, Hara explains that his execution for war crimes is scheduled for the next day. Lawrence reveals that Yonoi passed along Celliers' hair and asked that Lawrence place it in a shrine in his home village in Japan. Hara shares memories about Celliers and Yonoi, and it is confirmed that Yonoi was killed before the end of the war.

Reception

Merry Christmas, Mr. Lawrence premiered at the 36th Cannes Film Festival on 11 May 1983 and won a Palme D'Or nomination for Ôshima. Ryuichi Sakamoto subsequently won a BAFTA Award for Best Score. The film also garnered a number Japanese film nominations and awards but was not successful at the box office. Reviews were mixed. Roger Ebert gave the movie a tepid two and a half stars out of four, opining that it was "even stranger than it was intended to be" (Ebert, 1983). Janet Maslin found the movie "sometimes tense and surprising, sometimes merely bizarre . . . an intriguing if inconsistent effort" (Maslin, 1983). Laurens van der Post gave the film high marks, calling it "a great and deeply moving film." Not widely seen outside of Japan, *Merry Christmas, Mr. Lawrence* remains a favorite with cultists. In the astute words of one reviewer, "*Merry Christmas* is not the story of the West's civilizing influence on the East, but rather of individuals reaching past the flotsam of repression common to all societies and daring to touch the human being buried beneath" (Erdman, 2010).

Real History Versus Reel History

Laurens van der Post supposedly based his POW fiction on his real-life experiences during World War II, so certainly many aspects of prison camp life as depicted in *Merry Christmas, Mr. Lawrence* have a respectable degree of authenticity. Malnutrition, pervasive sickness, back-breaking work, the brutality of the Japanese toward their prisoners of war—all these things are well documented elsewhere. Other than Col. Lawrence, who is clearly based on the author himself, there is no way of knowing whether the principal characters correspond to actual persons who van der Post knew during his captivity. Given van der Post's well-documented penchant for creative storytelling to serve didactic purposes (or his own agenda), it seems likely that much of the film's narrative, which closely follows his fiction, is fanciful. Certainly viewers will recognize parallels to David Lean's *The Bridge on the River Kwai*, especially the vexed character and personality of prison camp commandant Yonoi, who bears considerable resemblance to *Kwai*'s Col. Saito, played by Sessue Hayakawa.

MIDNIGHT CLEAR, A (1992)

Synopsis

Based on the eponymous novel by William Wharton, *A Midnight Clear* is an American war drama set toward the end of World War II in Europe. Adapted and directed by Keith Gordon, the movie stars an ensemble cast: Ethan Hawke, Gary Sinise,

Peter Berg, Kevin Dillon, and Arye Gross. A low-budget independent feature, *A Midnight Clear* tells the story of an isolated American intelligence squad that encounters a German unit trying to surrender.

Background

William Wharton (real name: Albert William Du Aime, 1925–2008) was an American writer and expressionist painter who served in the U.S. Army in WWII. A product of the Army's Specialized Training Program (ASTP) for G.I.s with genius IQs, Wharton was severely wounded in the Battle of the Bulge and many of his ASTP comrades were killed. In the prologue to his war memoir, *Shrapnel*, Wharton says he wrote his third novel, *A Midnight Clear*, because he thought the U.S. under bellicose President Ronald Reagan was about "to re-establish the draft of young men, to send them off to kill or be killed. I felt an obligation to tell something about war as I knew it, in all its absurdity . . . War for me, though brief, had been a soul-shaking trauma. I was scared, miserable, and I lost confidence in human beings, especially myself" (Wharton, 1982, p. ii). While Wharton's anti-war novel was still in galleys, A & M Film's president Dale Pollock purchased the movie rights. Initially, British playwright Trevor Griffiths (*Reds*) was hired to write an adaptation and John Mackenzie (*The Long Good Friday*) was hired to direct but Pollock remained unsatisfied. In 1987 he hired Patrick Sheane Duncan (*84 Charlie MoPic*) to write another version of the script and Randa Haines (*Children of a Lesser God*) to replace Mackenzie as director, but the project remained unworkable. After viewing Keith Gordon's *The Chocolate War* (1988), Pollock hired Gordon to bring the project to fruition.

Production

Originally planned to be filmed in Yugoslavia (present-day Slovenia) in 1990, a lack of snow there necessitated a change of location and a year's delay. Snowy evergreen forests near Park City, Utah, substituted nicely for the Ardennes Forest near the French-German border in the winter of 1944–1945. The exterior of the chateau was actually a three-wall set, which was built in the secluded hills of Utah, and the interiors of the chateau were built in the gymnasium of a local high school. The attic set was constructed on the stage of the school's theater. Shooting the outdoor scenes, especially the night scenes, proved grueling as Utah experienced its coldest winter in 83 years.

Plot Summary

Just before the Battle of the Bulge in December 1944, U.S. Army Major Griffin (John C. McGinley) sends a small I&R (Intelligence and Reconnaissance) squad to inhabit an empty chateau near the German lines to keep an eye on enemy deployments. Losses from an earlier patrol have reduced the squad from 12 to 6 men: Sgt. Will Knott (Ethan Hawke), Bud Miller (Peter Berg), Mel Avakian (Kevin Dillon), Stan Shutzer (Arye Gross), Vance "Mother" Wilkins (Gary Sinise), and Paul "Father" Mundy (Frank Whaley). On their way to the chateau in two jeeps, they encounter an eerie, surreal sight on the road: the frozen corpses of a German and American soldier poised in a standing embrace, evidently arranged by the Germans as some sort of dark joke—or ominous threat. Settling into the chateau, they soon discover they are not alone. A group of Wehrmacht soldiers nearby reveals their presence that night with ominous laughter and taunting shouts of "Schlafen Sie gut!" (Sleep well!). Out on patrol, Knott, Mundy, and Shutzer are suddenly confronted by a trio of German soldiers aiming their weapons at them. The Americans panic and put their hands up in surrender but the enemy just as suddenly vanishes. At first the Americans think the Germans—a small group of teenagers commanded by a middle-aged noncommissioned officer (NCO)—are mocking them, but then realize the Germans want to surrender to survive the war. They ask the Americans to pretend to have captured them in combat to protect their families back home from retribution. The Americans agree, but elect not to inform Wilkins, who has become half-crazed since learning of the death of his child stateside. The two groups meet at a forest cabin and proceed to fire their weapons into the air to simulate a skirmish, as planned. Unfortunately Wilkins, nearby, hears the gunfire. Thinking the engagement is real, he rushes to the scene and opens fire at the Germans. Naturally, the Germans start to shoot back. As the situation spirals out of control, Knott's men are forced to eliminate all enemy soldiers, but not before Mundy is fatally shot and Shutzer badly wounded. As he is dying, Mundy begs the others not to tell Wilkins that the skirmish was staged. The always petulant Major Griffin arrives, harangues Knott, and takes Shutzer back for medical treatment (who later dies). The four remaining soldiers ritualistically bathe Mundy's body. The soldiers are then left with no choice but to flee from the chateau as German forces advance. Knott's men dress themselves as medics and carry Mundy's corpse back to American lines. There Knott learns that Wilkins has been recommended for the Bronze Star and transferred to the motor pool, while the rest of the squad will be sent into the frontline to fight as regular infantry.

Reception

A low-budget independent production, *A Midnight Clear* received minimal theatrical exhibition when it was released in April 1992 (only seven theaters) and initially earned a mere $1.5 million—less than half of what it cost to make. Shown occasionally on television and eventually released on DVD and Blu-ray (an enhanced 20th anniversary edition), the movie has since found a somewhat larger and more appreciative audience. Though war film traditionalists dislike *A Midnight Clear* due to its surreal qualities, lack of combat heroics, use of religious imagery, and decidedly cerebral and pacifist leanings, reviews were mostly positive, like Roger Ebert's: "*A Midnight Clear* is a little too much of a parable for my taste—there are times when the characters seem to be acting out of the author's need, rather than their own—but it's a good film, and Gordon is uncanny in the way he suggests the eerie forest mysteries that permeate all of the action" (Ebert, 1 May 1992).

Reel History Versus Real History

It is well known that during World War I some 100,000 British and German troops called a truce and fraternized in sectors of the front at Ypres and Saint-Yvon,

Belgium, on Christmas Day 1914: "live and let live" behavior that was not repeated, per strict orders of the British High Command. Truces were almost unheard of during WWII but a small-scale Christmas truce did occur during the Battle of the Bulge. At a remote cabin in the Hürtgen Forest three American and four German soldiers—all lost, tired, and hungry—were treated to an impromptu Christmas Eve supper by a German woman named Elisabeth Vincken, who told them all, "Es ist Heiligabend und hier wird nicht geschossen." ["It is the Holy Night and there will be no shooting here."] She insisted they leave their weapons outside. The soldiers complied and enjoyed a brief respite from the war (Hunt, 2017).

P

PATHS OF GLORY (1957)

Synopsis

Paths of Glory is an American anti-war film by Stanley Kubrick based on the 1935 novel of the same title by WWI combat veteran Humphrey Cobb. Set during World War I, the film stars Kirk Douglas as Colonel Dax, the commanding officer of a French regiment involved in a failed attack on a German stronghold. Dax, a lawyer in civilian life, attempts to defend three of his subordinates against a charge of cowardice in an ensuing court-martial.

Background

Humphrey Cobb (1899–1944) was an American expatriate who served with the Canadian Expeditionary Forces (CEF) in the First World War and was wounded and gassed at the Battle of Amiens in August 1918. In 1934 Cobb read a news item about the posthumous exoneration of five French soldiers who had been executed by firing squad after their unit refused to join a suicidal attack in the St. Mihiel sector on 19 April 1915 (Anonymous, 2 July 1934). Incensed by the absurd injustice of the original incident, Cobb was inspired to write *Paths of Glory*, a highly acclaimed anti-war novel published by Viking Press in 1935. That same year Sidney Howard staged an unsuccessful Broadway play based on Cobb's book and Paramount won a bidding war for the film rights, but let its option lapse. In 1956 James B. Harris and Stanley Kubrick bought the rights from Cobb's widow for $10,000 and tried to interest Dore Schary at MGM but he refused, citing the recent box office disaster that was John Huston's *The Red Badge of Courage*. Undeterred, Harris hired Jim Thompson to write a screen adaptation of Cobb's novel. Kubrick, Thompson, and Calder Willingham had a second draft completed by late November 1956. Kubrick and Harris wanted Gregory Peck to play the lead role of Col. Dax but he was not immediately available. They tried to interest Charlton Heston but he signed with Orson Welles to star in *Touch of Evil* (1958), so they secured Kirk Douglas instead, who demanded a $350,000 salary, profit sharing, and other perks. On the strength of Douglas's involvement, United Artists (UA) agreed to provide a modest $954,000 production budget, a third of which would pay for Douglas's salary.

Production

Though supposedly taking place in France, *Paths of Glory* was filmed in and around Munich, Bavaria, in the spring of 1957. Most interior scenes were filmed at Bavaria's Geiselgasteig Studios. The court-martial scenes were shot at New Schleissheim

Palace outside Munich, and the execution scene was shot in the palace's baroque gardens. UA wanted to film the battlefield scenes on Geiselgasteig Studios' backlot but it proved too small. Eventually a cow pasture 25 miles west of Munich was rented from a German farmer, and some 60 crew members worked long hours for three weeks to create a muddy, debris-strewn World War I battlefield, complete with trenches, barbed wire, ruined buildings, denuded trees, and huge shell craters. World War I trenches were four feet wide but Kubrick's trenches had to be made six feet wide to accommodate the camera dolly for the film's famous reverse tracking shots in the opening sequence. For the main combat scene Kubrick used a half-dozen cameras set up sequentially on a long dolly that ran parallel to the assault. The battlefield was divided into five "dying zones," and each extra (all German policemen) was given a number ranging from 1 to 5 and told to "die" in that zone, if possible, near an explosion. Hedging his bets on the film's commercial potential, Kubrick wanted an upbeat ending, but Kirk Douglas insisted that the movie stay true to Cobb's somber vision. Fortunately, Douglas won out.

Plot Summary

The film begins with a voice-over describing trench warfare up to 1916. At his headquarters in an elegant château, Gen. Georges Broulard (Adolphe Menjou), a member of the French General Staff, asks his subordinate, Gen. Mireau (George Macready), to send his division against a well-defended German fortress dubbed the "Anthill." Convinced the attack is doomed to fail, Mireau initially refuses, but when Broulard mentions a potential promotion, Mireau reverses himself. On an inspection tour of the trenches, Mireau asks several soldiers, "Ready to kill more Germans?" Encountering a dazed, shell-shocked private (Fred Bell), Mireau ejects him from out of the regiment for alleged cowardice. Mireau then meets with the 701st Regiment's commanding officer, Colonel Dax (Kirk Douglas), to plan the attack. During a recon mission before the assault, an inebriated lieutenant named Roget (Wayne Morris) sends out a scout to check the terrain, but panics and accidentally kills the man with a grenade upon his return. Another soldier—Corporal Paris (Ralph Meeker)—discovers the scout's body and later confronts Roget, who does not admit to the crime and provides a false report to Dax. The next day, Dax leads the first wave of soldiers on the attack on the Anthill amidst intense fire, but the assault fails. None of the troops make it to the German trenches, and the B men of Company decline to leave their trenches. Mireau commands his artillery to open fire on the "cowards" to encourage them into battle. However, artillery commander Rousseau (John Stein) won't fire without confirmation. In the meantime, Dax comes back to the trenches and attempts to spur B Company into action. In the aftermath of the failed attack, Mireau chooses to court-martial 100 of his own soldiers for alleged cowardice, as he does not want to take on any blame for himself. Broulard urges him to reduce the number to three: one from each company. Mireau chooses Corporal Paris, Private Ferol (Timothy Carey), and Private Arnaud (Joe Turkel). Dax, who served as a criminal defense lawyer before the war, volunteers to defend the men in court. The trial soon devolves into a farce. Despite Dax's best efforts, the three hapless soldiers are found guilty and handed a death sentence. Captain Rousseau the commander who had earlier refused to shoot at Mireau's own men, shares his story with Dax. Dax approaches Broulard with witness statements incriminating Mireau, but he is waved away dismissively. The three condemned men are later brought outdoors, with their fellow soldiers and commanding officers surrounding them. All three men are then executed by firing squad. After the sentence is carried out, Broulard meets Mireau for breakfast and finds him giddy with the result of the court-martial. Dax interrupts them, and Broulard tells Mireau that he will be investigated for his actions. Mireau departs in a fury, and Broulard then offers Dax Mirau's post. A disgusted Dax calls Broulard a "degenerate, sadistic old man." After the execution, Dax joins his soldiers on leave, drinking at an inn. Their mood shifts from antagonism to empathy as they listen to a captive German girl (Christiane Harlan) sing "The Faithful Hussar," a sentimental folk song. They are unaware that orders have come for them to return to the front. Dax lets the men enjoy a few minutes while his face hardens as he returns to his quarters.

Reception

Paths of Glory premiered on 1 November 1957 in Munich, West Germany, and opened in the United States the following month, but the movie's class-inflected anti-war politics made it box office poison throughout much of Europe. UA did not even bother to submit the film to the French censorship board, knowing that it would be banned for its unflattering depiction of France's military (*Paths* would not be shown in France until 1975). When the movie was screened in Berlin in June 1958 it caused an uproar with French occupation troops stationed there and had to be withdrawn from the Berlin Film Festival when the French threatened to withdraw altogether if it was exhibited. Weeks later the movie was banned at all American military bases in Europe. In Spain, Francisco Franco's government also banned the film as anti-military. It was not shown until 1986, 11 years after Franco's death. In Switzerland, the film was censored at the request of the Swiss Army until 1970. Because it was so often banned, box office returns were modest (less than $1 million) and *Paths of Glory* did not quite break even.

Reel History Versus Real History

As noted earlier, Humphrey Cobbs' novel was initially inspired by postwar revelations about the execution of five French soldiers from 5th Company, 63rd Infantry Regiment, after their unit refused to join an attack in the St. Mihiel sector on 19 April 1915. Many similar injustices were perpetrated by the French Army during the First World War—France carried out some 550 military executions—but Cobb's novel and Kubrick's film both derive from a particularly egregious incident known as the "Souain Corporals Affair." On 10 March 1915, near the Marne village of Souain, Gen. Géraud Réveilhac, commander of France's 60th Infantry Division, ordered his artillery to fire on his own trenches when the 21st company of the 336th Infantry Regiment refused to go over the top and attack after a first wave was mowed down by German machine-gun fire. As depicted in the movie, the artillery commander (the real man's name was Col. Raoul Berube) refused to obey his general's command without a written order. Réveilhac did not issue one, but in the wake of the failed attack he demanded that action be taken against the soldiers of the 21st Company. Réveilhac ordered its commander, Capt. Equilbey, to produce a list of names that included six corporals and 18 enlisted men, randomly chosen by lot from the two youngest members in every squad. Six days after the failed attack, the 24 men were court-martialed for cowardice by a military tribunal, quickly convicted, and sentenced to death. Though 20 were subsequently granted stays, 4 of the soldiers—Cpls. Théophile Maupas, Lefoulon Louis, Louis Girard, and Lucien Lechat—were executed by firing squad on 17 March 1915. Two of the four were married, three had children, and Maupas had been repeatedly cited for bravery in battle. Like Mireau in the film, Réveilhac did not escape repercussions. In 1916 he was relieved of command and later reassigned to rear echelon duty. In 1921 public outrage ensued when Réveilhac's callous actions at Souain were revealed in the press. Nonetheless, Blanche Maupas and Eulalie Lechat, two of the victims' widows, would have to wait another 13 years to gain any satisfaction from the French legal system. Finally, on 3 March 1934, a judge with the Cour spéciale de justice (Special Court of Justice) ordered the French Army to exonerate the four men and restore their ranks so their widows and dependents could receive pensions. The story told by Cobb and Kubrick distills the history to achieve both greater dramatic concentration and deeper sociopolitical resonance. In book and film only three men are court-martialed, convicted, and executed. Their defense attorney, the fictional Col. Dax, is also their regimental commander, which was not the case in actuality—though the perfunctory nature of the court martial proceedings is true to the historical reality. A brave and caring officer and an articulate advocate for legal justice, Dax expresses civilized moral ideals that were entirely absent at the actual court-martial in 1915. Both book and movie also address questions of social caste elitism and careerism in the military that are merely implicit in the historical source material. Finally, book and movie elide the widows' protracted fight to have their martyred husbands' names cleared—an interesting historical footnote but one that would dilute the admonitory power of both works.

PATTON (1970)

Synopsis
Patton is an American biopic/war epic directed by Franklin J. Schaffner from a script by Francis Ford Coppola and Edmund H. North. The film focuses on General George S. Patton (played by George C. Scott) during his World War II service as commander of the U.S. Seventh and Third armies.

Background
General George Smith Patton Jr. (1885–1945), commander of the U.S. Seventh Army in North Africa and Sicily and the U.S. Third Army in France and Germany during World War II, was one of the most colorful and controversial figures in modern American military history. Known as "Old Blood and Guts," Patton was a strutting, profanity-spouting, war-loving egomaniac, but also an effective military leader much feared by America's enemies—and sometimes feared and reviled by

George C. Scott portrays General George S. Patton in Frank Schaffner's epic biopic, *Patton* (1970). (20th Century Fox/Photofest)

his own men. Frank McCarthy (1912–1986), a staff officer with Gen. George C. Marshall during World War II and a Hollywood producer after the war, knew Patton and regarded his story as eminently screen-worthy. When he proposed a Patton film to his boss, Darryl F. Zanuck, at 20th Century Fox in October 1951, Zanuck gave the go-ahead, but it would be another 19 years before the project came to fruition. Patton's widow and other members of the Patton family obstructed McCarthy, fearing that a Hollywood biopic would caricature Patton and sully his memory (Toplin, 1996, pp. 158–159). McCarthy was only able to move forward after Ladislas Farago's biography, *Patton: Ordeal and Triumph* provided a source copious enough upon which to base a biopic without recourse to family sources. 20th Century Fox bought the film rights to Farago's book and to Gen. Omar Bradley's *A Soldier's Story*. In 1965, after rejecting several script drafts by other writers, Frank McCarthy hired an up-and-coming 26-year-old screenwriter named Francis Ford Coppola, paid him $50,000, and gave him six months to carve a coherent narrative out of Patton's complex life and military career. Coppola wisely made two tactical decisions early on that allowed him to create a fine script. After doing his research, Coppola concluded that "Patton was obviously out of his mind" (Phillips, 2004, pp. 31–32). A script that celebrated George Patton's bizarre war-mongering would be ridiculous but one that merely vilified him would be rejected out of hand, so

Coppola split the difference by writing an ambiguous script that emphasized Patton's dual nature—part lunatic, part super-warrior—and depicted him as an anachronistic, Quixotic figure who really belonged to a bygone era. Coppola's other choice was an easy one: to focus exclusively on Patton's life during the Second World War, a span of only two years and ten months (ten months of which he was sidelined), that kept the narrative tightly focused and action packed. McCarthy engaged William Wyler (*The Best Years of Our Lives*) to direct the picture but Wyler didn't like Coppola's unconventional script, so James Webb (*Cheyenne Autumn*) was brought in to write a new version. To play Patton, McCarthy and the studio wanted George C. Scott, a superb actor and ironically an avowed pacifist, but Scott found Webb's script too reductive so he bowed out. Robert Mitchum, Burt Lancaster, Rod Steiger, and Lee Marvin all turned down the role. John Wayne badly wanted to play Patton but his utterly dissimilar appearance, laconic manner, and narrow range as an actor made him a poor choice to play the shorter, more volatile, and markedly more educated and intelligent Patton. Fortunately, George C. Scott consented to do the film when McCarthy agreed to revert back to Coppola's script, though veteran screenwriter Edmund H. North (*Twelve O'Clock High*) made further revisions. Scott then proceeded to do exhaustive research on Patton, watching newsreels and reading and re-reading every Patton biography in order to master his character. In the meantime Wyler dropped out as director and was replaced by Frank Schaffner (*Planet of the Apes*). By early 1969, after five years of shuffling and reshuffling, Frank McCarthy finally had a script, a star, and a director.

Production

Principal photography began outside of Segovia, Spain, on 1 February 1969. *Patton* was filmed at 71 locations in six countries, but most of it was shot in Spain because Francisco Franco's Spanish Army could provide the needed WWII equipment—though the rental of troops and equipment consumed half the film's $12 million production budget. The film's opening, showing the aftermath of the American defeat at the Battle of the Kasserine Pass, was shot at the ruins of Tabernas Castle in Almeria Province on the coast of southern Spain. The place where Patton halts Rommel's advance towards Messina is located just below the village of Turillas, 12 miles east of Tabernas. Some 600 Almeria residents worked as extras for the scene depicting Patton's arrival in Palermo, Sicily, which was actually filmed in Nicolás Salmerón Park in the City of Almeria. After the Battle of El Guettar, Patton meets his new aide de camp at his headquarters, which was in reality the Governor's Palace of Almeria, and when Patton marches down a long corridor after the slapping incident, he is actually in La Granja Palace near Madrid. The winter scenes in Belgium were actually shot near Segovia. The scene depicting Patton driving up to an ancient city that is implied to be Carthage was actually shot in the ruins of the ancient Roman city of Volubilis in northwest Morocco. Patton's speech to the troops that opens the movie was shot at Bob Hope Patriotic Hall in downtown Los Angeles.

Plot Summary

Gen. George S. Patton (George C. Scott), in full military regalia, strides on to a stage at some undisclosed location in Europe during World War II. With a giant American flag behind him, he addresses an unseen group of American troops to rally them in support of the war, zeroing in on the importance of "winning" American style. The film proper begins with the humiliating American defeat at the Battle of the Kasserine Pass (19 February 1943–25 February 1943). Replacing Major General Lloyd Fredendall, Patton is put in charge of the U.S. Army's II Corps in North Africa. Upon his arrival, he cracks down on the soldiers and enforces rules, for example, demanding that soldiers wear ties and fining a cook for not wearing his Army-issue uniform. At a meeting with RAF Air Vice-Marshal Sir Arthur Coningham (John Barrie), Patton takes issue with Coningham for having discredited the notion that lack of air cover contributed to the American defeat. Coningham apologizes and promises Patton that he will see no more German planes. Seconds later Luftwaffe planes bomb and strafe the area, and Patton emerges from cover to fire his .45 at them. In the next scene, Patton defeats a German attack at the Battle of El Guettar in Tunisia (23 March–3 April 1943), but his aide-de-camp, Major Richard N. Jenson (Morgan Paull), is killed in the battle. Lt. Col. Charles R. Codman (Paul Stevens) replaces him. Patton is disappointed to learn that Field Marshall Erwin Rommel, Commander of the Afrika Korps, was on medical leave with diphtheria. Codman reassures him that "If you've defeated Rommel's plan, you've defeated Rommel." After victory in the North Africa campaign, Patton and Sir Bernard Montgomery (Michael Bates) formulate competing plans for the Allied invasion of Sicily. Patton's plan is to lead his Seventh Army to the northwest sending Montgomery to the southeast area of the island in an attempt to trap German and Italian units. Their superior officer, Gen. Alexander (Jack Gwillim), likes Patton's plan, but Gen. Dwight Eisenhower (not portrayed on screen) opts for Montgomery's conservative approach. As a result, Patton's army heads southeast to cover Montgomery's troops. All land without a hitch, but the Allied advance is sluggish, and Patton takes matters into his own hands. Going against his superiors, Patton leads his men to Palermo in the northwest, then continues on to Messina, outpacing Montgomery to their objective (17 August 1943). Patton states that his contention with Montgomery stems from Montgomery's inability to admit his own vanity and glory-seeking ambitions. However, Patton's methods do not go over well with the men he commands, Major Gen. Omar Bradley (Karl Malden) and Major Gen. Lucian Truscott (John Doucette). While on a visit to a field hospital (early August 1943) crowded with battle casualties, Patton sees a shaken soldier weeping (Tim Considine). Angrily labeling the soldier a coward, Patton assaults him and threatens to kill him, then concludes the interaction by insisting that the soldier return to the frontline. When Eisenhower learns of the incident, he relieves Patton of his command and orders him to offer apologies to the wronged soldier, to all occupants of the field hospital, and to his command, one unit at a time. Eisenhower also sidelines Patton during the D-Day landings (6 June 1944), placing him in command of the phantom First U.S. Army Group in southeast England as a decoy, which works; German Col. Gen. Alfred Jodl (Richard Münch) posits that Patton will lead the charge through Europe. Afraid he will miss out on the rest of the war, Patton pleads with his former subordinate, Omar Bradley, for a leadership role, and he is put in charge of the Third Army. Patton excels at his post and rapidly advances through France, but his tanks are halted when they run out of fuel, which is mostly consigned to Montgomery's Operation Market Garden (17–25 September 1944), much to Patton's disgust. Later, during the Battle of the Bulge (16 December 1944–25 January 1945), Patton's forces relieve the besieged town of Bastogne and then punch through the Siegfried Line and into Germany. In an off-the-record short speech at a war-drive event in Knutsford, England (25 April 1944), Patton said "it is the evident destiny of the British and Americans (and, of course, the Russians) to rule the world." Media coverage omits the reference to Russia, so Patton's remarks are viewed as an insult to the Soviet Union. After Germany capitulates (5 May 1945), Patton, through an interpreter, insults a Russian general to his face at a postwar dinner. The Russian amuses Patton by insulting him in kind, and the two officers proceed to have a drink together. Later, Patton makes the mistake of comparing the Nazi Party to American political parties. Patton's comments lead to his second loss of command. Patton is then seen away from the war, talking his dog, Willie. In voice-over, Patton describes how a returning hero of ancient Rome was honored with a "triumph," a victory parade in which "a slave stood behind the conqueror, holding a golden crown, and whispering in his ear a warning: that all glory is fleeting."

Reception

Patton had an East Coast premiere in New York City on 4 February 1970 and a West Coast premiere two weeks later. During its domestic theatrical run the movie made $61.75 million ($389 million in 2017 dollars). *Patton* earned an additional $28.1 million in video rentals later on—a grand total of almost $90 million against an estimated production cost of $12 million (i.e., a $78 million profit, minus promotion and advertising expenses). *Patton* received 10 Oscar nominations and won 7 Oscars at the 43rd Academy Awards (April 1971), including Best Picture and Best Original Screenplay. George C. Scott won the Best Actor Oscar for his portrayal of General Patton, but declined to accept the award on the grounds that acting should not be treated as a competitive enterprise. Reviews were overwhelmingly positive, with many critics citing George C. Scott's performance as one of the greatest ever committed to celluloid.

Reel History Versus Real History

In his book, *History by Hollywood: The Use and Abuse of the American Past*, Robert Brent Toplin includes a chapter on *Patton* entitled "*Patton*: Deliberately Planned as a Rorschach Test" (1996, pp. 155–175). Evidently unaware of Francis Ford Coppola's pragmatic reasons for writing an ambiguous script, Toplin argues that, given its time of release—at the height of the Vietnam War in 1970—*Patton* had to be carefully calibrated so as to present a balanced depiction of George S. Patton; at a time when anti-war sentiment was raging in the United States, an epic biopic about a gung-ho WWII general had to be constructed in ambiguous terms in order to appeal to the widest possible demographic. Hence, Patton is portrayed as a very capable military commander, pleasing Vietnam-era hawks, but also as an egomaniacal crackpot, confirming the biases of doves who abhorred war-mongering. In the end Toplin judges *Patton* as historically quite accurate and a "balanced" portrait. *Patton* is not, however, the "balanced" cinematic portrait that Toplin contends that it is. It contains contrived events and false characterizations designed to skew viewer identification toward George Patton. For example, George C. Scott's Patton speaks in a raspy growl whereas the real Patton had a high-pitched, squeaky voice that did not exude Scott's machismo. The movie also misrepresents the relationship between Patton and Gen. Omar Bradley. Depicted as close friends in the film they were, in reality, distant; Bradley found Patton's personality grating and offensive. The movie also suggests that Patton and Gen. Dwight Eisenhower were distant, whereas they had been close friends for decades. Oddly, Eisenhower is barely represented in the movie. The film depicts a sustained a rivalry between Patton and Field Marshall Montgomery. In reality, the rivalry was one-sided; Montgomery was less concerned about his reputation relative to Patton than Patton was to his. All of these touches tend to humanize Patton and make him more sympathetic. Patton was an avowed anti-Semite—an unsavory aspect of his character that the movie chooses to overlook. The film portrays George Patton as a largely solitary figure, barely mentioning his wife and family and completely omitting the fact that Patton had a long-term extramarital affair with his niece, Jean Gordon. The film also omits the fact that Patton set up a disastrous secret raid on a Nazi prison camp in Hammelburg, Germany, in a failed attempt to liberate his son-in-law, John K. Waters. The film excludes this incident to protect the myth of Patton as a military genius. Another key omission concerns the infamous slapping incident. The movie depicts just one slapping incident, but in point of fact, there were two separate incidents, and Patton bragged about them to Bradley, showing a pattern of disrespect for subordinates. In his book, *American Films of the 70s: Conflicting Visions*, film historian Peter Lev notes that *Patton* consistently enlists viewer identification with the film's protagonist: "General Patton is the focus of identification because he is the only character available for audience sympathy. We experience what he experiences; we share his hopes and dreams [because] we really have no alternatives for emotional investment" (Lev, 2000, p. 115). For corroboration, Lev reports the reaction of WWII veteran and war scholar Paul Fussell, who also noted the film's tendency to manipulate viewer identification. Fussell says that he would have preferred "a more complex" view of Patton "as a dangerously out-of-control individual, instead of the eccentric but brilliant leader of myth." Fussell adds that "there are other real moments that the film wouldn't think of including, such as the sotto voce remark of one disgruntled junior officer to another after being forced to listen to a vainglorious Patton harangue: 'What an a—hole!' That would be an interesting historic moment. I know it took place," says Fussell, "because I was the one who said it" (quoted by Lev, 2000, p. 115).

PIANIST, THE (2002)

Synopsis

The Pianist, a co-production between France, the United Kingdom, Germany, and Poland, is a war survival drama. Scripted by Ronald Harwood, co-produced and directed by Roman Polanski, and starring Adrien Brody, the film is based on the World War II memoirs of Polish Jewish pianist-composer Władysław Szpilman, who managed to survive the Warsaw Ghetto.

Background

Władysław Szpilman (1911–2000), a Polish pianist and classical composer of Jewish descent, was a popular performer in concert and on Polish radio before and after World War II. He miraculously survived the Warsaw Ghetto, the Ghetto Uprising, and final destruction of the Ghetto (19 April–16 May 1943). After the war, Szpilman resumed his career on Polish radio and wrote a memoir about his war years that was published under the title *Śmierć Miasta* [*Death of a City*] (1946), but it was suppressed by the Stalinist Polish authorities. With de-Stalinization in the mid-1950s the book was republished and became known to a wider readership. Decades later, Szpilman's son, Andrzej, again republished his father's memoir, first in German as *Das wunderbare Überleben* [*The Miraculous Survival*] and then in

Adrian Brody as Władysław Szpilman, a Polish-Jewish pianist-composer and Holocaust survivor, in Roman Polanski's *The Pianist* (2002). (Focus Features/Photofest)

English as *The Pianist*. Translations into 30 other languages soon followed. When director Roman Polanski, also of Polish Jewish extraction, read Szpilman's book, he saw deep affinities to his own story. After his parents were sent to concentration camps (his father survived Mauthausen, but his mother did not survive Auschwitz), Polanski escaped from the Kraków Ghetto and lasted out the war by hiding out in the countryside. He had always wanted to make his own film about the Holocaust; Szpilman's book presented the perfect source material. After putting together $35 million in financing from a dozen European production companies, Polanski hired playwright/screenwriter Ronald Harwood (*Cry, The Beloved Country*) to adapt Szpilman's memoir to the screen. Polanski wanted Joseph Fiennes for the lead role, but Fiennes was unavailable. Over 1,400 actors auditioned for the role of Szpilman at a casting call in London but none proved suitable. In the end, Polanski cast Adrien Brody (*The Thin Red Line*) for the part. To prepare for the six-month shoot, Brody spent six weeks dieting (and lost 35 pounds), growing a beard, working on a dialect, and learning to play the piano, of which he already had a basic knowledge. Władysław Szpilman met with Polanski socially a few times but did not make any specific suggestions as to how the movie should be filmed. Sadly, Szpilman did not get to see the film of his life; he died in Warsaw on 6 July 2000 at the age of 88, while the movie was still in its pre-production phase.

Production

Principal photography on *The Pianist* began on 9 February 2001 in Babelsberg Studio in Potsdam, Germany. The film's first scenes were shot at a complex of multistory Soviet Army barracks buildings. Already slated for demolition, the barracks were selectively wrecked by Polanski's production designer, Allan Starski, to simulate the ruins of Warsaw. The film crew then moved to a villa in Potsdam, which served as the house where Szpilman meets Hosenfeld. On 2 March 2001, filming relocated to an abandoned Soviet military hospital in Beelitz, Germany, near Potsdam, where scenes featuring German soldiers destroying a Warsaw hospital were shot. Between 15 and 26 March, filming took place on a backlot of Babelsberg Studios, where Starski skillfully re-created streets in the Warsaw Ghetto as they would have looked during World War II. On 29 March 2001, the production moved to Warsaw for the final three months of filming. The rundown district of Praga, on the east side of the Vistula River, was the location chosen because of its many pre-WWII buildings (the rest of Warsaw, completely destroyed during the war, had been rebuilt). Polanski's art department added WWII-era signs and posters. The Umschlagplatz scene where Szpilman, his family, and hundreds of other Jews wait to be deported to the death camps was filmed at the War Studies University of Warsaw. Principal photography ended in July 2001, followed by months of postproduction in Paris.

Plot Summary

In September 1939, Władysław Szpilman (Adrien Brody), a Polish Jewish pianist, is playing a Chopin piece live on the radio in Warsaw when the station is bombed by the Luftwaffe during Hitler's invasion of Poland. At home with his family,

Szpilman is happy to learn that Britain and France have declared war on Germany, but hope is short-lived; the Allies do not intervene as promised. Hostilities last only 35 days before Poland is crushed by the Nazi invasion from the west and Soviet invasion from the east. The conquering Nazis prohibit Jews from working or owning businesses and also require them to wear blue Star of David armbands. By November 1940, Szpilman and his family are evicted from their home and forced into the teeming Warsaw Ghetto, where starvation and Nazi brutality rule—during a round-up, the Szpilmans watch helplessly as the SS kills a family in a house across from them. In August 1942, Szpilman and his family are awaiting transport to Treblinka extermination camp at the Umschlagplatz as part of Operation Reinhard (the secret Nazi plan to exterminate all Polish Jews) when a friend in the Jewish Ghetto Police recognizes Władysław and separates him from his family. Szpilman toils as a slave laborer but also helps the Jewish resistance by smuggling weapons into the ghetto. He eventually manages to escape and goes into hiding with help from non-Jewish friends Janina Bogucki (Ruth Platt) and her husband, Andrzej (Ronan Vibert). In April 1943, Szpilman watches the Warsaw Ghetto Uprising unfold in the streets below his window. A neighbor finds Szpilman, forcing him to escape to a new secret hideaway. In August 1944, during the Warsaw Uprising, the Armia Krajowa (AK) attacks a German building across the street from Szpilman's hideout. Gunfire from tanks forces him to flee once again. The Uprising fails, Warsaw is utterly destroyed, and Szpilman is left alone to search for food and shelter in the ruins. He treks through the streets and manages to locate a home containing an unopened can of cucumbers. As he attempts to open the can, Wehrmacht officer Wilm Hosenfeld (Thomas Kretschmann) finds him and discovers that Szpilman is a pianist. He requests that Szpilman play and, despite extreme hunger and fatigue, the pianist obliges with Chopin's "Ballade in G Minor." Hosenfeld allows Szpilman to hide in the attic of the empty house and brings him food on a regular basis. In January 1945, the Germans are in retreat from the Red Army. Hosenfeld meets Szpilman one last time, giving him a greatcoat to keep warm. In the spring of 1945, former prisoners of a Nazi concentration camp pass a Soviet prisoner of war (POW) camp holding captured German soldiers. Hosenfeld, one of the prisoners, hears a fellow inmate complain about his past violin career. The violinist confirms knowing Szpilman, and Hosenfeld asks that the pianist aid him in his release. By the time Szpilman is brought to the site, it is deserted. Later, Szpilman works for Polish Radio and performs Chopin's "Grande Polonaise brillante," Op. 22, to a large, appreciative audience. An epilogue says that Szpilman lived to 88 and Hosenfeld perished while in a Soviet prison in 1952.

Reception

The Pianist premiered at the 55th Cannes Film Festival on 24 May 2002, where it won the Palme D'Or. The movie's American premiere was in Los Angeles on 4 December 2002. It went into wide release in the United States on 28 March 2003. The film did well commercially, grossing $121.1 million at the box office—a result bolstered by a good showing at the 2003 Academy Awards, where *The Pianist* garnered seven nominations and three of the most prestigious Oscars: Best Director (Polanski), Best Actor (Brody), and Best Adapted Screenplay (Harwood). Among a slew of other awards, *The Pianist* won two BAFTAs, eight César Awards, and ten Polish Film Awards. Reviews were almost unanimously favorable. A. O. Scott wrote, "Perhaps because of his own experiences, Mr. Polanski approaches this material with a calm, fierce authority. This is certainly the best work Mr. Polanski has done in many years . . . and it is also one of the very few nondocumentary movies about Jewish life and death under the Nazis that can be called definitive" (Scott, 2002).

Reel History Versus Real History

Writing his memoir right after the war, Władysław Szpilman still had detailed recall as to the harrowing events of the previous six years. Assuming that Szpilman is telling the truth about his experiences—and there is no reason to doubt him—*The Pianist* in book form is a highly accurate first-person glimpse of life in Warsaw under the Nazi occupation. Closely following the narrative contours of Szpilman's book, excerpting much of its dialogue, and replicating its detached tone, the movie version of *The Pianist* is, likewise, an unusually faithful historical representation. Though Polanski's scripting contribution went uncredited, he worked closely with screenwriter Ron Harwood in adapting Szpilman's book and brought his own memories to bear, which coincided with Szpilman's in many ways. Polanski and Harwood also watched documentary footage from Warsaw together to grasp the look and feel of life in Warsaw during the war. Allan Starski's superb production design ensured a high degree of visual verisimilitude.

PLATOON (1986)

Synopsis

Platoon is an American anti-war film written and directed by Vietnam War combat veteran Oliver Stone, starring Willem Dafoe and Tom Berenger as two sergeants—one decent and humane, the other a hateful nihilist—vying for the hearts and minds of a U.S. Army platoon during the Vietnam War. *Platoon* is the first film of a trilogy of Vietnam War films directed by Stone, followed by *Born on the Fourth of July* (1989) and *Heaven & Earth* (1993).

Background

A young man from privileged circumstances, Oliver Stone could have avoided the Vietnam-era draft. Instead he volunteered for military service as a way to experience something profound. As Stone later put it, "I could think of no greater reality than war" (*A Tour of the Inferno: Revisiting Platoon*, 2001). After finishing a tour of duty in Vietnam in April 1968, Stone returned home to New York City and wrote "Break" (1969), an allegorical film script that limned his existential and political transformation. A big fan of The Doors, Stone sent the script to Jim Morrison in hopes he would play the lead but Morrison never responded. Though he could not get "Break" produced, Stone pursued a career in film anyway. He attended NYU film school, made a short 16-mm film about the war (*Last Year in Vietnam*, 1971), and wrote a number of other screenplays, among them *Seizure* (1974; his first one made into a film) and "The Platoon," a Vietnam War film script that recycled characters and structure from "Break." Sidney Lumet wanted to direct it in 1976, but producer Martin Bregman was not able to secure studio backing; the script was deemed too grim and realistic a vision of the Vietnam War. Stone next wrote Alan Parker's *Midnight Express* (1978). The film was a hit, but the studios continued to pass on "The Platoon." A frustrated Stone soldiered on, writing the scripts for *The Hand* (1981, a low-budget horror film that he also directed), John Milius's *Conan the Barbarian* (1982), Brian De Palma's gangster epic *Scarface* (1983), Michael Cimino's *Year of the Dragon* (1985), and Hal Ashby's *8 Million Ways to Die* (1986). In 1984 Dino De Laurentiis secured financing for "The Platoon." Pre-production work began but soon ground to a halt when De Laurentiis could not find a distributor. "The Platoon" and another Oliver Stone script for what would become *Salvador* were then passed onto John Daly, the head of Hemdale, a British production company. Daly read both scripts, pronounced them "great stuff," and offered Stone the choice as to which he preferred to film first. Superstitious that something would again go wrong with "The Platoon," Stone opted to shoot *Salvador* first. After finishing *Salvador* at the end of 1985, Stone began pre-production on *Platoon*, as it was now called. He assembled a stellar cast: Martin Sheen's son, Charlie Sheen, in the lead role as Pfc. Chris Taylor; Tom Berenger as the Ahab-like Sgt. Barnes; Willem Dafoe as Barnes' nemesis, Sgt. Gordon Elias (hired over Denzel Washington); and John C. McGinley, Forest Whitaker, and Johnny Depp. James Woods, who had starred in *Salvador*, was also offered a part in *Platoon* but, sated on jungle shoots, turned it down. Oliver Stone realized that his actors would need to be subjected to extreme discomfort if they were going to look and behave like U.S. soldiers in Vietnam, so he hired Vietnam veteran Dale Dye (founder of Warriors, Inc., a company that provides military expertise to Hollywood war films). As *Platoon*'s technical advisor, Dye's mandate was to put the principal cast members through a rigorous, immersive 14-day military training regimen that included forced marches in full combat gear and schooled them in weapons, ordnance, tactics, ambushes, first aid, medevac, radio use, etc. He also limited food and water intake and had his tired actors take turns keeping a two-hour watch at night, as real soldiers would have done in Vietnam. The object was "to mess with [the actors'] heads so we could get that dog-tired, don't give a damn attitude, the anger, and the irritation . . . the casual approach to death" (Saporito, 2015).

Production

Just days before the *Platoon* shoot was scheduled to start in the Philippines, production was nearly canceled because of political unrest. A "People's Revolution" had suddenly erupted, which paralyzed the nation and rendered filmmaking out of the question. Luckily, Ferdinand Marcos, the Philippines' unutterably corrupt president, was persuaded to flee the country for asylum in Hawaii on 25 February 1986. Filming began on 27 February as scheduled and lasted nine weeks (54 shooting days). The studio made an agreement with the Philippine army, allowing crew members to use Philippine military equipment and cast local Vietnamese refugees. Scenes were shot in Mount Makiling (for the forest scenes), Cavite (for the river and village scenes), and Villamor Air Base near Manila. Stone put himself in the picture, making a cameo as a battalion commander in the last battle scene, which was based on the New Year's Day Battle of 1968. Stone had served during the real battle while he was with the 25th Infantry Division in Vietnam.

Plot Summary

In 1967, U.S. Army volunteer Chris Taylor (Charlie Sheen) arrives in Vietnam and is posted with a U.S. Army unit near the border of Cambodia. The troops are commanded by an inept Lt. Wolfe (Mark Moses), but the platoon members take their cues from their better-qualified subordinates: the battle-worn and brash Sgt. Robert "Bob" Barnes (Tom Berenger) and the more temperate and humane Sgt. Elias (Willem Dafoe). Taylor's first assignment is to join Barnes, Elias, and veteran soldiers on a surprise attack on a North Vietnamese Army (NVA) unit. After Gardner (Bob Orwig), another new recruit, falls asleep on night watch, NVA soldiers are able to sneak up on the slumbering U.S. unit in advance of a firefight. Gardner perishes in the exchange of bullets, and Taylor sustains injuries. After a brief trip to the field hospital, Taylor returns and gets close with Sgt. Elias and his relaxed

Chris (Charlie Sheen, left) and Rhah (Francesco Quinn) assist Crawford (Chris Pedersen), a wounded comrade, in Oliver Stone's Vietnam War epic, *Platoon* (1986). (Orion Pictures Corporation/Photofest)

crew. Meanwhile, three soldiers die during a patrol, inciting anger among the troops as they uncover stored enemy supplies in a neighboring village Barnes uses an interpreter to question the village chief (Bernardo Manalili) about his peoples' involvement with the NVA and then shoots the chief's wife when she speaks out of turn. Elias enters the scene and comes to blows with Barnes in response to the senseless killing. Wolfe ends the fight and orders the soldiers to trash the supplies and tear down the village. During the destruction, Taylor saves two female villagers from being sexually assaulted by two of Barnes' men. When the unit arrives back at camp, Capt. Harris (Dale Dye) states that he will investigate the claims of an illegal killing and will initiate a court-martial if he finds the claims to be true. Barns worries that if he is found out, Elias might testify against him. The next patrol endures heavy gunfire, some of which is friendly fire mistakenly ordered by Lt. Wolfe. While Elias, Taylor, and a few other soldiers enter the jungle to hunt down enemy combatants, Barnes sends his unit to retreat and, finding Elias alone, shoots him. He tells the other men that Elias was killed by enemy soldiers. While the troops are airlifted away via helicopter, they see a gravely injured Elias stumble out from the trees, pursued by NVA soldiers, who shoot him down. Seeing Barnes' facial expression as they watch the scene unfold below, Taylor realizes what Barnes has done. Once at base camp, Taylor shares his theory with the other soldiers and encourages them to retaliate. Barnes, drunk, overhears Taylor and provokes an attack. Barnes cuts Taylor with a knife before stumbling away. The soldiers are ordered back to the frontline, and during the first night, the NVA launch a large-scale attack against the Americans. Wolfe dies in the attack, along with most of Barnes' crew. Amidst the madness, Taylor finds Barnes wounded and ranting. Barnes moves to kill Taylor, but the two are knocked out by an aerial bombing. Taylor awakens the next day, grabs a gun, locates Barnes, and then kills him. A helicopter evacuates Taylor and a fellow soldier, who has wounded himself in order to secure a leave of absence. As Samuel Barber's deeply mournful "Adagio for Strings" plays on the soundtrack (also used elsewhere in the film), Taylor looks down on a huge crater full of corpses. In some future time he ruminates (in voice-over), "I think now, looking back, we did not fight the enemy, we fought ourselves, *and the enemy . . . was in us.* The war is over for me now, but it will always be there, for the rest of my days, as I'm sure Elias will be, fighting with Barnes for what Rhah called possession of my soul. There are times since I've felt like the child born of those two fathers. But be that as it may, those of us who did make it have an obligation to build again, to teach to others what we know, and to try with what's left of our lives to find a goodness, and meaning, to this life."

Reception

Platoon had its American premiere on 19 December 1986 in New York and Los Angeles and expanded to its widest release (1,564 theaters) over the next five weeks. *Platoon* was also screened at the 37th Berlin International Film Festival, where Oliver Stone won the Silver Bear for Best Director. The movie proved to be a major commercial success. Foreign grosses are unknown, but domestic receipts at the end of its 27-week theatrical run totaled $133.8 million—more than 20 times its production budget. Ticket sales were sharply boosted by eight Oscar nominations in February 1987 and four wins in March: Best Picture (Arnold Kopelson); Best Director (Oliver Stone); Best Editing (Claire Simpson); and Best Sound (John Wilkinson, Richard Rogers, Simon Kaye, and Charles Grenzbach). *Platoon* was also honored with two BAFTAs, three Golden Globes, and the DGA Award for Outstanding Directing. The critical response was, likewise, overwhelmingly positive. Roger Ebert gave it the maximum four stars and praised Stone for making a war movie devoid of "false heroics," "standard heroes," or a "carefully mapped plot," but one that dares to show an American atrocity perpetrated against Vietnamese civilians. Ebert: "After seeing *Platoon*, I fell to wondering [how] Stone was able to make such an effective movie without . . . making it [merely] exhilarating. Here's how I think he did it. He abandoned the choreography that is standard in almost all war movies. He abandoned any attempt to make it clear where the various forces were in relation to each other, so that we never know where 'our' side stands and where 'they' are" (Ebert, 1986). In his review, Vincent Canby described *Platoon* as a "singular achievement . . . possibly the best work of any kind about the Vietnam War since Michael Herr's vigorous and hallucinatory book *Dispatches*" (Canby, 1986).

Reel History Versus Real History

As one of only a handful of bona fide Vietnam veterans involved in the making of major motion pictures about the Vietnam War—Gus Hasford, Patrick Sheane Duncan, and James Carabatsos are others—Oliver Stone was able to bring a high degree of authenticity to *Platoon*. Viewers may wonder if there really was as much internecine conflict and drug use among American soldiers in Vietnam. Certainly, in some platoons, there were—though heavy drug use was more common in rear echelon areas. Viewers should not wonder, though, about anti-civilian atrocities committed by U.S. troops, which became notorious after the My Lai Massacre (16 March 1968) was exposed to the nation by *New York Times* reporter Seymour Hersh in October 1969. More recently, American war crimes in Vietnam have been exhaustively documented by Nick Turse in his controversial book, *Kill Anything That Moves: The Real American War in Vietnam* (2013). Whatever the actual scope of these atrocities, they did happen, as they do in all wars. Regarding the film's historical veracity, TV journalist Ted Koppel (*Nightline*) assembled a group of six Vietnam combat veterans in Chicago for a private screening of *Platoon* on 3 January 1987, just after the film was released, and all of them readily confirmed the film's truthfulness. Frank Kauzlarich, who served in 1968–1969 as a helicopter crew chief, told Koppel, "The character portrayals were outstanding; they didn't 'Hollywood it up.' They had the details right about the leeches—and the dust everywhere when (the college kid) arrived in Vietnam in the very first scene. I saw the same dust and the body bags when I first got there, and I thought to myself, 'What the hell am I getting into?' The characters were all right on: the good, the bad, and the ugly, you might say. Also it showed the things you had to do—the people you had to leave behind." Another veteran, Terry Tidd, who served in 1966 with the Marine I Corps near Da Nang, said "I want to get my ma and dad to see this movie. I got a 13-year-old boy I might want to take. It may be too heavy, but he's asked me a lot about Vietnam, and I probably should take him to see this. If anyone wants to know what the war is like, this would be a good one for them." A third veteran, Bill Burton, a Marine who fought in 1968–1969, said, "It was almost real. There were some things I saw in the film that I did." Asked what they were he said, "No, I'd rather not say. It affects me to this day" (Siskel, 1987).

PORK CHOP HILL (1959)

Synopsis

Pork Chop Hill is an American war film written by James R. Webb; produced by Sy Bartlett; directed by Lewis Milestone; and starring Gregory Peck, Rip Torn, and George Peppard. Based on the book by U.S. military historian Brigadier General S.L.A. Marshall, the film depicts the first Battle of Pork Chop Hill between the U.S. Army's 7th Infantry Division and Chinese and North Korean forces in April 1953 in the final days of the Korean War.

Background

The so-called Battle of Pork Chop Hill actually comprises two related Korean War battles fought during the spring and summer of 1953 in the midst of cease-fire negotiations at Panmunjom that would end the war on 27 July—and make these costly engagements militarily pointless. Military analyst and historian, U.S. Army Brigadier General S.L.A. "Slam" Marshall depicted the first battle (16–18 April 1953) in his 1956 bestseller, *Pork Chop Hill: The American Fighting Man in Action Korea, Spring 1953*. Screenwriter James Webb brought Marshall's book to the attention of Gregory Peck, who agreed to turn it into an anti-war film that would show war realistically, that is, in all its nerve-wracking carnage, waste, and futility. Peck purchased the screen rights from S.L.A. Marshall for a pittance: a lopsided deal that Marshall rued for the rest of his life. Peck then hired Lewis Milestone (*All Quiet on the Western Front*) to direct the picture for Melville Productions, Peck's new production company, formed with his friend, screenwriter Sy Bartlett (*Twelve O'Clock High*).

Production

A casting call yielded some 640 applicants for about 40 screen roles. Many of the young actors who won parts in the film went on to have distinguished film and/or TV careers (e.g., Rip Torn, Woody Strode, Harry Guardino, George Peppard, Norman Fell, Robert Blake, Martin Landau, James Edwards, Gavin McLeod, Harry Dean Stanton, Bert Remsen, and Clarence Williams III). Under the supervision of production designer Nicolai Remisoff and set decorator Edward G. Boyle, crews turned a 300-foot outcropping at Albertson Ranch, Thousand Oaks, California (10 miles north of Malibu), into a realistic facsimile of Pork Chop Hill, with trenches, bunkers, and concertina wire. Track was laid down to accommodate a rolling camera platform for tracking and following shots by cinematographer Sam Leavitt—an arrangement similar to the one that Lewis Milestone had deployed in *All Quiet on the Western Front* 28 years earlier. The filmmakers also benefited from the support of the Pentagon, which lent them the services of Joseph Clemons, Jr. himself as technical advisor (Fishgall, 2002, pp. 205–208). Budget-conscious Peck had insisted that the picture come in at $1.3 million. Casting unknowns and shooting in black and white near Los Angeles helped keep costs down, but what was supposed to be a 40-day shoot (26 May–18 July 1958) went 15 days over schedule. The film wrapped in early August, $450,000 over budget. Ironically, the actual battle lasted just two days and two nights. In post-production, Peck, Sy Bartlett, and James Webb took over the final editing and cut the film by nearly 20 minutes to make it tauter. An unhappy Lewis Milestone attributed the last-minute excisions to Gregory Peck's wife, Veronique, who felt that her husband made his first entrance too late into the picture, an unconfirmed but plausible assertion.

Plot Summary

In a surprise attack on the night of 16 April 1953, near the end of the Korean War, a Chinese battalion overruns U.S. defensive positions on Pork Chop Hill: an exposed outpost that projects into Chinese lines. The Chinese quickly capture most of the hill except for a few isolated bunkers. King Company, 31st Infantry Regiment, commanded by Lt. Joseph Clemons, Jr. (Gregory Peck), is tasked with recapturing the hill, with two platoons of Love Company mounting a supporting attack on the right flank. Subjected to demoralizing propaganda via loudspeaker (spoken by Viraj Amonsin) and withering artillery, mortar, and automatic weapons fire, both units take extremely heavy casualties. Love Company's advance is stymied, but King Company ultimately manages to capture most of the bunkers and trenches on the hill's summit. Of the 197 men who began the assault on Pork Chop Hill, only 35 men from King Company and 12 men from the two platoons of Love Company make it up the hill unscathed. After further casualties Lt. Clemons has only 25 men left to hold the hill against impending Chinese counterattacks. George Company arrives to help but is mistakenly ordered down off the hill. All of Clemons' men are exhausted, low on ammo, and under constant and heavy enemy fire. Clemons requests reinforcements to stave off annihilation but none are forthcoming. Unknown to him, the merits of holding Pork Chop Hill are being debated at every command level, from battalion, to Eighth Army headquarters, all the way up to the peace talks table at Panmunjom. Finally realizing that the Chinese had attacked Pork Chop Hill to test American resolve (not for its strategic value), the American negotiators at Panmunjom authorize 7th Infantry Division commanding officer, Major General Arthur Trudeau (Ken Lynch), to send in reinforcements for Clemons and his beleaguered men, who descend the hill as fresh troops climb it.

Reception

Released on 29 May 1959 (just before the Memorial Day weekend), *Pork Chop Hill* received no Oscar nominations but earned rave reviews for its gritty realism. For example, Bosley Crowther praised the filmmakers' willingness to depict the "resentments and misgivings" of the American troops: "The readiness to incorporate these resentments in the account and demonstrate the application of this new brainwash technique [i.e., an enemy battlefield loudspeaker broadcasting psychological abuse to attacking U.S. infantrymen] are worthy of highest commendation in James R. Webb's bone-bare script, which has been taken from S.L.A. Marshall's factual account of the fighting for Pork Chop Hill. And the audacity of Sy Bartlett to produce such a grim and rugged film, which tacitly points the obsoleteness of ground warfare, merits applause" (Crowther, 1959). Good notices notwithstanding, *Pork Chop Hill* did lackluster business at the box office. A relentlessly grim picture about a bloody battle at the end of an unpopular war, the movie generated $1.7 million in ticket sales—just enough to recuperate its production costs, despite an 11-city pre-release promotional tour by Gregory Peck.

Reel History Versus Real History

In general terms *Pork Chop Hill* is a fairly accurate depiction of the actual battle, albeit somewhat simplified for narrative coherence. As depicted in the movie, American G.I. morale at the time of the Battle of Pork Chop Hill was low. The Chinese did use loudspeakers as a means of psychological warfare but not quite as depicted in the film; the Chinese often welcomed arriving units by name via their loudspeakers but did not broadcast a greeting to King Company as it moved up the hill, as the film shows. At any rate, ongoing peace talks and impending prisoner exchanges made it clear that the war would soon be over; no one was anxious to be the last combatant to die in an unpopular conflict about to end in stalemate. Gregory Peck's rendition of Lt. Joseph Clemons is, however, more problematic. Lt. Clemons was 24 in 1953, whereas Peck was 42 in 1958 when he played Clemons—far too old to be playing a junior officer just two years out of West Point. In his book, S.L.A. Marshall characterized Lt. Clemons as still inexperienced and prone to confusion, a characterization that Lewis Milestone wanted to capture on film but Milestone was overridden by Gregory Peck. In keeping with his well-established star persona as an always righteous and invincible hero, Peck played Clemons as unshakably stalwart and decisive (Fishgall, 2002, p. 207). Despite the obvious age discrepancy and an idealized portrayal, the real Joe Clemons pronounced *Pork Chop Hill* "so realistic that it seems the battle itself is being refought before your very eyes" (Payne, 1959).

RAN (1985)

Synopsis

Ran is a Japanese-French war film/period tragedy directed, edited, and co-written by Akira Kurosawa, adapted from Shakespeare's tragedy, *King Lear* and the legends surrounding daimyō Mōri Motonari. The film stars Tatsuya Nakadai as Hidetora Ichimonji, an aging Sengoku-era warlord who abdicates for his three sons—with disastrous results.

Background

Akira Kurosawa first conceived of the idea for the film that would become *Ran* (Japanese for "chaos" or "discord") in the early 1970s, when he read about Mōri Motonari (1497–1571), a powerful daimyō in the Chūgoku region of Japan who is remembered as one of the greatest warlords of the Sengoku period (mid-16th century). Though a brilliant diplomat and strategist, Motonari is best known for an event that probably never happened: the "lesson of the three arrows," a parable that Motonari illustrated by giving each of his three sons an arrow to break. He then gave them three arrows bundled together and pointed out that although one may be easily broken, three bundled together are impossible to break. Motonari actually had nine sons (two of whom died in childhood) but most prominent of them were the three sons the parable concerns: Mōri Takamoto (1523–1563), Kikkawa Motoharu (1530–1586), and Kobayakawa Takakage (1533–1597). Formulating a scenario that could generate real drama, Kurosawa imagined trouble among the three brothers rather than unity and reasonableness. As he later told an interviewer, "What might their story be like, I wondered, if the sons had not been so good? It was only after I was well into writing the script about these imaginary unfilial sons of the Mōri clan that the similarities to [Shakespeare's 1606 tragedy, *King*] *Lear* occurred to me. Since the story is set in medieval Japan, the protagonist's children had to be men; to divide a realm among daughters would have been unthinkable" (Grilli, 2008, p. 126). Kurosawa and two co-writers—Hideo Oguni and Masato Ide—had a draft of a screenplay completed by 1975, but Kurosawa would not be able to arrange financing for an expensive, large-scale epic set in medieval Japan for another seven years. In the meantime, he painted storyboards of every shot in *Ran* and made *Dersu Uzala* (1975) and *Kagemusha* (1980), the latter of which he described as a "dress rehearsal" for *Ran*. In 1982 Kurosawa finally secured funding for *Ran* from two sources: Japanese producer Masatoshi Hara (Herald Ace Productions) and French producer Serge Silberman (Greenwich

Film Productions). After the box office success of Jean-Jacques Beineix's *Diva* (1981), Silberman was able to put up most of the money needed to back *Ran*, which ended up costing ¥2.4 billion (i.e., $12 million), the most expensive Japanese film produced up to that time. Kurosawa cast Tatsuya Nakadai (who played the dual lead roles in *Kagemusha*) as Hidetora Ichimonji, an aging Sengoku-era warlord based on Mōri Motonari who decides to abdicate as ruler in favor of his three sons. Prior to production, several hundred elaborate costumes had to be created by hand, an arduous process that took two years to complete. Pre-production also involved extensive location scouting and set construction, for example, a castle destroyed in the middle of the movie had to be specially built on the slopes of Mount Fuji, only to be burned down.

Production

Akira Kurosawa was 75 years old when he directed *Ran* (June 1984–February 1985) and was nearly blind when the initial photography started. He required assistance in order to frame his shots, and his assistants used hundreds of his storyboard paintings as templates to construct and film scenes. Almost the entire film is done in long shot, with only a handful of close-ups. An enormous undertaking, *Ran* used some 1,400 extras, 1,400 suits of armor (designed by Kurosawa himself), and 200 horses, some of them imported from the United States. Over his long career, Kurosawa worked with the same crew of technicians and assistants. Toward the end of the shoot, Kurosawa lost two of his old stalwarts. In January 1985, Fumio Yamoguchi, the sound recordist on nearly all of Kurosawa's films since 1949, and Ryu Kuze, action coordinator on many of them, died within a few days of each other. A month later (1 February 1985), Kurosawa's wife of 39 years, Yôko Yaguchi, also died. Kurosawa halted filming for just one day to mourn before resuming work on the picture.

Plot Summary

[Act I] Hidetora Ichimonji (Tatsuya Nakadai), a powerful warlord near the end of his life, decides to divide his kingdom among his three sons: Taro (Akira Terao), Jiro (Jinpachi Nezu), and Saburo (Daisuke Ryu). The oldest son, Taro, is bequeathed the sought-after First Castle and is named commander of the Ichimonji clan. Jiro and Saburo are given the Second and Third Castles, respectively. Hidetora retains his title of Great Lord, and the two younger sons are expected to rally behind Taro. Saburo calls his father a fool, stating that he can't expect loyalty from sons who grew up watching their father use the most cruel, heartless methods for power and domination. Hidetora is threatened by his son, but his servant, Tango (Masayuki Yui), defends Saburo. Hidetora responds by exiling both men. Nobuhiro Fujimaki (Hitoshi Ueki), a visiting warlord, sees Saburo's fervor and forthrightness and asks him to wed his daughter. [Act II] After Hidetora divides his remaining lands between Jiro and Saburo, Taro's wife, Lady Kaede (Mieko Harada), encourages Taro to gain control of the entire clan. Emboldened, Taro tells Hidetora to give up his title of Great Lord. Hidetora, now betrayed by two sons, runs to Jiro's castle only to discover that Jiro plans to use him in his own scheme for power and influence. Unsure of where to go, Hidetora and his company depart from Jiro's castle. Tango finds his father and informs Hidetora of Taro's new decree: anyone who assists Hidetora will be sentenced to death. Hidetora flees to Saburo's castle, which was left empty when Saburo went into exile. [Act III] Hidetora and his samurais are attacked by Taro's and Jiro's forces. In the ensuing battle, almost all of Hidetora's men are killed and the Third Castle is set on fire. Hidetora, alone and losing his mind, leaves the castle as it is consumed by flames. During the siege on the castle, Taro is killed by a bullet from Jiro's general, Shuri Kurogane's (Hisashi Igawa) gun. Meanwhile, Hidetora wanders the wilderness and is found by Tango, who tries to assist him. The pair take shelter in a peasant's home, but realize that the peasant is Tsurumaru (Mansai Nomura), the brother of Lady Sué (Yoshiko Miyazaki), Jiro's wife. Tsurumaru was a victim of Hidetora's regime: he was blinded and left for dead after Hidetora murdered his father and conquered their land. [Act IV] After Taro's death, Jiro takes on the title of the Great Lord, moving into the First Castle and commanding the Ichimonji clan. Jiro returns to the castle to find Lady Kaede, unbothered by Taro's death, waiting to blackmail Jiro into an affair. Lady Kaede uses her influence with Jiro to call for Lady Sué's death. Jiro orders Kurogane to carry out the task, but he declines, stating that Kaede will be the ruin of both Jiro and the clan. Kurogane runs to tell Sué and Tsurumaru to leave. Meanwhile, two ronin are captured by Tango, who coerces them to reveal plans for assassinating Hidetora. Tango leaves to share the news with Saburo. Hidetora is overtaken by madness and runs off into a volcanic plain while Kyoami (Pîtâ) runs after him. Saburo and Jiro meet on the battlefield and agree on a truce, and Saburo becomes concerned by the report of his father's onset of madness. While Saburo meets with Kyoami and takes 10 warriors along to rescue Hidetora, Jiro takes advantage of the situation and sends gunners to ambush his brother and father. Jiro also attacks Saburo's army, which falls back into the woods as the soldiers go on the defensive. As the family is warring, a messenger shares news that Ayabe, a rival lord, is headed towards the First Castle. At the same time, Saburo locates Hidetora, and the father experiences a reprieve from his insanity and begins to heal his relationship with his son. However, in the midst of the reconciliation, one of Jiro's snipers kills Saburo. Hidetora dies out of sadness. Fujimaki arrives with his troops to see Tango and Kyoami grieving. [Act V] In the meantime, Tsurumaru and Sué get to the ruined castle, but realize that they forgot a flute at Tsurumaru's home, one that Sué had gifted to Tsurumaru at the time of his banishment. She goes back for the flute, but is discovered and murdered by one of Jiro's assassins. Simultaneously, Ayabe's army attacks the First Castle. When Kurogane hears that Lady Sué has been killed by Jiro's assassin, he corners Kaede and pushes her for information. She comes clean about her plot to obliterate Hidetora and his clan to avenge the deaths of her family members. Kurogane decapitates Kaede for her treachery. As Ayabe's army overtakes the First Castle, Jiro, Kurogane, and all of Jiro's men are killed. Tsurumaru is left amidst the rubble, alone.

Reception

Ran had its world premiere in Tokyo on 25 May 1985. It was subsequently screened at a number of film festivals before going into staggered general release in about two dozen countries. *Ran* did not do very well at the box office, initially making only enough to break even. It did, however, receive Oscar nominations for Best Director, Best Art Direction, Best Cinematography, and Best Costume Design (which it won), among many other international nominations and awards. Reviews were, for the most part, adulatory. Vincent Canby wrote, "Though big in physical scope and of a beauty that suggests a kind of drunken, barbaric lyricism, *Ran* has the terrible logic and clarity of a morality tale seen in tight close-up, of a myth that, while being utterly specific and particular in its time and place, remains ageless, infinitely adaptable . . . Here is a film by a man whose art now stands outside time and fashion" (Canby, 1985). Roger Ebert called the film "visually magnificent" and said he realized on seeing it again in 2000 that "the action doesn't center on the old man, but has a fearful energy of its own, through which he wanders. Kurosawa has not told the story of a great man whose sin of pride drives him mad, but the story of a man who has waged war all his life, hopes to impose peace in his old age and unleashes even greater turmoil" (Ebert, 2000). Decades after its release, most film critics and scholars view *Ran* as Akira Kurosawa's masterpiece.

Reel History Versus Real History

The story that *Ran* tells is, of course, entirely fictional. One can only judge its historical accuracy in terms of its depictions of medieval Japanese castles; the look, dress, and demeanor of the Ichimonji clan; the conduct in battle of the samurai; etc. On these counts, *Ran* has extraordinary verisimilitude.

S

SAHARA (1943)

Synopsis
Sahara is an American war film directed by Zoltán Korda that stars Humphrey Bogart as an American tank commander in Libya during the Western Desert Campaign of World War II. Bogart and his small tank crew dig in to defend an isolated desert water well against an Afrika Korps battalion desperate for water.

Background
A rousing Bogart actioner that does not seem derivative, Zoltán Korda's *Sahara* (1943) actually has a long, complicated genealogy. The film's ultimate source is Philip MacDonald's *Patrol*, a 1927 novel about a group of WWI British soldiers lost in the desert in Mesopotamia (modern-day Iraq) and surrounded by the enemy. British writer-director Walter Summers brought *Lost Patrol*, a silent film version of *Patrol*, starring Cyril McLaglen, to the screen in 1929. Five years later John Ford crafted *The Lost Patrol* (1934), a solid American remake starring Cyril McLaglen's older brother, Victor, in the lead role. Three years later Russian director Mikhail Romm made a third film version entitled *Trinisdat* (*The Thirteen*) that made the soldiers Russians, transferred the setting to Central Asia during the Basmachi Revolt (1916–1924), and substituted Afghani bandits for John Ford's stereotypically loathsome Arabs. The fourth of six films to recycle MacDonald's Alamo-like scenario (followed by André de Toth's *Last of the Comanches* in 1953 and Brian Trenchard-Smith's *Sahara*, aka *Desert Storm*, in 1995), Zoltán Korda's *Sahara* was adapted from its immediate predecessor, *Trinisdat*, by Korda with the help of screenwriters James O'Hanlon, John Howard Lawson, and Sidney Buchman. Transferring the action from WWI-era Afghanistan to WWII-era Libya, Korda and his writing team set *Sahara* in June 1942, after the Battle of Al Gazala, when Tobruk fell to Erwin Rommel's Afrika Korps and Allied forces were in full retreat into Egypt. Released on 11 November 1943—during the "Operation Torch" landings in Tunisia that signaled the final, victorious phase of the North African Campaign—*Sahara* is a crafty pro-Allied propaganda film that uses the backdrop of impending Allied victory in North Africa to reflect on a time in the recent past when things were grim but the requisite American grit and Allied solidarity were fully in evidence.

Production
Columbia Pictures offered the lead role in *Sahara* (originally titled "Somewhere in Sahara") to Gary Cooper, Glenn Ford, and Brian Donlevy but the role finally went

to Humphrey Bogart after he and Donlevy traded movies. With the full cooperation of the War Department, shooting took place from early March to mid-May 1943, in 90° heat, in Anza-Borrego Desert State Park, a 600,000-acre preserve in the Mojave Desert just west of California's Salton Sea that was from the days of Rudolph Valentino, Hollywood's go-to locale for shooting desert pictures. Art Director Lionel Banks had 2,000 tons of sand trucked in, spray painted, and blown around by giant fans to make the terrain look more like the towering sand dunes of the Sahara Desert in Libya. The U.S. military supplied a 28-ton M3 "Grant" medium tank, a P-51 Mustang fighter (repainted to pass for a Messerschmitt 109 used in a strafing scene), various other tanks, half-tracks, weapons, equipment, and the 250 men of "C" Company, 84th Recon Battalion, 4th Armored Division, to play German soldiers in the film. During principal photography, cast and crew resided at the (now defunct) Planter's Hotel in Brawley, California, about 50 miles east of the shooting location, while the soldiers lived in tents at Anza-Borrego. Bogart's working relationship with Zoltán Korda was strained but not as much as his relationship with his then-wife, Mayo Methot, whom he sardonically nicknamed "Sluggy" (they were known in Hollywood as "the battling Bogarts"). Marital troubles notwithstanding, Bogart delivered one of his strongest performances, despite the fact that, at age 43, he was at least 17 years older than the average G.I. in World War II. He considered *Sahara* one of his best films.

Plot Summary

Separated from its unit during the latter stages of the Battle of Al Gazala, a U.S. Army M3 tank (dubbed "Lulubelle") commanded by Master Sergeant Joe Gunn (Humphrey Bogart) is trying to rejoin the retreating British Eighth Army. Arriving at a bombed-out field hospital, Gunn and his remaining crew, Jimmy Doyle (Dan Duryea) and Waco Hoyt (Bruce Bennett), pick up a motley group of stragglers, among them British Captain Jason Halliday (Richard Nugent), four Commonwealth soldiers, and Free French Corporal Jean "Frenchie" Leroux (Louis Mercier). Though he outranks Gunn, Halliday cedes command to him. Later, they come upon Sudanese Sergeant Major Tambul (Rex Ingram) and his Italian prisoner of war, Giuseppe (J. Carrol Naish). Initially, Gunn opts to leave Giuseppe behind—a sure death sentence—but humanitarian instincts prevail and the Italian is also taken aboard the tank. Tambul offers to take the group to a well at Hassan Barani. On the way, Luftwaffe pilot Captain von Schletow (Kurt Kreuger) fires at the tank and kills a British soldier, but is subsequently shot out of the air and captured. The men reach the well to find it bone dry. Low on water, Gunn and his ragtag outfit are forced to seek water at another desert well at Bir Acroma, 50 miles away. Capably led by Tambul through a blinding sandstorm, they find the well but it is almost dry. When German troops arrive soon afterwards, Gunn and his men attack the vehicle. A German survivor reveals that the Afrika Korps battalion is nearby, struggling to find water. Gunn convinces his fellow soldiers to fight the Germans as a distraction while Waco Hoyt searches for backup. The two German survivors are released to their battalion with an offer of water in exchange for food, despite the fact that Gunn barely has water for his own soldiers. When the German battalion shows up, Gunn changes the arrangement, demanding "guns for water." Though the well has run dry, Gunn buys time by pretending that the well is full of water while negotiating with Major von Falken (John Wengraf), the German commander. The Germans attack the sparsely defended well in waves and are repeatedly beaten back, but the defenders are killed off one by one. Giuseppe, Tambul, and an escaping von Schletow all perish. To Gunn's amazement, the Germans' final assault turns into a mass surrender as they drop their weapons and crawl across the sand towards the well. To Gunn's further amazement, a direct hit on the well by a German artillery shell has accidentally released abundant amounts of water. Gunn and Osmond "Ozzie" Bates (Patrick O'Moore), the only other Allied survivor, disarm the Germans while they quench their ravenous thirst. As Gunn and Bates march their column of POWs east, they encounter Allied troops guided by Waco and receive news of the Allied victory at the First Battle of El Alamein (1 July 1942–27 July 1942).

Reception

Box office receipts for *Sahara* were good and reviews were strong. For example, Bosley Crowther called Sahara "a real he-man picture . . . a laudable conception of soldier fortitude in this war, and it is also a bang-up action picture, cut out to hold one enthralled" (Crowther, 1943). The film earned Academy Award nominations for Best Sound (John Livadary), Best Cinematography (Black-and-White), and Best Supporting Actor (J. Carrol Naish).

Reel History Versus Real History

The Office of War Information (OWI) advised Hollywood that, for propaganda purposes, the ideal combat movie should show "an ethnically and geographically diverse group of Americans [who] would articulate what they were fighting for, pay due regard to the role of the Allies, and battle an enemy who was formidable but not a superman" (quoted in Kornweibel, Jr., 1981, p. 8). *Sahara* exceeds the OWI's mandate by featuring an international and interracial cast of Allies willing to fight and die as a cohesive force. It also shows the Germans as ruthless—von Schletow and von Falken are stereotypically arrogant and treacherous Nazis—but vulnerable to defeat on the battlefield. Finally, and most importantly, *Sahara* contains allegorical elements and set speeches that rationalize the war against fascism in emotionally compelling terms. Joe Gunn, a Yank, takes over from British Captain Halliday, neatly symbolizing the familiar U.S. role as rescuer of embattled Europe from German tyranny (a role that Bogart just dramatized with great success in *Casablanca*). Major Tambul's chasing down and vanquishing von Schletow subliminally reminds audiences of Jesse Owens' track victories over German competitors in the 1936 Berlin Olympics or Joe Louis's victory over Max Schmeling in June 1938: blows against the myth of Aryan supremacy. J. Carrol Naish's Oscar-nominated turn as the Italian POW, Giuseppe, is equally crucial to the film's meaning. Saved by Joe Gunn only to be later murdered by von Schletow, Giuseppe epitomizes Italy as Hitler's reluctant ally, repentant in defeat and awakened to the evils of fascism. Just before his death, Giuseppe recaptures his full humanity by denouncing the Axis powers in moral and religious terms: "But are my eyes blind that I must fall to my knees to worship a maniac [Mussolini] who has made of my country a concentration camp, who has made of my people slaves? . . . As for your Hitler, it's because of a man like him that God—my God—created hell!" Finally, the siege of the well at Bir Acroma conjures all the heroic but hopeless defensive battles of history, from Thermopylae to Wake Island. Unlike its historical precedents, Sahara delivers, deus ex machina, a miraculous albeit preposterous victory.

SAND PEBBLES, THE (1966)

Synopsis

The Sand Pebbles is an American adventure epic/war film directed and produced by Robert Wise. Based on the 1962 novel of the same title by Richard McKenna, the film tells the story of a U.S. Navy machinist's mate (played by Steve McQueen) aboard the fictional gunboat USS *San Pablo* in 1920s China: a country in the throes of anti-Western fervor and civil strife.

Background

In 1953, following a 22-year career in the U.S. Navy as a chief machinist mate, Richard McKenna (1913–1964) undertook a second career as a writer. After dabbling in science fiction, McKenna wrote his only novel: *The Sand Pebbles*, a 597-page epic about the travails of an American gunboat on China's Yangtze River in 1926 (McKenna had served on such a gunboat, but a decade later, in 1936). The book proved to be a huge hit: a condensed version was serialized in three issues of the *Saturday Evening Post* in November 1962; it won the $10,000 1963 Harper Prize Novel, was chosen as a Book-of-the-Month Club selection, and became a national bestseller. Furthermore, McKenna sold the movie rights to United Artists (UA) for $300,000 ($2.4 million in 2017 dollars). Shortly thereafter 20th Century Fox acquired the rights from UA and studio head Darryl F. Zanuck greenlit the project for producer-director Robert Wise in September 1962. The search for suitable filming locations in Asia, script writing, and other pre-production work would keep the project on hold for another three years. Paul Newman was tapped for the lead role of Jake Holman but turned it down. Teen crooner Pat Boone lobbied hard for it but it finally went to Steve McQueen (who was paid $650,000), after he achieved true stardom in John Sturges' *The Great Escape* (1963). A former Marine with a rebellious streak and lover of all things mechanical, McQueen was perfectly suited to play a feisty Navy machinist mate. When Julie Christie turned down the role of Shirley Eckert, it went to Candice Bergen (who was just 19). Richard Attenborough (an Englishman playing an American who had appeared with McQueen in *The Great Escape*), Mako (a Japanese American actor playing a Chinese man), and Richard Crenna (in his first major film role) filled out the rest of the main cast. Pre-production work on *The Sand Pebbles* included the construction of the movie's most important and expensive prop: the *San Pablo*, a 150-foot, steel-hulled gunboat closely modeled on the USS *Villalobos* (PG-42), an 1898 gunboat captured from Spain during the Spanish-American War and used on Yangtze River patrol from

1903 to 1928. Built in Hong Kong by Vaughn & Yung Engineering Ltd. at a cost of $250,000, the *San Pablo* was powered by reliable Cummins diesel engines, not a period steam engine liable to break down and cause production delays. The *San Pablo* emitted black smoke from her smokestack that came from old tires and other rubbish burned in a special compartment on the boat. Jake Holman's beloved engine—a working 20-ton, 1,000-horsepower, triple expansion steam engine built by Vickers in 1920 and salvaged from a Norwegian whaler in Vancouver, British Columbia—was actually located in an engine room set built on Stage 16 at 20th Century Fox studios in Burbank, not on the *San Pablo*.

Production

Shooting in mainland China, where the novel was set, was out of the question, so much of *The Sand Pebbles* was filmed on the Keelung and Tam Sui Rivers at Taipei, on the island of Taiwan. The narrow, crowded streets of Taipei were used for street scenes supposedly taking place in Shanghai, *San Pablo*'s home port. In the Tamsui district of Taipei, 900 of the 5,000 locals were recruited as extras to storm across the "Changsha Bund" and hurl lighted torches at the *San Pablo*. Po-Han's poignant death scene was also filmed in Tamsui. Filming on Taiwan lasted four and a half months (22 November 1965–21 March 1966). The company then moved on to Hong Kong to film the movie's climactic fight between the *San Pablo* and 30 Chinese junks blockading it, supposedly on the Chien River in mainland China, but it was actually shot on a narrow inlet in Hong Kong's Sai Kung district—the massive 1,000-foot bamboo rope that linked the junks together weighed 25 tons. Filming of the battle scene, which took two months, was completed 15 May 1966. The 135-person cast and crew then returned to California to shoot interior scenes at the studio in Burbank and some additional exteriors at Malibu Creek State Park in Calabasas in June and July. The grueling nine-month shoot was finally concluded on 2 August 1966 at the USS *Texas*, near Houston, where what was supposed to have been the film's opening scene was shot (i.e., Jake's departure from an American battleship in Shanghai harbor). Included in a test rough cut, that scene and some other scenes ended up on the cutting room floor in order to trim the film's running time from 196 minutes down to 182 minutes. Due to production delays, mostly caused by inclement weather but also due to the language barrier in Taiwan, unpredictable tides, etc., the film greatly exceeded its $8 million budget, coming in at $12 million. Steve McQueen was so exhausted that he took a year off to rest.

Plot Summary

In 1926, Machinist's Mate 1st Class Jake Holman (Steve McQueen) transfers to the Yangtze River Patrol gunboat USS *San Pablo* (nicknamed the "Sand Pebble" and its sailors are dubbed "Sand Pebbles"). The officers have hired coolies to do most of the routine work, leaving the sailors free for military drills or just lounging about. An industrious individualist and avid mechanic, Holman takes over the operation and maintenance of the ship's engine—inadvertently insulting the chief engine room coolie, Chien (Tommy Lee) in the process. Holman also alienates most of his fellow sailors, who are lazy, but he does become close friends with a waterten-der named Frenchy Burgoyne (Richard Attenborough). Holman discovers a serious problem with a crank bearing on the boat's engine and informs the captain, Lt. Collins (Richard Crenna), but Collins refuses to have it repaired until his execu-tive officer declares an emergency. Chien asks to complete the repair and is acciden-tally crushed to death when a jack slips. The chief coolie, Lop-eye Shing (Henry Wang), blames Holman, believing that a "ghost in the machine" killed Chien. Holman selects Po-Han (Mako) as a replacement for Chien, and the two men soon become friends. Po-Han is harassed by "Ski" Stawski (Simon Oakland), a brutish sailor, and the two box while the rest of the crew places bets on the outcome. Po-Han wins the fight, creating greater friction between Holman and the other crew members. Lt. Collins orders the crew to refrain from any hostilities with the Chi-nese, as they don't want to add fuel to the propaganda fire. The boat embarks, but Po-Han is sent ashore to avenge Chien's death. Po-Han is run down, taken cap-tive, and tortured by Chinese peasants while the crew watches from the boat. The Chinese refuse to release Po-Han, and Collins shoots him to relieve his suffering. The *San Pablo* moors on the Xiang River due to low water levels, and Lt. Collins begins to fear a mutiny. Frenchy dies from pneumonia after too many swims ashore to visit his new wife Maily (Emmanuelle Arsan). Kuomintang (Chinese National-ist Party) army soldiers locate Holman as he tries to comfort Maily, beat him, and drag the grieving woman away. The next day, the Chinese claim that Holman has "murdered" Maily and her unborn baby and demand that he is turned in as a crimi-nal. The crew worries for their safety and asks Homan to surrender, but then Col-lins shocks the Chinese with a gunshot to their boat, and Holman is left alone. In the spring, Collins begins river patrols anew, but is then ordered back to the Yangtze River. Before heading to his new post, Collins steams upstream to rescue Jameson (Larry Gates), an idealistic missionary and his schoolteacher assistant, Shirley Eckert (Candice Bergen), from their remote China Light Mission. After a good deal of fighting between the sailors and the Chinese near Dongting Lake, Collins leads three sailors, including Holman, ashore. Jameson does not want to be rescued, claiming that Eckert and he have renounced their U.S. citizenship and are com-mitted to their post. Collins orders Holman to evacuate Eckert and Jameson, but just as Holman declares that he is going to stay with them, Jameson is suddenly killed by Nationalist soldiers in a surprise attack. Collins is killed trying to pro-vide cover for Holman, leaving him in command. He tearfully parts from Eckert and is then fatally wounded right as he goes to join the others on his boat. His last bewildered words are: "I was home [free] . . . what happened . . . what the hell hap-pened?" as the *San Pablo* sails away.

Reception

Four years in the works, *The Sand Pebbles* finally premiered on 20 December 1966. Proving a hit at the box office, the film grossed $30 million ($226.4 million in 2017 dollars). It received seven Oscar nominations, eight Golden Globe nominations, and one win (a Golden Globe for Richard Attenborough as Best Supporting Actor). Reviews were, however, mixed. Philip K. Scheuer called it "a stirring movie . . .

adventure on the grand scale" (Scheuer, 1966). Richard Schickel found *The Sand Pebbles* to be "a clumsy and lumbering film, but it has a way of haunting the corners of your mind, as historical footnotes are sometimes wont to do" (Schickel, 1967). Many reviewers complained about the film's sheer length; at 3 hours it was judged too long to be consistently engaging.

Reel History Versus Real History

Having served in the China River Patrol in 1936, novelist Richard McKenna brought a good deal of authenticity to *The Sand Pebbles* in his rendition of daily life on an American gunboat plying the waters of the Yangtze River in pre-revolutionary China. The novel is set between June 1925 and June 1926, whereas the film is set in 1926–1927, but both settings encompass a particularly volatile moment in China's modern history: a time when the country was a powder keg, seething with anti-imperialist ardor and internecine political conflict. During the setting of the novel, the Kuomintang (KMT or Nationalist Party of China) was in the throes of a power vacuum following the death of its founder, Sun Yat-sen, in March 1925. On 5 June 1926 Chiang Kai-shek was named commander-in-chief of the National Revolutionary Army (NRA). Five weeks later he finally launched Sun's long-delayed Northern Expedition, aimed at conquering the northern warlords and uniting China under the KMT. Chiang disapproved of Sun Yat-sen's alliance with the Soviet Union and the Communist Party of China (CPC) but he still needed Soviet aid, so he could not break up the alliance at that time. The film shifts the novel's temporal framework forward about a year and distills and streamlines McKenna's fictional saga, but still manages to capture the politically explosive political climate, an uneasy time for gunboats of foreign powers on the Yangtze, with their very presence stirring intense resentment among Chinese nationalists and communists sick and tired of "gunboat diplomacy," that is, thinly disguised imperialist intervention. The culminating attack on the USS *San Pablo* may have been inspired by the so-called "USS *Panay* incident" (12 December 1937), when Japanese forces invading China bombed, strafed, and sank a U.S. gunboat on the Yangtze River, killing 3 and wounding 43, a sinking that caused a diplomatic rift between the United States and Japan and presaged Pearl Harbor. The plot element involving the killing of missionary Jameson at China Light Mission may have been inspired by the killing of American Christian missionaries John and Betty Stam (8 December 1934) by Chinese communists during the Chinese Civil War. Another possible antecedent: the "China Martyrs of 1900": hundreds of American and European Christian missionaries and converts who were killed during the Boxer Rebellion (1899–1901). One final note: a number of film critics erroneously assumed that *The Sand Pebbles* was meant to be an implicit critique of American intervention in Southeast Asia—the Vietnam War was in full swing when the film came out at the end of 1966—but that was never Richard McKenna's intention when he published the book in 1962, or the intention of the filmmakers four years later.

SANDS OF IWO JIMA (1949)

Synopsis

Sands of Iwo Jima is a war film written by Harry Brown and James Edward Grant, directed by Allan Dwan, and starring John Wayne. The film follows a group of U.S. Marines from training camp to the Battle of Iwo Jima during World War II.

Background

In 1948 Republic Pictures producer Edmund Grainger encountered the phrase "sands of Iwo Jima" in a newspaper. He recalled Joe Rosenthal's iconic photograph of the flag raising on Mount Suribachi and decided to make a movie on the notoriously bloody battle (February–March 1945) that took 6,821 American lives and nearly wiped out the Japanese defending force of some 20,000 men. Grainger wrote a 40-page treatment that was developed into a screenplay by Harry Brown, author of *A Walk in the Sun*. The script was then refined by James Earl "Jimmy" Grant, John Wayne's favorite screenwriter, after Wayne agreed to star in the picture. Initially slated to star Forrest Tucker and cost a very modest $250,000, the movie's budget was more than doubled after Wayne was hired but to the chagrin of studio owner Herbert Yates, still went $400,000 over budget. Upon release, however, it soon recouped all its costs and made a healthy profit.

Production

Avid to commemorate its pivotal role in securing America's Pacific Theater against Japan in World War II, anxious also for profile-raising publicity to ward off a congressional attempt to merge it with the U.S. Army, the U.S. Marine Corps provided full support. After vetting and approving the script, the Corps supplied technical advisors, demolition engineers, an entire regiment (2,000 Marines) as extras, copious amounts of war matériel (including planes and ships), thousands of feet of actual combat footage, and the use of the sprawling Marine Corps base at Camp Pendleton (including Camp Del Mar and El Toro Marine Air Station) in southern California, assistance that saved Republic huge sums of money and bolstered the film's putative authenticity. To re-create reasonable facsimiles of Tarawa and Iwo Jima, set dressers working for Art Director James Sullivan installed fake palm trees, gun emplacements, pill boxes, and miles of barbed wire. They also coated the white sand at Oceanside beach (where the Iwo landing sequence was shot) with oil to make it resemble the dark volcanic sands of Iwo Jima. At director Allan Dwan's request, General Graves B. Erskine (commander of Camp Pendleton) sent his toughest drill sergeant to the set to whip the actors into shape. *Sands of Iwo Jima* was filmed in July and August 1949.

Plot Summary

At Camp Paekakariki in New Zealand Marine Sergeant John Stryker (John Wayne) subjects his rifle squad to a grueling training regimen and is despised for it. His greatest detractors are Pfc. Pete Conway (John Agar), a haughty son of the admirable Colonel Sam Conway, under whom Stryker served, and Private Al Thomas (Forrest

Tucker), who sees Stryker as responsible for his demotion in rank. As Stryker commands his unit during the Tarawa invasion, his unit falls in line and accepts him with the exception of Conway, who is critical of Stryker's decision to leave a wounded soldier behind. Mid-battle, Thomas is tasked with getting more ammunition, but causes a delay by taking a coffee break, one that results in the death of Hellenopolis (Peter Coe). Stryker and Thomas come to blows over the incident, and while a passing officer sees the incident and goes to intervene, Thomas covers for Stryker. Later, a conscience-stricken Thomas asks forgiveness for dereliction of duty, thus completing his moral rehabilitation. While on leave in Honolulu Stryker, a married man whose wife has left him, reveals a softer side. After picking up a bargirl named Mary (Julie Bishop) and returning with her to her apartment, Stryker hears sounds emanating from an adjacent room which turns out to be the cries of Mary's infant son whom she is struggling to support. Stryker gives Mary some money and leaves without seeking any sexual favors. Afterwards, as the soldiers train, a new recruit mistakenly drops a live hand grenade. Everybody takes cover, but Conway is reading a letter and does not realize that his life is in danger. Stryker tackles him to the ground, saving him from certain death, and then berates him for being inattentive. Thereafter, Stryker's squad hits the beach at Iwo Jima and takes part in the fierce battle for the island. With victory at hand and the squad at rest, Stryker is killed by a hidden Japanese sniper. The surviving squad members find an unfinished letter he was carrying addressed to his estranged young son. Thomas reads it, and an emotional Pete Conway vows to "finish it for him." After the squad solemnly witnesses the American flag being raised on Mount Suribachi, Conway admonishes his men to "Saddle up! Let's get back in the war!"

Reception

A government-sponsored Cold War paean to military duty, honor, and patriotism, *Sands of Iwo Jima* was essentially a recruiting movie. Released six months before the outbreak of the Korean War, it did well with most film critics, though some reviewers found the film cliché-ridden. *Sands* also proved to be a solid hit at the box office, earning $3.9 million in receipts for a $2.9 million profit, making it Republic's most successful movie. Four Oscar nominations followed, for Best Actor in a Leading Role (John Wayne); Best Writing, Motion Picture Story (Harry Brown); Best Sound, Recording (T. A. Carman and Howard Wilson); and Best Film Editing (Richard L. Van Enger). Furthermore, *Sands of Iwo Jima* cemented John Wayne's status as a major movie star. His role as Stryker also made him an exemplar of the sort of forlorn American masculinity popular with adolescent boys in the post-war era: a lonely, romantic figure—woman-abandoned but stoical—that would be best epitomized by Alan Ladd a few years later in *Shane* (1953). In his 1976 memoir, *Born on the Fourth of July*, disabled Vietnam veteran and anti-war activist Ron Kovic cites *Sands of Iwo Jima* as one of the films that inspired him to enlist, with disastrous results. Ironically, and to his lasting embarrassment, John Wayne was strictly a make-believe war hero who never served in the military. In a 1987 article in *The New York Times Magazine*, ex-Marine William Manchester recalls having "the enormous pleasure of seeing [John] Wayne humiliated in person" at Aiea Heights

Naval Hospital in Oahu, Hawaii. One evening in 1945 Wayne made a personal appearance before badly wounded survivors of the Battle of Okinawa: "the curtains parted and out stepped John Wayne, wearing a cowboy outfit . . . He grinned his aw-shucks grin, passed a hand over his face and said, 'Hi ya, guys!' He was greeted by a stony silence. Then somebody booed. Suddenly everyone was booing. This man was a symbol of the fake machismo we had come to hate, and we weren't going to listen to him. He tried and tried to make himself heard, but we drowned him out, and eventually he quit and left" (Manchester, 1987, p. 84). Five years later Manchester and another Marine were ejected from a movie theater for laughing hysterically during a screening of *Sands of Iwo Jima*. In the end, though, hegemonic pro-war, pro-patria ideology prevailed. At an American Legion Convention in Miami, Florida (17 October 1951), six months after being sacked by President Truman for insubordination, Gen. Douglas MacArthur demonstrated he was laughably oblivious as to the real combat experiences of rank-and-file U.S. servicemen in WWII when he told John Wayne, "You represent the American serviceman better than the American serviceman himself" (quoted in Davis, 1998, p. 118). Wayne himself remained equally oblivious to his real status as a faux warrior. In later years he disingenuously declared "The Marines and all the American Armed Forces were quite proud of my portrayal of Stryker" (Suid, 2001, p. 129).

Reel History Versus Real History

There is surprisingly little combat depicted in *Sands of Iwo Jima* but some of it consists of actual footage taken by Signal Corps cameramen during the fighting on Tarawa and Iwo Jima. Furthermore, a number of actual soldiers portrayed themselves in the film: Lt. Gen. Holland M. Smith (ret.), the 5th Amphibious Corps commander (also one of the film's technical advisors); Medal of Honor winner Col. David M. Shoup, USMC; Capt. Harold G. Schrier, USMC, who commanded the Marines on Mt. Suribachi; Lt. Col. H. P. Crowe, USMC, a battalion commander on Tarawa; and Pfc. Rene A. Gagnon, Pfc. Ira H. Hayes, and PM 3/c John H. Bradley, three of the flag raisers on Mt. Suribachi. At 42, John Wayne was rather old to play the part of a WWII Marine sergeant, but screenwriters Harry Brown and Jimmy Grant make Stryker a believably flawed character—not quite the cardboard hero he so often played.

SAVING PRIVATE RYAN (1998)

Synopsis

Saving Private Ryan is an American war epic set during and immediately after the invasion of Normandy (June 1944) in World War II. Written by Robert Rodat and directed by Steven Spielberg, the film follows U.S. Army Rangers Capt. John H. Miller (Tom Hanks) who commands a squad (Tom Sizemore, Edward Burns, Barry Pepper, Giovanni Ribisi, Vin Diesel, Adam Goldberg, and Jeremy Davies) searching for paratrooper James Francis Ryan (Matt Damon), the last surviving brother of four U.S. servicemen.

Background

The Niland brothers—Edward ("Eddie"), Preston, Robert ("Bob"), and Frederick ("Fritz")—were four brothers from Tonawanda, New York, who served in the U.S. military during World War II. Of the four, two survived the war. For a time, though, it was believed that only one brother, Sgt. Fritz Niland, 501st Parachute Infantry Regiment (PIR), 101st Airborne, had survived. Eddie was shot down over Burma and reported missing on 16 May 1944; Bob was killed on D-Day; Preston was killed the day after. To spare his family further grief, Fritz Niland was pulled off the frontline near Normandy and returned to the United States to complete his service. Almost a year after D-Day, Fritz learned that Eddie, missing and presumed dead, had actually survived and had been held captive in a Japanese POW camp in Burma. Fifty years later, screenwriter Robert Rodat (*Fly Away Home*) saw a monument dedicated to the four sons of Agnes Allison of Port Carbon, Pennsylvania, all killed in the Civil War. Struck by the tragedy of a single family's huge loss in war, Rodat began to research WWII instances and read a slightly incorrect account of the Niland saga in Stephen Ambrose's *D-Day June 6, 1944: The Climactic Battle of World War II* (1994) and decided to use the Niland story as the rough basis for a film script. Rodat's first draft included an opening Omaha Beach sequence, altered the number of brothers killed from two to three, and added a search and rescue mission. In the spring of 1995 Rodat successfully pitched his script idea to producer Mark Gordon (a partner with Gary Levinsohn in Mutual Film Co., a newly formed production firm). Over the next two years Rodat and Gordon collaborated on 15 drafts of a script before shopping it around to the studios. Initially they met with rejection; the prevailing view was that WWII movies were passé. Things changed in 1997, however, when Gordon sent the script to Tom Hanks and got an enthusiastic reception. Gordon also sent the script to Creative Artists Agency (CAA) agent Karen Sage, who then pitched the concept to Steven Spielberg, a close friend of Hanks. Having an abiding interest in the Second World War, Spielberg embraced Rodat's script. Spielberg's studio (DreamWorks SKG) subsequently signed a distribution deal with Paramount and hired its own line producer, Ian Bryce, thus limiting the further involvement of Gordon and Levinsohn (though relations between parties remained cordial). Spielberg also followed suit with other directors making war films since 1984 and hired former Marine Dale Dye's Warriors, Inc., to put his principal actors through a tough six-day boot camp to familiarize them with standard military operating procedure, but also to have them gain respect for the arduous life of a soldier. Matt Damon was exempted to make the rest of the group feel resentment towards the Pvt. Ryan character. Tom Sanders, Spielberg's production designer, who was Mel Gibson's designer on *Braveheart* (1995), went to Ireland and once again struck a deal to use 1,000 Irish Army reservists as extras. Ian Bryce located 10 WWII-era landing craft in Palm Springs, California, and had the vessels transported to St. Austell, Cornwall, England, where they were made seaworthy by Robin Davies' Square Sail Ventures. As for the film's visual style, Janusz Kamiński, Spielberg's regular director of photography since *Schindler's List*, opted for a look "very much like color newsreel footage from the 1940s, which is highly desaturated and very

grainy and extremely low tech" (www.tcm.com/tcmdb/title/335178/Saving-Private
-Ryan/articles.html). To further suggest the shaky quality of newsreel footage, combat scenes were filmed with handheld cameras and, as was done for Mel Gibson's
Braveheart, some frames were deleted in the editing process to underscore a sense
of the jarring immediacy of combat.

Production

The two-month shoot on *Saving Private Ryan* began on 27 June 1997 with the filming of the 23 minute D-Day landing sequence, which was shot over a three-week
period (27 June–17 July) on Curracloe Strand in Ballinesker, Ireland, about 70 miles
south of Dublin: a beach not as broad as the real Omaha Beach in France so wide-
angle lenses were used to visually extend the length of the flats on the sandy beach
before the soldiers reach the shingle. Beforehand, hundreds of workers spent two
months building facsimile German coastal fortifications, trenches, and beach obsta-
cles (e.g., steel anti-tank "Czech hedgehogs," wooden ramps, posts with mines,
etc.). The shoot then moved to the grounds of a former British Aerospace factory
in Hertfordshire, about 20 miles north of London, where the fictive, ruined French
village of Ramelle was built (a set later reused for Spielberg's 2001 TV miniseries
Band of Brothers) and the final battle was filmed, described by Spielberg as a "very
complicated sequence which took weeks and weeks to plan out on paper" (Pizzello and Spielberg, 1996, p. 4). The Ryan farmstead where Mrs. Ryan receives news
of three of her sons' deaths was allegedly in Iowa but was actually built near West
Kennet, Wiltshire, 85 miles west of London. Two scenes—the costly skirmish with
the German machine-gun nest near a ruined radar installation, and the ambush of
the German half-track—were filmed on the grounds of Thame Park, about 15 miles
east of Oxford. The chapel on the grounds of Thame Park was used for the French
church where Miller's squad rests overnight. The only shooting actually done in
Normandy was for the present-day scenes bookending the film that take place at
the American Cemetery and Memorial in Colleville-sur-Mer.

Plot Summary

On the morning of 6 June 1944, American soldiers land on Omaha Beach as part
of the D-Day Normandy invasion. Exposed to withering artillery and machine-
gun fire from German coastal positions, they suffer extremely heavy losses. Capt.
John H. Miller (Tom Hanks) of the 2nd Ranger Battalion puts together a unit to
break through the German defenses. Meanwhile, on the beach, a deceased soldier
lies face down in the sand, with "Ryan, S." printed on his belongings. Back at the
U.S. War Department in Washington, D.C., General George Marshall (Harve
Presnell) hears that three out of four brothers serving in the war have perished in
battle, while the fourth brother, James Ryan, has gone missing in Normandy, France.
Taking inspiration from Abraham Lincoln's Bixby letter, Marshall demands that
the remaining Ryan be located and returned to his family. Capt. Miller is tasked
with bringing Ryan home, and so forms a unit of six troops from his platoon:
T/Sgt. Mike Horvath (Tom Sizemore), Pfcs. Richard Reiben (Edward Burns) and
Adrian Caparzo (Vin Diesel), Pvts. Stanley Mellish (Adam Goldberg) and Danny

Capt. Miller (Tom Hanks, left) confers with Pvt. Ryan (Matt Damon) in a still from Steven Spielberg's World War II epic, *Saving Private Ryan* (1998). (DreamWorks Distribution/Photofest)

Jackson (Barry Pepper), medic Irwin Wade (Giovanni Ribisi), and T/5 Timothy Upham (Jeremy Davies), a cartographer and interpreter—to find the missing soldier. Once in Neuville-au-Plain, they connect with the 101st Airborne Division. Caparzo is shot and killed by a German sniper, who is in turn killed by Jackson. Stopping later for a short break while a runner goes to search for Capt. Hamill (Ted Danson) to ask him about Ryan, Sgt. Hill (Paul Giamatti), who briefly joins Miller's men, inadvertently knocks over an unstable brick wall, revealing a group of German soldiers. A frantic standoff between the two armed parties ensues but comes to an abrupt end by the timely arrival of Hamill and another paratrooper, both of whom unload their automatic weapons into the unsuspecting Germans. Soon thereafter, Miller's squad locates a Pvt. James Ryan, but they soon figure out that he is not the person they're looking for. Soon after, they come across one of Ryan's friends, who informs the unit that Ryan is defending a bridge in Ramelle. Not wanting to waste an opportunity, Miller opts to overtake a German machine-gun position en route to Ramelle. The men protest, but Miller insists. Wade dies in the ensuing firefight. Miller decides against killing one of the German survivors, nicknamed "Steamboat Willie" (Joerg Stadler), and instead sends him away with instructions to surrender to the next Allied troops that cross his path. Losing confidence in Miller's leadership for not circumventing the machine-gun nest, Reiben, still unsettled over the decision to infiltrate the German machine-gun position, announces that he is going to desert, but after a confrontation and intervention by Miller, Reiben changes his mind and stays with his unit. Before they reach Ramelle, Miller and the soldiers encounter a unit of paratroopers ambushing a German Sd.Kfz. 251 half-track. One of them turns out to be Pvt. James Ryan (Matt Damon). Miller breaks the news about Ryan's deceased brothers and informs Ryan that he has orders to bring the private home. He also tells Ryan he has lost two men trying to find him. Though bereaved at the loss of his brothers, Ryan refuses to be led back to safety, so Miller relents, joining his team with the paratroopers to defend the bridge. Miller sets up defenses throughout the town. Tanks and infantry from the 2nd SS Panzer Division arrive. The American soldiers put up a valiant fight, but the majority of the paratroopers, along with Horvath, Mellish, and Jackson, die. Upham is frozen in fear and avoids the fight. Miller makes an effort to blow up the bridge, but he is shot by Steamboat Willie, who has arrived on the scene with his comrades. As a Tiger tank comes up to the bridge, an American P-51 Mustang suddenly appears in the sky and blows up the tank, and American armored troops appear and push back the Germans. Having witnessed Miller's shooting, Upham confronts Steamboat Willie and his group as they attempt to retreat. Steamboat Willie raises his hands in surrender, believing that Upham will let him go because of their earlier encounter. Instead, Upham, having seen Steamboat Willie shoot Miller, finds Willie and shoots him to avenge Miller. Reiben and Ryan are close to Miller as he dies and take in his final words: "James . . . Earn this. Earn it." Flash-forward 50 years to the present day, late 1990s: the elderly James Ryan, accompanied by his family, visits the American Cemetery and Memorial in Colleville-sur-Mer, Normandy, and discovers Capt. John Miller's gravestone among the thousands of others. A tearful James Ryan mentions how grateful he is to Miller and his unit for saving his life. He wonders whether he is worthy of their sacrifices, and his wife comforts him and confirms that he is indeed a "good man." Ryan then salutes Miller's grave. The final image is of the American flag fluttering in the wind over the cemetery.

Reception

Saving Private Ryan had its world premiere on 21 July 1998 and went into wide release in North America three days later (widest release: 2,807 theaters). Staggered releases in foreign markets took place that fall. During its initial 17-week domestic run, the movie earned $190.6 million at the box office. After *Saving Private Ryan* garnered 11 Oscar nominations in February 1998, the movie was re-released (widest release: 1,140 theaters) to take advantage of its enhanced profile. It ran until 27 May 1998 and earned another $25.7 million, bringing the total domestic gross to $216.3 million—the highest-grossing film of 1998 in the United States. Foreign ticket sales came in even higher, at $268.7 million. Overall, the movie grossed $485 million versus a $70 million production budget, making it a blockbuster hit. Though it lost the Best Picture Oscar to John Madden's *Shakespeare in Love*, *Saving Private Ryan* won five Oscars: Best Director (Steven Spielberg); Best Cinematography (Janusz Kamiński); Best Editing (Michael Kahn); Best Sound (Gary Rydstrom, Gary Summers, Andy Nelson, and Ron Judkins); and Best

Sound Effects Editing (Gary Rydstrom, Richard Hymns). It also won two Golden Globes, three BAFTAs, and numerous other awards and received mostly high praise from film critics. For example, Peter Rainer singled out the Omaha Beach sequence for special praise: "This opening sequence, in which thousands of men are splayed and pulverized, is perhaps the most wrenching battle scene ever filmed. It goes way beyond what we're used to in war movies." For Rainer, *Saving Private Ryan* "doesn't offer up the homilies that have drenched the morale-boosting WWII movies . . . By going back to a Good War and focusing so clearly on its carnage, he's putting forth the most obvious of positions: War is about killing people" (Rainer, 1998). There were, however, dissenting opinions. Although Ella Taylor praised *Saving Private Ryan* for using "screen brutality just the way it should be used—to deglamorize the undiscriminating overkill of modern combat, in which survival is governed far more by dumb luck than by derring-do, and heroism is beside the point," she also criticized the film for ending "in a burst of schmaltzy ritual. [James Ryan], now an old man, falls to his knees in a cemetery filled with white crosses, then begs his wife to tell him that he's a good man. With this hopelessly cloying coda, Spielberg, having won his battles, loses sight of the war" (Taylor, 1998). Still, the most damning reviews were by WWII veterans Paul Fussell and Howard Zinn. A decorated U.S. Army combat veteran (103rd Infantry Division) but also an intellectual who wrote authoritatively on war (*The Great War and Modern Memory*), Fussell praised Spielberg's 2001 mini-series *Band of Brothers* as "authentic" but found *Saving Private Ryan* conventional Hollywood fare: "After an honest, harrowing, 15-minute [sic] opening, visualizing details of the unbearable bloody mess at Omaha Beach, [the movie] degenerated into a harmless, uncritical patriotic performance apparently designed to thrill 12-year-old boys during the summer bad-film season. Its genre was pure cowboys and Indians, with the virtuous cowboys of course victorious" (Fussell, 2001). A veteran of the air war over Europe (Eighth Air Force, 490th Bombardment Group), but also a political science professor (Boston University), author (*People's History of the United States*), and lifelong social activist, Howard Zinn admitted to being taken in by the film's "extraordinarily photographed battle scenes" but further noted that he "disliked the film intensely. I was angry at it because I did not want the suffering of men in war to be used—yes, exploited—in such a way as to revive what should be buried along with all those bodies in Arlington Cemetery: the glory of military heroism" (Zinn, 1998, p. 39).

Reel History Versus Real History

Though widely regarded as historically authentic, *Saving Private Ryan* is problematic in many areas, including its famed Omaha Beach sequence. Though it uses fictional names, the movie accurately depicts the carnage and chaos at Dog Green, Omaha Beach, where elements of the U.S. 116th Regiment, 29th Infantry Division, and the 2nd and 5th Ranger Battalions took extremely heavy casualties from German automatic weapons fire and artillery and the sea ran red with blood, as the film shows. Tom Hanks's Capt. Miller is based in part on Capt. Ralph Goranson (1919–2012), the commanding officer of Company C, 2nd Ranger Battalion. What the film doesn't indicate is that this was the absolute worst sector of the landings and not typical of the invasion as a whole. Overall, D-Day was no walk-over but the operation's 3,000 fatalities were far fewer than the 10,000 anticipated. Military historian Antony Beevor (*D-Day: The Battle for Normandy*) points out that the "real fighting and the real casualties came in the Battle of Normandy" further inland, in the weeks following D-Day (Carey, 2009). Other aspects of the D-Day sequence are not wrong but also tend to be misleading. Front and side view following shots of the Higgins Boats approaching the shore show lots of open water right to the horizon. The D-Day naval operation, code-named Operation Neptune, involved history's largest armada: 6,939 vessels (including 4,126 landing craft); any view toward the sea that day would have disclosed myriad ships and boats as far as the eye could see. At 23 minutes running time, the movie's Omaha Beach segment also suggests that the American breakout from the beach occurred quite quickly. In reality, it took U.S. troops, aided by further naval bombardment not depicted in the film, some four hours to capture frontline German positions and get clear of the beach. Even then, Omaha wasn't entirely secure until the early afternoon of 6 June—more than seven hours after the first wave landed. During the battle at the fictive town of Ramelle, the film wrongly depicts the 2nd SS Panzer Division in the vicinity of Normandy just days after the landings; it was not. Also, the movie's final battle is rife with unlikely tactical errors for an elite German unit (e.g., sending in armor ahead of ground troops). Finally, in a broader sense, *Saving Private Ryan* implicitly reiterates the popular but erroneous American notion that the United States almost singlehandedly won the war against Hitler's Germany and that D-Day was the decisive turning point. In point of fact, it was the Soviet Union, not the Western Allies that defeated Hitler's war machine (and lost 8.7 million soldiers and 17.9 million civilians in the process). By June 1944, Germany had already been militarily beaten by the Red Army, was in steady retreat on the Eastern Front, and was about to suffer a military catastrophe far greater than D-Day: the total destruction of the Wehrmacht's Army Group Center during Operation Bagration (22 June–19 August 1944), the Soviet strategic offensive that liberated Belorussia and cleared a path for Berlin.

SCHINDLER'S LIST (1993)

Synopsis

Schindler's List is an American historical epic scripted by Steven Zaillian and directed and co-produced by Steven Spielberg. Based on *Schindler's Ark* (1982) by Australian novelist Thomas Keneally, the film tells the story of Oskar Schindler, a German business professional who protected over 1,000 mostly Polish Jewish refugees from certain death during the Holocaust by giving them jobs in his factories during World War II. It stars Liam Neeson as Schindler, Ralph Fiennes as SS officer Amon Göth, and Ben Kingsley as Schindler's accountant, Itzhak Stern.

Background

Leopold Page (real name: Leopold "Poldek" Pfefferberg, 1913–2001), a Polish American Holocaust survivor who ran a small Beverly Hills leather goods store, was one

Oskar Schindler (Liam Neeson, left) intervenes to save a Jewish family from the Nazis in Steven Spielberg's celebrated Holocaust epic, *Schindler's List* (1993). (Universal/Photofest)

of 1,098 Polish Jews (801 men and 297 women) saved by Oskar Schindler (1908–1974), a Roman Catholic, a member of the Nazi Party, and war profiteer in Kraków, Poland, who paradoxically risked his life to save Jews during World War II. Pfefferberg made it his life's mission to honor Schindler's memory. In 1963 he told Schindler's story to the wife of film producer Marvin Gosch, obtained a meeting with Gosch, and eventually sold the film rights to MGM for $50,000. Delbert Mann was slated to direct and Howard Koch (*Casablanca*) was contracted to write the script but somehow the deal fell through. In October 1980, during a layover while on a book tour, Australian writer Thomas Keneally (*The Chant of Jimmie Blacksmith*) stopped in to Pfefferberg's store to buy a briefcase and Pfefferberg regaled him with Schindler's remarkable story, also showing him materials from two filing cabinets full of information he had collected about Schindler. Intrigued, Keneally spent the next two years researching the story, which also involved interviewing 50 Schindler-juden ("Schindler's Jews"). The resulting historical novel, *Schindler's Ark* (1982), became a Booker Prize–winning bestseller. Sent a review of the book by Music Corporation of America president Sidney Sheinberg, director Steven Spielberg expressed interest, whereupon Universal Pictures bought the film rights for $500,000. Spielberg met with Pfefferberg in the spring of 1983 and told him he would start filming in 10 years, when he felt he was mature enough to make a movie about the Holocaust. True to his word, Spielberg let almost a decade elapse before he undertook his Schindler movie, during which time he hired Keneally to adapt his own book to the screen. In the meantime Spielberg directed a string of other pictures and struggled with ambivalence about tackling the Holocaust. At one point he tried to pass the project on to director Roman Polanski. Having survived the Kraków Ghetto—and lost his mother, who was gassed at Auschwitz—Polanski could not face the task either (though he eventually directed his own Holocaust film, *The Pianist*, 2002). Dissatisfied with Keneally's script, which he found too long and not evocative enough, Spielberg hired Kurt Luedtke (*Out of Africa*) to write the next draft in 1984. Luedtke gave up almost four years later, finding Schindler's change of heart too unbelievable to convincingly depict. In 1989 Martin Scorsese took over as director and hired Steven Zaillian to write another draft of the script, but soon had second thoughts. Scorsese swapped pictures with Spielberg, handing the Schindler project back to him in exchange for a remake of *Cape Fear* (1991). Finally in full control of his Schindler movie, Spielberg asked Zaillian to extend his 115-page draft to 195 pages, fill out depictions of the Schindlerjuden, extend the ghetto liquidation sequence to full effect, and make Schindler's moral transition more gradual and ambiguous. Spielberg also did extensive research on his own. Kevin Costner, Mel Gibson, and Warren Beatty all offered to play Schindler, but Spielberg wanted Swiss actor Bruno Ganz (who would later play Hitler in *Downfall*, 2004). Failing to secure Ganz, Spielberg offered the part to Harrison Ford, who also turned it down. Spielberg ended up casting the relative unknown Liam Neeson in December 1992, after watching him portray Mat Burke in a preview of Eugene O'Neil's *Anna Christie* on Broadway. For Amon Göth (1908–1946), a psychopathic SS officer who was Schindler's influential friend, Spielberg cast Ralph Fiennes after seeing him play T. E. Lawrence in *A Dangerous Man: Lawrence after Arabia* (1992). In uniform Fiennes looked so much like Göth that when survivor Mila Pfefferberg met him, she found herself shaking uncontrollably. Spielberg cast Ben Kingsley (*Gandhi*) as Itzhak Stern—a character embodying Schindler's conscience that is actually an amalgam of three real persons: Schindler's accountant, Stern (1901–1969); his factory manager, Abraham Bankier (1910–1956); and Göth's personal secretary, Mietek Pemper (1920–2011).

Production

Schindler's List was shot at or near actual locations in and around Kraków, Poland, over 72 work days (1 March–1 June 1993), wrapping up four days ahead of schedule. Spielberg decided to film in black and white at the suggestion of his cinematographer, Janusz Kamiński, who was inspired by an album of photographs by Roman Wiśniak, a photographer of Jewish settlements in 1920–1939. To heighten a sense of cinema vérité immediacy, nearly half of the movie was filmed with handheld cameras. Spielberg considered filming entirely in German and Polish but decided to keep the dialogue in English, partly because he felt he wouldn't be able to assess performances in unfamiliar languages but also to avoid the distraction that subtitle reading would provide to viewers. The site where the Kraków-Płaszów concentration camp stood is now a nature preserve, so Spielberg had a replica of the camp built at the abandoned Liban Quarry outside Kraków, which was also a Nazi labor camp during the war. Exterior shots of Schindler's enamelware factory, 4 Lipowa Street, in the Zabłocie district of Kraków, were filmed at the actual site (which is now a museum). Interior shots were filmed at a similar facility in Olkusz, Poland, 25 miles northeast of Kraków. The World Jewish Congress successfully lobbied against any film production at Auschwitz, so Spielberg had a partial replica of the camp constructed just outside its entrance. In the midst of the shoot, Spielberg envisioned the epilogue, where 128 survivors pay their respects by placing stones on Schindler's grave in Jerusalem. The producers had to scramble to find the Schindlerjuden and fly them in to film the scene.

Plot Summary

German Oskar Schindler (Liam Neeson) arrives in Kraków, Poland, aiming to profit from the war. A Nazi Party member, Schindler pays SS officials under the table and secures a large factory to make enamelware. Schindler hires Itzhak Stern (Ben Kingsley), a local Jewish official with ties to both the black market and the Jewish business community, to assist him with his finances. For a time, Schindler keeps up a cordial friendship with the Nazis and basks in his new wealth, embracing the title of "Herr Direktor" while Stern manages the day-to-day operations. Schindler makes the decision to take on Jewish workers because they are cheaper, and Stern pushes to hire as many people as can be afforded, because if they are seen as essential to the German war effort, they will survive the awful fate of the death camps. SS-Untersturmführer Amon Göth (Ralph Fiennes) travels to Kraków to manage the construction of Płaszów concentration camp. After the camp is built [December 1942], Göth demands that the Kraków Ghetto be destroyed, a brutal process involving widespread killing [13–14 March 1943]. Schindler witnesses these crimes against humanity and is appalled. He is specifically moved by a young child wearing a red coat (Oliwia Dabrowska) whom he notices as the Nazis are rounding people up and then recognizes later (identifiable by the red coat) on a cart piled high with corpses. To continue to enjoy SS support for his business, Schindler carefully maintains his friendship with Göth—even though he is quite aware that Göth is a moral monster who constantly degrades his Jewish maid, Helen Hirsch (Embeth Davidtz), and shoots Jewish camp inmates from the lofty balcony of his house. As the terrors of the war increase, Schindler abandons his goal of becoming rich for the more pressing need to save as many lives as he can. To allow his workers as much protection and safety as possible, Schindler bribes Göth and convinces him to allow Schindler to create a subcamp. The Germans lose ground in the war, and Göth is told that all remaining Jews at Płaszów must be transferred to the Auschwitz concentration camp. Schindler, not wanting to turn over his workers to Auschwitz, proposes instead that he relocate his employees to his new munitions factory being constructed in Zwittau-Brinnlitz, 210 miles to the west. Göth allows Schindler to proceed after a sizeable bribe. Schindler works with Stern to compose "Schindler's List": a register of approximately 850 people who will travel to Brinnlitz and be spared the horrors of Auschwitz. When the train transporting the women and children on Schindler's List is mistakenly sent to Auschwitz-Birkenau, the women are let into a cavernous shower room, where they fear for their lives. For a moment, they do not know if they are going to be showered with water or asphyxiated by poison gas; fortunately, water is delivered. Schindler offers a bribe to Rudolf Höss, the commandant of Auschwitz, and secures their release. Once settled in the new factory, Schindler stops SS guards from entering the factory floor and supports the Jews in observing their Sabbath. Over the course of the next seven months, Schindler uses his wealth to bribe Nazi officials and purchase shell casings from outside businesses in order to ensure that his own factory does not contribute to the Nazi war effort. Schindler runs through his entire fortune in May 1945, just as Germany surrenders. As a registered member of the Nazi Party and war profiteer, Schindler is forced to run from the Red Army. The SS soldiers guarding Schindler's factory are tasked with exterminating the Jewish workforce, but Schindler appeals to their humanity and persuades them to keep the workers alive. He then bids farewell to his employees and prepares to head west, with the aim of surrendering to the Americans. The factory employees present Schindler with a signed statement confirming his part in saving Jewish lives during the Holocaust and give him a ring engraved with a Talmudic quotation: "Whoever saves one life saves the world entire." When the workers awaken the next morning, a Soviet soldier arrives and tells them that they are free. Stunned, the Jewish factory workers leave their place of refuge and move to a nearby town. Final scenes depict Göth's execution [13 September 1946] and summarize Schindler's remaining years after the war. An epilogue shows Schindler's actual workers, side by side with the actors who portrayed them, placing stones on Schindler's grave—a Jewish act of reverence for the dead. In the final shot, Neeson places a pair of roses on the grave.

Reception

As befitting its cultural status as a major cinematic statement on the Holocaust, *Schindler's List* had four successive North American premieres: one in Washington, D.C., on 30 November 1993, another in New York City on 1 December; a third in Los Angeles on 9 December; and a fourth in Toronto on 15 December 1993. Theater openings were gradually ramped up in the United States, peaking in the film's 14th week toward the end of March 1994, with its widest release in 1,389 theaters and highest weekly gross $8.2 million (18–24 March 1994). Ultimately, *Schindler's List* remained in American theaters for eight months. By the time it closed out on 28 July 1994, the film had grossed $96 million in the United States. The foreign total amounted to $225 million, for a grand total of $321 million, versus a modest $23 million production budget. Given its exceedingly grim subject matter, Spielberg feared the movie would flop, but it turned out to be a major box office success. *Schindler's List* also earned a dozen Oscar nominations and won seven Oscars for Best Picture, Best Director (Spielberg's first Oscar), Best Screenplay, Best Cinematography, Best Editing, Best Original Score, and Best Art Direction. It also won four Golden Globes, nine BAFTAs, and numerous other international film awards. Reviews were almost uniformly approving in the highest terms, and other film directors—Robert Altman, Billy Wilder, Roman Polanski—lavished praise on Spielberg publicly and privately. There were, however, some dissenting opinions. His thunder stolen by Spielberg, a disgruntled Stanley Kubrick was forced to abandon his own Holocaust project. When scriptwriter Frederic Raphael suggested that *Schindler's List* was a fine representation of the Holocaust, Kubrick retorted, "Think that's about the Holocaust? That was about success, wasn't it? The Holocaust is about 6 million people who get killed. *Schindler's List* is about 600 [sic] who don't" (Raphael,

1999, p. 67). No less an authority on Holocaust cinema than Claude Lanzmann (*Shoah*) voiced a similar view: "There is this building of bridges now. Very strange. A film like *Schindler's List* builds bridges. It is an absolute distortion of historical truth, despite the fact that the story of Oskar Schindler is true. It is not what happened to the vast majority of Jews. The truth is extermination. Death wins" (quoted in Fisher, 1999).

Reel History Versus Real History

Published 11 years after *Schindler's List*, David M. Crowe's authoritative biography, *Oskar Schindler: The Untold Account of His Life, Wartime Activities, and the True Story Behind the List* provides a revisionist portrait that reveals some fairly serious inaccuracies perpetrated by the film. The movie paints Schindler as nothing more than a hedonistic carpetbagger when he arrives in Kraków, but Crowe fills out the backstory, noting that Schindler was actually a spy for the Abwehr (German military intelligence) in the late 1930s who compromised Czechoslovak security in advance of the Nazi occupation and was sent to prison as a result. Schindler was also the de facto head of a unit that mapped out the Nazi invasion of Poland. Crowe points out that there was no "Schindler's List"; in an interview, Crowe observed that "Schindler had almost nothing to do with the list" because he was in jail for bribing Amon Göth, the brutal SS commandant played by Ralph Fiennes in the film when the list was composed. Crowe contends that the legend of "the list" partly originates with Schindler himself to embellish his heroism when he was trying to win reparations for his wartime losses (Smith, 2004). Schindler's manager, Itzhak Stern (Ben Kingsley), was not even working for Schindler at the time. Furthermore, there was not one list but actually nine of them. The first four were drawn up primarily by a Jewish clerk named Marcel Goldberg. A corrupt assistant to the SS officer in charge of transporting Jews, Goldberg took bribes of diamonds from wealthier Jews to get their names put on the list. Crowe notes that Schindler suggested a few names but did not even know most of the people on the lists. The authors of the other five lists are unknown. Crowe also dismissed some scenes in the book and film as mythology. For example, the film shows Schindler horseback riding with his mistress on Kraków's Lasota Hill in March 1943. From that vantage point, Schindler watches the clearing of the ghetto and sees the little girl in the red coat, aimless and alone, seeking shelter. He later observes her corpse on a wagon. Crowe calls the scene "totally fictitious," noting that it would have been impossible to see that part of the ghetto from the hill. The girl in the red coat is, in fact, based on a real person—Gittel "Genia" Chill (1939–1943), a four-year-old Jewish girl murdered during the liquidation of the Kraków Ghetto—but Schindler never saw her that day. Crowe contends that Schindler's moral transformation was more gradual; even before the ghetto was cleared he was appalled by the Nazi mistreatment of the Jews. Another scene, fabricated for its devastating emotional impact, is the Auschwitz shower scene. Holocaust survivor Ernest S. Lobet notes: "Oskar Schindler's Jews almost certainly did not arrive at the Auschwitz-Birkenau gas chambers, and Edith Wertheim, whom you quote, is mistaken if she thinks the shower room in which she found herself on arrival was the gas chamber. Such a mistake is understandable, since none of us who arrived at Auschwitz and survived the initial selection at the 'ramp' knew where we were or knew that death by gassing was the Nazi method for bringing about the 'final solution'" (Lobet, 1994). With regard to Emilie Schindler (1907–2001), the film portrays her as an aggrieved and frequently cheated-upon spouse—which she most certainly was—but gives her humanitarian work on behalf of the Schindlerjuden short shrift. According to her 1996 memoir, *Where Light and Shadow Meet*, she was very much involved with her husband in aiding his Jewish workers in the last two years of the war. None of the foregoing cancels out Oskar Schindler's heroic acts in saving hundreds of Jewish lives but does suggest that Spielberg and his screenwriters could have taken greater risks and hewed closer to the admittedly incredible historical reality by letting Schindler be more fully himself.

SERGEANT YORK (1941)

Synopsis

Sergeant York is a biopic about the life of Alvin C. York, one of the most-decorated American soldiers of World War I. Co-produced and directed by Howard Hawks and starring Gary Cooper as Alvin York, the film recounts York's initial reluctance to serve in the military on religious grounds, his acceptance of his duty, his Medal of Honor–winning actions in combat, and his public recognition afterwards.

Background

Alvin Cullum York (1887–1964), a poor, unlettered farmer from rural Tennessee, was one of the most decorated American soldiers to serve in the First World War. On 8 October 1918, during the Meuse-Argonne Offensive, York (a corporal in Company G, 328th Infantry Regiment, 167th Infantry Brigade of the 82nd Infantry Division) led seven other soldiers in an attack on German positions near Chatel-Chehery, France, taking out 35 machine guns, killing at least 25 enemy soldiers, and capturing another 132. York's stunning display of marksmanship, courage, and resourcefulness under fire

Medal of Honor winner Sergeant Alvin C. York (Gary Cooper) surveys the battlefield in Howard Hawks's popular biopic, *Sergeant York* (1941). (Warner Bros./Photofest)

earned him a promotion to sergeant, the Medal of Honor, France's Croix de Guerre, and many other military decorations. His combat exploits also made him a celebrated national folk hero. After the war, York's business advisor hired New York author Sam K. Cowan to write a biography: *Sergeant York and His People* (1922). York also cooperated with Gallipoli veteran Tom Skeyhill, who essentially wrote York's "autobiography" based on interviews: *Sergeant York: His Own Life Story and War Diary*. Over a 20-year period starting in 1919, Hollywood producer Jesse L. Lasky begged York to sell the film rights to his life story, but York drew the line on a movie; films were literally against his religion (he belonged to Churches of Christ in Christian Union, a strict Evangelical sect). In the late 1930s altered circumstances prompted York to change his mind. He needed money to finance a planned Bible school. Moreover, war had broken out in Europe again, igniting a fierce national debate between interventionists (the minority position York favored) and isolationists (the popular "America First" stance advocated by another national hero and Medal of Honor winner, pro-German aviator Charles A. Lindbergh). Worried about the threat of fascism and hoping that a cinematic rendering of his WWI military service would help bolster interventionist sentiment, York finally agreed to sell Lasky the movie rights in March 1940. The studio tested Pat O'Brien and Ronald Reagan to play Alvin York but Lasky and York had always envisioned Gary Cooper as Alvin York. Cooper initially refused the role but York made a personal appeal to him, and Cooper signed on in September 1940. Lasky struck a production deal with Hal B. Wallis at Warner Bros., William Keighley was assigned to direct (later replaced by Howard Hawks), and studio head Jack Warner arranged to borrow Cooper from Samuel Goldwyn of MGM. To play York's wife, Gracie, Lasky wanted Jane Russell, a sexy 19-year-old ingénue, but York insisted the part go to a nonsmoking teetotaler. The studio tested Helen Wood, Linda Hayes, and Suzanne Carnahan but ultimately hired Joan Leslie, a wholesome 15-year-old—24 years younger than her male co-star (the real Grace Williams York was 13 years younger than her husband). Working closely with the filmmakers, Alvin York demanded that they adhere to high standards of accuracy. Accordingly, the screenwriters—Abem Finkel, Harry Chandlee, Howard Koch, and John Huston—relied on the books by Cowan and Skeyhill to fashion a true-to-life screenplay. They did, however, add the usual sorts of Hollywood embellishments to enliven the narrative (e.g., modeling York's religious conversion on St. Paul's sudden illumination when it was actually a gradual process prompted by his wife, Grace). Eugene P. Walters was hired as military technical director and William Yetter, a former sergeant major in the Imperial German Army, advised the filmmakers on the German military. The film's working title was *The Amazing Life of Sergeant York*, and the project was budgeted at $2 million.

Production

Sergeant York was mostly shot on Stages 6, 9, 16, and 24 at Warner Bros. Studios in Burbank. On Stage 16 (the biggest in North America, 98 feet tall and providing 32,000 square feet of production area) a set was built to represent a section of the Tennessee Valley at Three Forks of the Wolf, where Alvin York was born. It featured a 40-foot mock Appalachian mountain made of wood, plaster, rock, and soil and included 121 live trees and a 200-foot stream mounted on a giant turntable to allow for 16 basic camera angles. For the combat scenes, 300 workers under the supervision of Art Director John Hughes spent three weeks turning an 80-acre site at Warner Ranch in Calabasas, 20 miles west of Burbank, into a facsimile of the war-torn battlefield at Chatel-Chehery. They used five tons of dynamite to blast shell craters, installed 400 denuded tree trunks and stumps, and used 5,200 gallons of paint to blacken them. Other battle scenes were filmed in the Simi Hills and the Santa Susana Mountains (Toplin, 1996, pp. 82–101 and "Sergeant York (1941)," n.d.). Principal photography on *Sergeant York* ran 13 weeks (3 February–1 May 1941).

Plot Summary

Alvin York (Gary Cooper), a hardscrabble farm boy from backwoods Tennessee, is an expert marksman but also a wastrel fond of drinking and fighting, to the chagrin of his long-suffering mother (Margaret Wycherly). One day York meets Gracie Williams (Joan Leslie), is smitten, and works night and day to accumulate the payment for a coveted "bottomland" (i.e., good soil) farm so she'll marry him. The land's owner makes a verbal agreement with York, giving him an option on the land, on the condition that he produces the rest of purchase price in 60 days. When the due date arrives, York wins the amount that he needs during a target-shooting contest, but then finds that the land owner has gone against him and instead sold the land to York's nemesis, Zeb Andrews (Robert Porterfield). York turns to drink and plots his revenge for the betrayal he has suffered. As he moves to assault the man who has swindled him, York is struck by a bolt of lightning later in the night. He survives, but he loses both his mule and his gun in the process. He enters a local church to find a revival in progress, and then has a religious experience. The United States enters World War I [6 April 1917], and York soon receives his draft notice. York attempts to evade the draft by claiming conscientious objection, but his church is not officially recognized so he is forced to report to Camp Gordon, Chamblee, Georgia, for basic training. His commanding officers soon realize his superior marksmanship, and York is promoted to corporal and given the job of rifle range instructor, but York is still against the war and the killing that comes with it. Major Buxton (Stanley Ridges) attempts to sway York in the other direction, giving him a history lesson about the long tradition of American sacrifice. He grants York a leave of absence to think over his options, promising the corporal a recommendation for exemption due to conscientious objection if he does not change his mind. While York is fasting and mediating on a mountaintop with competing texts—an American history book and his Bible—the wind blows his Bible open to a famous verse that appears in the gospels of Matthew, Mark, and Luke: "Render therefore unto Caesar the things which are Caesar's; and unto God the things that are God's." York chooses to return to his unit, confirming that he is willing to fight in the war. York's unit is soon shipped to France, and he takes part in an assault led during the Meuse-Argonne Offensive on 8 October 1918. Facing heavy machine-gun fire, the unit's lieutenant tells Sergeant Early (Joe Sawyer) to get a group of men together and ambush the machine-gun nests. Casualties winnow down the detachment, making York the last remaining unwounded non-commissioned officer, so Early puts him in charge of the squad making the attack.

By stealthy maneuvering, York manages to flank the main enemy trench and picks off Germans with deadly accurate sniper fire, causing the survivors to surrender. At gunpoint, York also forces a prisoner (Charles Esmond) to demand the surrender of German forces mid-battle in a different part of the line. He and his fellow survivors capture a cohort of 132 German soldiers. York is subsequently awarded the Medal of Honor and celebrated for his heroism. When Major Buxton questions why he proceeded in the way that he did, York says that his only goal was to save the lives of his fellow soldiers. Upon his arrival in New York City, York is feted with a ticker tape parade and handed a key to the city before being lodged at the elegant Waldorf-Astoria hotel. Congressman Cordell Hull (Charles Trowbridge) gives him a tour of the city and informs him that he has lots of offers for endorsement deals totaling $250,000. York mentions the land he wanted to purchase before the war began, and Hull confirms that he could use the money for the property. However, York turns away the money, saying that he did his duty during the war, but was not proud of his actions. York returns to Tennessee and discovers that his neighbors and fellow residents have bought the land for him and built him a house.

Reception

Sergeant York had its world premiere at the 1,141-seat Astor Theatre at Broadway and West 45th Street, New York City, on the Wednesday before the July Fourth weekend in 1941. Alvin York attended the screening, accompanied by Jesse Lasky and Hal Wallis and greeted by a Veterans of Foreign Wars (VFW) band and a Tennessee state delegation headed by Col. George Buxton, York's former commanding officer. Gary Cooper also attended. The film went into wide release on 27 September 1941 and did phenomenal box office business; it was the top-grossing film of 1941 with $16,361,885 in ticket sales ($427 million in 2017 dollars) and was still in theaters when the Japanese attacked Pearl Harbor on 7 December, which further boosted ticket sales. *Sergeant York* also excelled in the awards department, garnering 11 Academy Award nominations and posting 2 wins: a Best Actor Oscar for Gary Cooper and a Best Editor Oscar for William Holmes. Contemporary reviews were almost uniformly adulatory.

Reel History Versus Real History

At the insistence of Alvin York, *Sergeant York* achieved an impressive degree of historical accuracy. The movie does, however, indulge in some truth-bending and sheer fabrications. A 39-year-old playing a man a decade younger, Cooper was three inches taller than York and did not much resemble him. Nor did he attempt to replicate York's somewhat higher voice and thick Southern drawl. Furthermore, the script indulges in country bumpkin stereotyping that makes Cooper's Alvin York more childlike and naïve than he really was. York was one of 11 children but in the interest of narrative streamlining, the movie depicts only two siblings. Joan Leslie's Gracie Williams is far prettier and more spirited than the real Gracie. The movie does not whitewash York's youthful propensity for booze and brawling, but it does elide the fact that Grace Williams' parents forbade their courting, so they had to meet in secret. To make its story more palatable to a general audience, the movie also tends to downplay Alvin York's intense religiosity. Instead, it focuses on his yeoman-like efforts to earn money farming and his prowess with a rifle—Adamic traits that identify York with legendary frontier heroes like Daniel Boone. As mentioned earlier, the film foreshortens York's religious conversion and makes it much more dramatic. Its rendition of York's other key conversion, from pacifist to armed combatant, is quite accurate but also highly stylized with its warring voices alternately championing God and State in York's head, Max Steiner's stirring mood music and the ethereal beauty of the mountainous landscape suffused in misty light evoked an Edenic America well worth fighting for. The battle scenes are putatively accurate, though the single-handed nature of York's amazing exploits was challenged by some of his comrades-in-arms who felt that their role in the battle was slighted. Finally, the film's culminating depiction of York being gifted outright with his dream farm by grateful Tennesseans brushed aside the fact that the actual 400-acre farm was not really a "gift." In 1919 the Nashville Rotary Club raised money for a $6,250 down payment on a farm that cost $25,000. York was saddled with an $18,750 mortgage that he couldn't afford. He ended up deeply in debt later in life—a somber reality that would have undercut the film's affirmation of the Cincinnatus-like citizen-soldier who reluctantly goes off to war, becomes a hero, returns safely, and is richly rewarded for his efforts: Warner Bros.' propagandistic message to an American public not eager to fight another war in Europe.

SLAUGHTERHOUSE-FIVE (1972)

Synopsis
Slaughterhouse-Five is an American anti-war/science fiction film based on Kurt Vonnegut's eponymous 1969 novel. Adapted for the screen by Stephen Geller; directed by George Roy Hill; and starring Michael Sacks, Ron Leibman, and Valerie Perrine, the film tells the story of Billy Pilgrim, an American soldier in World War II who is captured during the Battle of the Bulge. As a prisoner of war (POW) Pilgrim witnesses the aftermath of the Allied firebombing of Dresden. He is later abducted by aliens which causes him to become "unstuck in time," constantly reliving his World War II experiences: an apt metaphor for post-traumatic stress syndrome.

Background
On 22 December 1944, during the sixth day of the Battle of the Bulge, Kurt Vonnegut, Jr., a 22-year-old battalion scout with the 423rd Regiment, 106th Infantry Division, was captured (along with 7,000 other G.I.s) by advancing German forces and imprisoned at Dresden, Germany. Though Dresden was an open city with no military installations or air defenses, the Allied High Command decided to firebomb it anyway, presumably as payback for the Nazi bombing of Coventry earlier in the war. In three separate air raids on 13–14 February 1945 (ironically Shrove Tuesday and Ash Wednesday), Royal Air Force (RAF) and United States Army Air Forces (USAAF) bombers dropped more than 700,000 phosphorous bombs on "the Florence on the Elbe." The resulting firestorm, reaching temperatures of 3,000° F, obliterated 1,600 acres in the center of the city and incinerated some 25,000

civilians. One of only seven Allied POWs in Dresden to survive the bombing, Vonnegut was assigned to corpse recovery and burial detail. The overwhelming horror he experienced in Dresden would forever haunt him, indelibly coloring his worldview and his work as a writer. After returning to Dresden on a Guggenheim Fellowship in 1967, Vonnegut wrote *Slaughterhouse-Five, Or The Children's Crusade: A Duty-Dance with Death*, a fatalistic anti-war novel that blends fact, fiction, and science fiction in inimitable Vonnegut fashion. Though critically acclaimed, a National Book Award winner, and a runaway bestseller, *Slaughterhouse-Five* was often banned and condemned, allegedly for its frank language and sexual references, but mostly because it repudiated the myth of World War II as "The Good War" by dramatizing an Allied war crime of truly monstrous proportions. In March 1969, at the height of the Vietnam War, producer Paul Monash purchased the screen rights for Universal Pictures and was allotted a $3.2 million budget to make the film. Director George Roy Hill, Monash's partner on *Butch Cassidy and the Sundance Kid* (1969), signed on to direct in May 1970. Screenwriter Stephen Geller (*Pretty Poison*) was assigned the daunting task of adapting Vonnegut's complex novel to the screen. Michael Sacks, a 22-year-old stage actor, was hired in March 1971 to play Billy Pilgrim, the hapless main character. Hill also recruited Miloš Forman's cinematographer, Miroslav Ondříček, to shoot the picture.

Production

Slaughterhouse-Five was filmed in the early months of 1971 in the Czech Republic, in Minnesota, and at Universal Studios in Hollywood. Hill shot most of the film at Prague's Barrandov Studios and in the city, which doubled for Dresden, while Prague's Praha hlavní nádraží (Main Railway Station) stood in for Dresden's main railway station. Billy Pilgrim's otherworldly home—a geodesic dome on the mythical planet of Tralfamadore—was built on a Universal sound stage. Scenes supposedly taking place near Billy's postwar home in upstate New York were actually filmed at various locations in the Minneapolis-St. Paul area. Because its plot involved constant time disjunctive shifts between three disparate settings—World War II, postwar suburban America, and another planet—*Slaughterhouse-Five* hinged on elaborate cross-cutting that demanded an expert editor. Fortunately, Hill employed Dede Allen, widely acknowledged as one of Hollywood's best.

Plot Summary

In March 1968 a young lady and her husband pull up to a lakefront home in upstate New York near the (fictional) town of Ilium, looking for her father. In the basement of his home, Billy Pilgrim (Michael Sacks), a balding middle-aged man, is typing a letter to his local newspaper, describing his involuntary time travels (i.e., being "unstuck in time"). While he is typing his letter, he finds himself back at the Battle of the Bulge in Belgium in December 1944: a 22-year-old U.S. infantryman, dressed in motley attire, unarmed, and running through the snow. He is accosted by two other American soldiers, Paul Lazzaro (Ron Leibman) and Roland Weary (Kevin Conway), as an enemy attack is in progress. Briefly, Billy finds himself back on the planet Tralfamadore in a geodesic dome with Montana Wildhack (Valerie

Perrine), a beautiful young porn star. She suspects Billy is time traveling again and offers him a distracting kiss. Suddenly Billy is back at the Battle of the Bulge. Shortly thereafter, two German soldiers capture the trio. It is the summer of 1946, at Cape Cod, Massachusetts. Billy and his overweight bride, Valencia Merble Pilgrim (Sharon Gans), are on their honeymoon. She says she thinks he had girlfriends during the war but is glad they waited to have sex and that he married her. Back in World War II Billy, Weary, and Lazzaro, along with many other war captives, are marching through the streets of a war-torn town. Flirted with by two young prostitutes while marching, Billy accidentally steps on Weary's gangrenous feet. This enrages Lazzaro, who beats Billy for his clumsiness. Suddenly it is the late 1950s and Billy and his family are dedicating a new optometry office in Ilium. Back in the war, Billy enters the boxcar, goes to sleep, and finds himself at a Veterans Administration (VA) hospital in the spring of 1946 being treated for shell shock. His mother (Lucille Benson) is talking to fellow patient, Elliot Rosewater (Henry Bumstead) about Billy's war experiences. Then Billy is back in the boxcar, with Weary blaming him for his death. Lazzaro cradles him in his arms as he dies. Billy finds himself back in the VA hospital being given shock treatment. Billy's train pulls up to a POW camp somewhere in Germany. Billy is given a blue, fur-collared overcoat by German soldiers as a joke. The men are processed by a German officer and then led into a shower room to be deloused. Afterwards, Billy finds himself at age eight (Bob "Tiger" Hemond) at the YMCA, where his father throws him into the pool to either sink or swim. In WWII Billy and other soldiers are marched to the POW camp mess hall. The English officer escorting Billy tells him the coat was a joke but to wear it with pride. Billy is at his new home in Ilium in 1947 playing with his new puppy, Spot. There is a party going on at his house, celebrating the birth of his daughter, Barbara. Leaving the party, Billy and his dog are by the lake when he sees a strange beam of light coming toward him and then leaving. Next he is back to the POW camp. Lazzaro threatens Billy for Weary's death, but a kindly fellow soldier, Edgar Derby (Eugene Roche), intervenes. It is Billy and Valencia's anniversary at their home in the summer of 1964. Billy catches his son in the bathroom looking at a porn magazine. Later, Billy looks at the magazine himself and ogles the centerfold of Montana Wildhack. Back at the POW camp the men are assigned to Dresden. Billy and his family are watching a soft-core porn movie on TV with Montana Wildhack in it. Billy and fellow soldiers are in a boxcar on their way to Dresden. Circa 1965, Billy and his wife pull up to a cemetery with a police officer who has caught his now-delinquent son, Robert (Perry King) vandalizing tombstones. Billy offers to pay off the officers for the damages. It is February 1968. Billy and fellow optometrists, including his father-in-law, are about to take a chartered flight to Montreal for a convention. Billy sees visions of skiers in the crowd when waving goodbye and tells the pilots that the plane is going to crash—which it does. Back to Dresden, the elderly German officer tells them of their quarters, Slaughterhouse-Five, where they will be staying and what to shout in German in case of emergency. Injured and buried in the snow in the Green Mountains, Billy is rescued by a group of skiers. After hearing that he is alive at a hospital in Vermont, Billy's wife attempts to rush to his side but in her haste, drives crazily, causing accidents and damaging the exhaust on her own car. Ironically, Billy survives the plane crash but his wife dies from carbon monoxide poisoning. Billy is in his room recovering with an arrogant professor/historian for a roommate named B. C. Rumfoord (John Dehner) complaining to his much-younger wife about being stuck in a room with such a weak and worthless man. Rumfoord is writing about the bombing of Dresden. When Billy says he was there, Rumfoord tells Billy the bombing was justified. At dinner, the night of the bombing, Howard W. Campbell, Jr. (Richard Schaal), an American attired in a garish Nazi uniform with American flag décor, tries to recruit the POWs for the Free American Corps: an anti-communist and anti-Semitic outfit allied with the Germans. As Derby is denouncing Campbell as a traitor, an air raid siren sounds and the men are ordered to evacuate to an underground shelter just before Dresden is firebombed. In March 1968, Billy is taken home by his daughter Barbara (Holly Near). She pleads with him to stay with her and her husband but he refuses. He takes his elderly dog Spot and shuts the door in her face. The bombing is over, and the soldiers go up the stairs to inspect the damage. Billy is lying in bed at his home with Spot when his son Robert (Perry King) comes to visit him. The former delinquent, now a Green Beret fighting in Vietnam, is home on emergency leave. Robert is caring, but Billy is distracted. Right after Robert leaves, the beam of light he saw in the sky while at the lake in 1947 reappears and takes him away to a geodesic dome on the planet Tralfamadore. The Tralfamadorian elder tells him he cannot see them because they live in the fourth dimension and that he cannot leave the dome. An elderly German officer (Friedrich von Ledebur) orders Billy and the other POWs to process the corpses from the rubble of the bombed city and to collect their personal remains. He also warns them that looters will be summarily shot. While Billy and the soldiers are collecting the bodies, he is on Tralfamadore telling the elder about the bombing and how it affected him. The elder assures that everything that happens always has and always will happen; past, present, and future are always happening at the same time in their world, which also gets destroyed and destroys the entire universe because of a mishap with one of their test pilots. Porn actress Montana Wildhack has now been added to the exhibit with Billy, and the Tralfamadorian elder insists that they mate. Billy, always a gentleman, expresses reluctance but Montana lets him go to bed with her. Some days after the bombing, Derby finds an undamaged Hummel figurine in the rubble that is an exact replica of one his son once broke—a joyous find that gets him immediately shot to death by a firing squad. Billy is back on Tralfamadore with Montana in her new wardrobe. They want to have a baby together. It is back to March 1968 and Billy's daughter finds him in his house. When Billy speaks about Tralfamadore she thinks he has lost his mind. His son-in-law suggests that Billy see a psychiatrist. He assures them that the Tralfamadorians do not see past, present, and future the way Earthlings do and also reveals to them disappeared porn star Montana Wildhack is his love interest there and that he has seen his death. An elderly Billy Pilgrim addresses a crowd in Philadelphia about Tralfamadore and their lack of concept about time when an elderly Paul Lazzaro shoots him dead with a sniper rifle. Billy wakes up to find himself in the ruins of Dresden in April 1945 with Lazzaro and fellow soldiers attempting to steal a grandfather clock. In the process the clock topples onto Billy. It turns out the war in Europe is over. Russian soldiers give Billy a drink to celebrate but he gags on it. Billy and Montana have a baby on Tralfamadore, with the entire planet celebrating with applause and an array of fireworks.

Reception

Slaughterhouse-Five premiered in the United States on 15 March 1972 and was screened at the 25th Cannes Film Festival in May 1972, where it won the Jury Prize. The film also won a Hugo Award and Saturn Award, and Michael Sacks was nominated for a Golden Globe. A hard film to market, it received very limited distribution and did not do well at the box office. Reviews were mixed. Vincent Canby called *Slaughterhouse-Five* "probably the most perfectly cast film in months" but went on to observe that the "problem with the film, as it was with the novel, is that it's really not outraged or outrageous enough, much like its time-tripping gimmick" (Canby, 1972). Conversely, film critic Frank Getlein termed *Slaughterhouse-Five* "an extraordinary movie, a totally successful fusion of grim 20th century history and science fiction fantasy in far outer space." Unlike Canby, Getlein took the film's implicit message seriously: "With [the fire-bombing of] Dresden, the movie says, we, the Allies, passed over into Hitlerian violence against the innocent for the sheer love of violence. Even as they were defeated the Nazis won, for they converted us to their barbaric doctrine of destruction for its own sake, a doctrine we still adhere to" (Getlein, 1972). Vonnegut himself was thrilled with what the filmmakers had accomplished: "I love George Roy Hill and Universal Pictures, who made a flawless translation of my novel *Slaughterhouse-Five* to the silver screen . . . I drool and cackle every time I watch that film, because it is so harmonious with what I felt when I wrote the book" (Vonnegut, 1972, p. xv).

Reel History Versus Real History

A moral indictment of war's insanity, *Slaughterhouse-Five* never purported to be an informative historical novel about the 1945 firebombing of Dresden. Vonnegut broadly based Billy Pilgrim's experiences on his own war experiences; being captured during Hitler's Ardennes offensive and later witnessing the terrible aftermath of the Dresden firebombing as an American POW. The film follows the book quite closely but omits the book's first-person prologue, thus omitting Vonnegut himself from the narrative. In the novel, the Tralfamadorian response to death and destruction—"so it goes"—is repeated 106 times but is never spoken in the film.

SOLDIER OF ORANGE [DUTCH: *SOLDAAT VAN ORANJE*] (1977)

Synopsis

Soldier of Orange is a Dutch war film directed and co-written by Paul Verhoeven, produced by Rob Houwer, and starring Rutger Hauer and Jeroen Krabbé. Based on the 1970 autobiography *Soldaat van Oranje* by Dutch war hero Erik Hazelhoff Roelfzema, the film is set during the World War II German occupation of the

Netherlands and follows the lives of a number of Dutch students who assume different roles in the war.

Background

Erik Hazelhoff Roelfzema (1917–2007) was a Dutch writer who became a much decorated resistance fighter and Royal Air Force (RAF) pilot during World War II. In 1970 he published *Het Hol Van De Ratelslang* (*The Cave of the Rattlesnake*), a memoir of his war years that was later retitled *Soldaat Van Oranje* (*Soldier of Orange*), denoting Roelfzema's association with the Dutch royal family (he was Queen Wilhelmina's personal assistant). The book became an international bestseller and cemented Roelfzema's stature as Netherlands' greatest hero of the Second World War. A few years later the Dutch filmmaking team of Rob Houwer (producer), Paul Verhoeven (director-screenwriter), and Gerard Soeteman (screenwriter) secured the rights to the book. Verhoeven, Soeteman, and Kees Holierhoek collaborated on a screen adaptation, and Houwer eventually raised part of a production budget of 3.5 million guilder ($9.25 million). A then-unknown Rutger Hauer was cast as Erik Hazelhoff Roelfzema (called Erik Lanshof in the film). The real Hazelhoff Roelfzema was on the set as a consultant, and he and Verhoeven became lifelong friends. Prince Bernhard, Prince Consort to the Dutch Queen Juliana, and the Inspector General of the Dutch armed forces at the time of the shoot, became the film's patron, arranging for military support, temporary road closings, and other logistical necessities.

Production

Even with full government support, the shoot proved complicated and grueling. Lots of WWII-era weapons and 50 period autos were procured, 3,000 costumes and uniforms were made for extras, a modern Leopold I tank was disguised to look like a German Panther tank, and the correct model seaplane was found in Norway—but after seven weeks in the fall of 1976, the production had to be suspended for five months when it ran out of money. It resumed in the spring of 1977 after Houwer signed a deal with The Rank Organization and a Dutch television company (Excelsior) to provide additional financial support, under the condition that the material also be adapted into a four part mini-series, which was retitled *For Koningin en Vaderland* (*For Queen and Fatherland*). The second half of the shoot wrapped up seven weeks later.

Plot Summary

Before the opening credits, the film begins with mock black and white newsreel footage, narrated in voice-over, showing the Netherlands' Queen Wilhelmina (Andrea Domburg), accompanied by her personal assistant, Erik Lanshof (Rutger Hauer), arriving home from London shortly after the end of World War II. After the newsreel, the film starts in the late 1930s in Leiden, where freshmen university students submit to fraternity hazing. Thereafter the film follows the lives of some of these six affluent students: Erik Lanshof (Rutger Hauer), Guus LeJeune (Jeroen Krabbé), Jan Weinberg (Huib Rooymans), and Alex (Derek de Lint). Robby Froost (Eddy Habbemal) is a friend of Erik, and Esther (Belinda Meuldijk) is Robby's girlfriend. Some become collaborators; others join the Dutch Underground. Part of the story is set in London, where Queen Wilhelmina is living in exile during the war. Erik and Guus start a friendship, and Guus offers him housing in a private student dormitory in Leiden. In this house, the students (Erik, Guus, Jacques, Jan, and Alex) drink and toast their friendships. On 3 September 1939, a BBC radio broadcast interrupts the students at a tennis match, announcing that the United Kingdom has declared war on Germany. At first the students take the news lightly, believing that the Netherlands will likely remain neutral. Jan (a Jew) and Alex leave to enlist in the Dutch army. On 10 May 1940, Germany invades the Netherlands; Erik and Guus attempt to enlist, but they are rejected. Four days later, after the "Rotterdam Blitz," the Netherlands gives in. Erik and Esther have an affair. Robby uses a radio transmitter to get in contact with the Dutch resistance in London and set Erik up on a plane to join the group. Jan stands up for a Jewish salesman by fighting some anti-Semites and finds himself in hot water, so Erik gives his seat on the plane to his friend. Unfortunately, as they are being picked up, the pair fight with German soldiers and Jan is taken. Erik manages to escape, and upon meeting Alex at a military parade, discovers that Alex has joined Hitler's SS. Eventually, Erik is also imprisoned. Once captured, Jan tells him that an individual named Van der Zanden (Guus Hermus) is the traitor in London. The Gestapo executes Jan at the Waalsdorpervlakte, a desolate spot in "Meijendel" dune area, The Hague. The Gestapo discovers Robby's radio and blackmails him to work as a double agent (his fiancée, Esther, is a Jew). Meanwhile, Erik, having been released from jail, joins up with Guus and flees to London on the Swiss cargo steamer, *St. Cergue*. In London, Erik meets Van der Zanden and discovers that he is not a traitor but actually head of the Dutch Central Intelligence Service. Erik returns to the Netherlands to retrieve a group of resistance leaders. However, they find Robby amidst the group on the beach; the Germans have found the group, but Erik is unable to warn them about Robby. Meanwhile, en route to the beach, Erik sees Alex at a party, then eventually leaves the party and escapes to the beach to meet his fellow resistance members. When Robby realizes that Erik knows that he is working for both sides, he fires a signal flare and runs away. While the resistance group attempts to make an escape, their leaders are shot and killed. Guus and Erik flee by jumping into the sea, but only Erik makes it to the British ship and returns to London. Guus later encounters Robby on the street and kills him. Guus is then apprehended and killed for his crime. Alex is killed by a hand grenade thrown by a small Russian child who he mocked and refused to feed earlier in the day. Erik becomes an RAF pilot, flies combat missions over Germany, and then becomes Dutch Queen Wilhelmina's assistant. Erik follows the queen back to the Netherlands after the war. The film ends with Erik reunited with Esther, whose hair has been cropped short as a punishment for her collusion with the Nazis. Erik then toasts the end of the war with another student, Jacques ten Brinck (Dolf de Vries), who also managed to make it out alive.

Reception

Soldier of Orange had its world premiere in the Netherlands on 22 September 1977. Though the film would do well in terms of international box office receipts, it met with considerable controversy in its home country. As Johan Swinnen writes, "Many viewers in the Netherlands saw it [as] an insult to the efficiency of the Resistance, the character of the Dutch, and the impact the Dutch made as a whole on the outcome of the War . . . [It] also suggests that the Resistance's activities were little more than diversions to keep the Germans from focusing their entire efforts on the War." Swinnen further notes that the film "did not shy away from nudity and sexuality," another element that met with disapproval in some quarters (Mathijs, 2004, p. 147). Released in the United States on 16 August 1979, *Soldier of Orange* won the Los Angeles Film Critics Association Award for Best Foreign Film in 1979. A year later it received a Golden Globe nomination for Best Foreign Language Film. Not personally invested in the history it invoked, American film audiences and critics tended to regard the film as an engrossing war epic, though not without some obvious flaws. Janet Maslin's review is typical: "*Soldier of Orange* may not be great art but it's a good yarn. And the combined effects of Mr. Verhoeven's comfortingly old-fashioned storytelling and Mr. Hauer's unexpectedly brittle performance keep it moving at a fast clip." But Maslin also remarked on the film's two main English characters, "an officer (Edward Fox) and his trampy, ridiculous assistant (Susan Penhaligon), are so weirdly caricatured that they may make a great comic impression on American viewers" (Maslin, 1979). In a 1999 election for best Dutch film of the 20th century at the Netherlands Film Festival, *Soldier of Orange* was voted second greatest, right after another Paul Verhoeven film, *Turkish Delight* (1973).

Reel History Versus Real History

Though names have been changed, *Soldier of Orange* is a faithful distillation of its source material. However, in an interview when *Black Book*, his fourth film about the Dutch Resistance, appeared in 2006, Paul Verhoeven admitted that he needed to embellish the facts of Erik Lanshof's adventure to make it "more heroic and patriotic . . . And these events were embellished to begin with. Embellishment is unavoidable when you're turning actual events into a film." Verhoeven and Gerard Soeteman discovered "darker and shadowy material" about the Resistance during their research for *Soldier of Orange* but suppressed it until *Black Book*, almost 30 years later: "That the Dutch underground was marbled with anti-Semitism, that some high-ranking Nazis knew they were trapped in a matrix of insanity, that war can be fun, that liberation can be terrible, that revenge against Nazi collaborators can unleash new forms of ugliness no less horrific than Nazism itself" (Koehler, n.d.). As an exercise in conventional heroic storytelling, *Soldier of Orange* had to avoid such ambiguities.

STALAG 17 (1953)

Synopsis

Stalag 17 is an American war film produced and directed by Billy Wilder. Adapted from a Broadway play, starring William Holden and featuring Robert Strauss,

Neville Brand, Harvey Lembeck, Peter Graves, and Otto Preminger, the film tells the story of a group of American airmen held in a German World War II prisoner of war (POW) camp who come to suspect that there is an informant among them.

Background

Sgts. Donald Bevan (1920–2013) and Edmund Trzcinski (1921–1996) were two of the thousands of American airmen shot down over Germany during World War II. Both men ended up as "Kriegies" (short for Kriegsgefangener, i.e., German for POW) at Stalag 17, a POW camp at Krems-Gneixendorf in Austria. During their imprisonment Bevan and Trzcinski wrote *Stalag 17*, a three-act play based on their Kriegie experiences that they actually presented at the camp. Actor-director José Ferrer put the play on Broadway for a highly successful year-long run at the 48th Street Theatre (8 May 1951–21 June 1952; 472 performances), produced by Richard Condon and starring John Ericson as Sgt. J. J. Sefton. Film director Billy Wilder saw the play on Broadway, decided to purchase the rights for $50,000 of his own money, and hired screenwriter Edwin Blum to help him adapt it into a film script. In the transition from stage to screen Wilder and Blum altered the work considerably, making it funnier, adding Oberst von Scherbach, a cheerfully sadistic camp commandant, and transforming Sefton from a troubled loner into a selfish, cynical hustler disliked and distrusted by the other prisoners. The role was originally meant for Charlton Heston but as Sefton became more dislikeable, Heston bowed out. Kirk Douglas was offered the part but turned it down, to his lasting regret. Wilder's third choice, William Holden, reluctantly took on the role. Four actors from the Broadway play—Robert Straus, Harvey Lembeck, Robert Shawley, and William Pierson—were hired to reprise their roles in the movie version, and director Otto Preminger signed on to play von Scherbach. Extras allegedly included 14 former POWs, 7 of whom had been interned at Stalag 17, among them co-playwright Edmund Trzcinski, who was given a small speaking part.

Production

After a week of rehearsals, exterior scenes were shot during the first two weeks of February 1952 at a realistic seven-acre replica of the camp built at the John H. Show Ranch in present-day Woodland Hills, 20 miles northwest of Hollywood, an elaborate set complete with rows of prisoners' huts, guard towers, high fences topped with barbed wire, and an administration building. Thereafter, all the interior shots were filmed in a simulated barrack room on a Paramount sound stage. Wilder shot the film in sequence and kept the identity of the undercover German informant secret from most of the cast until the end, in order to elicit more authentic performances. He also chose not to open up the scenario beyond the confines of the camp. As he told an interviewer, "I wanted the audience to experience the confinement of the prisoners and therefore shot no scenes outside of the prison compound" (Horton, 2001, p. 106). The 47-day shoot wrapped on 29 March 1952 and ended up costing $1.66 million—about 21 percent over the projected budget, money later recouped through brisk ticket sales.

Plot Summary

Voice-over narration by Sgt. Clarence Harvey "Cookie" Cook (Gil Stratton, Jr.) sets the scene. It is the week before Christmas 1944 in the small American compound of a Luftwaffe POW camp near the Danube that holds about 630 gunners, radio-men, and flight engineers—all sergeants—from shot-down United States Army Air Forces (USAAF) bombers. As Manfredi (Michael Moore) and Johnson (Peter Baldwin) attempt to escape through a hidden tunnel, Sgt. J. J. Sefton (William Holden) bets the other 72 inmates of Baracke 4 a large quantity of cigarettes that the two escapees won't make it out of the forest. Sefton wins his bet; the pair is shot by waiting guards. The other prisoners conclude that an informant in their midst must have tipped off the Germans. Suspicion naturally falls on Sefton, an enterprising grifter who eschews all escape attempts as futile while devising various schemes to hustle his fellow Kriegies and bartering openly with the German guards for better food and other creature comforts. After von Scherbach displays the bodies of Manfredi and Johnson to the assembled POWs as an object lesson, routine daily life at the camp is depicted in a series of vignettes. Baracke 4 guard, Feldwebel Johann Sebastian Schulz (Sig Ruman), confiscates a clandestine radio in another success for the "stoolie." Sgt. Stanislaus "Animal" Kuzawa (Robert Straus) is obsessed with Betty Grable and becomes despondent when he hears that Grable and Harry

U.S. Army Air Force POWs Sgt. Stanislaus "Animal" Kuzawa (Robert Strauss, left), Sgt. J. J. Sefton (William Holden, middle), and Sgt. Harry Shapiro (Harvey Lembeck, right) peer through the barbed wire of their World War II prison camp in Billy Wilder's *Stalag 17* (1953). (Paramount Home Video/Photofest)

James, a musician, have wed. Harry "Sugar Lips" Shapiro (Harvey Lembeck) gets several letters in the mail, and when Kuzawa notices the professional financial letterhead, Harry tells his friends that they've repossessed his car. Sefton pays off the guards in order to sneak into the Russian women's barracks, but his fellow prisoners speculate that his temporary release is a reward for giving information to the German authorities. When he returns, Sefton discovers that his barrack mates have searched his footlocker. They accuse him of being a spy when Oberst von Scherbach (Otto Preminger) shows up and has Lt. James Schuyler Dunbar (Don Taylor) removed (Dunbar had told his fellow POWs that he had destroyed a German train containing ammunition—a secret the barrack spy has relayed to von Scherbach). The men in Baracke 4 are convinced that Sefton betrayed Dunbar, so they beat him severely. The next morning, the day before Christmas, the Red Cross delivers packages to the American compound while Sefton, alone in the barrack recovering from his beating, tries unsuccessfully to bribe Schulz to get him to release the name of the real spy. In the midst of a fake air attack, Sefton stays in the empty barracks and hears the security head, Sgt. Frank Price (Peter Graves), speaking with Schulz in German and describing how Dunbar was able to blow up the train. Sefton ponders his next move. If he tells the other POWs about Price, then the Germans will relocate him to another camp, putting others at risk. If he kills Price, he could put the entire camp in danger of execution. On Christmas Day, the men hear that the SS is set to relocate Dunbar to Berlin for what they assume will be extended interrogation-torture sessions. They use a diversion to free Dunbar and hide him elsewhere in the camp. Despite strenuous efforts, the Germans cannot locate Dunbar. Von Scherbach says that the camp will be destroyed, along with the people in it, if Dunbar isn't turned in, so the men decide that one of them must remove their comrade from harm's way. Price says that he will do it, but Sefton accuses him of being the spy. As a test, Sefton asks, "When was Pearl Harbor?" Price knows the date, but Sefton swiftly follows up, asking at what time he heard about the attack. Immediately, and without fully considering his answer, Price says that he heard at 6 o'clock p.m., while eating dinner. This mistake unmasks him: 6 o'clock was the proper time in Berlin, but not in Cleveland, Ohio, where Price is supposed to hail from. Sefton searches Price's pockets and finds a hollow chess piece that Price was using to send secret messages to his German unit (messaging them using a light bulb cord). Sefton opts to guide Dunbar out of the camp, anticipating a hefty reward from Dunbar's family for his role in the escape. Sefton and Dunbar escape out of a water tower above the latrines, while the other men punish Price by using him as a diversion: he is thrown into the yard with cans tied to his legs. The alerted tower guards fix Price in their searchlights and open fire. Despite his protestations, he is quickly shot dead. Amidst the chaos, Sefton and Dunbar make it out. A pleased Cookie whistles "When Johnny Comes Marching Home."

Reception

Stalag 17 opened in the United States on 6 June 1953 and proved to be a major box office success, earning $10 million. It was an even bigger hit in Europe. The movie also received Academy Award nominations for Best Director, Best Supporting Actor

(Robert Strauss), and Best Actor. William Holden won for Best Actor—an award widely thought to compensate for his *not* having won an Oscar for his brilliant rendition of Joe Gillis, the doomed gigolo in Wilder's noir classic, *Sunset Boulevard* (1951). Reviews were adulatory, and many decades later, the film continues to be held in high esteem—though there are dissenting opinions, such as Mike Mayo's: "Billy Wilder's highly honored adaptation . . . really does not live up to its reputation. It's less a realistic look at life inside a German prison camp than an improbable suspense tale that depends on some clumsy contrivances. Worse yet, the moments of comic relief are appalling." Mayo also astutely notes that "*Stalag 17* is really more a Cold War film than a World War II film. Its questions about informants, loyalty, and the tyranny of the group over the individual are concerns of the 1950s, not the 1940s" (quoted in Nixon and Stafford, n.d.). Unfortunately, *Stalag 17* also inspired the execrable TV 1960s comedy series, *Hogan's Heroes*.

Reel History Versus Real History

In the movie, the overall look of the American compound is quite authentic, but the sign over its entrance reads "Stalag 17-D." The real camp was designated Stalag XVII-B (short for Stammlager Luft, or prison camp for airmen, and the Germans used Roman numerals). The camp's actual commandant was Oberst Kuhn, a Wehrmacht officer—not Luftwaffe—who was every bit as tough as his fictional counterpart, von Scherbach. The bare, muddy ground conditions shown in the film are inauthentic. There was snow on the ground in Krems, Austria, in December 1943 and it was extremely cold—weather not convincingly replicated in balmy southern California in the spring of 1952. Indeed, one would expect to see the men exhale breath vapors outdoors in the freezing air, but none appear in the film. Living conditions at the real Stalag 17, exacerbated by severe overcrowding, were far more difficult than those shown in the film; prisoners were often beaten by brutal guards and a few were shot and killed, while complaints to the commandant fell on deaf ears. The prisoners did build a radio but it was never confiscated. The Germans did not plant spies in POW camps, as depicted in the movie. The Price character was likely inspired by a mysterious inmate—not a German "mole" but rather much the opposite: Dr. Reuben Rabinovitch (1909–1965), a Jewish Canadian resistance fighter who was given the cover identity of Staff Sgt. Harry Vosic, USAAF, to keep him out of the gas chambers. The action in *Stalag 17* is entirely fictional but it is based on at least one real incident. Frank Grey (aka "The Grey Ghost," 1915–2006), a U.S. Eighth Air Force B-17 tail gunner, pulled off the only escape from Stalag 17-B in January 1945. Temporarily at the camp on his way to the Gestapo for repeated escapes and acts of sabotage, Sgt. Grey was hidden by comrades in a tunnel as soon as he entered the compound. After a fruitless three-day search by camp guards and the Gestapo, the Germans became convinced he had escaped. Grey then resurfaced, made it into the adjoining Russian POW compound, escaped from there, and ultimately reached Yugoslavia, where anti-Nazi partisans assisted him in getting back to England. It was Grey's seventh escape. On a previous escape, Grey sabotaged a German freight train headed to the Russian front by disabling anti-aircraft guns and equipment on a flatcar. Grey's daring exploits obviously inspired the movie's Lt. Dunbar character, who also sabotaged a German train (albeit in a highly unlikely manner), is hidden at Stalag 17 to protect him from the Gestapo, and then escapes with Sefton's help. Frank Grey's incredible saga is recounted by fellow Kriegie Ned Handy in his memoir, *The Flame Keepers*.

STALINGRAD (1993)

Synopsis

Stalingrad is a German war film directed by Joseph Vilsmaier. Starring Thomas Kretschmann as Lt. Hans von Witzland, the movie follows a platoon of World War II Wehrmacht soldiers from Italy in the summer of 1942 as they are transferred to the German Sixth Army, which finds itself surrounded and besieged by the Red Army during the fateful Battle of Stalingrad during the winter of 1942–1943.

Background

The Battle of Stalingrad (23 August 1942–2 February 1943) was one of the largest (nearly 2.2 million personnel involved) and bloodiest battles ever fought. After 13 weeks of street-to-street combat in the fall of 1942, the Germans had taken most of the city—reduced to rubble from aerial bombardment and shelling—but they had neglected to shore up their weak flanks to the north and south. On 19 November 1942 the Russians launched Operation Uranus, a surprise massive counterattack on those flanks that quickly surrounded and ultimately destroyed the German Sixth Army in a giant pincer movement. Total Axis casualties (Germans, Romanians, Italians, and Hungarians) are believed to have been more than 250,000 dead, 450,000 wounded, and 91,000 captured—a devastating defeat that essentially sealed the doom of Hitler's Third Reich. Over the ensuing decades a number of documentary and fiction films, German and Russian, have been made about this decisive WWII battle, but the best of them remains Joseph Vilsmaier's *Stalingrad*. The film originates with Christoph Fromm, a young German screenwriter who wrote a screenplay (c.1990) based on extensive research, including numerous interviews, that places fictive characters in the 336th Pioneer Battalion, 336th Infantry Division, a real unit that fought at Stalingrad. Producers Günter Rohrbach and Hanno Huth acquired Fromm's script and hired director Joseph Vilsmaier to turn it into a movie for Bavaria Film. Vilsmaier and co-writers Jürgen Büscher and Johannes Heide retained Fromm's characters and basic narrative structure, but extensively reworked the material, making it less a documentary and more of "a movie with feelings," as Vilsmaier later put it—so much so that Fromm took his name off the project and later published his version as a novel (*Stalingrad—Die Einsamkeit vor dem Sterben* [*Stalingrad—The Loneliness Before Dying*]).

Production

In order to show the declining health and weight loss of its main protagonists, *Stalingrad* was shot in sequence between October 1991 and April 1992. The opening moments were filmed on location in Cervo, Liguria, Italy, while the Stalingrad scenes were shot in Prague and in Kurivody, Ceská Lípa District of Czechoslova-kia (now the Czech Republic), and in Kajaani and Kemijärvi, Finland. Additional interiors were shot on sets at Bavaria Studios, Geiselgasteig, Germany. There was no filming at Stalingrad itself (now Volgograd); destroyed during the Nazi siege, the city was completely rebuilt after the war so there were no period buildings. Vilsmaier's production team made every effort to ensure authenticity; they found 9,000 original World War II uniforms, period weapons, and a number of World War II–era Soviet tanks that were still operational. In addition to the 40 actors with speaking roles, the movie employed a production team of 180 technicians, 12,000 extras (mostly Czechs and Germans), and 100 stunt persons. Vilsmaier also combed a veterans' hospital near Prague for extras missing arms and legs. The world's largest snowmaking machine was used during the filming of the winter scenes, some of which were shot in the dead of winter with temperatures as low as −22° F (−30° C). The production budget was an estimated 20 million Deutschemarks ($13.2 million).

Plot Summary

In August 1942, after the First Battle of El Alamein (1–27 July 1942) ends in a stale-mate, German soldiers who fought with Rommel's Afrika Korps enjoy leave in Cervo, Liguria, Italy. At an assembly of the battalion, some of the men are awarded the Allgemeines Sturmabzeichen [General Assault Badge], including Unteroffizier [Sgt.] Manfred "Rollo" Rohleder (Jochen Nickel) and Obergefreiter [Senior Lance-corporal] Fritz Reiser (Dominique Horwitz). Both men meet Lieutenant Hans von Witzland (Thomas Kretschmann), a platoon commander on his first leadership posting, and the squadron travels by train to participate in the Battle of Stalingrad. Witzland's unit links up with a group led by Hauptmann [Captain] Hermann Musk (Karel Heřmánek), who takes them on an attack of a factory building, resulting in a large number of deaths and injuries. During a ceasefire, the unit retrieves their injured soldiers and manages to take a prisoner: Kolya (Pavel Mang), a young Russian boy. However, Russian forces swarm the next day, and the boy escapes. Without a working radio, von Witzland, Reiser, Rollo, Emigholtz (Heinz Emigholz), "GeGe" Müller (Sebastian Rudolph), and Wölk (Zdenek Vencl) take to the sewers to find their way back to the German front. Witzland is soon on his own, having lost his unit underground, but is able to capture a Russian soldier named Irina (Dana Vávrová), who lures him into a sense of safety by offering to help him, but betrays him by pushing him into the water before running off. Witzland is saved by his men, but Emigholtz is severely wounded when he unwittingly detonates a booby trap. His comrades take him to a crowded aid station full of severely wounded soldiers screaming in agony, and Reiser orders an aid worker to help his friend, pointing a gun at the orderly. Emigholtz dies, despite their efforts. Hauptmann Haller (Dieter Okras) captures the men and sets them up in a penal unit forced to disarm landmines. By late November 1942, a brutally cold winter season has arrived, and the Soviet forces have outflanked the Germans. Hauptmann Musk sends the penal unit to the frontline, and Witzland's squadron has some initial success defending their position, but Wölk dies in the process. Witzland, GeGe, and Reiser then decide to desert. They steal medical tags from corpses to feign being wounded and head towards Pitomnik Airfield, in the center of the "cauldron" (pocket), in hopes of catching a medical evacuation plane out of Stalingrad. However, they arrive too late and watch as the final transport heads out without them and the airfield is riddled with bullets from the Russian forces. They return to their unit in a shelter and see that Musk is afflicted by a bad case of trench foot. When a German plane arrives with supplies, the unit hurries out to secure provisions. Haller accosts them at gunpoint and is taken down, but he kills GeGe as he hits the ground. Making a desperate play for his life, Haller tells the men that he has a stash of supplies hidden at a local house, but Otto executes him. The men find the house in question full of provisions, but they also find Irina bound to Haller's bed as his sex slave. Von Witzland frees Irina, and she tells the men that she collaborated with the Germans. The squad help themselves to food and drink, while a feverish and dying Musk tries to convince them to fight on. Otto commits suicide instead. Once Musk dies, Rollo brings his body outside and sees the remaining members of the German Sixth Army conceding to the Russian forces. Irina, Witzland, and Reiser make their way through the snow to escape, but shots from the Soviets kill Irina and mortally wound Witzland. The Germans manage to get away. Witzland eventually succumbs to his wounds and perishes in Reiser's arms. Reiser holds his dead commander, thinking about North Africa as he eventually freezes to death.

Reception

Stalingrad premiered in Munich, Germany on 21 January 1993 but was not released in the United States until 24 May 1995, after it had already gone to video. Box office numbers are unknown, but anecdotal information suggests that the movie was not profitable—perhaps not surprising, insofar as *Stalingrad* is one of the bleakest movies ever made. It did, however, receive mostly positive reviews. Stephen Holden notes that *Stalingrad* "has some of the most virtuosic battle scenes to be found in a modern war film" but also observes that the movie "is so determined to show the horrors of war that [it] doesn't devote quite enough time to its major characters" (Holden, 1995, p. C19). Peter Stack called the film "grimly beautiful" and found the soldiers depicted as "anything but reverent toward their leaders . . . *Stalingrad* is rough yet fascinating viewing. Delving into the brutal realities of war with an almost docudrama style, it renders a bitter, almost choking sense of the futility of war through the destruction not only of bodies, but of the human spirit" (Stack, 1995).

Reel History Versus Real History

In its display of uniforms, weapons, and tanks and its visceral rendering of combat in urban and open settings, including severe casualties, atrocities, and the abysmal conditions faced by the trapped remnants of the Sixth Army, *Stalingrad* achieves a high degree of historical accuracy. Focused at the squad level, the film is not able to convey or even suggest the enormous scope and complexity of the Battle of Stalingrad (a task better left to documentaries).

STEEL HELMET, THE (1951)

Synopsis

The Steel Helmet is an American war film produced, written, and directed by Samuel Fuller. An examination of racial bigotry set during the Korean War, the film is about U.S. Army Sgt. Zack (Gene Evans), the sole survivor of a prisoner of war (POW) massacre, who forms a survival pact with a Korean orphan (William Chun).

Background

The Steel Helmet was writer-producer-director Sam Fuller's third movie, the last installment in a three-picture deal with independent producer Robert Lippert (the first two were *I Shot Jesse James*, 1949, and *The Baron of Arizona*, 1950). In the summer of 1950, just after the outbreak of the Korean War, Fuller wrote *The Steel Helmet* script in a week, setting it in Korea for topicality but largely basing it on his own WWII war diaries. As he recounts in his autobiography, *A Third Face*, Fuller was determined to challenge racial prejudice and bring realism to a film genre rife with jingoistic clichés: "Whatever the confrontation and wherever it's happening, the underlying story [of war] is one of destruction and hatred. I wanted an opportunity to show that war was more complex than the front-page newspaper articles. You never saw the genuine hardship of soldiers, not ours nor the enemy's, in movies. The confusion and brutality of war, not phony heroism, needed to be depicted. The people who chanted 'We are right, they are wrong,' needed to be debunked" (Fuller, 2002, p. 256). A major studio expressed interest but wanted John Wayne to star in the picture—casting that would have sabotaged Fuller's vision of what a realistic war movie should be. Fuller approached Mickey Knox to take the lead role of Sgt. Zack but Knox turned him down. Eventually Fuller hired a gruff and burly cigar-chomping WWII veteran named Gene Evans to play Sgt. Zack, a choice affirmed by Bob Lippert but overruled during rehearsals by associate producer William Berke, who tried to fire Evans and replace him with Larry Parks, then a genuine movie star. It was widely rumored that Parks would be summoned to testify at upcoming Hollywood House Un-American Activities Committee (HUAC) hearings in 1951. Berke cynically reasoned they could now hire Parks on the cheap and that he would, in Fuller's words, "be worth a fortune in free publicity when the s— hit the fan" (Fuller, 2002, p. 258). Fully committed to Evans and genuinely sympathetic to Parks's plight, Fuller refused to hire Parks for purposes of exploitation. He threatened to boycott his own movie unless Lippert promised that there would be no more tampering with his cast. Lippert agreed and Evans kept his job. The next day Fuller hung a sign on the sound stage door that read: "NO ASSOCIATE PRODUCERS, CO-PRODUCERS, EXECUTIVE PRODUCERS OR ANY PRODUCERS ADMITTED HEREIN." Just before filming got underway, Fuller sought cooperation from the U.S. military by submitting his script to Bernard Baruch, chief of the newly established Motion Picture Production section of the Public Affairs Office, Department of Defense (DOD). Baruch's office initially refused to cooperate with Fuller on the grounds that *The Steel Helmet* "contained no informational value and had a number of objectionable sequences" (Chung, 2006,

p. 125). After Fuller submitted a rough cut of the film in November 1950, the DOD relented and allowed Fuller to use some archival footage.

Production

Using a no-name cast, a plywood tank, stock combat footage, and 25 UCLA students playing both American and North Korean soldiers, Sam Fuller shot *The Steel Helmet* in 10 days in October 1950. The abbreviated shoot and a very modest production budget ($104,000) called for highly efficient filmmaking (i.e., one or two takes per shot). Interiors (a simulated Buddhist temple) were filmed in a rented Hollywood studio, while exteriors were shot in L.A.'s Griffith Park using direct sound and natural light. The only major glitch occurred when actor Steve Brodie required an emergency appendectomy after collapsing on the set on 14 October 1950. He returned to the shoot five days later.

Plot Summary

Part of a U.S. Army unit captured, tied up, and then massacred by the North Korean People's Army (NKPA), Sgt. Zack (Gene Evans) survives when an enemy bullet aimed at his head is deflected by his helmet. A South Korean orphan boy (William Chun) happens upon Zack, frees him of his bonds, and tags along thereafter, despite Zack's annoyance. Nicknamed "Short Round" by Zack, the boy challenges American racial bigotry by insisting that Zack refer to him as South Korean, not as a "gook." They soon encounter Cpl. Thompson (James Edwards), an African American medic—also the sole survivor of his unit—before merging with a patrol led by an untested Lt. Driscoll (Steve Brodie). Racial bigotry is again manifest when the white soldiers express suspicion that the black medic might be a deserter. Soon, however, race is rendered a moot point when the squad is pinned down by snipers; Zack and Nisei Sergeant Tanaka (Richard Loo) join forces to neutralize the enemy snipers. Thereafter, the small unit sets out to establish an observation post at a Buddhist temple, but not before one of their number is killed while inspecting a booby-trapped corpse. They reach the temple but Joe (Sid Melton) is killed that night by a North Korean major (Harold Fong) hiding inside. Subsequently captured, the enemy officer tries but fails to win over Thompson and then Tanaka by pointing out the racism they face in their own country. Sergeant Zack prepares to take his prisoner of war (POW) back for interrogation, anticipating the reward of a furlough. Before he leaves, Lt. Driscoll asks to exchange helmets for luck, but Zack refuses his request. Short Round is the next to die, killed by another sniper. After the NKPA major mocks the wish that the boy had written down (a prayer to Buddha that Zack will like him), Zack flies into a rage and shoots his prisoner. The unit then spots the North Koreans attacking in force, and Driscoll has Pvt. Baldy (Richard Monahan) call in artillery support. When the enemy soldiers realize that artillery is being directed from the temple, they attack en masse, supported by a tank. The Americans repel the assault, but only an obviously shell-shocked Zack, Tanaka, Thompson, and Baldy survive. When they are relieved, Zack is asked, "What outfit are you?" He responds simply but grandly: "U.S. infantry." As they leave the temple, Zack goes to Driscoll's grave and exchanges his helmet with the one marking the grave. Instead of the standard closing title, "The End," the film concludes with "There is no end to this story," a somber avowal that the human race is hopelessly addicted to war.

Reception
In Sam Fuller's words, "all hell broke loose" when *The Steel Helmet* opened nationally in January 1951, at the height of the second "Red Scare." Victor Riesel, a nationally syndicated columnist and a staunch anti-communist crusader, denounced the film as pro-communist and anti-American. Fuller also noted that "One of the country's most reactionary newspapermen, Westford Pedravy [i.e., Westbrook Pegler] wrote that I was secretly financed by the Reds and should be investigated thoroughly by the Pentagon" (Fuller, 2002, p. 262). On the far Left, *The Daily Worker* characterized Sgt. Zack as a bloodthirsty "beast" and labeled Fuller a "reactionary" for making him the hero of the movie. For its part, the DOD strenuously objected to the scene in the movie that has Zack killing a POW, an act of freelance savagery expressly forbidden by the Geneva Convention. Called on the carpet, Fuller pointed out that he had personally witnessed such war crimes in WWII. Fuller then phoned General George A. Taylor, his former regimental commander, who verified the truth of Fuller's claim. Despite or perhaps because of all the controversy it generated, *The Steel Helmet* produced phenomenal box office results for a bare-bones independent production: $2 million in receipts—20 times more than it cost to make.

Reel History Versus Real History
Small-scaled and localized, *The Steel Helmut* does not attempt to represent any specific battles or incidents related to the actual history of the Korean War, of which Fuller knew little beyond contemporary newspaper accounts. What the film gets right is more generalized and perennial: American racism and xenophobia (e.g., antipathy toward nonwhite U.S. soldiers, calling Koreans "gooks"); the fatalistic stoicism of the American foot soldier; the gritty, exhausting life of the G.I., a life marked by filth, boredom, and the occasional experience of abject terror and death in combat. The superstitious fixation with Zack's helmet as a lucky talisman and the death of a soldier killed by a booby-trapped corpse were plot elements derived from real incidents that Fuller recorded in his WWII diary.

STORY OF G.I. JOE, THE (1945)

Synopsis
The Story of G.I. Joe is an American war film directed by William Wellman, starring Burgess Meredith and Robert Mitchum, and based on the newspaper columns of Pulitzer Prize–winning war correspondent Ernie Pyle. The film, a tribute to the American infantryman (aka "G.I. Joe") during World War II concentrates on one unit (C Company, 18th Regiment, 1st Infantry Division) that Pyle accompanies into combat in Tunisia and Italy.

Background

During World War II Ernie Pyle (1900–1945) was America's most famous and revered war correspondent. His plainspoken dispatches, reporting on the lives of frontline G.I.s, appeared in hundreds of Scripps-Howard newspapers six days per week and were eagerly devoured by millions of American readers stateside. In late October 1943 Henry Holt published *Here Is Your War*, a book derived from Pyle's columns that covered "Operation Torch," the North African Campaign (8 November 1942–13 May 1943), and "Operation Husky," the campaign in Sicily (9 July–17 August 1943). The book became a bestseller and earned Pyle a Pulitzer Prize. Months earlier, the U.S. Army's Public Relations Division contacted independent film producer Lester Cowan and tasked him with making a movie that would pay homage to the ordinary foot soldier. Referred to Ernie Pyle by colleagues, Cowan read his columns and quickly became convinced that they were the source material he was looking for. Cowan approached Pyle and persuaded him that *Here Is Your War* could be turned into a coherent film that would avoid the jingoistic hokum and sentimentality all too evident in the war film genre at that time (Tobin, 1997). After securing the movie rights from Pyle, Cowan hired playwright Arthur Miller to pen a screen adaptation. In the fall of 1943 Cowan and Miller paid visits to Pyle at his home in Albuquerque, New Mexico, while he was taking a two-month respite from the war. By mid-November 1943, Cowan had submitted Miller's film outline to Col. Falkner Heard of the Army Ground Forces. By March 1944 Miller had the first draft of a script completed. Bereft of fresh ideas, he dropped out of the project—though his script research into military life produced an interesting nonfiction book entitled *Situation Normal* (1944). Over the next year and a half United Artists screenwriters Leopold Atlas, Guy Endore, and Philip Stevenson took over. With uncredited help from Ben Bengal and Alan Le May, they wrote a series of revisions, partly to incorporate new material from Pyle's latest columns as the war dragged on (these were collected in a second book, *Brave Men*, published 20 November 1944).

Production

Production began on 13 March 1944 with director Leslie Fenton (replacing Richard Rosson) helming a location crew and soldiers from the 104th Infantry Division as they reenacted the Battle of Kasserine Pass at the California-Arizona Maneuver Area (CAMA) in the desert near Yuma, Arizona. By mid-May production had ground to a halt, with Cowan discouraged and his writers flummoxed by a script that stubbornly refused to cohere. Another major stumbling block: Lester Cowan could not find an actor to portray Ernie Pyle. He wanted Burgess Meredith but Meredith was a captain in the U.S. Army and unavailable. Gary Cooper signed on but then dropped out to join a USO tour. Lester Cowan put Leslie Fenton on another film project and, with Ernie Pyle's help, convinced William Wellman to sign on as director on 18 September 1944. In the weeks that followed Cowan considered a number of actors to play Pyle: Fred Astaire, Fred MacMurray, Walter Brennan, and Barry Fitzgerald. He even considered Pittsburgh Pirates radio announcer "Rosey" Rowswell and Pyle look-alike John M. Waldeck, a streetcar conductor from

St. Louis, but in the end Cowan came back to his first choice. In late October 1944, after much lobbying by Cowan, the Army granted Burgess Meredith permission to make the film on condition that Cowan turn all profits from it over to Army Emergency Relief (AER). After a six-month hiatus, production resumed on 15 November 1944 and wrapped up six weeks later, in mid-January 1945. The movie was in post-production when news arrived that Ernie Pyle had been killed by a Japanese machine-gun bullet on le Shima, an island near Okinawa on 18 April 1945.

Plot Summary

The new infantrymen of C Company, 18th Infantry, U.S. Army, travel to the front-lines for the very first time. Lt. Bill Walker (Robert Mitchum) allows a green war correspondent, Ernie Pyle (Burgess Meredith), to ride with the troops. Ernie shocks Walker and his unit by following them right to the frontlines. On the way, Ernie spends time getting to know the squadron: Private Robert "Wingless" Murphy (John R. Reilly), Private Dondaro (Wally Cassell), Sergeant Warnicki (Freddie Steele), and Private Mew (William Murphy). The men's first battle is that of Kas-serine Pass, which ends up being a major defeat with many casualties. Ernie and the company initially part ways, but further into the year, Ernie looks for them, having nurtured a fondness for the first outfit that he'd covered as a wartime reporter. He finds the battalion in Italy, set to stage an assault on a German-occupied town. Ernie discovers that Company C is now practiced at killing without mercy or guilt. The unit soon captures the town and tries to move on to Monte Cassino. However, their advance is blocked, and they are forced to live in caves. Casualties are heavy as replacement troops are killed before they can learn how best to sur-vive (which Walker confesses to Ernie makes him feel like a murderer). As a result, Walker finds himself short of lieutenants, and the veterans lose men, including Wingless Murphy. Ernie returns to the correspondents' quarters to discover that he has been awarded the Pulitzer Prize for his war reporting. Ernie again reconnects with the soldiers on their way to Rome. He greets some familiar unit members, but is shocked when a mule passes by carrying the dead body of Capt. Walker. One by one, the old hands reluctantly come forth to express their grief in the presence of Walker's corpse. Ernie joins the company as it goes down the road, narrating its conclusion: "For those beneath the wooden crosses, there is nothing we can do, except perhaps to pause and murmur, 'Thanks pal, thanks.'"

Reception

The Story of G.I. Joe was released on 13 July 1945, 51 days before the end of World War II. Nominated for four Oscars (Best Actor in a Supporting Role—Robert Mit-chum's only career nomination; Best Writing, Screenplay; Best Music, Original Song; Best Music, Scoring of a Dramatic or Comedy Picture), *G.I. Joe* was named one of the top 10 films of 1945 by the National Board of Review. It was also nomi-nated for the Grand International Award at the 1947 Venice Film Festival. Film critics were, likewise, enthusiastic. James Agee called the film "an act of heroism" for its honesty, courage and artistic integrity (Agee, 1945, pp. 264–265). Joseph Foster praised *G.I. Joe*'s emphasis on characterization rather than plot: "For a constant moviegoer exposed to the banalities of the superplotted feature, this picture is a luxurious experience. For once the soldier is treated as a human being, set apart by special circumstances rather than by oddities of character. There are no plot compulsions. The characters do not get pushed around by the demands of the stereotyped melodrama that usually go under the name of 'war pictures.' There is more drama here, in the GI easing his pack by the roadside, than in the loud heroics of a Robert Taylor taking on the whole Japanese army" (Foster, 1945, p. 27). Thomas Pryor noted that the movie won high praise from actual G.I.s: "When the men of the Fifth Army, many of whom participated in the picture, saw *The Story of G.I. Joe* in Italy, their verdict was 'This is it.' Lester Cowan, the producer, and all those others who contributed to this magnificent and so richly deserved tribute to the infantry soldier, could ask for no greater rewards" (*New York Times*, Oct. 6, 1945). No less an authority than General Dwight Eisenhower pronounced *The Story of G.I. Joe* "the finest war film I have ever seen."

Reel History Versus Real History

The characters in *The Story of G.I. Joe* are mostly fictitious, but the episodic events depicted in the film are based on actual experiences documented by Pyle in his frontline dispatches. Respectful of Ernie Pyle and obligated to the U.S. military for cooperation and support, Cowan, Wellman, and their screenwriters strove to ensure that the film achieved the highest level of authenticity possible. They even used 150 G.I.s as extras who actually participated in the battles depicted in the film. The movie's final scene, dramatizing the aftermath of Capt. Walker's death, is based on Pyle's most famous and widely reprinted column: "The Death of Captain Waskow" (10 January 1944), a poignant piece on Capt. Henry T. Waskow of Belton, Texas, a beloved company commander in the 36th Division who was killed in Italy by a German mortar round. In the movie, his men respectfully bid him farewell in much the same way as Pyle described the actual incident. Critics generally credit *The Story of G.I. Joe* as the most authentic war film of its era.

T

THEY WERE EXPENDABLE (1945)

Synopsis

They Were Expendable is an American war film directed by John Ford and starring Robert Montgomery, John Wayne, and Donna Reed. Based on the 1942 book by William L. White, the film recounts the exploits of Motor Torpedo Boat Squadron Three, a PT boat unit defending the Philippines against Japanese invasion during the Battle of the Philippines (1941–1942) in World War II.

Background

During World War II the U.S. Navy stationed a motor torpedo boat squadron in the Philippines from September 1941 to mid-April 1942. Composed of six boats commanded by Lt. (later Vice Admiral) John D. Bulkeley (1911–1996), MTB Squadron 3 participated in the doomed defense of Bataan and Corregidor during the Japanese invasion of the Philippines (8 December 1941–8 May 1942); conducted the evacuation of General Douglas MacArthur and other high-ranking officers from Corregidor to Mindanao (11 March 1942); and destroyed numerous Japanese ships and planes in August 1942, for which Bulkeley was awarded the Medal of Honor. Covering the exploits of MTB Squadron 3, journalist William L. White extensively interviewed Bulkeley, Lt. Robert Kelly, and two other PT boat officers. He then published their first-person accounts in *They Were Expendable* (1942), a bestseller condensed in *Reader's Digest* and chosen as a Book of the Month Club selection. Collaborating with the U.S. Navy to make a pro-war effort propaganda movie, MGM acquired the film rights to *They Were Expendable* in July 1942, a month after the decisive U.S. victory at Midway and two months before White's book was published. Frank "Spig" Wead, a disabled former U.S. Navy aviator turned writer, was hired to work on a screen adaptation; producer Sidney Franklin and staff screenwriters Jan Lustig and George Froeschel contributed revisions. A draft script was completed by April 1943 but didn't quite work because of the inherently gloomy nature of the material (only 5 out of the 68 men in the real squadron made it out of the Philippines alive). Bulkeley and his men were undoubtedly heroic—good fodder for propaganda—but they had fought a futile rearguard action against an enemy overwhelmingly more powerful, were ultimately defeated, and were nearly wiped out: an implicit acknowledgment that the United States had been woefully unprepared in the Pacific and that its insistence on defending the Philippines had been an ill-advised political gesture. Radio journalist/screenwriter Norman Corwin was then brought in, but also struggled to find a viable narrative approach. In the meantime Jim McGuinness, the MGM executive put in charge of the project, sought John Ford to direct the picture but had a hard time signing him. As head of the photographic unit for the Office of Strategic Services (OSS), Ford was busy filming documentaries for the U.S. Navy in war zones and had no interest in returning home to shoot a Hollywood war movie. He changed his mind, however, when he met John Bulkeley, now a U.S. Navy commander, who had been reassigned to the Atlantic theater of operations for the D-Day landings in June 1944. Ford joined Bulkeley on his PT boat as it patrolled the invasion beachheads and developed a strong rapport with the Medal of Honor winner. After spending time with Bulkeley, Ford finally committed to the *They Were Expendable* film project in October 1944 on the condition that Frank Wead be rehired to make the final revisions on the script. (Ford's fee was set at a record $200,000 but he didn't want the public thinking he was profiting handsomely from commercial filmmaking during wartime, so he used the funds to buy land and build Field Photo Farm, a recreation center in San Fernando Valley for the 180 veterans of his Field Photographic Unit.) Also in October, Sidney Franklin signed Robert Montgomery to play John Bulkeley (called "Brickley" in the movie)—perfect casting because Montgomery had served as a lieutenant commander in the U.S. Navy on PT boats at Guadalcanal and on a destroyer at Normandy. In January 1945 John Wayne was hired to play the supporting role, Lt. (J. G.) "Rusty" Ryan (loosely based on the real Lt. Robert Kelly), and 20-year-old starlet Donna Reed was cast as Army nurse Lt. Sandy Davyss, Wayne's love interest.

Production

Filming on *They Were Expendable* ran almost four months (23 February to 18 May 1945). Though some studio work was done at Culver City, California, most of the filming took place in Key Biscayne and the Florida Keys, substituting for the Philippines. The production was an unusually large one, employing a cast of 140 actors and some 150 technicians. On 17 January 1945, a month before filming started, workers started construction on sets that re-created Bataan and Corregidor, work that continued throughout much of the shoot. MGM had always had the full cooperation of the U.S. Navy, which supplied six real PT boats sent down from a naval depot in Melville, Rhode Island. Although Ford respected Montgomery's naval experience, he was openly contemptuous of John Wayne for staying out of the war on a 3-A (family deferment) exemption to pursue his acting career. Ford badgered Wayne continuously until Montgomery finally intervened on Wayne's behalf and got Ford to desist. On Monday, 14 May 1945, near the end of the shoot, Ford slipped off a camera scaffold and broke his leg, whereupon Robert Montgomery stepped in for the rest of the week and directed the one remaining sequence. He did such a capable job that Ford couldn't tell the difference between Montgomery's scenes and his own (Montgomery went on to direct four noirs and a war movie between 1947 and 1960). John Wayne also learned directing technique from Ford and would direct his own epic, *The Alamo* (1960), with Ford's assistance. When shooting wrapped, Ford returned to his Field Photographic Unit in Europe and left the post-production work and scoring of *They Were Expendable* to others but later objected to some of the "heavy music" added.

Plot Summary

The film begins with an opening credits prologue: "'Today the guns are silent. A great tragedy has ended. A great victory has been won . . . I speak for the thousands of silent lips, forever stilled among the jungles and in the deep waters of the Pacific which marked the way.' Douglas MacArthur, General of the Army." In December 1941, a squadron of six PT boats under the command of Lt. John "Brick" Brickley (Robert Montgomery) is ordered to Manila to defend the Philippines against Japanese attack. The do not receive a warm welcome. One of Brick's officers, Lt. J. G. "Rusty" Ryan (John Wayne), is incensed that his superiors refuse to see the small, fast boats as effective naval craft and is in the process of transferring when news arrives of the Japanese attack on Pearl Harbor. Ryan and Brickley demand real combat assignments for their PT boat squadron but are frustratingly relegated to messenger duties. All that changes, at least temporarily, when the Japanese launch a surprise attack with warplanes the day after Pearl Harbor and Brickley's squadron is hastily sent into combat to retaliate. After the crisis, they are again relegated to messenger duty, once again infuriating Ryan. Eventually, top echelon commanders recognize that the PT boats are effective and utilize them against larger Japanese ships. Brick's boats manage to sink the Japanese cruiser and go on to score more victories but also sustain mounting losses they can ill afford. The squadron is sent to evacuate General Douglas MacArthur, his family, and other persons of high rank. Afterwards, Brickley and his men resume their forays against the Japanese and continue to lose precious boats. As PT boats are destroyed, their crew members are reassigned to infantry duty. At last, the final boat is given to the Army for use as a messenger boat. Brickley, Ryan, and two ensigns are airlifted out on the last plane. The remaining enlisted men, led by Chief "Boats" Mulcahey (Ward Bond), stay behind to continue the fight.

Reception

They Were Expendable had its premiere on 19 December 1945 in Washington, D.C., four months and four days after the end of the Second World War—too late to serve its original purpose as wartime patriotic propaganda. Reviews tended to be highly positive, though there was grumbling about the leisurely pace and sheer length of the film, which came in at 2 hours and 15 minutes. Bosley Crowther wrote, "Mr. Ford, and apparently his scriptwriter, Frank Wead, have a deep and true regard for men who stick to their business for no other purpose than to do their jobs. To hold on with dignity and courage, to improvise when resources fail and to face the inevitable without flinching—those are the things which they have shown us how men do. Mr. Ford has made another picture which, in spirit, recalls his *Lost Patrol*. It is nostalgic, warm with sentiment and full of fight in every foot" (Crowther, 1945). James Agee thought it "John Ford's finest movie" (Agee, 1946). *They Were Expendable* earned two Oscar nominations (for Best Sound and Best Special Effects), but box office returns were predictably mediocre for a postwar release: $3.2 million for a picture that cost at least $2.5 million to make.

Reel History Versus Real History

Closely following William White's book, *They Were Expendable* achieves a high degree of historical accuracy. Still, it goes awry in at least three areas: 1) its depiction of General MacArthur; 2) its portrayal of Rusty Ryan, the character representing Robert Kelly; and 3) its inclusion of a romance subplot. An unabashed admirer of Douglas MacArthur, John Ford re-created the arrival of "The General" (played by Robert Barrat) on board Brickley's PT boat for transit from Corregidor to Mindanao as a kind of super-patriotic Second Coming in reverse, underscored by an off-screen orchestra playing "The Battle Hymn of the Republic" and punctuated by a series of reaction-shot cutaways of American soldiers and sailors in rapturous admiration. The scene is so excessively fawning that some critics wrongly detected an air of mockery. In the real world, MacArthur was not much admired by U.S. rank-and-file troops, who thought him an incompetent, imperious blowhard who lost the Philippines through a lack of preparedness. They sarcastically nicknamed him "Dugout Doug" for assiduously looking after his own safety during and after the fall of the Philippines while his troops died in droves. (MacArthur, against Army regulations, also accepted a $500,000 payoff from President Manuel Quezon of the Philippines in February 1942). John Wayne's real-life counterpart, Robert B. Kelly (1913–1989), sued MGM for libel for depicting him as a moody, undisciplined hothead and was awarded $3,000. Donna Reed's real-life counterpart, Beulah "Peggy" Greenwalt Walcher (1911–1993), also sued, contending that the film's portrayal of her in a fictitious extramarital romance damaged her reputation and was an invasion of privacy. A federal court jury in Missouri agreed and awarded her $290,000 in 1948.

THIN RED LINE, THE (1998)

Synopsis

The Thin Red Line is an American war epic written and directed by Terrence Malick. Based on the eponymous novel by James Jones, the film is a semi-fictionalized account of the Battle of Mount Austen during of the Guadalcanal Campaign of World War II. It stars Sean Penn, Jim Caviezel, Nick Nolte, and Elias Koteas as soldiers of C Company, 1st Battalion, 27th Infantry Regiment, 25th Infantry Division.

Background

James Jones, the author of *From Here to Eternity* (1952), earned a Purple Heart in combat on Guadalcanal: a lonely, soul-searing experience he transmogrified into his fourth novel, *The Thin Red Line* (1962). Virginia Kirkus called the book a "well-drawn battle narrative [that] provides take-off points for dozens of character studies, and the author describes emotional responses to battle, fear, death, homosexuality, along with detached, ironic comments on army organization and the workings of fate, luck and circumstance" (Kirkus, 1962). *The Thin Red Line* was first made into a film in 1964, directed by Andrew Marton and starring Keir Dullea and Jack Warden, a simplified adaptation that still managed to evoke some of the disturbing power of the original work. Flash forward to 1988. Well respected for two distinctively beautiful films—*Badlands* (1973) and *Days of Heaven* (1978)—director Terrence Malick hadn't made a movie in 10 years when producers Robert Geisler and John Roberdeau offered him funding to undertake a new project. Malick suggested either an adaptation of Molière's *Tartuffe* or of Jones's *The Thin Red Line*. The producers chose *The Thin Red Line* and acquired the rights from the author's widow, Gloria Jones. Malick laboriously developed his script, completing a first draft in May 1989. As Peter Biskind notes, "Malick ultimately fashioned a remarkable script, infused with his own sensibility. But he had made some questionable choices. He retained several of Jones's more conventional situations, but dropped some interesting elements, including the suggestion of a homoerotic undertow among some of the characters. Later, he changed Stein, a Jewish captain, to Staros, an officer of Greek extraction, thereby gutting Jones's indictment of anti-Semitism in the military, which the novelist had observed close-up in his own company" (Biskind, 1999). Geisler and Roberdeau formed an alliance with Phoenix Pictures, a production company started by Malick's former agent, Mike Medavoy, in 1995, and a financing deal was struck with Sony Pictures. After scouting locations in Panama and Costa Rica, Malick chose the rainforests of northern Australia, and crews began building sets in Queensland when the movie hit a major roadblock when Sony's new studio head, John Calley, cancelled funding, forcing Malick and Medavoy to pitch the project to other studios. Fox 2000 Pictures agreed to supply $39 million—the lion's share of the budget—stipulating that Malick cast five movie stars from a list of ten provided. Pioneer Films, a Japanese company, contributed $8 million and Phoenix added another $3 million. Other sources brought the total up to the original $52 million. Malick, a former Rhodes Scholar who had studied philosophy at Oxford with Gilbert Ryle, was held in high esteem by actors as a cerebral, visionary director, so he had no trouble attracting the best talent in the business for his new film. Many A-list actors, including Brad Pitt, Al Pacino, Gary Oldman, Leonardo DiCaprio, Johnny Depp, Nicolas Cage, Bruce Willis, Edward Burns, Matthew McConaughey, William Baldwin, Neil Patrick Harris, Josh Hartnett, Philip Seymour Hoffman, and Stephen Dorff, offered to work for a fraction of their usual fee. As a result of the heavy traffic in interested parties, casting took a full year. None of these actors were cast, but those who were (noted later) were of equal caliber. Others who were cast—Bill Pullman, Lukas Haas, Mickey Rourke, John C. Reilly—had their parts eliminated or radically pared down. Adrien Brody saw his part, Cpl. Geoffrey Fife, gutted. Fife had been the lead protagonist in Jones' novel and in Malick's 198-page screenplay but ended up a mere cameo, with two spoken lines and about five minutes of screen time, so that Jim Caviezel's role could be vastly expanded. Billy Bob Thornton recorded voice-over narration for the entire movie but it was eventually scrapped in favor of eight different narrators.

Production

Some background footage was shot at Guadalcanal, the actual setting for the film, but the island was malaria ridden and too rugged and remote to sustain a movie crew, so most of the filming, which involved 250 actors and 200 crew members, took place in the Daintree Rainforest and on Bramston Beach in Queensland, Australia, about 1,000 miles southwest of Guadalcanal, across the Coral Sea. After 100 days in Queensland, filming the set piece battle for Hill 210, the shoot then moved to the Solomon Islands for the next 24 days for the filming of jungle scenes. The last three days of filming took place on the Pacific Ocean near Santa Catalina Island (about 20 miles southwest of Long Beach, California). A mercurial director, Malick often confused his actors, who couldn't figure out what he was after in a particular scene, or with the film as a whole. Co-producers Geisler and Roberdeau, who had spent years nurturing the project, had it worse; Malick banned them from the production so he could operate without supervision or interference. The five-month shoot wrapped at the end of October 1997. Post-production took another 13 months. By early March 1998, editor Leslie Jones had fashioned a five-hour rough cut from cinematographer John Toll's voluminous footage. Further cutting by Malick's trusted editor, Billy Weber, rendered a film three and a half hours long. With Sean Penn's assistance, Malick spent another three months cutting an additional 45 minutes, with the final cut coming in at a still-epic 170 minutes. Veteran composer Hans Zimmer did the film score.

Plot Summary

U.S. Army Private Witt (Jim Caviezel) has gone absent without leave (AWOL) and lives with the natives of the South Pacific. He is eventually located and locked up on a vessel by First Sergeant Welsh (Sean Penn) of his company. The soldiers of C-for-Charlie Company, 1st Battalion, 27th Infantry Regiment, 25th Infantry Division, have been transported to Guadalcanal as backup in the effort to capture Henderson Field and take the island from the Japanese. Below decks of the Navy transport, they warily anticipate the upcoming invasion. Topside, aging battalion commander Lt. Col. Gordon Tall (Nick Nolte) converses with his younger superior officer, Brig. Gen. Quintard (John Travolta), about the invasion and its importance for his own career. Soon thereafter, Charlie Company lands unopposed on Guadalcanal and moves inland, only encountering natives and evidence of the Japanese presence. They soon arrive at their objective: Hill 210, where a well-concealed bunker at the top of the hill, bristling with machine guns, commands the approaches. At dawn the next day, after a brief and ineffectual American artillery barrage, Charlie Company attempts to capture the hill, covered in tall wind-blown grass, but is repelled by concentrated, accurate gunfire. Among the first killed is one of the platoon leaders, 2nd Lt. Whyte (Jared Leto). During the battle, a squad led by Sergeant Keck (Woody Harrelson) hunkers down behind a low ridge, safe from enemy fire to wait for reinforcements. Keck reaches for a grenade but accidentally pulls the pin and blows himself up. Lt. Col. Tall radios the company commander, Capt. James "Bugger" Staros (Elias Koteas), and orders him to take the bunker by frontal assault, whatever the cost. Staros refuses. After a tense radio exchange involving threats of disciplinary action, Tall decides to join Staros on the frontline to assess the situation. Pvt. Witt, having been assigned punitively as a stretcher bearer, asks permission to rejoin the company, and permission is granted. On Tall's orders a small detachment is sent on a reconnaissance mission to determine the strength of the Japanese bunker. Pvt. Bell (Ben Chaplin) reports back there are five machine guns in the bunker. He then joins another small squad (including Witt), led by Capt. John Gaff (John Cusack), on a flanking mission to take the bunker. Gaff's men are able to get in close and take out the bunker and neighboring spider holes, killing most of the Japanese defenders without taking any casualties. Soon, Charlie Company takes over one of the final Japanese forts on the island. The Japanese soldiers who they encounter are poorly fed and fighting death, so they do not resist. The men are granted a week's leave, but the airfield comes under attack. The company is instead sent on a mission up a river with the inexperienced 1st Lt. George Band (Paul Gleeson) leading the way. As the Japanese fire near their location, Band sends some men, including Witt, upriver to scout out the situation. The scouts are met with a group of Japanese soldiers attacking and try to draw them away from their unit. Corporal Fife runs back to tell the unit, and Witt sacrifices himself to make sure that his unit is able to retreat. Witt is later buried near the riverbank by Welsh and his squad mates. C-for-Charlie Company receives a new commander, Capt. Charles Bosche (George Clooney), boards a waiting LCT (tank landing craft), and departs the island.

Reception

The Thin Red Line was shown in a limited release (five theaters) at Christmas 1998 and grossed $282,534 that weekend. The movie went into wide release on 15 January 1999 (1,528 theaters) and grossed $9.7 million during its opening weekend. It ultimately earned $98.1 million in worldwide box office receipts. *The Thin Red Line* received numerous accolades, including seven Oscar nominations, six Satellite Awards from the International Press Academy, and a Golden Bear at the Berlin Film Festival. John Toll's cinematography was singled out for a number of film critics' awards. Reviews were mixed but mostly positive. On their TV review show, *Siskel & Ebert at the Movies*, Gene Siskel called *The Thin Red Line* the "finest contemporary war film I've seen, supplanting Steven Spielberg's *Saving Private Ryan* from earlier this year, or even Oliver Stone's *Platoon* from 1986. Malick . . . has an almost-unmatched eye for the landscape and for storytelling through pictures" (2 January 1999). Roger Ebert was slightly less enthused. On the air he noted that *Thin Red Line*'s rambling philosophical musings in voice-over too much resembled similar musings in Malick's *Days of Heaven* from 20 years earlier. In his newspaper review, he wrote, "The movie's schizophrenia keeps it from greatness (this film has no firm idea of what it is about), but doesn't make it bad. It is, in fact, sort of fascinating" (Ebert, 1999). The critical consensus was that *The Thin Red Line* contains scenes of extraordinary beauty and power, but the film as a whole doesn't quite cohere into a meaningful statement about war, reality, or human nature. Traditional war movie buffs dislike the movie, finding it too diffuse, ultimately ponderous and pretentious.

Reel History Versus Real History

James Jones' novel provides a semi-fictionalized account of the Battle of Mount Austen, the Galloping Horse, and the Sea Horse (15 December 1942–23 January 1943), a series of American assaults on hills at the northeastern end of Guadalcanal in the closing days of the campaign. Mounted by several U.S. Army and Marine regiments (part of a total American force of 50,000), these attacks pushed 10,000 defeated, starving, and disease-ridden enemy soldiers—the last remnants of Japan's invasion force—toward Cape Esperance, where they were evacuated by Japanese destroyers in early February 1943. The taking of Hill 210 in Malick's film is therefore synecdotal for what was actually a much larger, bloodier, and complex battle. The combat action in the film is suitably realistic, as is the film's depiction of the condition of the Japanese troops, but what's missing is any larger sense of situational context. As historian Kenneth Jackson points out, the "viewer learns too little about Guadalcanal, either as personal experience or as grand strategy. Why was that tiny island important? Why was the fighting on Guadalcanal different from most other Pacific campaigns? . . . [Nor] does Malick give us the kind of texture from the novel that would reveal the combat infantryman's perspective. For example, we learn nothing of taking souvenirs or gold teeth from dead and dying enemy soldiers, of trading such trinkets for whiskey from the Air Corps personnel in rear areas, of homosexuality in the shared darkness of a tent, of the ranking of wounds according to how far back from the front each type of disability would take a person, of the constant struggle for promotion and position within the company, and most especially of the kind of loyalty for small units and for each other that would help explain to the viewer why so many persons put their own lives at risk to help fallen comrades. All of those issues were at the core of Jones's book." Jackson further observes that *The Thin Red Line* probably does not even render nature the way that soldiers experienced it: "Malick gives us . . . paradise, replete with lush green mountains, tropical waterfalls, and glorious beaches . . . In fact, American servicemen regarded Guadalcanal as a tropical hell. Ninety-two miles long and thirty-two miles wide, it was mostly dense jungle, infested with ferocious ants, poisonous snakes, and malarial mosquitoes, not to mention lizards, crocodiles, spiders, leeches, and scorpions" (Jackson, 1999).

THIRTY SECONDS OVER TOKYO (1944)

Synopsis

Thirty Seconds Over Tokyo is an American war film produced by Sam Zimbalist, written by Dalton Trumbo, and directed by Mervyn LeRoy. It is based on the true story of the Doolittle Raid, the U.S. retaliatory airstrike against Japan four months after the Japanese attack on Pearl Harbor.

Background

On the morning of 18 April 1942 16 B-25B Mitchell twin-engine medium bombers were launched from the aircraft carrier USS *Hornet* (CV-8) about 650 nautical miles off the east coast of Japan. Commanded by Lt. Col. James H. "Jimmy" Doolittle, the planes set off on a top secret mission to bomb targets in Tokyo and other Japanese cities in order to (1) retaliate for the Japanese attack on Pearl Harbor four and a half months prior, (2) boost American morale, and (3) demonstrate that Japan was vulnerable to air attack. The plan was to land the bombers in China after the raid; landing them on an aircraft carrier was impossible. Unfortunately, the planes had to launch 170 miles farther out than was originally planned when the task force was spotted by a Japanese patrol boat. After bombing their targets in Japan, all 16 B-25s ran out of fuel well short of their recovery airfields in China and either crashed on land or ditched at sea. Of the 80 airmen deployed (5 to a plane), 3 were killed in action and 8 taken prisoner by the Japanese (of which 3 were executed, 1 died in captivity, and the other 4 eventually repatriated). With every bomber lost and damage inflicted on Japan minimal and easily repaired, the Doolittle Raid was, for all practical purposes, an abject and costly failure. It was, however, a resounding propaganda success that lifted American morale when news of the raid was splashed across America's newspapers on 19 May 1942. In January 1943, one of Doolittle's pilots, Capt. Ted Lawson—who lost a leg in the raid—began to write a book about the mission entitled *Thirty Seconds Over Tokyo* with the help of newspaper columnist Bob Considine. Lawson and Considine spent four nights and two days at the Mayflower Hotel in Washington, D.C., sketching out the story but were not allowed to publish it until after detailed information on the raid was released by the War Department on 19 April 1943, a full year after it occurred. The book-length story was first serialized in six successive issues of *Collier's* magazine (22 May–26 June 1943). In early July Metro-Goldwyn-Mayer producer Sam Zimbalist secured the movie rights from Lawson and assigned Dalton Trumbo to adapt Lawson's story to the screen. After meeting with Lawson and other military officials in Washington, D.C., Trumbo came to the conclusion that the raid had been staged for propaganda purposes only. Accordingly, he fashioned a propagandistic script that emphasized the skill and heroism of the bomber crews and the heroic role that Chinese guerillas played in rescuing their American allies from the clutches of the Japanese, the latter point meant to refute the notion pushed by the Hearst newspapers: that the conflict in the Pacific was at base an Oriental-Occidental race war (Ceplair and Trumbo, 2014).

Production

The filmmakers received the full cooperation of the U.S. Navy and U.S. Army Air Forces (USAAF) and worked closely with Air Force chief Henry H. "Hap" Arnold, Jimmy Doolittle, Ted Lawson, and other airmen who participated in the raid to achieve a high degree of authenticity. Location shooting took place at Mines Field in Los Angeles, at Mills Field in San Francisco, at the Alameda Naval Air Station near San Francisco, at Hurlburt Field (near Mary Esther, Florida), and at Eglin Field (near Valparaiso, Florida), present-day Eglin AFB, which was the actual base where the Doolittle Raiders trained. The filmmakers used USAAF B-25C and -D bombers, which were quite similar to the B-25B Mitchells used in the raid, further ensuring verisimilitude. Auxiliary Field 4 (aka Peel Field) was used for the short-distance take-off practice scenes. With the war still raging, an aircraft carrier was unavailable—the USS *Hornet* itself had been sunk in the Battle of the Santa Cruz Islands on 27 October 1942—but a mix of realistic studio sets and archival footage accurately re-created the USS *Hornet* scenes. Second-unit aerial cinematography featured Los Angeles masquerading as Tokyo and Santa Maria (between Pismo Beach and Santa Barbara) simulating the coast of China. The film was shot in sequence between April and June 1944.

Plot Summary

An opening title card reads: "One-hundred and thirty-one days after December 7, 1941, a handful of young men, who had never dreamed of glory, struck the first blow at the heart of Japan. This is their true story we tell here." After the attack on Pearl Harbor, the U.S. Army Air Force quickly hatches a plan to retaliate by bombing Tokyo and four other Japanese cities: Yokohama, Yokosuka, Nagoya, and Kobe. Tapped to lead the mission, Lt. Col. James Doolittle (Spencer Tracy) assembles an all-volunteer force. Their top-secret training involves learning to get their B-25 bombers airborne in the extremely short take-off distance of 500 feet or less—the deck length of an aircraft carrier. After depicting the training process at Eglin Field, Florida, and Naval Air Station Alameda (San Francisco Bay), the film depicts the raid and its aftermath. While en route to Japan, a Japanese picket boat detects the *Hornet*'s task force and reports its location by radio. The boat is sunk, but the bombers are forced to take off at the outer limit of their fuel range. Nonetheless, they make it to Japan and drop their bombs. After the attack, all but one of the bombers run out of fuel before reaching their recovery airfields on mainland China, either ditching in the sea or crash-landing along the coast. Lt. Ted Lawson (Van Johnson) tries to land his B-25 on a China beach but crashes in the surf in bad weather and darkness. Seriously injured, Lawson and his crew face a grueling transit back to American lines, led and aided by Chinese allies. While he is en route, Lawson's injuries are so severe that the mission's flight surgeon, Lt. Thomas "Doc" White (Horace McNally) has to amputate one of his legs. The story ends with Lawson being reunited with his wife, Ellen (Phyllis Thaxter), in a Washington, D.C., hospital.

Reception

Released on 15 November 1944, *Thirty Seconds Over Tokyo* enjoyed widespread critical acclaim and did well at the box office, eventually earning $6,247,000 in domestic and foreign ticket sales against a production budget of $2.9 million—a $1,382,000 profit, minus promotional expenses. Likewise, reviews were effusive. For example, Bosley Crowther called the movie "a stunning picturization of an episode crammed with drama and suspense. And so expert are the re-enacted film scenes that it is hard to distinguish them from a few news shots cut in. As a matter of fact, all of the production involving planes and technical action is so fine that the film has the tough and literal quality of an Air Force documentary . . . it is certainly a most stimulating and emotionally satisfying film" (Crowther, 1944).

Reel History Versus Real History

In general terms, the movie version of *Thirty Seconds Over Tokyo* is a faithful adaptation of Lawson's book, though the film widens its focus and presents a more evenly paced procedural history that recounts the planning of the raid, the pilot training, the voyage of the *Hornet*, the raid itself, and its aftermath. Lawson's understandably more subjective account devotes much more time to his ordeal in China after crash-landing and his recovery stateside. Other changes were made to conform to Hays Code strictures and for propaganda purposes. Trumbo's script passes over the extremely risky, even foolhardy, nature of the Doolittle mission that put half the U.S. Pacific Fleet in jeopardy on a mission of negligible military value. Accordingly, in the movie, the bomber pilots are excited to leave early when the task force is spotted by a Japanese patrol boat. In reality, the sighting meant that they would not have enough fuel to reach their destination airfields in China (i.e., the raid suddenly became a de facto suicide mission). An early departure also meant that the raid would have to occur in daylight hours, when the bombers were more vulnerable to being spotted and attacked by Japanese anti-aircraft fire and fighters. The film's depiction of Lawson's crash landing is historically accurate, though his injuries were actually far worse. Although the movie does pays tribute to the Chinese for their invaluable help in rendering medical aid to American fliers and getting them to safety, it completely elides the fact that Japanese occupation forces exacted a terrible retribution, costing a quarter million Chinese lives so that Americans could enjoy a short-lived boost in morale.

317TH PLATOON, THE [FRENCH: *LA 317ÈME SECTION*] (1965)

Synopsis

During the final days of the First Indochina War in Vietnam in 1954, a French army platoon isolated behind enemy lines tries to rejoin friendly forces farther south. It is led by an inexperienced, idealistic sous-lieutenant (played by Jacques Perrin), assisted by adjutant Willsdorf (Bruno Cremer), a battle-hardened WWII veteran of the Werhmacht.

Background

A volunteer cameraman for the French Army's Cinematographic Service during the First Indochina War, director Pierre Schoendoerffer (1928–2012) was at the Battle of Diên Biên Phu (1954) and was captured when it fell to the Viet Minh. After spending four months as a prisoner of war, Schoendoerffer was repatriated to France and worked as a journalist for *Paris Match* and other magazines before becoming a filmmaker in the late 1950s. In 1963 Schoendoerffer published *La 317e section* (*The 317th Platoon*), a novel inspired by his war service in Indochina. Shortly thereafter, he undertook a film version of his book. Explaining his motivation many years later, Schoendoerffer said, "I was there with the troops on their long marches . . . I was injured, taken prisoner, and hit the rock bottom of human misery: three-quarters of my comrades didn't come back. They died on the road [and] in the camps . . . I lived through more than most people see in a lifetime. I felt a need to bear witness to that" (Museum of Modern Art, 2010). Schoendoerffer secured a modest production budget from French and Spanish co-producers Georges de Beauregard (Paris) and Benito Perojo (Madrid). He also managed to gain permission from Cambodian authorities to shoot his film in landscapes closely resembling the actual settings in Vietnam, though actually hundreds of miles farther south.

Production

To shoot *The 317th Platoon*, Schoendoerffer brought together a few actors and a dozen technicians, including his former his comrade-in-arms, Raoul Coutard (1924–2016), Jean-Luc Godard's cinematographer. Cambodian extras were hired to comprise the bulk of the "317th Platoon." The shoot occurred in 1964, in remote locations in northeastern Cambodia not far from where the borders of Cambodia, Laos, and Vietnam converge—and just a few miles from an American military base in Vietnam. Constrained by a low budget and influenced by French New Wave stylistics, Schoendoerffer opted to use guerilla shooting techniques. Everyone camped out at a forest location many miles from the airstrip where they landed, ate mostly rice, and shot mostly live ammunition because they had only been able to get a limited supply of blanks into Cambodia. The extreme economy of means imposed an aesthetic as well as moral rigor to the film that resulted in a stunning sense of realism. With his small crew in the middle of nowhere, Coutard was limited to bare-bones essentials: two Éclair Cameflex CM3 35-mm cameras (sometimes handheld, sometimes on a tripod, with night shots lit by a single magnesium flare), a Nagra III NP reel-to-reel tape recorder, and a generator to recharge batteries.

Plot Summary

On Tuesday, 4 May 1954, during the First Indo-China War, the 317th Platoon is ordered to abandon its isolated post at Luong Ba, on the Vietnam–Laos border, and proceed south to join up with another unit at Tao Tsai (a fictional version of Diên Biên Phu), a key French outpost. The 45-man 317th Platoon is led by 2nd Lt. Torrens (Jacques Perrin), a young and inexperienced officer who has arrived from training at Saint-Cyr, France, only a fortnight earlier. The rest of the unit is composed of two other Frenchmen, Sgt. Roudier (Pierre Fabre) and Cpl. Perrin (Manuel Zarzo); an Alsatian ex-Wehrmacht soldier, Warrant Officer Willsdorf (Bruno Cremer); a Laotian auxiliary sergeant, Ba Kut (Boramy Tioulong); and 40 other Laotian regulars. Tao Tsai is 150 kilometers (93 miles) to the south, and the long, dangerous trek involves traversing mountainous jungle terrain; crossing rice paddies, rivers, and enemy lines; and dealing with deadly enemy ambushes, monsoon rains, mud, and dysentery. Though he is smart and well trained, the idealistic Torrens is inexperienced in guerilla warfare. He often clashes with the tough, pragmatic Willsdorf, who has been in Vietnam for years and possesses a wealth of combat experience; he is not shy about challenging Torrens' decisions in the field. Willsdorf, who wants to avoid contact with the enemy and get to Tao Tsai as soon as possible, emphatically disagrees with Torrens' decision to mount a surprise attack on a Viet Minh column. The platoon wins the resulting firefight but now has several seriously wounded men on its hands. Anxious to get away from the enemy, Willsdorf tries to get Torren to leave the wounded behind but Torrens refuses. Taking along the wounded slows down the platoon and soon the enemy is barking at their heels. The group splits up, with Torren and the wounded going one way while Willsdorf and several Cambodian soldiers try to lead the enemy off their trail. Several days later the two parties meet farther down the trail. Willsdorf has managed to throw the pursuers off the scent, though he knows it will not be for long. Torrens now realizes that Willsdorf was right about the wounded; they have all died, and the platoon is now two days' hike behind where they should be on the trail. The group starts out again, only stopping for rest and food and to try and make radio contact to order a supply drop. The platoon is losing men with every clash they have with their pursuers. The soldiers finally reach Tao Tsai, only to discover that it has already fallen to the Viet Minh. They now need to head farther south to the next base and hope they can outpace the enemy. While stopping for a much-needed rest on Monday afternoon, 10 May 1954, the platoon is attacked by a large enemy force. Only five men—Willsdorf, a badly wounded Torrens, and three Cambodian troopers—escape the massacre alive. Torrens orders Willsdorf to leave him behind. Willsdorf complies, hands Torrens a grenade, and fades into the jungle with the three remaining troopers.

Reception

The 317th Platoon was released in France on 31 March 1965 and was screened at the 18th Cannes Film Festival three months later, where it shared the prize for best screenplay with another war film: Ray Rigby's *The Hill* (1965). *The 317th Platoon* opened in a few other European countries and film festivals and was shown on West German TV in 1968. Everywhere it played, the film garnered excellent reviews. Indeed, British war historian Antony Beevor rates it the best war movie ever made (Carey, 2009). But the film never had a theatrical screening in the United States during the time of its initial release, made no money, and was largely forgotten—until 45 years later, when La Cinémathèque Française and StudioCanal, with the support of The Franco-American Cultural Fund, undertook a painstaking digital restoration overseen by Schoendoerffer and Coutard, now elderly men near the end of their lives.

Reel History Versus Real History

A survivor of the Battle of Diên Biên Phu, Pierre Schoendoerffer was intimately familiar with the look, smell, and feel of combat in Vietnam. With *The 317th Platoon* Schoendoerffer and his cinematographer, Raoul Coutard, created an utterly convincing cinematic representation of the First Indo-China War that achieves the highest level of historical authenticity.

THREE KINGS (1999)

Synopsis

Three Kings is an American war film/black comedy written and directed by David O. Russell from a story idea by John Ridley. The film stars George Clooney, Mark Wahlberg, Ice Cube (aka O'Shea Jackson Sr.), and Spike Jonze as four U.S. Army soldiers on a quest for stolen gold in the midst of the 1991 uprisings in Iraq against Saddam Hussein following the end of the First Gulf War.

Background

In the annals of Hollywood the creative genesis of *Three Kings* is unique. In July 1995 John Ridley, an African American stand-up comic turned screenwriter, undertook an experiment to see how fast he could write and sell a film. He wrote a screenplay entitled "Spoils of War" in seven days. Eighteen days later he sold it to Warner Bros. In May 1997 filmmaker David O. Russell (*Flirting With Disaster*) saw a brief description of Ridley's script ("Heist set in the Gulf War") in the Warner Bros.' script log. Inspired by the concept, Russell spent the next 18 months researching and writing his own, original script based on the same broad premise (Russell claims he never read Ridley's screenplay but the two reached a private agreement, with Ridley being given a "story by" and co-producer credit for his idea). After securing a $48 million production deal with Warner Bros., Russell sought to cast the lead role of Archie Gates, which was originally written with Clint Eastwood in mind. After Eastwood passed on it, it was offered to Nicolas Cage, Mel Gibson, Jack Nicholson, Nick Nolte, and Dustin Hoffman. They all turned it down, whereupon Russell revised the role as a younger character and reluctantly cast George Clooney. A star on the hit television series *ER* since its inception in 1994, Clooney was ready to quit TV and transition to film work. He was very much taken with the *Three Kings* script and lobbied hard for the role. Russell wrote the part of Conrad Vig for film and music video director-producer Spike Jonze, even though he had never acted in a film before. The rapper Ice Cube (*Boyz n the Hood*) was cast as Chief Elgin, Mark Wahlberg (*The Basketball Diaries*) as Troy Barlow, and *Saturday Night Live* alumna, Nora Dunn, as Adriana Cruz.

Production

The opening scene of *Three Kings* was filmed on a dry lake bed outside Mexicali, Mexico, but most of the film was shot in Arizona, near the abandoned Sacaton Copper Mine, about six miles northwest of Casa Grande, between Tucson and Phoenix, where toxic mining chemicals had wiped out all vegetation. Facsimile Iraqi villages were constructed on a high plateau composed of tailings left over after the extraction of the mineral ore. Many of the extras were played by actual Iraqi refugees, all of whom were recruited from the Iraqi community in Dearborn, Michigan (called

"The Arab Capital of North America"). The shoot proved to be an unusually rocky one. Still filming episodes of *ER* in Los Angeles three days a week, an increasingly exhausted Clooney was working on the shoot in the Arizona desert the other four days. For his part, Russell was under enormous pressure, shooting his first big-budget Hollywood film—a nerve-wracking challenge that made him irritable and petulant, especially toward extras and crew members. Clooney came to loathe Russell, whom he would later describe as "vulnerable and selfish," and the two began to clash verbally. Eventually the on-set tension erupted into a fistfight. Witnessing the altercation, a disgusted Paul Bernard (assistant director) walked off the set, never to return. The conflict was kept under wraps at the time but word of it later surfaced in the October 2003 issue of *Vanity Fair* in a cover story on Clooney.

Plot Summary

In March 1991, following the end of the Persian Gulf War, U.S. soldiers are sent over for mop-up operations. They throw rowdy parties out of boredom—a result of inaction. Maj. Archie Gates (George Clooney), a U.S. Army Special Forces soldier, swaps sex for stories with a news journalist, Cathy Daitch (Judy Greer). While processing a captured Iraqi officer, U.S. Army Reserve Sergeant First Class Troy Barlow (Mark Wahlberg) and his best friend, Pfc. Conrad Vig (Spike Jonze), find a hidden map on the captive's person. Troy consults with Staff Sergeant Chief Elgin (Ice Cube) to interpret the map. Maj. Gates joins in and convinces the others that the map shows the way to stolen gold bullion from Kuwait and that they should steal the gold for themselves. To keep meddling TV news reporter Adriana Cruz (Nora Dunn) at bay, Gates has Specialist Walter Wogeman (Jamie Kennedy) give her an incorrect lead to follow. The next day the men arrive at the bunker indicated on the map, where they find the gold and luxury goods plundered from Kuwait and stumble on Amir Abdullah (Cliff Curtis) being interrogated and tortured. The crew stays to fight for the Iraqi prisoner's freedom and gets involved in a firefight. They retreat right before reinforcements arrive, but happen upon a minefield and become separated. Troy is captured by Iraqi soldiers, and the remaining Americans are rescued by local rebels and ushered to an underground hideout. There, Conrad, Chief, and Archie make a deal with the rebels, offering to help their families if they are first allowed to rescue Troy. Troy is brought back to a bunker and tossed in a room filled with Kuwaiti cell phones. He is able to phone his spouse and ask her to report his location, but he is cut off when the soldiers drag him to an interrogation room and have Iraqi Captain Saïd (Saïd Taghmaoui) torture him. The other Americans eventually free Troy, who spares Saïd, and finds Shi'ite dissidents being imprisoned in a dungeon. A few of the Iraqi soldiers who initially fled return, shooting Conrad and Troy. Conrad dies, but Troy survives the shots. Archie arranges transport, while the inept officers in the camp try to find the three soldiers after hearing from Troy's wife. Each of the rebels receives a bar of gold for his services, and the remaining gold is buried. The convoy reaches the Iranian border, and the Americans attempt to escort the rebels to Iran, but new American officers arrive and arrest the three soldiers while recapturing the rebels. Archie tries to bribe the officers, but they respond by saying that charges will be brought against Archie, Troy, and Chief Elgin. In an epilogue, the film states that the three surviving soldiers (Archie, Troy, and Chief Elgin) have been cleared of the charges and honorably discharged, thanks to Adriana's reporting. The epilogue goes on to show Archie and Chief working for Hollywood as military advisors and Troy back home with his family, running a carpet store. The stolen gold has been given back to Kuwait, which claims that some is missing, implying that some pilfering has occurred.

Reception

Three Kings had its U.S. premiere on 27 September 1999—eight years after the first Gulf War (1990–91) and three and a half years before the Second Gulf War (2003–2011). The movie went into general domestic release on 1 October 1999. It grossed $60.7 million domestically and $47.1 million in foreign markets for a worldwide total of $107.8 million: a very handsome profit. *Three Kings* also received almost universal critical acclaim. Roger Ebert gave the film four stars out of four and said that "*Three Kings* is one of the most surprising and exciting movies I've seen this year . . . a weird masterpiece, a screw-loose war picture that sends action and humor crashing head-on into each other and spinning off into political anger" (Ebert, 4 October 1999). David Edelstein also sang the movie's praises and noted that its exciting, audacious visual style has already been expropriated by the U.S. military for promotional purposes: "Even if someone regards Mr. Russell as a propagandist for the enemy, it hasn't stopped the military from swiping his visual palette and his syntax [for recruitment ads] . . . Whatever elements of *Three Kings* may have been appropriated for militaristic ends, however, the original will never lose its power to shock. It remains the most caustic anti-war movie of this generation" (Edelstein, 2003). President Bill Clinton screened *Three Kings* at the White House on 14 October 1999 and, according to Roger Ebert, instantly became one of its biggest fans. "'I loved it,' Clinton said, 'because it accomplished all these different things. It's a great cheap-thrills movie. Clooney's unbelievable—the screen loves him, and all the other guys are good. It's a tragedy as well as a comedy . . . And they tell the very sad story that our country has to come to terms with—of how we falsely raised the hopes of Shiites in the south of Iraq. And what has been done to them since then . . . It's an atrocity what Saddam Hussein did to them'" (Ebert, 3 February 2000). Clinton's successor, George W. Bush, had a different take on the outcome of the First Gulf War. When Russell met Bush in 1999 and said he was editing a film he'd made that would question his father's legacy in Iraq, Bush replied, "Then I guess I'm going to have to finish the job, aren't I?"

Reel History Versus Real History

Three Kings tells a fictional story but from a historically truthful premise. David O. Russell:

> When I started investigating the war I only knew the official story—that we went to the Middle East and kicked Saddam Hussein out of Kuwait. But when

I looked at it more closely, I saw that Hussein was left in power and George Bush encouraged the Iraqi civilians to rise up against Hussein and said 'We'll help you do it.' And the people did rise up, and we didn't support them . . . and they got massacred by their own army. I thought that this would be an interesting backdrop for a story about a band of soldiers who go into this sur-real, corrupted Iraqi atmosphere after the war. They think Iraq is littered with cell phones, luxury cars and booty stolen from rich Kuwait, and they want to steal something for themselves. But they suddenly find a situation that com-pletely confronts their humanity and demands that they re-think what they're doing and who they are. Almost everything in the film is true. Saddam did steal all the gold from Kuwait, and it was missing for a long time. When he had to return it, some was missing . . . And many American soldiers were dissatis-fied about leaving Saddam in power and seeing him beat up his own people. (://urbancinefile.com.au/home/view.asp?a=3186&s=Features).

What Russell could not acknowledge is that his story constructs a Western liberal wish-fulfillment fantasy that uncritically posits a "white savior" cinematic trope, that is, the portrayal of a white character (Clooney's Archie Gates) rescuing people of color from their plight: an example of a paternalistic Orientalism that subtly undermines the film's putative good intentions.

TO HELL AND BACK (1955)

Synopsis
To Hell and Back is an American war film directed by Jesse Hibbs and starring Medal of Honor recipient Audie Murphy as himself. Based on Murphy's 1949 autobiog-raphy, the film recounts his combat exploits in the European Theater during World War II.

Background
Medal of Honor winner Audie Leon Murphy (1924–1971) killed 250 enemy sol-diers; he was the most decorated U.S. combat soldier in WWII and a celebrated national hero. When Universal-International purchased the film rights to Audie Murphy's memoir, *To Hell and Back* (1949, ghost writer: David "Spec" McClure) in June 1953, the studio approached Murphy to play himself. Concerned that taking the role would be perceived as self-aggrandizing, he initially declined, recommend-ing Tony Curtis instead, with whom he had previously co-starred in three West-erns. Producer Aaron Rosenberg and director Jesse Hibbs pressured Murphy to star in the picture, despite the fact that 31-year-old Murphy would be portraying himself as he was at ages 18 to 20—actually not a problem inasmuch as Murphy still had an unusually youthful appearance. Eventually Murphy relented and signed on.

Production
The movie was filmed at Fort Lewis and the Yakima Training Center, near Yakima, Washington, in the fall of 1954 with soldiers from the base serving as extras.

Murphy received 60 percent of the $25,000 the studio paid for the rights, as well as $100,000 and 10 percent of the net profits for starring in the picture and acting as a technical advisor. Several U.S. generals who served in World War II were considered for the role of performing the voice-over introduction to the movie, among them Maxwell Taylor and Omar Bradley. General Walter Bedell "Beetle" Smith was finally chosen for the role.

Plot Summary
Young Audie Murphy (Gordon Gebert) grows up in a large, poor sharecropper family in east Texas. His father deserts the family around 1939–1940, leaving his mother, Josie Belle (Mary Field), struggling to feed her nine children. Murphy starts working early in life to make money for his mother and siblings. When his mother dies, his siblings are sent to live with his oldest sister, Corrine (to whom Murphy will send his G.I. allotment pay). Following the attack on Pearl Harbor, Murphy attempts to enlist but is turned away by everyone except the Army. Murphy completes basic training and is posted with the 3rd Infantry Division in North Africa. As a result of his youthful appearance, he is the butt of many jokes about "infants" being sent into battle. Murphy proves himself, however, and is quickly promoted up the ranks. Having earned the distinction of second lieutenant, Murphy leads men into combat in Sicily, Italy, and France, forming friendships with fellow soldiers Johnson (Marshall Thompson), Brandon (Charles Drake), and Kerrigan (Jack Kelly). In January 1945, near Holtzwihr, France, Murphy's company is forced into a retreat by the Germans, but Murphy stays behind to cover for his men. As the Germans surround him, Murphy commandeers an abandoned M4 Sherman tank and riddles the enemy with machine-gun fire. Murphy single-handedly foils the German attack and saves his entire company. After being hospitalized for his wounds, Murphy returns to active duty. The film concludes with Murphy's Medal of Honor ceremony shortly after the war ends.

Reception
To Hell and Back had its gala world premiere at the Majestic Theatre in San Antonio, Texas, on 17 August 1955. The date was the 10th anniversary of Murphy's Army discharge at Fort Sam Houston, also in San Antonio. Surpassing expectations, the film garnered critical accolades, was an enormous commercial success—Universal's highest-grossing release until *Jaws* (1975)—and was a great boon to Murphy's film career and personal finances; it was estimated the actor earned $1 million from the film. The movie also popularized "dogface," a slang term for U.S. Army foot soldiers, mostly through the use of the 3rd Infantry Division song, "Dogface Soldier," written by Lt. Ken Hart and Cpl. Bert Gold. Many of the film's battle scenes were reused in the Universal film *The Young Warriors* (1967). Murphy tried to make a sequel called *The Way Back*, dealing with his postwar life, but could never produce a script that attracted financing.

Reel History Versus Real History
In general terms, *To Hell and Back* is a fairly accurate depiction of Murphy's war experiences. The only glaring departure from fact is the use of a Sherman tank in

place of what should have been an M10 "Wolverine" tank destroyer for the Medal of Honor combat scene (though more than 6,700 M10s were built during WWII, none were available in 1954, much to Murphy's chagrin). The film omits Murphy's two Silver Star–winning battles and renders the combat deaths of a number of his friends in rather melodramatic terms. The movie's main weakness, though, is due to the repressive requisites of patriotic Cold War ideology and the strictures of the Motion Picture Production Code (aka "Hays Code"), which forbade foul language and violence that was too explicitly bloody. Consequently the film sanitizes everything: American infantryman, the reality of combat, even the landscape and weather. Suffice to say that real soldiers are often grimy and their language is often bitterly profane. The soldiers' uniforms in *To Hell and Back* are always too clean and well pressed, and their banter is unrealistically genteel. Likewise, the combat scenes are action packed but largely devoid of blood and suffering; war-torn Europe seems far less damaged than expected; the weather conditions are too temperate and dry for Anzio in 1944 or Holtzwihr in 1945. Having tried his best to make the movie as authentic as possible, Audie Murphy was disappointed with the film, which he dismissed as nothing more than a "Western in uniform" that "missed by a mile." Most irksome to Murphy was the film's concluding scene, showing him being awarded the Medal of Honor and a raft of other Allied military decorations. His autobiography had excluded this event, and he would have preferred it omitted from the film as well, but he was overruled by the commercially savvy producers who knew that audiences would want to see the film end in triumphal celebration. Ultimately, though, what's most misleading about *To Hell and Back* is that it gives the impression that great heroism comes without devastating psychological damage. In point of fact Audie Murphy suffered from severe "battle fatigue" (post-traumatic stress disorder [PTSD]): lasting and deep psychological trauma manifested by chronic insomnia, survivor's guilt, a gambling addiction, mood volatility, scrapes with the law, and other problems that dogged him the rest of his life. He slept, or tried to sleep, with a loaded .45 under his pillow. "To become an executioner, somebody cold and analytical, to be trained to kill, and then to come back into civilian life and be alone in the crowd—it takes an awful long time to get over it," he told journalist Thomas Morgan in 1967. "Fear and depression come over you" (quoted in Martone, 2010, p. 151).

TWELVE O'CLOCK HIGH (1949)

Synopsis

Twelve O'Clock High is an American war film produced by Darryl F. Zanuck, directed by Henry King, and adapted by Sy Bartlett and Beirne Lay, Jr. from their 1948 novel of the same title. Starring Gregory Peck, Gary Merrill, and Dean Jagger, the film is about aircrews in the U.S. Army's Eighth Air Force flying daylight bombing missions against Nazi Germany and occupied France during the Second World War.

Background

In February 1942 United States Army Air Forces (USAAF) Brigadier General Ira C. Eaker was sent England to establish the U.S. Eighth Air Force to conduct daylight, high altitude "precision" bombing of Nazi Germany that was often far from precise. One of the staff officers accompanying Eaker was Bierne Lay, Jr., who served briefly as the Eighth Air Force's historian and film unit commander. Lay went on to command the 487th Bomb Group, was shot down, managed to evade capture, and returned to friendly lines and further service. After the war Lay, a freelance writer, resumed his civilian trade. In the spring of 1946 Sidney "Sy" Bartlett (born Sacha Baraniev), a screenwriter and another Eighth Air Force veteran, approached Lay and proposed that they collaborate on a novel and screenplay based on their war experiences. While Bartlett and Lay were in the midst of their labors, the air war in Europe was dramatized by yet another Eighth Air Force veteran, William Wister Haines, whose *Command Decision* appeared as a serialized novel in *Atlantic Monthly* (1946–1947), then as a successful Broadway play (1947–1948), and finally as an acclaimed 1948 movie, appropriately starring Clark Gable, a decorated air combat veteran in real life. Scooped but undaunted, Bartlett and Lay finished their work and sold the screenplay, entitled *Twelve O'Clock High*, to Darryl F. Zanuck's 20th Century Fox in February 1948 for a hefty $100,000. Four months later Harper & Bros. published the novel version, which earned mostly rave reviews and became a bestseller.

Production

The casting of the film's lead character, General Frank Savage, turned out to be an involved process. John Wayne was offered the part but turned it down, as did Clark Gable, who had already played essentially the same role in *Command Decision* (1948). Dana Andrews lobbied hard for the part but was ultimately passed over. Edmond O'Brien, Ralph Bellamy, Robert Preston, Burt Lancaster, James Cagney, Van Heflin, Robert Young, and Robert Montgomery were also considered before the role finally went to Gregory Peck in January 1949. Peck had initially refused the part because he found the script too similar to *Command Decision* but director Henry King persuaded him to change his mind. King also literally went the extra mile for location scouting. Flying his own private plane, King visited Eglin Air Force Base in the Florida panhandle on 8 March 1949 and found the perfect location for most of the shoot a few miles north of the main base, at Eglin Auxiliary Field No. 3 (aka Duke Field), where a control tower and 14 other buildings were later constructed to create the fictional RAF Archbury. On the recommendation of the film's technical advisor, Col. John deRussy, King chose Ozark Army Airfield near Daleville, Alabama, as the site for filming B-17 takeoffs and landings, including a spectacular B-17 belly-landing sequence, because the light-colored runways at Eglin did not match wartime runways in England, which were black macadam less visible to enemy aircraft. Additional background photography was shot at RAF Barford St. John in Oxfordshire, England, and at other locations around Eglin AFB and Fort Walton Beach, Florida. The crew used a dozen B-17s for filming, borrowed from Eglin and elsewhere, courtesy of the U.S. Air Force, which had pledged its full cooperation after vetting the script. Principal photography took place from late April to early July 1949. Though color would have been preferred, the film was shot in black and white to allow for the inclusion of actual air combat footage.

Plot Summary

Twelve O'Clock High focuses on the "hard luck" 918th Bomb Group stationed at Archbury in the English midlands. With the lowest bombing effectiveness, most aborted missions, and highest loss rates in the Eighth Air Force, the 918th suffers from abysmally low morale. Brigadier General Frank Savage (Gregory Peck), the tough-as-nails operations officer for General Pritchard (Millard Mitchell), head of Bomber Command, identifies the problem as emanating from the group's commander, Col. Keith Davenport (Gary Merrill), an otherwise "first-rate" commanding officer who has come to over identify with his men, fostering lax discipline and a group culture of self-pity. Accompanied by Savage, Pritchard visits Archbury, relieves the popular Davenport of command, and replaces him with Savage. A "by-the-book" disciplinarian—almost to the point of being a martinet—Savage

In a scene from *Twelve O'Clock High* (1949), Brig. Gen. Frank Savage (Gregory Peck, right) suffers a stress-induced nervous breakdown as (from left) Capt. Twombley (Lawrence Dobkin), Maj. "Doc" Kaiser (Paul Stewart), Maj. Harvey Stovall (Dean Jagger), and Col. Keith Davenport (Gary Merrill) look on. (Twentieth Century Fox/Photofest)

cracks down on the men of the 918th and is soon roundly despised. When all of the pilots ask for transfers, Savage has his trusted adjutant, Major Stoval (Dean Jagger), drag his feet on the paperwork in order to buy the time needed for the men to acclimate to Savage's new morale-building regimen. As the group recovers its self-confidence and combat effectiveness improves, the pilots change their minds and begin to warm to Savage's leadership. Piloting the lead plane, Savage leads the 918th on a crucial mission: to destroy a German ball bearing factory deep in enemy territory. The B-17s inflict heavy damage on their target, but a second strike is needed to finish it off. As Savage attempts to climb into his bomber to lead a second strike, he suffers a mental breakdown after many months of intense stress and emotional self-repression. As Major Stovall notes, "He swept his feelings under the carpet. It had to spill out." Nonetheless, 19 of 21 planes return from their mission, having "clobbered" their target: welcome news to Savage who begins to come out of his psychological fugue as the film ends.

Reception

Twelve O'Clock High had three U.S. premieres: one for the studio, at Grauman's Chinese Theater in Hollywood, on 21 December 1949 (with Gens. Armstrong, Eakins, and Curtis LeMay in attendance); another for the Air Force, at Offutt AFB in Omaha, Nebraska (hosted by Gen. LeMay, chief of the newly formed Strategic Air Command) on 16 January 1950; and an East Coast debut at the Roxy in New York City on 28 January 1950. The film went into general release in February 1950 to rave reviews and robust box office returns. The *Times* picked *Twelve O'Clock High* as one of the 10 Best Films of 1949. After attending the first premiere, General LeMay averred that he "couldn't find anything wrong with it." It was once required viewing at all the U.S. service academies, where it was used as a teaching example for Hersey-Blanchard Situational Leadership Theory. The film is still widely used in both the military and civilian worlds to teach the principles of supposedly effective leadership.

Reel History Versus Real History

Though a work of fiction, *Twelve O'Clock High* is firmly rooted in Eighth Air Force history, and many of its characters are loosely based on real people. The actual "hard-luck" group was the 306th Bomb Group at Thurleigh, which, multiplied by three, became the 918th at mythical Archbury. Gregory Peck's General Savage is based on General Frank A. Armstrong, Jr. (aka "The Fireman"). A troubleshooter for Eighth Air Force chief Ira Eaker, Armstrong was assigned to rebuild two underperforming Bomb Groups: the 67th in the fall of 1942 and the 306th in early 1943. (Unlike Savage, Armstrong did not crack up but was sidelined with bleeding ulcers.) Major General Pat Prichard is based on Eaker. Col. Keith Davenport is a kinder and gentler version of Col. Charles B. "Chip" Overacker, the obstreperous, incompetent first commander of the 306th Bombardment Group, who was fired by Eaker and replaced by Armstrong on 3 January 1943. Lt. Jessie Bishop (Robert Patten) is based on Lt. John Morgan, a B-17 co-pilot who was awarded the Medal of Honor for landing his B-17 after his pilot was severely wounded during a bombing run over Hanover, Germany, on 28 July 1943. Major Joe Cobb (John Kellogg) is based on Major (later Col.) Paul Tibbets, who later became famous as the pilot of the B-29 "Enola Gay," which dropped the atomic bomb on Hiroshima in 1945 (Tibbets himself served as a technical advisor for this movie). Sgt. McIlhenny (Robert Arthur) is based on Sgt. Donald Bevan, who was shot down over Germany in April 1943 and became a prisoner of war (POW). Bevan and fellow POW, Edmund Trzcinski, later co-wrote the play *Stalag 17*, which was made into a hit movie by Billy Wilder in 1953.

WALK IN THE SUN, A (1945)

Synopsis

A Walk in the Sun is a World War II American combat film based on the epony-mous novel by *Yank* writer Harry Brown. Adapted to the screen by Robert Rossen; directed by Lewis Milestone; and starring Dana Andrews, Richard Conte, George Tyne, John Ireland, Lloyd Bridges, and Sterling Holloway (with narration by Bur-gess Meredith), the film follows a U.S. Army platoon as it fights its way inland dur-ing the 1943 Allied invasion of Italy.

Background

Just after D-Day (June 1944), Alfred A. Knopf published *A Walk in the Sun*, a grip-ping combat novel by a 27-year-old *Yank* magazine staff writer named Harry Brown (1917–1986). Written in just two weeks, the book generated excellent reviews and impressed actor Burgess Meredith, who persuaded his friend, producer/director Samuel Bronston (coincidentally a nephew of Leon Trotsky), to undertake produc-tion of a film version. An adaptation was rushed out by screenwriter Robert Ros-sen (*Body and Soul*) so the film could appear before the war ended—an ambition unrealized; the movie was released on 3 December 1945, three months after VJ Day ended the Second World War.

Production

Upon review by Joseph Breen at the Hays Office, Rossen's script was cleansed of words like "virgin," "geez," "chunk of hell," and "bloody." Also vetting the script, the War Department called for changes that explained why a U.S. infantry platoon would assault a farmhouse defended by Wehrmacht machine gunners without recourse to bazookas to destroy the building. Scenes were added showing all the platoon's bazooka rockets being used up beforehand to take out enemy armor. Directed by Lewis Milestone (*All Quiet on the Western Front*), *A Walk in the Sun* was shot in the winter of 1944–1945 at Malibou Lake and the Conejo Valley between the Simi Hills and Santa Monica Mountains, 30 miles northwest of Los Angeles—terrain suitably similar to the topography near Salerno—but the shoot ran into unexpected production snafus at the outset: four straight days of rain in an area where precipitation is extremely rare. Money proved to be another headache. Just days into shooting Samuel Bronston ran out of funds, abrogating a distribution deal with United Artists and forcing a shooting hiatus as Milestone scrambled to find alternative financing and distribution. Luckily, he secured a new backer: Johnny

Fisher, a con man and former bootlegger turned bookie and Beverly Hills bar owner (he owned The Nineteenth Hole on Melrose Avenue). Fisher came up with the money—probably laundered gambling proceeds from Las Vegas—but stipulated that he populate the film with his own extras in order to keep his investment under surveillance (Lloyd and Parker, 1993, pp. 95–96). With $750,000 in financing secured, Milestone brokered a new distribution contract with Darryl Zanuck's 20th Century Fox and the shoot resumed. Principal photography on *A Walk in the Sun* wrapped on 5 January 1945.

Plot Summary

During the pre-dawn hours of 3 September 1943 the 53 soldiers comprising Lee Platoon of the 26th Infantry ("Texas") Division are on a landing barge approaching the beaches near Salerno, Italy, as part of the Allied invasion of Italy ("Operation Avalanche"). The platoon commander, Lt. Rand (Robert Lowell), is hit by shrapnel that takes off half of his face. Platoon Sgt. Pete Halverson (Matt Willis) assumes command and orders Sgt. Eddie Porter (Herbert Rudley) to lead the men to the beach while he tries to find the captain and confirm their orders. McWilliams (Sterling Holloway), a medic, remains with Rand while the rest of the unit disembarks and digs in, doing what he can to avoid machine-gun fire. At sunrise, the men are ordered into the surrounding woods to seek shelter from the strafing by Nazi fighter planes. Tyne intends to wait on the beach for his comrades, but is informed that both Rand and Halverson are dead. Soon after, McWilliams dies in a strafing attack. Entering the woods, Tyne finds three men hit by gunfire, including Sgt. Hoskins who was the senior surviving noncommissioned officer (NCO). Hoskins' wound takes him out of the war, and Porter, as senior NCO, is forced to take command. Hoskins warns Tyne to keep an eye on Porter, who is showing signs of combat fatigue. Porter, Tyne, and Sgt. Ward (Lloyd Bridges) then lead the men in three squads along a road toward a bridge six miles inland that they're ordered to destroy. An enemy fighter plane strafes the platoon; they run for cover to a nearby ditch but sustain several casualties. The men encounter two Italian soldiers in retreat, who surrender and warn the squads that German troops control the road and surrounding area. Soon thereafter, the platoon meets a small reconnaissance patrol of U.S. soldiers. A patrolman takes a motorcycle to a nearby farmhouse to investigate, offering to report back. Tyne tells the men to "take ten" while he sits with Porter, who is beginning to break down completely as the motorcyclist fails to return, and tells Ward that he is putting Tyne in charge. When a German half-track approaches, Tyne commands his men to attack it with hand grenades and machine-gun fire. The bazooka men, who had been sent ahead, destroy two tanks and another half-track, but use all their bazooka rockets in the process. Leaving a man to guard Porter, Tyne orders his men to advance. The soldiers make it to the farmhouse, but Germans open fire and two men are killed. Tyne and Ward are stymied. Windy (John Ireland) suggests going around the farm by way of the river and blowing up the bridge. Tyne sends two patrols, one headed by Ward and another by Windy, to reach the bridge. Once Rivera opens covering fire Tyne and his men go over the stone wall and into the field in a frontal assault on the farmhouse. On his way to the house, Tyne discovers the body of Rankin (Chris Drake), one of the men killed earlier, still holding his Thompson submachine gun lovingly in his arms. The bridge is destroyed, and the platoon manages to capture the farmhouse as well. Then, at exactly noon, Windy, Ward, and the surviving men wander through the house as Ward fulfills his dream of eating an apple while Tyne adds another notch to the butt of Rankin's Tommy-gun.

Reception

Because it was released after the war ended, *A Walk in the Sun* did not do as well at the box office as was hoped; having just lived through four savage years of it, Americans were sick of war—and war films. Most reviews were favorable, but Bosley Crowther's assessment in the *New York Times* was more measured. Crowther pronounced *A Walk* "unquestionably one of the fine, sincere pictures about the war" but one that "falls considerably short of the cumulative force" of the novel upon which it was based: "the transcendent bomb-burst of emotion which forms the climax of the book is not achieved" (Crowther, 1946).

Reel History Versus Real History

Due to wartime exigencies the U.S. military could supply Milestone's film with only a single U.S. Army M3 half-track masquerading (poorly) as a German Sd.Kfz. 251 half-track and a P-51 fighter imitating a German fighter plane. The film gets some smaller details wrong, for example, the actors keep their helmets on with chinstraps fastened: a practice shunned by real G.I.s for fear that a strapped-on helmet might snap a man's neck if shock waves from a nearby shell explosion pulled it away with enough force. The film also depicts soldiers pulling out grenade pins with their teeth. In reality, strong steel cotter pins made this Hollywood cliché an impossible feat that would only result in severe dental damage. Sam Fuller, a decorated WWII veteran (and future director-producer of *The Steel Helmet* and other war films) found more egregious violations of verisimilitude. In June 1946 Fuller wrote to Lewis Milestone to express his "keen disappointment" with *A Walk in the Sun*. Hoping *A Walk* would be a World War II version of Milestone's superlative *All Quiet on the Western Front*, Fuller found the latter movie rife with "shabby forced remarks made by riflemen," a lack of suspense, and lots of implausible action: "A bridge? A bridge six miles from the beach with two Krauts pulling guard duty? On the morning of the invasion? A house . . . with Kraut machine-gunners? When the Krauts had months, years to put up a camouflaged pillbox, move in with women and kids? A house with Krauts manning a couple of machineguns six miles from the beach the morning of an invasion? Advance armored recon car tearing through a road, evidently Kraut armor somewhere in the rear—all that hell—and two Kraut guards on the bridge, goose-stepping. Oh Mr. Milestone!" (Quoted in Cull, 2000, pp. 82–84).

WE WERE SOLDIERS (2002)

Synopsis

We Were Soldiers is an American war film that dramatizes the Battle of Ia Drang in November 1965, during the Vietnam War. Directed by Randall Wallace and starring Mel Gibson, the film is based on the book *We Were Soldiers Once . . . And Young* (1992) by Lieutenant General (Ret.) Hal Moore and reporter Joseph L. Galloway, both of whom were at the battle.

Background

The Battle of Ia Drang (14–18 November 1965) was the first major set-piece battle between U.S. Army forces and regulars of the Vietnam People's Army (PAVN) during the Vietnam War. The two-part battle took place at two adjacent landing zones (LZs) west of Plei Me in the Central Highlands of South Vietnam. While being ferried to LZ X-Ray by Huey helicopters, the 450 men of 1st Battalion, 7th Cavalry were attacked by a much larger force of PAVN. After two days and nights of heavy fighting (14–16 November 1965), the Americans were able to hold out and survive as a unit. On 17 November the North Vietnamese ambushed and obliterated the 2nd Battalion, 7th Cavalry near LZ Albany. In the end, both sides suffered heavy casualties; the U.S. side had about 300 soldiers killed, and the North Vietnamese lost more than 1,000 men. Twenty-five years later, after a research trip to Vietnam with Lt. Gen Harold "Hal" Moore (USA-Ret.), the commander at LZ X-Ray, Joe Galloway (the only journalist present at the battle), published "Vietnam Story," a detailed account in *U.S. News & World Report* that earned a 1990 National Magazine Award. Galloway and Moore expanded Galloway's article into a book: *We Were Soldiers Once . . . And Young: Ia Drang—The Battle That Changed the War in Vietnam* (1992). Published a year after the stunning success of "Operation Desert Storm"— when renewed pride in American military prowess made the public more receptive to the ideological rehabilitation of the Vietnam-era soldier—*We Were Soldiers* sold an astonishing 1.3 million copies. Randall Wallace, a former seminarian from Tennessee turned novelist/filmmaker, read the book and was captivated by it. He approached Moore and Galloway to option the film rights in the fall of 1993, which they sold to him in 1995, some months before the release of Mel Gibson's *Braveheart*, a property written by Wallace, which made him a Hollywood force to reckon with.

Production

Having written the screenplay, Randall Wallace co-produced *We Were Soldiers* (with Mel Gibson's partners at Icon Entertainment, Bruce Davey and Stephen McEveety). Wallace also directed the film—his second directorial effort after *The Man in the Iron Mask* (1998)—and cast Mel Gibson, the star of *Braveheart*, to play Lt. Col. Moore. After Wallace had his key players meet their real-life counterparts, he put the cast through a Hollywood version of boot camp at Fort Benning, Georgia. With cinematography by Dean Semler (an action movie specialist and frequent Mel Gibson collaborator), *We Were Soldiers* was shot between 5 March and 30 June 2001. The battle scenes were filmed at Fort Hunter Liggett, a 167,000-acre Army training reservation in Monterey County 150 miles south of San Francisco that doubled for South Vietnam's Central Highlands. Training scenes were filmed at Fort Benning, and domestic scenes were shot in Pasadena.

Plot Summary

Prologue: during the final year of the First Indochina War (1954), Viet Minh forces ambush a French army unit on patrol and wipe it out. Cut to Fort Benning, 12 years later. U.S. Army Lt. Col. Hal Moore (Mel Gibson) is chosen to train and lead a newly created air cavalry battalion. Soon after arriving in Vietnam, Moore's unit is ferried into the Ia Drang Valley by helicopters at a site that turns out to be the base camp for North Vietnamese Army units totaling some 3,000 men. After arriving in the area, a platoon of soldiers led by 2nd Lt. Henry Herrick (Marc Blucas) is ambushed. Herrick and several others are killed and the surviving platoon members are surrounded. Sgt. Ernie Savage (Ryan Hurst) takes over the command and utilizes the darkness to keep the Vietnamese from taking over their position. Meanwhile, helicopters constantly drop off reinforcements. On the second day of the battle, the outnumbered U.S. force keeps the enemy at bay using artillery, mortars, and helicopter airlifts of supplies and reinforcements. The PAVN commander, Lt. Col. Nguyen Huu An (Duong Don), orders a large-scale attack on the American position. On the verge of being overrun by the enemy and with no options left, Moore orders 1st Lt. Charlie Hastings (Robert Bagnell), his Forward Air Controller, to call in "Broken Arrow" (an emergency call for all available combat aircraft to attack enemy positions, even those close to U.S. lines). The aircraft strafe, bomb, and napalm the enemy, killing many PAVN and Viet Cong troops. The second Vietnamese attack is stopped, and the surviving U.S. soldiers, led by Sgt. Savage, are brought to safety. Back in the United States, Hal Moore's wife, Julia (Madeleine Stowe), has taken on a leadership role among the soldiers' wives on base. Meanwhile, Moore's unit organizes, stabilizes the area, and waits at the bottom of a hill. Lt. Col. An organizes a final siege on the American troops and sends most of his own to stage the assault. The Vietnamese get in position, but Hal Moore and his men go on the offensive, charging forward with fixed bayonets. Before the Vietnamese can fire, Major Bruce P. "Snake" Crandall (Greg Kinnear) and other men in helicopters gun down the Vietnamese. An is forced to evacuate his headquarters. With their objective reached, Moore and his men return to the LZ for pickup. The film ends with the revelation that the landing zone reverted to the North Vietnamese as soon as the American troops departed.

Reception

Made at an estimated cost of $75 million, *We Were Soldiers* did quite well at the box office: $78 million in domestic receipts and $36.5 million in foreign ticket sales for a total of $114.6 million—a healthy profit after promotion expenses. The critical response was, however, mixed. Many mainstream film reviewers lauded the movie's graphic simulated realism, narrative coherence, and even-handed depiction of the soldiers on both sides of the fighting. However, some critics found *We Were Soldiers* clumsy and ideologically suspect, that is, rife with John Wayne–era war clichés and nationalistic righteousness obviously designed to revise the image of the Vietnam War in the popular imagination and glorify the U.S. soldier—while studiously avoiding any hint that the war was misguided or, worse yet, a catastrophic exercise of American imperialism. Indeed, the film's right-wing pedigree was amply demonstrated when President George W. Bush held a private screening of *We Were Soldiers* at the White House on 26 February 2002 (three days before its national release). In attendance were Moore, Galloway, Wallace, Gibson, and other cast members, spouses, and studio executives, as were Vice President Dick Cheney, Secretary of State Colin Powell, National Security Advisor Condoleezza Rice, and Secretary of Defense Donald Rumsfeld. In all the patriotic hoopla, no one seemed to notice the exquisite irony of the occasion. Whereas Moore, Galloway, and Powell were genuine Vietnam War veterans ("heroes," if you will), hawkish ideologues Wallace, Bush, Cheney, and Rumsfeld carefully avoided Vietnam, though all of them could have served.

Reel History Versus Real History

Although much of the relentless combat action depicted in the film is accurate in broad terms, the decisive, culminating bayonet charge led by Lt. Col. Moore is a total, absurd fabrication. In point of fact, the North Vietnamese broke off the engagement of their own accord but not before wiping out Moore's sister battalion, the 2/7, at LZ Albany—a crushing American defeat expunged from the movie for obvious reasons. Historian Maurice Isserman plausibly suggests that the mythical bayonet charge in *We Were Soldiers* was meant to evoke *Gettysburg* (1993): "Actor Sam Elliott, who plays a tough and gravelly voiced master sergeant [Basil L. Plumley] in *We Were Soldiers*, had played a tough and gravelly voiced cavalry officer [Brigadier General John Buford] in the earlier film. As a casting choice, Elliot's presence works at a subconscious level, and probably intentionally, to link the two films and the battles they depict in the audience's mind" (Isserman, 2002). Isserman goes on to characterize *We Were Soldiers* as an "idealized, abstracted, and ultimately cynically manipulative fantasy of generic American heroism under fire."

WINTER WAR, THE [FINNISH: *TALVISOTA*] (1989)

Synopsis

The Winter War is a Finnish war film written and directed by Pekka Parikka. Based on *The Winter War*, a novel by Antti Tuuri, the film tells the story of a platoon of reservists from Kauhava (central Finland), part of an infantry regiment from Southern Ostrobothnia, fighting the Red Army on the Karelian Isthmus.

Background

Just after the start of the Second World, the Soviet Union tried to bully neighboring Finland into ceding territory. The Finns chose to fight instead. The resulting Winter War (30 November 1939–13 March 1940) between Finland and Russia was the ultimate David and Goliath conflict—except, of course, that Goliath won. Actually it was a foregone conclusion that the Soviets would win, given their overwhelming superiority in war matériel and manpower, but the Finns put up a remarkable fight. During the war's 105 days, they inflicted a third of a million casualties (including at least 150,000 dead) on the Russian invaders—five times that of Finnish losses. Nearly a half-century later prolific Finnish writer/filmmaker Antti Tuuri published *Talvisota* [*The Winter War*] (1984), a terse and gripping historical novel about the conflict that follows soldiers from his hometown of Kauhava as they fight and die on the Mannerheim Line in Karelia. Based on authentic war diaries, interviews with veterans, and other firsthand sources, Tuuri's book strove for a high degree of historical accuracy. Taken with Tuuri's novel, Finnish TV director Pekka Parikka secured the film rights and teamed with Tuuri to adapt his book to the screen, in collaboration with producer Marko Röhr through the Helsinki-based studio, National-Filmi Oy.

Production

Filming of *The Winter War* began in October 1988 and ended in April 1989. The film was shot on location at the following sites: Kauhava (the Hakalas' hometown, in the Southern Ostrobothnia region of Western Finland); Kankaanpää (in southwestern Finland); Seinäjoki (in Southern Ostrobothnia); Ristiina (in southeastern Finland); Keuruu (in south-central Finland); Lapua (in Southern Ostrobothnia), and Hyvinkää (in the Uusimaa region, 30 miles north of Helsinki). The original budget of 13 million Finnish marks went up to 19 million FIM (€5.3 million in 2017 or $6 million in 2017 dollars): the most costly Finnish film to date.

Plot Summary

The date is 13 October 1939. The Soviet Union has demanded territorial concessions from Finland. The Finns have sent J. K. Paasikivi, their ambassador to Sweden, to Moscow to negotiate with the Russians to try to avert a war. In the meantime, Finland mobilizes its armed forces. Martti Hakala (Taneli Mäkelä) and his younger brother, Paavo (Konsta Mäkelä), report to their local military induction station in Kauhava, where they are outfitted with uniforms and weapons. They then join the rest of the Finnish Army's 23rd Regiment. An officer informs them they'll be going on training maneuvers. After bidding farewell to loved ones, the men board a train headed to Seinäjoki, 25 miles south. Yrjö "Ylli" Alanen (Esko Nikkari) a 50-year-old veteran of the Finnish Civil War (1918), counsels the young soldiers, teaching them a few fundamentals about warfare (e.g., that the men will have to fight waves of Soviet attacks one after the other). Upon arrival, Martii asks his commanding officer if his brother, Paavo, can be placed in his squad with him; permission is granted. Their half-brother, Vilho Erkkilä (Heikki Paavilainen), is also assigned to the same unit. The soldiers vie for possession of a field kitchen, are issued dog tags, attend religious services, and then march off to board their train again, which now takes them 360 miles southeast to Karjalankannas (the Karelian Isthmus). Over the next day the men march to the Mannerheim Line and camp. Martii is attracted to a local woman. He ploughs her field—her husband had to report to the front before he had a chance—but discovers that Arvi Huhtala (Martti Suosalo) is also courting her. Paavo is also attracted to a local woman whose fiancé is at the front. The soldiers shore up fortifications as civilians are evacuated. Vääpeli Hannu Jutila (Kari Sorvali) tells Martti that the Soviet Union has invaded Finland and the war has started (30 November 1939). Lt. Col. Matti Laurila (Esko Salminen) addresses the men of Ostrobothnia six days later (6 December, i.e., Finland's Independence Day) and emphasizes that the Finns did not want war but vows that they will "not yield an inch" of ground to the invaders. The Finns come under Russian artillery bombardment, and "Ylli" Alanen is killed by shrapnel. After more shelling, the Soviets attack the Finnish lines across an open field with infantry, tanks, and air support. Ahti Saari (Ari-Kyösti) is shot dead but the attack is repelled. The next morning the Russians attack again, this time digging their way into the Finnish trenches. Hand-to-hand combat with bayonets ensues as the Finns retake the trenches. The Soviets launch another massed attack and drive the Finns back, but they soon mount a successful counterattack. During a night artillery barrage, Vilho Erkkilä panics and abandons his post—but returns to action after getting a placebo that calms his nerves. Paavo, slightly wounded, is given leave to Ostrobothnia. He tells his mother that "none of us will come back alive." After returning to the front, Paavo is blown to bits by a direct hit from an artillery shell as Martii looks on. The Finns repel more massed Soviet frontal assaults. At Christmas (1939), the men gather round a campfire and sing the "Angel of Heaven." At this point, Lt. Jaakko Rajala (Ville Virtanen) has become the new company commander, replacing Lt. Yrjö Haavisto (Vesa Mäkelä), who has been killed in combat. War-loving soldier Aatos Laitila (Markku Huhtamo) dies from a grenade explosion. After more attacks the Soviets have begun to occupy the Finnish lines. Rajala sends Martii to battalion headquarters to request reinforcements. The Soviets continue their assaults and Huhtala is killed. On 27 December the Russians halt their attacks on the Taipale front, and the Finns go to Yläjärvi for rest and recuperation. Martti goes on leave in Ostrobothnia and tells the family about Paul's death. When Martti returns to the front, the unit goes to Vuosalmi on the Vuoksi River near the village of Äyräpää. There the men fend off more Russian human-wave attacks. The film shows the ill-fated attack by the Men of Nurmo (5 March 1940). The fighting abruptly stops at eleven o'clock on the morning of 13 March 1940, when the armistice takes effect.

Reception

Released in Finland on 20 November 1989—the 50th anniversary of the start of The Winter War—*Talvisota* proved to be a major box office hit in its own country, posting 628,767 admissions in a nation of just 5 million people. It fared less well in other countries, where Finnish films have minimal profile. For example, although National-Filmi Oy lobbied hard with lots of advertisements in the American print media at Oscar time, the film did not receive a hoped-for Academy Award nomination for Best Foreign Film. Reviews, though scant, tended to be highly complementary. Film critic Kevin Thomas called the movie "a grueling, superb and altogether rewarding achievement, with glorious cinematography and exceptional sound. It has a tremendous, agonizing immediacy yet preserves a detached perspective throughout. It has a whopping 196-minute running time, yet is so absorbing that it does not seem overly long" (Thomas, 1989).

Reel History Versus Real History

Talvisota, both book and film, are historically accurate to an unusual degree; both are meticulously based on the actual combat history of 4th Company, 23rd Infantry Regiment, commonly known as "Laurilan Rykmentti" ["Laurila's Regiment"] after its commanding officer, Lt.-Col. Matti Laurila. As depicted in the film, Infantry Regiment 23 was mobilized by the Southern Pohjanmaa Military District; its 4th Company was a rifle company composed mostly of reservists from the municipality of Kauhava. As also depicted in the film, the regiment fought in the frontlines in Taipale for a total of 36 days in four separate stints: 17–27 December 1939; 7–16 January 1940; 27 January–5 February 1940; and 11–19 February 1940, spending the time in between these periods at rest. As also shown in the film, the 23rd was transferred to Äyräpää-Vuosalmi on the 27–28 February 1940, where it fought in the frontline for another 14 days, from 29 February–13 March 1940. In sum, the 23rd Regiment fought on the frontlines for a total of 50 days—almost half the duration of the war. At full strength it numbered 2,955 men. Of that number, 682 men were killed in action: a 23 percent fatality rate. The movie's depiction of constant shelling and a seemingly endless series of frontal assaults by Soviet troops is true to history. Excessive Russian losses due to poor tactics can be pinned on Stalin; he had many of his best officers killed off in political purges in the 1930s. As also reflected in the movie, Finnish soldiers were exceptionally well trained, resourceful, and disciplined; they made the Soviet invaders pay a terrible price.

Z

ZULU (1964)

Synopsis

Zulu is a 1964 war epic written by Cy Enfield and John Prebble, directed by Enfield, and produced by Enfield and Stanley Baker. Starring Stanley Baker and Michael Caine, the film depicts the Battle of Rorke's Drift (January 1879) when a small British Army detachment held off a much larger force of Zulu warriors during the Anglo-Zulu War.

Background

On 22–23 January 1879, during the Anglo-Zulu War (in the Natal Province of Cape Colony, part of present-day South Africa), a small British garrison of 150 men at Rorke's Drift—many of them sick and wounded—successfully held off a force of some 4,000 Zulu warriors bent on annihilating them. British casualties numbered 17 killed and 15 wounded, whereas the Zulus lost some 350 dead and 500 wounded. Ultimately 11 Victoria Crosses were awarded to the defenders of Rorke's Drift—a record number for a single engagement up to that time. Britain's Alamo-like victory was trumpeted in the home press, especially because it offset a humiliating defeat at the Battle of Isandlwana, which immediately preceded it. In that encounter a Zulu army of 20,000 attacked and destroyed a force of 1,800 British and colonial troops. Seventy-nine years later British journalist and popular historian John Prebble (writing under the pseudonym John Curtis) revived the memory of Rorke's Drift with an article entitled "A Slaughter in the Sun" (*Lilliput* magazine, April 1958). Inspired by Prebble's account, blacklisted expatriate American screenwriter-director Cyril "Cy" Enfield approached his friend and filmmaking colleague, Welsh actor Stanley Baker, and won Baker's enthusiastic support. After Endfield and Prebble completed a script, Baker showed it to American movie mogul Joseph E. Levine while both men were making Robert Aldrich's *The Last Days of Sodom and Gomorrah* in Italy in 1961. Seeing the potential for a blockbuster epic, Levine agreed to supply the lion's share of the picture's $1.75 million production budget under the aegis of Baker's production company, Diamond Films, Ltd.

Production

Photographed in "Super Technirama 70," an anamorphic process less grainy than Cinemascope that uses a wide-screen 2.35:1 aspect ratio, most of *Zulu* was shot on location in Royal Natal National Park in South Africa, about 90 miles southwest of the actual battle site, during the spring and summer of 1963. A replica of the

Lt. Gonville Bromhead (Michael Caine, left) and fellow British soldiers fight off attacking Zulu warriors in Cy Endfield's *Zulu* (1964). (Photofest)

mission depot at Rorke's Drift was constructed beneath the Amphitheatre (an imposing crescent-shaped massif of sheer basalt cliffs in the Drakensberg Mountains) while the set for the field hospital and supply depot at Rorke's Drift was built near the Tugela River with the Amphitheatre in the background. Interiors and some other scenes were shot at Twickenham Film Studios near London. South Africa's Apartheid government assisted in the production by supplying 80 white South African National Defence Force (SANDF) soldiers as extras. The Zulu nation also assisted by supplying hundreds of paid extras to portray their ancestors, but first Stanley Baker had to show the Zulu what a film was, as they had never seen one. He showed them a Gene Autry Western, at which they laughed hysterically. Baker also had to convince the Zulu that blank cartridges were harmless. Once they mastered the basics of acting (especially faking death in simulated combat), they performed extremely well.

Plot Summary

Opening voice-over narration by Richard Burton recounts the Zulu rout of Lord Chelmsford's British forces at the Battle of Isandlwana. In the aftermath, the victorious Zulus are shown walking among the scattered corpses of British soldiers and expropriating their Martini-Henry rifles. Messengers interrupt a mass Zulu marriage ceremony at Cetewayo witnessed by missionary Otto Witt (Jack Hawkins) and his daughter (Ulla Jacobsson) to inform Zulu King Cetshwayo kaMpande (Chief Mangosuthu Buthelezi) of the stunning victory. An understrength company of the British Army's 24th Regiment of Foot is using the missionary station of Rorke's Drift as a supply depot and army hospital for their invasion force across the border from Natal into Zululand. Natal Native Contingent (NNC) commander Lt. Gert Adendorff (Gert van den Bergh) brings news of the disaster at Isandlwana and warns that an impi (detachment) of 4,000 Zulu warriors is advancing on Rorke's Drift. Lt. John Chard (Stanley Baker) of the Royal Engineers assumes command of the tiny garrison when he determines that he is slightly senior to army officer Lt. Gonville Bromhead (Michael Caine) due to a slightly earlier commission date. Burdened with dozens of wounded soldiers, the men at Rorke's Drift cannot outrun the Zulus. Chard therefore decides to make a stand, using upended wagons and stacked mealie sacks and biscuit crates to improvise a defensive perimeter wall. Rev. Witt gets drunk and demoralizes the men with his dire predictions of wholesale slaughter, causing the small Natal Native Contingent to desert. Chard orders Witt locked in a supply room. As the Zulu army approaches, a 100-man detachment of Boer cavalry arrives but soon ride off to safety, after advising Lt. Chard that defending the station is hopeless. The Zulu army finally arrives on the scene and immediately attacks at multiple points. The British open fire and kill scores of Zulu warriors, but Adendorff informs them that the Zulus are only testing the strength of British firepower. Rev. Witt issues more dire predictions before escaping the battle with his daughter. Chard realizes that the next attack will likely come from at least two sides at once. Worried that the northern perimeter wall is undermanned, he orders soldiers from the southern perimeter to fill in the gaps. To the surprise of the British, Zulu warriors on the adjacent bluff start firing on the station with rifles captured from the British dead at Isandlwana. Throughout the day and into the night, wave after wave of Zulus attack but are always repelled. The Zulus succeed in setting fire to the hospital's thatched roof, leading to intense hand-to-hand combat between British patients and encroaching Zulu warriors. Private Henry Hook (James Booth) takes charge and leads the other patients to safety. The next morning, the Zulus approach Rorke's Drift and begin singing a Zulu war chant, prompting the British to respond by singing "Men of Harlech," a Welsh military march. Another attack ensues. Just as it seems the Zulus will finally overpower the exhausted defenders of Rorke's Drift, the British soldiers fall back to a small inner redoubt with walls constructed from stacked mealie bags. A reserve cadre of soldiers hidden within the redoubt form into three ranks and fire volley after volley at their onrushing foe; while one rank kneels to reload, another behind it stands and fires, and so on: a devastating machine-like barrage that inflicts carnage, causing the Zulus to break off the fight. After a pause of three hours, the Zulus reorganize into yet another phalanx. Expecting another assault that will likely destroy them, the British are astonished when the Zulus instead sing a song to honor the bravery of the defenders before quitting the field. The film ends with another solemn voice-over by Richard Burton, listing the 11 defenders who received the Victoria Cross for their courageous and resourceful defense of Rorke's Drift.

Reception

Zulu premiered at the Plaza Theatre at Piccadilly Circus in London on the 85th anniversary of the battle (22 January 1964). In general release, the movie received rave reviews and was one of the biggest box office hits of all time in the UK (U.S. box office returns were solid but not as spectacular). Remarkably, *Zulu* remained in constant theatrical circulation in Britain for the next 12 years before making its first appearance on television. It remains a favorite among war film aficionados on both sides of the Atlantic.

Reel History Versus Real History

Zulu represents the 24th Regiment of Foot as mainly Welsh. It was based at Brecon, South Wales, but only a quarter of its soldiers were actually Welsh; a third were British and the rest were from other parts of the UK. No one sang "Men of Harlech"; the regimental march in 1879 was "The Warwickshire Lads." The film depicts the entire battle as occurring in daylight hours, but much of the fighting transpired at night. Rev. Otto Witt, the Swedish missionary who originally owned Rorke's Drift, was unpopular, but not a drunk, and his daughter was a young child in 1879, not a grown woman. Nor was she present at Rorke's Drift. Actually present but omitted from the movie was the British padre, George "Ammunition" Smith (1845–1918), who played a vital part in the battle. The film also mischaracterizes a number of the combatants. Lt. Bromhead was quite deaf and not very bright. Commissary James Dalton (Dennis Folbrigge) is portrayed as weak and inept. In reality Dalton was instrumental in the decision to stay and fight and in the preparation of the defensive works. Pvt. Henry (Harry) Hook is depicted, at least initially, as a drunken malingerer when, in fact, he was an exemplary soldier and a teetotaler. Colour Sergeant Frank Edward Bourne was 5'6" and just 24 years old in 1879, but Nigel Green, the actor who portrays him, was 6'2" and 40 years of age. As for the battle itself, the Zulu attacks were more relentless and less coordinated than depicted in the film. Nor did the Zulu sing in praise of the courage of the defenders of Rorke's Drift at the end of the battle; they quietly withdrew from the field when Lord Chelmsford's approaching column was spotted in the pre-dawn hours. The movie also omits the fact that the British finished off scores of wounded Zulu warriors left behind on the battlefield: a grim reality that, if shown, would have detracted from British glory.

Bibliography

Adamovich, Ales. *Khatyn*. Tilburg, Netherlands: Glagoslav Publications Ltd., 2012.

Adamovich, Ales, Yanka Bryl and Vladimir Kolesnik. *Out of the Fire*. Moscow, USSR: Progress Publishers, 1980.

Adams, Guy. "The Real Hero of Dunkirk: Courage of the Pier-Master Who Manned a Crucial Jetty to Organise Evacuees for Six Days and Five Nights Without a Break." *Daily Mail*, 24 July 2017.

Agee, James. Review of *The Story of G.I. Joe*. *The Nation*, 15 September 1945.

Agee, James. Review of *They Were Expendable*. *The Nation*, 5 January 1946.

Alba, Victor and Stephen Schwartz. *Spanish Marxism versus Soviet Communism: A History of the P.O.U.M.* New Brunswick, Canada: Transaction Books, 1988.

Alexander, Harriet. "Why *Beasts of No Nation* Fails to Tell the Whole Story about Child Soldiers." *The Telegraph*, 16 October 2015.

Allen, Jim. "Bringing the Lessons Home: An Interview with Jim Allen Conducted in 1995." *World Socialist Web Site* (WSWS), 11 August 1999, www.wsws.org/en/articles/1999/08/alle-a11.html.

Ambrose, Stephen. *D-Day June 6, 1944: The Climactic Battle of World War II*. New York: Simon & Schuster, 1994.

Anonymous. "French Acquit Five Shot for Mutiny in 1915: Widows of 2 Win Awards of 7 Cents Each." *New York Times*, 2 July 1934.

Anonymous. Review of *The Cruel Sea*. *London Times*, 25 March 1953.

Anonymous. Review of *The Dam Busters*. *London Times*, 17 May 1955.

Anonymous. Review of *The Bridge on the River Kwai*. *London Times*, 2 October 1957.

Anonymous. Review of *The Dam Busters*. *London Times*, 29 December 1955.

Anonymous. Review of *The Guns of Navarone*. *London Times*, 27 April 1961.

Anonymous. Teachers Notes, *Land and Freedom*, Film Education, www.filmeducation.org/pdf/film/LandFreedom.pdf.

Anonymous. Review of *Cross of Iron*. *Variety*, 1 January 1977.

Anonymous. Review of *The Big Red One*. *Variety*, 31 December 1979.

Arnold, Edwin T. and Eugene L. Miller, eds. *Robert Aldrich: Interviews*. Jackson, MS: University Press of Mississippi, 2004.

Ballard, J.G. *Empire of the Sun*. London: Victor Gollancz, 1984.

Ballard, J.G. "The Real Empire of the Sun: JG Ballard on How His Childhood Inspired the Gripping War Film." *London Daily Mail*, 24 April 2009.

Baron, Lawrence. *Projecting the Holocaust into the Present: The Changing Focus of Contemporary Holocaust Cinema*. New York: Rowman & Littlefield, 2005.

Bean, C.E.W., ed. *Official History of Australia in the War of 1914–1918*. Volume I—The Story of ANZAC from the outbreak of war to the end of the first phase of the Gallipoli Campaign, May 4, 1915 (1921); Volume II—The Story of ANZAC from 4 May, 1915, to the evacuation of the Gallipoli Peninsula (1924). Sydney, Australia: Angus and Robertson/Australian War Memorial.

Beevor, Antony. *D-Day: The Battle for Normandy.* New York: Viking, 2009.

Berg, Rick. "Losing Vietnam: Covering the War in an Age of Technology," *Cultural Critique* 3, Spring 1986.

Biskind, Peter. "The Runaway Genius." *Vanity Fair,* August 1999.

Biskind, Peter. "The Vietnam Oscars." *Vanity Fair,* 19 February 2008.

Blay, Zeba. "How *Beasts of No Nation* Perpetuates Hollywood's Skewed View of Africa." *Huffington Post,* 16 Aug. 2015.

Boldt, Gerhard. *Hitler's Last Days: An Eye-witness Account.* Translated by Sandra Bance. London: Arthur Baker, 1973.

Bolloten, Burnett. *The Spanish Civil War: Revolution and Counterrevolution.* Chapel Hill, NC: University of North Carolina Press, 1991.

Boulle, Pierre. *The Bridge on the River Kwai.* London: Secker & Warburg, 1954.

Bowden, Mark. *Black Hawk Down: A Story of Modern War.* New York: Atlantic Monthly Press, 1999.

Bradley, James and Ron Powers. *Flags of Our Fathers.* New York: Bantam Books, 2000.

Bradley, Omar. *A Soldier's Story.* New York: Henry Holt, 1951.

Brickhill, Paul. *The Dam Busters.* London: Evans Brothers, Ltd., 1951.

Brickhill, Paul. *The Great Escape.* London: Faber and Faber, Ltd., 1950.

Brody, Richard. "Mel's Gibson's *Hacksaw Ridge*: Religious Pomp Laced with Pornographic Violence." *The New Yorker,* 3 November 2016.

Brooks, Norman. *Fragile Fox.* New York: Dramatists Play Service, 1980.

Brown, Harry. *A Walk in the Sun.* Reprint of 1944 edition: New York: Carroll & Graff, 1985.

Brownlow, Kevin. *David Lean: A Biography.* London: Faber & Faber, 1996.

Bruce, John. "How Lawrence of Arabia Cracked Up." [London] *Sunday Times,* 9 June 1968.

Buchheim, Lothar-Günther. *The Boat.* New York: Alfred A. Knopf, 1975.

Burchard, Peter. *One Gallant Rush: Robert Gould Shaw and His Brave Black Regiment.* New York: St. Martin's Press, 1965.

Canby, Vincent. Review of *A Bridge Too Far. New York Times,* 16 June 1977.

Canby, Vincent. Review of *Full Metal Jacket. New York Times,* 26 June 1987.

Canby, Vincent. Review of *Hamburger Hill. New York Times,* 28 August 1987.

Canby, Vincent. Review of *Platoon.* New York Times, 19 December 1986.

Canby, Vincent. Review of *Ran.* New York Times, 27 September 1985.

Canby, Vincent. Review of *Slaughterhouse-Five. New York Times,* 23 March 1972.

Canby, Vincent. Review of *The Big Red One. New York Times,* 18 July 1980.

Canby, Vincent. Review of *The Killing Fields. New York Times,* 2 November 1984.

Carey, Matthew. "D-Day Historian: 'Ryan' Not Best War Film." *CNN Entertainment,* 11 November 2009, http://edition.cnn.com/2009/SHOWBIZ/books/11/11/beevor .movies.dday/index.html.

Carlyon, Les. *Gallipoli.* New York: Doubleday, 2001.

Carmody, Jay. Review of *Men in War. Washington Evening Star,* 9 March 1957.

Cavagna, Carlo. "Interviews: *Downfall.*" AboutFilm, March 2005, http://www.aboutfilm .com/features/downfall/feature.htm.

Ceplair, Larry and Christopher Trumbo. *Dalton Trumbo: Blacklisted Hollywood Radical.* Lexington, KY: University Press of Kentucky, 2014.

Chung, Hye Seung. *Hollywood Asian: Philip Ahn and the Politics of Cross-ethnic Performance.* Philadelphia, PA: Temple University Press, 2006.

Clark, James. "Here's Why 'The Hurt Locker' Is the Worst War Movie of All Time." 2 July 2016, http://taskandpurpose.com/heres-hurt-locker-worst-war-movie-time/.

Clavell, James. *King Rat.* Boston: Little Brown & Company, 1962.

Cobb, Humphrey. *Paths of Glory.* New York: Viking Press, 1935.

Conrad, Joseph. *Heart of Darkness.* Reprint of 1899 edition: Limited Editions, New York, 1969.

Cooper, James Fenimore. *The Last of the Mohicans: A Narrative of 1757.* Philadelphia: H. C. Carey & I. Lea, 1826.

Cowan, Sam K. *Sergeant York and His People.* New York: Grosset & Dunlop, 1922.

Coward, Noël. *Noël Coward Diaries.* Edited by Graham Payne and Sheridan Morley. New York: De Capo Press, 2000.

Craig, William. *Enemy at the Gates: The Battle for Stalingrad.* New York: Reader's Digest/ Dutton, 1973.

Crist, Judith. Review of *The Great Escape. New York Herald Tribune,* 6 July 1963.

Crowe, David M. *Oskar Schindler: The Untold Account of His Life, Wartime Activities, and the True Story Behind the List.* New York: Westview Press, 2004.

Crowther, Bosley. Review of *A Walk in the Sun. New York Times,* 12 January 1946.

Crowther, Bosley. Review of *Battleground. New York Times,* 12 November 1949.

Crowther, Bosley. Review of *Guadalcanal Diary.* 18 November 1943.

Crowther, Bosley. Review of *Heaven Knows, Mr. Allison. New York Times,* 15 March 1957.

Crowther, Bosley. Review of *In Which We Serve. New York Times,* 24 December 1942.

Crowther, Bosley. Review of *Kanał. New York Times,* 10 May 1961.

Crowther, Bosley. Review of *King Rat. New York Times,* 28 October 1965.

Crowther, Bosley. Review of *Lawrence of Arabia. New York Times,* 17 December 1962.

Crowther, Bosley. Review of *Paths of Glory. New York Times,* 20 March 1957.

Crowther, Bosley. Review of *Pork Chop Hill. New York Times,* 30 May 1959.

Crowther, Bosley. Review of *Sahara. New York Times,* 12 November 1943.

Crowther, Bosley. Review of *The Bridge. New York Times,* 2 May 1961.

Crowther, Bosley. Review of *The Bridge on the River Kwai. New York Times,* 19 December 1957.

Crowther, Bosley. Review of *The Great Escape. New York Times,* 8 August 1963.

Crowther, Bosley. Review of *The Guns of Navarone. New York Times,* June 23, 1961.

Crowther, Bosley. Review of *The Longest Day. New York Times,* 5 October 1962.

Crowther, Bosley. Review of *Thirty Seconds Over Tokyo. New York Times,* 16 November 1944.

Cull, Nicholas J. "Samuel Fuller on Lewis Milestone's *A Walk in the Sun* (1946): The Legacy of *All Quiet on the Western Front* (1930)." *Historical Journal of Film, Radio and Television* 20.1 (2000).

Dapkus, Liudas. "On Location in Eastern Europe; the Region's Landscape and Its Cost Savings Entice Filmmakers to Scout There." *Los Angeles Times,* 21 December 2007.

Dargis, Manohla. "*Dunkirk* Is a Tour de Force War Movie, Both Sweeping and Intimate." *New York Times,* 20 July 2017.

Darrack, Ed. *Victory Point: Operations Red Wings and Whalers—the Marine Corps' Battle for Freedom in Afghanistan.* New York: Berkley Books/Penguin, 2009.

Darrack, Ed. "Operation Red Wings—What Really Happened?" *Marine Corps Gazette,* January 2011.

Davis, Ronald L. *Duke: The Life and Image of John Wayne.* Norman, OK: University of Oklahoma Press, 1998.

Deseler, Graham. "Kangaroo Court: On Bruce Beresford's *Breaker Morant.*" *Bright Lights Film Journal,* 30 April 2013.

Des Vallières, Jean. *Kavalier Scharnhorst, Tender Germany.* Paris: Albin Michel, 1931.

Devine, Jeremy M. *Vietnam at 24 Frames a Second: A Critical and Thematic Analysis of Over 400 Films About the Vietnam War.* Austin: University of Texas Press, 1999.

De Vries, Hilary. "At Home with Samuel Goldwyn, Jr.; With an Epic Effort, the Scion Roars." *New York Times*, 26 February 2004, F1.

Diehl, Jackson. "The Sheep in Wolf's Clothing" [Review of *Europa Europa*]. *Washington Post*, 25 March 1992.

Dunlop, John. Review of *Land and Freedom*. International Brigade Memorial Trust, n.d., www.international-brigades.org.uk/content/land-and-freedom-review.

Ebert, Roger. "A Seat in the Balcony with Bill Clinton." *Chicago Sun-Times*, 3 February 2000.

Ebert, Roger. Review of *A Midnight Clear*. *Chicago Sun-Times*, 1 May 1992.

Ebert, Roger. Review of *84 Charlie MoPic*. *Chicago Sun-Times*, 28 April 1989.

Ebert, Roger. Review of *Enemy at the Gates*. *Chicago Sun-Times*, 16 March 2001.

Ebert, Roger. Review of *Flags of Our Fathers*. *Chicago Sun-Times*, 29 November 2007.

Ebert, Roger. Review of *Full Metal Jacket*. *Chicago Sun-Times*, 26 June 1987.

Ebert, Roger. Review of *Johnny Got His Gun*. *Chicago Sun-Times*, 1 January 1971.

Ebert, Roger. Review of *Kagemusha*. *Chicago Sun-Times*, 1 January 1980.

Ebert, Roger. Review of *Master and Commander: The Far Side of the World*. *Chicago Sun-Times*, 14 November 2003.

Ebert, Roger. Review of *Merry Christmas, Mr. Lawrence*. *Chicago Sun-Times*, 16 September 1983.

Ebert, Roger. Review of *Platoon*. *Chicago Sun-Times*, 30 December 1986.

Ebert, Roger. Review of *Ran*. *Chicago Sun-Times*, 1 October 2000.

Ebert, Roger. Review of *The Big Red One*. *Chicago Sun-Times*, 21 November 2004.

Ebert, Roger. Review of *The Hurt Locker*. *Chicago Sun-Times*, 8 July 2009.

Ebert, Roger. Review of *The Last Samurai*. *Chicago Sun-Times*, 5 December 2003.

Ebert, Roger. Review of *The Thin Red Line*. *Chicago Sun Times*, 8 January 1999.

Ebert, Roger. Review of *Three Kings*. *Chicago Sun-Times*, 4 October 1999.

Edelstein, David. "Edelstein on the Crude Propaganda of *Lone Survivor*." *Vulture*, 10 January 2014, www.vulture.com/2014/01/lone-survivor-movie-review-david-edelstein.html.

Edelstein, David. Review of *Three Kings*. *New York Times*, 6 April 2003.

Eley, Geoff. "Finding the People's War: Film, British Collective Memory, and World War II." *The American Historical Review* 106.3 (June 2001).

Epstein, Jason. "*Master and Commander*: On the Far Side of Credibility." *New York Times*, 16 November 2003.

Erdman, Dan. "Merry Christmas Mr. Lawrence: David Bowie in Nagisa Oshima World War II Drama." 2010, www.altfg.com/film/merry-christmas-mr-lawrence-david-bowie-nagisa-oshima/.

Evans, Martin. "*The Battle of Algiers*: Historical Truth and Filmic Representation." 18 December 2012, https://www.opendemocracy.net/martin-evans/battle-of-algiers-historical-truth-and-filmic-representation.

Farago, Ladislas. *Patton: Ordeal and Triumph*. New York: Ivan Obelensky, 1963.

Farber, Manny. Review of *From Here to Eternity*. *The Nation*, 29 August 1953.

Fest, Joachim. *Inside Hitler's Bunker: The Last Days of the Third Reich*. New York: Picador, 2005.

Fick, Nathaniel. "How Accurate Is *Jarhead*? What One Marine Makes of the Gulf War Movie." *Salon*, 9 November 2005.

Fisher, Marc. "The Truth That Can Only Hurt." *Washington Post*, 25 June 1999.

Fishgall, Gary. *Gregory Peck: A Biography*. New York: Scribner, 2002.

Flatley, Guy. "Thirty Years Later, Johnny Gets His Gun Again." *New York Times*, 28 June 1970.

Foster, Joseph. Review of *The Story of G.I. Joe*. *The New Masses*, 23 October 1945.

French, Phillip. Review of *Land and Freedom*. *The Observer*, 8 October 1995.

French, Phillip. Review of *Flags of Our Fathers*. *The Guardian*, 24 December 2006.

Fuller, Samuel. *A Third Face: My Tale of Writing, Fighting, and Filmmaking*. New York: Applause, 2002.

Fussell, Paul. "Uneasy Company: *Band of Brothers* Is *Private Ryan* for Grown-ups." *Slate*, 7 September 2001.

Galbraith, Jane. "Half a Score and Three Years Ago . . . Movies: Writer Ron Maxwell Fought 13 Years to Make 'Gettysburg.' An Assist from Ted Turner Pushed the Film-miniseries over the Top." *Los Angeles Times*, 5 October 1993.

Gammage, Bill. *The Broken Years: Australian Soldiers in the Great War*. Canberra, Australia: Australian National University Press, 1974.

Getlein, Frank. Review of *Slaughterhouse-Five*. *Washington Evening Star*, 28 August 1972.

Gibson, Guy. *Enemy Coast Ahead*. London: Michael Joseph Ltd., 1946.

Gonzalez, Ed. Review of *Beasts of No Nation*. *Slant Magazine*, 11 October 2015.

Greenhous, Brereton. *The Making of Billy Bishop: The First World War Exploits of Billy Bishop, VC*. Toronto, Ontario, Canada: Dundurn Group, 2002.

Gregor, Manfred. *The Bridge*. New York: Avon Books, 1960.

Grilli, Peter. "Kurosawa Directs a Cinematic Lear." In *Akira Kurosawa: Interviews*. Edited by Bert Cardullo. Jackson, MS: University Press of Mississippi, 2008.

Grzelecki, Stanisław. Review of *Kanał. Życie Warszawy* [*Warsaw Life*], 24 April 1957.

Haase, Christine. *When Heimat Meets Hollywood: German Filmmakers and America, 1985–2005*. Rochester, NY: Camden House, 2007.

Haber, Joyce. "'Johnny' Wins a Prize and Trumbo Gets Praise." *Cleveland Plain Dealer*, 4 June 1971.

Handy, Ned. *The Flame Keepers*. New York: Hachette Books, 2004.

Harper, Sue and Vincent Porter. *British Cinema of the 1950s: The Decline of Deference*. London: Oxford University Press, 2007.

Hartl, John. "'Hurricane Script Blows Out; War Veterans Protest Oscar." *Seattle Daily Times*, 13 April 1979.

Hasford, Gustav. *The Short-Timers*. New York: Harper & Row, 1979.

Haskell, Molly. *From Reverence to Rape: The Treatment of Women in the Movies*. 3rd ed. University of Chicago Press, 2016.

Heinrich, Willi. *The Willing Flesh*. London: Corgi Books, 1974.

Herndon, Booton. *The Unlikeliest Hero*. Oakland, CA: Pacific Press, 1967.

Herr, Michael. *Dispatches*. New York: Alfred A. Knopf, 1977.

Hinson, Hal. Review of *Hamburger Hill*. *Washington Post*, 28 August 1987.

Hoberman, J. Review of *Downfall*. *The Village Voice*, 8 February 2005.

Holden, Stephen. Review of *Stalingrad*. *New York Times*, 24 May 1995.

Horton, Robert, ed. *Billy Wilder: Interviews*. Jackson, MS: University Press of Mississippi, 2001.

Howe, Desson. Review of *Empire of the Sun*. *Washington Post*, 11 December 1987.

Howe, Desson. Review of *Glory*. *Washington Post*, 12 January 1990.

Howe, Desson. Review of *The Last of the Mohicans*. *Washington Post*, 25 September 1992.

Hoyle, Brian. *The Cinema of John Boorman*. Lanham, Maryland: Scarecrow Press/Rowman & Littlefield, 2012.

Hunt, David. "About World War 2: A Small Christmas Truce." 5 September 2017, https://owlcation.com/humanities/About-World-War-2-A-Small-Christmas-Truce.

Huston, John. *An Open Book*. New York: Knopf, 1980.

Isserman, Maurice. "We Were Soldiers Once . . . But Hollywood Isn't Sure in Which War," *History Matters*, 18 March 2002, http://historymatters.gmu.edu/d/6579.

Iweala, Uzodinma. *Beasts of No Nation*. New York: Harper Perennial, 2005.

Jackson, Kenneth. "Not Enough History." *Perspectives on History: The Newsmagazine of the American Historical Association*, April 1999.

James, Caryn. Review of *Land and Freedom*. *New York Times*, 6 October 1995.

Jepps, Rebecca. "Johnny Johnson." 13 May 2013, https://www.raf.mod.uk/news/archive /johnny-johnson-13052013.

Johnson, Sharon. "Living Together Legally." *New Orleans Times-Picayune*, 29 July 1980.

Johnson, Vida T. and Graham Petrie. *The Films of Andrei Tarkovsky: A Visual Fugue*. Bloomington, IN: Indiana University Press, 1994.

Jones, James. *From Here to Eternity*. New York: Charles Scribner's Sons, 1951.

Jones, James. *The Thin Red Line*. New York: Charles Scribner's Sons, 1962.

Jones, J.D.F. *Storyteller: The Lives of Laurens van der Post*. London: John Murray, 2001.

Jones, Kaylie. "Was a WWII Classic Too Gay?" *Daily Beast*, 10 November 2009.

Junge, Traudl. *Until the Final Hour: Hitler's Last Secretary*. New York: Arcade Publishing, 2004.

Kastor, Elizabeth. "Vets Join List of 'Casualties' Critics: De Palma's Film Draws Protest." *Washington Post*, 24 August 1989.

Katsuta, Tomomi. Review of *The Last Samurai*. *Mainichi Shimbun*, 2004, part of "A Sampling of Japanese Comment" on *The Last Samurai* at UCLA Asia Pacific Center website (translated by Fumie Nakamura), www.international.ucla.edu/apc/article/6157.

Kemp, Phillip. Review of *Dunkirk*. *Sight and Sound*, 21 July 2017.

Keneally, Thomas. *Schindler's Ark*. London: Hodder & Stoughton, 1982.

Kessel, Joseph. *Army of Shadows*. Translated from the French by Haakon Chevalier. New York: Alfred A. Knopf, 1944.

Kershaw, Ian. "The Human Hitler." *The Guardian*, 17 September 2004.

Khan, Yasmin. "Dunkirk, the War and the Amnesia of the Empire." *New York Times*, 2 August 2017.

Kirkus, Virginia. Review of the novel, *The Thin Red Line*. *Kirkus Review*, 1 September 1962.

Kirstein, Lincoln. *Lay This Laurel: An Album on the Saint-Gaudens Memorial on Boston Common Honoring Black and White Men Together Who Served the Union Cause with Robert Gould Shaw and Died with Him July 18, 1863*. New York: Eakins Press, 1973.

Knappe, Siegfried, and Ted Brusaw, with Susan Davis McLaughlin. *Soldat: Reflections of a German Soldier, 1936–1949*. New York: Orion Books, 1992.

Koehler, Robert. "Vulgar Moralism: Paul Verhoeven's Black Book." http://cinema-scope .com/cinema-scope-magazine/interviews-vulgar-moralism-paul-verhoevens-black -book/.

Koestler, Arthur. Letter to the Editor in *Tribune* magazine, 15 September 1944, reprinted in *I Have Tried to Tell the Truth: 1943–44, The Complete Works of George Orwell*, vol. 16.

Kornweibel, Theodore, Jr. "Humphrey Bogart's *Sahara*: Propaganda, Cinema and the American Character in World War II." *American Studies* 22.1 (Spring 1981).

Kovic, Ron. *Born on the Fourth of July*. New York: McGraw-Hill, 1976.

Kyle, Chris, Scott McEwen and Jim DeFelice. *American Sniper: The Autobiography of the Most Lethal Sniper in U.S. Military History*. New York: Harper, 2012.

Kyne, Phelim and Al Rockoff. "Being Al Rockoff: Shooting from the Hip in Cambodia." *Taipei Times,* 16 April 2000, http://www.taipeitimes.com/News/asia/archives/2000/04 /16/32498.

Landon, Christopher Guy. *Ice Cold in Alex.* London: Heinemann, 1957.

Lane, Anthony. Review of *Beasts of No Nation. The New Yorker,* 14 November 2005.

Lang, Daniel. *Casualties of War.* New York: McGraw-Hill, 1969.

Lardner, David. "The Current Cinema." *The New Yorker,* 27 November 1943.

Larsen, Andrew. "Why Historical Accuracy in Film Matters." 18 April 2014, https:// aelarsen.wordpress.com/2014/04/18/why-historical-accuracy-in-film-matters/.

LaSalle, Mick. Review of *Jarhead. San Francisco Chronicle,* 4 November 2005.

LaSalle, Mick. Review of *The Hurt Locker. San Francisco Chronicle,* 10 July 2009.

Laurier, Joanne. Review of *Jarhead. WSWS,* 18 November 2005.

Lawrence, T. E. *Seven Pillars of Wisdom: A Triumph.* London: Jonathan Cape, 1935.

Lev, Peter. *American Films of the '70s: Conflicting Visions.* Austin, TX: University of Texas Press, 2000.

Lindeman, Edith. Review of *Men in War. Richmond Times Dispatch,* 4 March 1957.

Lloyd, Norman and Francine Parker. *Stages of Life in Theatre, Film, and Television.* Honolulu, Hawaii: Limelight, 1993.

Lobet, Ernest S. "Letter to the Editor." *New York Times,* 15 February 1994.

Low, Mary and Juan Brea. *Red Spanish Notebook: The First Six Months of the Revolution and the Civil War.* San Francisco: City Lights Books, 1979.

Lowe, Walter. *Hyde Park Herald,* 15 September 1971.

Luttrell, Marcus. *Lone Survivor: The Eyewitness Account of Operation Redwing and the Lost Heroes of SEAL Team 10.* Boston: Little, Brown and Company, 2007.

Macdonald, Scott. "*The Longest Day.*" 2 July 2004, www.eyeforfilm.co.uk/review/the-longest -day-film-review-by-scott-macdonald.

MacLean, Alistair. *The Guns of Navarone.* London: Collins, 1957.

MaLone, Peter. Transcript of phone interview with Bruce Beresford (15 May 1999) at: https://archive.is/20121220180451/http://www.signis.net/malone/tiki-index.php ?page=Bruce+Beresford&bl.

Manabe, Noriko. "Rewriting Someone Else's History: The Japanese Reaction to *Letters from Iwo Jima.*" http://historynewsnetwork.org/article/35739.

Manchester, William. "The Bloodiest Battle of All." *New York Times Magazine,* 14 June 1987.

Mandelbaum, Jacques. Review of *Dunkirk. Le Monde* [Paris], 19 July 2017.

Marshall, S. L. A. *Pork Chop Hill: The American Fighting Man in Action Korea, Spring, 1953.* New York: William Morrow and Co., 1956.

Martone, Michael. *Unconventions: Attempting the Art of Craft and the Craft of Art - Writings on Writing by Michael Martone.* Athens, GA: University of Georgia Press, 2010.

Maslin, Janet. Review of *Empire of the Sun. New York Times,* 9 December 1987.

Maslin, Janet. Review of *Gallipoli. New York Times,* 28 August 1981.

Maslin, Janet. Review of *Merry Christmas Mr. Lawrence. New York Times,* 26 August 1983.

Maslin, Janet. Review of *Soldier of Orange. New York Times,* 16 August 1979.

Mathijs, Ernest, ed. *The Cinema of the Low Countries.* London: Wallflower Press, 2004.

McCarten, John. Review of *Battleground. The New Yorker,* 19 November 1949.

McElvey, Tara. "*The Hurt Locker* as Propaganda." *American Prospect,* 17 July 2009.

McKenna, Richard. *The Sand Pebbles.* New York: Harper & Row, 1962.

Mclaughlin, William. *War History Online,* 13 January 2016.

McPherson, James M. "The 'Glory' Story." *The New Republic,* 8 and 15 January 1990.

Meade, James. "'Guns of Navarone' Problem to Shoot but Finished Product Should Be Feather in Cap of Carl Foreman." *San Diego Union*, 29 January 1961.

Miller, Arthur. *Situation Normal*. New York: Reynal & Hitchcock, 1944.

Milton, Nicholas. "A Tank Veteran on *Fury*: 'Very realistic, but it can't show the full horror of war.'" *The Guardian*, 24 October 2014.

Mitchell, Elvis. Review of *Black Hawk Down*. *New York Times*, 28 December 2001.

Modine, Matthew. *Full Metal Jacket Diary*. New York: Rugged Land, 2005.

Monsarrat, Nicholas. *The Cruel Sea*. London: Cassell, 1951.

Moore, Harold G. and Joseph L. Galloway. *We Were Soldiers Once. And Young: Ia Drang: The Battle That Changed the War in Vietnam*. New York: Random House, 1992.

Morrow, Felix. *Revolution and Counter-Revolution in Spain*. New York: Pathfinder Press, 1974.

Murnaghan, Brigid. Review of *The Dam Busters*. *Village Voice*, 9 November 1955.

Murphy, Audie. *To Hell and Back*. New York: Henry Holt, 1949.

Murray, Al. *Watching War Films with My Dad*. New York: Century, 2013.

Museum of Modern Art. "MoMA's Eighth Annual International Festival of Film Preservation Showcases Newly Restored Masterworks and Rediscoveries" [press release]. 2010, http://press.moma.org/wp-content/press-archives/PRESS_RELEASE_ARCHIVE/TSAP10 ReleaseUpdated_FINAL.pdf.

Nixon, Rob and Jeff Stafford. "*Stalag 17* (1953)." http://www.tcm.com/tcmdb/title/4237 /Stalag-17/articles.html#topofpage.

Norman, Michael. "War's Face, Seen Intimately." *New York Times*, 19 March 1989.

NPR's *Weekend Edition Sunday*, 12 January 2014.

O'Brian, Patrick. *The Far Side of the World*. London: Collins, 1984.

Orr, Christopher. Review of *Fury*. *The Atlantic*, 17 October 2014.

Orwell, George. *Homage to Catalonia*. London: Secker & Warburg, 1938.

Payne, William A. "Pork Chop Hill Battle Refought for Movie." *Dallas Morning News*, 28 May 1959.

Paz, Abel. *Durruti: The People Armed*. Translated by Nancy MacDonald. Montreal, QC, Canada: Black Rose Books, 1996.

Pearson, Mike. Review of *84 Charlie MoPic*. *Arkansas Democrat*, 31 December 1989.

Peary, Gerald, ed. *Samuel Fuller: Interviews*. Jackson, MS: University of Mississippi Press, 2012.

Perel, Solomon. *Europa, Europa: A Memoir of World War II*. New York: Wiley, 1999.

Perry, Tony. "Experts' Opinion on *Jarhead*? Mixed; Marines Like the Film's Depiction of the 'First-to-Fight' Spirit but Call It a Relic of a Pre-9/11 World." *Los Angeles Times*, 7 November 2005.

Phillips, Gene D. *Godfather: The Intimate Francis Ford Coppola*. Lexington, KY: University Press of Kentucky, 2004.

Pizzello, Stephen and Stephen Spielberg. "Five Star General." *American Cinematographer*, August 1996.

Pomerantz, Margaret. Review of *Beneath Hill 60*. *At the Movies* [Australia], 19 August 2010.

Pryor, Thomas. Review of *The Story of G.I. Joe*. *New York Times*, 6 October 1945.

Rainer, Peter. Review of *Saving Private Ryan*. *San Francisco Weekly*, 22 July 1998.

Rainer, Peter. Review of *Defiance*. *Christian Science Monitor*, 17 January 2009.

Ramsden, John. *The Dam Busters*. London: I. B. Tauris, Ltd., 2003.

Raphael, Frederic. *Eyes Wide Open: A Memoir of Stanley Kubrick and Eyes Wide Shut*. London: Phoenix, 2000.

Remarque, Erich Maria. *All Quiet on the Western Front*. Boston: Little Brown, 1929.

Rich, Motoko. "Hollywood's Land of the Rising Cliché." *New York Times*, 4 January 2004.

Rich, Motoko. "He Lived to Tell the Tale (and Write a Best Seller)." *New York Times*, 9 August 2007.

Richie, Donald. *The Films of Akira Kurosawa*. 3rd ed. Oakland, CA: University of California Press, 1996.

Ringle, Ken. Review of *Gettysburg*. *Washington Post*, 10 October 1993.

Robertson, Nan. "On the Tumult in Tobago for 'Mr. Allison.'" *New York Times*, 18 November 1956.

Robbins, David L. *War of the Rats*. New York: Bantam, 1999.

Roelfzema, Erik Hazelhoff. *Soldier of Orange*. New York: Ballantine Books, 1980.

Rosenbaum, David. Review of *Cross of Iron*. *Boston Herald*, 19 May 1977.

Rosenbaum, Jonathan. "Born on the Fourth of July." n.d., https://www.chicagoreader.com/chicago/born-on-the-fourth-of-july/Film?oid=1063760.

Rottman, Gordon L. *US Army Infantryman in Vietnam 1965–73*. Oxford, UK: Osprey Publishing, 2005.

Rubin, Steven Jay. *Combat Films: American Realism 1945–2010*. 2nd ed. Jefferson, NC: McFarland, 2011.

Rusinko, Susan, ed. *Shaw and Other Matters: A Festschrift for Stanley Weintraub on the Occasion of His Forty-First Year at the Pennsylvania State University*. University Park, PA: Penn State University, 1998.

Ryan, Cornelius. *The Longest Day: 6 June 1944 D-Day*. New York: Simon & Schuster, 1959.

Ryan, Cornelius. *A Bridge Too Far*. New York: Simon & Schuster, 1974.

Saporito, Jeff. "How Did Oliver Stone's Approach to 'Platoon' Differ from Other War Films?" 28 October 2015, http://screenprism.com/insights/article/how-did-oliver-stones-approach-to-platoon-differ-from-many-other-war-films.

Sartre, Jean Paul. "Discussion on the Criticism of *Ivan's Childhood*." [Open letter to Mario Alicata dated 9 Oct. 1963]. Reprinted in: *Situations, tome VIII: Autour de 68* [*Situations, Volume VIII: Around 1968*]. Paris: Gallimard, 1965. English translation: https://people.ucalgary.ca/~tstronds/nostalghia.com/TheTopics/Sartre.html.

Schanberg, Sydney. "The Death and Life of Dith Pran." *New York Times Magazine*, 20 January 1980.

Scheuer, Phillip K. Review of *The Sand Pebbles*. *Los Angeles Times*, 25 December 1966.

Schickel, Richard. Review of *The Sand Pebbles*. *Life*, 6 January 1967.

Schindler, Emilie and Erika L. Rosenberg. *Where Light and Shadow Meet: A Memoir*. New York: W. W. Norton, 1997.

Schoendoerffer, Pierre. *La 317e section* [*The 317th Platoon*]. Paris: La Table ronde, 1963.

Scott, A. O. Review of *The Pianist*. *New York Times*, 27 December 2002.

"Sergeant York (1941)." *TCM Notes*. http://www.tcm.com/tcmdb/title/1386/Sergeant-York/notes.html.

Seydor, Paul. "Peckinpah," *Sight and Sound* 5.10 (1995).

Shaara, Michael. *The Killer Angels*. New York: David McKay, 1974.

Shaw, Charles. *Heaven Knows, Mister Allison*. New York: Crown, 1952.

Sheffield, Clayton Odie. *The War Film: Historical Perspective or Simple Entertainment*. Master's Thesis, U.S. Army Command and General Staff College, 2001.

Siegel, Robert. "'Flags of Our Fathers' Stays True to History." National Public Radio broadcast, 19 October 2006.

Siskel, Gene. "A Test for *Platoon*: Battle Vets Say the Film Lacks Only the Taste and the Smell of Death." *Chicago Tribune*, 4 January 1987.

Siskel & Ebert at the Movies. Season 13, Episode 17, 2 January 1999.

Smith, Denitia Smith. "A Scholar's Book Adds Layers of Complexity to the Schindler Legend." *New York Times,* 24 November 2004.

Stack, Peter. Review of *Stalingrad. San Francisco Chronicle,* 27 October 1995.

Stanley, Fred. "Hollywood Bulletins." *New York Times,* 1 August 1943.

Suid, Lawrence H. *Guts and Glory: The Making of the American Military Image in Film.* Lexington, KY: University of Kentucky Press, 2001.

Summers, Julie. "The Colonel of Tamarkan: Philip Toosey and the Bridge on the River Kwai." National Army Museum, Chelsea, London, UK (8 March 2012) [lecture video].

Speer, Albert. *Inside the Third Reich: Memoirs.* New York: Macmillan, 1969.

Steffen, James. "*Kanal* (1957)." www.tcm.com/tcmdb/title/80082/Kanal/articles.html.

Swofford, Anthony. *Jarhead: A Marine Chronicle of the Gulf War and Other Battles.* New York: Scribner, 2003.

Szpilman, Władysław. *The Pianist.* London: Victor Gollancz, 1999.

Taibbi, Matt. Review of *American Sniper. Rolling Stone,* 21 January 2015.

Taylor, Ella. Review of *Saving Private Ryan. LA Weekly,* 22 July 1998.

Tec, Nechama. *Defiance: The Bielski Partisans.* London: Oxford University Press, 1994.

Terry, Wallace. *Bloods: An Oral History of the Vietnam War.* Novato, CA: Presidio Press, 1985.

Thomas, Kevin. Review of *The Winter War. Los Angeles Times,* 8 December 1989.

Tobin, James. *Ernie Pyle's War: America's Eyewitness to World War II.* New York: Free Press, 1997.

Tong, Allan. "'The only place to execute some kind of power was the film set': Agnieszka Holland on Her Career." *Filmmaker Magazine,* 3 April 2014.

Toplin, Robert Brent. *History by Hollywood: The Use and Abuse of the American Past.* Champaign, IL: University of Illinois Press, 1996.

A Tour of the Inferno: Revisiting Platoon. Charles Kiselyak and Jeff McQueen, directors. MGM Home Entertainment, 2001. [Video documentary]

Travers, Peter. Review of *Enemy at the Gates. Rolling Stone,* 16 March 2001.

Tregaskis, Richard. *Guadalcanal Diary.* New York: Random House, 1943.

Trumbo, Dalton. *Johnny Got His Gun.* Philadelphia: J. P. Lippincott, 1939.

Turse, Nick. *Kill Anything That Moves: The Real American War in Vietnam.* New York: Metropolitan Books, 2013.

Tuuri, Antti. *The Winter War.* Translated by Richard Impola with an Introduction by Borje Vahamaki. Beaverton, Ontario, Canada: Aspasia Books, 2003.

Van der Post, Laurens. *A Bar of Shadow.* London: The Hogarth Press Ltd., 1972.

Van der Post, Laurens. *The Seed and the Sower.* London: The Hogarth Press Ltd., 1963.

Van der Post, Laurens. *The Night of the New Moon.* London: The Hogarth Press Ltd., 1970.

Van Praag, Van. *Day Without End.* New York: William Sloane, 1949.

Vogler, Christopher and Michele Montez. *The Writer's Journey: Mythic Structure for Writers.* 3rd ed. Michael Wiese Productions, 2007.

Von Busack. Review of *Courage Under Fire. Metro: Silicon Valley's Weekly Newspaper,* 11–17 July 1996, http://www.metroactive.com/papers/metro/07.11.96/courage-9628.html.

Von Tunzelmann, Alex. "The Battle of Algiers: A Masterpiece of Historical Accuracy." *The Guardian,* 26 March 2009.

Vonnegut, Kurt. *Slaughterhouse-Five, Or The Children's Crusade: A Duty-Dance with Death.* New York: Delacorte, 1969.

Vonnegut, Kurt. *Between Time and Timbuktu; or Prometheus-5: A Space Fantasy.* New York: Delacorte, 1972.

Walker, Alexander. Review of *The Cruel Sea. New York Times,* 11 August 1953.

Walker, Alexander. Review of *Lawrence of Arabia*. *London Evening Standard*, 12 December 1960.

Weddle, David. *If They Move . . . Kill 'Em!: The Life and Times of Sam Peckinpah*. New York: Grove Press, 2000.

Weiler, Abe H. Review of *From Here to Eternity*. *New York Times,* 6 August 1953.

Wenders, Wim. Review of *Land and Freedom*. *Daily Telegraph*, 12 July 2003.

Wenders, Wim. "Tja, dann wollen wir ma" ["Well, then we want ma"]. *Der Zeit*, 21 October 2004.

Wharton, William. *A Midnight Clear*. New York: Knopf, 1982.

Wharton, William. *Shrapnel: A Memoir*. New York: William Morrow, 2012.

White, William L. *They Were Expendable*. New York: Harcourt, Brace, 1942.

Witton, George. *Scapegoats of the Empire: The True Story of Breaker Morant's Bushveldt Carbineers*. Oxford, England: Benediction Classics, 2010.

York, Alvin C. *Sergeant York: His Own Life Story and War Diary*. Garden City, NY: Doubleday, Doran, 1928.

Zinn, Howard. "Private Ryan Saves War." *Progressive* 62.10 (October 1998).

Zinnemann, Fred. *Fred Zinnemann: An Autobiography*. New York: Scribner's, 1992.

Zwick, Edward. "Shadows of Valiant Ancestors." *New York Times*, December 24, 2008.

Index

Bold indicates the location of main entries.

About the Author

Robert Niemi, PhD, is professor of English and American Studies at St. Michael's College, Colchester, Vermont. He is the author of *History in the Media: Film and Television* (ABC-CLIO, 2006), *Inspired by True Events: An Illustrated Guide to More Than 500 History-Based Films* (ABC-CLIO, 2013), and *Robert Altman: Hollywood Maverick* (Columbia University Press, 2016).